WORLD WITHIN WALLS

Other Works by Donald Keene Published by Grove Press

Anthology of Chinese Literature Vol. I (with Cyril Birch, ed.)
Anthology of Japanese Literature: Earliest Era to Mid-Nineteenth Century
Japanese Literature: An Introduction for Western Readers
Modern Japanese Literature: An Anthology

DONALD KEENE

WORLD WITHIN WALLS

JAPANESE LITERATURE OF THE PRE-MODERN ERA, 1600–1867

Grove Press, Inc.
NEW YORK

First Edition 1978
First Printing 1978
ISBN: 0-394-17074-1
Grove Press ISBN: 0-8021-4220-6
Library of Congress Catalog Card Number: 78-66793

Library of Congress Cataloging in Publication Data

Keene, Donald.
World within walls.
Reprint of the 1st ed. published by Holt, Rinehart, and Winston, New York.
Includes bibliographies and index.
1. Japanese literature — Edo period, 1600-1868 — History and criticism. I. Title.
[PL726.35.K4 1978] 895.6′09′003 78-66793
ISBN 0-394-17074-1

Manufactured in the United States of America

Distributed by Random House, Inc., New York

GROVE PRESS, INC., 196 West Houston Street, New York, N.Y. 10014

To Benjamin A. Kurakata

CONTENTS

PREFACE

Japanese scholars usually refer to the poetry, prose, and drama written in their country between 1600 and 1867 as Edo literature because the shoguns, who ruled the country, had their capital in Edo, the modern Tokyo. Another way of describing this literature is to say that it is of the *kinsei*, meaning "recent times." Finally, the same period is sometimes also called Tokugawa, after the name of the family who served as shoguns. None of these appellations is entirely satisfactory. To use the name Edo for the literature of the first half of the period is inappropriate because most of it was composed elsewhere in Japan. "Recent times" is too vague in English, though *kinsei* refers to a special period. "Tokugawa literature" might be the best solution, but modern scholars tend to avoid using a political designation for a literary period. For want of a more suitable term I have called this section of my history of Japanese literature the "pre-modern period."

It is my hope that the book will be of interest to a wider audience than just the small group of scholars outside Japan who are professionally concerned with Japanese literature. For this reason I have translated or explained even elementary terms known to everyone with the slightest acquaintance with the Japanese language. Only when the translation of a title would involve sentences of explanation—unfortunately, not a rare occurrence—or when the title is of a minor work mentioned in passing, have I left it in the original. A few words like *shū*, meaning "collection," occur so often that I have not felt it necessary to translate them each time. All Japanese terms used in the text are otherwise explained in a glossary. Japanese terms are given in italics on first appearance, but in roman type subsequently.

Again, in the belief that it would make the book more pleasurable to read, I have relegated to an appendix the plots of certain works of the theater which are of great historical importance but do not make absorbing reading when compressed into the page or two of a summary. The notes indicate which works have been dealt with in this manner.

I have followed throughout the Japanese practice of referring to persons by their surnames followed by their personal names, rather than in the normal Western order. I realize that this may confuse a few readers, but it seems as absurd to me to say Monzaemon Chikamatsu as it would be to say Shakespeare William. There is, alas, another problem involved. Most writers were known by their literary names (*gō*), rather than by either their surnames or the names by which their mothers called them. I have referred to writers in the way followed by the Japanese today, rather than attempt to impose uniformity. Thus, Matsuo Bashō and Ihara Saikaku are called Bashō and Saikaku (Matsuo and Ihara would be unintelligible); but Chikamatsu Monzaemon is called by his surname Chikamatsu, following the universal but never explained practice.

I have whenever possible converted dates to the calendar used in Western Europe during the period covered. Chikamatsu died at the end of the eleventh lunar month of a year corresponding to 1724; but if this event had been reported in the European press it would have been in January 1725. I have therefore given 1725 as the year of his death. The ages of Japanese at this time were also calculated by a system different from the one prevailing in Europe. A baby was one year old at birth, and became two years old at the following New Year. It might happen, therefore, that an infant less than a month old by Western reckoning was considered to be two years old by the Japanese of this period. I have followed the Western practice except where noted.

Because I realize that some readers will be interested in a particular chapter and may not read all that precedes it, I have not hesitated to repeat certain essential information, rather than oblige such readers to search for earlier references. For the same reason, I have supplied bibliographies for each chapter. However, I have included in the index the names of persons and works mentioned in the text, together with the main topics.

This book was written over a period of years during which I received generous support from different organizations. I gratefully record my indebtedness to the East Asian Institute of Columbia University, the Guggenheim Foundation, and the American Council of Learned Societies, who made it financially possible to carry on this work. The understanding shown by the Columbia University administration, who provided me with the time I needed, was no less important. My thanks to all are profound.

WORLD
WITHIN
WALLS

INTRODUCTION

The literature of the pre-modern period (1600–1867) was pre-eminently popular in character. Of course, there had been poetry and prose written by commoners long before, some of it of high literary merit, and many genres associated with the court had originated in popular entertainments; but compared to most other literatures of the world, or to Japanese literature after 1600, the earlier literature was aristocratic in its tone, and both authors and readers for the most part belonged to the nobility.

It seldom happens that the beginning of a new political era so exactly coincides with the creation of a new literature as in Japan about 1600, the year of the decisive Battle of Sekigahara. If we include the developments of the last decade of the sixteenth century, we can say that almost every form of poetry, prose, and drama that would flourish for the next 270 years had largely been determined, even as the Tokugawa rulers were strengthening their hold over the country.

The most important single development was the adoption of printing, without which a popular literature could hardly have been created. The Japanese had known the art of printing from at least the eighth century A.D. Paper slips printed with *dharani* (Buddhist charms) were placed in the one million tiny pagodas built by order of Empress Shōtoku in 770, and during the following centuries Buddhist texts were printed from time to time. The art of printing from blocks was never lost but, contrary to Chinese tradition, secular works were not printed. No explanation was offered as to why the Japanese classics—the *Kokinshū*, *The Tale of Genji* and even the *Chronicles of Japan*—were preserved only in manuscript form. Perhaps the demand for copies was so small it could be satisfied with manuscripts, costly though they were, or perhaps Buddhism and printing were so closely associated in people's minds that to print other texts might have seemed sacrilegious. Perhaps, however, aesthetic considerations induced the Japanese to prefer the inconvenient and expensive manuscripts: the calligraphy and illustrations may have been considered so integral a part of literary works that a bare printed edition would have seemed as incomplete as a theatrical work without music.

Be that as it may, it is astonishing how many works of Japanese literature survived in one or two manuscripts that could easily have perished in the flames of warfare. Not until 1591 was a nonreligious work printed, the *Setsuyō-shū*, a dictionary giving Japanese pronunciations for the Chinese characters. This work, compiled during the middle years of the Muromachi period, was the first of a group of practical books to be printed by merchants in the commercial city of Sakai. About the same time the Jesuit Mission Press at Amakusa, near Nagasaki, was printing books from movable type in the roman alphabet; they included a few works of Japanese literature, such as *Heike Monogatari* (The Tale of the Heike). These developments, though indicative of the enterprising, uninhibited spirit of the times, were not directly responsible for the growth of printing that contributed so largely to the popular literature of the seventeenth century.

In 1593, in the wake of the Japanese invasion of Korea, a printing press with movable type was sent from Korea as a present for Emperor Go-Yōzei. Movable type was apparently invented in China in the eleventh century, but its use was much expanded and improved by the Koreans, especially after cast-metal types were first made in 1403.[1] The printing press may have been offered to the emperor more as a curiosity than as a practical invention, but that same year he commanded that it be used to print an edition of the Confucian *Kobun Kōkyō* (Classic of Filial Piety). Four years later, in 1597, a Japanese version of the Korean printing press was built with wooden instead of metal type, probably because of the difficulties of casting; and in 1599 this press was used to print the first part of the *Nihon Shoki* (Chronicles of Japan).

By this time printing was developing into the hobby or extravagance of the rich. Editions of medical books, Confucian works, and Buddhist doctrine, as well as examples of Japanese literature (including fiction, diaries, poetry, dictionaries, and histories) began to appear in small printings, probably fewer than one hundred copies each. These editions, associated with Emperors Go-Yōzei and Go-Mizunoo and with such figures as Toyotomi Hideyoshi and Tokugawa Ieyasu, were intended for presentation and not for sale.[2] The finest printed books of the time were designed by the artist Hon'ami Kōetsu (1558–1637) for the rich Kyoto merchant Suminokura Soan (1570–1632). They included Nō texts, *Hōjōki* (Account of My Hut), *Shin Kokinshū*, and various other works of classical Japanese literature. The masterpiece of this press was the illustrated edition of *Ise Monogatari* (Tales of Ise) published in 1608.

Commercial publication seems to have begun in 1609 with the popular anthology of Chinese poetry *Kobun Shimpō* (New Treasury of Old Writing).[3] Gradually the demand for printed books increased, and in the three great cities—Kyoto, Osaka, and Edo—men started to publish for profit. As a first step in transforming publication from the avocation of the rich into a commercial enterprise, it was found necessary to abandon movable type in favor of block printing. It has often been stated that this retrograde step was taken because printing from type was more expensive than from blocks, or else that it was unsuited to editions larger than one hundred copies, but no really convincing reason has been advanced. More likely, aesthetic reasons were responsible. The Japanese writing, especially the *hiragana* script, was normally connected, unlike the Chinese printed characters which stand in isolation. Movable-type printing of hiragana left each symbol detached, and this looked unnatural and ugly to readers accustomed to the fluid calligraphy of the manuscripts; some *kana* (symbols) were long and some very short, and to allot the same amount of space for each type made for an unattractive appearance. In order to remedy this aesthetic failing, two or three kana were sometimes combined on a single type, but the effect was still not pleasing.[4] Moreover, the illustrated books, particularly those produced in Nara, were at the height of their popularity in the early seventeenth century, and readers undoubtedly expected books to be illustrated. It was possible even with movable type to include illustrations, but it was simpler to make a block for a whole sheet including both writing and illustrations. Once block printing became general in the 1620s almost all works of Japanese literature were printed with numerous illustrations.[5]

The development of commercial publishing in the 1620s was closely related to the increased interest displayed by the samurai class in cultural matters. The earliest works of the seventeenth-century literature may have been written by members of the court aristocracy; many works were formerly credited to the nobleman Karasumaru Mitsuhiro (1579–1638), and even though such attributions are now generally rejected, the lingering importance of the court writers cannot be denied. Nevertheless, most authors and readers of the seventeenth century belonged to the samurai class.[6]

After long years of warfare the country was at peace, and the government accordingly encouraged the samurai to take up the way of letters. Initially the authorities must have feared that men accustomed to bloodthirsty exploits might prove rebellious, and therefore looked kindly even on the establishment of pleasure quarters as a means of dissipating surplus energies. Before many years had passed, the effeminacy and degeneracy of the samurai caused many statesmen to lament; but in the 1620s the participation of the samurai in the cultural life was actively welcomed.

The aristocrats among the samurai, the daimyo, kept literary men in their entourage. These storytellers and poets, known as *otogishu*, sometimes composed works celebrating the military exploits of their masters or their masters' masters; a notable example was *Shinchō-ki* (Chronicles of Nobunaga) by Ōta Gyūichi (1527–1610), who served as an otogishu to both Oda Nobunaga and Toyotomi Hideyoshi.[7] Humorous stories, related to amuse a daimyo, were also composed by the otogishu.

Haikai poetry, the most typical verse form of the period, originated in the milieu of a daimyo's salon. After a long session of composing serious linked verse (*renga*), the participants often concluded the evening on a lighter note in the frivolous haikai manner. The most important haikai poet at the beginning of the seventeenth century was a member of a distinguished samurai family, Matsunaga Teitoku, who served the daimyo Hosokawa Yūsai.

Only in the eighteenth century would literature pass from the samurai class to the townsmen, though the latter's tastes had dominated the theater since the end of the sixteenth century, when Kabuki and Jōruri, the two representative forms of the new drama, were created.

It is customary to divide the pre-modern literature into two main periods: from 1600 to about 1770, when the Kamigata region (Kyoto, Osaka, and the vicinity) was the center of most literary production; and from 1770 to 1867, when the center shifted to the shogun's capital in Edo. The literature can otherwise be divided into the main genres: waka poetry, haikai poetry, fiction, and drama. A few men like Saikaku wrote well in two or more genres, but on the whole the genres remained distinct. I have therefore taken up each genre separately and divided the literature chronologically only once, about 1770.

In addition to the works discussed in the following pages there were innumerable other books published during the pre-modern period, thanks both to the spread of printing and to the steady rise in literacy. Some are totally devoid of literary interest, but others, chiefly the collections of miscellaneous jottings (*zuihitsu*) occasionally include passages of distinction, and are of great importance in providing the background to indisputably literary works. No human being in the course of his lifetime could read *all* this material, and the literary level on the whole is not high enough to justify systematic treatment. For similar reasons the body of Confucian philosophical works, though they sometimes have literary significance, must remain outside the scope of this history.

The great works of pre-modern literature tended to appear in clusters. During the Genroku (1688–1703), Temmei (1781–88) and Bunka-Bunsei (1804–29) eras many writers and artists burst into creative activity, seeming to inspire one another. Some in-between periods were bleak, but this did not involve a diminution in quantity, only in quality. A scholar might read everything that survives of Heian literature, but the bulk of pre-modern literature is so large that it cannot be known in entirety to any one man. The best the historian can do is to distinguish the members of the great clusters of literary figures and the men on their periphery who once in a while were brushed by genius.

The historical and philosophical background of the literary works will be touched on only in passing. Readers who wish to pursue these aspects should consult the works listed in the bibliography below.

NOTES

1. For a description of the history of movable type, see Thomas Francis Carter, *The Invention of Printing in China*, chap. 23.
2. Richard Lane, "The Beginnings of the Modern Japanese Novel," p. 648.
3. Hamada Keisuke, in Ichiko Teiji and Noma Kōshin, *Otogi Zōshi, Kana Zōshi*, p. 282.
4. Hamada, p. 282.
5. Lane, p. 648.
6. Hamada, p. 283.
7. Hamada, p. 284. See also Okuno Takahiro and Iwasawa Yoshihiko, *Shinchōkō Ki*, pp. 476–78; and Matsuda Osamu, *Nihon Kinsei Bungaku no Seiritsu*, pp. 28–41.

BIBLIOGRAPHY

FOR INTRODUCTION

Carter, Thomas Francis. *The Invention of Printing in China.* New York: Columbia University Press, 1931.

Ichiko Teiji and Noma Kōshin. *Otogi Zōshi, Kana Zōshi,* in Nihon Koten Kanshō Kōza series. Tokyo: Kadokawa Shoten, 1963.

Lane, Richard. "The Beginnings of the Modern Japanese Novel," *Harvard Journal of Asiatic Studies*, vol. XX, no. 3–4 (1957).

Matsuda Osamu. *Nihon Kinsei Bungaku no Seiritsu*. Tokyo: Hōsei Daigaku Shuppankyoku, 1963.

Okuno Takahiro and Iwasawa Yoshihiko. *Shinchōkō Ki*, in Kadokawa Bunko series. Tokyo: Kadokawa Shoten, 1969.

FOR PRE-MODERN PERIOD

Sansom, George. *A History of Japan, 1615–1867*. Stanford: Stanford University Press, 1963.

———. *Japan, a Short Cultural History*. London: The Cresset Press, 1946.

Tsunoda, Ryusaku, Wm. Theodore de Bary, and Donald Keene. *Sources of Japanese Tradition*. New York: Columbia University Press, 1958.

Varley, H. Paul. *Japanese Culture*. New York: Praeger, 1973.

PART ONE
LITERATURE FROM 1600–1770

CHAPTER 1
HAIKAI POETRY
THE BEGINNINGS OF HAIKAI NO RENGA (COMIC LINKED VERSE)

The art of *renga* (linked verse) originated as a kind of elegant parlor game. Each participant was expected to display his readiness of wit by responding to the lines of verse composed by another man with lines of his own, copying the first man's contribution in such a way as to make a complete *waka* (verse form) of thirty-one syllables in five lines. The more absurd or puzzling the content of the first man's lines, the greater the achievement of the second man if he managed to add two or three lines that, perhaps by a clever play on words, made sense of the whole.[1]

This primitive display of ingenuity was soon left behind by the serious renga masters of the fifteenth and sixteenth centuries. They went beyond composing a single poem in thirty-one syllables, extending their joint efforts to a hundred or even a thousand "links" bound together into a single chain by overtones and evocations rather than by plays on words or clever shifts in meaning, and their art was universally revered.

Renga masters were constantly traveling around the country, staying with local potentates for weeks or even months at a time, enjoying hospitality in return for the lessons they gave in renga composition. However, the lofty conceptions of renga enunciated by Sōgi and other masters were far beyond the understanding of most amateur poets, whose preferences in renga ran to coarse humor, especially the salaciousness of the double entendre. In order to accommodate these patrons most renga poets were obliged to become as accomplished in the frivolous (*mushin*) variety of renga as in the serious (*ushin*), though normally they did not preserve their lighter compositions. The collection of renga *Tsukuba Shū* (1356), it is true, had included a *haikai* (or comic) section, as indeed had the waka collection *Kokinshū* (905), but the haikai style of renga was omitted from the next major renga collection, *Shinsen Tsukuba Shū* (1495), and henceforth was always excluded. This narrowing of the range of renga, to the point of denying its original purpose, occasioned the development of the comic renga in the sixteenth century as a light but literary outlet for humorous expression.

The poet invariably associated with the rise of comic renga as a recognized literary form was Yamazaki Sōkan. Extremely little is known about his life, and many contradictory dates are given for his death. One firm item of biographical data is the manuscript of a Nō play he copied in 1539, suggesting that the commonly given dates for his life, 1464–1552, may be correct. Some accounts state that Sōkan became a monk after the death of the shogun Yoshihisa, whom he served as a samurai, in 1487. There are also traditions that Sōkan, originally from the province of Ōmi, lived in the town of Yamazaki, west of Kyoto, during his middle years, supporting himself as a poet and teacher of calligraphy. Sōkan apparently died on the island of Shikoku where a grave, said to be his, may still be seen in the town of Kannonji. But the scraps of information concerning Sōkan hardly permit us to form a picture of the man or his life.

The first reference to Sōkan is found in the transcript of a renga session held in 1488. Sōkan, then a young man, participated along with the great masters of the day: Sōgi (1421–1502), Shōhaku (1443–1527), and Sōchō (1448–1532). One verse composed by Sōkan on that occasion has been preserved:

kasumi ni mo	Even in the spring mists
iwa moru mizu no	One hears the sound of water
oto wa shite	Trickling through the rocks.[2]

This verse in itself was conventional, but it acquired a comic quality by its association with the verse composed by the previous man:

tsuyu mono iwanu	The dew lies silent over
yamabuki no iro	The color of yellow roses.

The overly close parallelism between mist and dew would have struck renga poets as comic, as would the contrast between the water that makes a sound and the dew that says nothing. This probably was the kind of haikai verse popular with traditional renga masters in their moments of relaxation; even the great Sōgi composed in this vein. But Sōkan's haikai writing was marked not by a mere quibbling with words but by an earthiness and even indecency that set it apart from the genteel renga of Sōgi and his school.

The first collection of haikai-style renga, *Chikuba Kyōgin Shū*, was compiled in 1499 by a priest whose name is unknown.[3] The collection includes 217 examples of *tsukeku*, or second verses supplied to the first verses of another man. The dominant importance of the tsukeku, as a display of ingenuity or sensitivity, persisted until renga, whether of the serious or comic variety, was finally killed late in the nineteenth century; in most collections of renga the composer of the tsukeku, but not of the preceding verse (*maeku*) is identified. *Chikuba Kyōgin Shū* also includes twenty *hokku*, opening verses of a linked-verse series. Although the hokku was considered to be the most important verse, and was normally composed by the senior poet present at a renga session, the fewness of the hokku in this collection, as compared to the tsukeku, indicates plainly where the art of comic renga was most conspicuously displayed.

The humor in *Chikuba Kyōgin Shū* has been characterized as "tepid."[4] The same might be said of the haikai poetry composed by Arakida Moritake (1473–1549), a Shinto priest from the

Great Shrine at Ise who turned from serious to comic renga late in life, and has been customarily styled (together with Sōkan) as a founder of haikai no renga. Moritake's chief work, the celebrated *Dokugin Senku* (A Thousand Verses Composed by One Man), compiled between 1536 and 1540, is marked by a gentle humor quite distinct from the outspoken, coarse witticisms of Sōkan. Moritake's poetry seems to have exercised little influence in its own day, but it was rediscovered by Matsunaga Teitoku early in the seventeenth century. A typical example of Moritake's manner is his tsukeku to the following maeku:

abunaku mo ari	It is dangerous
medetaku mo ari	But also makes us joyful.

Moritake added:

muko iri no	The log bridge
yūbe ni wataru	We cross in the evening
hitotsubashi	To welcome the groom.[5]

The former verse, a typical maeku, presents the elements of a riddle: what is at once dangerous and felicitous? The answer is given by Moritake: the members of a family cross a shaky single-log bridge when going to welcome the young man they will take into their family. There is certainly nothing offensive about Moritake's humor, but consider a famous tsukeku by Sōkan in response to a similar maeku:

niganigashiku mo	Bitter, bitter it was
okashikarikeri	But it was also funny.

Sōkan's tsukeku was:

wa ga oya no	Even at the time
shinuru toki ni mo	When my father lay dying
he wo kokite	I still kept farting.[6]

The speaker's bitter grief over his father's death does not prevent him from being aware of the totally inappropriate but also totally unavoidable act he performs. This tsukeku may be in bad taste, but it is brilliant. Teitoku, however, was outraged by this example of Sōkan's wit:

> There can be no excuse for shaming one's parents in the interests of a comic effect. Unfilial behavior is condemned even

by Buddhism, let alone by Confucianism. It should be evident that all forms of poetry—renga and haikai included, to say nothing of waka—should serve as a means of instructing and admonishing people, and if a poet does not realize this, nothing will do him any good, no matter how famous he may become. If this poem is interpreted as referring to someone else's father, it might still be tolerated, though another tsukeku would surely be better. But if it refers to one's own father, how could it possibly be funny? Anyone who could consider this funny would not be human. He would be worse than a brute beast. Unless the poet gives due consideration to such matters, he will be scorned by later men, and he will be worse off than someone who does not compose haikai at all.[7]

The criticism by Teitoku was natural for his age, when Confucianism, the state philosophy, held the principles of filial piety and loyalty in particular esteem, but in Sōkan's age, a turbulent period of warfare, fathers and sons were frequently set against one another, and perhaps the unquestioning reverence expected of a Confucian son, regardless of his father's behavior, was foreign to the temper of the times. Or it may simply have been that Sōkan's humor was so unbridled he rejected the normal inhibitions as mere pretense and insincerity.

The collection associated with Sōkan's name, *Inu Tsukuba Shū* (Mongrel Renga Collection), was probably compiled over an extended period of time, as the numerous variant texts suggest. It was long supposed that the compilation was completed in 1514, the thirteenth anniversary of Sōgi's death, but evidence now suggests it must have been later. No doubt the collection was originally intended to serve as a selection of effective tsukeku and hokku for the private use of Sōkan's disciples. From time to time, however, it was augmented by verses chosen either because of their excellence or because some patron had paid for the privilege of having his verses included in the anthology. Persons with access to the collection probably used it as a source for their "extemporaneous" displays of wit when they put on a show of haikai no renga before their hosts at castles and temples throughout the provinces. A diary entry written in 1539 relates how in the course of a visit to the Kōfuku-ji in Nara three renga masters composed verses almost identical with those in present-day editions of *Mongrel Renga Collection.* Quite possibly they were merely "borrowing" verses written long before.

The title *Mongrel Renga Collection* was apparently not given to the work until it was first printed about 1615. It consists mainly of tsukeku arranged under such categories as the four seasons and love, plus a small number of hokku, making 268 verses in all, most of them anonymous.[8] The opening tsukeku at once set the tone for a "mongrel" collection. The maeku preceding it was:

kasumi no koromo	The garment of mist
suso wa nurekeri	Is damp at the hems.

The meaning of this verse is that now, when mist lies over the mountains, the scenery at the bottom fringes of the mist looks darker than that above; it is as if a person wears a garment with hems wetted by the damp ground. To this verse Sōkan supplied the tsukeku:

saohime no	The Goddess Sao
haru tachinagara	Now that spring has come, pisses
shito wo shite	While still standing.[9]

Sōkan unquestionably intended to startle people by the audacity and novelty of his verse. Never before had the goddess of spring been spoken of in such terms: she makes water standing, and that is why her garment of mist is damp at the hems!

To appreciate the boldness of Sōkan's tsukeku we need only examine the tsukeku later written by Sōchō for the same maeku. Sōchō was an especially free and imaginative renga master who excelled in the haikai style, but this was his tsukeku:

nawashiro wo	Chased away from
oitaterarete	The bed for rice-plants,
kaeru kari	The wild geese depart.

The humor in Sōchō's tsukeku is certainly feeble when compared to Sōkan's iconoclasm; apart from the reference to the wet rice-planting beds, which carries over the image of the wet hems, the verse offers little to amuse readers today.[10]

The *Mongrel Renga Collection* consists largely of displays of ingenuity in resolving the riddles posed by the maeku. Sometimes the maeku is almost wantonly difficult:

uma ni noritaru	Look at Hitomaro
Hitomaro wo mi yo	Riding on a horse!

The problem is to add a tsukeku which makes sense of this cryptic remark. (Why should the poet Hitomaro be riding a horse?) The successful tsukeku was:

honobono to	Palely, palely
Akashi no ura wa	Over the Bay of Akashi
tsukige ni te	The moon seems to linger.

The tsukeku refers to the celebrated poem by Hitomaro about a boat on the Bay of Akashi disappearing behind Awaji Island, but at first glance does not seem to mention Hitomaro's being on a horse. However, the word *tsukige* (there seems to be a moon) is a homonym of "moon-colored hair," a color used exclusively of horses. The pun met the challenge of the maeku.[11]

Another common variety of riddle is typified by the example to which Matsunaga Teitoku objected so violently. It is found in less sensational form in the following maeku and two different tsukeku added to it:

kiritaku mo ari	I would like to cut,
kiritaku mo nashi	But I would also rather not cut.

The first tsukeku was:

nusubito wo	When I caught the thief
toraete mireba	And examined him, I found
wa ga ko nari	It was my own son.

The father, discovering a thief, wants to cut him down with his sword; but now that he realizes the thief is his son, he would rather not kill him. The alternate tsukeku was:

sayaka naru	The branch of blossoms
tsuki wo kakuseru	That conceals from my view
hana no eda	The bright moon.

The speaker would like to cut down the branch which obscures his view of the moon, but he is reluctant to cut down the blossoms.[12]

Some of the verses are so crude or even obscene as to embarrass modern Japanese commentators:

birō ni miyuru	How uncouth it appears,
aki no yūgure	This autumn evening.

The word *birō* had at the time a meaning of uncouth or crude, as well as its present meaning of indecent. Like the maeku on Hitomaro, it is intended to pose an almost insuperable problem: how can one add a tsukeku that justifies speaking of an autumn evening, traditionally a time of lonely beauty, as "uncouth"? The tsukeku was:

tebakari wa	Measured by hand
rokusun bakari	Just six inches big
tsuki idete	The moon appears.

The surface meaning of the two poems taken together would seem to be that the bigness of the moon makes it seem uncouth on this autumn evening. This is neither humorous nor effective in terms of adding a tsukeku, but puns increase the range of expression. Fukui Kyūzō explained the pair:

> *Birō* means to commit a lapse in manners; it was considered *birō* to thrust out one's hand six or more inches. *Tsuki* for "thrust" is a pun on *tsuki* for "moon" and was a response to "autumn evening."[13]

Fukui interpreted *tsuki idete* as meaning "thrusting out" as well as "the moon appears." Undoubtedly both meanings were intended, but Fukui did not explain why holding out the hand six or more inches was considered to be so rude. Suzuki Tōzō first interpreted the tsukeku in these terms: "To thrust your hand, six inches in length, into somebody's face was rude, giving concrete form to the *birō* mentioned in the maeku."[14] But the same commentator, writing a few years later, now believed that the object which is six inches long and suddenly thrust out is not the speaker's hand but the "symbol of his virility."[15] This interpretation makes the best sense. The surface link between the maeku and the tsukeku is the mention of the word "moon" after the "autumn evening" of the maeku. The moon may have appeared to be six inches big, the surface meaning, but the humor of the tsukeku surely lay in the indecent overtones of the pun.

It may appear strange that Sōkan, who had taken orders as a

priest, should have composed such crude verses, but a renga master had no choice but to amuse his host wherever he accepted hospitality. The cruder the verse the more likely it was to please the parvenu military lord who had invited him to the castle in the hopes of acquiring some culture. Besides, Buddhist robes signified little at a time when most male entertainers habitually wore them, even if they were not priests, and Sōkan was unlikely to have been inhibited by his appearance. It was taken for granted that renga masters would serve as buffoons and sing for their supper; the surprising thing is that their quips at times attained the distinction of some verses in the *Mongrel Renga Collection*. Coarse humor tended always in Japan to get pushed out of sight; a comparison of medieval Japanese and European farce would certainly show how much more refined even this most plebeian form of Japanese literature was than its closest European counterpart. The very fact that the *Mongrel Renga Collection* was written down and preserved, instead of being pruned or completely hidden, like most works of earthy humor, suggests that its literary worth was recognized early.

Extremely few books of a nonreligious nature were printed before this time, and it is not surprising, therefore, that this frivolous collection of verse should have remained in manuscript until the 1610s, almost a century after it was compiled. Rather, it is noteworthy that it was selected as the first collection of haikai writing ever to be printed; and the next published haikai collection, *Enoku Shū* (1633), edited by Matsue Shigenori (1602–80), plainly revealed in its title (which means "Puppy Collection") its line of descent from Sōkan's "Mongrel Collection." Haikai anthologies soon were being published in large numbers, and haikai poetry itself entered the mainstream of Japanese literature. *Mongrel Renga Collection*, both admired and criticized by Matsunaga Teitoku and his school, was favored especially by poets of the Danrin school, who imitated its ready wit. But its humor, heavily dependent on puns and word associations, is now so obscure that it provokes little laughter. No doubt Yamazaki Sōkan would have appreciated the irony of his collection of puns and indecent jokes having become the object of the scholarly attention of specialists delving into the documents of the distant past.

NOTES

1. Originally, the former verse (*maeku*) was in three lines of five, seven, and five syllables, and the capping verse (*tsukeku*) in two lines of seven and seven syllables, the two parts combining to make a *tanka*. However, most examples in the standard collections are reversed: the two-line link is followed by the three-line link, perhaps an indication of the importance of the tsukeku.

2. Yoshikawa Ichirō, *Yamazaki Sōkan Den*, pp. 2–3.

3. The text is reproduced photographically with a commentary and other scholarly materials by Kimura Miyogo in *Biburia*, no. 43, pp. 1–111.

4. Suzuki Tōzō, *Inu Tsukuba Shū*, p. 270.

5. Suzuki Tōzō, "Inu Tsukuba no Renga," p. 399.

6. Suzuki, *Inu*, p. 133.

7. *Ibid.*, p. 250. The original quotation is in *Yodogawa* by Matsunaga Teitoku.

8. See Fukui Kyūzō, *Inu Tsukuba Shū*, pp. 449–56, for a discussion of the authors.

9. Suzuki, *Inu*, p. 11.

10. Suzuki, "Inu," pp. 410–11.

11. Suzuki, *Inu*, p. 35.

12. *Ibid.*, p. 76.

13. Fukui, p. 33.

14. Suzuki, *Inu*, p. 34.

15. Suzuki, "Inu," p. 416.

BIBLIOGRAPHY

Fukui Kyūzō. *Inu Tsukuba Shū: Kenkyū to Shohon*. Tokyo: Chikuma Shobō, 1948.

Okami Masao and Hayashiya Tatsusaburō. *Bungaku no Gekokujō*, in Nihon Bungaku no Rekishi series. Tokyo: Kadokawa Shoten, 1967.

Suzuki Tōzō. "Inu Tsukuba no Renga," in Okami and Hayashiya, *op. cit*.

Suzuki Tōzō. *Inu Tsukuba Shū*, in Kadokawa Bunko series. Tokyo: Kadokawa Shoyen, 1965.

Yoshikawa Ichirō. *Yamazaki Sōkan Den*. Tenri (Nara): Yōtokusha, 1955.

CHAPTER 2

HAIKAI POETRY

MATSUNAGA TEITOKU AND THE CREATION OF HAIKAI POETRY

It would be impossible to write a history of haikai[1] poetry without mention of Matsunaga Teitoku (1571–1653). Most accounts, however, content themselves with a brief description of Teitoku and his school, and with a few generalizations about their contributions to the art that would be perfected by the great Bashō. Little is said about Teitoku's own poetry or prose, and it is seldom quoted. Of the thousands of verses he wrote in his lifetime, hardly a dozen are included in the standard collections.

It is unquestionably as a historical figure that Teitoku merits study today, when his writings have largely lost their appeal. Not many people now can appreciate haikai poetry that is so dependent on poetic conceits and plays on words, and that provides so few flashes of insight or emotion. Teitoku was famed also in his day for his waka and his renga, but they are depressingly bland and lacking in character. His prose writings, with the exception of the autobiographical *Taionki* (A Record of Favors Received, *c.* 1645), give little pleasure. But Teitoku for a half century was the leading literary figure in Japan, and he commands attention not only because of developments in poetry that he initiated but because he was the pivotal figure of the Japanese literary world during an extraordinary era.

Teitoku was born in the age of the warlord Oda Nobunaga, the first unifier of Japan after the long warfare. While a young man, he served as a scribe to Nobunaga's successor, Toyotomi Hideyoshi, studied with nobles of the emperor's court and with daimyos, and was the intimate friend of Hayashi Razan, the Confucian adviser to Tokugawa Ieyasu, the founder of the shogunate. He also knew many people who did not share the Confucian philosophy of the state, including Christian converts. One of his brothers was exiled for violent Nichiren Buddhism, and another engaged in trade with the Portuguese and died in the "South Seas." He himself rose to be the first important man of letters of the Tokugawa era. Though a conservative, he became the acclaimed leader of the newest and most controversial movements in poetry; though he bitterly regretted that his birth did not permit him to share fully in the court traditions he passionately admired, he devoted himself to the education of classes lower than his own, and has been acclaimed as a *philosophe*, a man of the Enlightenment.

Little in Teitoku's background presaged a career as a *philosophe*. He was born in Kyoto, the second son of Matsunaga Eishu (1538?–1600?), a professional renga poet. Teitoku's family was distinguished. His paternal grandfather, the daimyo of Takatsuki (an important castle town between Kyoto and Osaka), had a family that could be traced back to the twelfth century, when his ancestors fought on the side of Minamoto Yoritomo. His father's excellent education and family connections enabled him to associate on familiar terms with the important poets of the day. Thanks to his father's acquaintances, Teitoku was to receive instruction as a child from the best scholars.[2]

Eishu recognized Teitoku's precocious gifts as a poet and sent him first to study waka with the courtier Kujō Tanemichi (1507–1594), revered as the repository of the authentic poetic traditions. Tanemichi must also have been impressed by the boy prodigy. Not only did he instruct Teitoku in the art of poetry, but he transmitted to the eleven-year-old the secret traditions of *The Tale of Genji*. If we had no firm evidence it would be difficult to believe Tanemichi had entrusted a child with such jealously guarded secrets; fortunately we have not only Teitoku's own testimony but the manuscript of the renga sequence in one hundred links composed on March 11, 1582, to celebrate Teitoku's induction into the mysteries.

Teitoku was profoundly grateful for the instruction Tanemichi gave him. He recalled in his autobiography, "When I went to study under him he was already eighty years old, but not in the least senile."[3] Tanemichi's scholarship was traditional: he devoted great attention to explanations of unusual words and pronunciations, relishing the unpredictable, highly irregular readings. But he genuinely loved *The Tale of Genji*, as we know from Teitoku:

> After his meals he would always spend hours leaning over his desk reading *Genji*. He often said, "Nothing gives me as much pleasure as this novel. I have been reading it for over sixty years, but I never tire of it. When I am reading this book I feel as if I were living in the reign of the Engi emperor."[4]

Like the medieval commentators, Tanemichi searched for Buddhist meanings behind *The Tale of Genji*, finding in the novel the embodiment of the doctrine of Concentration and Insight (*shikan*). His scholarship belonged to an earlier age.

Tanemichi believed he was the guardian of the orthodox traditions of the court, and displayed his contempt for any departures from them. Teitoku recorded:

> When I read *The Tale of Genji* aloud to Lord Kujō [Tanemichi] I thought I was pronouncing the words correctly, but he laughed at me, and said everything I uttered had a provincial ring. He added, "It's not your fault. Ever since Lord Nobunaga came here from Owari everyone in the capital, noble and commoner alike, has tended to change considerably in his speech habits."[5]

Tanemichi's insistence on the standard court speech, especially proper intonation, impressed Teitoku so much that he later induced a disciple to compile the pioneer study of this subject.

By the standards of the time Teitoku was fortunate to have studied under Tanemichi, but the content of the instruction would be of little interest today. A knowledge of the peculiar readings in *The Tale of Genji* is no longer believed to constitute a profound understanding of the work, and the mind boggles at the thought of the boy Teitoku spending months memorizing the secret traditions of how to pronounce the names of the successive emperors and the reign-names (*nengō*). Yet Teitoku, at least until late in life, never questioned that this was what scholarship meant. Nor had he any doubts about the value of the kind of waka in which Tanemichi guided him, the lifeless, formalistic poetry of the Nijō school. He accepted Tanemichi's teachings as the sole legitimate tradition in poetry. But Teitoku was aware, even as a boy, that he could never be recognized as a master of waka, no matter how skillful he became. This art was considered to be the privilege of the nobility, and a samurai of modest standing could not hope to acquire the aura that birth alone conferred. This tendency became more pronounced after the establishment of the Tokugawa regime. The court nobles in Kyoto, shorn of every other form of authority, were officially ensconced as the guardians of the waka.

One means the nobles employed to enforce their monopoly of waka was to control the transmission of the secret traditions of the *Kokinshū*, known as the *Kokin Denju*. The origins of these traditions are obscure, but they acquired their great authority with Sōgi, though he, paradoxically, was of humble origin. The climax to the steady exaltation of *Kokin Denju* occurred in 1600 when Hosokawa Yūsai (1534–1610) presented a new compilation of the three existing traditions to the emperor Go-Yōzei, thereby lending the prestige of the imperial family to the almost stupefyingly inconsequential bits of lore that made up a large part of the work. Teitoku undoubtedly would have given anything to be inducted into these secret traditions, but the closest he came was when, some years earlier, he was shown the covers of the volumes. He recorded:

> On the twenty-fourth of November, 1593, I went with my father to call on Hosokawa Yūsai. He took us to the back room of his house where he opened a box and showed us the contents, saying, "These are all the secret books of the Tradi-

> tion. Look at them." There were four books of different sizes with the words "transmitted texts" on the covers.[6]

Teitoku felt especially chagrined because he knew that in an earlier day, before *Kokin Denju* became the exclusive privilege of the nobility, he might have received instruction. He knew moreover that without this instruction he could never gain recognition as a fully qualified practitioner of the art of waka.

It may have been for this reason that Teitoku's father sent him at the age of eleven or twelve to study renga with Satomura Jōha (1524–1602), the leading renga poet of the day, although the two men were on bad terms. Jōha gladly accepted the boy, even though he apparently could not pay the usual fees. Eishu's decision to have his son study with Jōha may have reflected not only his awareness that Jōha was a superior renga poet but also his desire for Teitoku to associate with the nobles who frequented Jōha's house, craving his instruction. In any case, Teitoku showed such great aptitude for renga that he was allowed when he was barely eighteen to participate in sessions with the acknowledged masters.

Even though by this time the differences in themes and language between renga and waka had largely disappeared, these differences seemed of immense importance to a conservative poet like Tanemichi, who was convinced that any departures from the strict limits of the vocabulary of *Kokinshū*, a collection seven hundred years old, were intolerable. Teitoku probably shared these views. Although in later years he acknowledged his indebtedness to the many waka poets under whom he studied, however briefly, he seemed somewhat embarrassed about his long association with Jōha. Once Tanemichi criticized Jōha, saying he was "clever at renga but has never attained an understanding of the old poetry." Teitoku, though only a boy, thought this criticism was justified.[7] Far from attempting to "return to renga," as has frequently been claimed, Teitoku undoubtedly felt that the art was beneath him. He took greatest pride in his waka.

Close to three thousand waka by Teitoku have been preserved, most of them in the posthumous collection *Shōyū Gusō*. Although these poems were written over a period of sixty years, in the absence of prefatory notes it would be impossible to assign them to particular periods in his life or to detect stylistic development.

Some were written before he was twenty, but the impetuosity of youth did not occasion any challenge of the established conventions; he used precisely the same vocabulary and allusions as the countless other poets of the traditionalist Nijō school. A modern biographer of Teitoku, Odaka Toshio, who otherwise displayed the greatest enthusiasm for Teitoku's writings, said of the waka that they were all "mediocre and platitudinous, utterly monotonous."[8] Teitoku would not have been upset by this judgment of an outsider. He believed that only the expert, the man absolutely familiar with the traditions of waka, could judge the value of a poem; and that the poem itself merited praise not by its unique expression of emotions or unusual phrasing, but by its exact conformance to tradition and total avoidance of the innumerable "faults" defined by the compilers of the Japanese poetic canons. The restrictions imposed on his range of expression by the Nijō school assuredly did not frustrate Teitoku. He had no burning emotions that demanded voice in his waka. Composing poetry required no justification, and he was satisfied with the praise of his peers. In any case, his placid disposition did not dispose him to choose the course of controversy in poetry or in life.

After the death of Tanemichi in 1594, Teitoku continued his studies of waka under Hosokawa Yūsai. Yūsai's virtuosity, extending to many arts, excited Teitoku's admiration, but he revered him above all for his unique knowledge of *Kokin Denju*. In 1600, as the Battle of Sekigahara was looming, Yūsai was besieged for two months in Tanabe Castle by a vastly superior force. Some of Yūsai's disciples at the emperor's court, fearful that if Yūsai died in the siege "the profound inner truths of the Way of the Japanese Gods, the secrets of the Art of Poetry, would disappear forever and the teachings of the Land of the Gods come to naught," arranged for the siege to be lifted.[9] It is small wonder that Teitoku should have worshiped a man whose knowledge of *Kokin Denju* was considered to be more precious than victory in a siege! No doubt it flattered the young man to associate intimately with a celebrated daimyo, and he gladly humored the old man's taste for idle chatter.

In 1603 Teitoku made an important friend twelve years younger than himself, Hayashi Razan (1583–1657). Razan, who had been studying the Ch'eng-Chu texts of Confucianism for several years at Kennin-ji, a Zen monastery in Kyoto, decided to offer public lectures on their interpretations for the benefit of friends, mainly young Confucian scholars and physicians. They in turn requested Teitoku to lecture on *Tsurezuregusa* (Essays in Idleness). Teitoku was reluctant to take the unprecedented step of lecturing publicly on teaching he had received privately. Only after Razan's father and uncle had joined in the persuasion, urging Teitoku to make the experiment of giving public lectures respectable by participating himself, did he finally consent.[10] As so often in his life, Teitoku's initial negative reaction, the product of his naturally conservative and cautious attitudes, was shaken in the end by other people's enthusiasm. The man who so enjoyed hobnobbing with the nobility found himself in the role of a bringer of enlightenment to the general public. Odaka Toshio remarked that "unlike Hayashi Razan who captured the spirit of the new age, Teitoku was overcome by it."[11] Teitoku was to find his most lasting fame as the guiding spirit of the new popular culture, though it would have mortified him had anyone predicted it.

Teitoku delivered lectures "to the crowd" on two works, *Essays in Idleness* and the famous collection of poetry *Hyakunin Isshu* (A Hundred Poems by a Hundred Poets). He himself had only recently heard lectures on the former from Nakanoin Michikatsu (1558–1610), a courtier and expert on classical literature, and on the latter from Hosokawa Yūsai. Both works, though they were to be of enormous importance in the education of all classes during the Tokugawa period, had up to this time been relatively obscure.[12]

Teitoku's commentary on *Essays in Idleness*, called *Nagusamigusa*, seems also to have been prepared largely at this time, though it was not published until 1652. It ranks among the best commentaries of the Tokugawa period, because it goes beyond explaining the meanings of isolated words in the traditional manner and reveals an excellent understanding of the intrinsic value of the work. As for *A Hundred Poems*, it had formerly been taught with the usual secrecy, and even emperors had composed commentaries, but its extraordinary popularity with the general public, retained to this day, can be traced to Teitoku's lectures. It is perhaps no accident that Teitoku chose for his lectures the two literary works which were to exercise the greatest influence on popular culture for several hundred years.

The nobles' reactions to Teitoku's lectures were predictable. Nakanoin Michikatsu, his teacher of *Essays in Idleness*, was furious that Teitoku should have revealed secret traditions to the "vulgar public." Teitoku, far from resenting this criticism, felt deeply ashamed of himself. He wrote about Michikatsu: "If he had been a base person like myself, he would have called me to him and struck me, but being a member of the upper classes, he did not even reveal his anger on his face when he saw me."[13] Despite this embarrassment, the course of Teitoku's future activities as a bringer of the "enlightenment" had been set.

The impulse for his public lectures, as we have seen, came from a Confucianist, Hayashi Razan. Confucian studies had been pursued in Japan since the Heian period, but contrary to their original intent, they were transmitted mainly as secret traditions, the property of the Kiyohara and Nakahara families. The heads of these families jealously preserved their secrets, in some cases passing them on only to their eldest sons, just as the secrets of Japanese poetry or the arts were transmitted. Free inquiry into the interpretation or even the Japanese pronunciations of the texts was prohibited. Even the Zen Buddhist priests who had imported from China works of Sung Confucian scholarship showed no desire to break away from the esoteric mode of teaching the Confucian doctrines. The first departure occurred in 1599 when Fujiwara Seika (1561–1619, an uncle of Teitoku) had at the request of Akamatsu Hiromichi punctuated some of the Chinese classics for Japanese reading. This unsensational event is considered to mark the emergence of the new spirit of Tokugawa Confucian scholarship and the end of medieval secrecy. Razan, quite independently of Seika, had been studying the commentaries by Chu Hsi and others, borrowing books wherever he could find them, and passing on his knowledge in private lectures, beginning in 1600. (He would not meet Seika until 1604.) It was by a stroke of irony that Razan, whose enthusiasm so contrasted with the caution of Teitoku, became in later years the pillar of orthodoxy, even as Teitoku moved steadily in the direction of becoming the central figure in the new, unorthodox culture. Razan's influence may have induced

Teitoku to reject the secret traditions to which he had so long aspired.

Razan's influence may also have been responsible for Teitoku's founding a school about 1620. His school was situated in his house in Kyoto, and was apparently quite distinct from the instruction he gave in waka, renga, and haikai. The pupils were children ranging in age from four to eleven, most of them from the samurai class. A textbook called *Teitoku Bunshū*, compiled by Teitoku about 1628, was apparently intended for use in his school. The book, of the genre known as *ōraimono* (manuals of correspondence), consists of 174 brief letters on various subjects, supposedly sent by real or imaginary persons, dated and arranged through the course of a year. The pupils imitated the calligraphy of the text, written in both the running hand and the cursive, and learned incidentally how to compose letters in the epistolary style. The subjects included poetry, the tea ceremony, medicine, food, divination, and so on. *Teitoku Bunshū* is of special interest today for its glimpses into the daily life of the time, whether in the description of a festival or of opening a cask of foreign wine obtained from Nagasaki. *Teitoku Bunshū* is probably the best ōraimono of the early Tokugawa period.[14] Certainly it contrasted favorably with older textbooks like *Teikin Ōrai*, still widely used at the time though by now almost incomprehensible to schoolchildren.

Teitoku seems to have earned a comfortable living between his teaching and his guidance of aspiring poets. Gradually the latter occupation came to absorb most of his time, though he retained to the end of his life an interest in education of the young. Teitoku still considered his primary work to be composing and correcting Nijō-style waka, though for years he had also been composing comic poetry, both the comic waka (known as *kyōka*) and the comic renga (haikai). Kyōka had first attracted attention as a poetic form in 1595 with the publication of a collection[15] and continued to be a popular, if minor, genre throughout the pre-modern period. In time, Teitoku came to be considered the outstanding poet of kyōka.

Teitoku was hardly proud of this reputation, and treated his own positions with scant respect. He published altogether only one hundred of his kyōka (in 1636), never considering these "wild verses" to be more than a pastime. Teitoku's kyōka, lacking the sharpness or bite of true wit, consist mainly of ponderous plays on words or frivolous references to the classics.

Teitoku's heavy-handed drollery did not suit the genius of kyōka; his attitude remained equally unbending and conservative when he composed haikai. Teitoku, it should be remembered, never thought of his haikai as being *haiku* in the modern sense of independent verses, complete in themselves; the word and concept were invented late in the nineteenth century. On the contrary, he excelled especially at demonstrating his virtuosity by composing dozens of tsukeku (second verses) to the same hokku (opening verse). Teitoku's codes of haikai composition, which established him as the leader in this art, were concerned almost exclusively with the conduct of a session of comic linked verse.

Haikai might have remained for Teitoku no more than impromptu witticisms unworthy of being recorded had his disciples not been more aggressive than he. Two of them, Matsue Shigeyori (1602–80) and Nonoguchi Ryūho (1595–1669), asked Teitoku's permission to publish a collection of hokku and tsukeku. He refused, insisting that the word "collection" (*shū*) could not properly be used for so lowly a form of poetry as haikai. The two men persisted and eventually obtained Teitoku's consent to compile *Enoko Shū* (Puppy Collection), the "child" anthology after Sōkan's *Mongrel Renga Collection*. The two men at first collaborated on the project, gathering notable examples of haikai from all over Japan, especially from Ise, where Moritake's traditions still lingered on. During the process of compilation, which lasted from 1631 to 1633, Shigeyori and Ryūho quarreled, and Shigeyori alone published *Puppy Collection*, apparently at his own expense; needless to say, the selection represented his tastes. The collection included over fifteen hundred hokku and one thousand tsukeku by 178 poets. Teitoku refused to associate himself with the collection, even though he was the most prominent contributor. Shigeyori's afterword spoke merely of showing the work to "a certain old gentleman," as if embarrassed to mention Teitoku by name. The collection proved of major importance in the history of haikai. It encouraged poets everywhere, and attracted such favorable attention that Teitoku reconsidered his negative stand. Despite his wishes, he had become enthroned as the chief figure in the world of haikai.

The characteristic features of the haikai poetry included in the *Puppy Collection* may be illustrated by a few examples written by Teitoku.

1) *kasumi sae*	Even the mist
madara ni tatsu ya	Rises in spots
tora no toshi	This Year of the Tiger.[16]

The poetic convention of mist rising at the beginning of the year is given a new twist by suggesting that because this is the Year of the Tiger the mist is spotted. (The Japanese of Teitoku's time supposed that the leopard was the female of the tiger!)

2) *neburasete*	Let him lick them—
yashinaitate yo	That's the way to bring him up:
hana no ame	The flower sweets.[17]

This cryptic verse, presented to a man who had just had a child, depends for its effect on puns and allusions. It is typical of Teitoku at his best and worst. *Ame* means both "sweets" and "rain." *Hana no ame* is "rain on the flowers," recalling the line in the Nō play *Yuya* that calls rain the "parent" of the flowers; it also refers to the "rain of flowers" that fell when Shakyamuni Buddha was born. The verse is deliberately ambiguous, but the expanded meaning is something like: "Raise your child by giving him sweets to lick, as the rain raises the flowers, your child born as Shakyamuni was, amidst a rain of flowers."

3) *shioruru wa*	Do they droop because
nanika anzu no	Of some grief? The apricot
hana no iro	Blossoms' color.[18]

The key word is *anzu*, meaning "apricot" and also "to grieve"; it is used here in both senses as a *kakekotoba* (pivot word). *Hana no iro* (color of the blossoms) is probably an allusion to the famous poem by Ono no Komachi: "The color of the flowers faded, while meaninglessly I spent my days in the world and the long rains were falling." The poem thus combines a pun and a classical allusion.

4) *minahito no*	Is it the reason
hiru ne no tane ya	Why everyone is napping—
aki no tsuki	The autumn moon.[19]

People have been up until late the night before admiring the moon, and that is why everybody is sleepy today.

Each of the above four examples suggests a facet of Teitoku's haikai. The poems are all humorous, but the nature of the humor differs conspicuously. The humor in the second example depends on a *haigon*, or comic word. Here it is *neburasete* (let him lick). So earthy a word could not have appeared in the traditional poetry, but in Teitoku's haikai the presence of a haigon became the touchstone of whether or not a verse was truly haikai. The haikai poets were not merely allowed to use nontraditional vocabulary but absolutely required to do so.

The third example from *Puppy Collection* contains a variety of haigon that is neither comic nor mundane: it is the word *anzu*, derived from the Chinese. Only words of pure Yamato origin were permitted in the waka or the court renga, and the use of a Chinese-derived word, as well as the somewhat humorous pun, established this verse as being haikai.

It need hardly be said that these verses, among Teitoku's best, in no way compare to the superb creations in seventeen syllables of Bashō or Buson. We sense nothing resembling a world reduced to a microcosm, the poet's profound experiences given in their barest, most evocative essentials. The verses are, moreover, totally lacking in poetic tension. A *kireji* (cutting word), like the *ya* in the first example, generally divides the elements, but no attempt is made to suggest, in the manner of the later haikai poets, that it holds two worlds, one eternal and the other momentary, at once separated and in equilibrium. Such ideals were quite foreign to Teitoku. Even when he grudgingly came to admit that writing haikai could be more than a game, and even after he had been acclaimed to his discomfort the guiding spirit of the haikai movement, he never conceived that haikai poetry could be the vehicle for a man's deepest emotions. It was still essentially a comic form, and though it came increasingly to require skill in the choice of words, it aimed at no lofty ideals.

Teitoku's waka expressed more serious feelings, but even they contain little that is personal. The fact is, for Teitoku and most of his contemporaries, the expression of individual emotions was not a function of poetry. He considered haikai to be instead merely the form best suited to a plebeian age. Teitoku recounted how the waka had gradually been displaced in popularity by renga, only for the serious renga to prove even more remote from most men's lives; few people now aspired to write either waka or renga. "Then, just when sensitive people were lamenting this situation, thinking it must have arisen because people's hearts had become shallow, haikai quite unexpectedly gained popularity in recent days. It would seem that young and old, both in the capital and the countryside, are finding solace in this art. . . . Haikai is a form of waka. It should not be despised as a vulgar pastime. In these Latter Days of the Buddhist Law its virtue (*toku*) is broader even than that of the waka."[20]

Teitoku believed that Japanese poetry, first created by the gods, had changed in form with the times from waka to renga to haikai. The last, he felt, was most suited to his own age. Teitoku elsewhere expressed his conviction that unless the times are propitious, a work of literature cannot be appreciated. He felt that in the orderly but superficial world of his day haikai was more effective than waka in turning ordinary men to cultural pursuits which could rid them of the "three poisons" besetting humankind—greed, anger, and stupidity. Literature was a diversion that kept men out of worse mischief.

Teitoku's school was to publish over 260 collections of haikai before it finally petered out in the nineteenth century. The first two collections, Shigeyori's *Puppy Collection* and *Haikai Hokku Chō* edited by Ryūho, were welcomed by much the same readers as the early fiction (*kana zōshi*). Their popularity must have surprised Teitoku and induced him to reconsider his aversion to publishing haikai collections. In 1638, five years after the appearance of the first two collections, Teitoku authorized his disciple Yamamoto Saimu to publish *Taka Tsukuba*. The afterword indicates how greatly Teitoku's attitude had changed; far from being reluctant to publish, he now begrudged wasting any time arranging the contributions properly. He mentioned also how many haikai had been "difficult to reject," though at one time it would have seemed strange to preserve any. Teitoku attempted to bolster the authority of haikai by revealing how many great men had indulged in the art; the fifth volume of *Taka Tsukuba* includes verses by Hideyoshi, Yūsai, Sen no Rikyū, and other giants of the late sixteenth century. Only now, after the success of two unauthorized collections, had Teitoku decided to give haikai the dignity of a past.

Unlike his waka, Teitoku's haikai acquired depth with time, though their interest lies primarily in the increasing awareness they display of the legitimacy of haikai as a poetic form. It has often been asserted that Teitoku considered haikai to be merely a kind of stepping-stone to the composition of renga and eventually waka, but his writings do not substantiate this claim. At first he merely tolerated haikai as a poetic form written in a lighter mood than renga, but eventually he defended it as a medium with entirely distinct aims and rules.

The most important statement of his final position is found in the collection *Tensuishō*, edited after 1644 from Teitoku's manuscript by his disciple Kaedei Ryūtoku (1589–1679). *Tensuishō* seems to have been one of the most widely read books of haikai composition although it was never printed. Perhaps it was a concession to the deep-rooted medieval tradition of esoteric transmission of knowledge that the book circulated only in manuscript among members of Teitoku's school. Or perhaps the secrecy was dictated by Teitoku's dependence on fees from his haikai pupils, who insisted on being privy to secrets not known to outsiders. In any case, there were so many pupils of Teitoku that *Tensuishō*, even in manuscript, sufficed to establish his authority as the master of haikai theory.

In this work Teitoku insisted especially on the integrity of haikai as a poetic form:

> Some people believe that there is *haikai* present even in waka and that, in general, the proper way to write in this form is to imitate renga, merely adding a slightly comic flavor. But this is a most foolish and shallow criterion. The poetry written by men who have won fame because of their excellence—Sōkan, the priest Genri, Moritake from Ise—shares nothing in common with renga, nor has it the qualities of waka. These masters apparently considered that the words rejected by waka and renga were appropriate for their purposes, and created a new art, the comic linked verse.[21]

By "words rejected by waka and renga" Teitoku meant, of course, the haigon. He believed that the use of these words taken from daily life made haikai at once simpler and closer to the lives of ordinary men than the older forms. People who felt that poetry must be elegant should devote themselves to waka and renga; they had no need of the humble haikai.

At the same time that Teitoku defended the unpretentiousness of haikai he tried to establish the form as a serious art. The way he found most natural to achieve this end was to draw up a code of composition, similar to the old codes for waka and renga. As haikai gained in popularity Teitoku had repeatedly been urged to prepare a code, but he yielded now, only after many refusals. His first attempt was highly informal, consisting of the ten injunctions in the form of waka appended to the collection *Aburakasu* published in 1643. The general sense of Teitoku's prescriptions is that haikai, although an informal variety of renga, is subject to its own principles of composition. His emphasis was not on literary excellence but on the technical procedure of a sequence of comic linked verse. Here is one example:

oni onna	"Devil," "woman,"
tora ōkami no	"Tiger," or "wolf" may appear
senku mono	In a thousand verses
omote ni mo suredo	Even on the front page, but
ichiza ichiku zo	Only once in a session.[22]

Words considered too "frightening" for renga were permitted even on the front page of the transcript of a thousand-link haikai sequence, but could be used only once. This typical piece of advice could hardly have provided more than marginal assistance to a would-be haikai poet.

Teitoku was stimulated into preparing more detailed rules by the appearance in 1636 of the code compiled by his former disciple Ryūho. Teitoku and Yamamoto Saimu prepared the volume *Kururu* in response to many requests for guidance from poets who flocked to Teitoku's house "like children begging their father for something." The book was published only in 1651; until then it circulated privately among Teitoku's pupils. *Kururu* consists of specific advice on the use of words, as in this example:

> *Inazuma* (lightning). Not necessary to avoid mentioning "moon" or "sun" afterward. The sounds *tsuru* should not occur for two verses. Autumn.[23]

The principle of *sarikirau*, words that must be omitted or avoided after certain other words, was inherited by Teitoku from renga. After the word for "lightning," however, there was no need to avoid the words for "moon" or "sun." On the other hand, a poet who used the sounds *tsuru* in his link to a verse containing "lightning" revealed his incompetence, regardless of what *tsuru* might mean in context. The word "lightning" is further assigned to a season, autumn, though it occurs at other times, probably because of the importance of seasonal words in renga.

This typical selection from a haikai code indicates how much less Teitoku and his school were concerned about the content of their poetry than its technical correctness. All the same, the care Teitoku devoted to elaborating such codes enabled haikai to take a great step forward. If Teitoku had not established haikai as a legitimate occupation for a poet, Bashō and the other masters might never have chosen this form. Under Teitoku's leadership, as Howard Hibbett has said, haikai became a "well-regulated, demanding, and eminently respectable art."[24]

Teitoku's final efforts as a codifier of haikai resulted in the publication (in 1651) of the immensely long and detailed *Gosan*, a compendium of the usage and overtones of words likely to appear in haikai. *Gosan* did not represent any great advance on *Kururu*, but it gave the final stamp of authority to the medium and made Teitoku's views available to everyone interested. His school came to enjoy popularity even in remote parts of the country.

Teitoku's greatest contribution to Japanese literature, then, was to elevate haikai to the position of a recognized poetic form. Yamazaki Sōkan and his followers had created in *Mongrel Renga Collection* a work of crude exuberance, but their traditions were ephemeral. Most poets of the early seventeenth century supposed that haikai, as opposed to waka or renga, was a mere "spewing forth of whatever came to one's lips."[25] Teitoku, though he agreed at first with this opinion, came bit by bit to recognize the legitimate functions of haikai. His insistence on haigon not only enriched the vocabulary of poetry but opened up large areas of experience that could not be described except with such words. Haikai was especially popular with the merchant class which, though it retained a lingering admiration for the cherry blossoms and maple leaves of the old poetry, welcomed a variety of poetry that could describe their pleasures in an age of peace and prosperity. Teitoku's codes have sometimes been decried for their inhibiting effect on the liveliness of haikai, but without his formal guidance haikai poetry might have remained forever on the level of the limerick.

The haikai verses Teitoku wrote toward the end of his long career go beyond his customary plays on words, and sometimes he disregarded his own dicta on the importance of haigon. While even this more mature poetry is not of much interest in itself, it suggests the direction haikai would ultimately take in later generations. Teitoku failed as a poet. His verses are today seldom read, and most people hardly know his name. But his place in literary history is assured, as the reluctant innovator who founded the most popular form of Japanese poetry.

NOTES

1. The word *haikai*, written with various characters, was used as early as the *Kokinshū* for comic poetry. Here it stands for *haikai no renga*, or comic linked verse. For a discussion of this form, see Howard S. Hibbett, "The Japanese Comic Linked-Verse Tradition."

2. Teitoku's father, Eishu, never rose above the second rank of renga poets. He was by no means so highly esteemed as Satomura Jōha (1524–1602), a man of plebeian origins and appearance. Eishu and Jōha had a serious falling-out, probably in 1582 (when Teitoku was eleven). Eishu felt he had been insulted because he was asked to participate in a renga session after a man he considered his inferior. Jōha attempted to mollify him, but Eishu, conscious of his great dignity as the son of a daimyo, never permitted the dispute to be healed. Eishu with this proud gesture cut himself off from the main stream of renga composition, to the harm of both his career as a poet and his finances. Odaka Toshio (ed.), *Taionki* (henceforth abbreviated TOK), p. 66.

3. TOK, p. 41.

4. TOK, p. 44.

5. Odaka Toshio, *Matsunaga Teitoku no Kenkyū* (henceforth abbreviated MTK), p. 65. Much of the material in this chapter was derived from this study and its continuation, *Zokuhen* (henceforth abbreviated Z), by Professor Odaka.

6. *Teitoku Ō no Ki*, in Zoku Gunsho Ruijū series, *kan* 959 (p. 4 in 1927 edition).

7. TOK, p. 43.

8. MTK, p. 81.

9. MTK, pp. 108–109.

10. Hori Isao, *Hayashi Razan*, pp. 50–51.

11. Z, p. 36.

12. The first commentary on *Tsurezuregusa* was *Jumyōin Shō* by the physician Hata Sōha (1550?–1607), which appeared in 1604. It was followed in 1621 by Hayashi Razan's *Tsurezuregusa Nozuchi*. Razan's work was published before Teitoku's, but Teitoku's was in fact composed earlier. See Shigematsu Nobuhiro, "Tsurezuregusa Kenkyūshi."

13. TOK, p. 60.

14. The text is reprinted in the Kaihyō Sōsho series, and is analyzed by Okada Mareo in "Teitoku Bunshū no Jidai ni tsuite."

15. It was edited by Yūchōrō, a priest of the Kennin-ji, a Zen temple in Kyoto.

16. Abe Kimio and Asō Isoji, *Kinsei Haiku Haibun Shū*, p. 36.

17. *Ibid.*, p. 37.

18. *Ibid.* The poem by Komachi alluded to is *Kokinshū* 113.

19. *Ibid.*

20. Z, p. 140.

21. Z, p. 144.

22. *Teimon Haikai Shū*, I, in Nihon Haisho Taikei series, p. 102. See also MTK, p. 253. These waka, though first published in 1643, were apparently written in 1635.

23. Z, p. 171.

24. Hibbett, p. 86.

25. MTK, p. 255. The remark was made by the waka poet and novelist Karasumaru Mitsuhiro (1579–1638).

BIBLIOGRAPHY

NOTE: This chapter has been condensed from the essay "Matsunaga Teitoku and the Beginnings of *Haikai* Poetry," in my book *Landscapes and Portraits*. For full bibliographical information (and supplementary material) this work should be consulted.

Abe Kimio and Asō Isoji. *Kinsei Haiku Haibun Shū*, in Nihon Koten Bungaku Taikei series. Tokyo: Iwanami Shoten, 1964.

Hibbett, Howard S. "The Japanese Comic Linked-Verse Tradition," in *Harvard Journal of Asiatic Studies*, XXIII, 1960–61.

Hori Isao. *Hayashi Razan*, in Jimbutsu Sōsho series. Tokyo: Yoshikawa Kōbunkan, 1964.

Keene, Donald. *Landscapes and Portraits*. Tokyo and Palo Alto: Kodansha International, 1971.

Odaka Toshio. *Matsunaga Teitoku no Kenkyū.* Tokyo: Shibundō, 1953.

———. *Matsunaga Teitoku no Kenkyū, Zokuhen.* Tokyo: Shibundō, 1956.

Odaka Toshio (ed.). *Taionki, Oritaku Shiba no Ki, etc.*, in Nihon Koten Bungaku Taikei series. Tokyo: Iwanami Shoten, 1964.

Okada Mareo. "Teitoku Bunshū no Jidai ni tsuite," in *Geimon*, XXI, June, 1930.

Shigematsu Nobuhiro. "Tsurezuregusa Kenkyūshi," in *Kokugo to Kokubungaku*, VI, June, 1929.

Teimon Haikai Shū in Nihon Haisho Taikei series. Tokyo: Nihon Haisho Taikei Kankōkai, 1928.

Teitoku Ō no Ki, in Zoku Gunsho Ruijū series, *kan* 959, Tokyo: Zoku Gunsho Ruijū Kansei Kai, 1929.

CHAPTER 3
HAIKAI POETRY
DANRIN HAIKAI

As long as Matsunaga Teitoku lived he reigned supreme in the world of haikai. The art he established as a legitimate pursuit for educated poets and firmly buttressed with codes of composition was even after his death in 1653 in no danger of reverting to its origins as an after-dinner entertainment. But its dignity was impaired by the bitter struggles of his various pupils to gain recognition as his true successor. The unseemly spectacle of fellow disciples quarreling and engaging in mutual mud-slinging brought disrepute to the latter days of the Teitoku school.

Teitoku's most prominent disciple, Yasuhara Masaakira (1609–73), took the name Teishitsu in 1655 to indicate (by borrowing the first character of his master's name) his assumption of the role of leader of the school. After Teitoku's death he had composed, singlehanded, a thousand-verse sequence in mourning (*Teitoku Shūen Ki*), beginning:

fumaji nao	I shall not tread on it:
shi no kage uzumu	Still my master's shadow buries
matsu no yuki	The snow in the pines.[1]

Teishitsu, alluding to the Confucian proscription against stepping on one's master's shadow, gave it personal overtones by its implied meaning that Teitoku's greatness made it impossible to follow in his footsteps.

Not content with proclaiming himself Teitoku's successor, Teishitsu anonymously published in 1663 the work *Gojō no Hyakku* in which he denounced his rivals within the Teitoku school: Ryūho wrote in a manner too reminiscent of renga; Shigeyori had no character of his own; Ryōtoku and Saimu were outdated; Kigin had lost his senses.[2] Only Teishitsu was praised for his abundant talents and for following the orthodox traditions of Teitoku. This attack precipitated a series of rebuttals and counter-rebuttals, most of which were less concerned with the art of haikai poetry than with manifesting personal rancor. The quarrels of pupils after a teacher's death, no doubt in some sense an expression of impotent rage over a deep personal loss, also had an economic aspect: the pupil who could assert himself as the continuer of the legitimate traditions of the late master was likely to be in greatest demand as a teacher and corrector of haikai (a similarly unattractive series of quarrels would break out after Bashō's death in 1694). Perhaps the ultimate cause of these quarrels was the belief of some Buddhists, especially Shingon Buddhists, that the transmission of learning was necessarily esoteric, passed down from the teacher to a chosen disciple who had been adjudged worthy of the possession of the knowledge. The quarrels among Teitoku's successors also reflect the conviction that haikai was no longer a mere diversion indulged in by renga poets after they had finished a session of serious composition; it was a demanding art with secrets that only the most talented could fully absorb.

Teishitsu claimed to be squarely within the traditions of Teitoku, but his best verses are superior to Teitoku's not only in their display of skill but in their conception. The following verse was condemned by the eminent scholar of haikai, Ebara

Taizō, as typical of the Teitoku school's unfortunate predilection for intellectualization, but it is obviously more than a mere display of verbal dexterity:[3]

suzushisa no	A coagulation
katamari nare ya	Of coolness—is that what it is?
yowa no tsuki	The moon at midnight.

A more typical example of Teitoku school verse, depending on a knowledge of Japanese poetic tradition for its effect, runs:

uta ikusa	In song and warfare,
bumbu nidō no	Both civil and martial arts,
kawazu ka na	The frog excels.[4]

The *kawazu* frog was celebrated for its song, and the Battle of the Frogs was a familiar subject in comic painting. The verse acclaims the frog as a master of both civil and martial arts, like a model Tokugawa samurai. Teishitsu's most famous verse, quoted by Bashō with great admiration, is in quite a different vein:

kore wa kore wa	Look at that! and that!
to bakari hana no	Is all I can say of the blossoms
Yoshino yama	At Yoshino Mountain.[5]

Yoshino was of course celebrated for its cherry blossoms. When Teishitsu saw their full splendor he was rendered incapable of articulate poetic expression and could only cry out in astonishment. The verse has a naturalness, even artlessness, that contrasts with the ingenuity one might expect of a follower of Teitoku. Obviously, even for a man who styled himself an orthodox follower, the literary possibilities of the Teitoku school were rapidly being exhausted.

Among the less orthodox members of the school the divergence from the master's teachings became even more pronounced. Matsue Shigeyori (Ishū) (1602–80) had been, along with Nonoguchi Ryūho, one of Teitoku's chief disciples, but he quarreled bitterly with Ryūho over the publication of the *Puppy Collection*, as we have seen, and later demonstrated his irascibility by picking fights with almost everyone else in the school. He made fun not only of Teishitsu's poetry but of his plebeian face.[6] Needless to say, such a man had many enemies. Shigeyori eventually broke with the Teitoku school to found a subschool of his own that exhibited much of the impatience with tradition and formal rules that would characterize the Danrin school, founded after his death. He violated Teitoku's codes without compunction: for example, he wrote one haikai verse with a second line in thirteen instead of seven syllables, twisting the shape of the verse almost beyond recognition. He sometimes also demonstrated a freshness of conception that went beyond polished frivolity, as in:

junrei no	Only the staffs
bō bakari yuku	Of the pilgrims are seen going
natsuno ka na	Through the summer fields.[7]

This verse (unlike the quibbles typical of the Teitoku school) bears the marks of actual observation: the grasses are so tall that they conceal the pilgrims making their way through the fields; only their staffs can be seen. Again, a quality remote from the facetiousness of early haikai poetry emerges from such a verse as:

aki ya kesa	It's autumn—this morning
hitoashi ni shiru	I knew it from the first step
nogoien	On the wiped porch.[8]

From the first step on the newly wiped boards of the porch the speaker feels through the soles of his feet a chill that tells him autumn has come. The verse is not particularly humorous, but it captures with vividness a sudden awareness of the change of the seasons; this is the kind of subject that later haikai poets would favor. The humble imagery and the nature of the perception itself, not its use of haigon or any other such formal consideration, distinguishes this verse from waka or renga. In other verses Shigeyori depended more heavily on tricks of language in the conventional manner, and in still others he borrowed his imagery and style from the literature of the past, especially the Nō plays. The waka poets had often resorted to allusive variation on the poetry of the past, and the renga masters delighted in making oblique references to *The Tale of Genji*, but, in the words of Nishiyama Sōin, the founder of Danrin haikai, "Nō is the *The Tale of Genji* of haikai."[9] The Nō would be exploited especially by the Danrin poets, ever on the lookout for forms of expression not found in the waka or renga, but many Teitoku school poets, including Ryūho, Kigin, and Shigeyori, composed verses based on Nō, evidence that the differences between the two schools have generally been exaggerated. During this period, when haikai was rapidly evolving, only an arch-conservative would cling to the devices favored a decade before; and any successful innovation, like the use of the language of Nō, was at once taken up by all haikai poets, irrespective of school. This verse by Shigeyori in the Nō manner is particularly successful:

yaa shibaraku	Hey there, wait a moment!
hana ni taishite	Before you strike the temple bell
kane tsuku koto	At the cherry blossoms.[10]

We notice first of all that the poem contains two lines with six syllables each, a defiance of tradition in the manner for which the Danrin school became famous. The verse itself is based directly on a passage in the Nō play *Miidera*: the madwoman in the play, about to strike the temple bell, is stopped by the priest with the words: "*Yaa shibaraku*, kyōjin no mi nite, nani to te *kane* wo ba *tsuku* zo. . . ." (Hey there, wait a moment! What are you, a mad woman, doing striking the bell?) The italicized dialogue from the play was used in the first and third lines of the verse; the second line contains an allusion to a poem by the priest Nōin in *Shin Kokinshū* describing cherry blossoms that fall as the evening bell at a temple is struck. Shigeyori's verse is an appeal to the priest not to strike the temple bell, for fear that the cherry blossoms will fall. More than that, the verse evokes a scene: evening at a temple where blossoms are beginning to fall, and a poet and his friends who are loath to leave so lovely a spot.

Shigeyori earned a place in haikai history not only by his own poetry but by virtue of having persuaded Nishiyama Sōin (1605–82), the founder of the Danrin school, to take up haikai. Sōin was originally a samurai from the province of Higo in Kyushu. He might have remained an inconspicuous figure had he not had the good fortune to serve from the age of fourteen the lord of the fief, Katō Masakata, a man extremely fond of renga who not only recognized Sōin's literary gifts but helped him with his poetry. In 1622, with Masakata's encouragement, Sōin went to Kyoto to study renga with Satomura Shōtaku, a leading master. It was probably about 1625 that Sōin first met Shigeyori and formed a friendship that lasted throughout his life. While studying in Kyoto, Sōin continued to be supported by Masakata, even after the Katō family was deprived in 1632 of its samurai status. In the following year, however, Sōin decided to return to Kumamoto rather than drain the Katō family resources any further. His stay back home was brief; he soon realized that the only life possible for him was as a poet, and he returned once more to Kyoto, where he continued to associate with Masakata, now making a living as a professional renga poet.

In 1647 Masakata was granted the fief of Hiroshima. This may have been Sōin's reason for leaving Kyoto for Osaka, where he became the resident renga master at the Temmangū, a Shinto shrine dedicated to the memory of Sugawara no Michizane. Sōin's move to Osaka in 1648 meant that the Danrin school would henceforth he identified closely with the lively, down-to-earth atmosphere of the great commercial city. But Sōin was as yet far from founding a new school of haikai. He still considered himself to be primarily a renga poet, and composed haikai only as a diversion. Ebara described Sōin's verses of this period as being no more than poor imitations of Teitoku.[11] But gradually Sōin was beginning to reveal his own personality as a poet. One verse, first published in 1656 though written earlier, suggests his characteristic manner:

nagamu to te	Thanks to my gazing
hana ni mo itashi	I got a pain from the blossoms
kubi no hone	In the bone of my neck.[12]

Sōin's verse parodies a waka by Saigyō in the *Shin Kokinshū*: "I gazed so long at the blossoms they became dear to me, and when they fell, leaving me, I was sad."[13] Twisting the words of the famous old poem, Sōin created a moment of plebeian humor.

Sōin's interest in haikai became more pronounced in the 1660s, but he still had not gone much beyond the formalism of the Teitoku school. Only in his manner of linking one verse to another can a shift be detected from Teitoku's reliance on word plays to more subtle associations, but even then the manner was stiff, certainly when compared to the free-swinging manner of the later Danrin poetry. In the meantime Sōin was gradually establishing a reputation throughout the country, thanks in part to his extensive travels. He entrusted his routine work as a corrector of renga to his son, but we know from an essay written in 1670, when Sōin decided to take Buddhist orders, how greatly he was still esteemed. "There were always hundreds of people crowding around his house clamoring for instruction."[14] Sōin became a priest of the Ōbaku sect of Zen, which had its headquarters in Nagasaki. During a visit to that city, Sōin wrote:

oranda no	Is that Dutch writing?
moji ka yokotau	Across the heavens stretch
ama tsu kari	A line of wild geese.[15]

The conceit of mistaking the horizontal line of geese across the sky for Dutch writing was peculiarly apt for a verse written in Nagasaki, where the Dutch had their trading station.

In 1673 the famous collection *Saiō Toppyaku In* (One Thousand Verses by Sōin) was published; it consisted of haikai written by Sōin in all parts of Japan between the years 1663 and 1672. The collection has often been referred to as a typical expression of Sōin's style as a Danrin poet, but this opinion is misleading; most of the poems still reflect the conventions of Teitoku's school.[16] The real importance of this first-published collection of Sōin's verse was to establish him as an authority on haikai, and it would be around him that other haikai poets, eager to create a new style, would cluster. Younger poets, like Ihara Saikaku (1642–93) and Okanishi Ichū (1639–1711), accepted Sōin as their master, even though their own verses were far more radical. Indeed, one receives the impression that Sōin, like Matsunaga Teitoku before him, became the leader of a new movement almost in spite of himself, thanks to the energy and enthusiasm of his followers.

Saikaku first became a pupil of Sōin's when he was fourteen or fifteen. His oldest known verse appeared in a collection published in 1666, when he was twenty-four:

kokoro koko ni	Is my mind elsewhere?
naki ka nakanu ka	Or has it simply not sung?
hototogisu	*Hototogisu.*[17]

The verse refers to a passage in the Confucian classic *Great Learning*: "If one's mind is elsewhere one will look but not see, one will listen but not hear." In other words, Saikaku is asking if his failure to hear the *hototogisu* is because he is thinking of something else, or because the bird actually has not sung. The conception still shows no advance on Teitoku's style, but the clever use of alliteration gives the verse a buoyant rhythm that would typify Saikaku's more mature work.

In 1673, the same year that *One Thousand Verses by Sōin* appeared, Saikaku and his associates produced *Ikudama Manku* (Ten Thousand Verses at Ikudama). Over two hundred haikai poets are represented in this collection, and their characteristic style, which thumbed its nose at tradition, was called *Oranda-ryū*, or Dutch style, to indicate how eccentric and deviant it was. In the preface to the collection Saikaku mentioned his disgust with the poetry being written in his day—"most of the verses sound like the foolish pastimes of old men."[18] *Ikudama Manku*, a reaction against the triviality and tedium of contemporary haikai, challenged the authority of the Teitoku school not only by a fresh and unselfconscious use of colloquialisms, but by a new kind of linkage which depended on grasping the essence of the previous verse and responding to it with aptness and wit, rather than merely playing on some word in the previous verse. Saikaku, indeed, was to gain his lasting fame as a haikai poet not by his hokku, which show no conspicuous talent though some have been remembered, but as an unmatched writer of haikai linked verse. His fertility of invention was astounding. In 1675 he produced by himself one thousand verses in one day, at the rate of one hundred verses an hour, which gave him thirty-five seconds to think up each succeeding verse and write it down himself.[19] In 1677 he raised the total to sixteen hundred verses composed in a single day and night, a performance to which he gave the name *yakazu* after the archery matches at which arrow after arrow is fired into a single target. In 1680, in response to the challenge from two other *yakazu* poets, he lifted his solo performance to four thousand verses; and in 1684, at the Sumiyoshi Shrine in Osaka, he composed the incredible total of 23,500 verses in a single day and night, too fast for the scribes to do more than tally.[20]

In the afterword to *Ōyakazu*, published in 1681, the year after his four-thousand-verse performance, Saikaku declared that it was pointless to waste months and years perfecting a sequence of one hundred verses. His ideal instead was rapid and impromptu composition. The individual verses are generally colloquial in language and syntax, and rarely make reference to the literature of the past. The need for speed favored easy-to-understand witticisms rather than labored plays on words. Most of the verses, not surprisingly, have scant literary merit, but it was not Saikaku's intention to create works of lasting value. His exuberant displays of wit and technique were meant to vanish with the moment. Like so much of the artistic effort of the late seventeenth century, his poetry delighted in the present, in the rapidly shifting patterns of the "floating world" where the waves formed only to break.

Saikaku revered Sōin as the leader of the school, but Sōin moved cautiously. His first major step in the formation of a new style of haikai occurred in 1674, the year after the publication of *One Thousand Verses by Sōin*. Sōin composed a solo hundred links called *Kabashira* (Mosquito Pillar) which showed a marked increase in flexibility in linkage from the heavy-handed Teitoku style.[21] This first product of Sōin's new style was almost immediately denounced by the orthodox Teitoku adherents in *Shibuuchiwa* (Astringent Fan, 1674) which attacked Sōin from the standpoint, "Is not haikai after all a form of waka?" This first shot in the battle between the Teitoku school and future Danrin school ushered in a period of polemical criticism unrivaled in Japanese literary history.[22] Most of these works of so-called criticism consisted in nothing more than a defense of the writer's own school, generally on moral rather than literary grounds. (Sōin's *Mosquito Pillar* was denounced for leading beginners astray, and the use of "vulgar language" was held to be injurious to morals.) The long and unedifying exchange of blasts and counterblasts was to end only when the Danrin school finally triumphed in the 1680s. Occasionally in these writings, however, one finds a statement of literary principle, as in Sōin's remarks of 1674 after the first attack. He wrote:

> The art of haikai places falsehood (*kyo*) ahead of truth (*jitsu*). It is an apologue of waka, a kyōgen of renga. It is said to have been the teaching of the poets of old that one should make renga one's basis (*hon*) but also forget renga. . . . Whether in the old style, the current style, or the in-between style, a good poet is a good poet, and a bad one a bad one;

there is no such thing as distinguishing which style is the correct one; the best thing is to amuse oneself by writing what one likes; it is a joke within a fantasy (*mugen no gigen*).[23]

Sōin's attitude may strike us as being disappointingly frivolous. No doubt it was a reaction to the complicated codes evolved by Teitoku, but to state that haikai is nothing more than a jest composed in the dream that is human existence does not suggest he had gone much beyond the earlier conception of haikai as a game played after the serious composition of renga had been concluded. No doubt Sōin was aware of the anomaly of a man of his age (he was sixty-nine at the time he wrote the lines above) leading a movement of lively young poets. He wrote a friend, "If one writes haikai after one is sixty, one is likely to quarrel with young authors and engage in disputes unbecoming a man of that age. One is also likely to be despised by others for being old-fashioned in one's words, and that is humiliating."[24] Sōin to the end could not take haikai seriously as the primary occupation of a writer; it could only be a diversion. But Sōin imperceptibly changed the content of haikai from poetic conceits to descriptions of actual observation and feeling. A verse written in 1674, when he visited Oku no In, the enormous graveyard on Mount Kōya, has serious overtones despite the facetious attitude Sōin otherwise advocated:

tsuyu no yo ya	This world of dew!
banji no fumbetsu	The solution to all problems—
Oku no in	Oku no In.[25]

The following year, 1675, was of critical importance both for Sōin and for his school of poetry. That spring he went to Edo, where he was welcomed by Tashiro Shōi and his group of "eight or nine" haikai poets. This group had given itself the name Danrin—a Buddhist term, meaning literally "forest of sermons," which had acquired the meaning of an academy. Supposedly this name had originated with someone saying in jest, "The haikai written by people like us ought to be called poetry of the Academy."[26] Sōin was eagerly acclaimed by the group as its spiritual leader, and when asked to supply an opening verse for the session he wrote:

sareba koko ni	I have discovered here
Danrin no ki ari	There is a Danrin tree—
ume no hana	The plum blossoms.[27]

Mention of the plum indicates the season, early spring: it may also be a reference to Sōin's sobriquet Baiō (Plum Old Gentleman), and possibly to the fact that plum blossoms had long been associated with poets and scholars. A local poet responded with the second verse:

sezoku nemuri wo	The *uguisu* will arouse
samasu uguisu	The vulgar world from slumber.

The link is between plum blossoms and the *uguisu*, a bird traditionally depicted sporting among the plum blossoms; but the essential meaning of the two verses is that Sōin recognizes a new school with himself as its leader, and his friend announces that the school intends to waken vulgar poets from their slumbers.[28] The verses compiled during Sōin's visit were published by Tashiro Shōi in 1675 under the title *Edo Haikai: Danrin Toppyaku In* (Edo Taikai: One Thousand Verses of Danrin). The name Danrin caught on, and before long there was a group styling itself the "Osaka Danrin" as opposed to Edo Danrin. Sōin was now supported by most of the active young poets as the central figure of the new poetry. They all but forgot his advanced age. Even in Kyoto, which had been the bastion of Teitoku's school and conservatism in poetry, the atmosphere changed markedly after Sōin's visit of 1678. Sōin composed a first verse for his host, Suganoya Takamasa:

sue shigere	May it flourish forever,
Moritake ryū no	The great central temple of
Sōhonji	Moritake's style.[29]

Sōhonji (the chief temple of a sect) was a nom de plume taken by Takamasa; like other Danrin poets, he wished people to believe that his school was not merely a reaction against Teitoku's school but a revival of the older and superior traditions of Moritake. The afterword to *Edo Haikai: One Thousand Verses of Danrin* had declared:

> We the members of this group, though aware of our inadequacy, desire to preserve the essential qualities of the style of

> Moritake and Sōkan. . . . The haikai and manner of linking now generally practiced has become creaky, but since it is an aberration that developed after the times of Moritake and Sōkan, we call it a late manner.[30]

The announced partiality for Moritake is surprising, for Danrin was much closer to the earthiness of Sōkan than to the rather pedantic humor of Moritake. Presumably it was because Teitoku had openly expressed his admiration for Sōkan that the Danrin poets chose Moritake instead.

Takamasa was to become known as the most radical poet of the Danrin school, composing poetry that would be attacked as sacrilegious and indecent. He took the name Baterensha (Padre Club) as a parallel to Saikaku's "Dutch style" and delighted in shocking with such verses as:

shiroi ame	White rain
noki no kadoya ni	On the eaves of the corner house
tama nashite	Forms into beads.
kaze ni oto aru	There is a sound in the wind:
inu no shōben	A dog making water.[31]

The language of these verses is colloquial in its grammar and almost wantonly free in its syntax (the reversal of the normal *kadoya no noki* to read *noki no kadoya*); it presaged the later Danrin haikai which often delighted in obscurity for its own sake, as a kind of riddle. Mention in the second verse of a dog urinating, by way of amplification of "forming into beads," a hackneyed description of raindrops or melting icicles, was intended to surprise or shock.

The reactions to Takamasa's work were particularly violent. Nakajima Zuiryū, a partisan of the Teitoku school, published a volume entitled *Haikai Haja Kenshō* (Refuting the False and Demonstrating the True in Haikai) in 1679, the same year as Takamasa's collection. Zuiryū denounced Sōin's school as being the "Christians of haikai." He went on, "They form a heresy with respect to the Shinto of our country. They will definitely destroy Japan. A fake priest named Sōin is the ringleader of the Red-Haired School."[32]

Sōin by no means deserved such harsh condemnation. The scant remaining evidence of his theoretical views of haikai, for the most part contained in *Ōsaka Dokugin Shū* (Solo Collection of Poems Composed in Osaka, 1675), shows that the element he still prized most in haikai was novelty and surprise, as he demonstrated in his manner of linking one verse onto the previous one. He praised the following second verse for its novelty:

Toribeno no	At Toribeno
kemuri wa taenu	The smoke never ceases
sōreijo	Over the funeral pyres.
tobi mo karasu mo	Doesn't it make the kites and
kusame wa senu ka	Crows sneeze?[33]

Toribeno had been known for centuries as the site of the crematorium of Kyoto. Its name includes the word *tori*, "bird," which is the link with the birds in the second verse. Sōin was apparently impressed by the unusual conceit of having birds sneeze as the result of inhaling smoke. Another verse highly praised by Sōin for its clever twisting of a *Kokinshū* poem ran:

mugura hae	The kitchen
aretaru yado no	Of a desolate hut where
daidokoro	Rank goose-grass grows
tsurenaki kaka wo	While I called in vain
yobu to seshi ma ni	My heartless mother.[34]

The original poem, of which these two verses are a parody, was by the priest Henjō: "My house has become so ravaged one cannot even see the path to it; it happened while I waited for a heartless person."[35] Henjō's poem is written in the person of a woman who waits in vain for a lover who promised to visit her in the desolation of a neglected house; the two haikai verses describe a child who waits in the kitchen, so long that weeds sprout, for a mother who is neglecting him.

Sōin's praise, far from being bestowed on verses likely to overturn the country by their seditious thoughts, was reserved for flashes of wit that Teitoku himself might have admired. He deplored the excesses of such men as Takamasa, whose defiance of the old codes led them to ignore altogether the basic discipline of haikai in ever more frenzied efforts to achieve modernity. Sōin often reiterated his belief that haikai was a form of diversion, but his training as a renga master had instilled in him a respect for language and form that made it difficult to accept the license and disorder of the more extreme Danrin poets. By 1680 Danrin had triumphed, but Sōin had become disillusioned with the school he had long headed. Too old now to correct the excesses of his disciple, he gradually withdrew from the world of haikai and returned to renga.[36] He died in 1682 at the age of seventy-seven.

On the whole, Sōin's achievements as a haikai poet were not impressive. It is true that he (but more especially his disciples) restored to haikai the freedom that Teitoku had curbed in his efforts to impose order on the emerging form and raise its literary level. But Sōin's poetry has little appeal. Only in his late works does he suggest that if he had lived during the following age of haikai, that of Matsuo Bashō (1644–94), he might have been able to produce poetry of real literary value, as in this example:

na no hana ya	The rape-seed blossoms—
hito moto sakishi	A single stalk has flowered
matsu no moto	Under the pine tree.[37]

In such a verse, seemingly a product of observation rather than of cerebration, Sōin conveys the kind of overtones that would be typical of mature haikai—a single spray of brilliant yellow blossoms opens under the dark green of a pine, proclaiming the arrival of the spring.

The Danrin school's period of prosperity was brief, hardly more than the decade from 1675 to 1685, before it dissipated itself in extravagances. But it had served its function. Bashō himself years later was to declare, "If Sōin had not gone before us, our haikai would even now be licking the slobber of old Teitoku. Sōin brought about the revival of this art."[38] Bashō, who had studied the haikai of both schools, learned from both. From Teitoku he learned the importance of craftsmanship, from Sōin the importance of spontaneity and of describing the present moment. Both elements were to be essential in developing the mature haikai.

NOTES

1. Morikawa Akira and Shimai Kiyoshi, "Haikai Jinkō no Kakudai," in Imoto Nōichi (ed.), *Ningen Kaigan*, p. 114.

2. *Ibid.*

3. Ebara Taizō, *Haiku Hyōshaku*, I, p. 28.
4. *Ibid.*, p. 27.
5. *Ibid.* Bashō's comment occurs in *Oi no Kobumi*. See Sugiura Shōichirō *et al.*, *Bashō Bunshū*, p. 60.
6. Asō Isoji, *Haishumi no Hattatsu*, p. 157.
7. Ebara, *Haiku Hyōshaku*, I, p. 25.
8. *Ibid.*, pp. 25–26.
9. *Ibid.*, p. 36.
10. *Ibid.*, pp. 24–25.
11. Ebara Taizō, *Haikai Shi no Kenkyū*, p. 187.
12. Ebara, *Haiku Hyōshaku*, I, p. 33.
13. The *waka* by Saigyō is number 126 in the *Shin Kokinshū*.
14. *Saiō Inshi Sō to naru Jo*, quoted in Ebara, *Haikai Shi no Kenkyū*, p. 194.
15. *Ibid.*, p. 197.
16. *Ibid.*, p. 209.
17. Ebara, *Haiku Hyōshaku*, p. 44.
18. Quoted in Ebara, *Haikai Shi no Kenkyū*, p. 269.
19. Morikawa and Shimai, p. 124.
20. Jimbō Kazuya, "Saikaku no Ningen Tankyū," in Imoto and Nishiyama, p. 266.
21. Ebara, *Haikai Shi no Kenkyū*, p. 210.
22. See *ibid.*, pp. 33–132, for an exhaustive treatment of the dispute.
23. Quoted in *ibid.*, pp. 64–65.
24. *Ibid.*, p. 214.
25. *Ibid.*, p. 220.
26. *Ibid.*, p. 221.
27. *Ibid.*
28. *Ibid.*, pp. 221–22.
29. Morikawa and Shimai, p. 126. See also pp. 121–22 for the "Moritake style."
30. Asō, p. 164.
31. *Ibid.*, p. 175.
32. *Ibid.*, p. 176.
33. *Ibid.*, p. 182.
34. *Ibid.*
35. The poem is number 770 in the *Kokinshū*.
36. Ebara, *Haikai Shi no Kenkyū*, p. 232.
37. Ebara, *Haiku Hyōshaku*, p. 42.
38. Quoted in Ebara, *Haikai Shi no Kenkyū*, p. 171.

BIBLIOGRAPHY

Asō Isoji. *Haishumi no Hattatsu.* Tokyo: Tōkyōdō, 1943.

Ebara Taizō. *Haikai Shi no Kenkyū.* Kyoto: Hoshino Shoten, 1948.

Ebara Taizō. *Haiku Hyōshaku,* in Kadokawa Bunko series. Tokyo: Kadokawa Shoten, 1952.

Imoto Nōichi (ed.). *Ningen Kaigan,* vol. VII in Nihon Bungaku no Rekishi series. Tokyo: Kadokawa Shoten, 1967.

Jimbō Kazuya. "Saikaku no Ningen Tankyū," in Imoto.

Morikawa Akira and Shimai Kiyoshi. "Haikai Jinkō no Kakudai," in Imoto.

Noma Kōshin. "Sōin," in Ijichi Tetsuo, *et al. Haikai Daijiten.* Tokyo: Meiji Shoin, 1957.

CHAPTER 4
HAIKAI POETRY
THE TRANSITION TO BASHŌ

The bitter exchanges of manifestos between the supporters of Teitoku's school and the Danrin school reached their height around 1680. The volumes they published are unedifying when read today, and they must have been acutely distressing to haikai poets of the time who still clung to the ideals of the art, whether those enunciated by Teitoku or Sōin. But the unseemly exchanges of abuse produced a fortunate reaction. In both Edo and Osaka there were poets who, disgusted with the hopeless bickering of two schools which had already lost their momentum, began to search for some new reasons for writing haikai. Neither Teitoku nor Sōin had succeeded in making of haikai an important literary genre; for both men haikai was a diversion that had a place at festivities but could scarcely be the medium for conveying a poet's deepest emotions. Saikaku exploited to the full the exuberant possibilities of Danrin poetry, but he left an impression of energy rather than strength or beauty. If a small group of poets had not appeared at this time to rescue haikai from the frivolity that had become its hallmark, regardless of school, it would probably have sunk again into the inactivity of the period after Sōkan and Moritake, or else vanished altogether.

The year 1681 saw a remarkable series of developments. This was the year of the publication not only of Saikaku's *Ōyakazu*, perhaps the most typical of the Danrin products, but also of the collection *Azuma Nikki* (Diary of the East) published by Ikenishi Gonsui, which included this hokku by Bashō:

kareeda ni	On the withered branch
karasu no tomaritaru ya	A crow has alighted
aki no kure	Nightfall in autumn.

This verse, especially in the excessive number of syllables in the second line, clearly shows Danrin influence, but it is also totally unlike anything that had come before: it is the creation of a world and not simply a clever play on words. It was about this time too that Bashō wrote the first version of his celebrated poem on the frog jumping into the pond, acclaimed as the beginning of the *Shōfū*, the Style of Bashō. But the changes in haikai were not the work of a single man. A small group of poets, including Itō Shintoku (1634–98) and Ikenishi Gonsui (1650–1722), originally of the Teitoku school, and Uejima Onitsura (1661–1738), Konishi Raizan (1654–1716), and Shiinomoto Saimaro (1656–1738), of the Danrin school, were all actively writing haikai, and each contributed to the formation of the Style of Bashō. Though some of these men had little or no contact with Bashō himself, their works at best touch on Bashō's special domain. Viewed in this light, Bashō emerges not as a lonely figure creating his distinctive poetry in total isolation, but as incomparably the best of a group of poets gradually coming to write haikai similar to his own.

These poets were genuinely talented, and each is remembered today for a few verses invariably described as being "almost worthy of Bashō." Although all composed haikai no renga, their extended compositions are forgotten, and only their hokku are preserved in anthologies. Reading their poetry one gets the impression that if one poet had been born ten years later, or another had not had to depend on versemaking for a livelihood, or another had not become so wedded to a restricting concept of haikai, these might have been true rivals of Bashō instead of merely interesting transitional figures. Perhaps more important than the ultimate failure of these men is the evidence that each was traveling a road similar to Bashō's, one that led eventually to the creation of the serious haikai, a verse form that was short but could express more than an epigrammatic flash of wit; a haikai (or, to use the modern word, a haiku) came to represent the distillation of a great poet's thought.

Itō Shintoku was the oldest of the poets of the transition. He began studying Teitoku verse, but shifted to Danrin with an enthusiasm suggested by the following verse, perhaps the haikai with the most syllables ever composed:

yawaraka naru yō ni shite	The narcissus that seems gentle
yowakarazu suisen wa	Without being weak
hana no wakashu taran	Is the handsome hero of flowers.[1]

This verse, though not published until 1684, clearly belongs to an earlier period in its spirit. The narcissus, unlike flowers evocative of feminine beauty, has the somewhat aloof beauty of a handsome young man. Although the poem is highly irregular, Shintoku's intent was not to amuse by thumbing his nose at tradition, but to test the limits of the flexibility of the form; the underlying thought is not comic but perceptive, suggesting that Shintoku had really looked at a narcissus.

Shintoku was a rich merchant of Kyoto who traveled around the country on business. In 1677 he visited Edo where he joined with Bashō and Yamaguchi Sodō (1642–1716) to compose *Edo Sangin* (Three Poets at Edo). This haikai sequence is still much in the Danrin vein, but in 1681 Shintoku published the collection *Shichihyaku Gojūin* (750 Verses), which has been described as the "pioneer work of Shōfū."[2] Shintoku's association with Bashō extended over many years, and he probably influenced the younger man. A few poems will suggest Shintoku's mature style:

Fuji ni soute	Following by Fuji—
sangatsu nanuka	It was the seventh day or
yōka ka na	The eighth of April.[3]

This verse, entitled "Journey," was published in 1685. Shintoku suggests he enjoyed a leisurely journey in the pleasant spring weather of the third month (April) by mentioning the seventh (*nanuka*) and eighth (*yōka*) days, the sounds of which convey to Japanese ears an unhurried quality that would not be found, say, in the third and fourth days (*mikka yokka*). This care with words—and not for the sake of making a pun or allusion—is reminiscent of Bashō.[4]

meigetsu ya	The harvest moon!
koyoi umaruru	Tonight there must also be
ko mo aran	Children being born.[5]

This verse, written when Shintoku was old, has been interpreted as meaning that the children born that night will be as perfect as the full moon, unlike the waning Shintoku; but that even these children will some day experience old age, just as the harvest moon must wane.[6] It may seem implausible that such simple, unallusive language was intended to convey so much, but the full moon, rather than the young moon, in connection with the birth of a child is surely significant; it suggests Shintoku's real point, as well as his sadness at looking at the moon in old age.

Ikenishi Gonsui, like Shintoku, began his studies of haikai with the Teitoku style but shifted to Danrin. He knew Bashō early in his career and contributed to Bashō's rise to fame by publishing his verses in such collections as *Edo Shimmichi* (New Roads in Edo, 1678), *Edo Ja no Sushi* (Edo Snake Sushi, 1679), and *Azuma Nikki* (1681). At a time when almost everyone else was engaged in writing Danrin-style poems, Gonsui (in 1678) wrote this verse:

unohana mo	The verbena blossoms too
shiroshi yonaka no	Are white: in the middle of the night
ama no kawa	The Milky Way.[7]

The season is summer, when the white verbena blossoms open, but their whiteness suggests the cold nights of autumn when the Milky Way is in the sky. One Japanese authority commented, "It is worthy of note that he should already have been writing such Bashō-like verses as early as 1678."[8] We may wonder too if Gonsui himself did not play an important part in the creation of the new style. Another verse by Gonsui brings us to the threshold of Bashō's distinctive manner:

koi wa hanete	A carp leaps up
mizu shizuka nari	And now the water is still:
hototogisu	A nightingale.[9]

The resemblances to Bashō's famous poem on the frog are striking, and it is tempting to compare the two poems. Gonsui's is undated, but seems to have been the earlier. His note tells us:

> In the loneliness of the village I waited, hoping a nightingale might sing, but instead I heard the sound of a black fish leaping from the water. This made the loneliness all the more intense. Then finally I heard a nightingale.

The verse perfectly evokes Gonsui's experience, and it has the overtones of certain Chinese poetry, but it lacks the absolute authority of Bashō's verse.

Gonsui wrote many of his best verses about city sights and sounds, both of Edo and of Kyoto. There is something suggestive of such twentieth-century writers as Nagai Kafū or Yoshii Isamu in a verse like:

go wa shō ni	The chessboard upset
kuzusarete kiku	By my mistress, I hear outside
chidori ka na	The plovers crying.[10]

The scene is Kyoto, by the Kamo River, famous for its plovers. We can imagine the house by the river, the mistress playfully or angrily overturning the chessboard, and the moment of silence when the cries of the plovers are heard. But Gonsui's most famous verse, published in a 1690 collection, is hardly typical of the Bashō style:

kogarashi no	The winter wind
hate wa arikeri	Had a destination, I see:
umi no oto	The roar of the sea.[11]

The poet wonders where the savage winter wind goes after ripping through mountains and fields, then realizes it becomes one with the crash of the breakers. The poem is ingenious rather than profound, but as various commentators have pointed out, ingenuity has been the one quality most likely to win a haikai verse popular favor.

The most gifted of Bashō's predecessors was probably Konishi Raizan, a poet of rare sensitivity and originality, who apparently was frustrated in his career by the necessity of correcting popular verse to earn a living.[12] Raizan began studying Danrin haikai at the age of six (in 1660) and progressed so rapidly that at seventeen he was recognized as a qualified teacher. He took an active part in Danrin composition in Osaka, but his style gradually evolved in the direction of a perceptivity strikingly similar to that of Bashō.[13] His bold use of language, particularly of the colloquial, suggests that with Raizan the freedom of Danrin had at last been put to a legitimate poetic use.

aoshi aoshi	Green, dazzling green
wakana wa aoshi	The young shoots are so green:
yuki no hara	Snow-covered fields.[14]

The delight at discovering the first shoots of green in the barren, snow-covered fields is wonderfully conveyed by the repetition of the word *aoshi*. In haikai poetry each syllable is hoarded because the poet has only seventeen at his disposal, and anything suggesting repetition is normally avoided as a senseless waste of precious syllables. Here Raizan boldly squanders nine of his seventeen syllables on a single word, yet in no way gives the impression of a trick. Other poems approach even more closely the domain of Bashō:

shirauo ya	The whitebait—
sanagara ugoku	Just like the color of water
mizu no iro	Itself moving.[15]

The transparent fish swimming in the river swollen with spring rains seem to be the water itself. (A variant version of the last line has *mizu no tama*, meaning "spirit of the water.") Anyone familiar with Bashō's poetry will recall his haikai on the same small white fish: "The whitebait—At break of dawn an inch of whiteness." Perhaps one poet influenced the other, but because Raizan's poems are rarely dated, it is difficult to say which way the influence went.

mikaereba	When I look behind me
samushi higure no	How cold they look—the twilight
yamazakura	Mountain cherry blossoms.[16]

The traveler turns back on his lonely path to see in the twilight a cherry tree in blossom. The whiteness of the flowers, which seen in spring sunshine would have cheered him, now has a cold look that intensifies the loneliness of his journey. The tone and atmosphere of this verse are so far removed from the world of Danrin haikai that it is tempting to ascribe the change to the times—to a society that had lost some of its ebullience and had acquired instead a sense of tragedy. But in the absence of a date, we cannot place this verse in a historic setting; perhaps Raizan's genius enabled him to reach this poetic level even at a time when other Danrin poets were still playing with words.

Sometimes a prefatory note helps to establish the setting or time, as in this cheerful verse headed "Living in Osaka, right in the middle of the city":

o bugyō no	The year has ended
na sae oboezu	Without my learning even the name
toshi kurenu	Of the magistrate.[17]

The typical Osaka city-dweller is too busy with his own concerns, whether his shop or his visits to the licensed quarter, to bother to learn even the name of the representative of the shogun's government. A poem of an entirely different tone bears the headnote, "The Child Jōshun left the world early in the spring." This poem can be dated 1712, when Raizan was fifty-eight:

haru no yume	A spring dream—
ki no chigawanu ga	I am not out of my mind
urameshii	But how bitter I am.[18]

"Spring dream" was a familiar metaphor for the shortness of life, but here has a special meaning in that Raizan's son died in the spring. The colloquial tone of the poem gives it an almost unbearable note of poignancy, as if the last word is torn from Raizan in his own speech, rather than in the literary language normal in all varieties of poetry. Raizan and Onitsura were the only two poets, at least until the twentieth century, who used the colloquial language for serious, artistic purposes, rather than merely for fun.[19]

Sometimes Raizan alluded to the literature of the past, but not with the intent of parody or mere display. He enriched his own experience with that of poets of the past in a manner rare if not unique in haikai:

iku aki ka	How many autumns
nagusamekanetsu	Did she spend unconsoled?
haha hitori	My mother, alone.[20]

Raizan's father died when Raizan was nine, and he was brought up by his mother alone. The second line of the verse recalls a waka in *Kokinshū*: "My heart cannot be consoled at Sarashina, seeing the moon shining on the mountains." This waka in turn refers to the famous legend of the old woman abandoned on the mountain by the nephew she had raised.

In other instances Raizan's references to the past suggests the poetry of Buson:

honoka naru	I hear the faint cries
uguisu kikitsu	Of an *uguisu* by
Rashōmon	Rashōmon.[21]

Here the cries of a song thrush, associated with the early spring, bring a breath of new life to the ancient, dead gate at the south of the capital.

Raizan excelled above all in his ability to capture with a single image the essence of the subject announced in the first line, as in these examples:

harusame ya	The spring rain—
kotatsu no soto e	I move my legs outside
ashi wo dashi	The foot warmer.[22]

During the tedious days of the spring rains Raizan has remained at the *kotatsu*, a low table with a quilt over it reaching to the floor; but before he realized it, he has moved his legs outside, sensing the warmth of the spring.

harusame ya	The spring rain—
furu to mo shirazu	Reflected in the ox's eyes
ushi no me ni	Unaware it falls.[23]

The heaviness of feeling aroused in Raizan by the long rains is transferred to the dull eyes of an ox which reflect the rain without really perceiving it.

Raizan's fame as a writer of hokku, verses that were in effect complete poems, was obscured in his lifetime by his success as a teacher of *maekuzuke* and *zappai*, two popular varieties of haikai composition that harked back to the test of wits typical of the early renga. Many poems were distinctly unworthy of him; this may be why his works were not published until 1778. But at his best Raizan was surely one of the masters of haikai poetry.

The only other predecessor of Bashō whose haikai approaches his level was Uejima Onitsura.[24] As a young man Onitsura, a samurai by birth, served various daimyo, but he decided eventually to make haikai his life work. His training had begun early in his native town of Itami, where a branch of Danrin had been founded by a pupil of Sōin. At twelve Onitsura studied with Matsue Shigeyori, and at fifteen became a pupil of Sōin himself.[25] In his autobiographical *Hitorigoto* (Monologue, 1718) he spoke slightingly of his early verses with their typically Danrin fondness for lines with too many or too few syllables, and their tricks of imagery and form. Gradually, as he studied more about waka and renga, he began to doubt that the art of haikai consisted in a display of an ingenious or facetious use of language, as both Teitoku and Danrin schools contended. In 1681, the year of so many other developments in haikai, Onitsura reached the conclusion that haikai must be a means of expressing *makoto*. The word *makoto* became the key aesthetic criterion for Onitsura, and in 1685 he declared that "Haikai does not exist apart from makoto."[26] The precise meaning of makoto, which could mean "truth," "sincerity," "honesty," and the like, was not clearly defined, but Onitsura used the word again and again to describe his ideal in haikai composition. Makoto meant first of all simplicity, as opposed to the over-ingenuity of Teitoku and Danrin poetry; it meant also sincerity, as opposed to the superficiality of the early haikai; and it meant attempting to discover the true nature of the sights described, rather than using them merely as conventional props. Onitsura once likened makoto to an infant clinging to its mother's breast who smiles at a flower and points at the moon.[27] He urged poets to look at nature with the eyes of a baby, and rejected learning as a form of deception and evil. He felt that unless the poet could return to his original state without preconceptions and look on flowers and the moon with a baby's guilelessness, he could never compose true poetry. Once, when asked by a Zen priest how he would define truth, Onitsura composed this verse:

teizen ni	In the front of the garden
shiroku saitaru	It has whitely blossomed—
tsubaki ka na	The camellia.[28]

The poem is apparently an expression of the Zen concept of reality, otherwise expressed in the formula: "The willows are green and the flowers are red." The camellias are white and that is what the poet must say about them, rather than use the camellias as similes or metaphors or as shorthand signals for the season of year. This verse certainly has makoto, whether viewed as a reaction to earlier haikai or as the first step in the creation of a new haikai close to genuine human concerns, but it is curiously bland. This might not seem a fault to a Zen adept—it is unclear how deeply, in fact, Onitsura was influenced by Zen[29]—but the poem is excessively bare. Onitsura admired poems that seemed to be expressions of what had naturally come into the poet's mind, without any ornamentation or cleverness added. But it was not enough for the poet merely to look at a camellia and make a comment; he had to penetrate its essence. The infinity of the cosmos was to be discovered in a single camellia petal; we may be reminded of Tennyson's flower in the crannied wall—"If I knew what made thee, I could tell what God and man are." Onitsura believed that each element of creation had its own nature, and the task of the poet was to understand and distinguish it. He wrote:

> The fact that an uguisu sounds like an uguisu, and a kawazu like a kawazu is because each has its own song. The fact that the uguisu does not sing with the kawazu's voice nor does the kawazu chirp like the uguisu is makoto.[30]

The uguisu, or song thrush, and kawazu, or singing frog, were mentioned in the preface to the *Kokinshū*, and had since become conventional examples of sweet sounds; for Onitsura, however, the different natures of two equally melodious voices had to be distinguished.

Onitsura's dislike of pretension led him to use simple, sometimes even coarse language, and he was not averse to repeating words or to committing other "faults" of haikai. His poetry enjoyed popularity because of its simplicity, but Onitsura clearly did not cater to vulgar tastes; he impresses us instead as a man of exceptionally high principles who wrote simply, even when it would have been easier with his training as a Danrin poet to indulge in verbal display. At his best Onitsura can suggest with the barest means the peculiar atmosphere of a place or sight, as if he had truly absorbed its essence:

hana chirite	The blossoms scatter
mata shizuka nari	And it is tranquil again:
Onjōji	Onjōji.[31]

For a time, while the cherry trees are in blossom, the grounds of the Onjōji (also called Miidera) are filled with visitors, but once the blossoms have fallen the visitors disappear and the temple resumes its habitual calm.

yuku mizu ya	The flowing water!
take ni semi naku	Cicadas cry in the bamboos
Shōkokuji	At Shōkokuji.[32]

Here the atmosphere of a Zen temple in the city of Kyoto during the summer is evoked quite perfectly. Sometimes he chose to depict not the lonely grandeur of a temple but an almost imperceptible sight:

noki ura ni	Behind the eaves
kozo no ka ugoku	Last year's mosquitoes stir
momo no hana	In the peach blossoms.[33]
akebono ya	At break of day
mugi no hazue no	The spring frost at the tips
haru no shimo	Of the wheat leaves.[34]
yūgure wa	At the close of day
ayu no hara miru	You see sweetfish bellies
kawase ka na	In the river shallows.[35]

The tone is direct and colloquial, and the poems require little explanation. They succeed because the tone is so pure. In the last of the verses above, for example, the images fuse perfectly: the twilight hour, when things lose their color and become black and white; the flash of the white bellies of the sweetfish; the river shallows so clear we can see the fish unimpeded. Sometimes, however, Onitsura's simplicity is so lacking in overtones he hardly makes more than a flat statement:

fuyu wa mata	In winter, on the other hand,
natsu ga mashi ja to	People generally say,
iinikeri	"I prefer the summer."[36]

This verse is mildly amusing; it pokes fun at people's ability to forget in winter how miserable they were in the heat of summer, and to say now they prefer it to the cold. But the verse is little more than a wry observation. Onitsura's most popular verse was probably:

gyōzui no	Nowhere to throw
sutedokoro nashi	The water from my bath—
mushi no koe	The cries of insects.[37]

Onitsura, hearing the cries of the insects, is afraid to spill his bath water in the courtyard, for fear of disturbing them. The poem, like Kaga no Chiyojo's equally famous, "The well-bucket rope has been taken by morning-glories; I'll borrow water," is appealing because of the speaker's sensitivity to nature; but at the same time we cannot help but sense that the speaker is slightly too aware of his own sensitivity. A *senryū* (comic verse) made fun of the sentimentality of Onitsura's verse:

Onitsura wa	Onitsura
yachū tarai wo	Walked around all night
mochi ariki	A pail in his hand.[38]

Onitsura ultimately failed as a poet because he failed to realize that makoto alone was not enough to make a full poem out of seventeen syllables. Any kind of poetry of course demands skill, and skill inevitably runs the risks of turning into artifice or even artificiality; but the risk must be taken if verses are not to sound artless. Onitsura's verses have the unmistakable marks of sincerity, but sometimes they leave the reader slightly uncomfortable. Compare his verse on the death of his son (written in 1700) with the one by Raizan quoted above:

kono aki wa	This autumn
hiza ni ko no nai	I'll be looking at the moon
tsukimi ka na	With no child on my knee.[39]

Like Raizan, Onitsura uses colloquial rather than literary language to describe his loneliness, but one senses nothing of Raizan's anguish in this sincere but sentimental verse.

Yet whatever our judgment may be of Onitsura as a poet, his importance in the development of the art of haikai is unquestionable. Makoto alone was not enough, but without makoto a haikai could only be cerebral, a flash of humor or insight. Onitsura's insistence on makoto was an expression of the dissatisfaction with the old haikai that many other poets had come to feel by 1681, and he communicated it to Raizan and other poets, men better able than himself to make of makoto an element of great poetry.

The transition from the Teitoku and Danrin schools to Bashō's was part of the general literary developments attending the coming to maturity of Tokugawa literature. In prose, the appearance of Saikaku's *Kōshoku Ichidai Otoko* (The Life of an Amorous Man) in 1682, and in drama, the first performance in 1683 of Chikamatsu's *Yotsugi Soga* (The Soga Heir), provided evidence of a development similar to that in haikai poetry. Onitsura's word *makoto* is not inappropriate for describing the new element in literature, if by makoto is meant realism—the depicting of life as it actually is led. This element makes the haikai of such transitional poets as Gonsui, Raizan, and Onitsura more believable and affecting than the toying with language which earlier haikai writers had supposed was the essence of their art. These men gave to haikai the emotional quality found in earlier poetic forms, a makoto of feeling, but preserved also the plebeian quality that was the hallmark of haikai. Their craving for something deeper than conceits and quibbles made possible a new literature. With Bashō their efforts would be brought to fruition.

NOTES

1. Abe Kimio and Asō Isoji, *Kinsei Haiku Haibun Shū* (henceforth abbreviated KHHS), p. 64.
2. KHHS, p. 63.
3. KHHS, p. 63.
4. See Ebara Taizō, *Haiku Hyōshaku* (henceforth abbreviated HH), I, p. 59.
5. KHHS, p. 64.

6. HH, I, p. 60.
7. KHHS, p. 71.
8. HH, I, p. 72.
9. KHHS, p. 72. I have translated *hototogisu* here as nightingale because of the context, though the two birds are not the same.
10. HH, I, p. 71.
11. HH, I, p. 75.
12. Matsuo Yasuaki, *Kinsei Haijin*, p. 53.
13. Matsuo, p. 55.
14. KHHS, p. 67.
15. KHHS, p. 67.
16. KHHS, p. 71.
17. KHHS, p. 71.
18. KHHS, p. 69.
19. HH, p. 67.
20. KHHS, p. 70.
21. KHHS, p. 67.
22. KHHS, p. 68.
23. KHHS, p. 68.
24. The surname is read "Kamijima" by some scholars. See Kaneko Takeo, *Kinsei Haibun*, p. 10.
25. Asō Isoji, *Haishumi no Hattatsu*, pp. 189–90.
26. Quoted in Matsuo, p. 48.
27. Asō, p. 191.
28. KHHS, p. 76.
29. Asō, pp. 316–18.
30. Quoted in Asō, p. 317.
31. KHHS, p. 77.
32. KHHS, p. 77.
33. KHHS, p. 77.
34. KHHS, p. 76.
35. KHHS, p. 77.
36. KHHS, p. 78.
37. KHHS, p. 78.
38. HH, p. 85.
39. KHHS, p. 79.

BIBLIOGRAPHY

Abe Kimio and Asō Isoji. *Kinsei Haiku Haibun Shū*, in Nihon Koten Bungaku Taikei series. Tokyo: Iwanami Shoten, 1964.

Asō Isoji. *Haishumi no Hattatsu*. Tokyo: Tōkyōdō, 1943.

Ebara Taizō. *Haiku Hyōshaku*, in Kadokawa Bunko series. 2 vols. Tokyo: Kadokawa Shoten, 1952.

Kaneko Takeo. *Kinsei Haibun*, in Gakutō Bunko series. Tokyo: Gakutōsha, n.d.

Matsuo Yasuaki. *Kinsei Haijin*. Tokyo: Ōfūsha, 1962.

CHAPTER 5
HAIKAI POETRY
MATSUO BASHŌ
(1644–1694)

With rare exceptions the Japanese authors who lived before the middle of the seventeenth century exist today almost exclusively in terms of their own writings. However, the vastly increased output of books from this time onward include miscellaneous writings that enable us to see some writers from many angles with a clarity never before possible. This is true especially of Matsuo Bashō. In his own day he was idolized, and the interest he aroused wherever he traveled was without parallel. He himself left biographical evidence in the form of diaries and letters; over 165 letters enable us to trace his movements, sometimes with day-to-day accuracy, particularly during the last years of his life. The worship of Bashō was moreover so intense that not only were his casual writings treasured, but his utterances were faithfully transcribed and published by disciples.

Yet for all the information scholars have accumulated, many points about Bashō's life remain debatable.[1] It was long assumed, for example, that although Bashō never took Buddhist orders, he led a life of such rigorous devotion to his art that he never formed any romantic attachments. When, however, the scholar Nunami Keion (1877–1927) discovered in an eighteenth-century book of gossip written by the pupil of a pupil of Bashō's the statement that a nun named Jutei had been Bashō's mistress in his youthful days and that they had several children, he exclaimed in delight, "How wonderful of you, dear Bashō, to have had a mistress!"[2] Nunami, like many other Japanese critics, found it far more congenial to think of Bashō as a man with "human" weaknesses than as the austere saint of haikai. On the basis of this "discovery" (denied by other scholars[3]) some critics have read into Bashō's verses anguish over leaving his mistress and children and similar emotions appropriate to such an item of biographical data.

Obviously it is important to our understanding of Bashō to know if his life was consecrated to monastic devotion before the altar of haikai poetry, or if in fact, like most haikai poets of his day, he had a household with a wife and children. If the latter is the case, it is puzzling why he should have been at such pains to keep this family life a secret. Perhaps a Confucian sense of decorum inhibited his open admission of what he considered to be an unbecoming weakness; or perhaps his silence is negative testimony to a celibate life. It is the peculiar intimacy we feel with Bashō that makes such matters of interest; the more we know about him, the more we want to know.

Bashō was born in Ueno, a town in Iga province. The town itself dated back only to 1585, when a castle was built on a hillside overlooking the site. In 1608 the shogunate bestowed on Tōdō Takatora, the daimyo of Uwajima (on the island of Shikoku), the combined fiefs of Iga and Ise, and Ueno became the political and economic center of the region.[4] Bashō's father, Matsuo Yozaemon (d. 1656), a samurai of minor rank, moved to Ueno from the nearby town of Tsuge. The title of samurai meant little more than that he was expected to serve as a soldier in times of emergency; he received no stipend from the Tōdō household, and was forced to earn a meager living as a teacher of calligraphy.[5] Bashō's mother (d. 1683) was of samurai stock, perhaps somewhat superior to that of Bashō's father.

Bashō was the second son. His elder brother, Hanzaemon (d. 1701), served the Tōdō family in a minor capacity throughout his life, and Bashō's sisters married local men of the same lower-rank samurai class. Bashō's future career was determined at an early age when he had the good fortune to become friends with Sengin (Tōdō Yoshitada), a boy two years older than himself who was the heir of the head of an important branch of the Tōdō clan. It is not clear at what age the two boys became friends; some sources state that it was as children, others that it was only after Bashō had already demonstrated his skill as a haikai poet. In any case, Sengin's friendship and protection enabled Bashō to receive training in haikai composition from the outstanding literary figure Kitamura Kigin (1624–1705), a poet and critic of the Teitoku school. Bashō's earliest known verse, dating from 1662 (when he was eighteen), was:

haru ya koshi	Has the spring come
toshi ya yukiken	Or has the old year departed?
kotsugomori	The night before New Year's Eve.

The wording of this verse and its poetical conceit (the speaker cannot be sure, he says, whether one year is ending or a new one has begun) are derived from the *Kokinshū*,[6] and the verse clearly belongs to the artificial manner of Teitoku's school. It is hardly impressive, but it suggests that Bashō must already have had several years of training in haikai.

Bashō acquired about this time his first name as a haikai poet, Sōbō (or, to give it its Japanese rendering, Munefusa). There were nearly a hundred haikai poets in the province of Iga at the time, but only a few managed to publish regularly in the collections edited in Kyoto and other centers. Bashō and Sengin were so honored. In 1664 Matsue Shigeyori's collection *Sayo no Nakayama Shū* included two poems by Bashō[7] and one by Sengin, the first appearance for both in print. One of Bashō's verses ran:

ubazakura	Old-lady cherry blossoms—
saku ya rōgo no	Have they flowered? A final
omoiide	Keepsake for old age.

The language of this verse, again in the Teitoku vein, derives from a passage in the Nō play *Sanemori*. "Old-lady cherry blossoms" were so called because they bloomed when the tree was leafless, giving rise to the pun between *ha-nashi*, "leafless" and *ha-nashi*, "toothless." The verse indicates that Bashō, abreast of current fashions in haikai, borrowed phrases from the Nō plays with pedantic humor. He was still very far from being a master.

In 1665, the thirteenth anniversary of Teitoku's death, Sengin himself sponsored a memorial one-hundred-verse session of linked haikai, attended by Kitamura Kigin. Contributions were offered by Bashō and other Iga poets. Sengin gave the hokku (opening verse):

no wa yuki ni	The fields under snow
karuredo karenu	Have withered, but unwithered
shion ka na	Are the asters.

The focal point of this verse is the pun on *shion*, "asters" and *shion*, "the debt owed one's teacher" (in this case, Teitoku). In the light of Bashō's subsequent activity as a haikai poet we are apt to dismiss his "indebtedness" to Teitoku as minor; certainly his verses in the Teitoku manner do not remotely resemble those of the mature Bashō. But the care in the use of language insisted on by a learned poet like Kigin unquestionably influenced Bashō, and may have first revealed to him that haikai poetry should not only be of the moment but for all time, no less than a waka or renga. Bashō's early training lingered with him; even in his masterpiece *Oku no Hosomichi* (The Narrow Road of Oku), which describes his journey of 1689, we find:

Kisagata ya	Kisagata—
ame ni Seishi ga	In the rain Seishi sleeping,
nebu no hana	Mimosa blossoms.

Although this verse is infinitely superior to any Bashō wrote under the direct influence of the Teitoku school, the use of the *kakekotoba* (pivot word) on the word *nebu* ("to sleep," but also "mimosa") harks back to the Teitoku manner, as does the reference to Seishi (Hsi Shih), a Chinese beauty known for her perpetually melancholy expression. This is not the most appealing aspect of Bashō's poetry, but we must not forget it was part of his background.

In 1666 Sengin suddenly died at twenty-four. Bashō suffered a double blow: not only did he lose a friend and companion in the art of haikai, but a protector, the only person likely to secure him advancement as a samurai. Years later Bashō would remember Sengin with a famous verse, composed in the spring of 1688:

samazama no	How many many
koto omoidasu	Memories they bring to mind—
sakura ka na	The cherry blossoms.

After Sengin's death Bashō apparently remained in Ueno, even though he no longer enjoyed special favor within the Tōdō household. Evidently he threw himself more and more into haikai, as is evidenced by verses published from 1667 to 1672. He probably paid occasional visits to Kyoto during this period; his first work, *Kai-ōi* (Covering Shells, 1672) mentions his delight in the pleasures of the capital. *Covering Shells*, a collection of thirty pairs of humorous verses by local poets, matched and judged by Bashō with various comments, was published at Bashō's own expense. We may wonder where he obtained the funds. Perhaps he judged it necessary to publish a book before he embarked on a career as a professional poet and corrector of poetry (*tenja*).

In the spring of 1672 Bashō, aged twenty-eight, left for Edo to make his fortune. It is not clear why he chose this city. Perhaps he felt he had a better chance of establishing himself in a comparatively new city than in Kyoto or Osaka, where there was far greater competition from other poets. For his first three years in Edo he published little. About 1678 he took a minor post in the Department of Water Supply, probably as a means of augmenting his income rather than as a first step in an official career. Nevertheless, despite his country background and lack of influence, Bashō gradually began to build up a reputation.

At the time there were two main groups of haikai poets in Edo: those like Tashiro Shōi, the founder of Edo Danrin, who were natives of the region, and those who had come to Edo from the area of Kyoto and Osaka; Bashō belonged to the latter group. He frequented the literary salon of the daimyo of Iwakidaira,

Naitō Yoshiyasu (1619–85, known by his penname, Fūko), and his son the poet Rosen (1655–1733). Father and son enjoyed associating with Kigin, Shigeyori, and Sōin, and frequently entertained haikai poets at their house. In 1675 Fūko had invited Nishiyama Sōin to Edo, and Bashō took part in the haikai session welcoming him. On this occasion he first used the name Tōsei, which remained his official penname even after he came more commonly to be known as Bashō.[8]

Sōin's visit to Edo was of crucial importance, as we have seen, in establishing the local Danrin style; it also exerted considerable influence on Bashō and other poets not associated with Shōi's group. In 1676 Bashō and his friend Yamaguchi Sodō (1642–1716) joined in a *ryōgin,* or linked verse composed by two men, that proves they had already been affected by the new style. Sodō wrote:

ume no kaze	A plum-scented wind
haikai koku ni	In the land of haikai
sakan nari	Blows triumphant.

Here "plum" refers to Sōin's nom de plume, Baiō (Plum Old Man); the verse thus proclaims the success of the Danrin school. Bashō's response was:

kochitōzure mo	Even for the likes of us
kono toki no haru	This is the spring of the age.[9]

In the summer of the same year Bashō returned to Iga for a visit, bringing back to Edo with him a boy named Tōin, possibly a nephew, whom he may have intended to make his heir. In the winter of 1677, Fūko sponsored a haikai verse-matching contest, the largest affair of this kind ever held. The judges included Kigin, Shigeyori, and the priest Ninku, invited like many of the participants all the way from Kyoto and Osaka. Bashō submitted twenty verses. He made valuable acquaintances at the session, and in the following year became friendly with such visitors as Shintoku, Saimaro, and Gonsui, who included verses by Bashō in their published collections.

Bashō began to form his own school about 1677. His first pupils included such later stalwarts of the Bashō style as Sugiyama Sampū (1647–1732), Takarai Kikaku (1661–1707), and Hattori Ransetsu (1654–1707). These men associated with

Bashō not merely as pupils paying fees in return for their master's guidance, but as true disciples who propagated the new doctrines of haikai. Sampū, a rich merchant, proved again and again a generous patron when Bashō was in financial need. The school of Bashō grew manifold in the years that followed, but his first pupils retained a special place in his affections. In 1680 Bashō published *Tōsei Montei Dokugin Nijū Kasen* (Twenty Individual Kasen by Pupils of Tōsei). Each pupil was represented by a *kasen*, a thirty-six-verse haikai sequence composed entirely by himself, instead of by a small sampling of verse in a large collection, the usual practice. This was surely an expression of Bashō's confidence in his own school. In the same year Kikaku and Sampū each published collections. Bashō in 1680, at the age of thirty-six, had achieved top rank among the haikai poets of his day, both because of his own poetry, published in Kyoto as well as Edo, and because of the poetry written by his disciples.

Bashō's success did not, however, bring financial prosperity. Apparently he was reluctant to engage in correcting pupils' verses, the normal source of income for haikai masters, perhaps because of the obsequiousness this usually involved. He sold examples of his calligraphy and depended on gifts from his pupils. Nevertheless, a conspicuous number of poems composed during 1680–82 touch on the theme of poverty.[10] But this theme may have reflected less on Bashō's financial difficulties than on his increasing absorption with Chinese literature, in which honorable poverty, representing a rejection of worldly ambitions, plays such an important part in poetic traditions. In 1680 Bashō moved from Edo to Fukagawa, an inconvenient place on the outskirts of the city. The site, being close to the river, was subject to flooding, but its remoteness probably appealed to Bashō. He seems to have turned from the Danrin style, essentially a product of city life, and to have searched for something deeper than the flashes of wit and take-offs on contemporary mores at which the Danrin poets excelled. Yet he could not altogether desert the city to live in some lonely temple. The society of men was necessary, not only because Bashō depended on his pupils, but because haikai linked verse, an essential part of his poetry, demanded a group of like-minded poets. Bashō was influenced by Danrin poetry, even when he came to reject it, and its emphasis on the ever-changing nature of human society was perhaps its greatest contribution to Bashō's poetry, for it preserved him from the danger of losing vital contact with mundane life.

In 1681, the year after Bashō's move to his cottage in Fukagawa, a disciple, thinking to improve the rather desolate appearance of the place, planted a *bashō* tree in the garden. The bashō, a variety of banana tree that bears no fruit, was prized for its broad green leaves that are easily torn by the slightest wind, a ready symbol for the sensitivity of the poet. The bashō plant thrived so well in the damp soil that visitors began to refer to the place as the Bashō-an (Cottage of the bashō tree), and before long (probably 1682) Bashō was using the name for himself. Years later (in 1692) he would write a delightful essay describing how closely he associated himself with the tree. One verse from about 1681 describes the atmosphere of his thatched hut:

bashō nowaki shite	Bashō tree in the storm—
tarai ni ame wo	A night spent listening to
kiku yo ka na	Rain in a basin.

The long first line indicates Bashō was still under Danrin influence, but the lonely atmosphere—rain dripping through the roof into a basin—evokes not only the season of autumnal rain but the isolation of Bashō's retreat. From the same year dates Bashō's first masterpiece:

kareeda ni	On the withered branch
karasu no tomaritaru ya	A crow has alighted—
aki no kure	Nightfall in autumn.

The irregularity of the second line betrays Danrin influence, and scholars have pointed out that the theme is derived from a Chinese poem topic, "shivering crow in a withered tree." But the magic of this verse cannot be explained away. It is a superb example of Bashō's ability to evoke a world with a few words. The crow alighting on the withered branch is a moment of actual observation, the "now" of the poem, and it is equated silently with the coming of an autumn nightfall; each defines the other, not as a metaphor but as a moment "in and out of time." The last line can also be interpreted as meaning "the twilight of autumn" (late autumn), and surely this ambiguity was intended.

The scene is a monochrome: the black crow perched on a barren branch at the time of day and season of year when colors vanish. Like the best monochromes, it evokes more than bright colors. The stillness of the autumn dusk, the brooding intensity of the crow on the withered bough combine to present an unforgettable scene. The sounds too, especially the key words *karasu*, *kareeda*, and *kure*, contribute to the unique rhythm, and the long middle line was not merely a Danrin thumbing-of-the-nose at metrics but an attempt to convey the weight of the moment when the crow alighted. The importance of the verse was immediately recognized; it was listed as "one of the three verses of our style" in a collection published in 1681.[11]

About this time Bashō began studying Zen Buddhism with the monk Butchō, who was living in the neighborhood. It is difficult to measure Zen's influence in Bashō's writings. The flash of inspiration that enabled Bashō to detect in the quite ordinary sight of a crow alighted on a branch something of universal significance is of course akin to the spirit of Zen, but this particular verse seems to antedate his instruction from Butchō. Probably different streams were converging to produce his new style: his dissatisfaction with the superficial Danrin manner; indirect influence from late Danrin poets like Shintoku or Onitsura who were attempting to impart new depth to haikai; Bashō's growing interest in Chinese literature, especially the poetry of Tu Fu and Li Po and the philosophy of Chuang Tzu; and his equally growing admiration for the Japanese monk-poets of the past, above all Saigyō and Sōgi. His studies of Zen were probably occasioned by a similar deepening of his interests. In 1683 Bashō wrote the preface to Kikaku's collection *Minashiguri* (Empty Chestnuts) and praised the work for "tasting of the spiritual flavor of the wine of Li Po and Tu Fu and the religious broth" of the Zen poet Han Shan; for "searching for the style" of Saigyō's waka; and for "attiring in the garb" of the Japanese language the poetry of Po Chü-i.[12] No doubt these were precisely the qualities Bashō most wished for his own style. Haikai shared the literary spirit of the great Chinese and Japanese masters, and the Zen quality of a poet like Han Shan, but it had its own domain too, in the familiar and even vulgar activities of contemporary life.

At the end of 1682 one of the great fires for which Edo was famous swept through the city. It reached as far as Fukagawa, destroying Bashō's cottage. For six months he stayed with friends in Kai province, and not until the end of the year was a new cottage ready, built on approximately the same site as the old one. Sodō had been chiefly responsible for gathering the funds needed for the new house. In the meantime, in the sixth month of 1683, Bashō's mother died in Ueno. Bashō may have decided as soon as he heard the news to pay his respects at her grave, but he did not actually leave Edo until the eighth month of 1684.[13] It is not clear why he delayed so long, but perhaps a desire to visit his old home, where his mother had died, was not uppermost in his mind when he set out on the journey. Bashō seems to have felt that the time had come to make a dramatic change in his style, and that a journey might provide the impetus.

The journey of 1684 occasioned the first of five narratives that stand as markers in Bashō's career. He set out with professed feelings of dread, as if he had little hope of returning alive. Undoubtedly he considered it would not be a pleasant excursion but an arduous pilgrimage that would test him physically and mentally. This was in the tradition of the travelers of the past; Bashō well knew how many poets had died on the road. Certainly the long journey, most of it on foot, was infinitely more taxing than the modern equivalent, but by Bashō's day travel along the Tōkaidō, the main road between Edo and Kyoto, had become relatively easy and convenient. There was a steady flow of traffic, and at each station along the way comfortable inns and places of amusement catered to travelers. But Bashō, seeing himself as a poet-wayfarer, threw himself into the part. This was not so much a pose as an effort to savor to the utmost the essence of travel, and this meant not a cheerful room and a good dinner at an inn but the uncertainty, fatigue, and even danger that being alone and far from home implied.

The account of the journey of 1684–85 describes briefly highlights of the nine months he spent away from Edo, wandering through the provinces of Ise, Iga, Yamato, Yamashiro, Ōmi, and Owari. Bashō probably wrote this account soon after his return, but it was not published until 1698, after his death. It is not clear which title Bashō himself intended for the work, but two, *Nozarashi Kikō* (Exposure in the Fields, a Travel Account) and *Kasshi Ginkō* (Poetic Journey of 1684) are most frequently used in modern editions. The former title derives from the opening passage:

> When I set out on my journey of a thousand leagues I packed no provisions for the road. I clung to the staff of that pilgrim of old who, it is said, "entered the realm of nothingness under the moon after midnight." The voice of the wind sounded cold somehow as I left my tumbledown hut on the river in the eighth moon of the Year of the Rat, 1684.
>
> | | |
> |---|---|
> | *nozarashi wo* | Bones exposed in a field— |
> | *kokoro ni kaze no* | At the thought, how the wind |
> | *shimu mi ka na* | Bites into my flesh. |
>
> | | |
> |---|---|
> | *aki tō tose* | Autumn—this makes ten years; |
> | *kaette Edo wo* | Now I really mean Edo |
> | *sasu kokyō* | When I speak of "home." |

The prose passage, though assuredly reflecting Bashō's apprehensions as he set out on his journey, indicates how aware he was of his special role as a traveler, and his special interest in Chinese literature. His first words paraphrase Chuang Tzu: "A man who is going a thousand *li* should gather provisions three months ahead."[14] The second sentence quotes a poem by the Chinese Zen monk Kuang-wen (1189–1263),[15] and the pilgrim's staff was his, though Bashō may also have been thinking of Saigyō and Sōgi. The opening lines thus tell us indirectly that Bashō, like the Zen monks of the past, is about to journey into a realm untouched by mundane human concerns, the "village of Not-Even-Anything" of Chuang Tzu.[16]

The two verses follow from the prose: in the first Bashō wonders if his bones will not lie exposed in some field, after he has dropped of fatigue and hardship on his journey, and the thought sends a chill through him. In the second he relates (with less emotion) that although he is on his way to his birthplace, he now thinks of Edo as being home. Something of the apprehension of the first verse lingers into the second, with its overtones of uncertainty on leaving home, though Bashō is actually returning to his first home.

A certain awkwardness in the balance of poetry and prose is noticeable in this diary, occasioned perhaps by Bashō's inexperience in handling the poetic-diary form. First importance is given to the hokku composed on the way, and the prose sometimes consists of no more than prefatory notes. A shifting of the tone also makes the work seem a series of episodes rather than a unified whole; this may have been an unconscious product of Bashō's training in haikai linked verse, in which the prolongation of a given theme or mood beyond a couple of links was avoided. Only with his fifth and last travel account, *Oku no Hosomichi* (The Narrow Road of Oku), would Bashō achieve a balance between poetry and prose, and a structure that actually benefited from linked-verse usage.

The Chinese influence, apparent in the opening section, so dominates the prose of *Exposure in the Fields* that sometimes it reads like a translation from the Chinese. Even the thematic material often comes directly from a Chinese source, or is modified in the light of famous Chinese examples, as in the well-known passage describing the child encountered near the Fuji River:

> As we walked along by the Fuji River, we noticed an abandoned child, perhaps three years old, weeping pitifully. I wondered if its parents, buffeted by the swift currents of this river, and unable to withstand the rough waves of the floating world, had abandoned him here, thinking his life would last only as long as the dew. Would the tender clover blossoms scatter tonight in the autumn wind beneath the plant, or would they wither tomorrow? With these thoughts I took some food from my sleeve and threw it to the child as we passed.

saru wo kiku hito	What would poets who grieved
sutego ni aki no	To hear monkeys feel about this child
kaze ika ni	In the autumn wind?

It was a commonplace of Chinese poetry to express grief over the pitiful cries of monkeys but, Bashō suggests, such grief is as nothing compared to the feelings aroused by a child abandoned by its parents, no doubt because of poverty. Modern readers find it difficult, however, to understand why Bashō should have done no more than throw some food at the child. We may wonder why he could not have picked up the child or attempted in some way to save it from certain death by exposure or starvation. Such doubts have suggested to some scholars that the whole passage is a literary invention, a borrowing of a familiar Chinese example to lend weight to Bashō's original theme, death on a journey.[17] Others insist, instead, that an abandoned child was so common a sight at that time that Bashō could not have been expected to respond with the horror we would feel; besides, he was compelled by his consecration to his art to forsake normal obligations that might prevent him from accomplishing his journey. In any case, the use of Chinese material was intended to give depth and universality to the situation, whether real or imagined.

Some of the poetry composed on the journey reveals Chinese influence even more plainly:

uma ni nete	I dozed on my horse—
zammu tsuki tōshi	Half in dreams, the moon distant;
cha no keburi	Smoke of breakfast tea.

The meaning of this poem is clear: Bashō, dozing on his horse, awakens. Still under the spell of his dream, he notices the moon far off in the sky as the dawn comes, and smoke rising from houses where breakfast is being prepared. The prose passage that precedes this verse states:

> The waning moon could be seen only faintly, and at the foot of the mountains it was pitch black. Letting my whip dangle, I rode my horse several *ri* before cockcrow. The "lingering dream" of Tu Mu's "Early Departure" was suddenly shattered when I arrived at Sayo no Nakayama.

Both the hokku and the prose refer to the poem by Tu Mu (803–852) that begins:

> Dangling my whip, I let my horse go ahead;
> Even after several *li*, still the cocks do not crow.
> Under the forest trees I nod with a lingering dream;
> When a leaf flies I suddenly awaken.

Obviously Bashō was indebted to Tu Mu for his language,[18] but he was not a plagiarist. His experience was real, but it understandably gave him pleasure to realize it was one shared with a great Chinese poet of the past. The poem is given its point and special haikai quality by the last line, literally "smoke of tea," an experience of the moment which, by its closeness and humble nature, makes the perhaps second-hand experience of the first two lines come alive. Bashō's uses of Chinese materials were varied, but most often he sought to enrich his own experiences by associating them with those of Chinese poets; far from making his own experiences any less true, the references gave them an added dimension.

If the purpose of the journey had been to visit his old home, he should naturally have been eager to reach Ueno as soon as possible, even if he could not be present for the first anniversary of his mother's death, but he made no effort to hurry. Perhaps Bashō had felt when he set out on the journey that being a haikai poet, like being a Buddhist priest, involved the renunciation of family ties. He may even have hesitated to visit the scenes of his past. But when he actually reached Ueno his emotions were unmistakable. He wrote:

> I returned to my old home at the beginning of the ninth month. The day lilies in my mother's room had all been withered by the frost, and nothing was left of them now. Everything was changed from what it used to be. My brother's hair was white at the temples, and there were wrinkles on his brow. "We are still alive," was all he said. Then, without a word, he undid his relic bag and said, "Pay your respects to Mother's white hair! This is the jewel box Urashima brought back.[19] See how gray your brows have become!" For a while I wept.

te ni toraba kien	Taken in my hands it would melt,
namida zo atsuki	The tears are so warm—
aki no shimo	This autumnal frost.

The verse would be unintelligible without the passage preceding it. The brevity of the waka and haiku inevitably tended toward obscurity, and this occasioned the prefatory notes explaining the circumstances of a poem. The note (or title) thus became an integral part of the poem, and sometimes (even as far back as the *Manyōshū*) it was developed into an extended prose passage. Bashō took advantage of this tradition; through the medium of the travel account, a genre with a long history in Japan, he was able to present in a natural manner the information needed to understand his elliptic verses. Even a brief prefatory note can sometimes affect our interpretation of a poem, as in this example from *Exposure in the Fields*:

michinobe no	Mallow flower
mukuge wa uma ni	By the side of the road—
kuwarekeri	Devoured by my horse.

The title is found in two versions—"On horseback" and "Before my eyes." Both clarify the meaning. Bashō is riding his horse when suddenly it lowers its head to devour the flower near the road. In that moment of destruction he noticed its beauty for the first time. The poem describes something he witnessed before his eyes, not a reported or imagined event, and it is infinitely more effective if the horse that eats the flower is the poet's. An early translation illustrates what can happen when these two headnotes are ignored:

The mallow flower by the road
Was eaten by a passing horse.[20]

Surely no one reading the translation could guess that this poem had been acclaimed as a masterpiece! As it stands, the poem is no more than the statement of a fact; without the presence of Bashō on the horse, his surprise at the horse's sudden movement, and his realization that the beauty of the flower has gone, the verse is nothing at all. But its effortless, unaffected expression must have puzzled even Japanese of the Tokugawa period. Some commentators interpreted the poem as meaning that this particular flower, by choosing to bloom by the side of the road in a conspicuous place, rather than in the quiet anonymity of the fields, was inviting destruction; others, likening the poem to a line of Po Chü-i that mentions the "single day of splendor of the morning glory," decided that the poem was a philosophical reflection on the shortness of a mallow flower's life. But, like all good haikai poetry, this verse is a perception and not a moral lesson—certainly not a warning.

It has often been noted that the tone of *Exposure in the Fields* changes markedly once Bashō reaches the town of Ōgaki where, as he had long promised, he stayed with his disciple Tani Bokuin (1646–1725). He tells us:

When I left Musashi Plain and set out on my journey, it was with a vision of my bones lying exposed in a field. Now I wrote:

shini mo senu	I haven't died, after all,
tabine no hate yo	And this is where my travels led—
aki no kure	The end of autumn.

The apprehensions that marked the start of the journey had lifted, and from this point on Bashō's style becomes noticeably more cheerful.

Bashō and Bokuin traveled together to Kuwana and on to Nagoya, where they arrived in the tenth month. It was in Nagoya that *Fuyu no Hi* (A Winter's Day), the first of the seven collections of haikai most closely associated with Bashō's name, was composed. It consists of five kasen sequences of linked verse. The title of the collection comes from a waki, or second verse, composed by Bashō. The sequence had opened with this hokku by Yamamoto Kakei:

shimozuki ya	The eleventh moon—
kō no tsukutsuku	Storks listlessly
narabiite	Standing in a row.

Bashō added:

fuyu no asahi no	How touching the morning sun
aware narikeri	Of a winter's day.

A Winter's Day is considered to have been the first proclamation of the establishment of the Style of Bashō (*Shōfū*). The four principal poets taking part with Bashō were all well-to-do Nagoya merchants, an indication of the extent of Bashō's influence on poets of that city.[21] He continued to the end of his life to maintain a special interest in the Nagoya poets.

A Winter's Day represented a great advance over *Empty Chestnuts*, published only a year and a half before. The heavily Chinese influence everywhere apparent in the earlier collection has been absorbed, and the prevailing tone, though owing much to both Chinese poetry and the waka, is distinctively haikai.

Toward the end of 1684 Bashō returned again to Ueno, where he saw in the new year. Before leaving the area of Nagoya he had gone with friends to look at the winter sea at Atsuta, and composed this verse:

umi kurete	The sea darkens:
kamo no koe	The voices of the wild ducks
honoka ni shiroshi	Are faintly white.

The form of the verse (five, five, and seven syllables) is irregular. It would have been possible, without greatly altering the meaning, for Bashō to have transposed the second and third lines, but he broke the normal rules of haikai composition in order to emphasize the voices of the ducks. This was not a flaunting of the poet's independence of the rules, but a completely natural expression that imposed its own rules. The verse is at once brilliantly effective and moving: as the sea darkens, the sound of the ducks crying is apprehended in terms of pale flashes of white against the blackness. This transference of the senses occurs in some of Bashō's most famous verses, including:

kiku no ka ya	The scent of asters—
Nara ni wa furuki	In Nara all the ancient
hotoketachi	Statues of Buddha.

In this late (1694) verse Bashō evokes the quality of the old city of Nara in terms of the musty but noble scent of chrysanthemums and the dusty old statues with peeling gilt. The transference of smell to sight, and the union of the two senses, unforgettably evokes the city living in the past.

The whiteness also mentioned in the verse about the ducks was a familiar element in Bashō's poetry, and was generally used with a mystic meaning. Whiteness is used with special effect in this verse of 1689:

Ishiyama no	Whiter, whiter
ishi yori shiroshi	Than the stones of Stone Mountain—
aki no kaze	This autumn wind.

The transference of the senses heightens the experience: the cold touch of the autumn wind evokes the cold whiteness of stone.

After further travels in Kyoto and around the area of Lake Biwa, Bashō headed back to Edo, arriving at the end of the fourth month of 1685. This is the final verse of the journey:

natsugoromo	My summer clothes—
imada shirami wo	I still haven't quite finished
toritsukusazu	Picking out the lice.

This lighthearted comment contrasts markedly with the forebodings of the opening verse, and suggests how much fun the journey had been. The inconveniences and hardships of travel, symbolized by the lice picked up in some wayside inn, are forgotten as Bashō returns home at last.

The journey had indeed been a success. The sights had inspired Bashō to write a dozen of his best verses and, with these as the core, he had added an important work to the noble tradition of travel literature. He renewed his acquaintances in Ueno, and never again would permit so much time to elapse between visits. He also extended his circle of disciples wherever he went; for example, he accepted as disciples Mikami Senna (1651–1723) and Esa Shōhaku (1650–1722), two poets of Ōmi Province who would spread the Style of Bashō in that region. When Bashō had arrived in Kyoto in 1685 he had not a single disciple in the city, but soon Mukai Kyorai (1651–1704) had joined Bashō's "school," to become one of his most intimate disciples. The journey was thus important both for the breakthrough it marked in the development of Bashō's art and for the dissemination of his characteristic style. The haphazard manner of narration makes *Exposure in the Fields* somewhat unsatisfactory as a work of literature, but it was a necessary first step in Bashō's acquisition of mastery of the genre.

After returning to Edo in 1685 Bashō and his disciples strove to deepen still further the artistic achievement of *A Winter's Day*. In the first month of 1686 Bashō and sixteen disciples joined to produce the one-hundred-verse sequence *Hatsu Kaishi* (A First Manuscript Page) in the same mode. That spring Bashō wrote his most famous verse:

furuike ya	The ancient pond—
kawazu tobikomu	A frog jumps in,
mizu no oto	The sound of the water.

Bashō's disciple Kagami Shikō described in *Kuzu no Matsubara* (1692) the circumstances of composition of the verse:

> One day when the old gentleman of the Bashō-an was spending the spring in retirement north of Edo, the rain was gently falling, the cooing of the pigeons was deep-throated, and the cherry blossoms were slowly falling in the soft wind. It was just the kind of day when one most regrets the passing of the third month. The sound of frogs leaping into the water could

> frequently be heard, and the Master, moved by this remarkable beauty, wrote the second and third lines of a poem about the scene: "A frog jumps in,/ The sound of the water." Kikaku, who was with him, suggested for the first line "The yellow roses," but the Master settled on "The ancient pond."[22]

If this account can be trusted, the verse may have been written as far back as 1682, though not published until 1686. It is hard to imagine, however, that such a masterpiece would have been left in manuscript for four years. It was acclaimed as soon as it was published.

The effect achieved by Bashō in this and many of his best poems was to capture at once the eternal and the momentary. The ancient pond is eternal, but in order for us to become aware of its eternity there must be some momentary disruption. The leap of the frog, suggested by the splash of the water, is the "now" of haikai; but the pond immediately relapses into timelessness. A similar effect is found in a verse written in 1689, during his *Narrow Road of Oku* journey:

shizukasa ya	How still it is!
iwa ni shimiiru	Stinging into the stones,
semi no koe	The locusts' trill.

This verse is about stillness, yet only by sound can we know silence. The eternal stillness of the mountain temple is interrupted by the insistent trilling of cicadas, and when they stop the silence is penetrating. Bashō had been urged to visit the temple, famous for its tranquillity, but he comprehended it only through the momentary disturbance made by the insects.

Kikaku's suggestion as an opening line *yamabuki ya* (The yellow roses) was not bad; there probably were yamabuki roses blooming beside the pond, and the old waka had often associated frogs and yamabuki.[23] But although the picture of yellow flowers surrounding the frog as it jumps into the water is visually appealing, it lacks the eternity of "ancient pond." Even using the image of a pond, if it had been qualified as a "small pond" or a "garden pond," the effect would have been lost. Only by suggesting the age of the pond, its unchanging nature, is the momentary life of the frog evoked. This was the kind of understanding Bashō demanded. He believed that the smallest flower or insect if properly seen and understood could suggest all of creation, and each had its reason for existence. One verse by Bashō is headed "All things have their own purpose," a phrase borrowed from the Northern Sung philosopher Cheng Ming-tao. The verse runs:

hana ni asobu	Don't eat the horsefly
abu na kurai so	Playing in the blossoms,
tomosuzume	My friend, the sparrow.

The folksy tone of the verse, reminiscent of the nineteenth-century haikai poet Issa, is redeemed by the underlying thought: even the horsefly, which nobody likes, has a right to live. Another verse in a similar vein also dates from 1687:

yoku mireba	When I look carefully
nazuna hana saku	Purseweed flowers are blooming
kakine ka na	Right beneath my fence.

The inconspicuous purseweed flowers are normally not noticed, but Bashō, having made the effort to see them, discovers they too have their reason for existence. Again, attempting to capture the essence of the skylark, he wrote:

haranaka ya	In the midst of the fields,
mono ni mo tsukazu	Not clinging to anything at all,
naku hibari	A singing skylark.

The freedom of the skylark attracted Bashō and he discovered in it the bird's essential nature. These three poems indicate Bashō followed his own lesson: "Learn about pines from the pines, study about bamboos with the bamboos."

The year 1686 was relatively uneventful for Bashō, although the second of the *Shichibushū* (Seven Collections) by members of his school, *Haru no Hi* (A Spring Day), was published that year by Yamamoto Kakei (1648–1716). It contains only three verses by Bashō, including the one about the frog, but provides further proof of the eminence attained by his school.

In 1687 Bashō again set out traveling. He first made a short journey, to see the moon at the Kashima Shrine, northeast of Edo, leaving on the fourteenth day of the eighth month and returning about the twenty-fifth. This journey is described in *Kashima Mōde* (Pilgrimage to Kashima), a brief account in prose followed by a group of undistinguished poems by Bashō and various acquaintances, including his companion Kawai Sora (1649–1710).

Bashō apparently decided on the spur of the moment to visit Kashima and see the harvest moon, much in the spirit of those characters in Nō plays who journey to distant places merely to enjoy the scenery at a particular time of year; the style is accordingly light. Unlike *Exposure in the Fields*, which betrays marked Chinese influence, the language of *Pilgrimage to Kashima* is almost pure Japanese, written in kana. Even the occasional references to Chinese literature have been filtered through the medium of earlier Japanese renderings. The sentences are simple, with a minimum of the elliptic syntax that makes Bashō's prose so hard to understand: "Fune wo agareba, uma ni mo norazu, hosohagi no chikara wo tamesan to kachi yori zo yuku" (When I got off the boat I did not climb on a horse but, thinking I would test the strength of my skinny shanks, set out on foot.)

Probably the most interesting passage is a description of himself: "The other traveler was not a priest, nor was he a layman, but rather, might be described as a bat, being between a bird and a rat." Bashō, like other professional philosophers and poets, had shaved his head and wore black robes in the manner of a Buddhist priest, a tradition dating back to the Middle Ages, when literary men and entertainers were generally priests in name and appearance if not in reality. A verse dating from about this time described Bashō's appearance:

kami haete	My hair has grown back
yōgan aoshi	And my countenance is pale:
satsuki ame	Rainy month of June.

During the rainy season, he says, he has allowed his hair to grow back, and his face is pale from staying indoors. But normally Bashō maintained his "batlike" appearance, a *chauve-souris* attired in black.

The journey to Kashima was a disappointment: on the night of the full moon it rained. "It certainly was a shame to have come all this way to see the moon, all in vain." But he met his old friend, the Zen priest Butchō, who was residing at a Buddhist temple near the Kashima Shrine. The visit refreshed Bashō; perhaps the prospect of meeting Butchō had lured him to Kashima as much as the moon-viewing.

Little more than two months after returning from Kashima, on the twenty-fifth day of the tenth moon of 1687, Bashō set out again, this time on a much more ambitious journey. On the eleventh of that month a farewell party was held at Kikaku's house. Unlike the despondent atmosphere of his departure on his previous long journey, Bashō was now feted and provided with all necessities. "I made no effort to gather together three months' worth of provisions for the journey," he again wrote, but this time it may have been because everything had been provided. The hokku he composed at the farewell party contrasted with the whitened bones he imagined in 1684:

tabibito to	"Traveler"—is that
wa ga na yobaren	The name I am to be called?
hatsushigure	The first winter rain.

The journey was a happy one, and the account reflects Bashō's good spirits. He was met everywhere by disciples, old and new, as he traveled in the regions of Ise, Nagoya, his old home at Iga, Yoshino, Nara and, finally, Suma. The account, known usually as *Oi no Kobumi* (Manuscript in My Knapsack) was not published until 1709, twenty-three years after the journey and fifteen years after Bashō's death, by his disciple Kawai Otokuni. It is uncertain when Bashō completed the manuscript, but scholars have tentatively suggested 1690 or 1691.[24] The artistic views expressed in the work may therefore represent Bashō's thoughts several years later rather than during the journey.

Manuscript in My Knapsack opens with a celebrated passage:

> Within my frame of a hundred bones and nine apertures dwells a thing I have called for the moment Fūrabō—Gauze-in-the-Wind-Priest. Indeed, this must refer to the ease with which gauze is torn by the wind. This creature has for long enjoyed haikai, and in the end decided to make it his life work. Sometimes he had wearied of this art and has thought of abandoning it; at other times he has made strides and has prided himself to think he was better than other poets. Inside his heart the conflict has warred, and this art has deprived him of all peace. For a time he wished to establish himself in the world, but poetry prevented him; for a time too he thought of studying so as to dispel the ignorance in his mind, but for the

> same reason this hope also was frustrated. In the end, incapable and talentless as he is, he has been bound to this one thin line. One and the same thing runs through the waka of Saigyō, the renga of Sōgi, the paintings of Sesshū, the tea ceremony of Rikyū. What is common to all these arts is their following nature and making a friend of the four seasons. Nothing the artist sees but is flowers, nothing he thinks of but is the moon. When what a man sees is not flowers, he is no better than a barbarian. When what he thinks in his heart is not the moon, he belongs to the same species as the birds and beasts. I say, free yourselves from the barbarian, remove yourself from the birds and beasts; follow nature and return to nature!

The passage is remarkable not only for the correspondence Bashō senses in seemingly disparate arts (certainly unorthodox at a time when even similar literary forms like waka and renga were considered to be incompatible), but for his astute choices of the very men whose names we today would link with Bashō's at the highest artistic level. Bashō does not explicitly state that the thread that links the other arts also runs through haikai poetry, but surely this is implied. Perhaps he also meant to suggest that Fūrabō, as he comically styles himself, ranks with Saigyō, Sōgi, and the other supreme masters. Bashō was a modest man, but he had enormous confidence in his art.

A few lines later in *Manuscript in My Knapsack* is another revealing passage. Bashō discusses the genre of travel diaries:

> Nobody has succeeded in making any improvement in travel diaries since Ki no Tsurayuki, Chōmei, and the nun Abutsu wielded their brushes to describe their feelings completely; the rest have merely imitated. How much less likely it is that anyone of my shallow knowledge and inadequate talents could attain this goal. Of course, anyone can write a diary saying, "On that day it rained . . . it cleared in the afternoon . . . there is a pine at that place . . . the such-and-such river flows through this place," and the like, but unless a sight is truly remarkable one shouldn't mention it at all. Nevertheless, the scenery of different places lingers in my mind, and even my unpleasant experiences at huts in the mountains and fields can become subjects of conversation or material for poetry. With this in mind I have scribbled down, without any semblance of

> order, the unforgettable moments of my journey, and gathered them together in one work. Let the reader listen without paying too much attention, as to the ramblings of a drunkard or the mutterings of a man talking in his sleep.

Bashō was attempting in *Manuscript in My Knapsack* to blend poetry and prose in a work of artistic merit, but the curiously unfinished quality of some sections of the present text has caused scholars to suppose that Bashō abandoned the manuscript without completing intended revisions.[25] Even the poems included in the account have been criticized as being inferior, especially considering their number. But read with somewhat less finicky attention, the work is unusually appealing, a sunny counterpart to most of the other diaries; and although the verses may not match those in *The Narrow Road of Oku,* they include some masterpieces. The distinctive atmosphere is provided by the warmth of affection Bashō showed his disciple Tsuboi Tokoku, who accompanied him. One of the final verses in *Exposure in the Fields* is entitled "Sent to Tokoku":

shirageshi ni	For the white poppy
hane mogu chō no	The butterfly tears off its wings
katami ka na	As a memento.

This poem was written when Bashō said goodbye to Tokoku, who was going into exile for having sold "empty rice," a crime normally punishable by death. Bashō, far from turning from a disciple who had committed a serious crime, compares himself to a butterfly, so reluctant to leave the white poppy that it tears off its wings as a keepsake. The white poppy, a delicate flower that blooms only a day or two before withering, was an apt metaphor for Tokoku, who died in 1690 while still in his thirties. *Manuscript in My Knapsack* relates how Bashō made a special trip to Irako Point, where Tokoku was living in exile. The two men agreed to meet in Ise and to travel together to see the cherry blossoms at Yoshino. Tokoku, assuming for the journey a boyish name to accord with his functions as Bashō's helper, made this the most enjoyable of all Bashō's travels. Years later, in 1691, Bashō wrote in *Saga Nikki* (Saga Diary) that he had dreamed of Tokoku and recalled their journey to Yoshino: "Sometimes we joked, sometimes we were sad; his kindness touched me to the quick, and I can never forget it, I am sure. After waking, I again wrung tears from my sleeves."

Among the poems in *Manuscript in My Knapsack* are several of special interest:

kutabirete	Worn out by my travels,
yado karu koro ya	I rent a room at the inn—
fuji no hana	Just then, wisteria blossoms.

Here Bashō is not merely describing a scene, the glimpse of beauty when he arrives exhausted at an inn, but suggesting by the choice of the flower, the pale, drooping wisteria, something of his own feelings.

horohoro to	With a soft flutter
yamabuki chiru ka	How the yellow roses drop—
taki no oto	The roar of the falls.

This verse depends for its effect on the soft sounds of *horohoro*, suggesting the lazy scattering of the yamabuki petals, and contrasting with the roar of the waterfall. Bashō occasionally experimented with the use of the sound of words to reinforce their meaning, as in a verse already quoted:

shizukasa ya	How still it is!
iwa ni shimiiru	Stinging into the stones,
semi no koe	The locusts' trill.

In this verse the dinning of the cicadas is evoked by the repetition of the sound *i*, which occurs in seven of the seventeen syllables.

Another verse from *Manuscript in My Knapsack* achieves its special effect through a different use of sound:

hototogisu	There in the direction
kieyuku kata ya	Where the cuckoo disappeared—
shima hitotsu	An island, just one.

Here the movement of the verse—the eye follows the *hototogisu* as it disappears into the distance, only to turn into an island on the horizon—is emphasized by the word order and by the quiet falling of the voice.

The verse that evokes his feelings on meeting Tokoku at his lonely place of exile at Irako Point is of interest also because of its artistic evolution. In the final version it runs:

taka hitotsu	A solitary hawk—
mitsukete ureshi	How happy I was to find it
Irakozaki	At Irako Point.

Bashō, standing on the lonely shore, looks out over the expanse of ocean and sky, and sees in the distance a single hawk. Irako Point was known for its hawks, both from the *Manyōshū* and Saigyō's poetry, and Bashō is expressing pleasure at having seen a typical feature of the Irako landscape. But, as the critic Yamamoto Kenkichi pointed out,[26] his joy is tinged with sadness because the hawk he found, Tokoku, is an exile. Bashō's fondness for Tokoku is suggested even more explicitly by two earlier versions of the poem.

Irakozaki	Irako Point—
niru mono mo nashi	Nothing even resembles
taka no koe	The voice of the hawk.

The second version bore the headnote, "When I visited Tokoku, who was living in unfortunate circumstances at Irako Point, I happened to hear the voice of a hawk."

yume yori mo	Even more than the dream
utsutsu no taka zo	The hawk of reality
tanomoshiki	Reassures me.[27]

Mention of dreams implies that Bashō now, as in later years, dreamt about Tokoku; seeing him in reality was more comforting than any dream.

It may be seen by examining the three stages of the poem how Bashō, working with essentially the same materials each time, managed to add depth and grandeur to the verse by the use in the third version of precisely the right words, *taka hitotsu* (literally, "hawk, one"), suggesting a single moving spot seen against the vast expanse of the sky; the loneliness of exile is mitigated by the youth and strength of the hawk, and Bashō is overjoyed to find the hawk at Irako Point. In comparison, the first version seems flat in its statement "there is nothing which resembles it, the voice of the hawk," and the second version is almost embarrassingly direct.

The process of polishing and sometimes drastically altering an original verse was an essential part of Bashō's art. He wrote many impromptu verses, the equivalents of the greetings inscribed in guest books, complimenting a host on his entertainment or garden, but few have the artistry of the verses over which he struggled. Bashō's next diary, *Sarashina Kikō* (Sarashina Journey, 1688) gave an amusing picture of himself engaged in the act of creation. He described how, as he lay in his room at the inn, attempting with great effort to beat into shape the poetic materials he had gathered during the day, groaning and knocking his head in the effort, a priest, imagining that Bashō was suffering from depression, tried to cheer him with comforting stories about the miracles of Amida, thereby totally blocking Bashō's flow of inspiration.[28] A similar process must have accompanied the numerous recensions given to Bashō's best verses, some of which exist in four or five distinct versions. This endless polishing probably accounts for the fewness of his hokku—only a little more than a thousand were composed in his whole lifetime, though a facile haikai poet could easily produce that many in a week.

Manuscript in My Knapsack ends with a description of Suma and that place's association with *The Tale of Genji*, *Matsukaze*, and other works of literature. Bashō and Tokoku went from Suma to Kyoto, where they parted, Tokoku returning to his place of exile, and Bashō heading for Owari province by way of Gifu, where he wrote the famous verse:

omoshirōte	Delightful, and yet
yagate kanashiki	Presently how saddening,
ubune ka na	The cormorant boats.

Gifu had long been celebrated for the cormorant fishing on the Nagara River. Bashō's verse perfectly captured the excitement of the spectators watching the cormorants swoop into the water to catch the fish attracted by the blazing torches, and then the sadness that settles in afterward. The use of the colloquial form *omoshirōte* (instead of *omoshirokute*) gave an immediacy to the expression of pleasure in the spectacle, followed by the mournful sounds of *kanashiki*, "saddening," a rise and fall that parallels the experience.

Bashō decided in the middle of the eighth month to go to Sarashina in the mountains of central Japan. The place had been famous for its harvest moon ever since the *Kokinshū*. He was accompanied by his disciple Ochi Etsujin (1656–*c.* 1740). The account is short and, like *Pilgrimage to Kashima*, consists of a prose section to which various hokku are appended. *Sarashina Journey* was not published until 1704, and attracted relatively little attention afterward. Apart from the passage referred to above, in which Bashō described the agony of composing poetry, the chief interest of this work lies in its connections with the legend of Sarashina: the abandoning on a lonely mountainside of an old woman, a theme no doubt based on practices in the past when unproductive members of society were left on mountainsides because there was not enough food to go around. The legend of the old woman, coupled with the well-known association of the moon and Sarashina, inspired Bashō, when he saw the moonlight shining over the mountain, to this verse:

omokage ya	I can see her now—
oba hitori naku	The old woman, weeping alone,
tsuki no tomo	The moon her companion.

Bashō returned to Edo after an absence of almost a year. A verse composed on the thirteenth night of the ninth month suggested how fatigued he was by his travels:

Kiso no yase	Still not recovered
mada naoranu ni	From my thinness of Kiso—
ato no tsuki	The late moon-viewing.

Bashō's weariness makes it all the more surprising that he decided just a few months later, in the beginning of 1689, to embark on his most ambitious journey. He himself gave no reason why he felt impelled to leave again so soon after his return, other than to say that "the gods of the road" beckoned and he could not resist. In recent years, however, it has been suggested that Bashō, believing that 1689 was the five hundredth anniversary of the death of Saigyō, felt he should pay his respects by traveling to many of the same places as his great predecessor.[29] References to Saigyō are scattered through *The Narrow Road of Oku*, and it may be that Bashō saw himself, like Saigyō in such Nō plays as *Eguchi* or *Saigyō-zakura*, as the waki, visiting places mentioned in the poetry of the past, encountering the spirits of the dead and hearing their stories, then quietly praying for their repose. We know that before Bashō left on the journey he refrained from eating fish and otherwise prepared himself spiritually.[30]

Bashō's main purpose, however, was apparently to renew his

art by visiting the places that had inspired the poets of the past. This attitude accords with his famous prescription: "Do not seek to follow in the footsteps of the men of old; seek what they sought."[31] Bashō believed that standing before a river or mountain that had been described in some predecessor's poetry would enable him to imbibe the spirit of the place and thereby enrich his own poetry. Unlike most world travelers, he had no desire whatsoever to be the first man to set foot on some mountain peak or to behold some prodigy of nature; on the contrary, no matter how spectacular a landscape might be, if it had never attracted the attention of earlier poets Bashō was uninterested in it because it lacked poetic overtones. When, for example, he traveled along a stretch of the Japan Sea coast that had been neglected by the poets, he omitted mention of it in his account, alleging that he had been unwell and incapable of appreciating the scenery; but the journal kept by his companion Sora makes no mention of Bashō's illness. Bashō's failure to display more interest in unbeaten tracks was no doubt aesthetically inspired.

Sora's journal, first published in 1943, came as a bombshell to Bashō worshipers. The work, though devoid of literary merit, describes the circumstances of the *The Narrow Road of Oku* journey so convincingly that it is hard to dispute its veracity; nevertheless, Bashō's reputation as the "saint of haikai" was so firmly established that many people were loathe to believe that the discrepancies between Sora's unadorned account and Bashō's artistry proved that Bashō had resorted to fiction. Only gradually was it recognized that *The Narrow Road of Oku*, far from being the mere narrative of the events of a journey, is a work of art, and that Bashō was always ready, in the interests of art, to sacrifice the literal truth. The diary is by no means long—perhaps thirty pages in English translation—but it took Bashō about four years to write, from the autumn of 1690 to the summer of 1694. Such care was needed to create this masterpiece.

The name given by Bashō to his account was the name of a particular road leading north of the city of Sendai to the province of Oku; Bashō casually mentions the road in his work. But the choice of this place-name was surely not fortuitous: *oku* also means "within" or "inner recess," and the title thus suggests a narrow road—perhaps Bashō's art—leading to the inner depths of poetry. It was typical of Bashō to have for his title words that could be interpreted on two levels—the now of the journey, and the eternity of the poet's quest.

Each of Bashō's four earlier travel accounts had included passages of great beauty, but only in *The Narrow Road of Oku* did he succeed in fusing the prose and poetry into a unified composition, each element balancing and augmenting the other. The quality of the poetry is, moreover, exceptionally high; verse after verse figures today in every anthology of haikai masterpieces. Needless to say, the definitive versions of these poems are not always identical with what Bashō composed on his journey; as we have seen, Bashō revised his hokku again and again before he felt satisfied. The prose too, based on rough notes jotted down along the way, had to be considerably polished. Elaborate analyses of *The Narrow Road of Oku* have been prepared in order to demonstrate how closely Bashō followed the rules of composition and order of a renga sequence, despite the seemingly factual nature of his account.[32] At times he changed the order of places visited, or turned rainy days into sunny ones, or invented personages not mentioned by Sora, all in the interests of preserving the effect of a renga sequence. Sometimes too Bashō was forced to skip over experiences on the way, for fear of repeating similar kinds of material. The literal truth was of little interest to him, and he did not hesitate to embroider. The fact that Bashō had resorted to fiction—that it might even be said he lied—shocked some admirers, but impressed others by the fresh evidence it afforded of Bashō's devotion to literary excellence.

The Narrow Road of Oku is a kind of synthesis of the art of Bashō, containing every element that made up his distinctive style, from the artifice of his Teitoku and Danrin haikai to the simplicity of his late manner, and from the formal prose suggestive of Chinese influence to the most simple and melodious Japanese. But the variety should not suggest a mere hodgepodge; on the contrary, the work creates a wonderfully unified impression. It opens with a famous passage, derived in part from Li Po:

> The months and days are the passing guests of a hundred generations; the years that come and go are also travelers. Those who float their lives away aboard boats or who greet old age leading horses spend their days in travel and make travel their homes. Many of the men of old died on the road.

When Bashō set out on his *Exposure in the Fields* journey he envisioned his bones lying exposed in a field. That may have been an artistic convention, but five years later, now forty-five years old, Bashō undoubtedly felt closer to those poets of the past, both Chinese and Japanese, who had died on their travels, and he may even have felt pleasure at the prospect of joining them.

The journey was to take Bashō along the eastern coast of Japan as far north as Hiraizumi, the stronghold where a branch of the Fujiwara family had enjoyed a brief period of glory five hundred years before; then across the country to the west coast; then southeast again to Ise. Most of the way was on foot, though occasionally Bashō traveled by boat or on horseback. Wherever he went he was warmly welcomed by the local haikai poets, even those who still belonged to the Danrin or Teitoku schools. Almost invariably he was persuaded to join in composing a "roll" of linked verse, with one of his hokku composed on the journey as the first verse. Today if one travels along Bashō's route one sees stone monuments inscribed with the poems he composed at each stop; the descendants of the local celebrities with whom Bashō stayed proudly unfold poems in his handwriting; and the priests at the temples he visited recite, as part of their guided tours, the appropriate passages from *The Narrow Road of Oku*. The love this work has inspired testifies not only to its literary importance but to its peculiarly congenial nature, even for Japanese readers living in an age totally unlike Bashō's.

An analysis of a typical passage from *The Narrow Road of Oku* may suggest the distinctive qualities of Bashō's prose style. It occurs just after the introductory description of the different kinds of travelers in the world quoted above:

> *Yo mo izure no toshi yori ka, hen'un no kaze ni sasowarete, hyōhaku no omoi yamazu, kaihin ni sasurae, kozo no aki, kōjō no haoku ni kumo no furusu wo haraite, yaya toshi mo kure, haru tateru kasumi no sora ni, Shirakawa no seki koen to, sozorogami no mono ni tsukite kokoro wo kuruwase, dōsojin no maneki ni aite, toru mono te ni tsukazu.*

A fairly literal translation of the foregoing passage, which modern Japanese editors generally consider to constitute one sentence, would go:

> I too—from what year was it?—have been tempted by a solitary cloud drifting in the wind and, never ceasing in my thoughts of roaming, have wandered on the seacoast; in the autumn of last year, I brushed away the spider's old cobwebs from my tumbledown cottage on the river; gradually the year too came to a close; and when mists rose in the sky with the coming of spring, [I thought] I would cross the barrier of Shirakawa; the spirits of wanderlust took possession of things and bewitched me; being beckoned to by the gods of the road, nothing I took in my hands stayed put.

Closer analysis of some of the phrases reveals their complexity. *Hen'un no kaze ni sasowarete* means, "a solitary cloud is tempted (or led astray) by the wind"; but in context it also indicates that Bashō, seeing the cloud freely moving with the wind is himself tempted to wander. The phrase *kaihin ni sasurae* (I have wandered on the seacoast) is syntactically not connected to either what precedes or follows; an expanded version of this section would read something like, "I have never ceased my thoughts of roaming. In the spring of last year I wandered on the seacoast, and only in autumn did I return to my tumbledown cottage on the river, where I brushed away the old cobwebs that the spiders had spun during my long absence." Such amplification makes the meaning clearer, but obviously destroys the poetic beauty of Bashō's prose.

Again, a phrase like *haru tateru kasumi no sora ni* telescopes several distinct thoughts: spring has come (*haru tateru*); the mists which have risen (*tateru kasumi*); [under] a sky where the mists have risen (*tateru kasumi no sora ni*). The meaning of one phrase has been disputed for many years by the commentators: is it *sozorogami* (the spirits of wanderlust) or *sozoro kami* (somehow, the gods . . .)?

Such ambiguities and difficulties, far from discouraging readers, heightened the enjoyment of the work for Japanese, whose taste for such evocative prose was nurtured by the haikai poetry of Bashō and his school.

The method of narration consists essentially of prose passages, usually episodes or stages of the journey, followed by one or more verses related to the emotions or atmosphere of the incidents described. The verses are mainly by Bashō, but he included some by Sora and one by a merchant he met on the way. The prose is the masterpiece of the style known as *haibun*, the prose equivalent of the elliptic and evocative haikai poetry. Because there are no metric limitations governing this prose it is generally more relaxed than the poetry, but the deliberate ambiguities and unfinished phrases make *The Narrow Road of Oku* difficult to read even now, after hundreds of commentaries have appeared. Any attempt to pin Bashō down to a single meaning is surely mistaken, in any case; in his haibun, no less than in his haikai poetry, a suggestive vagueness, rather than a clear statement of fact, was his intent. Vagueness has not generally been admired in the West as a quality of prose, but one can no more criticize Bashō for his imprecision than the Japanese painters who deliberately obscured their landscapes with clouds and mist.

The most celebrated sections of *The Narrow Road of Oku* are the opening and the descriptions of three places: Matsushima, Hiraizumi, and Kisagata. Some in-between sections seem rather flat and colorless, at least on first reading, but this did not represent any failure on Bashō's part; consciously or unconsciously he was obeying the principles of renga composition that called for neutral "links" separating those of high emotional content. Bashō was at pains, for example, to avoid following one passage of an exalted religious nature with another, and for this reason he falsified the order of events surrounding his visits to Muro no Yashima and Nikkō, both holy sites; he inserted a thirtieth day of the third month (though this month had only twenty-nine days that year) on which he met the simple but honest Buddha Gozaemon, thereby breaking the sequence of religious descriptions.[33] The relatively dull sections were necessary also to give magnitude to his high points.

The great moments are carefully prepared, not only in terms of the renga conventions but dramatically. The rather conventional praise for Izumi Saburō, a warrior who five hundred years earlier had presented the Shiogama Shrine with a metal lantern, is followed by the lyrical beauty of the description of Matsushima:

> No matter how often it has been said, it is none the less true that Matsushima is the most beautiful place in Japan, in no way inferior to T'ung-t'ing or the Western Lake in China. The

> sea curves in from the southeast forming a bay three miles across. The tides flow in with great beauty. There are countless islands. Some rise up and point to the sky; the low-lying ones crawl into the waves. There are islands piled on one another or even stacked three high. To the left the islands stand apart, and to the right rise linked together. Some look like mothers with babes on their backs, and some as if the babes were at their breasts, suggesting all the affection of maternal love. The green of the pines is of a wonderful darkness, and their branches are constantly bent by winds from the sea, so that their crookedness seems to belong to the nature of the trees. The scene suggests all the mysterious charm of a beautiful face. Matsushima must have been made by the God of the Mountains when the world was created. What man could capture with his brush the wonder of this masterpiece of nature?[34]

We might have expected a poem by Bashō to follow this passage, a masterpiece equal to the subject, but instead we are given one by Sora, of no remarkable beauty. Bashō says, "I lay down without composing any poem, but could not sleep." The experience of Matsushima had stunned Bashō into speechlessness, at least as far as a poem was concerned. This was not the only such instance. He seemed often paralyzed by scenic grandeur; his most famous verse on Mount Fuji, for example, mentions *not* seeing Fuji on a day of mistiness. Bashō responded with great sensitivity to nature, but it was nature in the Japanese manner, seen in miniature—in a garden, a single flowering tree, or even in some almost invisible blossoms, rather than in the sweep of a landscape. When Bashō was inspired by some larger scene it was usually for its human meaning. At Hiraizumi, for example, he surveyed a site of long-ago battles that had now turned into a wilderness of grass, and he remembered the lines by Tu Fu, "The country has fallen, but its mountains and rivers remain; when spring comes to the city the grass turns green again." He added:

> Spreading my wicker hat under me, I wept, letting time go by.

natsukusa ya	The summer grasses—
tsuwamono domo ga	For many brave warriors
yume no ato	The aftermath of dreams.

This superb hokku, evoking the pathos of the vanished dreams of the past that have metamorphosed into the now of the waving summer grass, is given peculiar strength not only by the meaning but by the sound: the first line has only *a* and *u* vowels, the second interposes four successive *o* syllables into the repeated *a* and *u* sounds, and the final line, after one "light" word, *yume* (dreams), ends with *o a o*. One can test the difference in the effect of the poem by substituting a second line of identical meaning but different sound, *heitai tachi ga*.

Perhaps the most affecting passage of the entire work is a denial of the truth of the lines of Tu Fu quoted above. Somewhat earlier in the journey Bashō, visiting the ruins of the old castle at Taga, finds a monument dating back to the Nara period describing repairs to the castle completed in the year 762. The inscription is not in the least poetic, but the antiquity of the monument moved Bashō deeply. He wrote:

> Many are the places whose names have been preserved for us in poetry from ancient times, but mountains crumble and rivers disappear, new roads replace the old, stones are buried and vanish in the earth, trees grow old and give way to saplings. Time passes and the world changes. The remains of the past are shrouded in uncertainty. And yet, here before my eyes was a monument which none would deny had lasted a thousand years. I felt as if I were looking into the minds of the men of old. "This," I thought, "is one of the pleasures of travel and living to be old." I forgot the weariness of my journey, and was moved to tears for my joy.

In this unforgettable passage Bashō suggests that Tu Fu was wrong in supposing that even if a kingdom falls its mountains and rivers will remain; mountains and rivers are no less perishable than kingdoms. Only poetry remains, and the names mentioned in poetry last longer than the places themselves. The rare monument from the past confirms the precious nature of the written word. Bashō's belief in poetry was religious, and his bonds with Saigyō and the other poets of the past were expressions of his faith.

The technical virtuosity of *The Narrow Road of Oku* is easily overlooked because of this abiding impression of sincerity, but Bashō achieved in this work a dazzling mixture of themes and moods. Needless to say, this was the result of infinite polishing and his overall artistic conception. The second verse—the first after Bashō leaves Edo—runs:

yuku haru ya	Spring is passing by!
tori naki uo no	Birds cry, in the eyes of fish
me wa namida	Behold the tears.

The verse is ostensibly about the end of spring—Bashō left Edo on the twenty-seventh day of the third month, just three days before spring ended—but in context it is also a poem about leaving friends and departing on a dangerous journey. Ending the verse with the noun *namida* (tears) underlines this emotion, even though a weeping fish cannot be a wholly serious image. The verse is haikai, in Bashō's special vein—light, but with an underlying note of pathos. The final verse of the journey was:

hamaguri no	Parting at Futami,
Futami ni wakare	Dividing like clam and shells,
yuku aki zo	We go with the Fall.

This verse, filled with the ingenuity of expression associated with the Teitoku school, is a throwback to Basho's earliest training in haikai. The name Futami indicates that Bashō is bound for Ise, situated near Futami, but it contains the word *futa* (shell) of the *hamaguri* (clam). Futami was noted for its clams, and the final syllable of its name, *mi*, is used for the "flesh" of the clams. The verb *wakareyuku* means to "go parting," suggesting that the clam and its shells are being torn apart, like Bashō and the friends from whom he now parts. Finally, the last line, by mentioning the end of autumn, echoes the first line of the first verse of the journey, about the passing of spring. This verse also undoubtedly has undertones of grief over parting, but the emotions are less deeply felt than in the spring verse; it is as if Bashō, having completed his journey, is expressing his relief in the frivolous style of the past.

After the journey described in *The Narrow Road of Oku*, Bashō went to Ise to witness the renewing of the Great Shrine, an event that takes place only once in twenty years. At the end of the ninth month he again returned to Ueno in Iga. For the next two years Bashō wandered around the area of Kyoto and Lake Biwa, occasionally visiting his old home in Ueno. Various reasons have been adduced for his slowness in returning to Edo.

No doubt he was still tired after his long journey and reluctant to set forth on the Edo road. There were difficulties too in securing repossession of the Bashō-an, which he had relinquished when he left Edo in the spring of 1689. Perhaps also he now felt that his best disciples, those most capable of joining him in the search for an even deeper style of haikai, were in the Kamigata region, rather than in Edo. His position in Iga, for that matter, had been much enhanced by his growing reputation as a poet, and the Tōdō family had even offered to lodge Bashō in their mansion. He now had over forty pupils in Ueno, mainly samurai and rich merchants. He was the pride of the town, the local boy who had made good. After his experiences with poverty and the embarrassing necessity of depending on the largess of patrons in Edo, Bashō must have basked in the attentions bestowed on him at his old home.

Bashō had developed a particular fondness for the area south of Lake Biwa, especially the towns of Zeze and Ōtsu. He saw in the new year of 1690 in Zeze, and early that summer gratefully accepted the offer of his disciple Suganuma Kyokusui, a high-ranking samurai of the Zeze clan, to live in a summerhouse in the mountains south of the lake. Bashō remained there about three and a half months, celebrating his stay with the prose poem *Genjūan no Ki* (An Account of the Hut of Unreal Dwelling). This gem of his prose writings, in a style similar to that of *The Narrow Road of Oku*, describes his affection for the scenery, his pleasure in the sights and sounds of the season and, above all, his love of the unpretentious but somehow elegant cottage, where he lived in the traditions of *Hōjōki*.[35] This was undoubtedly one of the happiest periods in Bashō's life, and his fond memories of his stay may have accounted for the request in his will that he be buried in Zeze, rather than in Ueno with his parents. Bashō lived until the end of the autumn of 1690 in a cottage within the precincts of Gichū-ji, the temple in Zeze where he was to be buried.

It was about this time that Bashō's health began to deteriorate. He had long suffered from a "chronic complaint," an intestinal disorder, but his letters indicate that it had taken a sudden turn for the worse. He describes, for example, how he was obliged to watch the harvest moon of 1690 from his bed, being too feeble to go out into the garden.

Bashō returned to Iga for the new year of 1691, and after a few months there moved to Kyoto, where he stayed at Rakushisha (Hut of the Fallen Persimmons), the retreat of Mukai Kyorai. The small house was in Saga, to the northwest of the city, a place known for its scenic beauty. While living there Bashō wrote *Saga Diary*, his closest approximation to a true diary. The work lacks the artistic finish of his five travel accounts, and the verses included are not among his important works, but the informality of the writing and the attention devoted to minor details of Bashō's daily life give *Saga Diary* a special place in his works. Bashō mentions, for example, the books he brought with him, including the works of Po Chü-i, *The Tale of Genji*, *The Tosa Diary*, *Ōkagami*, and various collections of poetry. He records his excursions to places in the vicinity, the visitors who came from the capital to see him, his sleeping habits, and the time he spent polishing earlier writings (presumably both *The Narrow Road of Oku* and *Account of the Unreal Dwelling*).

After leaving Rakushisha Bashō went to stay with his disciple Nozawa Bonchō in Kyoto, assisting him and Kyorai to edit *Sarumino* (The Monkey's Raincoat), the chief collection of hokku and linked verse in the Bashō style. The two disciples had begun the compilation during the previous summer, and the book was now in its final stages. We can gather from passages in *Kyoraishō* (Conversations with Kyorai) that lively discussions took place as to which verses should be included in *The Monkey's Raincoat*. Bashō was evidently determined to make the collection exemplify his ideals of haikai poetry. The collection, published in the seventh month of 1691, was an immediate success, and it was acclaimed as "the *Kokinshū* of haikai."

The Monkey's Raincoat, the fifth of the Seven Collections issued by the School of Bashō, took its name from the verse that stands at the head:

hatsushigure	First rain of winter—
saru mo komino wo	The monkey too seems to want
hoshige nari	A little straw raincoat.

This verse is said to have been composed by Bashō in the ninth month of 1689, on his way from Ise to Iga. Overtaken by a *shigure*, the sudden shower that falls at the end of autumn and in early winter, Bashō noticed a monkey in the rain, and was moved by its forlorn appearance to make this comment with humor and compassion, the prevailing qualities of the entire collection.

The *renku*, or linked verse in the haikai manner, are the hardest part of Bashō's work for the modern reader to appreciate. Thanks to the patient work of many scholars it is now possible to grasp the meaning of each link in a sequence, to ascertain its relationship to the preceding and following links, and to catch any references to the literature of the past. Sometimes we may be struck with admiration by the skill and plastic imagination revealed by the movement from link to link. But without considerable grounding in the art of renku, including personal experience at composing these verses, it is difficult indeed to maintain one's interest very long. The old prescriptions of renga, observed for the most part by Bashō's renku, even at a time when the classical linked verse had fallen into disrepute, obliged poets to mention the moon and the cherry blossoms at certain places in the sequence, regulated the variations permissible in the number of successive links that had to be devoted to a particular season or theme, and determined the parts of speech with which the links had to end. Even if a modern reader took the trouble to memorize all these rules, it would be as hard for him to imagine the experience of composing renku as it would be to imagine what it is to waltz from reading a book on the subject.

Most of Bashō's best-known renku sequences are in thirty-six links, the form known as kasen. The form, reduced from the normal one hundred links of renga, goes back to the fifteenth century, but it first acquired importance in the seventeenth century with such men as Saitō Tokugen (1559–1647), who described the essentials of kasen composition in *Haikai Shogaku-shō* (1641). Kitamura Kigin in 1666 had published a solo kasen, and other Teitoku and Danrin poets also favored the form. The kasen, being shorter and more casual than the normal one-hundred-link sequences, was appropriate for informal gatherings of poets and for visits by Bashō and other haikai masters with poets in country towns. The kasen was divided into four sections of six, twelve, twelve, and six verses. As in formal renga, the opening verse, or hokku, had the greatest importance. It was usually composed by the most distinguished guest, and the response, the waki verse, was supplied by the host. By this time the hokku had so evolved as to be almost independent, as we know from the many examples by Bashō given without any verses appended to them. But we should not forget that the hokku was always potentially the first verse of an extended sequence; even after Bashō's death his disciples went on using his hokku for this purpose. The hokku was at once independent, a world in microcosm, yet dependent for the full realization of its implications on what other poets might add.

Bashō devoted considerable attention to explaining the principles of his style of renku. In the classical renga there were eighteen varieties of kireji, or cutting words, used to divide or set off sections of a verse; these included such familiar (and untranslatable) particles as *ya*, *ka na*, *keri*, etc., and were intended especially to establish the integrity of the elements of a hokku. Bashō, however, claimed to have increased the number of kireji to forty-eight.[36] The use of a word denoting the season (*kigo*), another requirement of the hokku, was also redefined and expanded.

Each verse in a sequence was governed by rules. After the hokku had announced the season, topography, time of day, and general atmosphere, the second verse confirmed the mood, sometimes strengthening the mention of the season. It usually ended in a noun. Bashō believed that the third verse, which ended in a participial form (*te*), should mark a bold switch in a new direction, even though the season remained the same. The fourth verse had to be simple and easy to understand; Bashō said of it, "Heaviness is not in the nature of the fourth verse. It should be like the second verse." The fifth verse was the "seat" of the moon, though it was not essential to mention the moon here if it had already appeared in the hokku. The sixth verse was another light one, and with it the first section of a kasen was concluded. The first section normally could not include verses on Shinto or Buddhist subjects, love, impermanence, personal feelings (growing old, regret over the passage of time, etc.), proper names of any kind, anecdotal material, mention of illness, or any other striking or unusual subjects.[37] A list of prescriptions runs through the structure of an entire kasen, making one wonder how it was ever possible to give an impression of spontaneity.

A typical kasen is the one known as *Ichinaka wa*, from the

first line, found in *The Monkey's Raincoat*. The participants were Bashō, Kyorai, and Bonchō.

1) *ichinaka wa*	In the city
mono no nioi ya	What a heavy smell of things!
natsu no tsuki	The summer moon.
	Bonchō

The first verse observes the formal requirements of a kireji (*ya*) and a seasonal word (summer moon). The place is the city, the time of day is night, and the atmosphere is sultry, even stifling. Even at night the heavy odor of dust and heat lingers, but the cool summer moon is in the sky. The verse is sensual and evocative of mundane experience, rather than conceptual, in the manner of the earlier hokku. This new attitude owes much to Bashō's insistence at this time on *karumi* (lightness), as well as to Bonchō's natural poetic inclinations.

2) *atsushi atsushi to*	How hot it is! How hot it is!
kado kado no koe	Voices call at gate after gate.
	Bashō

The second verse, strengthening the mood of the hokku, describes how people, now that the hot day is over, are standing by their gates, hoping for a breath of cool air, and complaining about the heat. The verse ends in a noun. It makes more specific the heat only suggested in the hokku.

3) *niban kusa*	The second weeding
tori mo hatasazu	Has not even been finished,
ho ni idete	But the rice is in ear.
	Kyorai

The third verse, obeying the prescription that it should mark a change, shifts the scene from the city to the country: the summer has been hot and therefore good for the rice crop. Usually the rice does not come into ear until after the third weeding of the fields, but this year, because of the fine weather, it is in ear even before the second weeding is completed. The verse ends in *te*, normal in the third verse. The season is summer, like the two preceding links. Summer and winter were usually mentioned in only two successive links, though spring and autumn had to be mentioned at least three times, but an exception was made here because the hokku was a summer verse.

4)	*hai uchitataku*	Brushing away the ashes,
	urume ichimai	A single smoked sardine.
		Bonchō

The country scene of the third verse is extended: busy with work in the fields, the farmer has time only for a quick lunch. He brushes the ashes from the sardine that has been smoked over the hearth, and makes a simple meal of it. The sardine was a seasonal word for autumn, the season when it is caught, but a dried sardine could be eaten in any season, so this verse is seasonless, and provides a necessary transition in shifting away from summer. The humble, graphic verse is typical of Bonchō.

5)	*kono suji wa*	In this neighborhood
	gin mo mishirazu	They don't even recognize money—
	fujiyusa yo	How inconvenient!
		Bashō

Bashō puts himself in the position of a traveler arriving at the remote, poverty-stricken neighborhood suggested by the fourth verse. People here have not even seen a silver coin before. The prosperity evoked by the third verse is no obstacle to the flow of the poem because in linked verse only the immediate preceding verse is taken into consideration. This verse is also without season. The fifth verse was traditionally occupied by the moon, but it is omitted here because the moon appeared in the hokku. The verse continues the theme of rustic life but points in a new direction by introducing a stranger, opening up a new avenue of exploration.

6)	*tada tohyōshi ni*	He just stands there stupidly
	nagaki wakizashi	Wearing a great big dagger.
		Kyorai

This verse suggests some country bully or gambler who has wandered into a village only to discover the people there are ignorant of money; he stands there foolishly, not knowing what to do with the dagger he intended to use in taking their money.

7)	*kusamura ni*	In the clump of grass
	kawazu kowagaru	A frog, and he jumps with fright
	yūmagure	At the twilight hour.
		Bonchō

The bully of the previous verse is mocked: although he wears a big dagger, he is terrified by the rustling of a frog in the grass.

This verse, the first of the second section of the kasen, is "lively," and "marks a change," as prescribed. From this verse on, the forbidden subjects—religion, love, etc.—can be freely mentioned. The season has been shifted to spring by mention of the frog, a seasonal word.

8) *fuki no me tori ni*	Going to pick butterbur shoots
ando yurikesu	The lamp flickers and goes out.
	Bashō

Bashō changes the unexpressed subject of the preceding verse; it is no longer a cowardly bully who is frightened by the rustling of a frog but someone, presumably a young girl, who has gone out at dusk to pick butterbur shoots. She is startled by the noise, her hands tremble, and her lantern goes out. The season is spring, indicated by the butterbur shoots.

9) *dōshin no*	The awakening
okori wa hana no	Of faith began when the flower
tsubomu toki	Was still in the bud.
	Kyorai

Kyorai in turn changes the unexpressed subject of Bashō's link; now it is someone in a religious order, presumably a nun, who as a girl went out one evening to pick butterbur shoots. When her lamp suddenly flickered out she became aware of the uncertainty of the world and turned her thoughts to the Buddhist awakening. She was then only a girl, a flower in the bud. This religious verse, appropriate in the second section, continues the season of spring by mention of flowers. Mention of flowers should not have occurred until the eleventh verse, but was permissible here because it constitutes a necessary third mention of spring. One could anticipate the requirement, but it was not permitted to delay the appearance of flowers beyond the eleventh verse.

10) *Noto no Nanao no*	The winters at Nanao
fuyu wa sumiuki	In Noto are hard to endure.
	Bonchō

Bonchō interprets the previous verse as referring to a priest who took up his vocation as a young man. After enduring the hardships of a winter at the lonely port of Nanao on the Noto peninsula, he now looks back on his past. There may be a reference to the holy man Kembutsu who once spent ten days in a cave at Nanao fasting. The verse belongs to winter, the shift in season implying that the flowers mentioned in the previous verse existed in the priest's recollection rather than in the world around him.

11) *uo no hone*	I have lived to see
shaburu made no	Such old age I can only
oi wo mite	Suck the bones of fish.
	Bashō

Bashō evokes here a wretched old man living on the lonely northern shore. When he was young his teeth could chomp through fish bones, but in his old age he can only suck the bones. The verse is without season.

12) *machibito ireshi*	He let my lover in
komikado no kagi	With the key of the side door.
	Kyorai

The old man of Bashō's verse is turned into the custodian of a palace gate. Kyorai himself said of this verse that when he wrote "he let my lover in" he was thinking of the old man, mentioned in *The Tale of Genji*, who lets Genji out of Suetsumuhana's palace one snowy morning with his key. Kyorai changed this to let the lover inside, so that the verse might be more romantic, the first love verse of the kasen.[38]

The foregoing is the first third of a representative kasen in *The Monkey's Raincoat*. The constant shifting of tone and subject was possible because of the vagueness of the Japanese language; the subject is generally unexpressed, and whether singular or plural, male or female, human being or animal, it can shift in retrospect as a link is added. The linkage is distinctive. Unlike the Teitoku school, which linked by verbal associations (mainly plays on words), or the Danrin school, which linked on the basis of meaning, Bashō and his school linked by the "perfume" of the preceding verse, the overtones of the mood and atmosphere. Bashō's criteria of haikai, expressed by such a word as *nioi* (perfume), were concerned with renku composition and the shifting of thought from one poet to the next, rather than with the qualities of a single verse. The School of Bashō meant more than a teacher surrounded by worshipful students; it was a group of men, each with his own characteristics as a poet, who were moved by the guiding spirit of the master to create together works of literature. As this kasen from *The Monkey's Raincoat* demonstrates, three men, catching the "perfume" of each other's verses, were moved to write complex and beautiful poetry.

After *The Monkey's Raincoat* had been completed Bashō moved back to the south shore of Lake Biwa and spent the three autumn months there, his health much improved. He left for Edo on the twenty-eighth day of the ninth month and arrived a month later. He had been away for two years and eight months. After his return his disciples Sora and Sampū unsuccessfully tried to get back Bashō's old house, but eventually decided to build a new Bashō-an near the old one. Sampū supplied most of the money. The new house was ready in the fifth month of 1692, and the bashō tree transplanted to the garden. Bashō led an extremely busy life, as new disciples arrived from all over the country to study with him. The most notable was Morikawa Kyoriku, a samurai from Hikone, who became Bashō's disciple in the eighth month of 1692. In the meanwhile the mysterious persons surrounding Bashō—his "heir" Tōin, the nun Jutei and her three children—were much on his mind. Tōin became seriously ill early in 1693 and died at the end of the third month. Bashō wrote of the exhaustion he felt after having watched over Tōin's sickbed. The strain of meeting a large number of pupils also began to tell. In the seventh month of 1693 he "shut the gate" of his cottage and for about a month refused to admit any visitors.

By the time Bashō resumed normal relations with his disciples he had switched his emphasis in haikai to a new principle, karumi (lightness), a word used in contrast to technical finish or decorative effects. It must have been a difficult ideal for Bashō to embrace; his verses, even of his mature period, are often exceedingly complex, requiring considerable exegesis before they can be understood. The hokku in *The Monkey's Raincoat*, however, had pointed in the direction of karumi, and shows that this touchstone of excellence had been in Bashō's mind for some time. A poem composed in 1690, when Bashō lay on a sickbed at Katada, on the shores of Lake Biwa, also conveyed a sense of karumi:

yamu kari no	A sick wild duck,
yosamu ni ochite	Falling in the cold of night:
tabine ka na	Sleep on a journey.

The unspoken comparison between the sick wild duck, dropping out of the formation of ducks flying over the lake, and himself, lying in travelers' lodgings on a cold night, is made with utter simplicity and effectiveness; this would be his goal in the poetry of his last years.

Bashō's insistence on karumi also included a preference for subjects drawn from daily life, rather than the loftier subjects of, say, *The Narrow Road of Oku.* A large number of verses mention food, humble dishes that are so peculiarly Japanese that their nature cannot easily be conveyed in translation. Street scenes in Edo also moved him to verse:

shiodai no	The salted bream
haguki mo samushi	Look cold, even to their gums,
uo no tana	On the fishmonger's shelf.

This verse, written in the winter of 1692, describes a fishmonger's in winter: there are no fresh fish on sale, and the shriveled salted bream bare their gums with the cold.

Bashō's last two collections of renku, *Sumidawara* (Sack of Charcoal, edited with Shida Yaba) and *Zoku Sarumino* (The Second Monkey's Raincoat, edited with Hattori Sempo, a Nō actor and poet), are both marked by the karumi manner. Bashō, however, encountered considerable resistance from his disciples in his efforts to propagate the new style. The ingenuity, conciseness, and obliqueness that had marked haikai poetry for many years were not easily abandoned. Perhaps the disciples realized also that a simple verse must be extremely good if it is not to be banal, but if a verse is cryptic or ambiguous, people may read meanings and depths into it that the original poet never imagined.

At the beginning of 1694 Bashō wrote a letter to an Iga disciple named Kubota Ensui (1640–1704) in which he expressed premonitions of death. He was now only fifty years old, but he seemed prematurely aged, and felt the approach of debility. This may be why he decided to undertake one final journey to Ueno. At the beginning of the fifth month a farewell party was held in Edo by his disciples, and Bashō again urged karumi. As he climbed into a sedan chair and took what proved to be his final look at his beloved disciples, he composed the verse:

mugi no ho wo	I clutch a stalk of wheat
tayori ni tsukamu	To support me—
wakare ka na	This is parting.

Presumably, wheat was visible nearby, and he tells his disciples, now that he is leaving them, even such frail support as a stalk of wheat will be the best he can hope for.

On this journey, unlike the earlier ones, Bashō did not stop here and there to compose poetry with the local poets. His only sojourn was a few days in Nagoya, where he preached karumi and patched up a quarrel among his disciples. He went on to Iga, arriving just seventeen days after leaving Edo. Two weeks later he left for the south shore of Lake Biwa, intending to enjoy the cool. But he was so mobbed by his disciples at Zeze and Ōtsu that he went to Kyoto, staying again at the Rakushisha. Disciples from all over Japan besieged him with requests to live with them, but Bashō could not consider new plans. His only thought now was karumi, exemplified by a verse composed at Rakushisha:

rokugatsu ya	The sixth month—
mine ni kumo oku	Clouds are resting on the peak
Arashiyama	At Arashiyama.

This summer scene (when clouds rest motionless on Arashiyama, the lovely mountain in the Saga area), evokes the breathless heat of a Kyoto summer. Another verse composed during his stay was:

Kiyotaki ya	Clear cascades—
nami ni chirikomu	Into the waves scatter
ao matsuba	Green pine needles.

Kiyotaki is a proper name, the name of a river near Kyoto, but is used here also for its meaning, "clear cascades."

Toward the end of the sixth month Bashō resided for a time at Gichū-ji in Zeze, then returned to Iga for the Bon Festival in the seventh month. He wrote:

ie wa mina	Everyone in the family
tsue ni shiraga no	Leans on a stick: a white-haired
haka mairi	Graveyard visit.

The white-haired mourners, assembled for the Feast of the Dead, are probably his elder brother and his family. Bashō stayed over a month in Ueno, living in the cottage built for him by disciples, writing poetry and editing *The Second Monkey's Raincoat.* He was determined to make the sequel not only as good as *The Monkey's Raincoat* but a model of karumi. Bashō was helped in the final stages of editing by his disciple Kagami Shikō, but did not live to see publication of the work in 1698.

On the eighth day of the ninth month Bashō left Ueno for Osaka, in response to the invitation of two disciples. His school, though triumphant elsewhere, had not made much headway in Osaka, perhaps because his two chief disciples were constantly bickering. Bashō decided he would reconcile the two men. His health was unfortunately not up to the journey. The distance to Osaka was only about forty miles, but Bashō was hardly capable of walking even a few miles at a time. He managed to struggle on, but the day after his arrival he developed a fever of unknown origin.* This illness, marked by chills and a headache, persisted, but nobody took it seriously. Bashō kept up with his work, attending receptions held by both factions of his school. On the twenty-seventh day of the ninth month, surrounded by disciples, he went on a brief excursion, composing two verses. The first was:

kono michi ya	Along this road
yuku hito nashi ni	There are no travelers—
aki no kure	Nightfall in autumn.

The lonely scene evoked is of the poet who travels a path without companions into the darkness of autumn.

His second verse of this occasion was:

kono aki wa	This autumn
nan de toshi yoru	Why do I feel so old?
kumo no tori	A bird in the clouds.

Bashō sees himself alone, a bird wandering in the clouds.

He was expected to attend another party on the twenty-ninth, and on the previous night prepared a hokku to deliver on this occasion:

aki fukaki	Autumn has deepened:
tonari wa nani wo	I wonder what the man next door
suru hito zo	Does for a living?

In his lonely lodgings the poet is cut off from the neighbor whose presence he shares but has never seen, and he feels a yearning for human company.

A sudden worsening of his illness on the twenty-ninth made it impossible for him to attend the gathering, and Bashō's condition continued to deteriorate. On the fifth day of the tenth month he was moved to a room rented from a florist. The news spread rapidly to his disciples, and they gathered around his bed. On the eighth of the month Bashō dictated his last verse. It bore the headnote "Composed in Illness."

tabi ni yande	Stricken on a journey,
yume wa kareno wo	My dreams go wandering round
kakemeguru	Withered fields.

On the night of the tenth he dictated to Shikō three letters in which he disposed of his manuscripts, books, and other possessions, and sent messages to pupils in Edo. Finally, he took a brush in his own hand and wrote a farewell note to his brother Hanzaemon. He refused further nourishment, but lay down quietly to await death. He died on the twelfth day of the tenth month. After the wake that night his body was sent the next day by boat to Gichū-ji in Zeze for burial, in accordance with his final instructions. At the service held on the fourteenth, over eighty disciples were present. Two Iga disciples were given a lock of his hair for interment in the family grave, but he made no provision in his will for even a token burial in Edo, the city where his art was perfected.

NOTES

1. The extremes to which scholars have gone in searching for biographical clues is typified by Shida Gishū, *Oku no Hosomichi, Bashō, Buson*. On pp. 31–36 he discusses the identity of a certain Hotoke Gozaemon, mentioned in *Oku no Hosomichi*; and on pp. 77–79 the merchant Teiji from Mino, also mentioned once in the work, is the subject of meticulous research.
2. See Asō Isoji, *Nihon Bungaku no Sōten*, V, pp. 137–39.
3. See especially Okamura Kenzō, *Bashō to Jutei-ni*.
4. Imoto Nōichi, *Bashō no Sekai*, p. 8.
5. *Ibid.*, p. 66.

6. Poem 1 in *Kokinshū* runs: "Spring has come before the old year ended; Shall we call the same year 'last year' or 'this year'?" Poem 645 in the same collection is: "Did you, I wonder, come here, or might I have gone there? I scarcely know. . . . Was it dream or reality—did I sleep or wake?" (Translated by Helen McCullough in *Tales of Ise*, p. 48.)

7. I have called him uniformly by this name, though at the time he was actually known as Sōbō.

8. The name Tōsei was apparently derived from Li Po, which is written with characters meaning "Plum White." Tōsei is written "Peach Green."

9. The peculiar word *kochitōzure* is explained in Iino Tetsuji, *Bashō Jiten*, p. 393, as a variant of *kochi tachi zure*, a word used when speaking disparagingly of oneself and one's associates. Text in Komiya Toyotaka, *Kōhon Bashō Zenshū*, III, pp. 69–70.

10. Imoto, p. 32.

11. So said by Suganoya Takamasa in his collection *Honobonodate*; quoted in Imoto, p. 98.

12. See Ebara Taizō and Yamazaki Kiyoshi, *Bashō Haibun Shū*, pp. 25–27.

13. Perhaps the fact that 1684 was the first year of the sixty-year cycle suggested to him that this was a time for renewal.

14. See Burton Watson, *The Complete Works of Chuang Tzu*, p. 30.

15. An illuminating discussion of the meaning for Bashō of the poem by Kuang-wen may be found in Akabane Manabu, "Nozarashi Kikō to Gōko Fūgetsu Shū," in *Renga Haikai Kenkyū*, no. 9, pp. 29–40.

16. See Watson, p. 93.

17. See Kuwabara Takeo, *Daini Geijutsu Ron*, p. 83. A complete translation of *Nozarashi Kikō* is given in my article, "Bashō's Journey of 1684."

18. In earlier versions of the poem the indebtedness to Tu Mu is even more pronounced. See Imoto, p. 268.

19. Urashima Tarō received a jewel-box similar to Pandora's; when he opened it he suddenly aged many years.

20. Translated by B. H. Chamberlain.

21. Among the Nagoya poets participating were Okada Yasui (1658–1743), Tsuboi Tokoku (perhaps twenty-seven at the time), Yamamoto Kakei (1648–1716), and Katō Jūgo (1654–1717). For background, see Imoto, pp. 125–28.

22. Quoted in Abe Masami, *Bashō Denki, Kōsetsu*, p. 114.

23. See Teruoka Yasutaka, *Kinsei Haiku*, p. 73.

24. See Asō, p. 152.

25. *Ibid.*, pp. 151–63.

26. Yamamoto Kenkichi, *Bashō*, I, pp. 148–52

27. Abe, pp. 303–304.

28. See the translation in my article, "Bashō's Journey to Sarashina," p. 66.

29. Asō, p. 165.

30. Abe, pp. 436–37.

31. See the translation in Ryusaku Tsunoda, *et al.*, *Sources of Japanese Tradition*, pp. 458–59.

32. See Yayoshi Kan'ichi, *et al.*, *Nozarashi Kikō, Kashima Mōde*, pp. 19–24.

33. *Ibid.*, pp. 13–14.

34. Translation from Donald Keene, *Anthology of Japanese Literature*, p. 367.

35. A translation of *Genjūan no Fu*, a somewhat earlier draft of *Genjūan no Ki*, may be found in my *Anthology*.

36. See Imoto, p. 209.

37. Maeda Toshiharu, *Bashō Meiku Seishaku*, p. 104.

38. The above interpretations follow Maeda, *op. cit.*, pp. 101–108. I have also consulted Andō Tsuguo, *Bashō Shichibushū Hyōshaku*, pp. 181–210. Slight variations are found in pronunciation of the characters. When in doubt I have followed Komiya, *Kōhon Bashō Zenshū*, IV, p. 244.

BIBLIOGRAPHY

Abe Masami. *Bashō Denki Kōsetsu*. Tokyo: Meiji Shoin, 1959.

Akabane Manabu. "Nozarashi Kikō to Gōko Fūgetsu Shū," in *Renga Haikai Kenkyū*, no. 9, November, 1954.

Andō Tsuguo. *Bashō*. Tokyo: Chikuma Shobō, 1971.

———. *Bashō Shichibushū Hyōshaku*. Tokyo: Shūeisha, 1973.

Asō Isoji (ed.). *Nihon Bungaku no Sōten*, V. Tokyo: Meiji Shoin, 1969.

Ebara Taizō and Yamazaki Kiyoshi. *Bashō Haibun Shū*, in Kadokawa Bunko series. Tokyo: Kadokawa Shoten, 1958.

Henderson, Harold G. *An Introduction to Haiku*. Garden City, N.Y.: Doubleday, 1958.

Iino Tetsuji (ed.). *Bashō Jiten*. Tokyo: Tōkyōdō, 1959.

Imoto Nōichi (ed.). *Bashō no Sekai*. Tokyo: Komine Shoten, 1968.

Keene, Donald. "Bashō's Journey of 1684," in *Asia Major*, no. 7, December, 1959.

———. "Bashō's Journey to Sarashina," in *Transactions of the Asiatic Society of Japan*, 3rd series, no. 5, 1957.

Komiya Toyotaka, *et al.* *Kōhon Bashō Zenshū*. 10 vols. Tokyo: Kadokawa Shoten, 1962–1969.

Kuwabara Takeo. *Daini Geijutsu Ron*, in Shimin Bunko series. Tokyo: Kawade Shobō, 1952.

Maeda Toshiharu. *Bashō Meiku Seishaku*. Tokyo: Katō Chūdōkan, 1963.

McCullough, Helen Craig. *Tales of Ise*. Stanford: Stanford University Press, 1968.

Okamura Kenzō. *Bashō to Jutei-ni*. Osaka: Bashō Haiku Kai, 1956.

Ōtani Tokuzō and Nakamura Shunjō. *Bashō Kushū*, in Nihon Koten Bungaku Taikei series. Tokyo: Iwanami Shoten, 1957.

Shida Gishū. *Oku no Hosomichi, Bashō, Buson*. Tokyo: Shūbunkan, 1946.

Sugiura Shōichirō, Miyamoto Saburō, and Ogino Kiyoshi. *Bashō Bunshū*, in Nihon Koten Bungaku Taikei series. Tokyo: Iwanami Shoten, 1959.

Teruoka Yasutaka. *Kinsei Haiku*. Tokyo: Gakutōsha, 1956.

Ueda, Makoto. *Matsuo Bashō*. New York: Twayne, 1970.

Watson, Burton. *The Complete Works of Chuang Tzu*. New York: Columbia University Press, 1968.

Yamamoto Kenkichi. *Bashō*, 2 vols. Tokyo: Shinchōsha, 1955.

Yayoshi Kan'ichi, *et al*. *Nozarashi Kikō, Kashima Mōde*. Tokyo: Meigen Shobō, 1967.

CHAPTER 6
HAIKAI POETRY
BASHŌ'S DISCIPLES

Takarai[1] Kikaku, perhaps Bashō's first pupil, by a strange accident of fate happened to be present at his deathbed, though he had arrived in Osaka not even knowing that Bashō was ill. In *Kareobana* (Withered Plumes of Grass, 1694), his moving account of Bashō's last hours, Kikaku mentioned that there were now more than two thousand disciples all over the country. The number kept increasing, even after Bashō's death, as everyone who had ever joined in making haikai poetry with even the least important of the original disciples proudly claimed to be a disciple himself. This naturally annoyed the "direct disciples" (who probably numbered no more than sixty), and one threatened to denounce all impostors. Mukai Kyorai answered him: "There's something in what you say, of course. But some of these men must surely have received instruction at least secondhand from disciples of the Master. Besides, the Master was so generous that he usually raised no objection when people styled themselves his disciples, making no distinction among them whether they were noble or humble, close to him or hardly known. . . . If the people you mention say they belong to the school of our master Bashō, you should let it go at that. It would be unwise to attempt to check up on them and get rid of the impostors."[2] Kyorai once stated why he thought so many men wanted to claim membership in the school: "I am sure that many different kinds of people worship the Master. Some look up to him because of the character he reveals in his poetry, for his qualities of serenity and sincerity, and are delighted to join with him in making haikai. Others are attracted by the reputation he has of being a great haikai poet, and follow him out of respect. And undoubtedly some people combine both feelings. It is impossible to ascribe his popularity to any one cause."[3]

The worshipful admiration inspired by Bashō owed much to his noble character, but he was above all respected for being incomparably the best poet of his day. His pupils included excellent poets, and some wrote eight or ten verses included today in the standard anthologies, but even their best efforts do not remotely compare with a hundred or more superb hokku by Bashō. He was a kindly teacher who attempted always to encourage his pupils by praising their poetry, but in his heart he must have known that none was his equal. His famous poem *Kono michi wa* (Along this road) suggests his loneliness when, nearing the end of his life, he realized he would have no successor.

After Bashō's death, various disciples tried to establish themselves as the true heirs to his traditions. Although their eager claims to special knowledge make unedifying reading today, we must be grateful to these men for having recorded their conversations with Bashō, even if it was in the hopes of demonstrating how highly he thought of them. Bashō's own critical writings are scanty; with a few exceptions his views on poetry have been preserved in the writings of the disciples, especially Kyorai, Morikawa Kyoriku, Hattori Tohō, and Kagami Shikō. It is not always certain how accurately Bashō's views were transmitted by these men; Shikō in particular was accused of having falsified

Bashō's opinions in order to lend greater authority to his own. But on the whole the salient points, no matter who recorded them, ring true. It is more as scribes than as poets that Bashō's disciples tend to be remembered.

TAKARAI KIKAKU (1661–1707)

Among the disciples, Kikaku was the most individual. Despite his long period of apprenticeship and the undoubted affection between him and Bashō over a period of twenty years, his poetry is distinctively his own, and not an evocation of the Master's. Kyorai, in a letter he wrote to Kyoriku after Bashō's death, criticized Kikaku for "not following in the same tracks as the writings of the Master."[4] But Kikaku was too unlike Bashō to follow him closely. He was a typical Edo man—a hard drinker, a frequenter of the licensed quarters (though one critic claimed Kikaku was physically excited only by fish![5]), a rather frivolous poet who to the end considered haikai a pastime rather than a means of expressing deep feelings.

Kikaku was a doctor's son and was himself trained to be a doctor. He received an excellent education in the Chinese classics, painting, and calligraphy. Even when he first became a pupil of Bashō he displayed a surprisingly quick wit and a skill at using his learning, though these qualities served mainly to mask a rather ordinary mind. Kyoriku once asked Bashō what he had been able to teach a poet so different from himself as Kikaku. Bashō replied, "My style favors solitude and is delicate; Kikaku's favors flashiness and is delicate. The delicacy marks him as belonging to my school."[6] Kikaku's verses, however dissimilar to Bashō's they may seem, undoubtedly owed much to his influence; the poetry he composed after Bashō's death shows Kikaku at his worst. His verses are often not merely obscure but totally unintelligible; and even if the riddle of a cryptic line is unlocked it may be of no interest. But his earlier style was much admired. Kyoriku wrote that "if any verses in the different collections attract one's attention, they generally turn out to be by Kikaku. I don't know of any other disciple in his class."[7] Kyorai answered, "I wonder if that is not an overstatement? If I were to rate him in terms of the magnitude of his talents, I would have to place him above my head. But if I rated him on the baseness of his verses, I would put him beneath my feet."[8]

Kikaku's greatest achievement may have been his success in arousing the interest of men of his class—the intellectuals of Edo, including doctors, Confucian scholars, and some samurai and merchants—in haikai poetry. At a time when Confucian studies enjoyed enormous prestige under the patronage of the shogun Tsunayoshi, the Chinese terms and allusions in Kikaku's haikai may have persuaded snobs that this was not necessarily a vulgar kind of poetry. The collection *Minashiguri* (Empty Chestnuts) compiled by Kikaku in 1683, when he was twenty-two, attracted the attention of men who had earlier been repelled by the Teitoku and Danrin schools. A typical example of Kikaku's erudition is this poem from *Empty Chestnuts*:

ka wo yaku ya	Burn the mosquitoes—
Hōji ga neya no	In Pao-ssu's bedchamber
sasamegoto	Lovers' whisperings.[9]

To understand this verse it is necessary to recognize the allusion to the story of Pao-ssu, the grim-faced consort of King Yu of the Chou Dynasty. When all other attempts to make her laugh had failed, the king, in desperation, lit the beacon fires to summon his feudal lords, even though he was not in any danger. The plan worked—Pao-ssu was moved to laughter by the sight of the vassals galloping up to rescue the king. But unfortunately, the king was soon overthrown as the result of his grand gesture. In Kikaku's verse, mention of the flame of mosquito incense (or possibly a lighted stick used to burn, rather than repel, mosquitoes) would have immediately evoked for his audience the beacon fires lit to amuse Pao-ssu, and her name in turn leads to a romantic scene, possibly in a brothel, of lovers whispering inside a mosquito netting. This kind of erotic atmosphere, not found in Bashō's poetry, helped to give Kikaku his unique place among the disciples. Bashō himself, in the postface to *Empty Chestnuts*, stated that he found in Kikaku's poetry a sensual beauty reminiscent of Po Chü-i. But although Kikaku's verses sometimes compel our admiration by their concentration and many layers of meaning, they lack the power to move us as Bashō's do. This is apparent when the two men wrote on similar themes.

shiodai no	The salted bream
haguki mo samushi	Look cold, even to their gums,
uo no tana	On the fishmonger's shelf.

This verse by Bashō, described in the preceding chapter, may ultimately owe something to the interest in the commonplace aroused when he read *Empty Chestnuts* years before, but how different it is from Kikaku's verse of 1694:

koe karete	Their voices are hoarse,
saru no ha shiroshi	And how white the monkey's teeth!
mine no tsuki	Moon over the peak.[10]

This verse bears the title "Gorges of the Yangtse." In Kikaku's usual manner, it incorporates a familiar Chinese literary theme, monkeys dolefully screaming in the gorges. The scene is late autumn and, as the monkeys cry, the moonlight catches the white flash of their teeth. Mention of the whiteness of the teeth, not found in Chinese poems on the subject, gave the verse its particular haikai quality. But there is something unpleasantly contrived about the image; it contrasts with Bashō's unaffected perception of the cold-looking fish, which he sees as the microcosm of the bleakness of the city in winter. Kikaku was so proud of his verse that in his collection *Kukyōdai* (Verse Brothers, 1694) he matched it against Bashō's and judged it superior—the "older brother." He wrote about his verse:

> The last line should have been "winter moon," but I said "moon over the peak" because I was associating it with the monkeys in the frightening gorges of the Yangtse, described in such Chinese verses as "monkeys scream in the mountains as the moon sinks." I think I have caught the suggestive power of the Chinese poetry describing those cries that cause listeners to wet their sleeves with tears.

But Kikaku also praised Bashō's verse:

> It captures the magic of living speech because the last line is "on the fishermonger's shelf" instead of "the last of old age" or "the end of the year," as one might expect. This is where he attains the realm of mystery and depth; the rest of his art can be deduced from this one example.[11]

Bashō, for his part, once said that it was the "ordinariness" of the last line that marked it as a poem in his style.[12]

The simplicity of the last line and, indeed, the unaffected quality of the entire verse, typifies the karumi of Bashō's last period. Kikaku refused to follow this new style, no doubt aware that his own talent consisted in the display of ingenuity of expression that Bashō was now trying to avoid.[13] Kikaku's verse on the Yangtse Gorges packed into seventeen syllables a whole cluster of desolate images: the hoarse voices of the monkeys; the chilly white of their teeth; the cold, distant moon; and beyond what is mentioned in the poem itself is the whole background in Chinese literature. Bashō's verse achieves an even more powerful effect because it stems from a single, uncontrived perception.

The devoted Kyorai, who remained absolutely loyal to the Master's ideals, rebuked Kikaku for refusing to make his poetry embody Bashō's karumi. He accused Kikaku of being indifferent to the importance of *ryūkō* (up-to-dateness), and pointed out how often Bashō's style had changed as his art matured. Kyorai was right in his charge: it is hard if not impossible to trace any development in Kikaku's poetry. But Kikaku was also right in rejecting Kyorai's advice. It was not that he failed to appreciate karumi—his comments on Bashō's verse on the salted bream prove he was sensitive to that manner of expression—but that he must have recognized a karumi verse without Bashō's genius behind it risked being nothing more than a bare statement.

Kikaku's cleverness, especially when applied to subjects well known to people of the time, won for his poetry a popularity that at one time even surpassed Bashō's.[14] Some of his verses have the lilt of a children's song or folk song, and are endearing even if the meaning is not entirely clear. But often his poetry is so contrived as to be unintelligible. The next great haikai poet, Yosa Buson (1716–83), was the disciple of a disciple of Kikaku's, and called his collection *Shin-Hanatsumi* (A New Flower Gathering, 1777) a title borrowed from Kikaku's *Hanatsumi* (1690). However, in the preface to the collection he called attention to Kikaku's failings, and only toward the end mentioned why he admired his predecessor. He wrote of *Gogenshū* (Poems of Five Eras), Kikaku's most celebrated collection, that it

> was compiled by Kikaku himself, and copied out in his own hand before delivering it to the printer. He must have been meticulous in his editing, since he intended that it have wide

distribution. Yet when one examines the collection one discovers that almost every verse is unintelligible, and very few seem of merit. The verses that have become popular are the ones that are easily understood. But though the author seems to have taken great pride in his achievements, for him to write such exceedingly obscure poetry is as useless as wearing brocade on a pitch-black night. . . . Kikaku has been called the Li Po of haikai, but of the many, many verses he has written not twenty sound impressive. Kikaku's collections contain many obscure verses, but somehow one never gets tired reading them. This is the sign of his excellence. It would seem to indicate that poetry should be open-hearted.[15]

It is probably true that Kikaku's verses had become far more difficult to understand in Buson's day than when originally written, but if this demonstrates how apt their expression was for their own time, it also suggests how quickly they dated.

The obscurity of Kikaku's verses is tedious to unravel, but a few samples will suggest the difficulties. The following poem, published in 1699, is entitled "Before the Dawn":

shinjō ni	For presentation
yami wo kanete ya	I have added the darkness—
ume no hana	The plum blossoms.

The main problem here is the word *kanete*, interpreted in the translation[16] as "added," meaning that the speaker has taken care to arrive before dawn, while it is still dark; this is a compliment to the person visited who, like the old poets, will be able to detect a spray of plum blossoms by the scent alone, even in the dark. But *kanete* also means "beforehand"; in that case the poem might mean, "For presentation (to you) I have broken off in the darkness, before it got light, the plum blossoms," suggesting the speaker's impatience to see his beloved.[17] It has also been suggested that plays on the words *ka* (fragrance) and *nete* (sleeping) were intended, meaning that the lover comes with his plum blossoms as an offering, only to find the beloved sleeping.[18] Perhaps *kane* is also used for the "bell" that sounds the dawn, and perhaps the character for *yami* (darkness) was deliberately written with the gate radical in order to suggest the gates of the house approached by the lover.[19] All this does not touch on the problem of the first word, *shinjō*, an extremely stiff word for "presentation," not normally used for lovers' gifts, and perhaps the sign of some arcane illusion. It seems impossible that Kikaku could have had *all* these overtones in mind, but the ambiguity has given commentators scope for their imaginations.

Even poems of lesser complexity have elicited detailed analyses. The following verse has a title in Chinese, "Regretting the blossoms, I do not sweep the ground," a line from a poem by Po Chü-i.[20]

wa ga yakko	My servant boy sleeps
rakka ni asane	This morning in falling blossoms—
yurushikeri	I have forgiven him.

There seems to be an allusion not only to Po Chü-i but to a waka by Minamoto no Kintada (888–948): "Keeper of the palace garden, if you have a heart forbear from sweeping it this morning, at least this spring." Following this allusion, we may conclude that Kikaku is glad that his servant has overslept and therefore spared the fallen blossoms instead of sweeping them. But one commentator analyzed Kikaku's reactions into six successive stages: (1) The servant is oversleeping. How disgraceful! (2) Look! The cherry blossoms are falling! (3) How uncouth of him not to be aware how lovely the garden is this morning! I'll wake him. (4) No, if I wake him he'll say something about being sorry to have overslept and then immediately sweep the garden. (5) Yes, the best thing he can do now is sleep. I'll keep quiet. (6) But perhaps he is deliberately oversleeping, knowing I would feel this way. I hadn't realized how intelligent he is![21] It is small wonder that a man whose verses inspire such detailed analysis should have resisted the claims of karumi!

Buson declared that he never wearied of reading Kikaku, even though most of his poems were obscure; this has been in general the judgment of posterity. He is the only one of Bashō's disciples whose complete poetry has been published with detailed commentaries, and his name immediately conjures up an exuberant if sometimes overly fanciful style. His most famous verse, perhaps, is one unmarred by his usual obscurity:

kiraretaru	Stabbed in a dream—
yume wa makoto ka	Or was it reality?
nomi no ato	The marks of a flea.

Kyorai commented on this poem, "Kikaku is really a poet. Who else would have composed a poem just about having been bitten by a flea?" Bashō replied, "That's right. He's a Teika. He lives up to his reputation of being able to put together an impressive poem even about a trifling incident."[22]

When Bashō called Kikaku a "Teika" he obviously meant to praise his craftsmanship, and not to suggest his poetry had mysterious depths. Even so, this was high praise for a disciple who squandered extraordinary gifts on poetry that was so unlike Bashō's own.

MUKAI KYORAI (1651–1704)

In the spring of 1684 (the year of Bashō's *Exposure in the Fields*) Kikaku made his first visit to Kyoto. Before going on to Osaka, where he was to participate as a scribe in Saikaku's celebrated composition of 23,500 verses in a day, he met Mukai Kyorai. Bashō's first Edo disciple was the agent for Kyorai's becoming his first Kyoto disciple.

Kyorai was born in Nagasaki, the son of a learned physician who boasted of an ancestry going back to Fujiwara no Kamatari.[23] One night toward the end of 1658 the father had a dream in which the spirit of Sugawara no Michizane appeared and delivered the oracle that he would enjoy great success if he moved to Kyoto and practiced there. The father, then a man of forty-nine, left at once with his family for the capital. True to the prophecy, he soon gained considerable renown, and eventually was appointed physician to the imperial family. Kyorai was a boy of seven when he arrived in Kyoto. At fifteen he was sent by his family to Fukuoka to study the martial arts under an uncle. He excelled in every variety, but he decided at the age of twenty-three to give up his career as a samurai and return to Kyoto. His reasons are not known, but perhaps he intended to help his brother, who had succeeded to his father's practice. In any case, Kyorai was able to lead a life of comparative affluence, devoting his leisure to haikai and extending hospitality to other poets. Alone among Bashō's disciples he had an entrée into court circles, and this was to color his poetry.

Kyorai was able, thanks to his wealth, to buy a country house at Saga, west of Kyoto, to which he gave the name Rakushisha (Hut of the Fallen Persimmons) after a storm in 1689 had stripped the forty persimmon trees around the house of their fruit.[24] Rakushisha was to become the home away from home for poets of Bashō's school whenever they visited the capital, and Bashō himself, as we have seen, wrote his *Saga Diary* there. Though it was only a modest retreat and Kyorai spent most of his time in the city, his verses never lost touch with nature, unlike those of the city-bred Kikaku, who could write:

Echigoya ni	At the Echigoya
kinu saku oto ya	The sound of ripping silk—
koromogae	Time to change clothes![25]

Kikaku evoked with this description the change of seasons in the city, without a single image drawn from nature; people are buying material for their summer costumes at the Echigoya, a big draper's shop in Edo. In contrast, Kyorai attempted to find something of nature even in a city scene. Here is a famous verse on the changing of the seasons:

hachitataki	Tonight I noticed
konu yo to nareba	The gong-beaters had stopped coming—
oboro nari	The moon was misty.[26]

The gong-beaters were a familiar feature of the winter in Kyoto. For forty-eight nights they wandered through the streets, but this night Kyorai realizes he hasn't heard their gongs. He looks out the window and sees that the moon is misty. Spring has come.

Kyorai's poetry at its best approaches Bashō's, and if faithful observation of Bashō's principles alone could have made for excellence, Kyorai would certainly have ranked a close second to the Master. But, except for an occasional verse recalling his military career or associations at the court, Kyorai lacked marked individuality. His verses that have enjoyed the most popularity are not the best, but those that display an uncharacteristic ingenuity:

hototogisu	Listen! The cuckoos
naku ya hibari to	Are calling—they and the skylarks
jūmonji	Make a crossmark.

Morikawa Kyoriku acclaimed this verse as one of Kyorai's two masterpieces (along with the verse on the lake given below), but Ebara Taizō wrote of it:

> The meaning of this poem needs hardly to be explained. It combines the flying habits of cuckoos and skylarks: the cuckoo flies horizontally across the sky at a medium height, whereas the skylark rises in a perpendicular line from the fields high up into the sky. The interest of the poem, then, is in the crossing of the two lines. One can only describe the interest of the poem as infantile, and the expression as primitive. If Kyoriku really meant it when he said he admired this verse, we have no choice but to doubt his critical faculties.[27]

The other poem acclaimed by Kyoriku was in an entirely dissimilar vein:

mizuumi no	How the waters
mizu masarikeri	Of the lake have swollen—
satsuki ame	The fifth-month rains.[28]

The effect of this verse is unfortunately lost in translation. The word *mizuumi* has a pattern of sounds in no way approximated by the English word "lake," and the *m* sounds are repeated in the second line and at the close, together with a *zu* or *tsu* sound that occurs in the second syllable of each line. The effect of the repetition is to suggest the slow swelling of the waters of Lake Biwa under the steady rains, and this is confirmed by the protracted syllables of *masarikeri*, "have swollen." The whole verse, in contrast to the ingenuity of the preceding one, breathes actual observation, and the two elements—the swollen lake and the rains—illuminate each other. This is clearly haikai poetry at its best. Kyoriku wrote about these verses, which first appeared in the collection *Arano* (Wilderness, 1689), "It would be hard to find poems, even among those by the Master, which are superior. There is not a poet but envies them."[29] The degree to which the second verse depends on its exact wording, as opposed to its imagery, conception, or structure, is revealed in another passage by Kyoriku:

> During the period when I first became a member of this school I was asked to write a verse about the fifth-month rains. I wrote this one:

mizuumi no	Even the waters
mizu mo masuru ya	Of the lake are swelling—
satsuki ame	The fifth-month rains.

But when I thought the poem over carefully I decided it was too direct and lacking in flavor. I reworked it, but only succeeded in making it worse. Some time afterward *Wilderness* appeared. I saw there your poem:

mizuumi no	How the waters
mizu masarikeri	Of the lake have swollen—
satsuki ame	The fifth-month rains.

I felt as if the dawn had come and that I had learned for the first time the meaning of haikai.[30]

Judged by normal standards Kyorai's poem—if not a fantastic coincidence—is plagiarized, at best a poem that could be printed only after due acknowledgment to Kyoriku. However, the poem is not only credited to Kyorai but acclaimed as his masterpiece, an indication of how crucial the difference seemed between *masarikeri*, a long, stately word for "has swollen," suggesting the steady flow of water into the lake, and the choppier *mo masuru ya.*

Kyorai's development as a poet is otherwise revealed in his most important work, *Kyoraishō* (Conversations with Kyorai).[31] The book is in four sections: Opinions of the Master; Opinions of Members of His School; Precedents; Training. The first section is deservedly the most famous, but the work is filled throughout with invaluable accounts of haikai poets at work. The format of the first two sections is to present a hokku by some member of the school, followed by the comments it aroused.

yūsuzumi	The cool of evening—
senki okoshite	I had a bout of colic
kaerinikeri	And went back home.
	Kyorai

When I was first studying hokku, I asked how one should be made. The Master replied, "The verse should be strong and the haikai element handled firmly." As an experiment I wrote this verse and asked his opinion. "You still haven't got the idea!" he said with a great laugh.[32]

Kyorai tended always to be literal in following Bashō's suggestions, obeying each recommendation as if it were an ultimate judgment. In this example he followed Bashō's prescriptions exactly, but what he wrote was unfortunately not a poem, merely a statement in five, seven, and five syllables.

Kyorai is endearing in his willingness to include conversations with Bashō that portray himself as foolish (or, at any rate, insufficiently perceptive), but in other conversations he proved he was a worthy disciple:

yuku haru wo	The passing of spring
Ōmi no hito to	With the men of Ōmi
oshimikeri	Have I lamented.
	Bashō

The Master said, "Shōhaku criticized this poem on the grounds that I might just as well have substituted Tamba for Ōmi, or 'passing of the year' for 'passing of spring.' How does that strike you?" Kyorai said, "Shōhaku's criticism misses the mark. It is proper that one regret the passing of spring when the waters of Lake Biwa are hazy. This is particularly so because this poem is based on actual observation." The Master said, "That's right. The men of old loved spring in this province hardly less than in the capital." Kyorai said, "I am most impressed by what you say. It's true—if you were in Ōmi at the end of the year, why should you regret its passing? And if you were in Tamba as spring was passing, such a feeling of regret would never arise. It's certainly true that the sights of nature have the power to stir men." The Master said, "Kyorai, you are a man with whom I can talk about poetry!" He was especially pleased.[33]

In this passage Kyorai, far from playing the role of the stumbling beginner, is acclaimed by Bashō as a worthy companion in haikai. Certainly Kyorai was pleased to report this progress. We have other evidence to indicate how much Bashō had come to respect Kyorai's judgment: when he completed the rough draft of *Genjūan no Ki* (Account of the Unreal Dwelling) he sent it to Kyorai for his criticism.[34]

However, this passage is of interest not only because of what it tells about Kyorai, but because it reveals an essential aspect of Bashō's poetry. He is insisting that each word of a hokku be absolutely unalterable. Shōhaku, a poet formerly of Bashō's school who had broken with him, was a native of Ōmi, the province mentioned in the verse, and his disparaging comment therefore had more than usual weight. But Kyorai's remarks were exactly to the point: spring is lovely in Ōmi and one is sorry to see it pass, but at the end of the year, when the cold, damp wind blows across Lake Biwa, one is not moved to the same regret; and Tamba could not be substituted for Ōmi because people in that isolated mountain region welcome the summer, the best time of year. Bashō's innumerable recensions of his verses were aimed at achieving, as here, the exact, immovable heart of his perception.

Every section of *Conversations with Kyorai* yields some valuable insight into Bashō's haikai aesthetic. His insistence that each verse be distinct in conception, his evaluation of the unspoken implications of a verse, or his judgment of which themes were suited to haikai poetry and which to waka are typical subjects of discussion. The book also contains interesting vignettes of the debates between Kyorai and Bonchō when selecting verses for inclusion in *The Monkey's Raincoat*.

Kyorai was known especially for his espousal of Bashō's doctrine of *fueki ryūkō*, which may be translated "permanence and change" or "unchanging and up-to-date." Bashō insisted that a worthwhile hokku must contain both elements: it had to have eternal validity and not be a mere flash of wit, but it must also be in tune with the moment and not a fossilized generalization. In other terms, a hokku had to be at once about the observed moment—the instant the horse eats the flower, or the frog splashes into the water, or the wind bends the bamboo—but also about the eternal element that was momentarily disturbed by the horse, frog, or gust of wind. The combination or juxtaposition of the two elements, one eternal and the other momentary, gives a tension to the verse, creating a field of tension between two electric poles that the spark of the reader's mind must leap across; the further the distance the poet can make the spark jump, the greater the effect of his poem.

Kyorai also used the term *fueki ryūkō* in a more restricted sense when he criticized Kikaku for lacking ryūkō. Kikaku's verses were certainly apt to be about the present moment, but Kyorai was condemning him for his failure to make karumi his new principle. This was not what Bashō meant by fueki ryūkō,[35] but Kyorai, searching for some expression of the Master's to use in rebuking Kikaku, twisted this term to fit the crime.

Kyorai was absolutely devoted to Bashō, but at times he seems unconsciously to have distorted Bashō's views to prove his own contentions. Falsification of the Master's views was a charge frequently exchanged by the disciples. Kyoriku, for example, disagreeing with Kyorai's insistence on fueki ryūkō, wrote:

> While the Master was alive I never troubled myself over ryūkō and fueki. Whenever I completed some verses I would show them to the Master, and he would decide which were the good ones and which the bad. In the case of the verses that he judged to be good, I never intentionally aimed at any particular quality, but fueki and ryūkō were naturally present. The same remains true today, when the Master is dead. I have never thought of ryūkō and fueki as holy.[36]

Kyoriku's bold assertion of his opinions contrasts with the modesty of Kyorai, who never pretended to be more than a transmitter of Bashō's opinions. He was an admirable man, self-effacing and earnest, but not an especially memorable poet.

MORIKAWA KYORIKU (1656–1715)

Kyoriku was a samurai of the Hikone clan. Unlike most of Bashō's other disciples of the samurai class, Kyoriku was on active duty, and not at liberty to leave his post in order to consult the Master. As a result, his association with Bashō lasted only for about nine months, beginning in the autumn of 1692; this did not prevent him, however, from claiming that he was the favorite disciple and the sole heir to Bashō's art.

Kyoriku began his study of haikai poetry when he was about eighteen, no doubt as part of the literary education a well-rounded samurai needed in addition to his martial skills. He evidently paid less attention to his hokku than to painting and writing poetry in Chinese, avocations he considered more suited to the austere samurai ideals. For a time, however, Kyoriku was turning out three hundred to five hundred verses a day, by his own estimates.[37] After some seven or eight years at haikai composition he abandoned the art, apparently disenchanted with his teacher.

Some years later he accidentally read some poetry by Bashō, whose fame was attracting increasing attention. Kyoriku tested himself by composing verses on the same themes as Bashō's and had to admit that he was no match for the master. He was eager to meet Bashō and discuss his poetry, but he had no opportunity to go to Edo. Kyoriku studied the volumes of Bashō he acquired, making them his teacher. A series of tragic deaths in his family led him to take up composition again, perhaps as an outlet for his grief. His earliest surviving verses, written in 1689, are childish in conception and execution,[38] but he devoted himself to the study of haikai poetry with such energy that he made astonishing progress. A year later he wrote:

daimyō no	I slept in a room
nema ni mo netaru	A daimyo himself had slept in—
samusa ka na	How cold it was![39]

This verse, written on an official journey, suggests the imposing bareness of a daimyo's rooms at some hostelry on the way; alone in the large suite, Kyoriku felt the cold more than in a junior officer's room.

After several frustrating near-meetings with Bashō, Kyoriku at last met him in the eighth month of 1693 at the newly rebuilt Bashō-an in Fukagawa. Kyoriku took along a sample of his recent poems. Bashō examined them and, according to Kyoriku, was astonished by their excellence. He was incredulous that so fine a poet could have been self-taught, and declared, "Kyoriku is the only one who has searched through my collections for my soul and found it. I have explained the nature of this soul day and night to my other pupils, but it has been difficult communicating with them. Today my deepest desire is realized." The setting and even the language is reminiscent of the first meeting of Kūkai and the Chinese priest Hui-kuo nine hundred years earlier: the Master, having despaired of ever finding a worthy vessel for the profound teachings of which he is the repository, is overjoyed to discover at last in a stranger the man he had so long been waiting for. Allowing for some exaggeration by Kyoriku, it seems certain that Bashō was indeed delighted to read these verses, particularly because he had long despaired of transmitting his philosophy of haikai. Bashō praised in particular this poem by Kyoriku:

tōdago mo	Dumplings on a string:
kotsubu ni narinu	They too are smaller this year—
aki no kaze	The winds of autumn.

Kyoriku wrote this verse at Utsunoyama, a hill on the Tōkaidō road. Dumplings, sold ten on a string, were the "famous product" of the place. Kyoriku had bought some on a previous visit; now, he notices they are smaller than they used to be, suggesting that the world has also contracted, grown harsher; at the moment of that realization he feels the autumnal wind.

Kyoriku wrote that he had spent two days polishing the second line. The perfection of its wording, as much as the meaning of the entire verse, no doubt accounted for the enthusiasm aroused in Bashō. He said that the poem had *shiori*, an indefinable quality akin to pathos, his highest term of praise.[40] The meeting with Kyoriku seems also to have snapped Bashō out of a mood of depression. He broke a silence of six months to participate in a kasen that has been called a first sounding of his karumi style.[41]

During the following months Kyoriku frequently visited the Bashō-an, and Bashō spent time with his new pupil at the mansion where Kyoriku served. Bashō wrote when Kyoriku left Edo the following year: "In painting you were my teacher; in poetry I taught you and you were my disciple. My teacher's paintings are imbued with such profundity of spirit and executed with such marvellous dexterity that I could never approach their mysterious depths."[42] The special intimacy Bashō felt for Kyoriku may have been owing to their both having come from the same provincial military class. Kyoriku claimed to be Bashō's spiritual heir, not only because of his poetic skill and understanding of the Master's art, but because Bashō allegedly gave him three secret works on haikai composition in the third month of 1693. Bashō was almost unique as a teacher in that age, when the tradition of esoteric transmission of secret teachings was so deeply rooted, in that he had so few secrets to impart to chosen pupils. Kyorai, it is true, once wrote, "I learned many things from the Master, but this was the only one he asked me to keep a secret, so for a time I refrained from letting others know."[43] The "secret" concerned the use of kireji. It is surprising that

Bashō retained this last trace of medieval secrecy, but the transmission of a secret, however unsensational, was a mark of special favor. That undoubtedly is how Kyoriku interpreted Bashō's gesture.

After Bashō's death Kyoriku was to insist on *kechimyaku* (blood lineage) as the most important factor in becoming a haikai poet. "If one is born with a particular blood lineage, one's eyes and nose are naturally formed."[44] By "blood lineage" Kyoriku seems to have meant something like tradition; he said that he first became aware of this connection between Bashō and himself when poring over the collections *Wilderness* and *The Monkey's Raincoat*. But he sometimes gives the impression that he alone among the disciples had the right pedigree to be Bashō's heir.

Kyoriku's certainty that he was Bashō's successor made him write arrogantly about other members of the school. He wrote about Hattori Ransetsu, generally esteemed as a senior disciple, "Extremely untalented. His poetry is essentially feeble. Though it seems to have surface charm, it is totally lacking in substance."[45] Even when he praised certain disciples there was a note of condescension, as if he were observing from his lofty eminence the merits of lesser men. He was especially unsparing in his criticisms of the manner in which other disciples transmitted the texts of Bashō's poetry and prose. For example, he violently attacked Itō Fūkoku (d. 1701) for the clumsy editing of *Hakusenshū* (1698), the first collection of Bashō's hokku. His criticisms were sometimes justified, but his intemperate expressions must have inspired terror.[46]

Apart from his insistence on blood lineage, Kyoriku was known for his espousal of juxtaposition (*toriawase*) as a basic principle of haikai composition. He quoted Bashō as saying, "The hokku is a matter of juxtaposition. A man who can bring two elements together and do it well is a skillful poet."[47]

A principle of juxtaposition, whether or not consciously practiced, was certainly basic to the haikai of Bashō and his school. A haikai normally had to contain two elements if it was not to be merely a short evocative statement; the juxtaposition of the two elements could stimulate the reader into re-creating the world which had been stripped down to these elements. As we have seen, one element is generally "eternal" and the other "fleeting," though this may not be immediately apparent. The two elements must not automatically follow one from the other, for in that case there would be no tension between them; on the other hand, they must not be totally disparate but "echo" each other, giving off similar overtones. Bashō's poetry contains many examples, such as the haikai on the statues of Buddha in Nara quoted in the preceding chapter. Kyoriku could also boast a few effective verses in this vein, such as:

ume ga ka ya	The scent of plum blossoms—
kyaku no hana ni wa	Under the visitor's nose
asagi wan	A celadon cup.[48]

The delicacy of the teacup and the faint perfume of the plum blossoms make a suitable pair of elements for juxtaposition, but the second line (which cost Kyoriku enormous trouble) is too unambiguous: the visiter lifts the teacup to his nose and catches a whiff of the scent of plum blossoms. In this case the gap between the two poles of the poem is insufficiently wide to induce a strong creative spark.

An excellent example of juxtaposition is given in *Conversations with Kyorai*, a poem by Bonchō to which Bashō contributed the telling line:

Shimogyō ya	The lower city—
yuki tsumu ue no	On the piled-up snow
yoru no ame	The night rain falls.

> This verse at first lacked an opening line, and everyone, from the Master on down, tried out various possibilities until the Master at length settled on this line. Bonchō said Yes to it, but he still did not seem satisfied. The Master said, "Bonchō, why don't you show what a good poet you are by writing a better line? If you can, I'll never write another haikai." Kyorai said, "Anyone can see what a good line it is, but it's not so easy to appreciate that no other line would do. If the members of some other school learned about this, they might think your claim was ridiculous, and make up any number of other first lines themselves. But the ones they considered good would seem laughably bad to us![49]

Kyorai does not specify what surpassing qualities the opening line possessed that made even Bashō depart from his customary modesty so far as to defy anyone to match it. It is clear, however, that mention of "the lower city" (Shimogyō), a quiet area of Kyoto where people of humble means lived, "echoed" exactly the mood of rain falling softly on the still undisturbed snow. Kyoriku's ideal of juxtaposition was nowhere more perfectly realized.

Kyoriku's poetry has lost most of its interest, but his high place among Bashō's disciples is assured, if only because of the effectiveness of his critical writings on haikai, especially *Haikai Mondō* (1697). He was also the editor of *Fūzoku Monzen* (1705), the first important collection of haibun. *Fūzoku Monzen* is a grab bag of prose pieces by Bashō and members of his school, including Kyoriku himself, Kikaku, Kyorai, Shikō, Bonchō, and Ransetsu. The prose of Bashō's travel diaries is known as haibun because its incise and elliptic style suggests his haikai poetry, not because it has any specifically humorous, "haikai" content; but many selections in *Fūzoku Monzen* are marred by the deliberate injection of an arch and pretentious humor, which the authors seem to have considered to be indispensable to haibun. The best pieces, apart from those by Bashō, are those in which the solemnity of the subject—an elegy for a dead poet, like the tributes to Kyorai by Kyoriku and Shikō—prevents the author from indulging in facetiousness or a ponderous use of allusions to Chinese and Japanese literature. In all, twenty-one "genres" of haibun are represented in the collection. These represent the various categories of elegy, preface, rhyme-prose, etc., derived from traditional Chinese collections like *Wen Hsüan* (*Monzen* in Japanese),[50] but little attempt was in fact made to distinguish one genre from another.[51]

Of the total of 114 selections in *Fūzoku Monzen*, ranging in length from a paragraph to eight or ten pages, Kyoriku, the editor, is represented by thirty-two, followed by Bashō with sixteen and Shikō with thirteen. The generous sampling Kyoriku gave of his own works is typical of his almost arrogant confidence, but may also indicate an awareness that he was better at prose than at poetry. His contributions include *Hyakka-fu* (*Fu* on the Hundred Flowers), which compares, in a manner that has reminded some critics of Saikaku, a variety of flowers with familiar figures of the licensed quarters; *Shiki-ji* (*Ji* on the Four Seasons), which, despite its title, is a humorous linking of money and the sights of the seasons; and *Gorōsei no Ki*, an allusion-filled account of his retreat near Hikone. Kyoriku emerges no more lovably in the prose poetry of *Fūzoku Monzen* than he does in his critical works, but he is clearly a master of haibun style.

Fūzoku Monzen was Kyoriku's most lasting monument. It was at once the first and best collection of haibun, and its influence was considerable, not only on writings specifically in this style but on much of the Japanese prose of the eighteenth century.

THE OTHER DISCIPLES

During Bashō's lifetime four disciples enjoyed special distinction: Kikaku, Ransetsu, Kyorai, and Naitō Jōsō (1662–1704). By 1705 Kyoriku was writing of the "ten philosophers who continue the art," likening the cream of Bashō's disciples to the ten famous disciples of Confucius. But the identity of the ten remained a matter of debate. The selection now generally adopted includes, in addition to the four men mentioned above, Kyoriku, Shikō, Shida Yaba (1663–1740), Tachibana Hokushi (d. 1718), Sugiyama Sampū (1647–1732), and Ochi Etsujin (1656–1739?). The list is arbitrary: many critics have expressed doubts that these ten men deserve to be singled out as the most distinguished of Bashō's disciples. Each man, it is true, is remembered for perhaps a half-dozen hokku, or as the compiler of an anthology or work of criticism.[52] But it is hard to justify the presence of Hokushi when the far more distinctive Nozawa Bonchō (d. 1714) is omitted, and we may wonder why Etsujin, who accompanied Bashō on one journey, was chosen instead of Kawai Sora (1649–1701), long his faithful companion. Even doubling the list of the "ten philosophers" would not accommodate all those who contributed to the glory of the School of Bashō; but if we restrict the list to the truly outstanding, Kikaku, Kyorai, and Kyoriku—with the possible addition of Shikō—might suffice.

Bashō's largest group of disciples was probably in his native town of Ueno in Iga. He always maintained special interest in these men, the most distinguished of whom was Hattori Tohō (1657–1730), a samurai who, like Bashō, gave up his calling in order to devote himself entirely to poetry. Tohō is best known as the compiler of *Sanzōshi* (Three Notebooks, 1704), a work of haikai criticism that ranks nearly as high as *Conversations with Kyorai*. Another notable disciple in Ueno was Kubota Ensui (1640–1704), a close friend to whom Bashō sent some of his best letters.

In Edo the disciples were headed by Kikaku and Ransetsu. Sampū, an early pupil, remained a benefactor over the years. Bashō's neighbor in Fukagawa, Sora, selflessly devoted himself to Bashō's well-being, as we know from *The Narrow Road of Oku*. Disciples from other parts of the country frequently visited Bashō in Edo, but toward the end of his life he preferred to live near Kyoto with his disciples there. Kyorai was his most intimate disciple in the capital, but Bashō was attracted to the Zen priest Jōsō, who also wrote poetry in Chinese; a combination of Buddhist discipline and deep devotion to Bashō gave Jōsō's poetry a depth that led later men to say that he alone of the disciples had inherited Bashō's *sabi*, an understatement hinting at great depths.

Although Bashō's disciples came from different social classes, none of them, with the possible exception of Kyoriku, ever seemed to consider that status was a matter of consequence, a remarkable phenomenon in the Tokugawa period, when the hierarchical structure of society was emphasized. Kyorai, who frequented the imperial court, joined with Bonchō, an impoverished physician, to compile *The Monkey's Raincoat*, and their discussions, as recorded in *Conversations with Kyorai*, suggest absolute equality. Bashō welcomed to his school Imbe Rotsū, said to have been a beggar, and broke with him only when Rotsū began to sell forgeries as "secret teachings" of the Master; in the end, however, Bashō forgave even Rotsū, and on his deathbed asked other members of the school to be kind to him. Perhaps Bashō's favorite disciple was Tsuboi Tokoku, who died young, leaving few verses of distinction; even after Tokoku had been exiled for fraud, Bashō continued to seek out his company, as we have seen. Bonchō was also convicted of a crime—smuggling, it seems—and was thrown into prison, but when he was released he was immediately again accepted into the circle of disciples. On the other hand, Ransetsu's high rank as a samurai did not protect him from criticism or give him any other special privileges among the disciples. One is tempted to speak of the "democracy of poetry" in connection with this school.[53]

In later years the reputations of the different disciples varied according to the critics. Bonchō's objective manner appealed to Buson and Shiki, as a forerunner of a less emotional poetry than Bashō's. Kagami Shikō (1665–1731), on the other hand, was generally remembered as an ambitious, even unscrupulous figure, eager to push himself and profit by his relations with Bashō. His books of criticism, disseminated throughout the country, helped to establish haikai as a national poetic avocation, and are dotted with useful observations, but they have often been condemned as a vulgarization of Bashō's teachings.

After Bashō's death his school splintered into many factions, each claiming to represent the authentic traditions. The competition for pupils sometimes became severe, and enterprising teachers, in the attempt to establish their authority, were not above producing spurious evidence of the confidence bestowed on them by the Master. Kyoriku, a samurai who took his calling seriously, naturally did not stoop to such practices, but his disciple Yamamoto Mōen (1669–1729) gave up his samurai status and became a Buddhist priest so that he might be free to travel around the country as a missionary for Kyoriku's school.[54] The name of the Master continued to be invoked, even after his teachings were thoroughly corrupted by self-seeking, inferior poets. Deprived of their teacher, many disciples fell silent, or else wrote conspicuously inferior verse. But the books of poetry and criticism that had appeared under Bashō's inspiration remained behind and, even when misunderstood, acquired the status of classics.

NOTES

1. Early in his career Kikaku used the surname Enomoto, and some scholars refer to him by that name. I have followed the preference of Imaizumi Jun'ichi, the author of the study of Kikaku, *Genroku Haijin Takarai Kikaku.*

2. Quoted in Yamazaki Kiyoshi, *Bashō to Monjin*, p. 5.

3. *Ibid.*, p. 4.

4. Yokozawa Saburō (ed.), *Haikai Mondō*, p. 43.

5. Kanda Hideo, "Kikaku," in Imoto Nōichi, *Bashō wo meguru Hitobito*, p. 120.

6. Yokozawa, p. 91.

7. *Ibid.*, p. 35.

8. *Ibid.*, p. 43.

9. Abe Kimio and Asō Isoji, *Kinsei Haiku Haibun Shū*, p. 88.

10. *Ibid.*, p. 89.

11. Ebara Taizō, *Shōmon no Hitobito*, p. 14.

12. See Kidō Saizō and Imoto Nōichi, *Rengaron Shū, Haironn Shū*, p. 408.

13. See Ebara, p. 15. Imaizumi devotes a whole chapter to the simplicity (*sobokusa*) in Kikaku's verse (*op. cit.*, pp. 32–58). Although this is useful in redressing the balance of criticism leveled against Kikaku for his overingenuity, the prevailing impression of Kikaku's verse is certainly not one of simplicity, and Imaizumi's own elaborate analyses of certain Kikaku verses (pp. 9–21) indicate the pitfalls awaiting modern readers, even if Kikaku's contemporaries had less trouble figuring out his poetry.

14. See preface by Abe Kimio in Imaizumi, *Genroku Haijin*.

15. Teruoka Yasutaka and Kawashima Tsuyu, *Buson Shū, Issa Shū*, p. 274.

16. Following Naitō Meisetsu in *Kikaku Kenkyū*, ed. by Samukawa Sokotsu and Hayashi Wakaki, p. 24.

17. Interpretation of Yamazaki Gakudō in *ibid.*

18. Iwamoto Shiseki, *Gogenshū Zenkai*, p. 6.

19. *Ibid.*

20. See Abe and Asō, p. 87.

21. Kanda, p. 111.

22. Kidō and Imoto, p. 313.

23. Sugiura Shōichirō, "Haijin Kyorai Hyōden," in *Mukai Kyorai*, p. 4.

24. Abe and Asō, p. 317.

25. *Ibid.*, p. 87.

26. *Ibid.*, p. 96.

27. Ebara Taizō, *Haiku Hyōshaku*, p. 256.

28. Abe and Asō, p. 98.

29. Yokozawa, p. 190.

30. *Ibid.*, p. 173. Imoto Nōichi (in Komiya Toyotake and Yokozawa Saburō, *Bashō Kōza*, III, p. 231) expressed the belief that the story must be taken with a large grain of salt.

31. This collection of discussions of poetry by Bashō and others of his school was not published until 1775, so long after Kyorai's death that some scholars doubted its authenticity; but the discovery of the rough draft of part of the manuscript makes it certain that the work was indeed written by Kyorai, probably toward the end of his life. See Imoto Nōichi in Kidō and Imoto, pp. 279–87.

32. See Donald Keene, *Anthology of Japanese Literature*, pp. 377–83 for a wider selection from *Kyoraishō*.

33. See Andō Tsuguo, *Bashō*, pp. 7–10, for the background to this section.

34. Sugiura, p. 65.

35. See Okamoto Akira, *Kyoraishō Hyōshaku*, pp. 253–56.

36. Yokozawa, p. 37.

37. *Ibid.*, p. 83.

38. See Ogata Tsutomu, "Kyoriku," in Imoto, *Bashō wo meguru*, p. 144.

39. Abe and Asō, p. 128.

40. See Kidō and Imoto, p. 377.

41. Ogata, p. 149.

42. Complete translation in Ryusaku Tsunoda, *et al.*, *Sources of Japanese Tradition*, p. 458.

43. Kidō and Imoto, p. 349.

44. Yokozawa, p. 97.

45. *Ibid.*, p. 202.

46. Ogata, p. 158.

47. Quoted in Yamazaki, p. 262.

48. Ebara, *Haiku Hyōshaku*, II, p. 15.

49. Kidō and Imoto, pp. 315–16.

50. See J. R. Hightower, "The *Wen Hsüan* and Genre Theory," in *Harvard Journal of Asiatic Studies*, XX (1957), pp. 512–33.

51. Kyorai did make a stab at rhymed prose in Japanese, but for the rest it is hard to tell the various *fu*, *ji*, etc., apart.

52. For translations of haiku by Bashō's disciples, see Harold G. Henderson, *An Introduction to Haiku*, pp. 49–67.

53. See Tsunoda, pp. 450–58.

54. See Yamazaki, pp. 318–43.

BIBLIOGRAPHY

Abe Kimio and Asō Isoji. *Kinsei Haiku Haibun Shū*, Nihon Koten Bungaku Taikei series. Tokyo: Iwanami Shoten, 1964.

Andō Tsuguo. *Bashō*. Tokyo: Chikuma Shobō, 1965.

Ebara Taizō. *Haiku Hyōshaku*, 2 vols. Tokyo: Kadokawa Shoten, 1947.

———. *Shōmon no Hitobito*. Kyoto: Ōyashima Shuppan KK, 1946.

Henderson, Harold G. *An Introduction to Haiku*. Garden City, N.Y.: Doubleday, 1958.

Ichihashi Taku. *Bashō no Monjin*. Kyoto: Ōyashima Shuppan KK, 1947.

Imaizumi Jun'ichi. *Genroku Haijin Takarai Kikaku*. Tokyo: Ōfūsha, 1969.

Imoto Nōichi, *Bashō wo meguru Hitobito*. Tokyo: Murasaki no Kokyōsha, 1953.

Iwamoto Shiseki. *Gogenshū Zenkai*. Tokyo: Haishodō, 1929.

Kidō Saizō and Imoto Nōichi. *Rengaron Shū, Hairon Shū* in Nihon Koten Bungaku Taikei series. Tokyo: Iwanami Shoten, 1961.

Komiya Yasutaka and Yokozawa Saburō. *Bashō Kōza*, 9 vols. Tokyo: Sanseidō, 1948.

Okamoto Akira. *Kyoraishō Hyōshaku*. Tokyo: Meicho Kankōkai, 1970.

Samukawa Sokotsu and Hayashi Wakaki. *Kikaku Kenkyū*. Tokyo: Arusu, 1927.

Sugiura Shōichirō (ed.). *Mukai Kyorai*. Nagasaki: Kyorai Kenshōkai, 1954.

Teruoka Yasutaka and Kawashima Tsuyu. *Buson Shū, Issa Shū*, in Nihon Koten Bungaku Taikei series. Tokyo: Iwanami Shoten, 1959.

Yamazaki Kiyoshi. *Bashō to Monjin*. Osaka: Kōbunsha, 1947.

Yokozawa Saburō (ed.). *Haikai Mondō*, in Iwanami Bunko series. Tokyo: Iwanami, 1954.

CHAPTER 7
FICTION
KANA ZŌSHI

Kana zōshi (kana books) is the general term for the prose literature between 1600 and 1682. The name originally was used to distinguish writings entirely in kana (the Japanese syllabary) —or in a mixture of Chinese characters and kana—from texts in Chinese. In the Meiji period, however, it came to be used to designate the wide variety of literary works that appeared prior to the publication of Saikaku's *Life of an Amorous Man* in 1682.[1] The genre embraces not only fiction but works of a near-historical nature, pious or moral tracts, books of practical information, translations from Chinese and European literature, guidebooks, evaluations of courtesans and actors, and miscellaneous essays.[2]

The first books printed from movable type had mainly been

works of classical literature, but a few kana zōshi, especially works of fiction in the traditions of the preceding century, began to be published in private editions. The most celebrated of these stories was *Uraminosuke*, written soon after 1612 by an unknown author. The story opens with the statement that the fateful meeting of the young samurai Uraminosuke and the beautiful Yukinomae occurred in the summer of 1604, on the occasion of the Festival of Ten Thousand Lanterns at the Kiyomizu Temple in Kyoto. Various attempts have been made to determine if there was a real-life model for Uraminosuke,[3] but even if there was not, it is noteworthy that the story was set in recent times. References to Kabuki and other features of life in seventeenth-century Kyoto give a contemporary flavor even to the hackneyed plot.

Uraminosuke describes how the hero, after falling in love at first sight wtih Yukinomae, prays to the deity Kannon of Kiyomizu for success in his affair. Eventually, in a dream, he is given instructions on how to reach the house of a certain widow. He meets the woman and persuades her to deliver a letter to Yukinomae. The girl, moved by his letter, sends a reply consisting of scraps of old poetry. Uraminosuke is unable to decipher the meaning. He takes the letter to a disciple of Hosokawa Yūsai, the great expert in poetry, and learns that the poems signify the girl is pleased with his love and is willing to meet him on the night of the harvest moon. That night he makes his way to her room, taking advantage of the covering noise from moon-viewing parties, and they sleep together.

The next morning, when Uraminosuke must leave, he asks when they can meet again. Yukinomae replies, "In the next life." She is soon to be married to a member of the imperial court and dares not see him any more. Uraminosuke is so despondent that he falls into a mortal illness. Before he dies, he sends a final letter to Yukinomae. When she learns that her seeming coldness has caused his death she is so horrified that she herself dies on the spot, and three ladies of her entourage commit suicide. The members of the court subsequently decide that Uraminosuke and Yukinomae should be buried together.[4]

The medieval elements in *Uraminosuke* are obvious: the first meeting in the grounds of a Buddhist temple, the dream revelation granted after long hours of prayer, the single night spent with the beloved, the wasting away of the hero because of thwarted love, the deaths of Yukinomae and her companions, and the courtiers' tribute to the couple's love are all themes found in earlier fiction. The style too shows hardly any evolution; for example, the beauty of Yukinomae when first she appears before Uraminosuke is evoked by comparison with over sixty famous beauties of Japan and China.[5] A heavily Buddhist flavor is also evident. Nevertheless, the story departs from tradition in being almost contemporary; no pretense was made, in the medieval manner, that this was a fugitive work from the remote past.

Another romantic work written about the same time, possibly under the influence of *Uraminosuke*,[6] was called *Usuyuki Monogatari* (The Story of Usuyuki). A young man, Sonobe no Emon[7] by name, visits the Kiyomizu Temple and sees there a marvelously beautiful young woman. He falls in love at first sight and prays to Kannon for his love to be fulfilled. Soon afterward Emon learns that the lady is called Usuyuki and that she lives in the house of a great noble. He addresses her a letter expressing his love. She at first dismisses his protestations as mere banter, but a battery of letters convinces her he is sincere. She reveals that she is already married, but he replies with instances from literature proving how often married women have taken lovers. Usuyuki at last yields, but after a brief period of happiness he must leave on a journey. When he returns he discovers she has died. Overcome by grief, he becomes a monk on Mount Kōya, where he builts a hermitage and practices religious austerities until his death, in his twenty-sixth year. The concluding paragraph suggests the tone of the entire work:

> Later on he built on the Eastern Mountain a hut of brushwood which he called Kansō Hermitage. The only visitors were the voices of the monkeys swinging in the trees on the peak, and the moonlight that streamed in through breaks in the eaves. In the loneliness of the season the wind through the pines invited melancholy thought, and the dripping of water from the eaves had a doleful sound. The smoke from incense recalled the fragrance of robes he had known long ago. His dwelling, with posts of bamboo and brushwood gate, was too frail even

to hold out the wind. In this manner Renshō, leading a life of exemplary devotion, passed away in his twenty-sixth year. This was truly an impressive example.[8]

The language is a pastiche derived from *The Tale of the Heike* (especially the description of the retreat of the former Empress Kenreimon'in) and the Nō plays. The name Renshō, assumed by Emon after he became a priest, is the same that Kumagai takes in the Nō play *Atsumori*. Other quotations reveal the author's indebtedness to works of medieval literature.[9] But *Usuyuki Monogatari*, despite its borrowings from the past, was welcomed by readers, not only for its story but for its practical use as a model for writing love letters! It was frequently reprinted in the seventeenth century, and exercised considerable influence on later literature.

Apart from such works in the traditional idiom as *Uraminosuke* and *Usuyuki Monogatari*, the kana zōshi included various other kinds of fiction that reflected the tastes of the samurai class, the principal market for these stories once printed books had become commercial wares in the late 1620s. The many didactic works printed showed how eager the badly educated samurai were for self-improvement. Their respect for knowledge may have been the result of the adoption of Confucianism as the state philosophy, but some of the most popular kana zōshi were strongly Buddhist in inspiration. The emphasis in these works, departing from the medieval legacy of secret traditions, was on acquiring through reading a practical knowledge of how to get along in the world or, even better, how to make money. The optimism of the times is suggested by such works as *Chōja-kyō* (The Millionaire's Gospel) which taught, "Even if you haven't got a *rin* to your name, if you make up your mind to become a millionaire you can do it."[10]

With the restoration of peace at the beginning of the seventeenth century there was a great awakening of interest in travel, especially to the cities of Kyoto, Nara, and Kamakura, or along the Tōkaidō, the road joining Edo and Kyoto. The writers of kana zōshi exploited this interest, including in their guidebooks not only useful information on where to spend the night or how much souvenirs cost, but the historical and poetical associations of each place. Travel accounts go back very far, to the *Tosa*

Diary written in the tenth century, but in the past they were primarily of literary interest, prized not so much for the information they supplied about conditions along the road as for the poetically recorded impressions of the author. Literary diaries also flourished in the Tokugawa period, but guidebooks that revealed nothing about the personality of the author and made no pretense to stylistic beauty were very popular both with people intending to make a journey and with armchair travelers.[11]

Some of these guidebooks were made even more enjoyable by being provided with the rudiments of a story, usually by giving names and attributes to the travelers who follow the route described. *Chikusai Monogatari,*[12] perhaps the best-known work in this form, is believed to have been the work of a physician named Tomiyama Dōya (1585–1634).[13] Originally written about 1622, it was printed from woodblocks five or ten years later. Chikusai, a quack doctor unable to make a living in Kyoto, journeys along the Tōkaidō to Nagoya, accompanied by a servant named Niraminosuke (obviously a parody of Uraminosuke). The two men have various adventures, but the text consists mainly of descriptions of sights on the way, in the manner of a guidebook. Unfortunately, the facetiousness of the style and the heavy-handed punning have not aged well; *Chikusai Monogatari* is of interest today mainly for the glimpses it provides of contemporary life: a renga salon, prostitutes playing the samisen, a performance of a Nō play.

Some famous travel accounts of the period, such as *Kyō Warabe* (Children of Kyoto, 1658) by Nakagawa Kiun, have almost no novelistic elements, but *Tōkaidō Meishoki* (Famous Sights of the Tōkaidō, 1659) by Asai Ryōi (d. 1691) still retains its interest as a story, even though its tips on local products and the carefully recorded distances between places are no longer of much use.

Other varieties of kana zōshi were intended solely as entertainment. *Inu Makura* (A Mongrel Pillow, *c.* 1596) is attributed to Hata Sōha (1550–1607), a physician and one of the eight hundred storytellers (*otogishu*) who served Toyotomi Hideyoshi. It consists of some seventy-three lists of "delightful things," "sad things," and so on in the manner of *The Pillow Book of Sei Shōnagon,* plus seventeen comic waka (*kyōka*). Sōha's lists are amusing, but by no means in the same class with Sei Shōnagon's:

Things Which Should Be Long
One's life, though old age brings many shames[14]
A woman's hair
Nights when one meets one's sweetheart
Other people's kindnesses

Things Which Should Be Short
The years after fifty
Visits to a sick person
The handle of a spear with a big blade
Nights one spends alone
Anecdotes[15]

Seisuishō (Laughter That Wakes You from Sleep, 1628) by Anrakuan Sakuden (1554–1642) is a collection of over one thousand humorous stories. Sakuden began listening to and recording funny stories when he was a boy; and perhaps, as a Buddhist priest, he used them to keep people awake during his sermons. The stories included some gathered by acquaintances, especially Matsunaga Teitoku. Apparently it was Teitoku who introduced Sakuden to the shogun's deputy in Kyoto, Itakura Shigemune. Sakuden began to serve Itakura as a storyteller about 1620, and *Seisuishō* may have reflected the hours he spent amusing his master.[16] The collection abounds in scraps of interesting historical information, and some of the stories are still funny:

> Someone, forgetting the adage that the walls have ears, once started to say, "So-and-so is simply not human," when, turning around, he noticed the man standing by him. In a panic, he finished the sentence, "He's a living Buddha."[17]

> A young *zatō* [blind musician] went courting a woman one night. He was about to climb over a wall when, the moon being very bright, he was discovered by the master of the house. "What are you doing there, *zatō*?" asked the master. "I'm ascending to heaven," was the reply.[18]

Parodies make up another part of the kana zōshi literature. The most famous example is *Nise Monogatari* (Fake Tales), based on *Ise Monogatari* (Tales of Ise) and written after 1640 by an unknown author. It closely follows its model in each of the 125 episodes, twisting the language and giving contemporary contexts to the situations. Unlike most parodies, however, the episodes in *Fake Tales* are sometimes grimly humorous, rather than lighthearted. Here is the twelfth episode:

> It is a funny thing, but once there was a man who, because of the edict against Christianity, was fleeing with his wife to Musashino when he was arrested by the city magistrate of Edo as a criminal. The man and his wife were led into a field and people were about to set torches to them when the wife cried out, imploring them:
>
> | | |
> |---|---|
> | *Musashino wa* | Do not today |
> | *kyō wa na yaki so* | Set fire to Musashi Field: |
> | *Asakusa ya* | In Asakusa |
> | *tsuma mo koroberi* | My husband has recanted |
> | *ware mo koroberi* | And I also have recanted. |
>
> Hearing this, the executioners spared the lives of husband and wife and released them.[19]

This episode, like most of the others in *Fake Tales*, opens with the words *okashi otoko arikeri* (It is funny, but once there was a man . . .), a close parody of *mukashi otoko arikeri* (Long ago there was a man . . .), the opening phrases in the episodes of *Tales of Ise*. Ingenuity is also displayed in altering the words of the original prose and poetry only slightly to yield quite different meanings. But the whole passage—a description of the persecution of the Christians and of the recanting that saved one couple on the execution grounds at Asakusa—no longer seems as funny as it probably did to Japanese of the time.[20]

The interest of most of the kana zōshi is nonliterary. We may be intrigued, it is true, by the glimpse into the minds of ordinary people at the time of the persecution of the Christians, or amused by the description of the youthful Oda Nobunaga walking along the street munching on chestnuts, persimmons, or melons,[21] and an enumeration of the hardships of the peasantry is certainly likely to move us more than Confucian philosophizing on the importance of agriculture to the nation. But these snapshots of life in the early seventeenth century are equally interesting even if the style or language is inept. Indeed, when the kana zōshi are consciously literary, as in the pastiche of classical phraseology of *Uraminosuke*, they tend to be almost comically tedious.

Only one writer of distinction is associated with the kana zōshi, Asai Ryōi, the author of many works.[22] Ryōi began life as a samurai but, like many others of his class, he discovered that his services were no longer needed in an age of peace, and he was forced to become a *rōnin*, a masterless samurai. Deprived of their stipends, the rōnin were forced to choose other professions. Most became farmers or merchants, but a few of the best educated (like Ryōi) tried to make a living as writers. The earliest kana zōshi appeared in such small editions that they could not have provided much income for their authors, but in 1638 *Kiyomizu Monogatari*, a popular Confucian work by Asayama Soshin (1589–1664) reputedly sold three thousand copies.[23] From this time on the publication of kana zōshi became a commercial enterprise, and their character changed; they were written with the intent of being published, not simply as a hobby. Asai Ryōi became at once the first popular and the first professional writer in Japanese history.[24] We know how eagerly people in the past had sought to obtain copies of *The Tale of Genji*, but as long as there were no booksellers and the books themselves were expensive manuscripts, no author could be said to be "popular." At the same time, only with the development of relatively cheap methods of printing and a marked increase in the reading public could anyone make a living as a writer. Ryōi appeared just at the moment when it became possible for a man to be a professional author.

Ryōi was a learned man, as his many Buddhist writings prove, but most of his books were intended for the general public. He wrote largely in kana, employing a style relatively free of the literary ornamentation of such works as *Uraminosuke*. His most famous book was *Ukiyo Monogatari* (Tales of the Floating World) written after 1661. The opening section, entitled "On the Floating World," describes the difference between the old meaning of *ukiyo* and the new one: in the past *ukiyo* was used as a term for the sadness of a world where everything went contrary to one's hopes; but now, taking the meaning "floating" for *uki* instead of "sad," it had come to designate the delightful uncertainties of life in a joyous age when people lived for the moment, merrily bobbing up and down on the tides of uncertainty like a gourd on the waves.[25]

The image of the gourd was echoed in the name of the chief

character, a rich young man named Hyōtarō (*hyō* means gourd). His delight in the floating world is described in detail: there is even a spirited account of the pleasures of gambling and fornication. Gradually, however, the tone becomes darker. Hyōtarō, impoverished as a result of his indulgence in worldly pleasures, accepts a position under a certain daimyo, serving as a storyteller and an adviser:

> Day and night he appeared before the daimyo and these were the things they discussed: how to tax the rice paid to retainers of the fief in such a way as to take back at least half; next, how to make sure that the farmers of the domain would remit their full yearly tribute without fail, even if it meant selling their wives and children, vacating their houses or running off to another province; next, how to levy miscellaneous taxes on every single object the farmers possessed, and to collect these taxes. Their discussions, based solely on greed, revealed no trace of compassion or human decency; they were restricted to the consideration of ways to seize everything in taxes from the retainers and farmers.[26]

Not surprisingly, Hyōtarō is hated by everyone.

A few sections later we learn that Hyōtarō has been forced to leave the daimyo's service and become a priest on account of the prank he has played on a samurai of the fief. The tone of indignation Ryōi employed when describing the hardships suffered by the retainers and farmers gives way at this point to farcicality. The offended samurai beats Hyōtarō and, we are told, "He was a born coward, just like his father, and afraid of being slashed down, he made his escape, crawling on the ground because his legs were limp with fear."[27] He decides he can no longer be a samurai, and shaves his head as a sign he has become a priest, though he certainly experiences no conversion. We may be disappointed that Ryōi failed to make a novel out of his kana zōshi by maintaining a tone of anger against a society in which men are so cruelly treated, but we must not expect too much of a work intended primarily for entertainment. When Hyōtarō becomes a priest he takes the name Ukiyobō, evidence that he still pays allegiance to the floating world he ostensibly renounced.

The episodic nature of *Tales of the Floating World* appealed to readers whose attention could not be kept very long, and the apparent frivolity of many scenes may have been necessary in order to sell the book, but Ryōi's serious intent is never completely forgotten. Again and again he describes the misery of the farmers oppressed by high taxes and forced to desperate expedients in order to stay alive. He attacked both the greed of the merchants and the extravagance practiced by the daimyos in the name of elegance. Ryōi, as a rōnin, was especially bitter about the harsh treatment his fellows received. In another work he stated, "They are not men who have abandoned the world; the world has abandoned them."[28] But he had no solutions to offer save the traditional appeals in the Confucian manner for greater humanity; his most powerful denunciations were likely to peter out into frivolity:

> Take the case of a man who is so hungry that he cuts a slice off his thigh and eats it. His stomach may feel satisfied, but his leg will collapse under him. The ruler of a country is like the belly, the farmers like the legs. It does no good for the belly to be swollen with food if the legs refuse to stand. Nor can a ruler successfully govern a country if the farmers are weak and exhausted, no matter how prosperous the ruler himself may be. Nevertheless, there are some extremely greedy men who fill their storehouses with huge quantities of rice, and refuse to sell it for years. In the old days people used to pray they would be spared droughts, floods or typhoons, but the merchants today pray for precisely these disasters, in the hopes that the value of the rice in their storehouses will increase. Because such men think only about profit, the poor people, who eke out a living from day to day, cannot earn enough to pay even for one *masu* of rice, no matter how hard they work. They pawn their mosquito netting and spend the summer nights sleepless; they sell their bedding and freeze to death on winter nights. They sell their children as servants, and they abandon their infants by the side of the road. The five grains ripen every year, but every year sees quite a few people die of starvation. What a pitiful state of affairs! [Ryōi concludes this story, related by Ukiyobō, with the comment of the owner of a wholesaler's establishment:] There are also plenty of people who are glad

> when the price of rice is high. I can't figure out what this priest is blubbering over. I suppose he wants some rice.[29]

Ukiyobō later becomes the adviser to a more receptive daimyo. He urges the daimyo never to let his samurai forget their calling, and advises him to shun all extravagance, but his pills of good sense eventually become too bitter for the daimyo to swallow, and he is dismissed. At the end he simply disappears: "his soul departed from his body." He uses magic so effectively that "nobody knew where he went. Was it up to Heaven? Or down into the Earth?" He left behind a poem written on a card. It said, "Now my heart has returned to the sky. My body, left behind, is the discarded husk of the cicada."[30]

In other works Ryōi sometimes rose to more bitter criticism. He described for example, the tortures administered to farmers who had been remiss in paying their taxes: beatings, the water dungeon, and worse.[31] It may be wondered how, under a despotic government that tolerated absolutely no public criticism of its policies and repeatedly confiscated books that it found offensive, it was possible for Ryōi to publish such criticism. The nature of his works—tales of comic adventures, ghost stories, guidebooks, and historical romances—probably disarmed the censors; books of a more obviously intellectual content would surely have been closely examined. Ryōi was careful also to phrase his criticism in such a way that it would seem as if he were attacking only certain greedy daimyos who forgot their true calling as samurai and gentlemen; he certainly did not oppose the institution of daimyos. Moreover, when Ryōi criticized a daimyo for wasting money on antiques for the tea ceremony, instead of saving his funds for some national emergency, he was saying no more than the government itself frequently said. His attacks on rapacious merchants were hardly more than echoes of the Confucian philosophers who despised the money-grubbing of the townsmen.[32] Indeed, it may be that readers of Asai Ryōi's works found his criticism of the cruel exploitation of the farmers the least interesting part of the stories, taking it for so much Confucian moralizing which they would cheerfully have done without.[33] It seems evident, however, that these parts meant most to Ryōi himself; they grew out of his painful experiences as a rōnin and reveal his discontent with a society that had abandoned its principles. Didactic works, whether Buddhist or Confucian, are common in the kona zōshi literature, but none is as vivid as Ryōi's descriptions of the ills of society. This element of criticism, abortively developed by Ryōi, was to disappear in the works of his great successor, Saikaku. The kana zōshi is usually considered a transitional literature between the medieval fiction and the novels of Saikaku, but we must consider not only what Saikaku borrowed from *Tales of the Floating World* and similar works, but what he failed to incorporate into his own works.[34] Ryōi's character Ukiyobō cannot be taken seriously as a literary creation, and the techniques of narration and plot in *Tales of the Floating World* are primitive, but Ryōi transcended these limitations to write a kind of criticism that Saikaku, always concerned with the individual rather than with society, never attempted.

Ryōi's literary techniques owed much to the Chinese fiction written in the classical language, which he adapted into Japanese, and apparently also to the Japanese translation of *Aesop's Fables.* The section from *Tales of the Floating World* that I have translated above gives a new twist to the fable "The Belly and the Members," but is recognizably derived from Aesop.[35] *Aesop's Fables* had originally been rendered into romanized Japanese and published by the Jesuits in 1593, but this version was not generally known. A later Japanese translation, into characters and kana, was published in 1639 under the title *Isoho Monogatari*, and became the one European literary work widely known in Japan before the country was opened in the nineteenth century. Fables recur in Ryōi's stories; in one episode of *Tales of the Floating World*, for example, a daimyo mercilessly whips his horse, only for the horse "speaking like a man" to reveal why he cannot gallop any faster.[36]

Ryōi's style is not easy, but it is free from the usual literary flourishes, perhaps because he depended more on foreign than Japanese literature. His collection *Otogibōko* (Hand Puppets, 1666), for example, was directly derived from a Korean work which in turn was inspired by the celebrated Chinese collection of ghost stories *Chien-têng Hsin-yü* by Ch'u Yü (d. 1433).[37] Ryōi departed freely from his sources, but his style was essentially a straightforward narration.

Most of the kana zōshi literature was written by and for members of the samurai class, but toward the end of the eighty years (1600–80) of this literature more and more works were aimed at the townsmen. The publication of *hyōbanki*, evaluations of prostitutes and actors, especially tended to narrow the distance between the townsmen and the world of books.[38] Their value as literature is slight, but because the hyōbanki were focused exclusively on the denizens of the pleasure quarters, rather than on upper-class samurai society, they were easy for townsmen to read and enjoy. The evaluations sometimes consist of no more than fragmentary remarks, but occasionally these are expanded into lyrical appreciations. The hyōbanki lead easily into the world of Saikaku; they were among the earliest literary products of the pleasure quarters that flourished throughout the Tokugawa period.

The growth of the licensed quarters in the principal cities of Japan was, paradoxically, a result of the adoption of Confucianism as the state philosophy. In the attempt to construct a society that would be stable and permanent, the Confucian philosophers prescribed a rigid order governed by codes of behavior that emphasized loyalty to the ruler and filial piety toward the father. Each household was considered a microcosm of the state, and the respect due its head was as absolute as the loyalty due the sovereign. The head of the household was expected to support his family, but any display of affection toward his wife and children was considered unseemly. His wife was a wholly submissive creature, forbidden to show jealousy and not encouraged even to speak; if dissatisfaction with life at home drove her into the arms of another man, the penalty was death.

The Confucian scholars condemned love as an irrelevant and possibly disruptive element in family relations, but they tacitly recognized the necessity of permitting men to amuse themselves on occasion. The government in fact deliberately established "bad places" as a means of dissipating the energies of unruly warriors. No disgrace surrounded a visit; indeed, a man who refused to go, preferring the sedate pleasures of his own household, would have seemed unattractively virtuous, possibly a miser, and certainly without taste. But the prohibition on love was even stronger there than within a household; a man was free to divert himself to the degree that his finances permitted, but if by mischance he fell in love with a prostitute it threatened the stability of his family and often led to disaster.

The outstanding panegyrist of the licensed quarters was the kana zōshi writer Fujimoto Kizan (1626–1704). He wrote his grand study *Shikidō Ōkagami* (The Great Mirror of the Art of Love) without a glance at emotional attachment. The love he described of course included physical pleasure—he was sure that a prostitute afforded infinitely greater pleasure than any amateur—but also the entire ambience of the licensed quarters. He became fascinated with the usages of the world of prostitutes and at an early age decided to consecrate his energies to learning and glorifying them, establishing a Way, in the manner of the Confucianists. Sometimes Kizan even spoke of himself in the self-laudatory tones of the founder of a new religion, reciting how he had turned his back on the humdrum lives led by the common mass of men so that he might devote himself to the difficult and time-consuming task of mastering the old traditions.

It took Kizan over twenty years to complete his masterpiece, *The Great Mirror* (1678). Leaving its subject matter aside, it is a model of learning. Quotations from the Chinese and Japanese classics sprinkle the pages, giving a dignified and even erudite tone to his account. Kizan devoted minute attention to every aspect of a courtesan's appearance and behavior. Each article she wore, each gesture she made had to be in keeping with tradition, no less surely than the performance of a Nō play. He wrote, for example:

> Laughter. It is most delightful when, something amusing having happened, a courtesan smiles, showing her dimples. . . . But for her to open her mouth and bare her teeth or to laugh in a loud voice is to deprive her instantly of all elegance and make her seem crude. When something is so extremely funny that she *must* laugh, she should either cover her mouth with her sleeve or else avert her head behind the customer's shoulder.[39]

The prostitutes were divided into classes, ranging from the great courtesans at the top, who demanded exorbitant fees from the customers and even then might not sleep with them, down to unfortunate women who expected no more than a small coin for their favors. Kizan devoted scant attention to the lower ranks. His interests lay in the upper reaches of the hierarchy, and the accomplishments he prescribed were for elegant women reigning over apartments in a lavish brothel.

> A courtesan should be able to write poetry. She should at least be familiar with the old language so that she can recite poems describing the changing of the seasons. It is a mistake to assume that only crude, ignorant men buy prostitutes. If a woman can converse adequately with a cultivated customer, why should he ever look elsewhere?

Again:

> It is unfortunate for *anyone* not to be able to write, but for a courtesan it is a disaster. They say that playing the samisen is the most important artistic accomplishment of a courtesan, but in fact writing comes first and the samisen only afterward. As long as a courtesan writes well it does not matter if she is incompetent at the samisen, but even for a samisen virtuoso it would be unfortunate if people said she wrote a bad hand or that her grammar was shaky.

A most interesting section of *The Great Mirror* deals with the pledges of love (*shinjū*) offered by courtesans to their customers. The supreme pledge was cutting off a finger. Kizan commented:

> The other four varieties of pledges—fingernails, oaths, locks of hair and tattooing—can be carried out, as part of a calculated scheme, even if the woman is insincere. But unless she really loves a man, it is hard to go through with cutting off a finger . . . Nails grow back in days, a head of hair in months, oaths can be hidden away, and tattooing can be erased when a woman no longer sees a man. But giving up a finger makes a woman a cripple for life, and she can never restore things to what they were. The act should therefore be performed only after grave deliberation.

But although Kizan urged caution, he asked, "If a man says he will forgive a prostitute her misdeeds, providing she clears up his doubts by cutting off her finger, what prostitute would refuse?"

Kizan's *Great Mirror* is of intrinsic interest because it so absorbingly described the ceremonies and traditions of the pleasure quarters at the time of their most brilliant flowering. It provides also the background for the important works of Japanese literature written toward the end of the seventeenth century, notably the novels of Saikaku.

NOTES

1. The first use of *kana zōshi* as a term designating the literature written between 1600 and 1682 occurs in a work published in 1897. See Hasegawa Tsuyoshi, "Kana Zōshi," p. 26.

2. For a classification of the different varieties of kana zōshi, see Noda Hisao, *Kinsei Shōsetsushi Ronkō*, pp. 84–85.

3. See especially Ichiko Teiji and Noma Kōshin, *Otogi Zōshi, Kana Zōshi*, pp. 186–90. Professor Noma identified Uraminosuke with Matsudaira Chikatsugu, the daimyo of Wakasa, who was found guilty of immoral relations with a court lady in 1606 and died while still confined to his quarters in 1612.

4. The text of *Uraminosuke* is given in Maeda Kingorō and Morita Takeshi, *Kana Zōshi Shū*, pp. 51–88.

5. Maeda and Morita, pp. 54–55.

6. Noda Hisao, *Kana Zōshi Shū*, I, p. 80.

7. The name is so given in Noda, *Kana Zōshi Shū*, but some editions give Saemon.

8. Noda, *Kana Zōshi Shū*, p. 212.

9. *Ibid.*, p. 79.

10. A complete translation of "The Millionaire's Gospel" is given by G. W. Sargent in *The Japanese Family Storehouse*, pp. 239–44. See also Munemasa Isoo, *Saikaku no Kenkyū*, p. 303.

11. Kishi Tokuzō, "Kana Zōshi ni okeru Meishoki Yūranki," in Ichiko and Noma, p. 290.

12. Partial translation by Edward Putzar in *Monumenta Nipponica*, XVI, pp. 160–95.

13. See Kishi Tokuzō, "Seikatsu no naka no Kana Zōshi," p. 88. Some scholars refer to the same man as Isoda Dōya. Earlier authorities attributed the work to the courtier Karasumaru Mitsuhiro.

14. An allusion to *Tsurezuregusa*, section 7. See translation by Keene, *Essays in Idleness*, p. 8. ("The longer a man lives, the more shame he endures.")

15. Maeda and Morita, pp. 44–45. A complete translation is found in Edward Putzar's article "Inu Makura: The Dog Pillow."

16. See Suzuki Tōzō, *Seisuishō*, II, pp. 226–44.

17. Suzuki, I, p. 47.

18. Suzuki, II, p. 90.

19. Maeda and Morita, p. 173; Ichiko and Noma, pp. 157–58. See Helen Craig McCullough, *Tales of Ise*, p. 78, for the original story. See Jack Rucinski, "A Japanese Burlesque: *Nise Monogatari*" for a complete translation together with parallels from *Ise Monogatari*.

20. For a discussion of how the Shimabara Rebellion, the last stand of the Japanese Christians, was treated in literature, see Ōiso Yoshio, "Shimabara no Ran no Kana Zōshi e no Hannō."

21. Okuno Takahiro and Iwasawa Yoshihiko, *Shinchōkō Ki*, p. 22.

22. The most interesting account of Asai Ryōi is contained in Matsuda Osamu, *Nihon Kinsei Bungaku no Seiritsu*, pp. 139–55.

23. Kishi, "Kana Zōshi ni okeru Meishoki Yūranki," p. 90.

24. Hamada Keisuke, "Kana Zōshi no Sakusha to Dokusha," p. 287.

25. Maeda and Morita, p. 244.

26. *Ibid.*, pp. 257–58.

27. *Ibid.*, p. 261.

28. Quoted in Matsuda, p. 129.

29. Maeda and Morita, pp. 277–78.

30. *Ibid.*, p. 354.

31. Matsuda, p. 152.

32. See Donald Keene, *The Japanese Discovery of Europe*, pp. 98–99.

33. Matsuda, p. 154.

34. *Ibid.*, p. 113.

35. For the Japanese translation of this fable, see Maeda and Morita, p. 427.

36. *Ibid.*, pp. 258–59.

37. Matsuda, p. 124. The Korean work is described by Peter H. Lee in *Korean Literature: Topics and Themes*, pp. 67–68. The Chinese work also influenced later writers like Ueda Akinari.

38. See Hamada, p. 288.

39. See Donald Keene, *Landscapes and Portraits*, p. 245. For the original text, see Noma Kōshin (ed.), *Shikidō Ōkagami*, pp. 140–41.

BIBLIOGRAPHY

Hamada Keisuke. "Kana Zōshi no Sakusha to Dokusha," in Ichiko Teiji and Noma Kōshin, *Otogi Zōshi, Kana Zōshi*.

Hasegawa Tsuyoshi. "Kana Zōshi," *Kōza Nihon Bungaku*, vol. VII.

Ichiko Teiji and Noma Kōshin. *Otogi Zōshi, Kana Zōshi*, in Nihon Koten Kanshō Kōza series, vol. XVI. Tokyo: Kadokawa Shoten, 1963.

Imoto Nōichi and Nishiyama Matsunosuke. *Ningen Kaigan*, in Nihon Bungaku no Rekishi series. Tokyo: Kadokawa Shoten, 1967.

Keene, Donald (trans.). *Essays in Idleness*. New York: Columbia University Press, 1967.

———. *The Japanese Discovery of Europe*. Stanford: Stanford University Press, 1969.

———. *Landscapes and Portraits*. Tokyo: Kodansha International, 1971.

Kishi Tokuzō. "Kana Zōshi ni okeru Meishoki Yūranki," in Ichiko and Noma, *op. cit.*

———. "Seikatsu no naka no Kana Zōshi," in Imoto and Nishiyama, *op. cit.*

Kōza Nihon Bungaku, vol. VII. Tokyo: Sanseidō, 1969.

Lane, Richard. "The Beginnings of the Modern Japanese Novel," in *Harvard Journal of Asiatic Studies*, vol. XX, nos. 3 and 4 (December 1957).

Lee, Peter H. *Korean Literature: Topics and Themes*. Tucson: University of Arizona Press, 1965.

Maeda Kingorō and Morita Takeshi (eds.). *Kana Zōshi Shū*, in Nihon Koten Bungaku Taikei series. Tokyo: Iwanami Shoten, 1965.

Matsuda Osamu. *Nihon Kinsei Bungaku no Seiritsu*. Tokyo: Hōsei Daigaku Shuppankyoku, 1963.

McCullough, Helen Craig (trans.). *Tales of Ise*. Stanford: Stanford University Press, 1968.

Munemasa Isoo. *Saikaku no Kenkyū*. Tokyo: Miraisha, 1969.

Noda Hisao. *Kinsei Shōsetsushi Ronkō*. Tokyo: Hanawa Shobō, 1961.

——— (ed.). *Kana Zōshi Shū*. Tokyo: Asahi Shimbun Sha, 1960.

Noma Kōshin (ed.). *Shikidō Ōkagami*. Kyoto: Yūsan Bunko, 1961.

Ōiso Yoshio. "Shimabara no Ran no Kana Zōshi e no Hannō," in *Kokugo to Kokubungaku*, December 1955.

Okuno Takahiro and Iwasawa Yoshihiko (eds.). *Shinchōkō Ki*, in Kadokawa Bunko series. Tokyo: Kadokawa Shoten, 1969.

Putzar, Edward (trans.). *Chikusai Monogatari*, in *Monumenta Nipponica*, XVI (1960–61).

———. "Inu Makura: The Dog Pillow," in *Harvard Journal of Asiatic Studies*, XXVIII, 1968.

Rucinski, Jack (trans.). "A Japanese Burlesque: *Nise Monogatari*" in *Monumenta Nipponica*, vol. XXX, no. 1. Spring, 1975.

Sargent G. W. (trans.). *The Japanese Family Storehouse*. Cambridge, Eng.: Cambridge University Press, 1959.

Suzuki Tōzō (ed.). *Seisuishō*, in Kadokawa Bunko series. Tokyo: Kadokawa Shoten, 1964.

CHAPTER 8
FICTION
IHARA SAIKAKU
(1642–1693)

Ihara Saikaku is revered today as a great novelist; some Japanese critics rank him second only to Lady Murasaki. His works have been edited with the painstaking care accorded only to classics, and learned articles have probed the underlying structure of his tales, their hidden meanings, and their connections with contemporary society. Such attention would surely have surprised Saikaku, whose fiction was dashed off almost as quickly as his legendary performances at linked verse, with seemingly little concern for the judgments of posterity.[1]

Saikaku's first "novel," *Kōshoku Ichidai Otoko* (The Life of an Amorous Man) was published in the tenth month of 1682. By this time Saikaku had already established himself as a leading haikai poet. After the death of Nishiyama Sōin earlier the same year, Saikaku ranked higher than any other poet of the Danrin school, and his reputation would be further enhanced in 1684 when he dazzled the world with his performance at the Sumiyoshi Shrine that earned him the nickname of "Master of the Twenty Thousand Verses." But in 1682 Saikaku suddenly produced a work in prose that created a new genre and changed the course of Tokugawa literature.

The first word in the title, *kōshoku*, meaning literally "to love love," designated a voluptuary, or at any rate a person with conspicuously amatory interests. Saikaku was probably not the first to give a work a title beginning with *kōshoku*, but earlier books (apparently pornography) that bore this word in their titles were quickly forgotten after Saikaku's book appeared. In his own day his works of fiction describing love affairs, whether in the licensed quarters or in the merchants' society, were known as kōshoku books, but soon after his death another term was invented that has lasted to this day, *ukiyo zōshi*.[2] The term *ukiyo*, as a designation for the floating world of pleasure (and not its homonym, the "sad world" of medieval literature), had been familiar since Asai Ryōi's kana zōshi, but with Saikaku the term acquired another shade of meaning: his first novel was devoted to the adventures of a hero named Yonosuke (a contraction for Ukiyo-nosuke) in the various licensed quarters, the floating world par excellence.[3] Indeed, the two terms, *kōshoku* and *ukiyo* came to mean much the same thing; the word *ukiyo* had strongly erotic overtones and the *ukiyo-e* began as pornographic prints.

The Life of an Amorous Man was read as a work of erotic content. It is not pornographic—indeed, Saikaku's works, with one exception, are far removed from pornography, regardless of their titles—but it traces in joyous detail the career of an amorous man from his precocious essays at love-making as a child of seven to his decision at the age of sixty to sail to an island populated exclusively by women. The novel is divided into fifty-four chapters, one for each year in Yonosuke's life. The number of chapters, the same as for *The Tale of Genji*, has suggested to many critics that Saikaku's intent was parody, and elaborate attempts have been made to trace parallels between the two works. Probably Saikaku, creating the first novel of his age, turned back to *Genji* for inspiration; in general he followed its pattern of describing the amorous involvements of a single hero. But surely there was no deeper influence. Yonosuke, unlike Genji, is untouched by any awareness of "the pity of things," and his relations with women are summed up by the number of conquests he made, rather than by the extent of his involvement with each woman. Yonosuke only intermittently gives signs of being a human being; for the most part he is an unremitting agent of lust who learns nothing about women he did not know as a child, even after the innumerable seductions he has achieved either by personal charm or by the use of abundant funds. There is nothing remotely endearing about him; he seems to exist only in terms of his one obsession. If for a moment adversity causes him to think of "abandoning the world" and leading a monk's life in some hermitage, it does not take long for him to revert to his old habits. Yonosuke becomes a priest at nineteen, having been disowned for his profligacy, but after a couple of days spent reading the Amida Sutra he realizes that the religious life has no appeal for him. He decides that the present world is much more to his taste and sells his rosary, using the proceeds to establish friendly relations with an itinerant peddler of perfume, a handsome lad whose perfume is only the pretext for selling his favors. Soon Yonosuke is established with three such boys. The chapter concludes:

> He spent day and night engaged in lustful pleasures with the three of them. Before he knew it, his hair had grown out long enough to comb. He tore up his Buddhist robe to make dustcloths. The kitchen was littered with the bones of wild ducks gnawed clean of flesh and with the remains from globefish soup. He had returned to his past as easily as a half-burned post to the flames.[4]

Everything happens to Yonosuke at the surface level. He does not even suffer the kind of disappointment in love that might have provoked a few moments of reflection, in the manner of the kana zōshi. When, at the age of thirty-four, he is informed of his father's death, he is hardly willing to spare the time even for a conventional moment of sadness: Yonosuke's mother, with an intuitive understanding of what really interests her son, hands him a document transferring to him an immense fortune. He cries, "The moment I have waited for so long has come at last! I will ransom all the prostitutes I want, or else I'll buy the services of every last courtesan worthy of the name. Now's my chance!" He gathers together a throng of jesters, and proclaims himself a great, great, great spender.[5]

Subsequent episodes describe Yonosuke's prodigality with his newfound wealth, but with the sixth of the eight books the nature of the narration abruptly changes. The center of attention shifts from Yonosuke to the various courtesans he encounters, and only at the very end of the work, when Yonosuke gives up his life in Japan to sail to the Island of Women, does he assume the center of the stage again. Noma Kōshin suggested that Saikaku, having reached the point in the narration where his hero (with whom he strongly identified) was the same age as himself, found it difficult to project the story into the future.[6] He could have abandoned his novel at this point, but at the end of the first chapter of the work he had promised, "He chose of his own to be tormented by love, and by the time he reached the age of fifty-four he had dallied with 3742 women and 725 young men."[7] If Saikaku had dropped Yonosuke at forty-one, that would have left at least thirteen years unaccounted for. Noma believes that it was while Saikaku was debating whether or not to continue the story that his pupil Saigin visited him and urged him to go ahead with it.[8] When Saikaku resumed the novel he mixed up the chronology: the year after Yonosuke is forty-one he reverts to being thirty-six. The error is corrected by having him skip from forty-two to forty-nine later on, but the significance of the year-to-year account has by this time been lost. Perhaps Saikaku had shifted the chronology in order to make Yonosuke die at fifty-four, as originally planned; instead, he has him set sail at sixty, thus completing a cycle, before his "rebirth" abroad. The last line tells us that he disappeared in the tenth month of the second year of Tenwa (1682), precisely the date of publication of *The Life of an Amorous Man*.

Judged in purely literary terms the work is a failure. The story is disjointed and the hero is a cardboard creation with scarcely a recognizable human feature. But the work was a brilliant success in other terms. Saikaku created in Yonosuke an emblematic figure who was immediately accepted as representing the ideals of the new society. He is a Robinson Crusoe, an exemplar of how a man can exploit his own potentialities; he is above all the man of the ukiyo, the world of delightful uncertainty, of pleasure, and of expertise. If *The Life of an Amorous Man* had been Saikaku's second or third book in this vein, or if it represented a more polished and skillful version of an already familiar type of writing, nobody would read it today; instead, it marks the creation of a new genre, the ukiyo zōshi, and of a new kind of hero.

Perhaps the most distinguished feature is the style. The novel opens with a sentence typical of Saikaku's manner: "Sakura mo chiru ni nageki, tsuki wa kagiri arite Irusa-yama." A fairly literal translation would go: "We grieve when cherry blossoms fall, and the moon, having its limits, sinks behind Irusa Mountain." The full meaning, however, is something like: "The sights of nature, such as the cherry blossoms or the moon, give us pleasure, but this pleasure is necessarily of limited duration: the blossoms fall and the moon disappears behind a mountain. But the pleasures of the flesh have no limits."[9] The sentence is characteristic of Saikaku's style in that it ends in a noun, contrary to normal Japanese usage; it also contains a play on the word *iru*, meaning both "to sink" of the moon and the first part of the name Irusa. But what gives the sentence its truly Saikakuesque flavor is the omission of the implied conclusion: "But the pleasures of the flesh have no limits." This elliptic kind of utterance surely owes much to Saikaku's training as a haikai poet of the Danrin school. We have only to compare this opening sentence with those of typical kana zōshi to recognize the startling achievement of Saikaku's style: "When did the story take place? It was during the first part of the last month of the summer of the ninth year of Keichō . . ." (*Uraminosuke*). "All under Heaven is calm; the mountains are still, the pines on the peaks are peaceful, the wind is gentle and orderly. This is an age of long rejoicing for the nation" (*Chikusai*).

Saikaku's style, perhaps even more brilliantly displayed in *The Life of an Amorous Man* than in later works, gave the work its eclat. He was at pains to make his diction "elegant."[10] The elegance showed itself in the borrowings from the classics, especially the Nō plays (it will be recalled that the Danrin poets considered these plays their "*Genji*"). Writing, initially at least, within the traditions of the kana zōshi, he no doubt felt that literary expression demanded the use of poetic phraseology. The most striking feature of his style, however, is its strongly colloquial flavor;

this is what makes *The Life of an Amorous Man* so difficult to read today. Necessary postpositions, indicating the subject of a sentence or the agent of the action, are cavalierly omitted, sometimes for euphonic reasons, sometimes because the meaning would be obvious in oral delivery. Readers of the texts are at a disadvantage because pauses that would clarify the sense are not indicated by punctuation, and inserted phrases interrupt the line of thought. The subjects of sentences are often left unexpressed, as if Saikaku assumed the reader could guess them; the first chapter of Book IV contains neither the name Yonosuke nor even a pronoun for him, though he is the subject throughout.

Saikaku's style often shifts without warning from a classical idiom suggestive of *Tales of Ise* to contemporary colloquial, from earthy descriptions to long passages meant to be understood by the ear rather than by the eye; the effect is to make *The Life of an Amorous Man* virtually impossible to translate. It must have been difficult to understand even for contemporary readers, but they were apparently captivated by the novelty of the subject, the interest of the story, and the expansive atmosphere, even if they could not follow the refinements of language. Saikaku's style became plainer in his later works; the success of *The Life of an Amorous Man*, despite its complexities, may have encouraged him to try to win an even larger body of readers.

Saikaku nowhere stated his purpose in writing his first novel. Many critics have interpreted *The Life of an Amorous Man* as a hymn in praise of the new, lively culture that had thrown off the gloom of medieval times and the hollow didacticism of kana zōshi. Perhaps Saikaku "had written for amusement, if not simply for money."[11] Critics today praise the work in terms of its picaresque hero, and his happy-go-lucky adventures set against a background reminiscent of the ukiyo-e. At the end of the work Yonosuke induces six of his cronies to join him in taking passage aboard a ship called the *Yoshiiro Maru* (the S.S. *Lust*); it is loaded with aphrodisiacs and other instruments of sexual pleasure, and sets sail for the Island of Women (Nyogo no Shima). This has generally been interpreted as a further statement of the inexhaustible nature of physical pleasures announced in the first line: Yonosuke, having visited all the houses of prostitution in Japan, has turned his attention abroad, seeking out an island that promises to provide unlimited numbers of females. This episode has seemed to most readers to epitomize the springtime of the merchant class, when all Japan seemed too small to hold their ambitions. But Noma has presented a quite contrary view. He insists that Yonosuke, having lost faith in his money, which had hitherto supported his adventures with prostitutes, had become so despondent about life in Japan that he had to make an escape. The name of his destination, the Island of Women, sounds appealing, but this was actually another name for Hachijō-jima, a bleak island "even birds avoided," a place of banishment. Noma reminds us too that Japan had been struck by a series of natural disasters—typhoons, floods, unseasonable frosts—culminating in the famine of 1681, which took many lives. Even worse than such disasters, Noma continues, were the cruel policies instituted by the new shogun Tsunayoshi, who took office in 1680.[12]

Noma's strictures provide a necessary corrective to the common impression of the period as a cloudless Renaissance when Japan basked in the warmth of a prosperity that erased all memory of the gloomy past. But *The Life of an Amorous Man* in no way suggests despondency or a veiled attack on the regime. The tone is cheerful, even ebullient, and even if Yonosuke has lost faith in money, he clearly retains his interest in sex.

If Saikaku had any intent beyond telling an entertaining story, it may have been to challenge the literature of the past, especially *The Tale of Genji* and *Tales of Ise*, by exalting the behavior of a contemporary lover. His hero, though no Genji or Narihira, possesses instead the qualities most admired in a contemporary man: he is *sui*, an expert in the gay quarters, and he has a great deal of dash. The laboriously traced parallels between Saikaku's hero and Genji are rarely convincing, but even in his day people seem to have felt that Saikaku had written a new *Genji*, as this verse by the haikai poet Sango, written in 1706, the thirteenth anniversary of Saikaku's death, implies:

aki no yo no	Now it has become
katami narikeri	A memento for autumn nights—
zoku Genji	The modern *Genji*.[13]

The Life of an Amorous Man was published by a nonprofessional house in Osaka, but sold about one thousand copies in its first printing, a best seller for those days.[14] The commercial success of the work, confirmed by the appearance of a pirated edition in Edo (with illustrations by the great Moronobu), may have made Saikaku consider for the first time the possibility of becoming a professional writer of fiction. *The Life of an Amorous Man* was an act of exuberance (it was described as *tengōgaki*, or "wild writing," in the afterword by Saikaku's disciple Saigin), but his next work, *Shoen Ōkagami* (Great Mirror of Various Amours, 1684), intended as a sequel, lacks this spontaneity, and gives the impression of having been written in order to capitalize on his earlier success.[15] The style is markedly simpler, an indication that Saikaku was abandoning his haikai disregard of normal syntax in favor of a more easily understandable prose.

Noma has established that Saikaku drew on his own experiences when writing the first half of *The Life of an Amorous Man*. Unfortunately, however, the surviving biographical details for Saikaku consist mainly of the dates when he published various works or participated in haikai meetings. Little more is known of his private life than the few lines in *Kembun Dansō* by Itō Baiu (1683–1745), the second son of Itō Jinsai:

> Along about the Jōkyō and Genroku eras there was a townsman named Hirayama Tōgo in Osaka of Settsu Province. He was well-to-do, but his wife died early, and his only child, a blind daughter, also died. He turned over his business to a shop-clerk and lived exactly as he pleased, though he never became a priest. He would wander for about half the year all over the country, a wallet slung around his neck like a pilgrim, then return home. He was extremely fond of haikai and studied with Isshō [1643–1707]. Later he founded his own school. He changed his name to Saikaku and wrote such works as *Eitaigura, Nishi no Umi, Sejō Shimin Hinagata*, etc.[16]

Saikaku's extensive travels, alluded to in Baiu's account, must have supplied him with the material for his next major work, *Saikaku Shokoku Hanashi* (Saikaku's Tales of the Provinces, 1685). The first thing that strikes the reader is the use of Saikaku's name at the head of the title, probably by request of the publisher, unmistakable evidence of his popularity.[17]

The thirty-five short tales included in the collection are all set in specific localities identified at the opening with such sentences as: "This is something that happened at a temple in Nara" or

"This is something that happened at Ichijō in Kyoto." The geographical area covered by the stories includes most of the island of Honshū and northern Kyushu, an indication of how widely Saikaku traveled. Some stories are clearly regional folk tales, but others have been traced to Japanese, Chinese, and even Indian literary sources.[18] Saikaku not only sets each tale in a specific place and time, but manages by the use of deftly chosen details and realistic touches to impart a moment of life to each; his mastery of the short story is apparent even in this early work.

Saikaku followed this collection with a minor work, *Wankyū Issei no Monogatari* (The Story of Wankyū the First, 1685), concerning the adventures in the licensed quarters of the rich townsman, Wankyū. Saikaku chronicles how Wankyū lost his fortune, sank in the world and, eventually losing his mind, drowned himself. The work bears evidence of hasty composition, but is of special interest because it was based on the life of an actual person, the first time Saikaku had used a model. The direct inspiration for the novel probably came, however, from a Kabuki play on the subject performed in Osaka at the end of 1684.[19]

Saikaku's interest in the theater, evidenced not only by this borrowing of a Kabuki plot but by the frequent mentions of actors in his early works, is confirmed by the puppet play he wrote in 1685, his only venture in the theater. Saikaku's Jōruri *Koyomi* (The Calendar) has a highly involved plot set in the reign of the seventh-century empress Jitō, and is concerned with the adoption of a new calendar. Perhaps the impetus to treat so seemingly undramatic a subject was provided by the change in the reign-name from Tenwa to Jōkyō in 1684. The play was apparently well received when first performed by Uji Kaganojō in Osaka during the spring of 1685, but when Takemoto Gidayū decided to compete for public favor by staging Chikamatsu's *Kenjo no Tenarai narabi ni Shinkoyomi* (The Wise Ladies' Writing Practice and the New Calendar), on a similar theme, he was triumphantly successful. This incident is often held up as proof of Chikamatsu's superiority as a playwright, but an examination of the texts does not necessarily bear out this contention; other elements of the performance—Gidayū's new style of chanting, the musical accompaniment, and the skill of the puppet operators—were largely responsible for the success of Chikamatsu's play. The contest was less between Saikaku and Chikamatsu as playwrights than between Kaganojō and Gidayū as chanters. Saikaku's play is possibly superior, but it is hard to be sure; both works are immature, and the language and manner are so similar one can hardly distinguish the two dramatists.[20]

The Calendar has none of Saikaku's characteristic humor or verve, but its language and the familiarity Saikaku displays with the historical background make it unique among his writings. It is sometimes assumed that Saikaku was poorly educated, but the allusions in *The Calendar* to Japanese and Chinese literary and philosophical works, and the ready use of all the stylistic mannerisms of the Jōruri theater prove that, whatever his formal education may have been, he could hold his own even with the learned Chikamatsu.

Saikaku's next work, *Kōshoku Gonin Onna* (Five Women Who Loved Love), was his masterpiece. The direct inspiration for the work may have come in the first month of 1685 when a barrelmaker's wife, having committed adultery, killed herself. This event, which occurred in a section of Osaka close to Saikaku's house, furnished him with the material for the second of the five stories. The third story—the most effective—about Osan, the wife of an almanac maker, and the clerk Moemon who became her lover, was based on an incident which occurred in 1683 in Kyoto, and the crucifixion of the guilty pair was still vivid in people's memories.[21]

The great success of *Five Women* has been ascribed to its strikingly dramatic quality, possibly a result of Saikaku's recent exposure to the world of the theater.[22] The stories are told superbly, with an irony and detachment that do not diminish Saikaku's obvious affection for the characters he observes, as it were, through the reverse end of a telescope. Seen at the distance he has chosen, the antics of the men and women, even their tragic misfortunes, do not excite our pity and terror but our smiles. Of the five main heroines four end unhappily, executed for adultery and other crimes or driven by despair into becoming nuns, and a sixth heroine kills herself. Yet the total effect is surely not sad. The last we hear of Osan is: "Today the name of Osan still brings to mind her beautiful figure, clothed in the pale-blue slip which she wore to her execution."[23] She has become a pale-blue dot in the distance, lovely to the end.

Saikaku emphasizes his distance from the story by the genial introductions to each section; certainly there is no suggestion of anger or despair. His wry comments, interjected into the tales, are in the same vein. Our feelings about Osan derive not only from the events of her life—the trick she played on Moemon that unexpectedly ended with her sharing a bed with him, the escape of the lovers, their hardships in exile, their capture and execution—but from Saikaku's attitude as narrator. The same general plot, dramatized by Chikamatsu in his play *Daikyōji Mukashibanashi* (The Almanac Maker, 1715), becomes oppressively gloomy, and the happy ending does nothing to relieve the tragedy. Saikaku makes every episode comic by his manner of narration and comments. Here, for example, is the description of the flight of Osan and Moemon through the mountains:

> Osan stumbled feebly along, so wretched that she seemed to be gasping for what might her last breath, and her face lost all its color. . . . Her pulse beat more and more faintly; any minute might be her last. Moemon could offer nothing at all in the way of medicine. He stood by helplessly to wait for Osan's end, then suddenly bent near and whispered in her ear: "Just a little further on we shall come to the village of some people I know. There we can forget all our misery, indulge our hearts' desire with pillows side by side, and talk again of love!"
>
> When she heard this, Osan felt better right away. . . .
>
> [Saikaku concludes,] A pitiful woman indeed, whom lust alone could arouse![24]

It might be argued that Saikaku in this passage is attempting to demonstrate how shallow and easily changed a woman is—to show "the pitifulness, fickleness, sadness and also the strength and indomitability of a woman's heart."[25] I prefer to think that the intention is comic. Saikaku has chosen a familiar, romantic situation (reminiscent of Manon Lescaut perishing in the deserts of Louisiana!) and having described it with the familiar details —"any minute might be her last"—he explodes it with a single sardonic touch. The result is not to make us despise Osan as a frivolous woman, but to make us love her precisely because she is so human. This effect was possible only because of Saikaku's detachment. Saikaku has frequently been called a realist, but his realism depends on a suspension of the normal rules of perspective: he is marvelously exact in small details when he captures the wanton streak in Osan or evokes the sights and sounds of a house in the slums, but the larger circumstances of the story are usually unbelievable. If, for example, Osan had really been close to death's door, the prospect of lying in her lover's arms would not have instantly cured her. But the lack of realism does not disturb us; on the contrary, it reveals to us something essentially true about Osan's character. Toward the end of the story the bodhisattva Manjusri appears to Osan in a dream and suggests that, despite her crime, she may be saved if she gives up her evil passion. But Osan replies, "Please don't worry about what becomes of us. We are more than glad to pay with our lives for this illicit affair."[26]

We feel affection for Osan, but not pity; in fact, we may even envy anyone so happy in her love that she gladly pays for it with her life. We feel equally sure that Oshichi the greengrocer's daughter, another of his five women, who sets the fire that burns down the city of Edo in order to be again with her sweetheart, does not regret her actions, even though they lead her to death at the stake. Saikaku does not dwell on her anguish: "As the evening bell was struck, Oshichi turned into sad wisps of smoke that hovered in the grasses by the Shinagawa road, a rare and cruel punishment."[27] We remember Oshichi not in terms of the agony of her execution, nor, for that matter, in terms of the suffering caused the people of Edo by her impetuous action, but in terms of a love so strong it would stop at nothing.

The harshness of the punishment meted out to Osan and Moemon was the direct result of Tsunayoshi's edict that in the case of adultery between the wife of a master and a shop assistant, or between persons of different classes, both guilty parties must be put to death. Tsunayoshi, despising such un-Confucian weakness of the flesh, issued this decree, imagining he was a sage ruler bringing order to a corrupt society.

One reason for the success of *Five Women* is that the women portrayed are not courtesans, the familiar heroines of Edo period romances, but women of the merchant class. Saikaku demonstrates that such women, normally depicted as faithful wives acquiescing to the demands of the family system, were sisters under the skin of the courtesans; they were moved by the same passions and caprices, and as willing to die for love as any courtesan who ever joined her sweetheart in a double suicide. We regret that these enchanting creatures must perish, but we neither wish that they had dutifully accepted their allotted position in life, nor condemn the Confucian morality that so confined them. The detached tone of the work keeps us from becoming involved with these women except at the surface level. At no point does Saikaku expect us to wish that Tokugawa society had been more lenient toward a wanton girl like Oshichi, though other writers (for example, Ki no Kaion in his play *Yaoya Oshichi*) emphasized the pathetic aspects of the incident. That is not where Saikaku's interest lay. Nor can we suppose he wished to criticize the regime: he is concerned only with the individual. "Liberation" meant for him only the opportunity to find oneself sexually, and for that privilege it was worth paying the price, as Osan states; Saikaku had no wish to liberate the *chōnin* (townsman) class from the restrictions imposed on it by the samurai.[28] Saikaku seems to have considered the society he lived in as eternal, unlikely ever to be changed, and probably not very different from society in the past. It was hard for some people to survive, but that was the condition of life itself; the best course was probably to give all for love. If Yonosuke is the chōnin hero, Osan is the chōnin heroine.

Saikaku's realism is light-years removed from the realism of nineteenth-century European fiction. It differs also from the realism of his contemporary, Chikamatsu, whose romantic tone is often contrasted with Saikaku's unsentimentality. Chikamatsu may have been romantic in portraying courtesans uniformly as women forced into their profession by the claims of filial piety, or in depicting them as ready always to prove their sincerity by joining in a lovers' suicide; most prostitutes were probably not quite so admirable. But when we compare the pictures drawn by Saikaku and Chikamatsu of the licensed quarters, certainly Chikamatsu seems the more realistic in his insistence on the essential sordidness of the sale of women's bodies. He is also more realistic in his evocations of the anguish of love. Saikaku's characters spend their lives at lovemaking, but one woman is much the same as another to a man like Yonosuke. Even the women who die for love seem to experience none of the mingled joy and anguish of love, but only a physical involvement.

Osen passively agrees to go on a secret pilgrimage to Ise with the cooper who is courting her, and eventually marries him. All promises well for the couple, but one day a bowl accidentally falls off a shelf, disarraying her hair. Osen is suspected by the wife of another man of having been in bed with him. Depressed by this unfounded rebuke, she declares, "Having suffered the shame, there is nothing to lose. I shall make love to Chōzaemon and teach that woman a lesson." Saikaku comments: "Dwelling upon this idea, she aroused in herself a passion for Chōzaemon which soon resulted in a secret exchange of promises between the two."[29] Osen, fully aware of the terrible penalty for adultery, decides out of pique to have an affair with a man in his sixties. She admits him to her bedroom where the cooper soon catches the guilty pair. There is surely nothing of realism here. We are amused, rather than touched, because Saikaku has not permitted us to take these people seriously. His final remark is: "This is a stern world and sin never goes unpunished,"[30] but we cannot even take the sin seriously. If Osen, knowing the likely consequences, nevertheless decided to sleep with the old man because she genuinely loved him, we might be prepared to accept the final adage, but Osen's actions are silly rather than sinful. Saikaku clearly did not intend for us to despise Osen or to condemn her either; she is one of those delightful, illogical, somehow lovable creatures we call human beings; seen from the reverse end of the telescope she is too far away to elicit more than our indulgent smiles.

One of Saikaku's most successfully employed comic techniques is enumeration. The miscellaneous objects dredged up when the cooper cleans a well are enumerated with marvelous precision;[31] each item suggests some facet of contemporary city life, recorded with realism and wit. Again, the objects in Osen's dowry are so tellingly chosen that we understand without further explanation what her life was like as a lady's maid.[32]

Another aspect of Saikaku's comic realism is his insistence on the voice of common sense even in situations that normally call for romantic impetuosity. When the cooper promises the old crone who serves as a go-between in his romance with Osen "a set of Nara-hemp clothes of second quality" the precision of "second quality" injects a prudent note that makes us smile at the level-headed cooper.[33] Shortly afterward we are told, "This set the flames of love burning more fiercely in the cooper's heart and he cried: 'My lady, I will supply you with all the firewood you will need to make tea the rest of your life.' "[34] The caution that kept the cooper from promising firewood for all occasions is humorous, and Saikaku underlines it with the comment: "In this world no one knows how long a person may live, and it is amusing to think that love should have made him promise so much."

Sometimes the situation itself is comic. The night spent at the inn with Osen lying between the two men, the cooper and the manservant Kyūshichi, each determined to keep the other from enjoying the girl, is irresistibly funny. So too is the scene when the fierce Zetarō the Rock Jumper proposes to Osan, not realizing that the man with her, Moemon, is her lover and not (as she had stated) her brother.

Finally, there is the humor of Saikaku the commentator, standing somewhat removed from the story, and making his dryly humorous observations on the antics of his characters. His manner is reminiscent of Fielding in *Tom Jones*, introducing each episode with a reflective piece, often in a mock-philosophical mode. Saikaku is apt also to undercut the tragedy of a situation by a single remark pointing out that it too is part of the human comedy. After Seijūrō is executed for a theft he did not commit, the seven hundred missing gold pieces are discovered in the course of a general housecleaning: "It just goes to show you how careful you must be," said an old graybeard in the family with an air of "I told you so!"[35]

The characters Saikaku creates in *Five Women* are two-dimensional, but not in the same sense that this is true of Yonosuke. He is a reduction to the extreme of an instinct common to all men, but he has no individuality, nothing to suggest that he was modeled on a human being with human complexities. He belongs to the world of the cartoon; the rather crude drawings made by Saikaku himself for the original edition suit Yonosuke perfectly. But the "five women" and their lovers call for different treatment. They are modeled on real people and themselves might serve as models for masterpieces of the ukiyo-e —lovely, entirely human, winning, though lacking the weight of flesh. Saikaku's style, at its most brilliant in this work, is perfectly suited to sketching with swift but unerring strokes figures of enormous charm.

Four months after *Five Women*, Saikaku published *Kōshoku Ichidai Onna* (The Life of an Amorous Woman). The novel does not appear to have been based on the experiences of any particular woman; probably after the success of *Five Women*, Saikaku decided to write a full-length work treating the love of a female voluptuary, the counterpart to his Yonosuke. The two novels are similar in their seriatim construction; only one character, the woman who relates (by way of confession) her many experiences in love, threads together the episodes.

The work begins as an unidentified narrator encounters two young men: one, though exhausted by excessive indulgence in fleshly pleasures nevertheless prays for the strength to continue them; the other, weary of these pleasures, desires only to escape from women altogether. The narrator accompanies the young men to a lonely hermitage, the habitation of an old crone. The setting is appropriate for a monk or nun who has renounced all worldly interests, but the old woman, despite her age and white hair, wears a sky-blue kimono, and her sash is tied in front, in the stylish manner of a courtesan. The hermitage is also given a special character by the plaque over the door bearing the inscription "The Hut of Fleshly Pleasures" and by the fragrance of a perfume quite unlike the incense burned at temples. These details warn us that whatever confession the old woman may make, however earnestly she may profess disillusion with the mundane world, her renunciation is far from complete.

The two young men, both plagued by love, though in opposite ways, ask the old woman about her past, hoping to learn from her experiences. They offer saké, and under its influence she begins the confession that occupies all the rest of the novel; the two young men and the narrator never reappear. Saikaku was undoubtedly influenced by earlier confessional literature, particularly the two kana zōshi *Shichinin Bikuni* (Seven Nuns, 1643) and *Ninin Bikuni* (Two Nuns, 1663) as well as by more recent, though less celebrated, confessional tales. The first-person narration immediately sets this novel apart from *The Life of an Amorous Man*. This manner of narration not only keeps the work from disintegrating into nearly unrelated episodes, but gives greater solidity to the portrayal of the central figure. The characterization as such, apart from the insistence on her nymphomania, is exceedingly vague. We are told at the beginning that the woman, of a good family, learned what was expected of a young lady—calligraphy, the dyeing of fabrics and the like; these accomplishments serve her in good stead in later years when she is obliged to making a living as a seamstress or teacher of penmanship. But her beauty is clearly of greater importance than her artistic talent.

Some Japanese critics have suggested that Saikaku intended in this work to describe the hard life to which a woman was condemned by the society. Certainly the various steps downward in the hierarchy of prostitution as the heroine loses her beauty and charm are graphically depicted; and when, toward the end, she becomes a common streetwalker, taking advantage of the darkness to make men think she is forty years younger than her actual age, we sense an element of pathos totally lacking in *The Life of an Amorous Man*. There are even two scenes bordering on sentimentality, a new note in Saikaku: in the first the heroine has a vision of "some ninety-five different childlike figures, each child wearing a hat in the form of a lotus leaf and each one stained with blood from his waist down."[36] She realizes that these were the children she had conceived but disposed of by abortion. The vision disappears, leaving her to wonder if it does not signify her life is drawing to an end. But she has another even graver shock: she spends one whole night walking the streets without a single man accosting her. At this she decides, ". . . this would be my last effort in the Floating World at plying the lustful trade, and I gave it up for once and all."[37] In her bleak old age she turns to Buddhism. One day she goes into a hall containing statues of the five hundred disciples of the Buddha. As she examines them, each face comes to resemble that of a man she has spent the night with, and she reflects, "Nothing in the world is so terrible as a woman who practices this calling." She withdraws to the lonely retreat where the young men visit her. The book concludes with her confident assertion that, thanks to her confession, she has freed herself of all taint. "I may have lived in this world by selling my body, but is my heart itself polluted?"[38]

Our final glimpse of the woman may suggest she has been degraded by society, but we must not forget that her repentance comes late in the day. Again and again she has been given the chance to become a respectable housewife, but a housewife's humdrum existence is evidently far more distasteful than any brothel. Her insatiable appetite cannot be satisfied except in her chosen career; even the visions at the end do not prevent her from styling her hermitage "The Hut of Fleshly Pleasures." There is no suggestion of a condemnation of society or even of this woman herself, only a record of an eventful life that ends, as all lives must, with physical deterioration. Saikaku manages, thanks to his fertility of invention and flashing twists of style, to keep us from being bored by repetition; but apart from the changes resulting from old age and loss of beauty, he does not develop the character. Saikaku's woman is as two-dimensional as his man, Yonosuke. We cannot even feel sorry for her. At one point she takes up residence in a temple. She tells us: "The priest to whom I had entrusted myself was a disagreeable man. He indulged ceaselessly in fornication, until all my interest in these matters stopped and all my pleasure died away." But, just as we are beginning to sympathize, she continued, "Howbeit, even this form of life is tolerable when once a woman has grown accustomed to it. Finally it came about that when my priest returned late at night from a death watch, I would wait impatiently for him, and that when he set out at dawn to gather the ashes, I would be plunged in sorrow at the parting."[39] The woman's lusting after the priest, even when he has just come from a wake or is about to attend a cremation, hardly strikes us as pathetic; it seems less an example of Saikaku's realism than of burlesque. The woman is depicted in such extravagant terms, uniquely and utterly devoted to sex, that she is comic even in her most sordid pursuits. Saikai surely did not intend her to stand as a representative of downtrodden womanhood; she led precisely the life she desired.

This is not to say that Saikaku romanticizes her career. Quite the contrary, her descent into the lower ranks of prostitutes is chronicled with the utmost objectivity. Money counts for everything in this world: without it, even Yonosuke would be frustrated in his craving for pleasure, and without it a prostitute is doomed to even harsher circumstances. Even during the woman's brief career as a teacher of penmanship, before she reverted to her calling, her craving for men never caused her to forget money. When she makes overtures to one young man, and he frankly informs her that he is too poor to offer any presents, she is indignant. He takes her, and by way of revenge she "subjugates" the man by inducing him to indulge in pleasure day and night; in the end he is a wreck, abandoned even by doctors.[40] But the woman never loses her good humor, even in adversity. We learn, for example, that once she had slipped from the highest to the second and then to the third rank of courtesans, "I was so glad to have a customer I didn't ask anyone to see what he looked like."[41] She spends little time brooding over past glories, but devotes herself instead to maintaining her reduced prestige.

The Life of an Amorous Woman is of most lasting interest in its picture of the pleasure quarters. Unlike the hyōbanki books, evaluations of prostitutes, it is largely concerned with the seamier side of the world of pleasure. The wretched women who have no choice but to catch at the sleeves of passersby are treated with detachment and humor, but the facts are there. Because *The Life of an Amorous Woman* is written almost entirely in the first person, Saikaku gives himself little opportunity for his usual sardonic comments, but his willingness to treat the lowest circle of prostitutes is indicative of his moral concern. He neither suggests any solution, nor does he blame the woman's misfortunes on anyone other than herself, but he surely was not a mere impassive witness.

Saikaku's special brand of morality is more conspicuous in his next work, *Honchō Nijū Fukō* (Twenty Cases of Unfilial Children in Japan), published in the eleventh month of the same year, 1686—truly a year of miracles for the author! This work, reverting to the pattern of *Saikaku's Tales of the Provinces*, consists of anecdotes collected in many parts of Japan. The title makes obvious reference to the famous Chinese work *Twenty-four Examples of Filial Conduct*, long familiar in Japan, and adapted by Asai Ryōi in *Yamato Nijūshi Kō* (1665). The Tokugawa government had placed great emphasis on the importance of filial piety, making it the cornerstone of education. In 1682 Tsunayoshi, learning of the extreme filial piety of a farmer's son in the province of Suruga, decorated the man and ordered his Confucian philosopher, Hayashi Nobuatsu, to compose a biography of this paragon. In the same year Tsunayoshi ordered that signboards be erected throughout the country encouraging loyalty and filial piety. In the 1683 version of the *Rules for the Military Houses*, the first article mentioned filial piety.[42]

In the preface to *Twenty Cases* Saikaku adopts his usual cynical tone:

> The bamboo shoots that Mêng Tsung sought in the snow can be found today at a greengrocer's. The carp that Wang Hsiang fished from the river is in a tank at the fishmonger's. Even if we cannot hope for conduct that goes beyond the call of normal duty, it is proper for people to be diligent in their respective family businesses and to use the income to keep their households in order and to carry out to the full the teachings. But decent people of their kind are rare, and bad people are many. Any human being ignorant of the Way of Filial Piety will surely incur the punishment of Heaven. Instances I have heard about all over the country reveal the unmistakable guilt of unfilial people. I have had them printed in the hope they will be helpful in encouraging filial conduct.[43]

The opening sentences, making light of famous Chinese examples of filial piety, suggest that this book will be a parody, perhaps thinly disguised as a moral lesson, in accordance with the government's encouragement of filial piety. But although there is humor in the work, particularly in the deft introductions to each episode, the tone on the whole is grim. Perhaps, as Noma has suggested, Saikaku resented Tsunayoshi's posing as a model Confucian ruler, despite his capricious and sometimes unspeakable actions, and was trying indirectly, by presenting instances of horribly unfilial behavior, to give the lie to the hollow platitudes of filial piety.[44] I believe it more likely that Saikaku, having described the sordid life of a common streetwalker, had shifted his attention to even lower forms of conduct, as if he had become fascinated by evil itself. His unfilial sons are not merely spendthrifts or rebels unwilling to follow the family business: they are ready to murder their fathers.

The most shocking story of the collection tells of an itinerant priest, exhausted by his long and painful journey, who asks some little girls in a remote mountain hamlet if they know of a house nearby where he could rest. All the girls but one run away, intimidated by his haggard appearance. The remaining little girl—she is only eight—offers to take him home, and the overjoyed priest goes with her. After he has rested a while he tells his hosts he must be off again on his journey. He describes his sad mission, traveling around the country to pray at different shrines for the repose of his parents. As he leaves he expresses the hope they will meet again. No sooner has he departed than the little girl informs her parents she has noticed a wallet filled with gold in the priest's pack. She urges them to kill the priest and take the money: "He's traveling alone—no one will ever know." The father, machete under his arm, sets off in pursuit. At this point Saikaku comments on the evil nature of a girl of eight who could incite her father to murder and expresses surprise that a girl who lived in such a wretchedly poor village should have recognized gold pieces. This sardonic remark, recalling the episode in *Five Women* when Osan and Moemon are refused lodging at an inn because the owner does not recognize that their gold pieces are money, is delivered in exactly the same tone as similar comments found in Saikaku's other works, but the intent could hardly have been comic.

The girl's father catches up to the priest and, even though the latter gives up his money without resistance, kills him with the words, "Your money was your enemy. Consider this is the floating world" (*ukiyo to omoe*). The priest, with his dying breath, predicts that retribution will soon strike. The murderer uses the money to establish himself in the world, and soon he and his family are leading prosperous lives.

Perhaps the intent up to this point was burlesque: the intelligence and sharp powers of observation of the little girl have provided her father and mother with a comfortable living—just what is expected of a filial daughter. But it would take a very special reader to laugh. Despite their newfound wealth, the family does not live happily ever after. The girl grows up to be a great beauty and is much sought, but she imposes so many conditions on her suitors that it seems she will never marry. When her parents complain she reminds them menacingly that the family owes its fortune to her. Eventually she marries a man, only to leave him on discovering he has an almost invisible scar under one ear. She accepts service in a samurai household, where she at once seduces the husband. The samurai's wife, fearful of gossip, tries to break up the affair, but the girl, enraged at the interference, stabs the wife fatally. She manages to escape, but her parents are held as hostages. The father is condemned to death when the girl fails to surrender herself, but he does not resent the sentence; he confesses that it was exactly six years before that he killed the itinerant monk. The day after her father is beheaded the girl is caught and executed.[45]

This story is so horrendous that we may not be able to take it seriously, simply because our mind refuses to admit the possibility of so odious a woman. But this is a far cry from the normal reaction to parody or burlesque. Other stories in the collection, it is true, are less macabre in tone, and a humorous element is not absent, but the work as a whole is unpleasant; this is no doubt why *Twenty Cases* has never been popular.

Saikaku's next work, *Nanshoku Ōkagami* (The Great Mirror of Manly Love), was published in the first month of 1687. Stories about homosexual love were common in the Muromachi period, and other isolated examples, usually telling of priests and young acolytes, date back much earlier. The kana zōshi literature includes such works as *Dembu Monogatari* (The Story of a Boor), written during the Kan'ei era (1624–43), which debates the relative merits of women and men as sexual partners. The evaluation books of actors also had homosexual overtones. Saikaku, however, went beyond his predecessors in his insistence that it was preferable to love a man, rather than a woman. The brief preface concludes: "There is nothing for which we should be more grateful than the love of youths; we should not hesitate to enter on this path."[46] The first episode, a piece of expository writing rather than a story, opens with a declaration of the superior pedigree of homosexual love, citing dubious instances from the ancient writings of both Japan and China, and naming famous writers of the past who, according to Saikaku, were practitioners of this kind of love. The merits and demerits of men and women are contrasted:

> It costs a lot of money whether you ransom a prostitute or buy a house for a man. If you lend your coat to an entertainer in Yoshiwara it's no more likely to come back than if you leave pocket money with the servant of an actor from Shijō.[47]

He concludes:

> When we compare and contrast the love of men and the love of women and wonder which to choose, we see that no matter how attractive or sweet-tempered a woman may be, and no matter how base and unattractive a man, it is in general insulting to the man to discuss the two different forms of love in the same breath. A woman can be likened to a plant which, for all its blossoms, has creeping tendrils that twist around you. A youth is aloof, but imbued with an indescribable fragrance, like the first plum blossoms. For this reason, if one discusses their relative merits one must end by discarding women in favor of men.[48]

Another episode begins:

> All men in the world are beautiful, but among women beauties are rare, or so Abe no Kiyoaki is reputed to have said.[49]

It is hard to know how seriously to take such remarks. Was Saikaku, who had written so differently of women in his earlier works, now revealing his true preferences? Noma has linked this work to Tsunayoshi's well-known fondness for young men, a public secret at the time. Saikaku had carefully excluded stories about Edo from his collection of unfilial children, presumably to avoid giving offense; in this work he may have gone further in an attempt to ingratiate himself with the government. Perhaps also Saikaku wrote this work, concerned in large part with the amours of the samurai, at the request of booksellers in Edo, whose customers were largely samurai.[50] In any case, *The Great Mirror of Manly Love* was the first work of a distinct class of writings by Saikaku, tales of the samurai. In this and subsequent works of the same genre Saikaku expressed almost uncritical admiration, even to espousing the variety of love many samurai preferred.

The Great Mirror of Manly Love has often been praised for its style, particularly of the first half, which describes love affairs of the samurai. The simpler manner Saikaku had adopted in *Twenty Cases* and other miscellaneous works, no doubt in order to please readers unable to follow the intricacies of his haikai prose, would predominate in most of his subsequent writings, but here he returns to the more complex and more beautiful style of his kōshoku stories. The second half of the book is devoted to the love affairs of Kabuki actors. The style drops to a more prosaic level, producing an uneven impression of the book as a whole. The samurai stories emphasize especially the fidelity of the pairs of lovers to their mutual vows of love, no matter how great the difficulties. Fidelity was an unusual theme for Saikaku, who more frequently described profligates; perhaps it was a further proof of his respect for the samurai. The stories about actors, lighter in tone, resemble Saikaku's works on the licensed quarters.

Most of Saikaku's samurai heroes are drawn without any trace of either criticism or humor. It is not clear how much personal contact Saikaku actually had with the samurai class. His townsmen have an authentic ring to their last detail, but his samurai tend to be schematized, and their love affairs are almost invariably portrayed in terms of flawless devotion. Conceivably Saikaku's only object was to cater to samurai readers, but more likely he believed the samurai did in fact possess virtues beyond the attainment of the merchant class. The samurai lovers are depicted in Grecian terms as warriors who scorn the love of women but are ready to die to prove their unwavering love for another man. Again and again these stories end with the *seppuku* (ritual disembowelment) of both young men, each determined not to seem less than a hero in the eyes of the other. Occasionally a different note is sounded. Sasanosuke is enraged to discover that his lover Haemon has shown interest in another boy. When Haemon returns home, Sasanosuke leads him to an inside courtyard and locks the doors around him. It is snowing, but Sasanosuke, not satisfied with keeping Haemon standing in the snow, demands that he hand over his swords, strip naked, and let his hair fall loose. Then Sasanosuke orders Haemon to stick a piece of paper marked with a Sanskrit letter to his forehead, like a corpse. The poor young man, trembling with cold and misery, raises his hands in prayer, and Sasanosuke, from his vantage point in an upstairs room, mockingly beats a drum accompaniment. But the punishment goes too far—Haemon dies, and Sasanosuke at once commits seppuku.[51] The cruelty of this episode suggests an element of sadism in such affairs Saikaku normally did not treat.

In times of peace there was no opportunity for the samurai to display their loyalty in battle. The supreme test of bravery and martial skill might be a vendetta to avenge an insult or an aggrieved father. *The Great Mirror of Manly Love* contains some stories in this vein, notably one describing the youth Katsuya who avenges his father's murder. The story, more complex and interesting than most, describes how Katsuya is noticed one day in the street by a daimyo going by in a palanquin. His beauty induces the daimyo to take Katsuya into his service, but the daimyo soon loses interest in his charms. One day Katsuya finds a letter from his mother, to be opened when he is grown, giving the name of his father's murderer and commanding him to exact vengeance. The daimyo encourages Katsuya to perform this filial act. Katsuya sets out and soon encounters a beggar whom he recognizes as an old friend, a samurai who has fallen in the world. That night he visits the friend, Gensuke, in the outcasts' section by the river; the scene has the vivid quality of actual experience otherwise missing from the work. Katsuya reveals that he is about to leave to avenge his father, and explains that in the past, when he had received letters of love from Gensuke he had been under obligations to another lover, the daimyo, but now is glad to spend the night with him. Gensuke is overjoyed. The next morning he gives Katsuya a valuable sword, a family heirloom, to use in carrying out his revenge. Katsuya travels to the distant province where his enemy lives, followed by Gensuke, who keeps out of sight. The two men return together to Edo after the successful vendetta and are acclaimed by the daimyo. Saikaku concludes: "This event was unprecedented; it deserves to be described as a mirror of *wakashu* conduct. The love of men must always be like this."[52]

Saikaku's next work, published two months after *The Great Mirror of Manly Love*, in the third month of 1687, was a minor work entitled *Futokoro Suzuri* (A Portable Writing Kit) which consists of twenty-five anecdotes heard in different parts of the country, by a man described as being "half priest, half laity."

The following month Saikaku published another collection of samurai stories, *Budō Denrai Ki* (The Transmission of the Martial Arts). The work bears the subtitle "Vendettas in the Various Provinces," and this in fact is the theme of most of the thirty-two stories, though the circumstances are sometimes stated only briefly. Some of the offenses that give rise to vendettas are so trifling we may wonder why the samurai's honor demanded satisfaction. Sometimes too a man carried out his vendetta even though he knew he was in the wrong, whether for the sake of his family's honor or his own reputation. Some stories have as a secondary theme the homosexual relations that are described in such detail in *The Great Mirror of Manly Love*, but other love affairs are between samurai and women.

One of the most memorable stories tells of a samurai who loses his wife in childbirth. People attempt to distract him by sending other women to him, and eventually he falls in love with a woman named Nozawa. He makes advances one day, only for her to refuse him, explaining it is the anniversary of her mother's death. Another woman, Koume, seeing her chance, goes to the man and becomes his mistress. His affections, however, are still held by Nozawa, and the enraged Koume, after resorting in vain to black magic and spells, poisons Nozawa and her six maids. Koume is apprehended and put to death in a most unusual manner: she is placed in a wooden box into which the families of the murdered women drive nails one at a time until, after eleven days, they finally kill her. Koume's brother, learning what has happened, decides he must avenge his sister. He disguises himself as a traveling merchant, and insinuates himself into the household. He waits for his chance; eventually he gets his hands on the samurai's small son and threatens to kill him. Fortunately for the boy, a young samurai, known for his skill with a gun, shoots and kills the kidnaper. Some years later the boy, now fourteen, notices a small scar when his hair is being combed. He learns it was caused by the bullet grazing him. He is so grateful to the samurai who saved his life that he offers to become his lover, and later joins him in a vendetta.[53]

The vendetta that earns this story its place in the collection is presumably the one described in the last few lines, rather than the abortive revenge of Koume's brother, but the interest of the story lies with Koume and her brother, and not in the conventional act of vengeance by the two young samurai.

Saikaku himself must have felt that his glorification of vendettas had gone too far. The third of his samurai collections, *Buke Giri Monogatari* (Tales of Samurai Duty), published in 1688, opens with this preface:

> Human beings by nature are all the same, whoever they may be, yet each reveals himself in his own way: the samurai by wearing a long sword, the Shinto priest by his court cap, the Buddhist priest by his black robes, the farmer by his mattock, the artisan by his adze, the merchant by his abacus. Each man has his own occupation and he must cultivate it as the most important thing in his life. Skill in using bows and horses is the mark of a samurai. For a samurai to forget the wishes of his lord, who has given him a stipend in return for service in an emergency, and throw away his life over some private matter—the quarrel or argument of a moment—is not the true way of a warrior. The proper behavior for him is to give himself completely to his duties as a samurai. I have collected here stories I have heard from old and recent times on this theme and formed them into this book.[54]

Tales of Samurai Duty, instead of glorifying vendettas, is devoted to accounts of consecration to samurai obligations (*giri*). The term *giri*, one of the key words in understanding all of Tokugawa culture, has a broad range of meaning. Minamoto Ryōen wrote: "*Giri* originates in the natural human feelings of wishing to respond to, and in some manner return, acts of kindness received from persons other than those in such special intimate relationships as parent and child, husband and wife or lovers."[55] Minamoto also distinguished a "cold" giri, acts performed out of obligation in response to social pressures, from a "warm" giri, which develops from emotional relationships; in the Tokugawa period when the relations between lord and vassal were strictly prescribed, giri of both varieties came to be considered a paramount samurai virtue. The samurai, following their mentors, the Confucian philosophers, believed that observing giri was their prime responsibility.[56] Minamoto's analysis of giri in the twenty-five stories making up *Tales of Samurai Duty* indicated that the great majority of the acts inspired by this principle are performed not because of any abstract or formal obligation but as the personal response to acts of kindness or a man's desire to prove that his motives are pure.[57] In contrast to the hotheaded reactions to trivial acts of offense recorded in *The Transmission of the Martial Arts*, the stories in this collection imply that the essential qualities of a samurai are gratitude, compassion, and generosity. Saikaku declared in his preface that all men, at one level, are the same: they feel hot in summer and cold in winter, they feel pain and pleasure in the same ways; they are physically the same. It is what they do that distinguishes different varieties of men. The performance of acts of giri is the mark of the samurai. Although the samurai virtues were at this time gradually being adopted by the rest of society, Saikaku did not welcome the breaking down of the class lines. In an age when the samurai could no longer achieve merit by service on the battlefield, their one claim to distinction lay in virtues which merchants, in their struggle for profit, could not and (according to Saikaku) should not imitate. All men were alike, but only in their least interesting aspects; in everything that counted the distinctions had to be maintained.

The stories in *Tales of Samurai Duty* are related with the economy and stylistic excellence we expect in Saikaku, but they seem too short for the material they contain, and the characters rarely come alive. One story begins:

> The span of human life is set by fate, but it happens also that men die for giri; this is the custom of those born in a warrior household. Rank makes no difference in human lives, but it is impressive when a man, deciding that the time has come, is willing to die.[58]

What a difference between this statement and the introductions to Saikaku's tales about prostitutes or townsmen! The story itself tells of the faithful retainer of a daimyo named Kansaki Shikibu. The daimyo's second son, Muramaru, decides he would like to go sightseeing in the Kurile Islands, and Shikibu is ordered to accompany him. Shikibu is permitted to take his son Katsutarō along. They journey under unfavorable conditions; when they reach the Ōi River it is so swollen that Shikibu urges Muramaru to wait until the water subsides. The impetuous youth insists on crossing, and there is no disobeying his commands. Shikibu is last to cross, first verifying that all are safely on their way. At the last moment, however, a third young man, the son of a colleague, is lost when his horse stumbles. Shikibu tells his son Katsutarō that if he survives when the other boy, who was entrusted to Shikibu's care by his father, has died, he will not be able to hold his head high as a samurai. Katsutarō, who is filled with the samurai spirit, at once turns his horse round, rides back into the current and disappears. "Shikibu for a time considered human life. Truly there is nothing sadder than giri." He realizes, now that his only son is dead, nothing in life can give him any pleasure, but he continues on the journey and makes sure that the young lord returns home safely. He and his wife then both take Buddhist orders, as do the parents of the other boy who was drowned. The story ends on a note of fatalism unusual in Saikaku: "They spent years in their devotions, but these people are all no more, and even those who then remained in the world are also no more."[59]

The overall structure of this story resembles such medieval tales as *The Three Priests*, which describes how a brutal murder caused people to leave the world and live together as fellow worshipers of Buddha. But the tone is entirely different. Shikibu orders his own son's death as an act of giri. This is extremely painful, but as a samurai he has no choice: the boy he had agreed to look after has drowned. If any fault is to be found, clearly it lies not with Shikibu but with Muramaru. It was merely a whim, not an urgent mission, that took him to the north, and there was no reason why he could not wait until the river subsided. But not only does Saikaku make no overt criticism of Muramaru, he does not seem even to disapprove. Saikaku accepts the caprice of a daimyo's son without question; probably, like others of the time, he considered that to serve a capricious or tyrannical master was a better test of a samurai's loyalty than serving a kind and just man.

Giri can take even more unusual forms. In another story two young samurai are lovers; when one is dying he begs the other, Muranosuke, to become the lover of a much older man, once his own lover. Muranosuke seeks out the old man, now retired from the world, and asks to be taken as his lover. Even though the man inspires not the least love in Muranosuke, he feels bound by giri to carry out his dying friend's request. The surprised old man refuses, whereupon Muranosuke declares he will kill himself unless he is accepted. The story concludes:

> From then on he secretly visited the man every night. People expressed their admiration that he had, entirely out of giri, formed an attachment with a man who did not please him,

because this foolish request had been made of him. "Muranosuke is truly sincere at heart," people said.[60]

Another story, almost at the end of the collection, begins:

> Someone once said that any decision taken on the spur of the moment will certainly be regretted. He claimed moreover that the true samurai delays deciding about today's events until tomorrow, and he determines the rights and wrongs only after a thorough examination of the facts.[61]

This opinion certainly flies in the face of the usual conception of a samurai as a man who acts instantly, scorning prudence as the virtue of merchants, but it accords with the basic attitude shown by Saikaku in this work.

After the mindless acts of vengeance chronicled in *The Transmission of the Martial Arts*, the prudence extolled in *Tales of Samurai Duty* comes as a pleasant surprise. It is as if Saikaku, initially fascinated by the stern code of vengeance of the warriors, had come to realize that the times had changed, and the actions appropriate for the age of warfare could no longer be permitted. The samurai became the incarnation of giri, this Confucian virtue taking the place of the immediate emotional reactions formerly expected of men who wore two swords.

Saikaku's samurai stories lack the wit or incision of his other works, but there is no mistaking his narrative skill or his effective use of language. These works have generally been given scant attention because they fail to convey Saikaku's comic genius, but they indicate how strongly he must have been attracted by the virtues he attributed to the samurai.

The month before publishing *Tales of Samurai Duty* Saikaku had brought out *Nippon Eitaigura* (The Japanese Family Storehouse, 1688), his most important collection of stories about the merchant class. The fact that he should have written these two works in such close conjunction suggests that he had pondered the appropriate behavior for each. He was not only contrasting the two classes, but implying that the distinctions must be firmly maintained. In *Tales of Samurai Duty* one story describes a samurai named Kuzaemon who, having fallen in the world (because of giri), has become a carpenter. One day some money falls from the possessions of a certain woman which were secretly being moved. He tells his wife of his lucky find. She suspects he is lying—people do not carelessly lose such large sums of money. Fearing she may become involved in her husband's crime, she tells an official, who arrests the husband. Signs are erected declaring that unless the person who lost the money identifies himself Kuzaemon will be punished. The owner of the money for various reasons is embarrassed to reveal herself, but does so out of compassion for Kuzaemon. The magistrate, releasing Kuzaemon, informs him that it was his wife who gave rise to the rumors. The angered Kuzaemon declares he intends to divorce her. The official suggests that the original owner of the money take Kuzaemon as a son-in-law, and everything is soon arranged. The story concludes:

> When the newlyweds discussed their ancestry with each other, it turned out that the woman had been raised in a samurai household, and the man, who was indisputably a samurai, acted as a filial son to his new mother, without ever showing any baseness. The household prospered.[62]

The lesson is that no matter how fallen in the world a samurai may be, he still remains a samurai. If he has married a woman of plebeian upbringing she probably will not appreciate his incorruptible character but suppose instead that he is just as deceitful as a man of her own class. Kuzaemon's new wife, on the other hand, having grown up among samurai and having been the wife of a gallant samurai who died in battle, will be able to value her husband properly. As a familiar expression of the period had it, "A horse goes with a horse, an ox with an ox"; samurai and merchants do not mix.

The corollary of this story, that merchants must not ape the samurai, is found in *The Japanese Family Storehouse* again and again. The man of a merchant family who uses his father's wealth to acquire the trappings of a samurai is likely to end up as a beggar. "At a loss in a samurai household, useless as a merchant's apprentice, his services were scorned by all."[63] A merchant's business, Saikaku repeatedly informs us, is to make money; his virtues include diligence, thrift, honesty, quickness of mind, resilience in adversity, and so on, but neither vengeance nor giri has any place in his life. Saikaku does not choose between samurai and merchant virtues. It is the function of a merchant to calculate sums on his abacus and choose a profitable course, just as it is the function of dogs to bark at strangers or cats to catch mice; it would be idiotic to hope for one all-purpose animal which could frighten off thieves, catch mice, and carry men on its back.

Obviously Saikaku in *The Japanese Family Storehouse* is more at home than in his samurai collections. His humor is abundantly in evidence and the characters, though only briefly sketched in the thirty episodes (none longer than a few pages), come alive and linger in our memories, unlike the many samurai who exist mainly as abstractions. The stories, on the other hand, are quite unlike the adventures recounted in *Five Women*. Each opens with a didactic passage, sometimes extending to more than half the length of the episodes, in which Saikaku gives his prescriptions for getting ahead in the world. The subtitle of the work *Daifuku Shin Chōja-kyō* (The Millionaire's Gospel Modernized) refers to *Chōja Kyō*, a kana zōshi of unknown authorship first published in 1627.

Chōja Kyō, less than ten pages long, is devoid of literary pretentions, but its insistence on the possibility of becoming a millionaire by unremitting efforts undoubtedly influenced Saikaku. The narrator of *Chōja-kyō* describes how, as a temple apprentice, he ate only half of the rice he received each day for his meals; when he had in this manner accumulated a fair amount of rice he started to lend it to people, charging ten percent interest. The amount of rice continued to increase, as did his interest rates, and eventually he became a millionaire, known for his success in all his plans. *Chōja-kyō* also contains lists of "principles to cherish at all times," such as "To regard every man as a thief, every fire as a conflagration," cautionary verses, and ironical comments on how to be poor—"you must be at everyone's beck and call, and be praised by all."[64]

Saikaku's heroes in *The Japanese Family Storehouse* are men like Fuji-ichi, about whom we are told, "He never passed by anything which might be of use. Even if he stumbled he used the opportunity to pick up stones for fire-lighters, and tucked them in his sleeves."[65] Of course, Saikaku recognized that not every hard-working person actually became rich: "To make a fortune some assistance from fate is essential. Ability alone is insufficient. There are highly intelligent people plagued with poverty, and fools blessed with riches."[66] But such cases do not detain him often; his interest is in those men who, by practice of the merchantly virtues, rise from poverty to affluence. The first virtue is thrift. Saikaku does not approve of miserliness—some of his most amusing sarcasm is directed against the man who "for fear of creating an expensive appetite would even remember not to hurry when inquiring about friends after a fire"—but the man who refrains from extravagance and puts away a little each day is on the right track to making a fortune. Next, he must be diligent in his work. The god of Kashima vouchsafes the message that "all must pay proper heed to their means of livelihood, and that poverty never gets the better of a busy man."[67] The worst sin is *yudan*, or negligence, whether indulgence in the pleasures of the licensed quarters or a simple failure to notice business opportunities. The great Fuji-ichi, Saikaku's hero, is not only thrifty with himself, but sees to it that his daughter, on whom he dotes, grows up to be a fit wife for a merchant:

> When the young girl grew into womanhood he had a marriage screen constructed for her, and (since he considered that one decorated with views of Kyoto would make her restless to visit the places she had not seen, and that illustrations of "The Tale of Genji" or "The Tales of Ise" might engender frivolous thoughts) he had the screens painted with busy scenes of the silver and copper mines at Tada.[68]

When, then, a man who by virtue of hard work and thrift has established himself and his family, it is proper for him to enjoy his wealth—never falling into extravagance, but remembering always that "though mothers and fathers give us life, it is money alone which preserves it."[69] Finally, when the man dies he can leave his fortune to a son, whom he has brought up so well he is confident the son will not squander the money. Saikaku's highest praise goes to the merchant city of Sakai:

> In Sakai newly-rich are rare. It is a place where fortunes have deep, firm roots, stretching back for three generations or more, and where goods bought on speculation centuries ago are still kept in stock, awaiting the favourable moment for sale.[70]

Money is everything, or almost everything. In the opening section, after ironically quoting some familiar platitudes, Saikaku reveals why money is so useful:

> People will tell us that when we die, and vanish in a moment's wisp of smoke, all our gold is less than dross and buys us nothing in the world beyond. It is true enough, and yet—is not what we leave behind of service to our sons and our posterity? And while we live (to take a shorter view) how many of life's desirable things is it not within the power of gold to grant us?[71]

The book concludes:

> Money is still to be found in certain places, and where it lies it lies in abundance. Whenever I heard stories about it I noted them in my great national stock-book, and, in order that future generations might study them and profit thereby, I placed them in a storehouse to serve each family's posterity. Here they now rest, as securely guarded as the peace of Japan.[72]

The Japanese Family Storehouse is fascinating as a portrayal of aspects of merchant life. Unlike Saikaku's samurai stories each episode, however broadly caricatured, has the ring of truth; and instead of a rather monotonous harping on the theme of vengeance or giri we have a lively variety of success and failure tales. Saikaku is careful to set each in a particular locality and give the characters names and traits, even though they may not be essential for the "lesson" of the episode. If we compare this work with Defoe's *Complete English Tradesman* (1725–27) we cannot but be struck by the superior literary quality of Saikaku. In place of Defoe's anonymous and featureless clerks, we have a gallery of men and women who remain in one's memory.

The work is optimistic, even though written in a time of depression, when merchantly virtues certainly were not enough for a man to prosper. The shogunate prohibitions on extravagance in clothing, promulgated in 1683, had threatened the large silk-weaving industry of Kyoto with disaster,[73] and the capricious financial policies of Tsunayoshi caused great anxiety among the merchants of the entire country. Saikaku does not allude to such disquieting factors. The prevailing impression the reader obtains is of a thriving merchant class, living almost unto itself, having few connections with either the samurai or the peasantry, and enjoying the fruits of prosperity while threatened only by over-indulgence. The ingenuity displayed by these merchants was called *saikaku*; Saikaku must have felt a strong bond of sympathy with men who exercised a virtue he chose for his name, and his stories in turn, whether based on originals or invented, provide splendid examples of how saikaku controls the destinies of men.

Saikaku followed *The Japanese Family Storehouse* and *Tales of Samurai Duty* with a series of definitely inferior works, including *Irozato Mitokoro Zetai* (1688), *Shin Kashō Ki* (1688) and *Kōshoku Seisui Ki* (1688). Saikaku's productivity was impressive, but the contents of the books are disappointing. *Irozato Mitokoro Zetai* (Households of Three Pleasure Quarters), an account of the debauchery of a rich patron of the brothels, has been characterized by Teruoka Yasutaka as "excessively vulgar and obscene,"[74] falling to the lowest level of any of Saikaku's works. Saikaku's novels, beginning with *The Life of an Amorous Man*, contain hardly a passage that could offend readers today. But in *Households of Three Pleasure Quarters* the mechanical descriptions of orgies become pornography, having neither the verve of *The Life of an Amorous Man* nor the love of *Five Women*. At the end the hero, Sotoemon, having squandered his fortune in the pleasure quarters of Kyoto, Osaka, and Edo (the places of the title), dies of sexual exhaustion, together with his companions in pleasure.

Shin Kashō Ki (The New Kashō Ki) derives its title from the *Kashō Ki* of Nyoraishi, published in 1642. Nyoraishi's book was didactic in intent, lamenting the decline in morality among samurai, and offering examples, from both China and Japan, of virtuous conduct; Saikaku's work, on the surface at least, also aims at illustrating the proper conduct for samurai, but in fact the twenty-six stories lack a unifying theme and seem little more than leftovers from Saikaku's bag.

Kōshoku Seisui Ki (The Rise and Fall of Love) borrows its title from the medieval *Gempei Seisui Ki* (Rise and Fall of the Minamoto and Taira), and its opening lines parody the famous "The bell (*kane*) of the Gion Temple . . . ," with "The money (*kane*) spent in the bad places of Gion. . . ." The first episode concludes with a boy being inducted into the mysteries of the pleasure quarters by his father; the last episode of the book concerns an aged man who on his death bed asks to be taken to a courtesan's establishment; with his dying breath he bemoans the fact he didn't meet her thirty years earlier.[75] The rise and fall of love, represented by these two episodes, seem the other side to the merchants' unremitting quest of money. In a society where the merchants officially ranked lowest among the four classes and where they could not hope to enjoy political power, the pleasures of the gay quarters were their highest ambition. Saikaku did not condemn them for this indulgence, providing it was within their means. Unlike *The Life of an Amorous Man*, which concerns a particular townsman who enjoyed to the full the fleshly pleasures, this work deals with the whole merchant class, suggesting its affinity with *The Japanese Family Storehouse*.

Though none of these three works is devoid of interest, they clearly rank low on the list of Saikaku's works. We may feel disappointed that Saikaku, having achieved the wit and warmth of *Five Women* should not have written even superior works in the same vein but, as Teruoka pointed out, Saikaku, unlike a modern intellectual writer, had no clearly defined artistic conceptions. He wrote as the spirit moved him, now surprising us with a work of high artistic value only to follow it immediately with one of shocking vulgarity.[76] His works of the years immediately following *The Japanese Family Storehouse* are of little interest today. *Hitome Tamaboko* (1669) is a kind of travelogue, describing sights on the way from the north of Japan south to Nagasaki, illustrated with anecdotes and songs about the places passed. *Honchō Ōin Hiji* (1689) is a collection of forty-four brief stories describing wise decisions made by two judges, apparently Itakura Katsushige (administrator in Kyoto 1601–19) and his son Shigemune (1619–55). These stories have sometimes been praised as being embryonic detective stories, but they have neither suspense nor excitement, and rarely rise above the commonplace.[77] *Arashi Mujō Monogatari* (1691) and *Wankyū Nisei no Monogatari* (1691) are both about actors; the materials suggest they have been left over from the first *Wankyū* or from *The Great Mirror of Manly Love*.

It is with relief that we reach *Seken Mune Sanyō* (Reckonings That Carry Men through the World, 1692), a series of tales describing the desperate expedients of men unable to pay their bills at the end of the year. Despite the grim nature of the characters—the relentless bill-collectors, the hapless debtors, and the unscrupulous debt-evaders—the prevailing tone is cheerful. Noma stated that, no matter how desperate the plight of the debtors, Saikaku avoids exaggeration and maintains an equanimity of tone approaching resignation. Some scholars, however, by carefully choosing the two or three gloomiest stories in the collection, have attempted to prove that *Reckonings* was a reflection of Saikaku's increasing bitterness toward life, as a result of the worsening condition of the Japanese economy. But, it will be remembered, Saikaku's first novel, *The Life of an Amorous Man*, was written at the time of a famine, though it is hard to find in this ebullient work any concern over the suffering of the hungry. Almost every period of Tokugawa history had its hardships and inequality, and Asai Ryōi's bitter comments on the predicament of the rōnin in the 1660s express far more indignation toward society than anything in *Reckonings*. Indeed, the most striking feature of this work is that, given the theme (which could easily have lent itself to the harshest descriptions of his time), Saikaku retains his affection not only for the debtors but for the clever bill-collectors; he still sees all his creatures as participants in the human comedy. It is possible to extract a philosophy of despair: the proverbial statement that "money begets money," quoted by Saikaku,[78] has been interpreted as proving that Saikaku believed no one could build a fortune who did not already possess some capital. No doubt this thought on occasion crossed his mind, but he also quotes the proverb "Poverty never catches up to the hard worker";[79] Saikaku was evidently still convinced, part of the time anyway, that ingenuity and thrift were enough for a man to prosper. In his favorite city of Sakai, there are no more than four or five really poor people.[80] He tells us also that "during the past thirty years the whole country has become noticeably prosperous,"[81] and follows this statement with a description of how houses, formerly thatched, are now shingled, and how even the barrier at Fuwa, famous in poetry for the moonlight pouring through the broken roof, now has new roof tiles and whitewashed walls.

Obviously Saikaku has no consistent philosophy. His various utterances on money or society are full of contradictions. It is foolish to blame him for these contradictions and it is wrong to attempt to bring order out of them by suppressing some of his opinions or deciding that they were not meant to be taken seriously. Saikaku, in *Reckonings* as elsewhere, is above all a storyteller, and his comments shift according to the story, not as the result of philosophic reflection. The closest he comes to enunciating a code of behavior fit for a merchant is given in *Reckonings*, Book II: from the time he is twenty-five he should avoid yudan (neglect of opportunities); at thirty-five strive to establish his fortune; at fifty strengthen the foundations of his fortune before turning it over to his heir; and the year before he reaches sixty he should retire and spend his time visiting temples.[82] A similar set of stages in a man's life was charted in *The Japanese Family Storehouse*,[83] but neither list suggests anything more striking than Saikaku's usual belief that the merchant's business is to build a solid fortune.

The stories in *Reckonings*, like those in *The Japanese Family Storehouse*, usually consist of long, didactic introductions followed by a brief story; one section devotes only its last few lines to the story proper after a long sermon on thrift and the desirability of staying at home rather than squandering money in the pleasure quarters.[84] A few episodes have gained fame as literary works, notably the chapter called "Lord Heitarō." This tells of the sermon given one New Year's Eve at a Shinshū temple about Heitarō, a follower of the founder of the sect. Only three people attend. The priest, after finishing the services, assures the three that their piety will be rewarded. Then each speaks up in turn and tells why he has come. The first, an old woman, has "disappeared" so as to give her son a plausible excuse for not meeting his creditors; the second describes how he has been chased out of his house by a wife who despises him for his failure to raise any money; the third admits that he had planned to steal the *zōri* left at the temple door by the crowds of worshipers, only to be disappointed by the miserable attendance. These confessions move the priest, but as he is deploring the uncertainties of this world, various people rush in to inform him of a birth, a death, and a theft, among other events. The story ends with a wry comment on how busy a priest is if he lives in the ukiyo.[85] The entire work concludes, one story later, with acclaim for the morning sun on New Year's Day shining over a prosperous and peaceful country. Perhaps this is the closest Saikaku could come to expressing overt criticism of the times and the regime; more likely, it was not his intent to express criticism but only to describe the endlessly absorbing ways of men. In some books he depicted them in reckless pursuit of pleasure, in others dominated by desire for revenge, or worse; in *The Japanese Family Store-*

house he showed how merchants made money, in *Reckonings*, how the unsuccessful fared.

Saikaku died in his fifty-second year, on September 9, 1693. He left behind various manuscripts posthumously published as *Saikaku Okimiyage* (1693), *Saikaku Oritome* (1694), *Saikaku Zoku Tsurezure* (1695), *Yorozu no Fumi-hōgu* (1696), and *Saikaku Nagori no Tomo* (1699).

These works vary considerably in content. One, *Yorozu no Fumi-hōgu* (Scraps of Letters of Every Kind), is unique among Saikaku's works in being cast in the form of letters. All five works seem to reveal a decline in the author's powers, despite passages of his old brilliance. The problem of authorship also arises at least in the cases of *Saikaku Okimiyage* (Saikaku's Parting Gift) and *Scraps of Letters.* After Saikaku's death his manuscripts were edited by his disciple Hōjō Dansui (1663–1711). Although Dansui professed merely to have assembled manuscripts he found in Saikaku's house, discrepancies of style strongly suggest that he made additions, perhaps in order to fill out the book to the size required by the publisher. Nakamura Yukihiko believed that five of the seventeen stories in *Scraps of Letters* were added, though probably not all by Dansui.[86] *Saikaku's Parting Gift* contains some marvelously effective descriptions of merchants reduced to poverty by over-indulgence in fleshly pleasures, but there are also clumsy passages that do not at all resemble Saikaku's usual style. The structure of some episodes is so disjointed as to be downright inartistic. Perhaps Dansui put this work together out of unfinished manuscripts, supplementing them with occasional additions of his own. *Saikaku Nagori no Tomo* (Saikaku's Parting with Friends), though published last of the posthumous works, seems the least tampered with. Munemasa believed that Dansui put it aside, intending to make additions, but finally published it as it stood.[87] The work as a result is obviously unfinished.

It is not clear why Saikaku left behind so many manuscripts. Noma suggested that Saikaku's reappearance at haikai gatherings in 1690 and his renewed contributions to haikai collections after years of silence as a poet may have been due to an eye affliction; composing haikai would have involved less strain on his eyes than writing a novel.[88] Perhaps it was this illness that obliged him to abandon his incomplete manuscripts. After he recovered his eyesight he wrote the two minor works *Arashi Mujō Monogatari* and *Wankyū Nisei Monogatari* in 1691, but evidently he had lost interest in the earlier manuscripts and devoted his attention to *Reckonings*, his last major work.[89] He apparently was working on *Saikaku's Parting Gift* when he died; it was published in the winter of 1693 with his portrait and valedictory haikai.

Saikaku's Parting Gift, a collection of fifteen stories, is one of Saikaku's shortest works. The style and subject matter—the weakness of men with respect to sex, etc.—are familiar, and the work deserves only a minor place in the Saikaku canon.[90] On the other hand, *Saikaku Oritome* (Saikaku's Last Weaving), published in the third month of the following year, though an uneven work, at its best is unique. The title appears to have been derived from Saikaku's preface, which concludes:

> I have strung out with my brush the foolish things of the world and given it the title "Hearts of Men in This World." This must surely be a fabric woven by the weaver bird of Naniwa.

Dansui's preface explains that Saikaku originally intended to write a trilogy consisting of *The Japanese Family Storehouse*, *Honchō Chōnin Kagami* (A Mirror of Japanese Townsmen), and *Yo no Hitogokoro* (Hearts of Men in This World); the latter two manuscripts being incomplete, he put them together to make up this volume. The date of composition is revealed by one episode that begins facetiously: "It has been 2,336,283 years in Japan from the first year of the Sun Goddess until the beginning of spring this year, the second of Genroku."[91] The complete book evidently was supposed to appear in the spring of 1689 and, as we know from an advertisement, there were to be stories of "model townsmen" divided into sections, each devoted to one of the five cardinal virtues.

The present text is in five books of which the first two are from *A Mirror of Japanese Townsmen* and the remaining three from *Hearts of Men*. It is difficult, however, to see how the various people described could be considered as "models." The main theme of many stories is the difficulty, and often impossibility, of getting ahead in the world without capital (*motode*);

only some remarkably clever discovery or a miraculous stroke of good fortune can remedy an intolerable situation:

> There are all kinds of ways to make your way in the world if you have to. But the merchant without capital can rack his brains to the utmost, yet end up nevertheless by spending his entire income on interest, working all his days for other people. The man with a good financial backer naturally is free to trade as he pleases. He can always judge when the time is right for buying, and he frequently makes a profit.[92]

Another story sardonically contrasts the prosperous present with the old days: in the Kan'ei era a certain business establishment had annual sales of less than seven *kan*, but this income was enough to support a household of six comfortably, and creditors were all paid between the twenty-fifth and twenty-eighth of the last month. On the last day of the year, when other people were frantically worried about bills, this family merrily gathered to celebrate, with nothing on their minds. Now the company, in the hands of the former owner's son, does over forty *kan* of business each year, and the establishment numbers eighteen people. But when they have paid their year-end bills there are only a few small coins left to spare. The house has been so thoroughly stripped of valuables that there is no need to put a lock on the door. Such is progress.[93]

The few "model townsmen" are somewhat dubious. The first is a profligate son who spends his time in the pleasure quarters of Kyoto. One night as he is about to get into the bed of a grand courtesan, he hears from the next room someone deliver a message to the customer there, reporting a bad rice crop in Edo; merchants will soon be arriving from there to buy up available supplies. The man in the next room says he will act the first thing in the morning, but our hero, with scarcely a word to the courtesan, leaves at once to corner the market before the Edo merchants arrive. In this way he successfully builds up the family fortune.[94] Another model townsman starts off unpromisingly. In the hopes of ingratiating himself with a temple sufficiently to borrow money at New Year he takes a present to the temple every five days; when mushrooms are worth their weight in gold he sends some, pretending they were a present from an uncle. He rushes to the temple even when he hears that the temple cat has fallen from a shelf and injured itself. But when he finally gets the money he discovers that he has already spent most of it on presents. He and his wife, convinced now that "in this world money begets money" and that all their labors have been for other people's sake, leave Osaka and go to live in the country. They set up a little school where they intend to teach the elements of reading, but they are asked instead to teach Nō plays (including the most obscure) and their pupils ask the meanings of Chinese characters not in any dictionary. In the end the pupils leave, one by one, and the couple is hard put to earn anything, struggle though they may. But one morning they notice that the flame they set the previous night under the cooking pot has not gone out. They investigate and invent a pocket heater (*kairo*) that earns them a fortune.[95]

The conclusion of the story is cheerful, and the hero indeed qualifies as a "model," but the happy ending is described in less than a page after many pages relating the couple's miseries. Contrary to Saikaku's usual practice of opening an episode with general remarks, then presenting a single unified story, here as elsewhere in *Saikaku's Last Weaving* unrelated stories have arbitrarily been lumped together after the same introduction. The story about the couple is preceded by one about a villainous moneylender who drives an innocent man to suicide and is punished when his child is born without arms. Another story has three entirely different plots, ending with the dismal tale of a man who at last obtains a sum of money which will enable him to escape his hand-to-mouth existence. When he reaches the shores of Lake Biwa he refuses to board the ferry, though the weather is perfect, for fear that the boat may capsize. He takes instead the long route around by land, only to be set upon by robbers. Impoverished once again, he is condemned to spending the rest of his days in misery. Surely he does not make much of a model!

Other stories, notably one about a noble salt peddler, are closer to the stated aim of portraying model townsmen, but even here the prevailing impression is of fragmentary materials hastily assembled. In the entire collection only one story (from the second part, *Hearts of Men in This World*) has the kind of brilliance we expect of Saikaku, though the tone is utterly unlike anything he previously wrote. The story, entitled "The Bridge of the Nose of the Landlord's Wife," opens with a typical enough remark: "It is never a good idea to change your accustomed dwelling, no matter whether you are a merchant or an artisan." The narrative relates closely to the announced subject; it tells about a man who learned to his regret he should never have moved. The man, a maker of paper garments, lives with his wife, who makes fans, in a rented apartment. One day at a party the wife makes fun of the landlord's wife, saying her nose looks big enough to decoy a *tengu* (a long-nosed goblin). This unflattering remark is quickly relayed to the landlord's wife, and the two women quarrel. The landlord's wife finally orders the couple to leave, and the other woman replies, "Kyoto's a big place, you know. As long as we pay the rent regularly every month, we'll have no trouble finding a house where the roof doesn't leak and where the landlady's nose is a normal size." The two women now begin to quarrel in earnest, abusing each other's ancestry, and they part as mortal enemies. When the husband hears what has happened he is furious. He orders the wife to apologize to the landlady, but she refuses. He then tells her that if she refuses to obey him he will divorce her. She answers, "I see. Well, I'll go then. But before you get rid of me I'll let people know the circumstances of your sister's sudden death." The husband at once becomes conciliatory, "Do you suppose that changing my lodgings means more to me than my own wife? I'm fed up anyway with the landlady's giving herself airs of importance. This is a good chance to leave the place."

Saikaku, in a manner at once strikingly modern and unlike himself, never fully explains the meaning of the wife's threat, though he later gives another hint that the husband stole his sister's money, perhaps after killing her. Both husband and wife are established as evil, and this impression is not altered by the amusing description of the various lodgings to which they move, each one worse than the last, until finally they exhaust their money in moving expenses. Having changed residence nine times in less than two years, they finally move in with the wife's brother. When the husband objects that their part of the house is in the unlucky direction, the brother sneeringly replies, "In this modern age do you still believe in such superstitions?" But sure enough, everything goes from bad to worse. The couple finally separates, to make their living in opposite parts of the country. At first it appears that their separation will be amicable, but the wife provokes a quarrel with the intention of leaving the husband permanently, and taunts him once again about his sister's death. The story concludes with the remark by Saikaku: "It's true, as they say, once a couple separates they become strangers. How frightening are the hearts of men!"[96]

This conclusion, in a work entitled originally, *Hearts of Men in This World*, reveals an embittered outlook quite foreign to the Saikaku of earlier days. Saikaku has often been described as a realist; the term is inappropriate for the genial observer of the human comedy, but it fits this episode exactly. Even the most Saikakuesque sections of the story, the enumeration of the various undesirable lodgings where the couple stay, are sinister rather than amusing. In their first new home they have a crazy woman for their neighbor who runs around at odd times with a knife; at another place, which seems quiet, they are bothered by the smell of smoke from a nearby crematorium; still another house is invaded by thousands of huge cockroaches that get into the food and water. These descriptions are filled not with humor, but with a kind of chilling realism. Saikaku has also lost his detachment from the characters; obviously he detests the wife of the story, and the husband, who may have murdered his own sister, hardly wins his approval. We may receive the uncomfortable feeling that this was Saikaku's final conclusion about the nature of men. The existence of evil, a theme he had first treated in *Twenty Cases of Unfilial Children in Japan*, had come to seem the truth about "the hearts of men."

Saikaku may have discarded *Saikaku's Last Weaving* because he could not face his own conclusions. Or perhaps the book was the product of a period when illness and possibly near-blindness had embittered him. But the unmistakable realism and the grim cynicism represent developments in Saikaku so important that we cannot but regret that he failed to explore this vein further. No one can read *The Life of an Amorous Man* as a realistic picture of life at the time. Even *Reckonings* has only a few touches of the brutal realism some scholars profess to see in it. But *Saikaku's Last Weaving* as a social document is unique. Perhaps Dansui wrote a larger part than commentators admit, but the most vivid sections not only represent Saikaku at an unhappy stage in his career; they have a depth otherwise lacking in his writings.

Saikaku is acclaimed today as one of two or three great Japanese novelists. When compared to the masters of the European novel—Balzac, Dickens, Turgenev, etc.—he obviously lacks weight and authority. He is certainly no match at characterization with Murasaki Shikibu, let alone Balzac. But his two-dimensional approach to a society, seen at such a distance that only its most salient features emerge, has a curious modernity. He excels as a comic writer, though his wit is sometimes tinged with bitterness. His work belongs to the same world as the woodblock prints, especially of the great Hishikawa Moronobu (d. 1694). As Howard Hibbett wrote: "Both Saikaku and Moronobu achieve their finest effects by sheer stylistic verve."[97] The works of the two men elicit the same kind of admiration; if Saikaku lacks the depth and intensity of Dickens, Moronobu seems shallow alongside Vermeer. But such comparisons are meaningless. To search for profundity in either Saikaku or Moronobu is to mistake their intent. Their wit and their ability to make a single line live account for their unique places in the world of art, and their works are just as fresh as when they were created.

Saikaku's popularity in his own day is demonstrated not only by the repeated editions of some works (including pirated versions) but by the use of his name in the titles, especially of his posthumous writings. His influence on later writers was enormous, as we shall see. Although he was preceded by Asai Ryōi as a popular writer, it is not much of an exaggeration to say that he reestablished prose fiction as an art after over four hundred years of anonymous writings. Writers of every age since Saikaku have turned to him for a style at once entertaining and poetic, and a content quintessentially Japanese.

NOTES

1. Ebara Taizō, *Edo Bungei Ronkō*, p. 25.
2. Noma Kōshin, *Saikaku to Saikaku Igo*, p. 4.
3. Ebara, p. 47.
4. Asō Isoji, Itasaka Gen, and Tsutsumi Seiji, *Saikaku Shū*, pp. 75–77.
5. *Ibid.*, p. 126.
6. Noma, *Saikaku*, p. 9.
7. Asō, Itasaka, and Tsutsumi, p. 41.

8. Noma, *Saikaku*, p. 10.
9. Asō Isoji, *Ihara Saikaku Shū*, p. 3.
10. Nakamura Yukihiko, *Kinsei Sakka Kenkyū*, pp. 7–46, gives a detailed analysis of the style of this work.
11. Howard Hibbett, *The Floating World in Japanese Fiction*, p. 3.
12. See Noma, *Saikaku*, pp. 13–14, for an account of Tsunayoshi's outrages.
13. Nakamura Yukihiko, *Kinsei Shōsetsu Shi no Kenkyū*, p. 63.
14. Noma Kōshin, *Saikaku Nempu Kōshō*, p. 4.
15. Noma, *Saikaku*, p. 18.
16. Noma, *Saikaku Nempu*, p. 148.
17. Noma, *Saikaku*, p. 21.
18. Kishi Tokuzō, "Saikaku Shokoku Hanashi," p. 79.
19. Noma, *Saikaku*, p. 22.
20. See Higuchi Yoshichiyo (ed.), *Kessaku Jōruri Shū*, I, for an annotated edition of *Koyomi*.
21. Noma, *Saikaku*, p. 24.
22. *Ibid.*, p. 25.
23. W. T. de Bary (trans.), *Five Women Who Loved Love*, p. 156.
24. *Ibid.*, pp. 142–43.
25. Noma, *Saikaku*, p. 25.
26. de Bary, p. 150.
27. *Ibid.*, p. 185.
28. Matsuda Osamu, *Nihon Kinsei Bungaku no Seiritsu*, pp. 114–15.
29. de Bary, pp. 109–12.
30. *Ibid.*, p. 113.
31. *Ibid.*, p. 77.
32. *Ibid.*, p. 103.
33. *Ibid.*, p. 79.
34. *Ibid.*, p. 82.
35. *Ibid.*, p. 69.
36. Ivan Morris (trans.), *The Life of an Amorous Woman*, p. 194.
37. *Ibid.*, p. 203.
38. *Ibid.*, p. 208.
39. *Ibid.*, pp. 150–51.
40. *Ibid.*, pp. 157–58.
41. Hibbett, p. 186.
42. Noma, *Saikaku Nempu Kōshō*, pp. 175–76.
43. Fujimura Tsukuru, *Saikaku Zenshū*, I, p. 39.
44. Noma, *Saikaku to Saikaku Igo*, p. 29.

45. Fujimura, I. pp. 101–12.
46. Ozaki Kōyō and Watanabe Otowa, *Saikaku Zenshū*, I, pp. 555–56.
47. *Ibid.*, p. 561.
48. *Ibid.*, pp. 561–62.
49. *Ibid.*, p. 565.
50. Noma, *Saikaku to Saikaku Igo*, pp. 34–35.
51. Ozaki and Watanabe, pp. 611–14.
52. *Ibid.*, pp. 583–89.
53. Fujimura, XIII, pp. 18–33.
54. *Ibid.*, XII, p. 1.
55. Minamoto Ryōen, *Giri to Ninjō*, p. 27.
56. *Ibid.*, p. 49.
57. *Ibid.*, pp. 77–78.
58. Fujimura, XII, p. 42.
59. *Ibid.*, p. 49.
60. *Ibid.*, p. 34.
61. *Ibid.*, p. 243.
62. *Ibid.*, pp. 187–88.
63. G. W. Sargent (trans.), *The Japanese Family Storehouse*, pp. 47–48.
64. *Ibid.*, pp. 241–43.
65. *Ibid.*, p. 36.
66. *Ibid.*, p. 72.
67. *Ibid.*, p. 120.
68. *Ibid.*, p. 38.
69. *Ibid.*, p. 13.
70. *Ibid.*, p. 101.
71. *Ibid.*, p. 13.
72. *Ibid.*, p. 146.
73. Noma, *Saikaku to Saikaku Igo*, p. 39.
74. Teruoka Yasutaka, *Saikaku Hyōron to Kenkyū*, II, p. 48.
75. Fujimura, XI, pp. 3–14.
76. Teruoka, II, p. 7.
77. A partial translation by Munemasa Isoo and Thomas M. Kondō is found in *Ryūkoku Daigaku Ronsō*.
78. Noma Kōshin, *Saikaku Shū*, p. 285.
79. *Ibid.*, p. 271.
80. *Ibid.*, p. 263.
81. *Ibid.*, p. 291.
82. Takatsuka Masanori and David C. Stubbs (trans.), *This Scheming World*, p. 42.

83. Sargent, p. 84.

84. Noma, *Saikaku Shū*, pp. 230–35.

85. *Ibid.*, p. 306.

86. Nakamura Yukihiko, *Kinsei Sakka Kenkyū*, pp. 45–46.

87. Munemasa Isoo, *Saikaku no Kenkyū*, p. 167.

88. Noma, *Saikaku to Saikaku Igo*, p. 40.

89. Professor Noma believed that *Ukiyo Eiga Ichidai Otoko*, published in the first month of 1693, was a genuine work by Saikaku, but most other scholars disagree. See Noma, *Saikaku Nempu*, p. 292.

90. Robert Leutner, the translator of *Saikaku's Parting Gift*, believed that "it surely ranks as one of his finer products." His introduction to the translation provides excellent background information. See Leutner, "Saikaku's Parting Gift," p. 361.

91. Noma, *Saikaku Shū*, p. 347.

92. *Ibid.*, p. 326.

93. *Ibid.*, pp. 331–32.

94. *Ibid.*, pp. 330–32.

95. *Ibid.*, pp. 325–30.

96. *Ibid.*, p. 402.

97. Hibbett, p. 44.

BIBLIOGRAPHY

Asō Isoji. *Ihara Saikaku Shū*, in Koten Nihon Bungaku Zenshū series, vol. XXII. Tokyo: Chikuma Shobō, 1966.

———, Itasaka Gen, and Tsutsumi Seiji. *Saikaku Shū*, in Nihon Koten Bungaku Taikei series. Tokyo: Iwanami Shoten, 1959.

de Bary, Wm. Theodore (trans.). *Five Women Who Loved Love*. Rutland, Vt.: Tuttle, 1956.

Ebara Taizō. *Edo Bungei Ronkō*. Tokyo: Sanseidō, 1937.

———, Teruoka Yasutaka, and Noma Kōshin (eds.). *Teihon Saikaku Zenshū*. Tokyo: Chūō Kōron Sha, 1949–76.

Fujimura Tsukuru. *Saikaku Zenshū*, 13 vols. Tokyo: Shibundō, 1947–61.

Hibbett, Howard. *The Floating World in Japanese Fiction*. New York: Oxford University Press, 1959.

Higuchi Yoshichiyo (ed.). *Kessaku Jōruri Shū*, I, in Hyōshaku Edo Bungaku Sōsho series. Tokyo: Dainippon Yūbenkai Kōdansha, 1935.

Leutner, Robert (trans.). "Saikaku's Parting Gift," in *Monumenta Nipponica*, XXX, 4, 1975.

Matsuda Osamu. *Nihon Kinsei Bungaku no Seiritsu*. Tokyo: Hōsei Daigaku Shuppanbu, 1963.

Minamoto Ryōen. *Giri to Ninjō*. Tokyo: Chūō Kōron Sha, 1969.

Morris, Ivan (trans.). *The Life of an Amorous Woman*. New York: New Directions, 1963.

Munemasa Isoo. *Saikaku no Kenkyū*. Tokyo: Miraisha, 1969.

——— and Thomas Mamoru Kondō (trans.). "Japanese Trials under the Shade of a Cherry Tree," in *Ryūkoku Daigaku Ronsō*, no. 386.

Nakamura Yukihiko. *Kinsei Sakka Kenkyū*. Tokyo: San'ichi Shobō, 1961.

———. *Kinsei Shōsetsu Shi no Kenkyū*. Tokyo: Ōfūsha, 1961.

Noma Kōshin. *Saikaku Nempu Kōshō*. Tokyo: Chūō Kōron Sha, 1953.

———. *Saikaku to Saikaku Igo*, in Iwanami Kōza Nihon Bungaku Shi series, X. Tokyo: Iwanami Shoten, 1959.

———. *Saikaku Shū*, vol. II, in Nihon Koten Bungaku Taikei series. Tokyo: Iwanami Shoten, 1960.

Ozaki Kōyō and Watanabe Otowa. *Saikaku Zenshū*, I, in Teikoku Bunko series. Tokyo: Hakubunkan, 1894.

Sargent, G. W. (trans.). *The Japanese Family Storehouse*. Cambridge, Eng.: Cambridge University Press, 1959.

Takatsuka, Masanori, and David C. Stubbs (trans.). *This Scheming World*. Rutland, Vt.: Tuttle, 1965.

Teruoka Yasutaka. *Saikaku Hyōron to Kenkyū*, 2 vols. Tokyo: Chūō Kōron Sha, 1953.

CHAPTER 9
FICTION
UKIYO ZŌSHI

Ukiyo zōshi, "stories of the floating world," is the name used to describe the fiction written between Saikaku's *Kōshoku Ichidai Otoko* (The Life of an Amorous Man, 1683) and the novel *Shogei Hitori Jiman* (Self-Satisfaction in the Various Arts) published in 1783 by the virtually unknown writer Fukugūken Asei. The choice of these two works for the opening and close of an era conveniently makes the period of the ukiyo zōshi last exactly one hundred years. Perhaps *Self-Satisfaction* does not deserve even the distinction of being the last echo of a literary movement, but the qualifications of *The Life of an Amorous Man* surely cannot be questioned. It is true that a few earlier works had treated the demimonde in the realistic manner that characterized the ukiyo zōshi, but even in its own time *The Life of an Amorous*

Man was recognized as the first work of a tradition. Nishizawa Ippū (1665–1731),[1] one of Saikaku's successors as a writer of ukiyo zōshi, wrote in 1700: "Novels about love (*kōshoku-bon*) have grown more popular every year since they originated in Osaka with Saikaku's *The Life of an Amorous Man*."[2] Another important writer of ukiyo zōshi, Ejima Kiseki (1667–1736), in 1711 facetiously referred to the "*Amorous Man Sutra*,"[3] implying that the first masterpiece in the genre has by this time acquired the dignity of a sacred text.

The writings of Saikaku influenced and even dominated the whole of subsequent ukiyo zōshi literature. Saikaku's most bitter opponent, Miyako no Nishiki (1675–1720?), borrowed so liberally from Saikaku that he felt it necessary to defend himself from the charge of plagiarism. He wrote about himself:

> It is a mistake to criticize Miyako no Nishiki because his writings include passages from Saikaku or phrases from popular songs. Even if his borrowings were unconsciously made, it would surely happen, quite naturally, that his books on occasion resembled Saikaku's. Are you unaware that Ono no Takamura borrowed from Po Chü-i, or that, to take an example from China, Ssu-ma Ch'ien used phrases from the *Tso Chuan* when he wrote *Shih Chi*, and that there were in turn men who wrote books based on the *Shih Chi*? . . . It was a teaching of the masters of the past that in Chinese poetry it was permissible to borrow the old themes, and in Japanese poetry the borrowing of the words of the old poets was positively encouraged. One can see, therefore, that Miyako no Nishiki is guilty of no great fault if he has used in his compositions some words tossed off by Saikaku. To take old materials and make them new is the work of a master.[4]

The ukiyo zōshi by Saikaku's successors were not merely inspired by the master but often directly derived, word for word, from his published books. There was no legal protection against plagiarism, and no particular opprobrium was attached to the practice. The booksellers, knowing that ukiyo zōshi were the most profitable items on their lists, eagerly published book after book to meet the demands of the public and enrich themselves. The ethical implications of plagiarism never seem to have bothered them. Indeed, the booksellers themselves were often the authors of these plagiarized stories. In any case, literary merit was of less importance in determining the popularity of an author or a work than the novelty of the presentation. A book on an unfamiliar theme or illustrated in an especially attractive manner might sell many copies even if the text was inferior. The authors, even those who were not booksellers themselves, wrote solely for the money; some were so far from aspiring to literary fame that they used pseudonyms that have never been penetrated. Unlike Saikaku, or Asai Ryōi before him, these authors had nothing to say. Their writings are conspicuously devoid of social concern, of any attempt to probe the workings of the heart or mind, or even of any evocation of real emotions. They show many signs of hasty composition, and some are almost formless. The tales at best are ingenious and amusing, and a few superior authors of ukiyo zōshi can be recognized by their style or skillful composition, but the interest remains always on the surface. No doubt this was what contemporary readers wanted. They were diverted by reading of the foibles of the denizens of the "floating world," and it never occurred to them that such writings should be of lasting literary value. The ukiyo zōshi are still amusing, at least intermittently, and even their crudities can be overlooked because of the tastes of the age, but the endless frivolity eventually palls. It is dismaying when we realize that these frothy writings constituted the bulk of Japanese fiction for a century.

The immediate successor to Saikaku was Hōjō Dansui (1663–1711), the editor of three posthumous collections of Saikaku. At one stage Dansui even styled himself "the second Saikaku," and some of his works not only bear such derivative titles as *Shin Nippon Eitaigura* (The New Family Storehouse of Japan, 1712) but incorporate whole passages from the master.[5] Dansui, though a haikai poet by training, wrote in a prosaic, matter-of-fact style, even when he was directly imitating Saikaku. He lacked the imagination to make any new departures. Saikaku's successors tended to be men like Dansui, content with reaping second and third growths from the seeds once sown by Saikaku, or else hired hacks who ground out trash of no literary pretension whatsoever.

The center of publishing activity remained in the Kamigata (Kyoto-Osaka) region, though there were Edo reprints of successful Kamigata works and original publication of a few local authors. Among the publisher-authors of the early period of ukiyo zōshi (from 1683 to 1703),[6] Nishizawa Ippū made the most important contributions. His company in Osaka had been publishing Jōruri texts from as far back as 1660, and his father had been one of the first publishers to try his hand at writing ukiyo zōshi.[7] Ippū published his first work *Shinshiki Gokansho* (New Love: Five Outstanding Examples) in 1698. The title indicates an indebtedness to Saikaku's masterpiece *Five Women Who Loved Love*, but also proclaims Ippū's belief that his book is "new" and not a mere reworking of familiar material. The five stories describe unhappy couples who lose their lives because of love, and all are based on actual occurrences. So far, this sounds exactly like a description of Saikaku's novel; the difference lies in the style and tone adopted by Ippū. We find in this work not the detachment and ironic manner of Saikaku, but the romantic qualities of the Jōruri, as we might expect of an author who not only published Jōruri texts but later wrote many of his own. The second story in the collection is about Sankatsu, a dancer, and her lover Hanshichi. Their love suicides in 1695 had already become famous from ballads and theatrical representations, but this was the first time they had been related in a work of fiction. The love-suicide theme itself was typical of Jōruri, and Ippū's manner of presenting his material is dramatic rather than novelistic. Saikaku's only Jōruri was so unlike his fiction as to suggest a totally different writer, but Ippū's fiction has the same theatricality as his plays. Using material that hitherto had been reserved for the theater was one way of ending the stagnation that had afflicted the novel after the death of Saikaku.

Ippū's most famous ukiyo zōshi, called *Gozen Gikeiki* (Yoshitsune's Story, as Told before His Excellency, 1700), represented another development in a direction away from Saikaku. This is essentially a retelling in modern dress of the story of the popular hero Yoshitsune. Saikaku apparently derived some inspiration from *The Tale of Genji* when writing *The Life of an Amorous Man*, but a knowledge of the source is in no way important to the appreciation of his work. In the case of *Yoshitsune's Story*, however, the title insists on the source, and without knowledge of the Yoshitsune legends, especially as related in the original *Gikeiki*, it would be impossible to recognize Ippū's skill in modernizing them. The book is written in the form of stories narrated by the familiar comic character Tarōkaja in the presence of a daimyo; this format, derived from the theater, became typical of the later ukiyo zōshi. Another innovation was its being a single long story, rather than a collection of short works in the manner of Saikaku in his later period or of his imitators.

A modernization of the classics, not necessarily with any intent of burlesque or parody, became a prominent feature of the ukiyo zōshi. A revival of the old literature, in part the work of the scholars of national learning, now became general after the long period of insistence on being up-to-date in the manner of Saikaku and the Danrin poets.[8] The public, sated perhaps by the realistic descriptions of the gay quarters, enjoyed a work like *Yoshitsune's Story*, with its heroes and ghosts, and felt as if their own world had been extended to include the past. There was no interest in historical accuracy; on the contrary, readers took pleasure in the ingenious ways that the old stories were modified by new and specifically modern elements. For those unfamiliar with the classics these new versions sometimes supplied basic, if anachronistic, knowledge of the story.

The vogue for modernized classics may have led Ippū to hire the author Miyako no Nishiki, an educated man with a wide knowledge of the Japanese classics. Ippū had published in 1701 *Kankatsu Soga Monogatari* (The Cheerful Tale of the Soga), and its success encouraged him to plan a sequel; but instead of writing it himself, he induced Miyako no Nishiki to write *Genroku Soga Monogatari* in 1702. This work was followed by *Fūryū Jindai no Maki* (Elegant Chapters on the Age of the Gods, 1702), a retelling of the legends in the first book of the *Kojiki*, and *Fūryū Genji Monogatari* (1703), a retelling of the first two books of *The Tale of Genji*. Miyako no Nishiki's best-known work, *Genroku Taiheiki* (Genroku Chronicles of Great Peace, 1701), is not, however, a Genroku version of the fourteenth-century *Taiheiki*, despite the title; it consists instead of a hodge-podge of fiction, fantasy, and learning only vaguely related to the "Era of Great Peace" (*taihei*) lauded in the preface. The main intent of the book seems to have been self-glorification, together with an attack on Saikaku; the most famous section describes Saikaku wandering through the circles of hell.

Genroku Chronicles opens with two booksellers meeting aboard a boat bound from Kyoto to Osaka. They talk about their businesses, to help pass the time; Miyako no Nishiki here displayed his inside knowledge of the book trade. The Osaka dealer (perhaps he is meant to be Ippū) insists that "ever since Saikaku's death erotic writings have come to a halt. . . . In all the years since Japanese writing was invented, there has probably never been an author superior to Saikaku."[9] The Kyoto bookseller denies this: "Saikaku is an illiterate who knows nothing about writing." The sole evidence he gives to support this bold statement is Saikaku's alleged failure to recognize that *inogozuchi* and *goshitsu* were two names for the same medicine. The Kyoto bookseller then goes on to praise Miyako no Nishiki for his perfect familiarity with both Japanese and Chinese literature, his flawless command of the traditional language, and his balanced expression.[10] The Osaka dealer counters by accusing Miyako no Nishiki of plagiarism, to which the Kyoto dealer responds in the terms already quoted above. Thus concludes the first of the eight books of *Genroku Chronicles*.

The story shifts to the account of a certain physician who claimed that in a dream he saw Saikaku in hell:

> Saikaku has fallen into the hell of *abi*, and has suffered months and years of torments. His tongue has been pulled out with iron pincers, causing him indescribable agony, for his crime of having, while in the mortal world, told inflammatory falsehoods about people he did not know and having pretended they were truth.[11]

Saikaku is specifically accused of the crime of having accepted an advance payment for a book that he failed to deliver.

Later in the dream some friends appear before Saikaku and inform him that he has been transferred to the Hell of Horrible Screams. Saikaku strikes up an acquaintance with a young demon who describes the brothels in hell frequented by the assorted devils. Saikaku expresses surprise that hell boasts such refinements, and the demon responds by saying that without such facilities hell would be dreary indeed. Eventually the physician wakens from his dream, and we return to the two booksellers on the boat. Their conversation turns to a discussion of the serious books on their lists. Quite unnecessarily detailed information is given on the authors they publish, a display of Miyako no Nishiki's erudition. The work limps to a close with an enumeration of the pleasures of the Osaka theaters.

Almost everything known about Miyako no Nishiki's life is derived from a petition he wrote in 1705 while under sentence of death for having escaped from prison.[12] A year or so earlier he had been picked up as a vagrant in Edo. It is strange that he should have been sentenced to distant banishment merely for having been without proper employment, but no other evidence explains this. Miyako no Nishiki was sent to a gold mine in Kyushu, from which he escaped after a few months, only to be caught again. His plea for clemency was allowed, but he was returned to the mine. He probably was released in the general amnesty after the death of the shogun Tsunayoshi in 1709, but apart from a work written under another pseudonym, nothing more is known about this talented liar and braggart.[13]

We know even less about the two other important writers of early ukiyo zōshi.[14] Umpūshi Rinkō is remembered for only one work, *Kōshoku Ubuge* (The Downy Hair of Love, before 1696), and Yashoku Jibun for three works, *Kōshoku Bankintan* (A Love Medicine Worth a Myriad Pieces of Gold, 1693), *Zashiki Banashi* (Drawing Room Tales, 1693), and *Kōshoku Haidokusan* (Love's Remedy, 1702). Both men were haikai poets, and this may account for their wit and invention, reminiscent of Saikaku's. Extremely little biographical information has been uncovered about Rinkō beyond his real name (Horie Shigenori) and his connections with the Kyoto haikai world. We know even less about Yashoku Jibun, whose pseudonym means "Supper Time." Some scholars have even conjectured the two may have been the same man.

In any case, both men published collections of anecdotes constructed rather in the manner of the O. Henry short story, with its surprise ending or effective punch line. A typical example is a story in Yashoku Jibun's *Love's Remedy*.[15] We are told of an elderly couple whose only son has died young, leaving a grandson named Genjirō, whom they themselves rear. Because the boy's father is not around to indulge in expensive luxuries, in the manner expected of a wealthy gentleman, the family fortune continues to increase. Genjirō grows into a young man of peerless beauty, like his near namesake Prince Genji, but he devotes himself exclusively to his studies until one day a companion takes him to a brothel. Word of this reaches a family retainer, who reports in alarm to the boy's grandfather, only to be given a lecture on how much more sensible and economical it is for the boy to indulge himself with their knowledge than for him to take his pleasures secretly. The retainer, entering into the spirit of the argument, cries, "That's right! The saké at the brothel is sure to be bad. I'll send some light saké of a good vintage, and tell them not to let him drink too much." Genjirō is encouraged to frequent the brothel without the least embarrassment, but he discovers that "the fun lies in visiting the quarter in secret, searching out devious ways and means, and if you take your pleasures too much out in the open, it ruins the fun." In the end Genjirō ceases to enjoy his visits and even feels disgusted with the licensed quarters. He begs to be allowed to visit some temples instead.[16] This is how the story ends. We are not expected to take it seriously of course, and the ingenious twist to the overly familiar tale of the young man who loses himself in the world of pleasure is both amusing and effective. Yashoku Jibun's success with the anecdote and Rinkō's with the salacious story were developments that went beyond the usual borrowings from Saikaku.

The most famous of Saikaku's successors as a ukiyo zōshi author was Ejima Kiseki. His career began in 1699 when he was commissioned by the Hachimonji-ya (Figure-of-Eight Shop) to write an actor-evaluation booklet. The Hachimonji-ya had been founded about 1650 to publish texts of plays. The third-generation owner, Andō Jishō, invited Kiseki, better known until that time as the owner of a prosperous cake shop than as an amateur writer of Jōruri texts, to write fiction for his firm. Kiseki's first book, *Yakusha Kuchijamisen* (The Actor's Vocal Samisen, 1699), was so popular that it established the Hachimonji-ya as the leading publisher. Kiseki followed this book with several works of theatrical criticism, which owed much of their success to the attractive presentation, especially the illustrations by Nishikawa Sukenobu. Readers also enjoyed the sharp, professional comments Kiseki directed at performances he had seen. Similar books of gossip and criticism continued to appear annually for many years to come. Kiseki's first ukiyo zōshi was *Keisei Irojamisen* (The Courtesan's Amorous Samisen, 1701), a collection of stories about courtesans from all over Japan. This book, along with Ippū's *Gozen Gikeiki* (Yoshitsune's Story) of 1701, has been praised as a "fresh breeze" that blew into the stuffy atmosphere of fiction,[17] though almost every story is a retelling, if not a plagiarizing, of a work by Saikaku.[18] Readers nevertheless welcomed Kiseki's book, undoubtedly because even secondhand Saikaku was preferable to the rest of the current fiction. Kiseki's crisp if not poetic, style and Sukenobu's illustrations created works of charm.

During the next ten years Ejima Kiseki wrote eleven books for the Hachimonji-ya. They were signed not by Kiseki who seems, initially at least, to have been reluctant to associate his name with such frivolous writings, but by Andō Jishō, the publisher. In the fourth month of 1711 Kiseki's masterpiece, *Keisei Kintanki*, was published, and as usual bore Jishō's signature. The title is difficult to translate: it consists of characters meaning "courtesans forbidden to have short tempers," and one section of the work is in fact devoted to this subject. But the real meaning of the title involves puns on *dangi*, popular Buddhist sermons delivered by streetcorner preachers to the accompaniment of samisens, and on the title of a work by the Tendai priest Shinyō, *Kindan Nichiren Gi* (1654).[19] Kiseki's book of scandalous gossip about the licensed quarters would not seem to have much relation to the disputations of learned monks, the subject of Shinyō's work, but the debate that opens the work, between a proponent of heterosexual love and one of homosexual love, parallels the dispute between the proponents of Pure Land and Nichiren Buddhism; Pure Land (Jōdo) Buddhism had been compared to "the way of women" and Nichiren Buddhism to "the way of men." After two chapters of burlesque theological debate on this subject, the book moves on to another, the comparative merits of licensed and amateur prostitutes. The remaining three chapters are devoted to sermons on the secrets of the art of love and on the wiles of courtesans. Neither the form nor the material of the book was entirely new: debates on the two "ways" of love are found in the kana zōshi, as we have seen, and many passages consist of scraps of Saikaku texts pieced together. *Courtesans Forbidden to Lose Their Tempers* nevertheless delighted readers with its lively style, and the learned poet and painter Yanagizawa Kien (1706–58) declared it was "fresher than Saikaku."[20] The Buddhist phraseology, familiar to the readers, lent the piquance of blasphemy to the totally mundane subjects debated so seriously.

Soon after delivering the manuscript of *Courtesans Forbidden to Lose Their Tempers* to the Hachimonji-ya, Kiseki established his own publishing firm, the Ejima-ya. Kiseki had grown dissatisfied with his share of the glory and thought of setting up a small publishing house for his son; when Jishō rebuffed his overtures, Kiseki decided to break entirely with the Hachimonji-ya. Jishō's competitors, who had suffered from the prosperity of the Hachimonji-ya, welcomed and encouraged the new company, but Kiseki found it extremely difficult, with only limited capital at his disposal, to rival his former employers. In the hopes of establishing a reputation for his company by its superior books, Kiseki plunged into furious literary activity. The period of his break with the Hachimonji-ya proved to be the most important in his career: Kiseki was compelled to write over twenty books in less than seven years, and to invent new types of fiction in the hopes of pleasing a public that always craved novelty. In 1712 he published *Akindo Gumbai Uchiwa* (The Merchants' Referee Fan), his first work derived from Saikaku's chōnin fiction, and in 1715 *Seken Musuko Katagi* (Characters of Worldly Sons), the first of the collections of character sketches that would be intimately associated with his name.[21] His desperate eagerness to produce more and more manuscripts is revealed by the extent of his borrowing and even stealing from other authors.[22]

Kiseki is an amusing writer who can exploit a comic idea, but his writing is thin, and we sense nothing of the personality of the author behind them. Saikaku is a real presence, interposing his comments and making us aware of his distinctive manner of looking at the world. Kiseki's comments are superficial and unrevealing. He wrote at first for fun; later (as his cake business waned), he wrote for money; but never does he make us feel that he wrote because of some internal compulsion. It is not inappropriate that Kiseki's books are usually known by the name of the publisher (Hachimonji-ya *bon*) rather than that of the author.

When we read, say, Kiseki's character of the rake,[23] we do not feel that he has captured anything quintessential about rakes; he has hit on an amusing predicament—his rake, whose only life is in the pleasure quarters, is deprived of his usual entertainment because of the New Year's preparations in the licensed quarter. The rake goes to the one available spot, a hot spring, but unfortunately for him, the other visitors are not revelers like himself but patients taking a cure, and they do not at all appreciate the noise. The episode concludes lamely with the innkeeper's suggestion that the party patronize some other hot spring. The story is insignificant, and it fails as a character sketch epitomizing all rakes. But its evocations of the gay quarters are amusing, and there are some surprising twists in the story. (When the customer announces with a mournful expression that he has something to inform the brothel-keeper, the latter jumps to the conclusion that, in the manner familiar from many books about the licensed quarters, the customer will be unable to meet his New Year bills, only to learn of the customer's distress that he must endure a week without parties.) This story may not be Kiseki at his best, but surely it is not atypical; it suggests the limitations of his world of fiction. Reading Kiseki makes one appreciate the achievement of Saikaku in the same domain, and suggests that without a touch of the tragic, or at least an awareness that tragedy exists, fiction of this kind easily palls or evaporates like so much froth.

In 1714, at the height of his estrangement from the Hachimonji-ya, Kiseki published his version of the events that had led to the break.[24] He revealed for the first time that he himself had been the author not only of the annual books of actor evaluations but of such popular works as *The Courtesan's Amorous Samisen* and *Courtesans Forbidden to Lose Their Tempers*. Jishō, however, continued to claim credit for the books published under the Hachimonji-ya imprint; even in his diary, published in 1747, he still made this false claim.[25] Jishō probably did write some books, particularly during his quarrel with Kiseki, but the works that can be assigned to Jishō are clearly inferior.

A reconciliation took place in 1718. Jishō apparently made the first overtures, but his position was actually the stronger. Even after the Hachimonji-ya had been deprived of its chief author, it still had the capital and organization to withstand the loss, but the Ejima-ya had from the start been on a shaky financial basis. The two men jointly signed the preface to a work published in 1718, expressing regret over their recent enmity and joy over their reunion.[26] On the surface, at least, harmonious relations had been restored, and the two companies were both able to publish works by Kiseki. But gradually the Ejima-ya discontinued publication, and in the end Kiseki's name disappeared even from the Hachimonji-ya books.

The last important writer of ukiyo zōshi was Tada Nanrei (1698–1750), the mainstay of the Hachimonji-ya during its final period. Most of Nanrei's works were signed by Jishō or by Jishō's successors; but Nakamura Yukihiko has identified some twenty-five ukiyo zōshi, ranging in date from 1737 to a posthumous work of 1753, as works by Nanrei.[27] Nanrei also wrote numerous studies on Japanese learning, philology, and traditional usages. A complete edition of his serious writings began to appear in 1780, an unusual honor at the time, but he is remembered today not for his *Kojiki* researches but for frivolous novels published under other men's names. At first glance his ukiyo zōshi have little to distinguish them. His two most famous, *Kamakura Shogei Sode Nikki* (1743) and *Seken Hahaoya Katagi* (Characters of Worldly Mothers, 1752) are both in the manner of Kiseki's character sketches. Other works belong to Ippū's style of modernizing the classics. Nakamura believes, however, that Nanrei's style, marked by an admixture of phrases derived from Chinese and Heian literature, not only reveals his superior education, but his attitude toward writing ukiyo zōshi; unlike Kiseki, a competent and prolific professional writer, Nanrei seems to stand apart from his own work, viewing it with wry amusement as an occupation unworthy of him in which he must indulge because he has no other outlet for his literary talent.[28] Despite the many surface resemblances to the earlier ukiyo zōshi writers, Nanrei shares much with the dilettante authors of the following period, when men of education deliberately wrote *gesaku* (playful compositions). The social criticism in these works did not take the form of indictments of injustice, but rather, the denial of the authors' capacity to treat society seriously; the authors take refuge behind the foolishness of their stories. This was the dispiriting end to the ukiyo zōshi tradition so vigorously initiated by Saikaku.

Character sketches continued to appear until the end of the century of ukiyo zōshi, turning to more and more far-fetched subjects, until the extreme was reached in 1770 with *Séken Bakemono Katagi* (Characters of Worldly Ghosts). Among the last of the ukiyo zōshi are two by Ueda Akinari (1734–1809); the minor place that they occupy in his works indicates that the form had outlived its usefulness, though the name "character sketches" (*katagi*) was still used by Tsubouchi Shōyō (1859–1935) for one of the pioneering works of modern Japanese literature.

NOTES

1. See Hasegawa Tsuyoshi, *Ukiyo Zōshi no Kenkyū*, pp. 59, 81, for dating.
2. Fujii Otoo, *Ukiyo Zōshi Meisaku Shū*, p. 122. *Ukiyo zōshi* were generally known as *kōshoku-bon* at this time.
3. Noma Kōshin, *Ukiyo Zōshi Shū*, p. 271.
4. Fujii, pp. 327–28.
5. See Munemasa Isoo, *Saikaku no Kenkyū*, pp. 294–301, for comparisons between Dansui's texts and passages in Saikaku he used as models.
6. Noma has divided the century of ukiyo zōshi into four periods: 1683–1703, 1704–11, 1712–35, and 1765–83. (See his *Ukiyo Zōshi Shū*, pp. 4–12.)
7. Noma, p. 40.
8. See Teruoka Yasutaka, *Kinsei Bungaku no Tembō*, p. 50.
9. Fujii, pp. 323–24.
10. *Ibid.*, p. 325.
11. *Ibid.*, p. 345.
12. Text given in *ibid.*, pp. 71–73.
13. The most detailed information about Miyako no Nishiki is found in two articles by Noma Kōshin, "Miyako no Nishiki Gokuchū Gokugai," in *Kokugo Kobubun*, XVII, nos. 8, 10.
14. See Noma, pp. 7–8.
15. Text in Fujii, pp. 490–94.
16. This story was plagiarized by Ejima Kiseki (see below, p. 224). An illustration to Kiseki's version is found in Howard Hibbett, *The Floating World in Japanese Fiction*, p. 140.
17. Noma, p. 9.
18. Hasegawa, pp. 100–109, lists 131 instances of direct borrowing from Saikaku.
19. Noma, pp. 22–23.
20. Noma, p. 26.
21. See Hibbett, pp. 59ff.

22. The story by Yashoku Jibun is reproduced almost word for word in *Seken Musuko Katagi*, V, 2.

23. Hibbett, pp. 139–44.

24. Text in Fujii, pp. 102–103.

25. *Ibid.*, pp. 112–13.

26. *Ibid.*, p. 109.

27. Nakamura Yukihiko, *Kinsei Sakka Kenkyū*, pp. 77–130.

28. *Ibid.*, pp. 85–86.

BIBLIOGRAPHY

Fujii Otoo. *Ukiyo Zōshi Meisaku Shū*, in Hyōshaku Edo Bungaku Sōsho series. Tokyo: Dainippon Yūbenkai Kōdansha, 1937.

Hasegawa Tsuyoshi. *Ukiyo Zōshi no Kenkyū*. Tokyo: Ōfūsha, 1969.

Hibbett, Howard. *The Floating World in Japanese Fiction*. New York: Oxford University Press, 1959.

Munemasa Isoo. *Saikaku no Kenkyū*. Tokyo: Miraisha, 1969.

Nakamura Yukihiko. *Kinsei Sakka Kenkyū*. Tokyo: San'ichi Shobō, 1961.

———. *Kinsei Shōsetsushi no Kenkyū*. Tokyo: Ōfūsha, 1961.

Noma Kōshin. "Miyako Nishiki Gokuchū Gokugai," in *Kokugo Kokubun*, XVII (1948–49), 8, 10.

———. *Ukiyo Zōshi Shū*, in Nihon Koten Bungaku Taikei series. Tokyo: Iwanami Shoten, 1966.

Teruoka Yasutaka. *Kinsei Bunkaku no Tembō*. Tokyo: Meiji Shoin, 1953.

Tsukamoto Tetsuzō (ed.). *Hachimonji-ya Sha Goshu*, in Yūhōdō Bunko series. Tokyo: Yūhōdō, 1927.

CHAPTER 10
DRAMA
THE BEGINNINGS OF KABUKI AND JŌRURI

During the Tokugawa period the two most important forms of drama were Kabuki, a theater of actors, and Jōruri (later known as Bunraku), a theater of puppets. Both began to evolve as popular entertainments toward the end of the sixteenth century and quickly secured a place in the hearts of the common people. Nō and Kyōgen continued to be staged, but increasingly as the ritual "music" of the courts of the shogun and the various daimyos. Only rarely were public performances permitted. Townsmen sometimes learned to sing the Nō plays, an accomplishment indicative of their eagerness to identify themselves with the upper classes, like performing the tea ceremony.[1] In this manner Nō and Kyōgen turned into petrified theaters, incapable of further development, even though assured of official support. Kabuki, on the other hand, became a mania with the townsmen, ever eager for novelty, and Jōruri enjoyed popularity with all classes, ranging from the court down to the lowliest commoners; in both instances the tastes of the commoners, not the patronage of the great, determined the characteristics of the theater.

The name Kabuki derived from a verb *kabuku* that meant "to bend forward"; by extension, the word came to describe the state of being twisted, deviant, or nonconformist. The period when the *kabuki* spirit flourished most conspicuously was probably the last thirty years of the sixteenth century, and the outstanding exemplar was the ruler himself, Toyotomi Hideyoshi.[2] Not only did Hideyoshi rise from humble origins to the highest power in the country—amazing even in an age of warfare and upheavals—but he deliberately defied the established conventions in every field. Like other parvenus, he delighted in wearing the trappings of the old aristocracy: he took the name Fujiwara and had himself appointed as the *kampaku*, or civil dictator, recalling the Heian court. He threw his energies into mastering the tea ceremony, the austere medieval rite, but enjoyed it most in the teahouse he built of solid gold. He also took pride acting in Nō, choosing the most difficult and lofty roles, and had special plays written at his command in which he performed as himself, a hero of legendary prowess with divine attributes.

We know from documents and from the large ornamental screens popular at the end of the sixteenth century what a variety of colorful entertainments was offered in Kyoto during Hideyoshi's day. Juggling, sleight of hand, stunts performed by dogs and monkeys, and the usual range of sideshow attractions were available at booths set up in the bed of the Kamo River, dry for most of the year. This peculiar site, a riverbed, may have been chosen because the flat land provided space for many booths, but probably the chief merit of the riverbed was that this land, being under water part of the year, did not belong to anyone. It has been suggested, moreover, that most varieties of theatrical entertainment were intimately associated with the *eta*, or pariah class, and because they were forbidden to enter ordinary buildings it was necessary to stage performances in places like the riverbed which they were free to visit.[3] Be that as it may, the bed of the Kamo River at Shijō in Kyoto is traditionally considered to be the birthplace of both Kabuki and Jōruri.[4]

The beginnings of Kabuki are traced back to the dances and skits performed by a troupe led by one Okuni, said to be a priestess from the Shinto shrine at Izumo. At the time, itinerant entertainers usually claimed to be performing as a means of raising funds for a temple or shrine; this connection with a religious organization served as a kind of passport in getting through the various barriers erected on the roads. Troupes of women entertainers—"women *sarugaku* and women *kyōgen*"—performed all over the country. Okuni and her troupe, thanks to their *kabuki* dances, were able to realize the dream of countless other performers, scoring a success in the capital.

Okuni's first appearance in Kyoto was at the Temmangū, the Shinto shrine dedicated to the memory of Sugawara no Michizane, on the twenty-fifth of the third month of 1603. The audience, we know from screens, included dandies dressed in Portuguese doublets and ruffs, fashionable ladies in kimonos made of velvet or batik cloth, samurai whose cloaks were decorated with cannonball patterns, and even a few genuine Europeans.[5] People jammed the shrine grounds, pressing around the small Nō stage for a better look at the Kabuki dances (*kabuki odori*).

Okuni entered, dressed in black monk's robes and a black lacquered hat that partially obscured her face. She banged on a small gong suspended around her neck on a crimson cord and sang in a lively voice:

> The holy light of the Buddha illumines the world in ten
> directions;
> Invoking his name brings salvation to all without fail.
> *Namu Amida Butsu. Namu Amida.*[6]

The words of the song and Okuni's attire suggest a solemn Buddhist incantation, appropriate to a priestess gathering funds for a pious cause, but despite the religious trappings, the songs and dances were of infectious vivacity.[7] The *nembutsu odori,* as they were called, were originally folk dances, and Okuni's success lay mainly in having introduced these rustic entertainments to the capital.[8]

Later in the same program Okuni wore an even more striking costume—a man's robe of crimson silk (the cloak embroidered in gold and fastened with a purple sash), a sword, and a dagger worked in gold. To top everything, she wore a gold crucifix around her neck, a proof not of Christian belief but of her being up-to-date on the latest, most exotic fashion. In this attire Okuni performed the role of a handsome young man who visits a teahouse and chats with the proprietress. Another of Okuni's skits featured her partner Nagoya Sanzaburō (1572?–1603), Sanza for short, a samurai of a distinguished family whose *kabuki* inclinations led him to appear with a troupe of dancers.[9] Some doubts have been raised as to whether or not Sanza actually performed on Okuni's stage, but he was killed soon afterward in a quarrel, and from then on his "ghost" definitely took part in Okuni's skits, lending the luster of his name to Kabuki.

Okuni's revue shows soon degenerated into mere come-ons for the prostitutes who sang and danced. A close association between Kabuki and the licensed quarters began at this time and was maintained until late in the nineteenth century. Both the theaters and the licensed quarters were categorized as "bad places" (*akusho*) by the government, and of the two the theaters ranked lower. Throughout the Tokugawa period there was the paradox of actors at once idolized by the public to a far greater degree than the film stars of today, and despised as belonging to an outcast group. The contradictory nature of the actor's position became increasingly apparent, but in the early part of the seventeenth century the spectators attended Kabuki shows for erotic excitement rather than for a display of histrionic ability.

It has often been stated that the relations that developed between the performers and members of the audience—a kind of unlicensed prostitution—finally decided the government, in 1629, to prohibit women from appearing on the stage. We may wonder, however, why the government, which had permitted and even encouraged the establishment of the licensed quarters, should have been distressed by such immorality. It seems more likely that quarrels over favorite actresses, especially among the upper ranks of samurai, displeased the government so much as to precipitate this action. Women were superseded on the Kabuki stage by young men known as *wakashu* who performed similar songs and dances with the addition of a few specialties (such as acrobatics). The wakashu were also available after the performances, and had their admirers. In 1652, after the death of the shogun Iemitsu, a conspicuous patron of wakashu Kabuki, it too was forbidden, apparently in the wake of quarrels and other disorderly incidents. The Tokugawa shogunate could condone immorality, but never disorder.

It may seem strange that the government, which so often expressed disapproval of the state of the Kabuki theater, did not simply ban it. Probably the enormous popularity among the townsmen made the government hesitate to take so drastic a step; or, it may have felt that Kabuki, like the circuses of Rome, provided needed distraction for the common people and kept their minds from turning to mischief.

The fortuitous result of the banning of women and boys from Kabuki was to make it into a dramatic art. Before 1652 Kabuki, though important in the history of the Japanese theater, had no connection with literature; but when it became necessary to interest audiences in the plots of plays, now that the beauty of actresses or young men could not be counted on to bring in customers, a literary element entered Kabuki. The early plays were no doubt rudimentary, mere vehicles to display the talents of the performers; even today the literary importance of Kabuki plays is still overshadowed by the audience's interest in the actors. But the prohibition on the wakashu led almost immediately to a new kind of Kabuki, although the name Kabuki itself was avoided: performances, known as *monomane kyōgen-zukushi* (imitative Kyōgen series), apparently consisting of two or three playlets, were staged by grown actors, some of whom wore wigs when taking the roles of women.[10] By 1664 "continuous plays" were first performed, meaning perhaps that four acts formed a single play, rather than four separate works.

Nothing is known about the authors of these plays or if, indeed, the texts consisted of anything more than rough scenarios that provided a framework for the actors' improvisations. Probably they borrowed the themes of the *Shimabara kyōgen*, plays about the Shimabara licensed quarter in Kyoto that were popular from 1655–60. For unknown reasons the government banned these plays; perhaps the name Shimabara, associated with the rebellion of 1636, still had undesirable political overtones.[11] The typical subject matter, a young man's visit to a brothel where he chats with the proprietor and watches a prostitute dance, would hardly have offended the censors.

Apart from plays describing the brothels, some drew their materials from anecdotes about celebrated people. Already in 1644 the government had decreed that "the names of actual people must not be used in plays."[12] This practice was observed throughout the period, the playwrights of Kabuki and Jōruri elaborately disguising names of people and places so as to foil the censors. The plots and dramatic structure of many Nō plays were borrowed to enrich the repertory. Plays in more than one act could be performed even without a curtain to divide the acts by adopting the Nō practice of an interval when the actors left the stage. The future division of the repertory of both Kabuki and Jōruri into "historical" and "domestic" plays was already present in embryonic form, as we know from a list of plays published in 1678 which enables us to infer not only the content but the length of each play, about half an hour.[13]

Our information on early Kabuki is extremely fragmentary, but nothing suggests that works of literary value were presented. Not until the Genroku era (1688–1703) were plays written whose texts have been preserved; from this time we can discuss Kabuki in literary terms, even if we recognize that the actors were free to disregard the texts whenever it suited their fancy. But before discussing these plays it is necessary to examine developments in the related art of Jōruri.

The term *jōruri* was derived from the name of Lady Jōruri, the leading character in the story *Jōruri Monogatari*, first mentioned in 1485.[14] Her brief love affair with the hero Minamoto Yoshitsune captured the imagination of the Japanese, and they never seem to have wearied of it. The tale, in many versions, was being recited by professional storytellers as early as 1531, and it continued to interest audiences well into the seventeenth century. One version, divided into twelve episodes and therefore known as *Jūnidan Zōshi* (Story Book in Twelve Episodes), acquired special authority.[15] There are many minor variations, but essentially the story relates how Yoshitsune, a fugitive from his brother Yoritomo, arrives at the village of Yahagi and hears rumors about Lady Jōruri, who lives there. He finds her house and peeps into the garden. One glance at Jōruri, seated among her attendants and making sweet music, and he falls in love. Noticing that the flute part is missing from the ensemble, he plays his own, so beautifully that Jōruri sends someone to induce him to join the others. Yoshitsune falls even more deeply in love, and late that night visits Jōruri. He persuades her to yield to him, despite her protestations, but the next morning they must part; it is dangerous for him to linger. Soon afterward, at a place called Fukiage, Yoshitsune falls seriously ill. The god Hachiman appears before Jōruri in the guise of an old man and informs her of Yoshitsune's plight. She rushes to him, finds him apparently dead, but succeeds in bringing him back to life. He now reveals his identity and promises to meet Jōruri again, but they are fated to remain separated forever.[16]

The story of Lady Jōruri is mildly interesting, and the romantic passages no doubt supplied a welcome addition to the standard fare of martial recitations from *The Tale of the Heike*, but the century-long success of so undramatic a story is puzzling. Later versions, far from heightening the drama, emphasize what are for us the least interesting sections—the descriptions of Jōruri's garden or of the furnishings of her apartments.[17] Nevertheless, for decades the work enjoyed such popularity when recited to the accompaniment of a biwa, that this story was chosen as the first text of the nascent puppet theater and gave it its name, Jōruri.

The puppet theater was created at the end of the sixteenth century, when the three distinctive elements—the texts, the samisen accompaniment, and the puppets—were combined. The samisen (or shamisen) had been introduced to Japan about 1570 from the Ryukyu Islands, and quickly gained popularity, especially among female entertainers. Its piercing, taut notes made it more effective than the gentler-sounding biwa as an accompaniment to dramatic recitations, and it seems to have been used for this purpose as early as 1580. The music employed for the early Jōruri recitations was apparently derived from the melodies that had been used earlier for *The Tale of the Heike*, the samisen merely replacing the biwa. The puppets were added somewhat later.

Puppets had been known in Japan at least from the eleventh century, but after a brief period they vanish from the records, reappearing only in the fifteenth century, when we read of them performing Nō plays and Kyōgen. They were also used during ceremonies at Shinto shrines and Buddhist temples to act out plays of religious content. Probably these puppets were used in *sekkyō-bushi*,[18] gloomy plays with a pronounced Buddhist intent, even before they were adopted into Jōruri recitations, but there is little reliable information on how the three elements were brought together in the 1590s. The combination proved an immediate success: by 1614 puppet performances had been held in the palace of the retired emperor Go-Yōzei. A screen painted in 1622 depicts two theaters of puppets playing side by side, one performing Jōruri, the other sekkyō-bushi.[19] The Jōruri play being staged is *Amida no Munewari* (The Riven Breast of Amida), written about 1614.[20] Even in this early work we can detect the first glimmerings of literary effort; in this respect Jōruri differed from Kabuki, as we have seen. The importance of the texts to the Jōruri theater must have been quickly recognized: the puppets, unlike actors, could not conquer audiences by their good looks or personalities. Instead, as Paul Claudel once pointed out, the puppets become words incarnate. Even today the chanters who recite the texts ceremoniously lift them to their foreheads before a performance to indicate their respect for the written word.

The literary qualities of Jōruri pose another problem: are they in fact plays? The chanter not only assumes all the roles, but narrates the circumstances of the story, characterizes the attitudes and behavior of the persons, and sometimes intones popular songs or poems suggestive of the atmosphere. The texts he reads from are not divided into parts, and sometimes he has only tradition to guide him as to which character is speaking. Unlike the chorus in a Nō play, which merely speaks for the characters, the chanter is an active storyteller who often makes comments in his own voice; only when in direct discourse does he imitate the voices of the characters. *The Riven Breast*, for example, begins, "Well, now, to proceed, once upon a time. . . ."[21] These phrases, traditional in Jōruri plays until Chikamatsu changed them in the late 1680s, suggest not the dialogue of true drama but the opening of a narrative; hardly anything distinguishes *The Riven Breast* from many kana zōshi. Even when the dramatic elements grew more pronounced, the person of the narrator was retained. The early Jōruri plays were like short works of fiction recited by one or more chanters and mimed by puppets. This remained true throughout the period of "old Jōruri," before Chikamatsu's *Kagekiyo Victorious* of 1686. In the Kimpira plays, describing the prowess and superhuman achievements of the warrior Kimpira, popular from the 1650s to 1670s, there is a higher proportion of dialogue than in *The Riven Breast*, but there is still little to differentiate the texts from prose fiction.[22]

Before the Genroku era, then, the two chief forms of popular theater, Kabuki and Jōruri, were strikingly dissimilar: the former consisted of songs and dialogue and relied more on impromptu remarks than on written texts; the latter was literary in intent and gave greatest attention to passages that were not dialogue but descriptions of the scene. The two arts eventually influenced each other considerably, to their mutual advantage.

During the early period of Kabuki, the manager of the troupe was also an actor and the chief playwright. The texts performed were no more than vehicles, altered at will by the actors, whose personal popularity, rather than the quality of the plays presented, attracted the customers. In 1680, however, one Tominaga Heibei was identified in a Kabuki program as the playwright, the earliest we know about.[23] He continued to write plays into the Genroku era, but he was soon overshadowed by Chikamatsu Monzaemon, the first dramatist not to have been an actor or manager and to have enjoyed a personal following.

Regardless of the author, almost all Genroku Kabuki plays dealt with the troubles within a great household, the genre being known as *oiemono*. These plays often described the attempts of a younger brother to usurp lands belonging to his elder brother. He is generally abetted by his wicked mother (the stepmother of his half-brother), an uncle, or a family retainer, who prefers the cause of the younger brother for selfish reasons. Some of these plays were based on actual events, but in order to escape censorship they were invariably set in the distant past.

Far from attempting to convince audiences by the use of authentic historical details that the action had occurred four or five centuries earlier, the actors and audiences delighted in the modernizing of the great figures of history. Sukeroku, the swaggering hero of the play that bears his name, appears as a high-spirited townsman who asserts his importance in the Yoshiwara licensed quarter; eventually, however, we learn that in reality he is Soga Gorō, a historical figure who lived five centuries before the Yoshiwara quarter was established. Readers of the ukiyo zōshi, written about the same time,[24] were intrigued by similar examples of famous men transformed into contemporaries.

In the *oiemono* plays, too, scenes set in a daimyo's mansion, where men plot to seize an inheritance, alternate with others set in the licensed quarters, where the rightful heir finds solace in the company of a courtesan. The plays came to consist of familiar elements, each with its own name, such as *wagoto* (romantic business), *ikengoto* (admonitory business), *budōgoto* (martial business), and *aragoto* (rough business).[25] Regardless of the ostensible plot of the play, room was always found for each of these elements, so as to display to the full the different facets of the main actors' talents and provide the variety that Japanese audiences have always craved in the theater. At the same time, stylization of the roles became usual, different parts being designated as "the young master," "the wicked stepmother," "the loyal retainer," etc., and actors tended to specialize in one or another category.

The contrast is often drawn between the Kabuki plays preferred in Edo and those preferred in the Kamigata. The Edo plays were likely to emphasize aragoto and feature such heroic figures as the Soga brothers, Kimpira, or the demon Shutendōji. In the Kamigata the preference was for wagoto, realistic dramas with tender scenes, often based on recent incidents that had caught the attention of the public. The first play about a lovers' suicide was performed in Osaka in 1683.[26] This kind of play, dealing with ordinary, contemporary life and not with the heroes of the past, came to be known as *sewamono*, a term that probably meant something like "gossip play." The term was used in contrast with *jidaimono*, or "period piece," the kind of plays popular in Edo.

The sewamono, usually about townsmen who are murdered or commit suicide, appealed to the public because of their topicality. The names of the persons were always changed, in compliance with the government edict of 1644, but it was not deemed necessary to change the period because the people involved were so unimportant. At first the sewamono plays were added at the end of a program of jidaimono, providing a touch of variety, but gradually they began to enjoy such popularity that a program was incomplete without one. Usually two period pieces were presented with one domestic piece; the former emphasized the "rough business" typical of Edo, the latter the "romantic business" of Osaka.

The Kabuki plays had developed by the Genroku period far beyond the simple skits of thirty years before. The texts had benefited by borrowings from Nō and Kyōgen, and finally the part of the narrator of the Jōruri plays, unnecessary in a theater of actors, was taken over by a singer who intoned the descriptions exactly like a Jōruri chanter. The texts themselves became coherent enough to warrant printing illustrated booklets outlining the plots; the earliest example dates back to about 1685.[27] When plays were adapted from Nō or Jōruri, they were much rewritten to enhance the possibilities for the actors to display their virtuoso talents.

An excellent description survives of how new plays were rehearsed in the era before the development of Genroku Kabuki:

> The normal way of working was that after the discussion of a new play and a decision upon it, the construction of each scene was worked out. Then the actors in a scene were called together, placed in a circle, and taught the speeches orally. They stood there until they made their exit, and then either rehearsed it again in what was termed the *kokaeshi*, "little going over," or the authors worked out the speeches for the next section, and got them fixed by repetition. The action in scenes in which a distinguished member of the company appeared was worked out by this member himself. With the revival of *kabuki* the plots of plays became more difficult, and then actors were told to take their writing brushes and write down the headings; they used to write about a line of the beginning of each speech which had been allotted to them.[28]

A text from 1683 indicates the dialogue and stage directions, but even after the texts had become more polished and complex, much of the dialogue was still left to the actor to improvise. Many of Chikamatsu's Kabuki plays were written with Sakata Tōjūrō's special talents in mind; one play leads up to and away from a climactic mad scene, which Tōjūrō was free to embellish as he pleased.

Kabuki during the Genroku era attained maturity as a theatrical art and was blessed with great actors. A collection of anecdotes called *Yakusha Rongo* (The Actors' Analects) fortunately preserves the opinions and gossip of these actors, and enables us to come within touching distance of the theater in a brilliant period.

Jōruri in this period continued to develop as a literary form of theater. The chanter Uji Kaganojō (1635–1711) was known especially for his determination to elevate Jōruri to the level of Nō by borrowing its language and themes. He had studied Nō in his youth and in his critical writings (*dammono*) he insisted on the closeness of the two arts: "In Jōruri there are no teachers. You should consider Nō as the only parent of your art."[29] His instructions to beginners were often vague, urging them to pay careful attention to innumerable points, but he was clearly attempting by his prescriptions to make Jōruri as serious and demanding an art as Nō. In order to guide chanters in the delivery of the vocal line he applied to the Jōruri texts musical symbols borrowed from Nō and invented still others.[30] The five-act structure that became typical of Jōruri was invented by the chanter Satsuma Jōun (1593–1672), who reduced the six acts of the old Jōruri (presumably half the number of episodes in *Story Book in Twelve Episodes*) to five; it was Kaganojō who equated the five acts of a Jōruri play with the five categories of Nō presented at a single performance. Kaganojō's preference for melodious and elegant plays helped to fashion tastes in the Kamigata region, but his greatest contribution to Jōruri was probably his having persuaded Chikamatsu Monzaemon to write for that theater.

NOTES

1. See Gunji Masakatsu, *Kabuki no Hassō*, pp. 157–58.
2. Matsuda Osamu, *Nihon Kinsei Bungaku no Seiritsu*, p. 7.
3. Gunji Masakatsu, *Kabuki Yōshiki to Dentō*, p. 110.
4. See C. J. Dunn, *The Early Japanese Puppet Drama*, p. 53.
5. Ogasawara Yasuko and Gunji Masakatsu, "Izumo no Okuni to kabuku Hitobito," pp. 134–35.
6. *Ibid.*, p. 135.
7. Gunji, *Kabuki no Hassō*, p. 7.
8. Toita Yasuji and Gunji Masakatsu, *Kabuki*, p. 11.

9. See Muroki Yatarō, "Nagoya Sanzaburō ni kansuru nisan no mondaiten ni tsuite."

10. Gunji Masakatsu, *Kabuki*, p. 26.

11. *Ibid.*, p. 30.

12. *Ibid.*, p. 32.

13. *Ibid.*

14. Dunn, p. 7.

15. See synopsis in Dunn, pp. 31–34.

16. See Keene, *Bunraku*, p. 32.

17. Dunn, pp. 36, 39.

18. *Sekkyō* means literally "explanation of the sutras." Probably the sekkyō plays originated as dramatized versions of the sacred texts, staged in order to teach doctrine in an interesting and easy-to-understand manner. *Sekkyō-bushi* (sekkyō music) were originally chanted to the rhythm of gongs and the *sasara*, an instrument made of bamboo that was scraped to produce a sound. However, these plays also adopted the samisen in time, and at the height of their popularity, in the middle of the sixteenth century, they were barely distinguishable from Jōruri. Sekkyō-bushi survive today in an etiolated form on the island of Sado.

19. The illustration is reproduced in Keene, *Bunraku*, p. 136.

20. Translated by Dunn as "The Riven Breast" in two versions, *op. cit.*, pp. 112–34; a summary is given in Keene, *Bunraku*, pp. 45–47.

21. Dunn, p. 112.

22. See the translations in Dunn, pp. 135–48.

23. Suwa Haruo, *Genroku Kabuki no Kenkyū*, p. 226.

24. See above, p. 220.

25. Gunji, *Kabuki*, p. 34. See also Masakatsu Gunji, *Kabuki* [in English], p. 22.

26. Gunji, *Kabuki*, p. 36.

27. Suwa, "Kabuki no Tenkai," p. 166.

28. C. J. Dunn and Bunzō Torigoe (trans.), *The Actors' Analects*, p. 118.

29. Yokoyama Shigeru, *Kaganojō Dammono Shū*, p. 31.

30. Yokoyama, p. 38; Dunn, *Puppet Drama*, p. 101.

BIBLIOGRAPHY

Dunn, C. J. *The Early Japanese Puppet Drama*. London: Luzac, 1966.

——— and Bunzō Torigoe. *The Actors' Analects*. New York: Columbia University Press, 1969.

Gunji, Masakatsu. *Kabuki* [in English]. Tokyo and Palo Alto, Calif.: Kodansha International, 1969.

———. *Kabuki*, in Nihon Bungaku Shi series. Tokyo: Iwanami Shoten, 1958.

———. *Kabuki no Hassō*. Tokyo: Kōbundō, 1959.

———. *Kabuki Yōshiki to Dentō*. Tokyo: Nara Shobō, 1954.

Keene, Donald. *Bunraku, the Puppet Theatre of Japan.* Tokyo and Palo Alto, Calif.: Kodansha International, 1965.

Matsuda Osamu. *Nihon Kinsei Bungaku no Seiritsu.* Tokyo: Hōsei Daigaku, 1963.

Muroki Yatarō. "Nagoya Sanzaburō ni kansuru nisan no mondaiten ni tsuite," in *Kokugo to Kokubungaku*, November 1955.

Ogasawara Yasuko and Gunji Masakatsu. "Izumo no Okuni to kabuku Hitobito," in Nihon Bungaku no Rekishi series, vol. VII. Tokyo: Kadokawa Shoten, 1967.

Suwa Haruo. *Genroku Kabuki no Kenkyū*. Tokyo: Kasama Shoin, 1967.

———. "Kabuki no Tenkai," in *Kōza Nihon Bungaku*, VII. Tokyo: Sanseidō, 1969.

Toita Yasuji and Gunji Masakatsu. *Kabuki: sono Rekishi to Yōshiki.* Tokyo: Nihon Hōsō Shuppan Kyōkai, 1965.

Yokoyama Shigeru. *Kaganojō Dammono Shū*. Tokyo: Koten Bunko, 1958.

CHAPTER 11
DRAMA
CHIKAMATSU MONZAEMON (1653-1725)

By the 1680s both Kabuki and Jōruri had developed into theaters with considerable verve and some polish, but the texts performed, as far as we can tell from surviving examples, were undistinguished, if not childish. Each theater exploited its special capabilities: Kabuki, performed by actors, provided maximum opportunities for the display of virtuoso acting techniques; Jōruri, taking advantage of the expendability of puppets, sometimes included scenes of mayhem or superhuman feats of strength. The atmosphere of Kabuki tended to be cheerful, even when the plot involved heroic or tragic deeds; but Jōruri, in part no doubt because of its heritage from the moralistic sekkyō-bushi, presented gloomier, more distinctly Buddhist scenes. In neither theater was it attempted to create dramatic works of permanent value. The managers were satisfied as long as the theaters were filled, and the audiences apparently craved nothing more than to watch their favorite actors or chanters perform new roles.

This situation was changed completely by one man, Chikamatsu Monzaemon. Chikamatsu excelled as an author of both Kabuki and Jōruri plays, but today he is known for his Jōruri, the finest works of that theater, and his Kabuki plays survive only in mutilated texts. Nevertheless, he wrote the first Kabuki plays of distinction, and it is not surprising that when critics of the Meiji era, eager to establish parallels between Japanese and Western literature, looked for a Japanese Shakespeare, they chose Chikamatsu.

Chikamatsu was born in Fukui, in the province of Echizen, the second son of a fairly prominent samurai family. He remained there until he was ten or eleven, when his father, having in the meantime become a rōnin for reasons we do not know, moved the family to Kyoto. In 1671, when Chikamatsu was eighteen, a collection of poetry called *Takaragura* (The Treasure House) was published by the poet Yamaoka Genrin (1631–72) and included some verses by Chikamatsu and other members of his family. It was his literary debut. Chikamatsu continued for some time to study haikai poetry and Japanese classical literature with Genrin. At the time he also served as a page in the household of a Kyoto nobleman. This may have been how he became interested in Jōruri: despite the humble status of Jōruri performers, their art was patronized by the aristocracy, and the nobleman Ōgimachi Kimmochi (1653–1733) even wrote plays for the chanter Uji Kaganojō. According to one tradition, Chikamatsu became acquainted with Kaganojō in the course of running errands for this nobleman, and the chance meeting determined his future career.[1]

Of course, it was one thing to dabble like Kimmochi in Jōruri, and quite another to devote one's whole life to a despised profession. Kaganojō's family felt so humiliated when he became a chanter that they disowned him. We can easily imagine how upset Chikamatsu's family was when this son of a samurai of aristocratic descent decided to take up so ignoble a calling. But Chikamatsu may have had no choice. Once his father had become a rōnin there was almost no chance for Chikamatsu to make a career as a samurai, and his period of service with the nobility, though it enriched his knowledge greatly, did not provide a means of earning a living. Of the limited variety of professions open to someone of his background, he might have become a teacher of waka or haikai, but perhaps his contacts with Kaganojō convinced him that an educated man could fruitfully work in the Jōruri theater.

It is hard to know when Chikamatsu began his career as a dramatist. Probably his first work was *Yotsugi Soga* (The Soga Heir), written in 1683 for Kaganojō, but some scholars credit Chikamatsu with as many as fifteen unsigned, earlier plays, for both Kabuki and Jōruri. In any case, it was the instant success of *The Soga Heir* that established Chikamatsu's fame.[2] A modern reader has trouble imagining why this crudely written play, so filled with grandiloquent gestures as to approach burlesque, should have won such acclaim. Probably it was owing to Chikamatsu's novel treatment of the familiar Soga story. Earlier Jōruri plays on the theme had not ventured beyond the material in the thirteenth-century *Soga Monogatari*, as if the dramatists feared that audiences, accustomed to the old story retold each time with only a slightly different emphasis, might resent drastic changes.[3] But Chikamatsu boldly set his play in the generation after the two heroic brothers, Jūrō and Gorō. Jūrō is already dead when the play begins, and Gorō appears only in the opening scene, just long enough for Minamoto no Yoritomo regretfully to order his beheading. The protagonists are instead the brothers Oniō and Dōsaburō, retainers of the Soga brothers. They learn from the mighty Asaina that when Yoritomo asked his men to enumerate their trophies after a hunt, two men had cast an unspeakable slur on the memory of Soga Jūrō by mentioning they had killed him, in much the same terms as other men had boasted of killing wild boars, rabbits, and other game. Oniō and Dōsaburō are naturally outraged, but when they must decide which man will avenge the insult and which one will remain at home to look after the aged mother of the Soga brothers, they fall to quarreling, each eager to be the one to exact vengeance. They part as sworn enemies.

In normal versions of the Soga story the vengeance of the two brothers, followed by their deaths, marked the end of their epic, but Chikamatsu prolonged the story in a transparently artificial manner. Still, to audiences who had never seen what happened after the successful revenge, the new developments were exciting. Chikamatsu also demonstrated his mastery of the puppets by having them perform such stunts as a beheading in full view of the audience (harder with actors!). Finally, the quarrel between two loyal retainers of the Soga provided an interesting counterpart to the fraternal affection invariably displayed by their masters.

The next scene was even more surprising. It was set in the brothel where Tora Gozen, the sweetheart of Soga Jūrō, and Shōshō, the sweetheart of Gorō, are both employed. The period is ostensibly the twelfth century, but when Tora speaks of her career as a prostitute ("We first became intimate when I was a novice"), or when she describes the pledges of love she exchanged with Jūrō (the severed fingertip, the shorn locks of hair, the tattoo), she clearly refers to the seventeenth-century practice of the licensed quarters. The scene opens with the two women relating their uneasiness over the failure of their lovers to write. The two men who had allegedly insulted the memory of the Soga brothers charge into the brothel at this point and demand rudely that the women lie with them. Oniō appears and chases off the obstreperous intruders, not realizing, however, that they were the very men he was searching for. Oniō informs the women of the deaths of his masters, only to discover what a great opportunity he has missed.

The third act opens with the *michiyuki* of Tora and Shōshō, that is, their journey to the village of Soga. This section, written in highly poetic language, is ultimately derived from the michiyuki (the travel descriptions) of the Nō plays, but is greatly expanded and far more complex. In Chikamatsu's plays, as we shall see, the michiyuki acquired the dramatic function of building the characters into the hero and heroine of a tragedy, but here the effect is lyric, teasing the ears with complexities of allusions and word plays. Some phrases in this early work anticipate the michiyuki of Chikamatsu's masterpieces, and the whole passage, evoking with poetic beauty the poignance of the fate of prostitutes and the brevity of their loves, has a tragic quality not found elsewhere in the play; it is as if the two women had been enabled through poetry to become human beings, instead of remaining childish puppets.

When Tora and Shōshō arrive in Soga, intending to inform the old mother of the death of her sons, they are urged not to break the news too abruptly. They therefore put on the court caps and cloaks left by their lovers and pretend to the dim-sighted mother that they are her sons who have returned in triumph. Then they act out the events that occurred in the fifth month of 1193, ending up with the brothers dying, one night apart, and "vanishing into the dews and frost of the grasses at the foot of Fuji." When the mother realizes at last that her sons are dead, Tora discloses that she has borne Jūrō a son, named Sukewaka, now safely in hiding with an aunt. The mother rejoices that the Soga family has an heir.

The fourth act opens as Oniō learns the whereabouts of his enemies. He and his brother again quarrel over who will strike the first blow. Each grabs the tail of his brother's horse and pulls. Oniō proves the stronger, jerking Dōsaburō from his horse; but he is solicitous toward his unhorsed brother who, when he revives, expresses gratitude that Oniō did not profit by this chance to kill the villains singlehandedly.

The scene shifts to the villains. They have heard about Jūrō's son, and decide to kidnap him, lest the Soga followers use him as the rallying point for a revolt. They go to Tora's house and demand the child. Tora and Shōshō pretend to have fallen in love with the villains, and insist that the attentions Oniō and Dōsaburō have foisted on them are unwelcomed. The villains gladly agree to dispose of their rivals. Shōshō promises to get Oniō and Dōsaburō drunk when they arrive. Until then, she suggests, the two men should hide inside large chests. They get in, but just as Shōshō is about to snap shut the lids, the men prudently insist on being given the keys. Soon afterward Oniō and Dōsaburō arrive with their powerful friend Asaina. He places two enormous boulders on the lids of the chests. One villain worms his way out only to be crushed flat; the other is taken alive. The party leaves in triumph for Kamakura.

This act, despite the grand theme of vengeance, is closer to farce than serious drama. The two punctilious brothers, more concerned about priorities in striking the first blow than about the vendetta itself, seem to burlesque the samurai ideals, and their mutual attempts to unhorse each other, an amusing exploitation of the puppets, cannot have been taken seriously by the audience. The scene at Tora's house is also farcical; the villains are only too ready to be deceived, even crawling into chests that can only serve as their coffins. The powerful Asaina, lifting a rock that not twenty men could lift, must also have amused the spectators as he struggled to hoist the cardboard boulder. Even the squashed villain is funny, at least when played by a puppet.

In the fifth and final act Yoritomo learns in Kamakura of the circumstances of the vendetta and expresses his approval. The surviving villain is released, so as not to mar this festive day with bloodshed, and the lands of the Soga are bestowed on the infant Sukewaka. Yoritomo's consort, impressed by the gallant behavior of Tora and Shōshō, declares she now understands that prostitutes, far from being base and fickle creatures, are models of fidelity in love. Yoritomo calls for a dance that will represent the history of courtesans, and the two women perform on an improvised stage. The words accompanying their dance are a pastiche of lines from the Nō plays, classical poetry, and *The Tale of the Heike*—every favorable thing ever said about prostitutes! The play ends as Tora and her child take their leave amid assurances that the Soga clan will flourish a myriad, myriad years.

The Soga Heir, despite its obvious crudity, contains beautiful passages, and the break with the long traditions of Soga stories suggests that Chikamatsu was trying to see how far he could expand the Jōruri form. His next important Jōruri, *Shusse Kagekiyo* (Kagekiyo Victorious) of 1686, written for Takemoto Gidayū (1651–1714), a younger rival of Kaganojō, was even more daringly experimental.[4] The tone of the play is almost uniformly dark; only occasionally, when Chikamatsu exploits the capacity of puppets to perform superhuman feats, is there the kind of fantasy that audiences so enjoyed. The most interesting character is Akoya, Kagekiyo's mistress. When she learns he is about to marry a woman of high birth, she is so furious she betrays Kagekiyo, revealing his hideout to his enemies. She regrets this act immediately, but to no avail; Kagekiyo is captured and, a tribute to his strength, he is clamped down by tree-trunks and enormous iron chains. Akoya appears with their children and begs his forgiveness, but he rebuffs her scornfully, saying he would kill her if he had even a single finger free. She tries to explain how jealousy drove her to an act she now bitterly regrets, but Kagekiyo will not listen. He declares, moreover, that he no longer recognizes her two little boys as her sons. Akoya, driven wild with despair, says she will kill the boys before his eyes. She quickly stabs one child, but the other, terrified, runs to Kagekiyo, imploring his protection. Kagekiyo remains impassive. Akoya at length persuades the boy to allow himself to be killed. She stabs him and then herself.

In the fifth act the news is reported that Kagekiyo has been beheaded, but then some excited witnesses reveal that his head, publicly displayed at a streetcorner, has been replaced by that of the bodhisattva Kannon. A miracle has occurred: Kannon, whom Kagekiyo assiduously worshiped, has substituted her own head for his, and he is safe. The play ends with rejoicing over the reconciliation of Kagekiyo and his old enemy Yoritomo.

Kagekiyo Victorious can hardly be called an artistic success. The miracle belongs to the Buddhist traditions of *The Riven Breast* and the other old Jōruri plays, and the happy ending defies historical fact in order to conform to stage requirements. In one respect, however, *Kagekiyo Victorious* is superior to anything Chikamatsu ever wrote again. The character Akoya has tragic intensity; she is, above all, a believable woman with the contradictions and complexities that distinguish a human being from a puppet, no matter how lifelike. Kagekiyo could be represented throughout as a powerful, good man; but if Akoya is performed with the head of a "good" puppet in the first scene, when she gives Kagekiyo refuge and comforts him, should she be shown with the same head when she kills her sons? The puppet theater, because it uses carved heads with unvarying expressions, must inevitably be a theater of types rather than of individuals. Akoya is a brilliant dramatic creation, but the role fails in the puppet theater; the intensity of the portrayal compels the admiration of anyone who reads the text, but it is out of place in a puppet play, not only because it fails to conform to a type, but because it reveals all too plainly the two-dimensional nature of the other characters. Moreover, the motivation of Akoya, though intelligible in terms of universal human sentiments (one thinks of Medea), was intolerable in terms of contemporary morality; if Akoya had killed her children so as to save those of a feudal lord she would have won the sympathy of the audience, but her act of despair was incomprehensible. That may be why *Kagekiyo Victorious*, though recognized today as the first work of the "new Jōruri," attracted little attention in its own day.[5]

It may be wondered if Kabuki would not have been a more suitable theater for the presentation of a complex character like Akoya. Chikamatsu's success with *The Soga Heir* had in fact been noticed by the Kabuki actors, perhaps because Sakata Tōjūrō was a friend of Kaganojō's. In 1684, the year after *The Soga Heir*, Chikamatsu wrote the Kabuki play *Yūgiri Shichinen Ki* (The Seventh Anniversary of Yūgiri's Death) for Tōjūrō. During the next four years he wrote mainly Jōruri, but from 1688 to 1703 he devoted himself to Kabuki,[6] and became in 1695 the staff playwright for Sakata Tōjūrō's theater. The reasons for his shift from Jōruri to Kabuki are not clear but, judging from the texts he wrote, it was probably not because he supposed his works would be displayed to better advantage by actors. His Kabuki plays, even such acclaimed works as *Keisei Hotoke no Hara* (1699) and *Keisei Mibu Dainembutsu* (1702), are inferior in every respect to the Jōruri plays he wrote at the same period. Not only are the characters stereotypes, but the range of the leading roles was determined by Tōjūrō's strengths as an actor: because he excelled at playing gentle, amorous young men involved in unhappy circumstances, Chikamatsu was obliged to build his plays around such roles. Chikamatsu's Kabuki plays, like most others of the period, were oiemono (about quarrels in a great family), and although his showed superior craftsmanship, they did not escape the conventions. Akoya would have been as much out of place in Kabuki as in Jōruri.

Keisei Mibu Dainembutsu (the title means something like "Courtesans and the Great Recitation of the Name of Buddha at the Mibu Temple"), the best of Chikamatsu's Kabuki plays, is distinguished by the number of elements from ordinary life that Chikamatsu introduced into a familiar oiemono story. Like many other plays of the time, it was written in conjunction with the public display of the secret Buddha at a well-known temple—in this case, the statue of Jizō at the Mibu Temple in Kyoto.[7] The success of this play did not result from a carefully constructed plot, nor the beauty of language, nor the development of the characters; it succeeded because it provided the actors maximum opportunities to display their particular talents in a variety of scenes.[8] The first scene of the first act, for example, includes a play within a play, a performance of the celebrated Mibu Kyōgen. Hikoroku, a faithful retainer, is chosen by lot to take the part of a woman, much to his discomfort. While dressed in woman's clothing and wearing a mask, he overhears the villainous stepmother and her brother as they attempt to force the youthful heir's sister to reveal the whereabouts of the family treasure, a statue of Jizō. They catch sight of Hikoroku, who identifies himself as Hikoroku's wife. The wicked brother informs the supposed wife that Hikoroku has been having relations with the heir's sister. The "wife" pretends to be furious, and is so convincing that the evil pair take "her" into the secrets of their plot. This scene obviously depends for its effect on the actor's being able to suggest an appropriate awkwardness when performing as a woman. The same effect would be impossible with a puppet; once a puppet puts on a woman's mask and clothes it becomes a woman.

In the next scene the maid Omiyo decides to steal the statue from the storehouse so that she can give it to Tamiya, the heir. She walks tightrope along the rope strung for the curtain of the Mibu Kyōgen performance. Halfway across to the storehouse window, she is discovered, and is obliged (while still standing on the rope) to deliver a long speech explaining her actions. Undoubtedly this trick scene also appealed to the Kabuki spectators and could not have been effectively performed by puppets.

Later in the act Omiyo is killed by an impostor posing as Tamiya, and her ghost reveals itself in a basin of water that proves to be hot as fire. When pursued, the ghost performs a variety of acrobatics, turning a scene of brutal murder into wholesome fun.

Tamiya's long monologue on the glories of prostitution provided Tōjūrō with a superb opportunity to exhibit his virtuosity as he mimed the words in a one-man show. The only moment in the play which departs from the realm of comic intrigue and approaches tragedy was given to the actor who played Hikoroku; no doubt he exploited to the full the dramatic possibilities of the scene when he kills his daughter in order to protect his master's reputation. Each actor, however, was furnished with a scene in which he could display his special talents, rather in the manner that the old-fashioned opera contained at least one aria each for the principal singers.

Keisei Mibu Dainembutsu was a perfect vehicle for Kabuki actors, but in its present form has little literary value. It is preserved only in the abbreviated form of an illustrated booklet, and the text in places is no more than a synopsis. Perhaps if Chikamatsu's original words were preserved, the play might exhibit more of his customary skill with language; even so, the set pieces for the different actors contrast poorly with the overall dramatic structure of his Jōruri plays.

Chikamatsu continued to write Kabuki plays from time to time in the following years, but his 1703 he shifted his main efforts back to Jōruri. This decision was probably made because of Tōjūrō's imminent withdrawal from the stage. Without Tōjūrō, for whom Chikamatsu had left the Jōruri theater, there was little inducement to remain with Kabuki. Perhaps also, as has frequently been suggested, Chikamatsu was dissatisfied with the liberties taken with his texts by the actors, and preferred puppets without personalities of their own to display. Or it may be that Chikamatsu, sensitive to the shifting tides of public taste, sensed that the rising star of the Jōruri chanter Takemoto Gidayū would soon obscure the fame of any Kabuki performer. In any case, this decision to return to Jōruri meant that for over a half century the puppet theater would be of predominant importance because it presented the works of the country's outstanding dramatist.

In 1703 Chikamatsu wrote for Gidayū the play *Sonezaki Shinjū* (The Love Suicides at Sonezaki). It scored such a tremendous success that Gidayū's theater, which had been threatened with bankruptcy, was firmly established, and it created the genre of lovers'-suicide plays.

At the end of the seventeenth century there was a sudden vogue for lovers' suicides. They were called *shinjū*, using the term that had formerly denoted milder pledges of love such as exchanging oaths or tearing out a fingernail. The vogue was soon reflected in Kabuki, in its capacity of serving as a "living newspaper" that displayed on the stage, as soon after the events as possible, the latest scandal or murder. The first shinjū play was staged as early as 1683, and Kabuki plays on the subject were often presented after 1700; but the more conservative Jōruri theater was slower to take up the theme. In the fourth month of 1703 the shinjū of Tokubei, a shop assistant, and Ohatsu, a prostitute, became the subject of gossip in Osaka. Chikamatsu, who happened to be visiting the city at the time, learned of the circumstances and decided to write a play. He worked with great speed, and the first performance of *The Love Suicides at Sonezaki* took place about three weeks later; nevertheless, his dramatization was preceded on the boards by a Kabuki play on the same subject, as we know from the apologetic remarks delivered at the opening night of Chikamatsu's play.

The story is simple. Tokubei, in love with the prostitute Ohatsu, has refused to marry the girl chosen for him by his uncle. He tells Ohatsu what has happened, explaining that he must return the girl's dowry money. Unfortunately, however, the good-natured Tokubei has lent the money to a friend, Kuheiji, who has pretended to need it desperately. Kuheiji succeeds in tricking Tokubei out of the money so successfully that nobody believes Tokubei's story. In despair over the consequences, which seem to involve their separation, Tokubei and Ohatsu commit suicide together.

The success of the play was instant and enormous. An account written not long afterward stated, "The whole town was happy, and the theater was packed to the bursting point. . . . They made a lot of money in a very short time."[9] The triumph of *The Love Suicides at Sonezaki* blotted out all remembrance of earlier plays on contemporary themes; Chikamatsu had not only effectively dramatized the subject of recent gossip, but transmuted it into a literary masterpiece.

The topicality of the play undoubtedly gave it immediate appeal, and Chikamatsu was able to convince the audiences that they were witnessing a recreation of actual events. The spectators at a performance of a jidaimono expected to see fantasy and enjoyed the unreality; they would have been bored by a faithful and literal rendering of the historical events, as we know from the unsuccessful experiments of the Meiji era. But at a sewamono the audience wanted every word and gesture to be believable. If Tokubei had thrashed Kuheiji and his cohorts when they tormented him, despite their numerical superiority and his unprepossessing appearance, the audiences which cheerfully accepted such scenes in a jidaimono (or in a samurai film today) would have been shocked by the implausibility; it was essential that Tokubei, faced with overwhelming odds, be defeated. The absurd plots of the jidaimono released the imaginative powers of the spectators, normally chained by the tedium of daily life, but the rodstick with which they measured the excellence of a sewamono was its exactness in portraying reality; they wanted to see their close neighbors, if not themselves, faithfully depicted. In practice this meant that the audience insisted on a true-seeming play rather than on the truth itself; nobody objected to Chikamatsu's invention of the villain Kuheiji, though no such person caused the suicides of the real-life Tokubei and Ohatsu.

Chikamatsu's genius as a dramatist made him able to detect, within the pathetic circumstances of the suicides of a clerk and a prostitute, the material of tragedy. This was not an inevitable treatment. The story of Tokubei and Ohatsu is treated in *Shinjū Ōkagami* (The Great Mirror of Love Suicides, 1704), a compendium of instances of shinjū, merely as an unusual event, a matter of public gossip. At the end of this account the two lovers decide that, since the world no longer holds any joy for them, they will commit suicide together, but with some flair, so that people will remember them. In the end, the narrative sternly informs us, "they polluted the wood of Sonezaki."[10] If Chikamatsu had merely reproduced the actual circumstances, he could never have created the hero and heroine of a tragedy out of two such insignificant people. He could not, on the other hand, transform Tokubei and Ohatsu into persons of grandeur, in the familiar manner of jidaimono, for they lacked the position, education, and stature for such distinction. Instead, Chikamatsu chose to make his hero a weakling, a well-meaning but inept young man who foolishly trusts a scoundrel. But Tokubei emerges as a hero all the same, thanks to the poetry Chikamatsu wrote for and about him. The same holds true of Ohatsu; she is a prostitute of the lowest class, an uneducated, impetuous woman whose thoughts fly to death even before other possibilities have been considered. The clerk and the prostitute are ennobled and redeemed by the purity of their love.

Tokubei provides a sharp contrast to Chikamatsu's previous heroes. Far from performing prodigies of strength like Kagekiyo or Asaina, Tokubei is pathetic when, having been battered by Kuheiji's henchmen, he tearfully assures the bystanders that he will one day prove his innocence, or when he creeps along the ground under Ohatsu's skirts to avoid detection. Chikamatsu nevertheless admired Tokubei's love, which was so strong he rejected an advantageous marriage and later chose death rather than give it up. This love made a weakling into a tragic hero.

The most dramatic moment in *The Love Suicides at Sonezaki* occurs when Tokubei, hiding under the porch of a brothel, hears Ohatsu ask for a sign that he is ready to die with her. He takes her foot, which hangs over the edge of the porch, and passes it across his throat. This gesture, though inspired by a woman, bespeaks Tokubei's emergence as a man, and he gains full tragic stature in the following scene, when he and Ohatsu journey to the wood of Sonezaki where they are to die. The michiyuki of the lovers is one of the most beautiful passages in Japanese literature. It begins:

> Farewell to this world, and to the night farewell.
> We who walk the road to death, to what should we be likened?
> To the frost by the road that leads to the graveyard,
> Vanishing with each step we take ahead:
> How sad is this dream of a dream![11]

Any love described in such language is likely to command not only our sympathy but our admiration. Tokubei, as he walks his last journey, grows taller before our eyes. His character is not transformed; rather, the purity and strength that have always been within him are now first exposed. From a pathetic figure, almost comic in his futility, he turns into a man who can kill the women he loves and then himself. Finally, Chikamatsu assures us, "The lovers beyond a doubt will in the future attain Buddhahood." Their suicides have become the means of salvation, and their whole lives given meaning by this one act.

A religious conviction that lovers who died together would be reborn together in paradise, though ultimately derived from the Amidist belief in universal salvation, was a popular accretion to Buddhist doctrine that contributed to the craze for love suicides. The deaths of the merchant Hanshichi and the courtesan Sankatsu in 1695 accelerated the craze. His suicide note declared:

> I am sure people will be shocked that Sankatsu and I have ended our lives this way, but I hope you will understand, even if I do not write all the circumstances in detail, that it is the intensity of our love that has made us take this step, at the cost of our precious lives. . . . I am sure too that you will not

> consider us to have been merely creatures of lust. . . . I am ashamed when I think that some may look on us as fools or debauchees, but all those who know what love and the uncertainty of life imply will understand us.[12]

It does not matter much whether this letter is genuine or a forgery by someone who merely imagined Hanshichi's feelings; it unmistakably reveals the current attitudes toward love suicides. There is no suggestion of guilt, but instead confidence that what they are doing is proper. Other documents indicate that lovers before their suicides felt cheerful and full of hope.[13] Stories about love suicides circulated not as gloomy or morbid tales but as the lively subjects of gossip, as we can tell from this passage in the michiyuki of *The Love Suicides at Sonezaki*:

> Some revelers, still not gone to bed,
> Are loudly talking under blazing lamps—
> No doubt gossiping about the good or bad
> Of this year's crop of lovers' suicides.[14]

From a commonsensical point of view it might seem that the lovers' suicide was a total disaster, bringing grief to their families, and snuffing out the lives of two people whose nobility has at last been revealed. The only person who can possibly rejoice is the villain, Kuheiji. But Chikamatsu, alone among the dramatists or novelists of his time, predicted salvation for the lovers who had killed themselves; other writers promised at best that the victims would be long remembered.[15] Chikamatsu attempted in this way not only to justify their act but to assure the lovers a happiness in the future world that they were denied in this life.

The play's ultimate promise of Buddhist salvation may suggest it is a throwback to medieval tales, but the atmosphere of the play is thoroughly in keeping with its time. The tragedy is directly caused by the wickedness of Kuheiji in swindling Tokubei out of his money, an inconceivable circumstance in, say, a Nō play. Money—or the lack of money—controls the lives of Tokubei and Ohatsu. Tokubei cannot return the dowry money he accepted from his uncle, and is therefore menaced by the threat of being driven from Osaka by the angry uncle. Ohatsu, who presumably became a prostitute because her family needed the money, cannot escape from her servitude unless a customer buys up her contract, but the customer she would wish to "ransom" her, Tokubei, is penniless. The one free act left them is to commit suicide. They die in the belief that they will be reunited in Amida's paradise, and in this sense they die happy, despite the agonies of their final moments. Money was everything in this life, but there would be happiness in the world to come, thanks to the strength of their love.

The success of *The Love Suicides at Sonezaki* cannot be measured solely in terms of its popularity or the imitations it inspired; it marked the creation of the sewamono, in literary terms the most important dramatic genre since Nō. Jōruri plays on love suicides formed an extremely conspicuous part of Chikamatsu's work; he wrote his last in 1722, three years before his death. Even in sewamono not strictly concerned with love suicides, the characters were often modeled on Tokubei and Ohatsu. The heroes are usually young men of undiluted emotions but weak characters, the heroines generous and passionate women.

Jihei, the hero of *Shinjū Ten no Amijima* (The Love Suicides at Amijima, 1721), Chikamatsu's masterpiece, is another Tokubei, but with two women in his life. He loves and needs both the prostitute Koharu and his wife Osan. Desperate at the thought of losing either, he lies in a state of tearful stupor, unable to resolve his conflicting love for the two women. Koharu, like Ohatsu, is utterly faithful and devoted to Jihei, even though she is a prostitute, and only a sense of duty toward Jihei's wife has made her pretend to be unwilling to join him in a lovers' suicide. Osan wants her husband back, but when she realizes this may cost Koharu's life, her sense of duty toward the generous prostitute leads her to urge Jihei to buy up Koharu's contract and save her. But the situation is hopeless. When Osan gives Jihei her savings and even her clothes, he can only weep.

> JIHEI: Yes, I can pay the earnest money and keep her out of Tahei's hands. But once I've redeemed her, I'll either have to maintain her in a separate establishment or bring her here. Then what will become of you?
>
> NARRATOR: Osan is at a loss to answer.
>
> OSAN: Yes, what shall I do? Shall I become your children's nurse or the cook? Or perhaps the retired mistress of the house?[16]

Jihei begs Osan's forgiveness, but she assures him, "I'd be glad to rip the nails from my fingers and toes, to do anything that might serve my husband. . . . But it's too late now to talk of such things. Hurry, change your cloak and go to her with a smile."

Their plan is frustrated by the arrival of Osan's father, who guesses something is amiss, and drags off Osan, declaring Jihei is unworthy to be her husband. Jihei now has no choice but to go through with a lovers' suicide with Koharu. Their journey to Amijima is described in another superlative michiyuki that sums up the tragedy and prepares the two of them for death at the end. Yet when they reach Amijima, their thoughts are mainly about Osan, and their actions are intended to fulfill their duty toward her. Jihei cuts his hair, signifying he has become a priest, and says, "Our duties as husband and wife belong to our profane past." Afraid, however, that Osan will suppose he and Koharu committed suicide together, he arranges that she die on land and he in the water. This transparent excuse shows that in form at least they have observed their obligations toward Osan.

The differences between Tokubei and Jihei or between Ohatsu and Koharu are not to be measured in terms of their characters, which are strikingly similar, but of Chikamatsu's greater maturity as a dramatist. Like every true tragedy, *The Love Suicides at Amijima* is inevitable, but the sad conclusion of *The Love Suicides at Sonezaki* could have been averted if only somebody had proved Kuheiji was lying. (A revised version of the play, possibly made by Chikamatsu himself, added a scene in which Kuheiji's guilt is disclosed.) The tragedy in *The Love Suicides at Amijima* is brought about not by the villain Tahei, who makes a comically maladroit exit, but by the fundamental goodness of the three main characters; each feels ties of duty and affection too strong to break, binding them in an impossible triangle. Lack of money is the immediate cause of misfortune; if Jihei had more money he could "ransom" Koharu. But what then? This is the question Osan asks Jihei, but he has no answer. Jihei's financial worries arose from his neglect of his shop, and this in turn was caused by his all-absorbing love for Koharu. At the time there was no objection to a man amusing himself in the gay quarters, but falling in love with a prostitute was extremely dangerous, for precisely this reason. Jihei and Koharu pay for this mistake with their lives, and Osan must suffer too.

The complex pattern of duty and affection that runs through *The Love Suicides at Amijima* helps to account for Chikamatsu's reputation as a dramatist who treated *giri* (obligation) and *ninjō* (human feelings). These two elements are indeed often taken to typify the morality of the Tokugawa period, and the conflict between the two, represented by a man who is torn between his personal desires and his social obligations, is central to Chikamatsu's sewamono.[17] Jihei's love for Koharu is complicated by his giri toward Osan; but this giri comes from within him and is not artificially imposed by society. Similarly, Osan's love for Jihei is complicated by her giri toward Koharu; when she realizes Koharu is likely to kill herself, feelings of giri make Osan insist that Jihei ransom Koharu, even though this can only bring unhappiness to herself. Koharu, for her part, is deeply in love with Jihei, but compassion for Osan induces her, first, to break with Jihei, by pretending she is reluctant to die with him, then later, when she and Jihei have reached Amijima, to worry about Osan's reactions when she learns of their suicides. Such "complications" give rise to the tragedy, not the wicked deeds of the blustering Tahei, nor even the financial problems besetting the hero.

Giri was not necessarily stern-voiced duty calling a man away from the natural inclinations of his heart. Often it was a natural, internal response, directed toward another person primarily out of gratitude.[18] But when critics speak of the theme of giri in Chikamatsu's plays they are generally referring to the instances when a fear of what society will think, or a feeling of obligation to another person, compels someone to give up what he most desires. This is common in Chikamatsu's sewamono plays about samurai. Shigenoi in *Tamba Yosaku* (Yosaku from Tamba, 1708) rejects her long-lost son, though it pains her exceedingly, because of giri to the princess she serves.[19] In the jidaimono such instances of giri become extreme. Many examples are likely to irritate the Western reader, who wonders why such enormous importance is given to conventions; modern Japanese readers are likely to be repelled by the "feudal" mentality. Giri not softened by ninjō may seem inhuman: it denies the individual's right to be happy at the expense of society. Ninjō unchecked by giri, however, is not only self-indulgent but can in the end destroy human society.

Western readers may find the manifestations of ninjō even harder to take than those of giri. To kill one's own child to save the child of one's master makes a kind of sense, unspeakable though the act is; but to abandon one's family without thought to their future may seem contemptible. Jihei deserts his children to die with Koharu, and she turns her back on her old mother, doing piecework in a back alley, to die with him. Koman in *Yosaku from Tamba* runs away with Yosaku, though she knows this action will send her father back to a terrible dungeon in a debtors' prison. But of course we are not expected to consider the characters in coldly rational terms. Chikamatsu wanted us to feel that Jihei's giri gave dimension to a love he could not master, and the strength of this love, which brings him to commit a lover's suicide, will in the end assure him of salvation. Purity of emotions excuses any weakness occasioned by ninjō. Yojibei in *Nebiki no Kadomatsu* (The Uprooted Pine, 1718) goes out of his mind, but since his madness is occasioned by love, he does not seem foolish, even in his incoherence. In *Onnagoroshi Abura Jigoku* (The Woman-Killer, 1721) Yohei's mother, a woman of samurai origins, obeys the dictates of giri in disinheriting her profligate son, but ninjō induces her to steal money that she gives him secretly; this weakness, far from making us despise the mother, makes her seem all the more admirable.

Chikamatsu's concern with giri and ninjō deprived his sewamono of some of the variety we expect of a great dramatist. He could not repeat himself too obviously before a public that demanded novelty, but the theme of the lovers' suicides with its "complications" of giri and ninjō did not allow for much invention. The audience knew in advance the conclusion to these plays from the title—the terrible moment when the hero kills his beloved and then himself—and the surrounding circumstances were often familiar from gossip or ballads. Chikamatsu was also obliged, as we have seen, to make types of his characters because of the limitations of puppet stage. He could create severe old men whose crabbed exteriors conceal hearts of gold, or wise old models of good sense, or evil old villains, but not a King Lear.

The interest in his plays lies first of all in Chikamatsu's

portrayals of the lives of townsmen. Saikaku excelled in his descriptions of the ways in which townsmen made or lost money, but because his intent was prevailingly comic he rarely touched on their deeper concerns. When Osan (in *Five Women Who Loved Love*) impetuously decides to run off with Moemon, we enjoy the author's wry realism, but Saikaku does not suggest that her actions stemmed from anything deeper than a sudden impulse. He may have been more realistic than Chikamatsu in describing prostitutes—Chikamatsu gives the impression that *all* prostitutes were faithful to the men they loved—but we must turn to Chikamatsu if we wish to know the anguish that merchants and samurai of the lower ranks suffered because of their passions or their times.

Chikamatsu's merchants have little to distinguish them, one from the other, but probably the models on which they were based did not possess much individuality either. One man might have a quicker temper than another, or be gentler or surlier, but the natural tendency of the puppet theater to portray types accorded with the society. Aristotle would have considered Chikamatsu's characters to be unsuitable as the heroes of tragedy, if only because their humble status rendered them incapable of determining their own fates. If urgent financial difficulties had distracted Orestes or Hamlet from avenging his father's death, there obviously would have been no tragedy in an Aristotelian sense. But such restrictions on the freedom of action of the characters were basic to the nature of Chikamatsu's domestic tragedies. The heroes could not aspire to the noble actions of their social superiors—avenging the death of a father, sacrificing a beloved child to save the child of a master, or making a painful choice between conflicting loyalties—but there was a kind of tragedy which was not only appropriate to their class but their exclusive privilege, death with the woman of their choice.

If Tokubei had been a samurai he might have killed Kuheiji, rather than endure his abuse, and committed seppuku afterward, in the manner expected of a samurai, but there would have been no love suicide with a prostitute, an action that would have brought disgrace and contempt. The little men who appear as the heroes of Chikamatsu's sewamono, like the heroes of many modern plays, are trapped by financial and other circumstances which they are powerless to alter, and in the end their daggers are turned against themselves, and not against an enemy. The resolution of their unhappiness is likely to seem pathetic or even sordid, rather than ennobling, in contrast to the deaths of the heroes of classical tragedy. A furtive escape from the licensed quarter, a frightened journey in the hours before the dawn to some temple, and the double death by a knife were the highest reaches of tragedy of which they were capable. The overpowering emotions which these men experience are not tragic flaws in otherwise exemplary men but the most distinctive and appealing aspects of otherwise largely undifferentiated creatures. They were typical of their society, though Hamlet was able not to be typical of any society. Shakespeare's tragedies were called by the names of their heroes, Chikamatsu's by the circumstances of their deaths. It is hard to distinguish Jihei from Tokubei or Chūbei, but the entire group of sewamono creates an unforgettable impression of what it meant to be an Osaka townsman at that time. The lack of variety in these plays is compensated for by the confirmation each work lends to the portrayal of Chikamatsu's chosen milieu. In the end the effect produced is undeniably tragic.

The sewamono alone do not, however, give a complete picture of Chikamatsu as a dramatist. Most were intended to be performed at the conclusion of a full-length jidaimono; the pleasure-loving audiences might not have appreciated the gloom of a love-suicide play if it had not followed the colorful posturing of the history plays. The jidaimono are difficult to appreciate as literature, however, because so much depends on the presentation. The lack of unity in the plots, which grew even more pronounced in the plays written after Chikamatsu, was no great fault as far as the spectators were concerned; they spent the entire day in the theater, and were unlikely in any case to maintain undivided attention. It was enough for each separate scene to be diverting and that there be a variety of effects. The looseness of the structure meant that a single act could be presented independently, and in later time it became a normal practice to present a program consisting of single acts from four or five different plays.

The only jidaimono with real literary value is *Kokusenya Kassen* (The Battles of Coxinga, 1715), Chikamatsu's most ambitious work and greatest success. It ran for seventeen months when first performed, and was repeated and imitated for many years afterward; it is the one play of Chikamatsu's for which the original music has been preserved, no doubt because it never left the stage for long. A complete performance of the work would take the best part of a day, and the five acts abound in variety. That is why it was the first of Chikamatsu's plays to be presented by itself, with no other entertainments on the bill.

The story of *The Battles of Coxinga* is complicated, and the fantastic elements are so prominent that it will seem childish unless we are ready to accept its conventions. The hero, the son of a Chinese man and a Japanese woman, leaves his native Japan, determined to restore the Ming rulers to the throne of China and overthrow the "Tartar" invaders. There is some historical basis to the play, but the career of the real Coxinga (the name by which Europeans knew Cheng Ch'eng-kung) provided very little of the plot. Chikamatsu used only elements that fitted in with his scheme for a drama of patriotic themes presented in an exotic setting.[20]

Judged by normal standards the play has many glaring faults, but it performs superbly, and its popularity has never waned. Chikamatsu devoted to this work his mastery of poetic and dramatic genius. The language displays every variety of style, ranging from the ostentatiously virtuosic to the simplest, most conversational. The play's structure suggests the different moods evoked by a full program of Nō plays, and its effects range from the solemn splendor of the Chinese court to earthy realism.[21] There is no mistaking Chikamatsu's intention of providing in *The Battles of Coxinga* a complete theatrical experience.

The characters in a sewamono are generally believable, if not especially striking; those in a jidaimono, where every action is pushed to extremes for theatrical effect, are such embodiments of particular virtues as to be only intermittently human. Coxinga is bravery itself: he can tackle a whole army, storm his way through a fortress, leap over castle walls. Chikamatsu does not allow us the time to consider whether or not these deeds are possible. We observe Coxinga with totally different standards than those we apply to Jihei. Coxinga has moments of human weakness—when, for example, he weeps after his mother commits suicide—but never for long. The puppet head used for the fierce warrior was incapable of showing fear, dejection, merriment, or any other emotion not directly related to his basic nature. Even when *The Battles of Coxinga* is performed by actors (who could make more subtle gradations), they follow the puppet stereotypes. Every laugh becomes a roar of contempt, every statement a defiant manifesto. We cannot accept Coxinga as a human being, but he definitely is a hero. His feminine counterpart, his sister Kinshōjo, has all the womanly virtues—devotion to her husband and father, compassion and, above all, a readiness to sacrifice herself. When Coxinga demands a signal indicating whether or not her husband, Kanki, will join him, Kinshōjo stabs herself and sends her blood flowing through a pipe into the garden. The extravagance of her gesture, like the extravagance of the villainous Ri Tōten gouging out his eye, does not belong to the world of mortals. Everything is larger than life and painted in strongest colors. That undoubtedly is why the play was so successful on the puppet stage.

The emphasis on the puppets, so conspicuous in *The Battles of Coxinga*, was maintained through most of the works written afterward. This was largely the result of the influence of Takeda Izumo (d. 1747), the manager of the Takemoto Theater from 1705 and an especially influential figure after the death of Gidayū in 1714. In the history plays the bravura display of the art of the puppeteer accorded well with the unreal stories, but some of the later sewamono are marred by situations that suggest trickery with puppets for its own sake, without respect to the play. In *The Woman-Killer*, Chikamatsu's only murder play, the carefully built up tension is shattered by a foolish stunt: mourners gathered at the house of the murdered woman are startled when a rat "races over the beams and rafters of the living room, kicking up a great quantity of soot and dust. It dislodges a scrap of paper before its rampage subsides."[22] The bloodstained paper proves to be a vital clue to the identity of the murderer. Remarkable coincidences occur even in daily life, and perhaps on occasion rats knock telltale pieces of paper from the rafters, but the scene is absurd as realistic drama. No doubt it was intended to provide relief, a bright touch in the darkness of the plot provided by an amusing puppet rat, but it is harder to accept the scene here than it would have been in *The Battles of Coxinga*.

Chikamatsu's views on the art of the puppet theater have

fortunately been preserved in the form of a conversation, recorded by his friend Hozumi Ikan in 1738, after Chikamatsu's death. It begins:

> Jōruri differs from other forms of fiction in that, since it is primarily concerned with puppets, the words must all be living and full of action. Because Jōruri is performed in theatres that operate in close competition with those of the Kabuki, which is the art of living actors, the author must impart to lifeless wooden puppets a variety of emotions, and attempt in this way to capture the interest of the audience.[23]

Chikamatsu realized that, since he was writing for puppets, he could not rely on actors to enhance the dialogue with the coloring of their personalities. The dramatist had to charge even narrative phrases with emotion or they would not produce much effect when acted out by a puppet. He distinguished, however, between making the words and situation moving in themselves and merely saying about some situation that it was moving, in the manner of the old Jōruri. "If one says of something which is sad that it is sad, one loses the implications, and in the end, even the impression of sadness is slight."[24] He noted that

> in writing Jōruri, one attempts first to describe facts as they really are, but in so doing one writes things which are not true, in the interest of art. In recent plays many things have been said by female characters which real women could not utter. Such things fall under the heading of art; it is because they say what could not come from a real woman's lips that their true emotions are disclosed. If in such cases the author were to model his character on the ways of a real woman and conceal her feelings, such realism, far from being admired, would permit no pleasure in the work.[25]

For Chikamatsu the art of Jōruri was to be found in "the slender margin between the real and unreal."

Chikamatsu's views are intelligent and surprisingly modern, but they are not always embodied in his works. Too often we are *told* of a character's grief, rather than having the emotion revealed through the dialogue alone: "The sad tears flow from the depths of her heart, from the depths of her soul, from her very entrails."[26] Chikamatsu's violation of his own principle may have been dictated by the needs of a particular play, but certainly the use of expressionless puppets tended in any case to require clarification and amplification by the narrator of the characters' emotions. Chikamatsu's mastery of the technical demands of the puppet theater enabled him to satisfy the expectations of his audiences, but a theater of actors who respected the texts (unlike the Kabuki actors) might have enabled Chikamatsu to develop into a playwright of worldwide importance, instead of merely into the greatest playwright ever to have written for puppets.

The puppet theater makes great demands on the spectator, but necessarily so. The chief danger is not that the puppets will be too awkward but that they will be too skillful, making them look like midgets performing the roles. Chikamatsu's jidaimono exploited the capacities of the puppets for the superhuman. There is no danger in these plays that the puppets will become boring, but in the sewamono, where there is often little action while the characters narrate their woes, it takes great skill on the part of the operators to keep the play inside the "slender margin between the real and the unreal."

Chikamatsu's plays were printed during his lifetime both for people who wished to practice singing parts and for readers who enjoyed the poetry. He took great pains with his texts, not only to ensure their success on the stage, but to give them literary distinction. The most beautiful passages are not in the dialogue but in the descriptions narrated by the chanter, which give the setting of an act, and in the fantastically complex tissues of puns, allusions, and half-finished phrases that make up the michiyuki.

No short extract from a michiyuki could reveal the whole gamut of complexities in an extended passage, but perhaps the following section from *Meido no Hikyaku* (The Courier for Hell, 1711) will suggest the typical manner:

> *Sore oboete ka itsu no koto, kano hatsuyuki no asagomi ni, nemaki nagara ni okurareshi, daimonguchi no usuyuki mo, ima furu yuki mo kawaranedo, kawarihatetaru mi no yukue, ware yue somete, itōshi ya moto no shiraji wo asagi yori, koi wa Konda no Hachiman ni kishō seishi no fude no bachi.*

A fairly literal translation would go:

> Do you remember? When was it? That morning of the first snow, when customers were pressing to get inside [the licensed quarter], and I was shown by you, still in your nightclothes, to the Great Gate: the light fall of snow then was no different from the snow falling now, but how completely altered is your fate! Because you have been dyed [with love] for me, my poor dear, you can never return to your former, uncolored state. But rather than a pale green, let our love be deep-hued. Such is our punishment for the [words we wrote with our] brushes when we vowed to the Hachiman of Konda we would be constant.

The entire passage is written alternating units of seven plus five syllables. Words necessary to an understanding of the meaning are omitted or else telescoped into the next phrase. For example, *moto no shiraji wo asagi yori* means "rather than dye the original uncolored material a pale green"; the verb "to dye" is not given, though it occurred a little earlier, and "pale green" is used to suggest any faint color, as opposed to deep passion. The next words, *koi wa Konda*, contain a pivot-word on *ko*: *koi wa ko* suggests *koi wa koshi*, "love is deep-hued," and *Ko*nda is the site of a famous shrine to the god Hachiman. Apart from such complexities of meaning, there is an adroit use of sound in such words as *usuyuki*, *yuki*, *yukue*, *yue* occurring close together. In other michiyuki passages one would find quotations of phrases from classical literature.

The spectators, though poorly educated, were able to grasp the meanings of Chikamatsu's intricate language, thanks to their general familiarity with the materials he quoted. Even if they could not fully grasp all the word plays, they could relax in the stream of beautiful language, carried along also by the musical accompaniment of the samisen.[27] Chikamatsu was proud of the beauty of his texts, and his deathbed verse seems to express confidence that his plays would live on in their printed form.[28]

Chikamatsu's popularity has not matched that of his great contemporaries Saikaku and Bashō. He has little of Saikaku's winning humor, and his poetry, though beautiful, rarely attains the heights of Bashō's best hokku. The plays, moreover, are rarely performed today in their original versions. Instead, nineteenth-century adaptations—which accentuate the pathos, give chanters many opportunities to weep and howl, and complicate the plots with additional surprises—are preferred by the audiences who, like their predecessors of the eighteenth century, attend the theater for dramatic rather than literary pleasure.

Chikamatsu's rival, the staff playwright at the Toyotake Theater, Ki no Kaion (1663–1742), is today remembered mainly in terms of the fruitful competition that spurred Chikamatsu into writing some of his masterpieces. Kaion is important not only for the few works whose names are still remembered, but because stories he first treated on the stage became great popular favorites in the adaptations of other men.[29]

Kaion was born in Osaka, the son of a merchant who dabbled in haikai poetry. His elder brother became a famous kyōka poet under the name Yuensai Teiryū. Undoubtedly this family background accounted for Kaion's early training in Jōruri.[30] As a young man Kaion took Buddhist orders, but returned to the laity to practice medicine in Osaka. He was attracted to the gay quarters and probably met there Toyotake Wakatayū, who founded the Toyotake Theater in 1703. The earliest datable work by Kaion was performed at this theater in 1708, when he was forty-five, and his last work was performed in 1723. During the fifteen or so years that he wrote for the Toyotake Theater he completed close to fifty plays, of which ten were sewamono. His forty jidaimono were mainly rewritings of works by Chikamatsu and other dramatists, and his own worth is revealed entirely in his sewamono.

Kaion's best play, perhaps, is *Yaoya Oshichi* (Oshichi, the Greengrocer's Daughter, 1714?). It has often been said that Kaion stressed giri to the exclusion of ninjō, making his plays seem coldly moralistic, but the story of Oshichi provided an irresistibly affecting heroine. Oshichi is the fourth of Saikaku's "five women"; in his version of her tale the girl Oshichi remembers that it was because of a fire that she and her family were evacuated to the temple where she met her lover. She therefore decides to set another fire, hoping to meet him again, but she is caught and put to death for arson. Her lover, Kichiza, learning of her death, at first wishes to kill himself, but he is persuaded to become a Buddhist priest, this having been her final wish. In Kaion's play the tone is much darker. Oshichi is transformed from an impetuous tomboy into a girl of great sincerity who gives way to her emotions under the strain of unbearable pressure. Her father, we learn, borrowed two hundred *ryō* in gold to rebuild his house after the Great Fire. The lender, one Buhei, suddenly demands either the return of his money or Oshichi's hand in marriage. The parents are reluctant to give their daughter to the unpleasant Buhei, but being unable to return the money, they have no choice. The mother begs Oshichi to marry Buhei. She even promises to help the girl to get a divorce immediately afterward so that she can marry the man she loves. Kichiza, who has overheard this conversation, decides that he would only be in the way of Oshichi's marriage, and leaves without seeing her. Oshichi is frantic when she learns that Kichiza has gone, and she conceives of setting a fire as the one way to avoid a hateful marriage and to rejoin her lover.

The greatest differences between Kaion's play and Saikaku's novel occur in the third act. Saikaku mentions, so briefly one almost misses it, that "Oshichi turned into sad wisps of smoke that hovered in the grasses,"[31] but in Kaion's play the horror of burning at the stake is evoked. Oshichi's parents blame themselves for having driven Oshichi to her crime by insisting on a repugnant marriage. They even express disillusion that their devout prayers over the years to Buddha and the Japanese gods have been powerless to save their daughter's life. In the midst of their grieving they learn that a sympathetic magistrate has ordered Buhei to forfeit the two hundred *ryō* to Oshichi's parents, and that Buhei himself has been jailed for attempted extortion. But Oshichi's sentence cannot be revoked because she has admitted there were no extenuating circumstances. The parents' momentary joy over the cancellation of the debt quickly gives way to despair over their daughter's impending death.

In the meantime, preparations are going ahead for the execution. The michiyuki is not a lovers' journey, but Oshichi being paraded from the prison to the execution grounds in the bright morning sunlight, despite her parents' prayers for rain. The passage is worthy of Chikamatsu, a moving blend of remembrances and present feelings:

> Let anyone who wishes call me human scum, let anyone laugh who wants to; my love was the first I ever knew, and it

> is undivided. Even if my body is transfixed, my bones ground to powder, my flesh turned to ashes, my soul will remain in this world and follow his shadow, clinging to his body. Hand in hand with my husband for two lifetimes or three, we will mount in the end the same lotus blossom.[32]

No sooner does Oshichi arrive at the execution grounds than Kichiza, whose absence has been much commented on, makes his way through the crowd. He is dressed in white, a sign that he is resolved to die. He begs the guards to execute him together with Oshichi, but she says:

> How foolish you are, dear Kichiza. I have nothing in the least to regret—my crime was of my own choosing. Now that I have seen you, I have nothing more to hope for before I die. Your life is precious. Please become a priest and pray for me, pray hard for me when I am gone. This is all I have to say. Please go, quickly.

But Kichiza still begs the officials to kill him instead, insisting that he was responsible. They refuse, and Kichiza, crying out that his life is meaningless now, declares that he will go before Oshichi and wait for her on the road of death. He plunges a dagger into himself and commits seppuku.

This play is saved from the stiffness of some of Kaion's other works by the unalterable elements in the story. Nothing could change the fact that Oshichi had been driven by love to set a fire. This tremendous, foolish act lifts Oshichi above the ranks of conventionally unhappy young women, and inspired Kaion to write in terms of a love so powerful that it would risk the most terrible consequences.

Kaion has been accused of a lack of poetic or dramatic imagination. It is true that his texts tend to be prosaic, and he repeatedly borrowed from Chikamatsu and other dramatists, but in one case at least Chikamatsu borrowed from him. Kaion's play *Shinjū Futatsu Haraobi* (The Love Suicides with Two Sashes) was performed at the Toyotake Theater in the fourth month of 1722; sixteen days later Chikamatsu's play *Shinjū Yoi Kōshin* (The Love Suicides during the Kōshin Vigil), describing the same lovers' suicide, was performed at the rival Takemoto Theater. The points of resemblance are numerous. This was probably not the first time Chikamatsu had borrowed from Kaion,[33] but on this occasion the popularity of Kaion's work had inspired a direct answer. Kaion emerged the victor in this contest, though neither play is of the first quality, either in language or in structure.

It might have been expected that with the death of Chikamatsu early in 1725 Kaion would have emerged as the undisputed leader in the world of Jōruri, but although he lived on until 1742, his last play was written in 1723. Apparently he succeeded his brother in 1724 as the owner of a prosperous cake business, and this led him to leave the theater.[34] Perhaps too the death of Chikamatsu deprived Kaion of a necessary stimulus, and he lost interest in the stage. In his late years he wrote haikai and even came to enjoy something of a reputation as a poet, but his surviving verses, redolent of the Teitoku variety of humor, retain little interest today.[35] We can only regret Kaion's failure to write for the theater during the last twenty years of his life. The generation after Chikamatsu had to start afresh.

NOTES

1. Mori Shū, "Giri to Nasake no Sakusha Chikamatsu," p. 296.
2. *Ibid.*, p. 297.
3. See Takano Tatsuyuki, *Kinsei Engeki no Kenkyū*, p. 40.
4. The play is summarized in Keene, *Major Plays of Chikamatsu*, pp. 12–14.
5. Mori Shū, "Jōruri to Chikamatsu," p. 134.
6. See Mori, "Giri," p. 298.
7. See Gunji Masakatsu, *Kabuki no Hassō*, pp. 165–85.
8. For a summary of the entire play, see Appendix, 1.
9. Quoted in Hara Michio, "Sonezaki Shinjū no Igi," p. 65.
10. *Ibid.*, pp. 68–69.
11. Keene, *Major Plays*, p. 51.
12. Quoted in Yokoyama Tadashi, *Jōruri Ayatsuri Shibai no Kenkyū*, p. 230.
13. *Ibid.*, p. 231.
14. Keene, *Major Plays*, p. 52.
15. Hara, p. 74.
16. Keene, *Major Plays*, p. 410.

17. Minamoto Ryōen, *Giri to Ninjō*, p. 151, contrasts external and internal pressure of giri.

18. *Ibid.*, p. 59.

19. Keene, *Major Plays*, p. 101.

20. For a study of the play's appeal see Keene, *The Battles of Coxinga*, pp. 2–9. The plot is summarized in Appendix, 2.

21. See Keene, *The Battles of Coxinga*, pp. 87–89, for a comparison of the five acts of the play with the five categories of Nō plays presented on a single program.

22. Keene, *Major Plays*, p. 469.

23. Keene, *Anthology of Japanese Literature* (Grove Press, 1955), p. 386.

24. *Ibid.*, p. 388.

25. *Ibid.*

26. Keene, *Major Plays*, p. 119.

27. See Keene, *Major Plays*, pp. 27–29, for details of Chikamatsu's literary style and the difficulties in comprehending the meaning.

28. *Ibid.*, p. 26.

29. His was the first dramatic treatment of such popular figures as Osome and Hisamatsu or of Sankatsu and Hanshichi.

30. Mori, "Giri to Nasake," p. 309.

31. Teruoka Yasutaka and Higashi Akimasa, *Ihara Saikaku*, I, p. 397.

32. Otoba Hiromu (ed.), *Jōruri Shū*, I, p. 99.

33. See Takano Masami, *Chikamatsu to sono Dentō Geinō*, pp. 278–97.

34. Otoba, p. 15.

35. See Ebara Taizō, *Edo Bungei Ronkō*, p. 126.

BIBLIOGRAPHY

Ebara Taizō, *Edo Bungei Ronkō*. Tokyo: Sanseidō, 1937.

Fujino Yoshio. *Sonezaki Shinjū: Kaishaku to Kenkyū*. Tokyo: Ōfūsha, 1968.

Gunji Masakatsu. *Kabuki no Bigaku*. Tokyo: Engeki Shuppan Sha, 1963.

———. *Kabuki no Hassō*. Tokyo: Kōbundō, 1959.

Hara Michio. "Sonezaki Shinjū no Igi," in *Chikamatsu Ronshū*, I, 1962.

Higuchi Yoshichiyo. *Kessaku Jōruri Shū: Chikamatsu Jidai*. Tokyo: Dainippon Yūbenkai Kōdansha, 1935.

Keene, Donald. *The Battles of Coxinga*. London: Taylor's Foreign Press, 1951.

———. *Major Plays of Chikamatsu*. New York: Columbia University Press, 1961.

Minamoto Ryōen. *Giri to Ninjō*. Tokyo: Chūō Kōron Sha, 1969.

Mori Shū. *Chikamatsu Monzaemon*. Kyoto: San'ichi Shobō, 1959.

———. "Giri to Nasake no Sakusha Chikamatsu," in Nihon Bungaku no Rekishi series, VII. Tokyo: Kadokawa Shoten, 1967.

———. "Jōruri to Chikamatsu," in Kōza Nihon Bungaku series, vol. VII. Tokyo: Sanseidō, 1969.

Otoba Hiromu (ed.). *Jōruri Shū*, I, in Nihon Koten Bungaku Taikei series. Tokyo: Iwanami Shoten, 1960.

Suwa Haruo. *Chikamatsu Sewa Jōruri no Kenkyū*. Tokyo: Kasama Shoin, 1974.

Takano Masami (ed.). *Chikamatsu Monzaemon Shū*, in Nihon Koten Zensho series. Tokyo: Asahi Shimbun Sha, 1950–52.

Takano Tatsuyuki. *Kinsei Engeki no Kenkyū*. Tokyo: Tōkyōdō, 1941.

Teruoka Yasutaka and Higashi Akimasa. *Ihara Saikaku*, I, in Nihon Koten Bungaku Zenshū series. Tokyo: Shōgakkan, 1971.

Urayama Masao and Matsuzaki Hitoshi (ed.). *Kabuki Kyakuhon Shū*, in Nihon Koten Bungaku Taikei series. Tokyo: Iwanami Shoten, 1960.

Yokoyama Shigeru (ed.). *Kaganojō Dammono Shū*, in Koten Bunko series. Tokyo: Koten Bunko, 1958.

Yokoyama Tadashi. *Jōruri Ayatsuri Shibai no Kenkyū*. Tokyo: Kazama Shobō, 1963.

Yuda Yoshio. "Sonezaki Shinjū no Kabukiteki Kiban," in *Shima Kyōju Koki Kinen*, Kokubungaku Rombun Shū, 1960.

———. *Zenkō Shinjū Ten no Amijima*. Tokyo: Shibundō, 1975.

CHAPTER 12
DRAMA
JŌRURI AFTER CHIKAMATSU

The death of Chikamatsu and the early retirement of Ki no Kaion deprived the puppet theaters of their outstanding playwrights. This double misfortune should have threatened the very survival of Jōruri but, paradoxically, the half century or so after Chikamatsu's death marked the period of greatest prosperity for the puppet theaters. In the words of an eighteenth-century account:

> Puppet plays are all the vogue, and Kabuki might just as well not exist. Outside the puppet theaters one sees hundreds of banners and innumerable gifts for the performers. To the east there is the Toyotake, to the west the Takemoto; the theaters are divided into east and west like sumō wrestlers.

> Patrons flock from the whole town and the nearby provinces.
> Words cannot describe the prosperity of the art of the puppets.[1]

The thriving state of Jōruri after Chikamatsu's death was not due so much to the abilities of the dramatists as to developments in the operation of the puppets and the art of recitation. Toward the end of his career Chikamatsu sometimes catered to the taste of his audiences for trick stage business, known as *karakuri*, but when we read his texts today these moments seem like temporary lapses. In the Jōruri of Chikamatsu's successors, however, no effort was spared to exploit the capabilities of the puppets, especially after 1734, when the three-man puppet came into general use. In the decade after Chikamatsu's death in 1725 various other improvements were made: in 1727 puppets with mouths that moved, hands that could grasp objects, and eyes that opened and shut were introduced; in 1730 the puppets' eyes were enabled to roll; in 1733 the puppets' fingers were jointed to permit movement; and in 1736 an ultimate refinement, the puppets' eyebrows could also be moved. These technical improvements, though they had nothing to do with the merits of the texts performed, intrigued audiences, and the two rival theaters devoted their efforts mainly to such innovations. Chikamatsu's plays dropped from the repertory, or else survived only in drastically revised forms that gave greater play to the new puppets and the new, more psychologically effective, style of chanting.

The effect aimed at by both puppet operators and chanters was realism, but it was achieved only within the framework of essentially unreal conditions of performance. Chikamatsu's sewamono represented the furthest development in the direction of realism that the texts of the puppet theater attained; the language is fairly close to contemporary speech and the problems faced by the characters are believable in terms of ordinary life. Even in the case of Chikamatsu's plays, however, the visible presence of operators and chanters and the awkward if artistic movements of the puppets established conventions of unreality that the audience cheerfully accepted. If realism had been the only goal of the performances, it would have been simple to keep the operators and chanters concealed, as at a European marionette show, but in fact each advance in terms of increasing realism tended to be balanced by the introduction of an additional element of unreality or even fantasy, especially of the variety called karakuri.

In the works of Chikamatsu's successors the social problems he treated tended to disappear. Love still brought suffering to heroes and heroines who could not stay together, but they were kept apart now by family strife, warfare, or the inflexible claims of duty, rather than by an insufficiency of money. Commoners still appear in these plays, but they are governed by samurai ideals. The merchant Gihei in *Chūshingura*, for example, earns our admiration not by his thrift or hard work (in the manner of a Saikaku hero), but by chivalrous behavior worthy of a samurai. Even the authors who followed in Chikamatsu's line at the Takemoto Theater tended to make righteous samurai out of their townsmen. The curious result is that Chikamatsu's characters not only seem more realistic but even more modern than those invented by his successors.

The simple lines of Chikamatsu's plays gave way to increasingly complicated plots in response to the demands of the spectators for novelty and profusion of incidents. The main effort of the dramatists during the seventy years after Chikamatsu's death was devoted to creating new situations (*shukō*). When plays by Chikamatsu or by Ki no Kaion were adapted, they were invariably expanded with such "sure-fire" additions. In the version of *The Love Suicides at Amijima* currently performed, the second act ends with Osan's little daughter Osue returning home alone attired in an unfamiliar black costume. She tells her father that her underrobe has something written on it, and Jihei removes the black robe to discover a message written by Osan on the white underrobe; it reveals that Osan has become a nun so that Jihei and Koharu can be together. This disclosure ties up the loose end of what happened to Osan after her husband committed suicide. At the same time, the shukō of having the message written over the child's kimono, rather than in a letter, surprised the audience and provided the operators with a chance to display their virtuosity as Jihei and Koharu eagerly scan the message written all over Osue's robe.[2]

Each act of the later Jōruri plays was usually built around one or more such situations. A self-sacrificing suicide, a father's killing his own child to save the life of his master's child, the inspection of the severed head of an enemy general, the anguished separation of a mother and child, the appearance of a vengeful spirit or a madwoman—any of these shukō afforded the chanter ample opportunities to emote, and were therefore welcome to the spectators. At first each dramatist had his own favorite shukō: Yokoyama Tadashi was able to assign authorship of the different acts of plays written jointly by Matsuda Bunkōdō and Takeda Izumo on the basis of the characteristic shukō of each man. Bunkōdō often concluded his third acts with a young woman displaying the purity of her feelings by sacrificing her life.[3] Another favorite shukō of his was to have a character sacrifice himself because he had been so moved by an enemy's display of duty or loyalty. Takeda Izumo, on the other hand, often ended his third acts with a character becoming a priest as a means of showing his sense of duty to another person.[4] The authorship of acts of plays written in the 1730s is more easily deduced from a statistical analysis of preferred situations than from the literary style or structure. However, playwrights tended to imitate one another, obscuring such distinctions. Yokoyama wrote: "It is comparatively easy to distinguish the characteristics of a particular dramatist in works written during the period of Chikamatsu and Kaion, but by the time we come to Bunkōdō's age the works almost all display similar structures and almost identical shukō, making it extremely difficult to recognize individuality."[5]

Joint authorship was extremely common in the later Jōruri. Once it became common to present only a single play on a given day, the plays grew longer, to fill up the time. A division of labor probably developed in order to turn out such long works more rapidly, so as to meet the incessant demands of the public for novelty. In the absence of telltale shukō, it is extremely difficult now to assign responsibility to the different acts of a play by three or more men, but we can assume that the principal dramatist wrote the crucial sections—the ends of the third, fourth, and second acts (in descending order of importance), and the opening scene of the first act.[6] The senior chanter of the company normally delivered most of these choice passages, and the dramatists wrote with his particular talents in mind. The collaborators of the principal dramatist might be assigned one or more crucial sections, but their task was chiefly to write the lesser parts of the play—the opening of the second act, the fifth act, and so on. Even if the collaborators were all talented men, the level of interest inevitably varied from act to act; the result was that most plays were never performed in entirety after their opening runs. A single act often came to enjoy a separate existence after the rest of the play had been forgotten. Today when a performance is advertised as being "full length" (*tōshi-kyōgen*) it usually means no more than that an exceptionally generous selection of the work is being presented, not the integral text.[7] The unevenness was the risk the collaborators took; their object in any case was to achieve a surprising diversity of effects, rather than the unity of a literary masterpiece.

The successes scored by the later Jōruri playwrights were due not to the beauty of their language or any other literary virtue but to their unfailing grasp of the theatrical. Reading a play by Chikamatsu is sometimes more satisfactory than seeing it performed; the plays by his successors have little of his poetry, but often run to bombast or grotesque exaggeration. Their characters rarely suggest believable human beings, but they are superbly effective on the stage. Perhaps the clearest way to show the differences between Chikamatsu and the later playwrights is by comparing parallel passages from Chikamatsu's masterpiece *The Love Suicides at Amijima* (1721) and the adaptation *Shinjū Kamiya Jihei* (1778) by Chikamatsu Hanji and Takeda Bunkichi. At the end of the first act Jihei, convinced by what he has overheard of the conversation between Koharu and his brother, Magoemon, that she is being untrue to him, flings at her the written oaths of fidelity she had given him. Koharu is also obliged to surrender Jihei's written oaths.

> MAGOEMON: One, two, three, four . . . ten . . . twenty-nine. They're all here. There's also a letter from a woman. What's this?
>
> NARRATOR: He starts to unfold it.
>
> KOHARU: That's an important letter. I can't let you see it.
>
> NARRATOR: She clings to Magoemon's arm, but he pushes her away. He holds the letter to the lamplight and examines

the address, "To Miss Koharu from Kamiya Osan." As soon as he reads the words, he casually thrusts the letter into his kimono.

MAGOEMON: Koharu. A while ago I swore by my good fortune as a samurai, but now Magoemon the Miller swears by his good fortune as a businessman that he will show this letter to no one, not even his wife. I alone will read it, then burn it with the oaths. You can trust me. I will not break this oath.[8]

This is the parallel version by Chikamatsu Hanji and Takeda Bunkichi:

MAGOEMON: I'm sure you've got the oaths written by Jihei. Give them back to me, please. Come on, what are you dawdling over? Hurry! Is this it?

NARRATOR: He thrusts his hand into her bosom and pulls out an amulet bag and a letter.

MAGOEMON: I'll take this wastepaper. I'm sure you don't mind parting with it now.

NARRATOR: So saying he reads the address with astonishment.

MAGOEMON: What's this? "To Miss Koharu from Kamiya's house"?

KOHARU: Ohh—that's an important letter. I can't let anyone see it.

NARRATOR: Magoemon holds off the hand that clutches at the letter.

MAGOEMON: Hmmm. Then you acted out of a sense of duty to the customer who wrote this letter?

JIHEI: Brother, which customer of hers sent her that letter? Show it to me for a moment.

MAGOEMON: What difference does it make to you who wrote the letter? You've given up that prostitute, haven't you? Go over there and stay out of the conversation. (*To Koharu.*) Koharu. A while ago I swore by my good fortune as a samurai, but now Magoemon the Miller swears by his good fortune as a businessman that he will not talk of this to anyone, not even his wife or children. Ah, I spoke coldly when I said that among professions none was so base and insincere as a prostitute's. But now that I know you received this letter, it all makes sense, it all makes sense. It wouldn't be too absurd to fear you might commit suicide together. The more I think of it, the funnier and the more pathetic it becomes. It's too much for me. I can feel the tears coming. Hahahahaha.

NARRATOR: Hiding his true feelings behind the laugh he forces, he thanks her in his heart with words his lips cannot pronounce.[9]

In Chikamatsu's play Magoemon says nothing openly to indicate that he is aware Koharu's apparent faithlessness was inspired by the letter from Jihei's wife begging her to save her husband's life. Of course we infer that Magoemon realizes the letter had special significance from his declaration that he will show it to no one, but he does not voice any appreciation, nor does the narrator comment on his feelings. In the revised version everything is spelled out. "Then you acted out of a sense of duty to the customer who wrote this letter?" Magoemon asks, pretending the letter was not from Osan. The mingled emotions he experiences—relief that his brother will not commit suicide, admiration for Koharu's generous gesture, embarrassment over his own denunciation of Koharu as a faithless prostitute—must all be revealed in the laugh he forces even as his tears flow. In literary terms this dramatic situation is bathetic, but on the stage it is unquestionably more exciting than Chikamatsu's understatement. The mixture of laughter and tears at the end afforded the chanter a splendid opportunity to display his virtuoso talents; these two nonliterary elements in a performance—the heroic roar of laughter and the convulsive sobs of despair—came to be considered by the public the ultimate tests of a chanter's ability. The adaptors of Chikamatsu's play also gave the puppet operators greater scope to display their techniques. Chikamatsu's heroine meekly surrenders the amulet bag with the papers, but in the revised version Magoemon must search in her bosom, the traditional hiding place for valuable papers. Jihei, who in the original shows no interest in the mysterious letter, here asks to see it, bringing that puppet into the action. Magoemon orders him to another part of the stage, then in his next speech says certain parts in a soft voice, so that only Koharu can hear, and others ("I spoke coldly . . .") loudly enough for Jihei also to hear. The effectiveness of the revisions is proved by the fact that although Chikamatsu's original version has from time to time been revived, it has never displaced the adaptation in public favor.

The continuing importance of Chikamatsu's dramas in the seventy years after his death is indicated by the many works that borrowed themes and situations from him, as well as by the innumerable, respectful references to him as the great master of the art. Chikamatsu never named a successor, but he had particularly close relations with two dramatists, Matsuda Bunkōdō and Takeda Izumo, the principal figures in Jōruri during the period 1725–45. Chikamatsu's name appears as the "reviser" of two works principally by Bunkōdō and one by Takeda Izumo. He also contributed a preface to the illustrated edition of Izumo's play *Shokatsu Kōmei Kanae Gundan* (1724) in which he praised Izumo's fidelity to his own style: "Everything accords with my own secret techniques; it is like transferring water from one bottle to another."[10]

This preface suggests that Chikamatsu considered Takeda Izumo as a disciple, and possibly as his successor, but Yokoyama believes that Bunkōdō more properly merits that distinction.[11] In any case, the two men were the chief authors at the Takemoto Theater during the period immediately after Chikamatsu's death. There was a problem, however, concerning the identity of Takeda Izumo which was at last resolved by Yuda Yoshio, who determined that there were in fact two men known by that name; the second Takeda (1691–1756) succeeded to the name after the death of the first Takeda Izumo in 1747, previously being called Takeda Koizumo.[12] The first Izumo became the manager of the Takemoto Theater in 1705, at a time when the great Gidayū, having satisfied all his ambitions with the success of *The Love Suicides at Sonezaki*, was threatening to resign from the company. Izumo persuaded him to remain, agreeing to take over administrative responsibilities. From then on Izumo's influence on the theater and on the plays of Chikamatsu became increasingly apparent. The success of *The Battles of Coxinga* has been attributed in part at least to Izumo's suggestions, and the conspicuous use of karakuri stage business in Chikamatsu's late works has even led some critics to consider them as joint ventures with Izumo. Possibly it was Izumo's realization that Chikamatsu was approaching the end of his career that induced him to start writing plays himself.

The first work signed by Takeda Izumo was *Ōtō no Miya Asahi no Yoroi* (The Prince of the Great Pagoda: Armor in the Morning Sunlight, 1723), written in conjunction with Bunkōdō and "corrected" by Chikamatsu. This work reveals the exaggerated complicated shukō and conceptions of duty (giri) that would play such an important part in the later Jōruri.[13]

Some of the shukō that run through this work can be traced back to Chikamatsu, but the connections with the Jōruri of later times are even closer. The substitution of one person for another as a victim, a theme in various plays by Chikamatsu, is here presented in the exaggerated form of child A substituting for child B who in turn is substituting for a young prince. The instant seppuku of one man, as soon as he realizes that another will not join his plot, is echoed again and again in later drama, where the samurai ideal is represented not as one of prudence or long service but as a fanatical insistence on honor which involves seppuku for the least miscalculation. Above all, it is giri, in its new sense, that colors the play. In *The Love Suicides at Amijima* the giri shown by Koharu toward Osan or by Osan toward Koharu arises from mutual respect and from an obligation to behave decently; but in the later Jōruri, giri becomes a formal set of requirements, usually opposed to normal human emotions. Tarozaemon, the aged hero of *The Prince of the Great Pagoda*, is responsible for the deaths of innocent people—his son-in-law, daughter, and grandchild—all because he is bound by a sense of giri toward a master he rejects in his heart. Giri in this play is what Minamoto Ryōen described as "an external social criterion that constrained people and forced them to comply with its dictates."[14] It is not a natural sentiment springing from natural affection or respect, but a painful obligation imposed from without.

Again and again in the later Jōruri we are presented with inhuman situations forced on the persons of the play by giri. Kumagai in *Ichinotani Futaba Gunki* kills his son in order to save Atsumori's life, though up until the last moments we have been led to believe that he took Atsumori's head. This shukō is connected with another characteristic device of the later Jōruri—the revelation of secret feelings quite the opposite of those we have hitherto associated with a particular person. Tarozaemon, who refused to join the plot against the Hōjō and even summoned Hōjō troops to quell the uprising of the Prince of the Great

Pagoda, reveals by his sacrifice where his deepest loyalties lie. Even in Chikamatsu's plays a gruff old man like Jōkan in *Nebiki no Kadomatsu* (The Uprooted Pine, 1718), may at a critical moment disclose the tenderness that actually fills his heart, but in the later plays everything is pushed to extremes: the most inhuman-seeming act often serves to conceal "true feelings" of compassion. Tamate Gozen in *Sesshū Gappō ga Tsuji* (1773) makes her stepson drink a poison that horribly disfigures him, but she does so in the hope that she will provoke her father into killing her, for she knows that the only cure for her stepson's disfigurement is drinking blood from the liver of a woman born, like herself, in the hour, day, month, and year of the Tiger. Her seemingly evil nature is revealed to have been the mask of true compassion.

The more unexpected the disclosure of the true motives of a character, the more the shukō was appreciated by the audiences. Disguised characters, a variation on the same theme, became numerous, and the moment when the true identity was revealed provided a thrill of surprise. When Kumagai, the severe and unbending warrior, removed his armor to disclose he was wearing a priest's robe underneath, the audience was expected to gasp with surprise. It was for such moments, rather than for the poetic beauty of Chikamatsu's masterpieces, that audiences were attracted to the puppet theaters in the eighteenth century.

Matsuda Bunkōdō (active 1722–41) resembled Chikamatsu in his avoidance of extremes of exaggeration and in the pathos he brought to his climactic scenes, but his works suffered in popularity precisely because of their restraint and their lack of startling dramatic incidents.[15] Undoubtedly he tailored his style to fit the talents of the principal chanter of his day, Takemoto Masatayū (1691–1744), for whom Chikamatsu had written the pathetic scenes in the third act of *The Battles of Coxinga,* and he serves as a transition between the age of Chikamatsu, when the play itself was of the greatest importance, and the following age when the dramatist served as the purveyor of vehicles for the chanters. The practice of several men collaborating on a play inevitably tended to weaken the importance of all of them.

The first Takeda Izumo introduced to Jōruri not only the striking stage effects of karakuri but lavish costumes and sets. The theater became a spectacle for the eyes, though in Chikamatsu's day it was primarily for the ears. Izumo's play *Ashiya Dōman Ōuchi Kagami* (1734) was the first to employ puppets operated by three men, as in Bunraku performances today. The second Takeda Izumo, together with his collaborators, wrote the most popular works of the entire repertory: *Natsumatsuri Naniwa Kagami* (Summer Festival, a Mirror of Osaka, 1745), *Sugawara Denju Tenarai Kagami* (Secrets of Calligraphy of the House of Sugawara, 1746), *Yoshitsune Sembonzakura* (Yoshitsune and the Thousand Cherry Trees, 1747), and *Kanadehon Chūshingura*, usually shortened to *Chūshingura* (The Treasury of Loyal Retainers, 1748), a dazzling sequence of masterpieces. With the exception of *Chūshingura*, these plays are today performed only in part, and it is rare to see a more or less complete performance of *Chūshingura*, which takes about eleven hours. But the excerpts, whether staged by puppets or by Kabuki actors, are beloved by audiences that have never seen or read the whole plays.

Secrets of Calligraphy, written by Takeda Izumo, Miyoshi Shōraku (1696–1772), Namiki Senryū (1695–1751), and Takeda Koizumo, has a long and most unwieldy plot.[16] Its materials include legends associated with Sugawara no Michizane (898–981), the scholar and statesman who was exiled because of a rival's machinations, but the main characters in the play are triplet brothers Sakuramaru, Umeōmaru, and Matsuōmaru. Their names, meaning cherry tree, plum tree, and pine, were inspired by the poem Michizane reputedly wrote in exile, in which he expressed his disappointment that although his favorite plum trees had followed him to Kyushu and his cherry tree had withered with grief, the pine tree in his garden seemed unaffected. In the play Matsuōmaru (the pine) seems indifferent to Michizane's exile. He serves Michizane's mortal enemy, Shihei, but at the end he reveals his loyalty by sacrificing his son; he has pretended to be disloyal only so that he might demonstrate in an hour of great need how deep his loyalty actually is.

The play is full of colorful and ingenious scenes that are often revived quite independently. The third act has one famous scene, the carriage-pulling episode, in which the triplet brothers quarrel, striking extravagant postures revelatory of their different personalities: the gentle Sakuramaru, the fierce Umeōmaru, and the seemingly treacherous Matsuōmaru. The act concludes with the seppuku of Sakuramaru. In the fourth act Michizane turns into a thunder god who ascends into the clouds belching fire, but later in the act we have the village-schoolroom scene, the climax of the entire work. Written and played with a realism that contrasts with the fantasy of the previous acts, it never fails to move audiences. The warrior Genzō, who learned the secrets of calligraphy from Michizane, was later disowned for having married without permission. He and his wife now run a village school where they are hiding Kan Shūsai, Michizane's son. The other pupils are all loutish country boys, and when Genzō is told that he must turn over Kan Shūsai's head to a deputy of the villain Shihei, he is desperate, for none of the other boys could pass as a nobleman's son. Fortunately, however, a new boy is brought to the school, and Genzō, noticing his aristocratic features, decides he must kill this boy in order to save Kan Shūsai. He does so, and the "head inspection" carried out by Matsuōmaru is successful. Just at this moment the mother of the slain boy arrives, and Genzō attempts to kill her, to keep her from revealing that the head belonged to her son. She wards off the blow with the son's desk, and a shroud falls out. Genzō and his wife are astonished, but Matsuōmaru cries, "Rejoice, wife! our son has served our lord." Genzō realizes now that the couple deliberately sent their son to the school, fully expecting that he would substitute the boy's head for Kan Shūsai's. Genzō tells the parents how bravely the boy stuck out his neck when told he was to die in Kan Shūsai's place. The parents, rejoicing and wretched at the same time, take the body of their son to a burial place, declaring to the end that it is Kan Shūsai's. The last act, a brief one, depicts how Michizane, now a lightning god, kills the villain Shihei; at the very end the scenery parts to reveal the Shinto shrine sacred to Michizane's memory.

It is hard to imagine any other theater but Jōruri in which this play could be presented in entirety. Not only is the thread of the plot tenuous, but there is no consistency in the characterization: the fierce Matsuōmaru of the earlier scenes becomes the suffering man of the fourth act without even any great lapse of time to account for the change. The decision he and his wife make to send their son to Genzō's school is based on their assumption that Genzō (1) will try to save Kan Shūsai's life by killing another child in his place; (2) will not have a son of his own or any other presentable child to kill; and (3) will not hesitate to kill a child who has just been placed in his care. So sure are they of what will happen that Matsuōmaru's wife packs a shroud for the boy in his desk; at the right moment, when she protects herself from Genzō's sword with the desk, it opens and the shroud drops to the floor. A few moments later Matsuōmaru and his wife both remove their outer robes to reveal they are dressed in mourning garments of white. Nothing is unforeseen.

Yet, however absurd the play may appear on the printed page, in performance it succeeds magnificently. Tradition has it that when the collaborating dramatists were first informed that their subject would be Sugawara no Michizane, Miyoshi Shōraku proposed that each man take as his theme the parting between a parent and child. The second act accordingly ended with Michizane going off into exile, leaving behind his daughter; the third act with Sakuramaru's suicide, leaving his father; and the fourth act with Matsuōmaru inspecting his son's head and giving him a final blessing.[17] Perhaps this is actually how the play was written; it would help account for the conspicuous lack of unity among the acts.

It may be wondered why audiences consisting mainly of townsmen so enjoyed plays depicting the lofty ideals of the samurai, and did not prefer works, like Chikamatsu's sewamono, that portrayed a world closer to them. Some critics have suggested that life was so hard in the Tokugawa period for townsmen that they could identify their sorrows with the extreme tragedies they witnessed in the theater. But surely head inspections were not common, and a merchant was rarely expected to kill his own child to save the child of a master. Such scenes may have struck chords in the subconscious, like the Greek dramas or Nō plays, but it is even more likely that the townsmen, no matter how little disposed to perform martial activity, fancied themselves as heroes ready to sacrifice everything in the service of a master. The humdrum, confined nature of daily life during the Tokugawa period inspired this special form of escapist fiction; a merchant could otherwise escape by visiting the brothels, where he could imagine he was Prince Genji, dallying with Lady Rokujō. In the theater the townsman could become a resolute martial hero, equally prepared to conquer an enemy army or to throw away his life, without a flicker of hesitation, to preserve his honor from any blemish.

Little in the behavior of contemporary samurai was likely to elicit the admiration of the townsmen. Some were impoverished and deeply in the merchants' debt, and others lived as rōnin, men with a sword to hire. The samurai virtues seemed definitely to belong to the past, the world of fiction. Suddenly word was spread about the vendetta executed on the fourteenth night of the twelfth moon of the fifteenth year of Genroku (January 30, 1703). Forty-six rōnin, formerly samurai of Lord Asano of Akō, had broken into the mansion of their late master's enemy, Lord Kira of Kōzuke, and killed him. Two months later these rōnin, headed by Ōishi Kuranosuke, were ordered by the government to commit suicide.

The story attracted wide attention. Twelve days after the rōnin committed suicide a Kabuki play on the subject was performed in Edo for three days before the authorities stopped it.[18] In the sixth month of 1706 Chikamatsu staged at the Takemoto Theater a one-act work on the theme called *Goban Taiheiki*, the first of many Jōruri about the loyal retainers. Although a slight work when compared to the later masterpieces, it established many of the conventions that would be followed when adapting the historical events for the stage. The period was shifted back to the days of the *Taiheiki*—the 1330s—and some of the characters were given names from that period: Kira became the historical Kō no Moronao, and Asano became Enya Hangan. Other names were only slightly disguised by Chikamatsu: Ōishi Kuranosuke became Ōboshi Yuranosuke, etc.

Chikamatsu's rival, Ki no Kaion, also treated the vendetta in *Onikage Musashi Abumi*, presented at the Toyotake Theater in 1713. It too exerted some influence on *Chūshingura*, but the most important source was *Chūshin Kogane no Tanjaku* (A Golden Poem-Card of Loyalty), by Namiki Sōsuke and others, performed at the Toyotake Theater in 1732. In this work we find some of the *Chūshingura* subplots, including the stories of Hayano Kampei and of the low-ranking samurai Heiemon, who at first was not permitted to participate in the vendetta.

All earlier works were eclipsed, however, by *The Treasury of Loyal Retainers*, presented at the Takemoto Theater in 1748.

Although the work extends to eleven acts and there are many subplots, the great central theme of the vendetta unifies the work in a manner unique among eighteenth-century Jōruri. The steadily increasing influence of Kabuki on the puppet theater is revealed by the emphasis on the dialogue, rather than on the descriptions recited by the narrator, and by the attention given to effective occasions for the display of the personalities of the characters. It is true that many of the characters are stereotypes, in the manner expected of the puppet theater. No distinction is made among equally virtuous samurai wives, and no shade of ambiguity is given to the totally loyal Yuranosuke or to the totally evil Moronao. The great variety of types makes us forget that each one is not a rounded character. Similarly, the same actions performed under different circumstances by persons of different status appear strikingly unalike; the seppuku scenes of Enya Hangan and of Hayano Kampei produce totally dissimilar impressions because the former is carried out with ritual dignity by a daimyo, but the latter takes place in the mean surroundings of a hunter's cottage. No matter how highflown the sentiment may be, they never lose contact with the reality of the speakers. Shukō are employed, but they are not the obvious ones (a head inspection, etc.), and they seem to grow naturally from the story. A realism that owes much to Kabuki, as well as to the nature of the main theme, gives the play its prevalent tone, even when it strays on occasion into exaggerated sentiments.

It is difficult to determine which of the three dramatists wrote which acts, but there is reason to believe that Namiki Senryū who (under the name Namiki Sōsuke) had written *A Golden Poem-Card of Loyalty* provided the general scheme of the play.[19] Other evidence is found in the informal book of criticism *Chūshingura Okame Hyōban* (A Bystander Looks at *Chūshingura*), written by Jippensha Ikku in 1803. Ikku states that Miyoshi Shōraku wrote the second act and Senryū the fourth. Probably each playwright was assigned one suicide scene; we may infer that Senryū wrote Enya's suicide in the fourth act, Izumo the sixth act with Kampei's suicide, and Shōraku the ninth act with Honzō's self-provoked death. The eleven-act structure of the play made it impossible to follow traditions evolved for the five-act jidaimono, but the eleven acts were apparently divided into five playing units.[20] The three dramatists had unequal abilities, but somehow the play not only holds together, it remains at a remarkably high level. The weakest parts in literary terms are the second and ninth acts, both by Shōraku, who was an experienced hack rather than a first-class dramatist. The prevailing style was that of Takeda Izumo.[21]

The qualities of Izumo's style most praised by Jippensha Ikku were the unpredictable twists he gave to the story of *Chūshingura* and the directness of his language, both being contrasted with Chikamatsu's poetic but natural style. Izumo is certainly a more prosaic writer than Chikamatsu, but he resorts to transparently theatrical effects. Quite apart from the style, however, his story is irresistible. The main theme is the loyalty of Ōboshi Yuranosuke. As it happens his master, Enya Hangan, is a good man (the historical Lord Asano was certainly less admirable), but even if he were wicked, the feudal obedience of Yuranosuke would have been no less absolute. Yuranosuke's loyalty is enhanced by his intelligence and foresight; the vendetta he organizes is brilliantly planned and not a rash attack.

It was a grave responsibility to be a samurai, but also a privilege. Kampei desperately wants to join the avenging league, but is rejected by the others because at a critical moment he failed his lord. The fact that Kampei's misdeed was unintentional does not render him less culpable. Only by his suicide, the ultimate proof of sincerity, can he qualify to join the league, as a ghostly presence. Heiemon, on the other hand, has committed no fault, but at first he too is ineligible to join the avengers because he is only an *ashigaru*, the lowest rank of samurai. He is accorded the privilege of dying like a samurai only after Yuranosuke has discovered the depth of his loyalty. Gihei, the unselfish merchant, to the end cannot be permitted to accompany the attackers, though he is no less imbued by loyalty than any samurai.

The loyalty of Honzō to his master, Wakasanosuke, is made to seem less attractive than Yuranosuke's, even though he saves his master's life. In the second act Honzō swears he will not interfere with Wakasanosuke's plan to exact vengeance of Moronao, and even demonstrates how his master should use his sword. But Honzō secretly approaches Moronao with a bribe that deflects his insolence and saves Wakasanosuke. It is impossible to think of Yuranosuke resorting to bribery. Later, after Enya Hangan has slashed Moronao, Honzō restrains him from further assault. Such prudence, a virtue in the eyes of most men, incurs not the gratitude but the hatred of the loyal retainers. Honzō redeems himself toward the end of the play by provoking Yuranosuke's son Rikiya into killing him; his death atones for conduct unworthy of a true samurai.

Although there are highly dramatic scenes involving other characters, the play owes its fame to the portrayal of Yuranosuke and his loyalty to his master. His breathless arrival, at the very moment of Enya's seppuku, is superbly conceived. Jippensha Ikku stated that Takeda Izumo suggested to Namiki Senryū, the author of this act, that Yuranosuke rush onto the scene in a state of utter confusion and wild agitation, quite at variance with his normal composure.

The great scene at the Ichiriki Teahouse shows Yuranosuke in every mood and attitude. It opens with three loyal samurai arriving at the house, hoping to discuss plans with Yuranosuke. One says, "At first I thought it was some trick of his to throw the enemy off the track, but he has been a little bit too convincing in the way he has thrown himself into his pleasures. I don't understand it." Yuranosuke appears, and the samurai ask when the league of avengers is to leave for Kamakura, but he puts them off with a foolish song. Next, Heiemon describes his own valiant efforts to join the league. Yuranosuke teases him: "It's quite true I felt a certain amount of indignation—about as big as a flea's head split by a hatchet—and tried forming a league of some forty or fifty men, but what a crazy notion that was!" He ends up with the cry, "Oh, when I hear the samisens playing like that I can't resist!" The loyal samurai leave, dismayed and disgusted. Then Rikiya, Yuranosuke's son, arrives and goes to the room where his father apparently lies in a drunken stupor. He clinks the hilt of his sword against the scabbard, and Yuranosuke instantly awakens, totally sober. He takes the letter Rikiya gives him and sends the boy away. Immediately afterward the villain Kudayū appears. Yuranosuke becomes a yet different man, the clever adversary.

KUDAYŪ: There's no point in pretending, Yuranosuke. Your disposition is, in fact—

YURANOSUKE: You think it's a trick to enable me to attack the enemy?

KUDAYŪ: Of course I do.

YURANOSUKE: How you flatter me! I thought you'd laugh at me, taking me for a fool, a madman, who's still a slave to physical pleasure even though he's over forty. But you tell me it's all part of a scheme so that I can attack the enemy! Thank you, good Kudayū. You've made me happy.

Kudayū tests Yuranosuke by offering him some octopus to eat with his saké. Yuranosuke cheerfully accepts a piece. Kudayū reminds him that the next day is the anniversary of Enya Hangan's death, and that it is particularly important to avoid eating fish the night before. He asks, "Are you going to eat that octopus and think nothing of it?" Yuranosuke replies, "Of course I'll eat it. Or have you had word that Lord Enya has turned into an octopus?"

Yuranosuke staggers off to join the women in the next room. He forgets his sword, unthinkable of a samurai. Kudayū examines the blade and discovers it is as "rusty as a red sardine." He leaves, more or less reassured that Yuranosuke is harmless. But he is still worried about the letter Rikiya brought, so he hides under the veranda to observe Yuranosuke further. Yuranosuke returns, singing, but once he is sure everyone has gone, he opens the scroll of the letter and reads. Startled by the sound of Okaru's hair ornament striking the ground, he looks up and sees that she has been reading the letter in her mirror. At once he changes again: this time he pretends to flirt with Okaru, exchanging rather obscene jokes before he finally proposes marriage. He goes off to pay the money for her "ransom." Heiemon appears and soon apprises his sister Okaru of the meaning of Yuranosuke's gesture. She decides to kill herself, in order to reassure Yuranosuke that she will not betray the secret contained in the letter she read, but Yuranosuke returns and prevents her. He has heard everything, and he praises the loyalty of brother and sister. Then he returns to the room where he read the letter and suddenly drives the sword he has wrenched from Okaru through the floor to stab Kudayū hiding below.

In this act Yuranosuke registers an extremely wide variety of attitudes, but his every action is dictated by his sense of loyalty and by the determination to carry through his mission. The role is certainly better suited to an actor than a puppet; it is probably the greatest of all Kabuki parts. The writing itself is not remarkably beautiful, but the character is drawn with exceptional skill. Even the sometimes mechanical tricks of staging serve the purpose of enhancing the role.

The success of *Chūshingura* was immediate. It was soon being performed by Kabuki actors in Kyoto and Osaka, and in Edo no less than three rival companies performed the work. At the Takemoto Theater, however, the run was cut short by the quarrel that broke out between the puppet operator Yoshida Bunzaburō and the chanter Takemoto Konodayū. Bunzaburō's skill had won him so high a reputation he was known as "the treasure of the Takemoto Theater," a sign not only of his competence but of the new prestige of the operators, who formerly had ranked far below the chanters. Bunzaburō asked Konodayū to alter his recitation of a passage in the ninth act so as to make it easier to move the Yuranosuke puppet. Konodayū, annoyed by this lack of respect for the chanter's prerogatives, bluntly refused. The quarrel eventually involved everyone in the company, and when a compromise proposal failed, Konodayū and the playwright Namiki Senryū, among others, shifted to the rival Toyotake Theater. These changes of allegiance not only obscured the differences in performance that had always distinguished the Takemoto and Toyotake styles of Jōruri, but in the end threatened the survival of both theaters.[22]

It is paradoxical that a great success should have had such disastrous consequences, but regardless of where *Chūshingura* was performed or by whom, its popularity was unshaken. It may have been the first major work of Japanese literature to appear in a foreign language: a Chinese translation into an elegant colloquial style was published in 1794.

Chūshingura represented the apogee of the great period of Jōruri. During the following decade Jōruri plays increasingly became display pieces for the virtuoso talents of chanters and operators. The chanters delivered with great expression and convincing realism the extremes of emotions, and the operators used the improved puppets to display delicate shadings of movement and emotion. The plays were full of ingenuity, with hidden meanings behind hidden meanings. A good example is *Ichinotani*

Futaba Gunki (An Account of the Battle of Young Sprouts at Ichinotani, 1751), of which Namiki Senryū wrote the first three acts before his death.

The story is ultimately derived from the famous episode in *The Tale of the Heike* describing how the warrior Kumagai killed the young Heike general Atsumori. In this play, however, Yoshitsune wishes Kumagai to spare the life of Atsumori because of his royal blood, and leaves for Kumagai's edification a cryptic signboard set before a cherry tree in bloom: *Isshi wo kiraba isshi wo kirubeshi.* The surface meaning seems to be, "If you cut off a branch, we will cut off a finger." But Kumagai, as we learn later, interprets the signboard as meaning, "If you are going to cut down a son, you should cut down your own son." Accordingly, he kills not Atsumori but his own son, Kojirō. This type of ingenuity is likely to seem absurd to modern readers—what if the surface meaning was in fact the correct one? But as part of a Jōruri or Kabuki play, and surrounded by its special atmosphere, the effect is electrifying when Kumagai, having presented for Yoshitsune's inspection the head of his own son, lifts the signboard that stood before the cherry tree and, showing it to Yoshitsune, asks if he has correctly interpreted its meaning. At the end Kumagai removes his helmet and armor to reveal that his head is shaven and he is wearing the black robes of a priest. He exits with the words, "Sixteen years—was it all a dream?" a reference to the life of his son.

The scene is further complicated by the presence of Kumagai's wife, Sagami, and of Atsumori's mother, Fujinokata. Each assumes the head, concealed in a box, must be Atsumori's. When Sagami finally sees it, she is horrified to discover it is her own son's, but she must hide her grief; when Fujinokata sees it she is astonished that the head is *not* Atsumori's, and she too must hide her emotions after the first, uncontrollable reaction of surprise. The dialogue is realistic, rather than poetic, and the whole work is clearly better suited to actors than to puppets. The innumerable twists in the original story of Kumagai and Atsumori were meant to surprise the first audiences by the revelations of what *really* had occurred. Even when these shukō became familiar through repeated viewings, they provided opportunities for matchless displays of histrionics.

During the years following the production of *Battle of Young*

Sprouts in 1751 many disasters struck the world of Jōruri. Takeda Izumo died in 1756 and Yoshida Bunzaburō in 1760. Both the Takemoto and Toyotake theaters were destroyed by fire, in 1759 and 1760 respectively, and even though subsequently rebuilt, they were beset by financial troubles. In 1765 the Toyotake Theater and in 1767 the Takemoto Theater was yielded to Kabuki troupes. Although both puppet theaters were reestablished, they were constantly in danger of collapse, and it is difficult now to trace their different reincarnations. Rival Jōruri companies were formed not only in Osaka but in Edo, and the competition from Kabuki became ever severer.

But there was still a silver age to come in the person of Chikamatsu Hanji (1725–83), whose career began in 1751 as one of five playwrights collaborating in a work presented at the Takemoto Theater. His first important work was *Honchō Nijūshi Kō* (The Japanese Twenty-four Examples of Filial Piety, 1766). He followed this success with *Keisei Awa no Naruto* (1768), *Ōmi Genji Senjin Yakata* (1769), *Imoseyama Onna Teikin* (Household Teachings for Women at Imo and Se Mountains, 1771), and *Shimpan Utazaimon* (1780). These works were marked by a further intensification of features already observed in Jōruri: complicated and exaggerated shukō, realistic language in the dialogue, a Kabuki manner of performance, elaborate settings, etc. Yokoyama Tadashi finds in the works of this period "an attitude toward the works created that reveals a loss of confidence as a writer and of seriousness, or else a negative, servile attitude toward the spectators."[23] No doubt the difficulties under which the Jōruri theater labored at this time induced a desperate seeking for the public's favor, even if it meant writing works that the dramatist himself knew were nonsense. The miracle is that Hanji's plays were so well written that they are still among the most popular plays of both Jōruri and Kabuki theaters.

Chikamatsu Hanji was the son of Chikamatsu Monzaemon's friend Hozumi Ikan, the Confucian scholar who wrote *Naniwa Miyage*. He grew up with such great admiration for Chikamatsu that he followed in his footsteps as a dramatist and even took his name. His talents were fostered by Takeda Izumo; beginning in 1751 he contributed in a minor capacity to plays written by Izumo and his associates. After a long apprenticeship he became the chief dramatist of the Takemoto Theater in 1763. Most of his dramas were jidaimono, but *Shimpan Utazaimon* shows what great talent he had for sewamono as well. By this time, however, the two genres tended to become mingled; part of each jidaimono or sewamono would be in the other style.[24] The plays are closer to Kabuki than to the earlier Jōruri in the ramifications of their endless subplots, which strike us today as annoyingly complicated. Each of the famous plays is known for one or two scenes: the incense-burning scene in *Filial Piety*, the scene at Moritsuna's camp from *Ōmi Genji Senjin Yakata*, the scene in the mountains from *Household Teachings*, and the Nozaki Village scene from *Shimpan Utazaimon*. These excerpts, deservedly celebrated, are today the mainstays of both Bunraku and Kabuki theaters. They are mutually different in every way, except for the brillance of their shukō; we remember the incense-burning scene for the moment when Lady Yaegaki, carrying a magical helmet over a bridge, sees reflected in the water below the fox spirit guarding the helmet; or the moment in the scene at Moritsuna's camp when Moritsuna, inspecting the head he supposes is that of his brother, an enemy general, discovers it is a stranger's; or the pathos of the Nozaki Village scene when Omitsu, dressed in bridal robes, removes her hat and outer kimono to reveal she has become a nun, in order that Osome and Hisamatsu may marry.

The most impressive of Hanji's plays is *Household Teachings for Women at Imo and Se Mountains*. The title refers to the mountains that figure importantly in the third act; their names mean "wife" and "husband," and the love of devoted wives for their husbands is suggested in the rest of the title.[25] *Household Teaching* was such a great success that it temporarily restored the fortunes of the Takemoto Theater, but it was no less successful on the Kabuki stage. One gets the impression that Hanji was gallantly supporting a dying theater and that he might more profitably have written for Kabuki. His last work, written in 1783, the year of his death, was *Igagoe Dōchū Sugoroku*, which was closely based on a Kabuki play of 1777. The long period of adaptation from Jōruri to Kabuki was coming to an end.

Hanji was the last important writer of Jōruri, but there were a few conspicuously successful works by minor dramatists. *Sesshū Gappō ga Tsuji* by Suga Sensuke and Wakatake Fuemi is famous for one scene that has distant overtones of the story of Phaedra and Hippolytus: Tamate Gozen makes advances to her stepson, but is spurned by him, arousing her fury.[26] *Hade Sugata Onna Maiginu* (1772), by Takemoto Saburobei and others, is known especially for Osono's monologue, one of the highlights of the entire Jōruri repertory. This play, based on the love suicides of the courtesan Sankatsu and the merchant Hanshichi in 1695, was the best of a long series of works inspired by the event. Although written in a realistic language close to everyday speech and telling an interesting story, the play has little literary interest; it has never been given in entirety since the first performances.[27]

Shinrei Yaguchi no Watashi (The Miracle at the Yaguchi Ferry, 1770), by Hiraga Gennai is also remembered mainly for one scene. Unlike most of Gennai's other writings, frivolous in tone, this is a deadly serious drama set in the Kamakura period. It was first performed in Edo, an indication that the shift of center of culture from Osaka to Edo had occurred even in Jōruri. *Ehon Taikōki* by Chikamatsu Yanagi and others, first performed in 1802, keeps its place in the repertory. Yanagi has been called the last author of Jōruri, and the description is very nearly literally true. Only two or three later works expressly written for the Jōruri theater are still staged, notably *Shō Utsushi Asagao Nikki* (1832), a posthumous work by Chikamatsu Tokusō (1751–1810), and *Tsubosaka Reigenki* (The Miracle at Tsubosaka, 1887) by Toyozawa Dampei (1827–98). None of them is of literary interest. Other "new" works for the Bunraku Theater have either been drawn directly from Kabuki or Nō or else are occasional pieces that have not survived their first runs.

Jōruri was overcome by Kabuki after several decades of flirting with its themes and techniques. This does not mean that the puppet theater ceased to draw customers, but that it became a provincial entertainment and its repertory no longer grew. It enjoyed a brief period of great popularity at the end of the nineteenth century, but it was wholly incapable of representing the new era, and it survived as a nostalgic reminder of a vanishing past. The puppet theater, thanks to governmental support, maintains an etiolated existence to this day, but it will not be necessary to refer to it again in this history. Its period of glory ended when Osaka was displaced as the cultural capital, but it had by then supplied Kabuki with about half the plays of its repertory and Japanese literature with many of its masterpieces of drama.

NOTES

1. Quoted by Yuda Yoshio, *Bunraku Jōruri Shū*, p. 8. The original work, *Jōruri-fu*, was written after 1767.
2. Tamura Nishio and Nakauchi Chōji, *Gidayū Zenshū*, I, pp. 354–55.
3. Yokoyama Tadashi, *Jōruri Ayatsuri Shibai no Kenkyū*, p. 594.
4. *Ibid.*, p. 597.
5. *Ibid.*, p. 594.
6. *Ibid.*, p. 593.
7. Yuda, p. 6.
8. Keene, *Major Plays of Chikamatsu*, p. 402.
9. Chikaishi Yasuaki, *Jōruri Meisaku Shū*, I, pp. 182–84.
10. Chikaishi Yasuaki, *Ayatsuri Jōruri no Kenkyū*, I, p. 243.
11. Yokoyama, p. 587.
12. See Yuda Yoshio, "Takeda Izumo no Shūmei to Sakuhin."
13. For a summary, see Appendix, 3.
14. Minamoto Ryōen, *Giri to Ninjō*, p. 155.
15. See Yokoyama, p. 612.
16. There is a free translation given in Earle Ernst, *Three Japanese Plays*.
17. Suwa Haruo, "Jōruri no Dentō," p. 410.
18. Tsurumi Makoto, *Jōruri Shū*, II, p. 55.
19. See Otoba Hiromu, *Jōruri Shū*, I, p. 35.
20. See Toita Yasuji, *Chūshingura*, p. 106.
21. Jippensha Ikku, *Chūshingura Okame Hyōban*, pp. 453–56.
22. Suwa, pp. 414–17.
23. Yokoyama, p. 626.
24. Tsurumi, p. 14.
25. For a summary, see Appendix, 4.
26. See Keene, "The Hippolytus Triangle East and West."
27. Yuda, *Bunraku Jōruri Shū*, p. 18.

BIBLIOGRAPHY

Chikaishi Yasuaki. *Ayatsuri Jōruri no Kenkyū*. Tokyo: Kazama Shobō, 1961.

———. *Jōruri Meisaku Shū*. Tokyo: Dai Nippon Yūbenkai Kōdansha, 1950.

Ernst, Earle. *Three Japanese Plays*. London: Oxford University Press, 1959.

Fujimura Tsukuru (ed.). *Nihon Bungaku Daijiten*. Tokyo: Shinchōsha, 1956.

Jippensha Ikku. *Chūshingura Okame Hyōban*, in Teikoku Bunko series, vol. 35, *Akō Fukushū Zenshū*. Tokyo: Hakubunkan, 1909.

Kawatake Shigetoshi. *Nihon Engeki Zenshi*. Tokyo: Iwanami Shoten, 1959.

——— (ed.). *Jōruri Kenkyū Bunken Shūsei*. Tokyo: Hokkō Shobō, 1944.

Keene, Donald. "The Hippolytus Triangle East and West," in *Yearbook of Comparative and General Literature*. No. 11. Bloomington, Ind.: Indiana University Press, 1962.

———. *Major Plays of Chikamatsu*. New York: Columbia University Press, 1961.

——— (trans.). *Chūshingura*. New York: Columbia University Press, 1971.

Kuroki Kanzō. *Chikamatsu Igo*. Tokyo: Daitō Shuppansha, 1942.

Minamoto Ryōen. *Giri to Ninjō*. Tokyo: Chūō Kōron Sha, 1969.

Otoba Hiromu. *Jōruri Shū*, I, in Nihon Bungaku Taikei series. Tokyo: Iwanami Shoten, 1960.

Shuzui Kenji. *Chikamatsu Hanji Shū*, in Nihon Koten Zensho series. Tokyo: Asahi Shimbun Sha, 1949.

Sonoda Tamio. *Jōruri Sakusha no Kenkyū*. Tokyo: Tōkyōdō, 1944.

Suwa Haruo. "Jōruri no Dentō," in Nihon Bungaku no Rekishi series, vol. VII. Tokyo: Kadokawa Shoten, 1967.

Tamura Nishio and Nakauchi Chōji. *Gidayū Zenshū*. Tokyo: Seibundō Shinkōsha, 1937.

Toita Yasuji. *Chūshingura*. Tokyo: Sōgensha, 1957.

Tsurumi Makoto. *Jōruri Shū*, in Nihon Koten Bungaku Taikei series. Tokyo: Iwanami Shoten, 1959.

———. *Takeda Izumo Shū*, in Nihon Koten Zensho series. Tokyo: Asahi Shimbun Sha, 1956.

Yokoyama Tadashi. *Jōruri Ayatsuri Shibai no Kenkyū*. Tokyo: Kazama Shobō, 1963.

Yuda Yoshio. *Bunraku Jōruri Shū*, in Nihon Koten Bungaku Taikei series. Tokyo: Iwanami Shoten, 1965.

———. "Takeda Izumo no Shūmei to Sakuhin," in *Kinsei Bungei*, vol. I, no. 1 (1954).

———. "Takeda Ōmi, Izumo no Daidai," in *Yamanobenomichi*, vol. I, no. 1 (1954).

———. "Takeda Ōmi, Izumo no Daidai Tsuikō," in *Yamanobenomichi*, vol. I, no. 2 (1956).

CHAPTER 13
WAKA POETRY
KOKUGAKU AND THE WAKA

The characteristic verse form of the pre-modern period was, of course, haikai, but immense quantities of waka were also composed by men at the court and in every part of the country. Most of this poetry is undistinguished, despite the care, scholarship, and intelligence everywhere apparent. In reading the works of even the most accomplished waka poets we find ourselves looking not for any particular qualities of either the men or their age but for telltale influences from the past, whether revealed in archaisms and other stylistic features or in the attempts to evoke ideals associated with distant epochs.

The orthodox court poets in Kyoto, known as *dōjō* (a term

designating nobles privileged to appear before the emperor), continued to write in the traditions of the Nijō school (a conservative school of waka) and to revere secret teachings; but elsewhere there were many waka poets, unable to participate in this exclusive society, who turned for guidance to other poetic traditions. The most important group, certainly from the beginning of the seventeenth century until the middle of the eighteenth century, were the poets who rediscovered the *Manyōshū* and attempted not only to absorb its poetry but to revivify its ideals. In most cases these men were associated with *kokugaku*, or "national learning," so called to distinguish it from Confucian or Buddhist learning. Later in the eighteenth century another important group of poets would insist on the supremacy of the *Kokinshū* as a source of poetic guidance, and a few notable poets made *Shin Kokinshū* their ideal. In a sense all these men, regardless of which ancient anthology they preferred, were expressing contemporary tastes, but their waka lacked the vibrant quality so apparent in haikai poetry. Only toward the end of the Tokugawa period do we begin to detect individual, recognizable voices, as even the docile waka poets showed their dissatisfaction with the hamstringing restrictions placed on their expression by the dead traditions of the past.

Japanese scholars often divide the waka of the period according to various schools, but it might be simpler to make a division into two unequal periods: from 1600 to about 1770, when the *Manyōshū* was a dominating influence; and from 1770 to 1867, when poets professed to be writing their own thoughts in their own language. This chapter deals with the former period.

The impression of sameness in the waka of the early Tokugawa period is deceptive. An expert can easily detect the differences in style and vocabulary between the dōjō poets of the conservative court traditions, headed by those entrusted with the secret transmission of the *Kokinshū* and other medieval lore, and the poets who displayed their dissatisfaction with the courtly traditions of the *Kokinshū* by turning to the *Manyōshū* or even more ancient poetry, and who sought to express their philosophic or political convictions in what they wrote. But no matter how divergent the views of the different poets, the imagery tended to be extraordinarily similar. Cherry blossoms and maple leaves, spring mists and autumn rains figured in the poetry of every school. Some poets, rebelling against the poetic diction approved at the court, used forgotten words from the ancient folk songs, but no one wished to follow the haikai poets in expanding their vocabulary with modern language or words of Chinese origin. The result was that a poem inspired by deeply felt emotions could hardly be distinguished from the most conventional expressions of grief over falling blossoms or deer separated from their mates.

Kamo no Mabuchi (1697–1769), perhaps the finest waka poet of the period, proclaimed "sincerity" (*makoto*) to be his poetic ideal, following the *Manyōshū*; but, because he chose to express his feelings in a language a thousand years old, his poems often seem tepid even when the occasion demands powerful, direct expression. A poem written in 1745, when Kamo no Mabuchi was forty-eight, bears this preface:

> When I was told that my mother had died I could hardly believe it was true: I had spent seven years away from her, able to see her only in dreams. But the person who informed me was in tears. I had supposed our separation would last only a little while longer, and had long looked forward to spending her old age with her, going together to different places, living in one house. But what a vain and sad world it proved to be! What am I to do now?

He appended this verse:

karigane no	I had hoped we would stay
yoriau koto wo	Close together as wild geese,
tanomishi mo	But my hopes were in vain:
munashikarikeri	The village of holy Yoshino.[1]
mi Yoshino no sato	

Read in conjunction with the preface we can tell that the waka is intended to suggest Mabuchi's grief that he will be unable to show his mother the sights of Yoshino, as he had long planned. This regret was undoubtedly heartfelt, but how much less the poem says than the prose! Mention of Yoshino, the historic site that figures in countless waka, adds no touch of personal grief; besides, the reference is unintelligible without the preface. The waka form itself was in a sense to blame, since it is too short to express all that Mabuchi said in his preface; but if his conception of what was "poetic" had not been so narrow and conventional he might have created a more moving and individual impression.

A disparity between literary theory and literary practice was typical of most pre-modern waka poets. However much Kada no Azumamaro—to name one poet—exalted the simplicity of the *Manyōshū*, his own poetry was dotted with pivot words, "related words," and the rest of the poetic baggage of the past. The waka poetry of the period, on the whole, is unsuccessful, despite flashes of life and excellence; on the other hand, the literary scholarship associated with the poetry, especially the recovery of the *Manyōshū*, ranks among the finest achievements of the pre-modern period.

The composition of waka at this time acquired a nonliterary significance that sometimes, even for the poets themselves, took precedence over artistic values. Poets admired the *Kojiki* and *Manyōshū* not so much for their literary beauty as for their uniquely Japanese qualities, and they imitated the ancient poetry because they believed this was necessary in order to understand the pristine Japanese virtues.[2] Most of the kokugaku scholars wrote poetry more as a duty than because deep emotions had demanded expression. The most important literary dispute—over *Kokka Hachiron* (Eight Essays on Japanese Poetry, 1742) by Kada no Arimaro (1706–51)—revolved especially around Arimaro's opinion that "Poetry is obviously of no value in governing the nation and does not help in daily life either."[3] This statement specifically denied a typical Confucian justification of poetry, as well as the kokugaku belief that studying and imitating the poetry of the Japanese past could inspire even a modern man with simple and noble virtues. The furor raged over an essentially philosophic question, rather than any challenge to established ideas on the language, form, or content of poetry. Writing waka, at a time when the best poets of the country were devoting themselves to haikai, was justified in terms of devotion to sacred Japanese ideals. Little of the passion engendered by the *Eight Essays* dispute showed itself in the poetry, suggesting the degree to which conventions and habits had deprived the waka of its vitality, even in the hands of men of consecrated purpose.

YŪSAI AND CHŌSHŌSHI

No sharp break divided the waka of the early Tokugawa period from the poetry of the past. Hosokawa Yūsai (1534–1610), the most respected poet and the leader of the dōjō faction, devoted his life to preserving tradition, as he sometimes stated in his poetry:

Shikishima no	I shall look up
michi no hikari mo	At the light shed by the Way
aogimin	Of Shikishima
kotoba no tama no	As I spread out the numbers
kazu wo hirogete	Of jewels of words.[4]

The Way of Shikishima—the art of Japanese poetry—inspired his reverential glance, and he expressed himself in the traditional vocabulary. In 1600 when Yūsai taught Prince Tomohito the *Kokin Denju*—the secret traditions of the *Kokinshū*—he wrote this poem:

inishie mo	Words preserve
ima mo kawaranu	Seeds of the heart
yo no naka ni	Unchanged in this world
kokoro no tane wo	Both in ancient times
nokosu koto no ha	And in the present.

The belief that men's emotions had not changed, despite the surface differences in the language used over the centuries to describe them, recurs often in writings on poetry of the period, sometimes as a reason for imitating ancient words and thoughts, sometimes to suggest the contrary, that language need not be archaic provided the sentiments are eternal.

Yūsai's poems rarely ventured beyond the low-keyed style of the Nijō school, but each departure, however slight, has been eagerly noted by commentators as evidence of a "new attitude."[5] In his poetic theories too Yūsai was a medieval poet; his greatest contribution to the poetry of his day was indirect: he owned a manuscript of the *Manyōshū* and interested his pupils in delving into this collection, though it had become almost unintelligible because of the long hiatus in the study of the peculiar script and diction. Two of Yūsai's pupils, Matsunaga Teitoku and Kinoshita

Chōshōshi, experimented with using *Manyōshū* archaisms in their poetry, and Chōshōshi even attempted to evoke the *Manyōshū* spirit, though his poems can hardly be said to resemble those in that great collection.

Kinoshita Chōshōshi (1569–1649), an appealing figure, was certainly the best waka poet of the early seventeenth century. He came from a minor samurai family that rose to great importance thanks to fortunate marriages: his aunt became Hideyoshi's wife and his younger sister married Tokugawa Ieyasu's fifth son. Chōshōshi's services to Hideyoshi were rewarded with the important castle of Obama in Wakasa, but Hideyoshi's death in 1598 cast a shadow over his career. At the time of the Battle of Sekigahara in 1600 Chōshōshi was faced with a hopeless dilemma: when ordered by Ieyasu to defend Fushimi Castle he could not make up his mind whether to obey this relative by marriage or throw in his lot with another relative, Hideyoshi's son. In the end he seems to have refused to make a choice, and fled instead to a place of retreat in Kyoto. He was deprived of his fief, but his Tokugawa family connections preserved him from greater harm. He led the rest of his life in genteel poverty at his retreat in the Higashiyama district, frequently visited by intellectuals of the day. Although he lived simply, he owned a library of fifteen hundred volumes of Chinese books and 260 volumes of Japanese writings, a first-class library for the time.[6]

Chōshōshi, unlike most talented waka poets, never attempted to turn his gifts to financial profit. Poetry was his avocation, his chosen way of passing the time in idleness. He once told an intimate, "I know nothing about the art of poetry. I merely express, for my own amusement, what I have thought in my heart."[7] Chōshōshi may have exaggerated his attitude of detachment; perhaps he was contrasting himself with the highly professional Teitoku, his adversary in many disputes. Teitoku spoke ill of Chōshōshi, apparently because certain rich disciples had deserted him to study with Chōshōshi. The latter, for his part, accused Teitoku of allowing his poetry to be defiled by the dust of the floating world; Teitoku's writings, he said, were "closer to vulgarity than to poetry. He conducts himself in the manner of a mendicant."[8] But, unlike Chōshōshi, Teitoku had no choice but to sell his talents, as a teacher and "corrector" of other poets.

Chōshōshi, having studied with Yūsai, was certainly not ignorant of the "maladies of poetry" and the rest of the traditional lore, but remained independent, accepting no pupils. His poetry nevertheless enjoyed unrivaled popularity in its day; we are told that village boys sang poems by Chōshōshi and townsmen inscribed them on fans.[9] People responded to a style that was much freer and more imaginative than the waka of Yūsai or of the dōjō poets. But even if his detachment and nonprofessionalism were appealing, they did not necessarily make for poetic excellence. Rather than search for individuality or freshness in Chōshōshi, it is best to savor the quiet nonchalance of a waka like:

kado sashite	The house I live in
yaemugura seri	Has its door bolted by weeds;
wa ga yado wa	It's east of the capital,
miyako no higashi	At the foot of Eagle Mountain.[10]
washi no yamamoto	

This is livelier than the dōjō poets, and even has a touch of realism, though it was a familiar convention to speak of a poet's house as being overgrown with weeds. Other poems have an even more distinctive note of actual observation:

matsukaze wa	The wind blowing
fukishizumarite	Through the pines has calmed
takaki e ni	And on the high branches
mata nakikawasu	Again the spring thrushes
haru no uguisu	Are calling to each other.[11]

Occasionally too we catch an unmistakably personal tone:

yoyo no hito no	When I realize
tsuki ni nagameshi	The moon is the memento
katami zo to	Of the brooding
omoeba omoeba	Of generations of men
mono zo kanashiki	How sad everything seems!

In his own day such verses attracted many poets to Chōshōshi, but they incurred the wrath and contempt of the dōjō poets, who viciously attacked his collection *Kyohaku Shū* (1649). One man sarcastically suggested that the book should have been called the "Repetitious Collection" because of the repeated use of the same words, or the "Broken Commandment and Stolen Words Collection" from the number of rules laid down by the ancients which Chōshōshi had broken and the number of other men's lines he had appropriated, or the "Nuisance and Vulgarity Collection" from the distressingly low level of the poems. "Persons interested in poetry should fear this book and stay away from it," he warned.[12]

Chōshōshi was also a perceptive if not systematic critic. He maintained a disconcertingly ironic or even farcical tone, but his points are sound. In his discussion of *The Tale of Genji*, characteristically cast by Chōshōshi in the form of a question-and-answer session with a tent caterpillar, the latter complains of the difficulty of understanding the great novel. The poet counters by urging the caterpillar to read the work without worrying about possible profound meanings. Direct experience will lead to perfect understanding even without any special instruction. Chōshōshi denied that *The Tale of Genji* should be considered a "treasure" in the sense that the Confucian Five Classics were treasures, or as a guide to good statesmanship; he insisted that it was meant not as a public but as a private book, to be read and enjoyed by oneself.[13] These views were to be expanded and given a more impressive presentation by Motoori Norinaga, but their break with medieval tradition was remarkable. We have only to remember the kind of instruction Teitoku received in *The Tale of Genji* to appreciate the freshness of Chōshōshi's interpretations.

Chōshōshi's poetry, reminiscent of that of the Kyōgoku-Reizei school which flourished in the fourteenth century, is more intellectual and complex than the bland simplicity of the dōjō poets. He also evinced great admiration for the *Manyōshū*, but unlike other disciples of Hosokawa Yūsai, whose interest in the *Manyōshū* tended to be restricted to the archaic language of the old poems, Chōshōshi was moved by the content, especially by his discovery that "in the distant past, and in this day too, human hearts are one."[14] The unconventional touches in poetry owe something to his explorations of the *Manyōshū*, though his waka could hardly be said to belong to the *Manyōshū* traditions.

CHŌRYŪ AND KEICHŪ

Chōshōshi formally recognized no disciples, but many poets felt his influence, including Bashō. The closest to being a disciple was Shimokōbe Chōryū (1624–86),[15] but the two men did not meet until shortly before Chōshōshi's death in 1649. Chōryū came of a samurai family. As a boy he demonstrated his literary talents by memorizing the *Kokinshū* in about a month, and by displaying such proficiency at renga when only seventeen as to win him nationwide fame. His skill at renga may have harmed his career as a samurai: he is said to have composed renga so much more proficiently than his master that the master got rid of him. Be that as it may, Chōryū became a rōnin and left his native province of Yamato for Edo, in the hopes of finding a more congenial master. He returned to Kyoto unsuccessful, but there began studying the *Manyōshū* under Chōshōshi's encouragement. At the time waka composition was recognized as a prerogative of the nobles, and Chōryū was aware that as an outsider he could not hope to gain admittance to the dōjō circles. That may be why he turned from the closed world of the court poets and plunged into serious study of the *Manyōshū*. Chōryū, perhaps more than any other scholar, should be credited with the revival of *Manyōshū* studies.[16]

Chōryū's reputation as a *Manyōshū* expert eventually attracted the attention of Tokugawa Mitsukuni, the daimyo of Mito, who was planning to sponsor an annotated edition. Mitsukuni invited Chōryū to direct this undertaking, but Chōryū, in the manner of his teacher Chōshōshi, worked only when he felt like it, and his commentary made little progress. When he took ill in 1683 a close friend, the Buddhist priest Keichū (1640–1701), substituted for him. Keichū's magnum opus, *Manyōshū Daishōki*, completed in 1688–1690, was to become the foundation of *Manyōshū* studies.

Keichū was the son of an upper-rank samurai, but his family was involved in the punishment meted out to the daimyo they served, and the boy became a priest at the age of twelve. As a young man, in his twenties, he was the resident priest of a temple in Osaka, and there formed a friendship with Chōryū that lasted until the latter's death. Keichū was apparently depressed by his life in the temple, and for several years wandered around the country. At the Murō-ji he felt so overcome by the scenic beauty that he attempted to commit suicide by bashing his head against a rock. Fortunately he failed, but having surmounted a spiritual crisis, he abandoned his aimless wanderings and returned to his studies of the Japanese classics. His consecration to the *Manyōshū* in particular was to bear fruit in *Manyōshū Daishōki*.

Both Chōryū and Keichū wrote many waka, but surprisingly little influence from the *Manyōshū* can be detected; their poems are graceful, usually in the manner of *Shin Kokinshū*, with sometimes an intellectual touch in the manner of the Kyōgoku-Reizei school. Here is a typical verse by Keichū:

sora no iro wa	The color of the sky
mizu yori sumite	Is clearer than water;
ama no kawa	How cool is this night
hotaru nagaruru	When fireflies are flowing
yoi zo suzushiki	Down the River of Heaven.[17]

The use of words related to the River of Heaven (Milky Way)—*mizu* (water), *sumite* (is clear), *nagaruru* (to flow)—suggests the Kyōgoku-Reizei influence. This waka, like many others of the period, has grace and elegance, but little content; it is hard to realize that about the same time Bashō was composing masterpieces that belong so distinctively to their age. If the *Shin Kokinshū* did not exist, Keichū's poetry might rank very high; reading one of his poems is likely to awaken the faded echoes of Teika, with no touch of a more modern sensibility.

shimo mayou	On the returning wings
sora ni shioreshi	Of the wild geese that had drooped
karigane no	In the frost-filled sky,
kaeru tsubasa ni	The spring rains are falling.
harusame zo furu	
	Teika (*Shin Kokinshū*, No. 63)

karigane no	Will it again
kaeru tsubasa wo	Sift through the wings
mata ya moru	Of the returning wild geese,
akatsuki samuki	That frost of a cold
kisaragi no shimo	Dawning in March?
	Keichū[18]

The literary contributions of Chōryū and Keichū were clearly less in their own poetry than in their *Manyōshū* studies, and their real disciples were men who read their commentaries, perhaps many years later. *Manyōshū* studies represented not only the exciting rediscovery of a forgotten treasury of poetry but a liberation from the medieval insistence on conformity, especially the observance of the "forbidden words" and other secret traditions. The sharpest attack on the monopoly of poetry by the dōjō poets was made by Toda Mosui (1629–1706), a member of the shogunate aristocracy who, having lost his official position, devoted his life to poetry. In book after book he denounced the dōjō poetics, pointing out the stupidity of the secret transmission of the *Kokinshū* and the rest of the heritage of poetic lore. His most violent attacks were in *Nashinomoto Shū* (Collection under the Pear Tree), written in 1698, when he was already sixty-nine. In this work Mosui tested 121 examples of prohibited locutions, demonstrating the meaninglessness of each.[19] Toda Mosui was probably influenced by Keichū's studies of the *Manyōshū*, and like many other scholars who admired the poetic achievements of the distant past, he became convinced that the Japanese had been spiritually superior before they became corrupted by foreign influence. He declared that Shinto was the root and source of Japanese civilization, Confucianism the branches and leaves, and Buddhism the flowers and fruit; he also opined that "the Way of the Gods is the Great Way; the Way of man lies at the end of the Great Way of the Gods."[20]

The rediscovery of the *Manyōshū* served as a weapon in the attack on the traditions of medieval scholarship; at the same time it became the focal point for the resistance to Confucian thought that had tended to exalt China at the expense of Japan. *Manyōshū* studies were initiated by men whose main interest was in poetry, but gradually they became associated with the emphasis on Japanese supremacy implicit in kokugaku (national learning).

KADA NO AZUMAMARO

The foundation of kokugaku is often credited to Kada no Azumamaro (1669–1736). Members of his family for generations had served as Shinto priests at the shrine of Inari in Fushimi, and they had gained renown as scholars of the Shinto traditions. Azumamaro studied both Shinto and waka composition as a boy; a poem written at the age of eight was acclaimed as a masterpiece: "At Inari Mountain today the birds have stopped singing; the sound we hear is the water in the valley stream." His talents attracted the attention of the imperial family, and for two years (1697–99) he was tutor in poetry to the fifth son of Emperor Reigen. Such recognition aroused his ambitions of establishing Shinto as a legitimate academic discipline. In 1699 he went to Edo, perhaps in hopes of finding support from officials of the shogunate. He made his living by teaching the Shinto classics, especially *Nihon Shoki* (Chronicles of Japan) and *Manyōshū*, his studies in the latter owing much to Keichū. Azumamaro remained in Edo for fourteen years, until 1713, delivering numerous lectures on the classics which were later edited as books by his disciples. The remainder of his life he divided between Kyoto and Edo, working tirelessly on behalf of kokugaku.

In 1728 Azumamaro submitted to the shogun Yoshimune, known as a patron of scholarship, a petition for the establishment of a School of National Learning. With the greatest eloquence, and with the greatest care lest the Confucian sensibilities of the shogun's court be offended, Azumamaro urged the importance of the preservation of the heritage of Japanese learning. He deplored the disappearance of old books and traditions, and described his own efforts over the years to preserve them. He wrote:

> Prostrate, I here make my humble request: that I be granted a quiet tract of land in Kyoto where I can open a school for studies of the Imperial Land. I have collected since my youth many secret and obscure writings and have corrected since I became old numerous old records and accounts. I propose to store them at this school to provide for the researches of future days.[21]

He suggested that texts of Japanese learning be lent to people throughout the country so that this study would not perish. The books he singled out for special attention were the *Chronicles of Japan*, the *Manyōshū*, the *Six Dynastic Histories*, and the *Kokinshū*. "The *Manyōshū*," he wrote, "is the pure essence of our national temperament."

Despite Azumamaro's care in phrasing his petition in the heavy antithetical prose of classical Chinese, he could not refrain from criticizing the emphasis placed on Chinese studies by the former academies of learning:

They taught Chinese history and the Chinese classics in these schools, even in those for the Imperial Family. Offerings were made to the spirit of Confucius. Alas, how ignorant were the Confucian scholars of the past, not knowing a single thing about the Imperial Japanese learning.[22]

By implication, of course, this criticism extended to the Confucian scholarship of his own day, and perhaps the advisers of the shogun were annoyed. In any case, the school Azumamaro requested was not to be established for another sixty years.

Azumamaro's poetry often reflected his moral and philosophical views:

fumiwake yo	Make your own way!
Yamato ni wa aranu	Is it proper for a man
Kara tori no	To look only at the tracks
ato wo miru no mi	Left by Chinese birds
hito no michi ka wa	Not found in Japan?[23]

This condemnation of scholars who devote themselves exclusively to the study of Chinese writings ("the tracks left by Chinese birds") can hardly be evaluated by the standards of the traditional waka, for it lacks any beauty of expression or tone. Unlike the poetry of Keichū, or even of Toda Mosui, however, Azumamaro's waka often have something to say; unfortunately, his poetic gifts were limited and the waka was an inappropriate medium for his sentiments.

Azumamaro's poetry, first published in 1795, distinctly reveals his indebtedness to the *Manyōshū*. The preface by Ueda Akinari reiterated the now popular opinion that the *magokoro* (true feelings) of people have not changed through the ages, even though the language has changed; Akinari praised Azumamaro for successfully mingling old and new words to express this magokoro. Experiments in the use of archaic *Manyōshū* words to enrich the poetic vocabulary go back to Teitoku and Chōshōshi, but Azumamaro used the old language to recapture what he imagined to be the simplicity and sincerity of the warriors of the *Manyōshū* age. He rejected femininity in poetry, and refused to write love poetry, distrusting the emotion.[24]

Azumamaro's aesthetic ideals were distinguished by his insistence on "manliness" (*masuraogokoro*); his equal emphasis on "truth" (*makoto*) as the touchstone of poetry was shared by others of his time, like the haikai poet Onitsura or the waka poet and Confucian scholar Tayasu Munetake (1715–78). Manliness was the quality most admired in the *Manyōshū*, not only by Azumamaro and his disciples but even, in later years, by the untutored public. The feminine delicacy of the later anthologies came to be compared unfavorably with the simple, masculine spirit of the *Manyōshū* poets, and the artistry of the *Kokinshū* or *Shin Kokinshū* poets was denounced as insincerity, or a lack of makoto.

When Azumamaro chose subjects other than ideology, his poetry is surprisingly conventional. Despite his conscious attempts to incorporate *Manyōshū* sentiments, his poetic style is characterized by a heavy use of *engo* (related words) and *kakekotoba* (pivot words), in the artificial manner of the late poetry he so often condemned.[25] It is evident that Azumamaro revered the *Manyōshū* not so much for its literary as its didactic qualities; he believed that a knowledge of this ancient anthology could teach present-day Japanese the proper way to behave. This view would have made sense to the Confucianists; and like many of them, Azumamaro composed poetry not because of powerful feelings but because it was expected of practitioners of the Way. The ancient way he searched for in the *Manyōshū* and in *Chronicles of Japan* was moral, not poetic, even though the documents he cited might be poems. His chief contribution to kokugaku was to explain the obscure texts and fashion the underlying thoughts into a kind of ethical system.

KADA NO ARIMARO

Azumamaro chose as his heir a nephew, Kada no Arimaro (1706–51), an expert on old customs and usages. On the basis of this recommendation Arimaro obtained employment with Tayasu Munetake, the son of Tokugawa Yoshimune and a poet of considerable attainments. In 1738 Arimaro was asked to write a description of the Great Purification Ceremony at the Imperial Palace in Kyoto. He made the mistake of publishing this account in the following year and for a time was kept under house arrest because of the lèse-majesté. This incident ultimately led to his resignation from service with Tayasu Munetake, but in the meantime he further incurred his master's wrath by composing in 1742 *Kokka Hachiron* (Eight Essays on Japanese Poetry). Munetake, a devoted admirer of the *Manyōshū*, commanded Arimaro to write an essay on the principles of Japanese poetry, assuming that a nephew of Azumamaro would exalt the *Manyōshū*. To his surprise and dismay he discovered that, in fact, Arimaro did not think so highly of the *Manyōshū*; the essay proclaimed his admiration instead for the *Shin Kokinshū*. This alone must certainly have annoyed Munetake, but when Arimaro stated that poetry, an art that existed for its own sake, was without significance when it came to ruling the country, he flew in the face of Munetake's Confucian beliefs. *Eight Essays* was immediately attacked by Munetake and, at his request, by Kamo no Mabuchi (1697–1769), but Arimaro did not yield; he insisted that Confucius made his selection of poems for the *Shih Ching* (Book of Odes) not because they especially encouraged virtue and chastised vice, but because they helped us to understand humanity. Arimaro believed that poetry and song were originally identical, but once these two arts divided, the writing of poetry came to demand greater and greater skill at "playing with words." He therefore preferred the polished style of the *Shin Kokinshū* to the simpler *Kokinshū*, and rejected the *Manyōshū* altogether as a model for modern poets.

Arimaro's views were attractively unconventional, and *Eight Essays* has been praised as the first systematic presentation of poetical criticism during the Tokugawa period, but a sizable part of the work is devoted to quibbling over minor details of diction and not to elucidating the main points. *Eight Essays* contains only a handful of provocative statements set in a tissue of placid and conventional reiterations of the lofty purposes of poetry. Nevertheless, it served to arouse the most celebrated controversy over the nature of the waka.

KAMO NO MABUCHI

The main lines of development in kokugaku and in poetry led from Azumamaro not to Arimaro but to Kamo no Mabuchi. Mabuchi came from a hereditary Shinto family that had fallen on hard times and was forced to support itself by farming. This early background may explain his fondness for rusticity in later life, as well as his determination to restore his family's fortunes by means of his literary talents. As a child in Hamamatsu, an important coastal town on the route between Kyoto and Edo, he showed proficiency at composing waka, and was trained in the Japanese classics. He also received a good education in Chinese learning and Confucianism, and enjoyed youthful celebrity as a prodigy at these studies.[26] Local scholars of Japanese learning (one of them married to Azumamaro's niece) encouraged Mabuchi and prepared the foundations for his future career.

Even as a young man Mabuchi apparently visited Kyoto from time to time to obtain instruction directly from Azumamaro, and after he moved to Kyoto in 1733 he fell deeply under his influence. Mabuchi moved to Edo in 1737, the year after Azumamaro's death, and became friendly there with Azumamaro's younger brother Nobuna and his nephew Arimaro, engaging with them and others in discussion meetings on the *Manyōshū* that lasted for ten months. Various studies by the participants, the products of these meetings, contributed much to Mabuchi's future work. In 1740 he began to deliver lectures on *The Tale of Genji* at his house, and took the occasion to hold poetry meetings as well.

Mabuchi also studied *Kokinshū, Hyakunin Isshu* (A Hundred Poems by a Hundred Poets), and other collections of Heian and Kamakura poetry. His own poetry at this time shows this influence, as in a charming example entitled "A Garden of Fallen Plum Blossoms":

tou hito no	I can hear the flute
fue mo kikoete	Of someone come to call;
kaki no uchi ni	Inside the fence
ume chiru kaze no	How delightful the wind is
omoshiroki ka na	As it scatters the plum blossoms![27]

In 1746 Mabuchi's house was destroyed in a great conflagration that swept Edo. He wrote a waka preceded by a long prose preface describing what had happened and his wild consternation as he attempted to rescue his precious books and manuscripts. The poem itself, however, is less exciting:

haru no no no	The spring fields have turned
yakeno no hibari	To scorched earth, and the skylark,
toko wo nami	Driven from its nest,
kemuri no yoso ni	Wanders uncertainly,
mayoite zo naku	Singing beyond the smoke.[28]

This was perhaps as close as the traditional waka could permit Mabuchi to evoke his emotions; in mentioning the skylark he no doubt was referring to himself, forced to take refuge in a friend's house. The poem fails because it is too "poetic" for the terrifying occasion, and the sixfold repetition of the syllable *no*, doubtless intentional, suggests a stylistic trick rather than heartfelt expression.

In the same year, 1746, Mabuchi replaced Arimaro in the service of Tayasu Munetake, having demonstrated his reliability by writing a rebuttal of *Eight Essays*. Munetake was pleased to get rid of the troublesome Arimaro and to consolidate *Manyōshū* studies. Mabuchi, in his capacity as Munetake's tutor in Japanese literature, presided over the education of Munetake's children, held poetry meetings in the palace, and wrote commentaries for Munetake, not only on *Manyōshū* but on *Tales of Ise* and *The Tale of Genji*. Mabuchi retired from service with the Tayasu family in 1760, leaving an adopted son in his place. After his retirement, by command of Munetake, he visited the Yamato region in 1763. The chief importance of this journey was that he met Motoori Norinaga in Matsuzaka and, after a night of conversation, Norinaga became Mabuchi's disciple, formally registering as such that year. Mabuchi returned to Edo in 1764 and built a house at a place he called Agatai (Rustic Cottage); this name came to be associated with the poetry written by Mabuchi and his disciples.

Mabuchi probably had the greatest literary talent of any kokugaku scholar. He himself considered that his poetry was of equal importance with his kokugaku studies; though he lacked Norinaga's depth of scholarship, his poetry was superior. Sometimes Mabuchi claimed he was interested in the ancient learning only as a means of penetrating the minds of the men of old, but he obviously responded to poetic beauty.

Mabuchi recognized that his poetry could be divided into three periods. The waka he wrote before he was fifty, when he took up employment with Tayasu Munetake, were mainly in the *Shin Kokinshū* vein. For the next fifteen years he cast his poetry into the noble style of the *Manyōshū*, probably in the hopes of persuading Muneyasu and other Confucianists that Japanese poetry need not be restricted to descriptions of love and other unworthy emotions.[29] Finally, his continued determination to lend age and dignity to kokugaku studies led him in the last years of his life to prefer, even to the *Manyōshū*, the ancient and unadorned poetry of the *Kojiki*.

Mabuchi's finest waka are a group of five composed on "the thirteenth night of the ninth moon," after moving to his rustic house.[30] The first two are:

aki no yo no	The plains of heaven
hogara hogara to	Are bright and serene
ama no hara	This autumn night;
teru tsukikage ni	Through the shining moonlight
kari nakiwataru	The wild geese cross, crying.

kōrogi no	Here in my dwelling
naku ya agata no	Rustic as it is,
wa ga yado ni	How the crickets sing!
tsukikage kiyoshi	The moonlight is so pure—
tou hito mo gamo	If only someone would visit me!

These waka have been praised in the highest terms: "They borrow words from the *Manyōshū*, the *Kokinshū*, and elsewhere, but they are the masterpieces of Mabuchi's whole life; the *Manyōshū* tone has become one, naturally and completely, with the poet, and there is not the slightest distance separating them."[31] If these poems fail to impress us so much, it is not because their words or sentiments are inadequate, but because the content is so familiar. We may feel that Mabuchi is saying not what his heart compels him to say but what the diction and mood he has prescribed for himself allows him to say. No doubt Mabuchi's pleasure in the moonlight was genuine, and his new house, built in keeping with his *Manyōshū* tastes, suited him perfectly; but why had he to pretend, in the conventional manner, that he wished someone would visit him? Surely his more than three hundred disciples wanted nothing better! Here, as elsewhere in his poetry, we are disappointed not by what he says but by what he fails to say. Was there nothing, we wonder, that a man living in the middle of the eighteenth century would have wanted to express that was unknown a thousand years before? It is true that the pleasure of an evening spent in one's garden with congenial friends had remained much the same, despite the great lapse of time, and a poet could be quite sincere in describing this pleasure in the old language, but a masterpiece surely should be more distinctive.

Mabuchi's admiration for the *Manyōshū* led him to revive the *chōka*, the long poems. The form had continued to exist vestigially, even after the *Kokinshū*, but it clearly belonged to an earlier age. In 1363 the two leading poets, Nijō Yoshimoto and Ton'a, had expressed the opinion that the chōka had first come into being because the poets of ancient times had so much to express they could not confine themselves to thirty-one syllables, but in modern times the chōka had become rare because poets had little to say.[32] Mabuchi nevertheless decided at about the age of forty that he would write chōka.[33] This involved not merely multiplying the alternating lines of five and seven syllables but also using the vocabulary and stylistic features of the *Manyōshū*, including pillow words. The chōka he wrote in 1752, mourning the early death of his female disciple Aburaya Shizuko (1735–52), is perhaps his most affecting work in this form. Despite the heavy burden of archaic language and style, it somehow manages to convey his grief:

chichi no mi no	Though I was not her father,
chichi ni mo arazu	
haha soba no	Though I was not her mother,
haha naranaku ni	
naku ko nasu	Like a crying child
ware wo shitaite	She followed after me;
itsukushimi	This child I thought of
omoitsuru ko wa	With warmest love.
hatsuaki no	One day in early autumn
tsuyu ni nioeru	When dew made the colors sparkle
mahagihara	In the fields of lavender,
koromo suru to ya	Perhaps thinking to dye her clothes,
maneku naru	Perhaps intending to visit
obana tou to ya	The beckoning plumes of grass,

kakojimono	She went off alone;
hitori idetachi	She went like a solitary fawn
uraburete	And, bowed with grief,
nobe ni iniki to	Disappeared into the fields.
kikishi yori	Ever since I heard the news
hi ni ke ni matedo	I have waited day after day,
utsutae ni	But never once
koto mo kikoezu	Have I heard a single word.
chichi naranu	Has she failed to visit me
ware to ya towanu	Because I am not her father?
haha naranu	Has she grown distant
mi to te ya utoki	Because I am not her mother?
koishiki mono wo	I miss her so much.[34]

Even a cursory examination reveals what a pastiche this is of *Manyōshū* phrases, from the meaningless *makura kotoba* (pillow words) at the opening, modifying father and mother.[35] This chōka, when compared to those in the *Manyōshū* mourning the death of a wife, child, or princess, is so feeble as to be almost ludicrous, but Mabuchi's effort to identify himself with the *Manyōshū* poets by composing their kind of poetry was, to his way of thinking, the sole justification for writing poetry at all. Besides, he did not do too badly, considering he was attempting to revive a form that had been dead for eight hundred years. Some critics even believe that his chōka influenced the modern poetry composed at the end of the nineteenth century.[36]

Mabuchi's greatest contribution to Japanese literature, however, lay in his scholarship and not his poetry. His elucidations of the *Manyōshū*, especially his masterpiece *Manyōshū-kō*, completed in 1768, are valuable even today because of the intuitive understanding he brought to the deciphering of the texts.[37] Not only did he explain individual words but he provided brief judgments of the major poets and a critical evaluation of the collection as a whole. His was without question the finest study of the *Manyōshū* before modern times.

Mabuchi is also famous for his nonliterary works in the kokugaku tradition. They are marked by an anti-Confucian, even anti-Chinese bias that stemmed not only from an exaltation of pure Japanese ways, but from a resolve to establish kokugaku as an eminently worthwhile pursuit. In his attempts to return to the past he undoubtedly was influenced by the Confucian philosopher Ogyū Sorai, who had devoted himself to the elucidation of the ancient meanings of the Confucian texts. Mabuchi also followed Sorai in asserting that literature (like music and rites) had a political significance in molding the minds of loyal subjects.[38] But Mabuchi's rejection of Confucianism recalls his youthful studies of Taoist literature. However much he may have owed to Sorai in his attempt to reconstruct the classics and the world that had produced the classics, his Shinto creed, like Taoism, emphasized spontaneity and simplicity, not the rationalism of Confucian scholarship.

Mabuchi's disciples continued his work in every field. Tayasu Munetake was his most distinguished successor as a poet, writing a kind of "warrior poetry" reminiscent of Sanetomo. His collection *Amorigoto* reveals that it was only after coming under Mabuchi's influence that Munetake shifted from a *Shin Kokinshū* style to a *Manyōshū* style.[39] Mabuchi had more than 330 disciples, a third of them women; they included daimyos, physicians, Shinto and Buddhist priests, merchants, and other men of repute. In retrospect, however, it would seem that his chief disciple was a man he met only once, for a single night, Motoori Norinaga.

MOTOORI NORINAGA

Motoori Norinaga (1730–1801) was certainly one of the greatest Japanese scholars, perhaps the greatest. His writings covered three main areas—literature, philology, and Shinto thought—though he himself would probably not have recognized distinctions among these different aspects of the Way. His essays on literature in particular are of genuine, abiding value, and not merely of historical interest or, like so much poetic criticism of the past, intriguing because of occasional flashes of understanding. Motoori's analyses of Japanese poetry or of *The Tale of Genji* are not only valid, but anticipate arguments still being advanced. His writings are colored by his conviction of the supreme importance of Japanese poetry and prose, but they display an erudition and a sensitivity that accord perfectly with his subjects.

Motoori is most celebrated for his reconstruction of the *Kojiki*, a task that engaged him from about 1764 to the completion in

1798. Other scholars, notably Kamo no Mabuchi, had tried to decipher the songs and prose, but Motoori obtained little assistance from his predecessors. His task was to restore the original pronunciations of the text, basing his work on the known vocabulary of the time, as revealed in phonetically transcribed materials. Motoori also studied the *Manyōshū* with great care, in the manner of his teacher, but his chief concern was to master its vocabulary and syntax, rather than to capture its spirit. His primary interest in reconstructing the *Kojiki* text, for that matter, was not literary. Although he amply demonstrated in his discussions of *The Tale of Genji* how profoundly literature moved him, his studies of *Kojiki* were conceived of in terms of an investigation into the Way of ancient Japan. The *Kojiki* was not only a sacred text, but contained the most reliable information on how the Japanese behaved before being infected with Chinese ideas. No amount of time was too great to devote to so important a task, and Motoori's reconstruction of the *Kojiki* pronunciations was so successful that they have been retained to this day with only minor modifications.

The third aspect of Motoori's activity, the establishment and proclamation of the Way of Japan, was closely linked with his *Kojiki* studies. The purely Japanese virtues—worship of the gods and of their descendant, the emperor—were contrasted with the superficial, meretricious reasoning of the Chinese and of Japanese infatuated with Chinese thought. A detailed examination of Motoori's political and theological views does not lie within the scope of a history of Japanese literature, but it should not be forgotten that even when Motoori wrote literary criticism of the greatest acumen, these nationalistic conceptions were never far from his mind.

Motoori spent most of his life in the small commercial city of Matsuzaka, near Ise. As a young man he studied medicine in Kyoto and profited from the opportunity to pursue his earlier interest in Japanese literature. His decision to take up medicine, like his changing of his surname from the plebeian Ozu to Motoori in 1752, probably indicated a desire to escape from the chōnin class of his father, a wealthy cotton merchant who had died in 1740. After his return to Matsuzaka in 1757 Motoori set himself up as a physician and practiced this profession even while deeply involved in kokugaku studies. Most educated Japanese enjoyed traveling, but Motoori rarely left Matsuzaka, apparently too absorbed in his work to leave his books.

Motoori's first published work, *Ashiwake Obune* (A Little Boat Breaking a Path Through the Reeds), seems to have been written during his stay in Kyoto. This essay is an honest attempt to confront the real problems involved in composing poetry, and not, like so many similar books, a mere restatement of platitudes. One event during Motoori's stay in Kyoto made this essay possible, a meeting with Keichū, which inspired Motoori to search for the truth about poetry and to make of himself "a little boat breaking a path through the reeds," the implied meaning of the title.[40] He was resolved to brush aside the encumbrances hindering his boat and sail directly to the heart of poetry. Motoori wrote of Keichū with the deepest respect, but he easily surpassed his master, thanks perhaps to the methodology of Ogyū Sorai which he learned (along with medicine) from his teacher Hori Keizan (1688–1757).

Ashiwake Obune fairly bubbles over with ideas. It is written in question-and-answer form, and covers a wide range of topics.[41] In 1763 Motoori wrote an expanded and far more systematic version of this essay, but most of the basic ideas that would remain characteristic of Motoori's writings on literature were present in his first work.

Ashiwake Obune opens with a statement and question:

> The *uta* is a Way for assisting the government of the country. It must not be thought of as a plaything to be toyed with idly. That is why one finds statements to this effect in the preface to the *Kokinshū*. What do you think of this opinion?

The questioner reveals a Confucian attitude toward literature and brings to mind the controversy over *Eight Essays* and the statement that the uta (waka poetry) was of no help in promoting good government. Motoori's answer to the question shows familiarity with Arimaro's arguments, but he introduced a distinctive note:

> Answer. This is incorrect. The basic function of the uta is not to assist the government, nor is it intended to improve the person. It is the outward expression of thoughts in the mind, and nothing else. Undoubtedly some poems do assist the gov-

> ernment, and others serve as a lesson to people. Some poems also are harmful to the country and others do damage to the person. These effects surely depend on the particular poem produced by the mind of a particular person. A poem can be used for evil or for good; it can be used to express excitement, depression, grief, joy, or any other mood. . . . And if, moreover, it is wondered why there are so few poems with a didactic message and so many about love, it is because that is the area in which the true nature of poetry is naturally expressed. No emotion is as powerful as love, and it is precisely because every single person desires to be successful in love that there are so many poems on the subject. Few sages in the world are so given to improving themselves and obtaining the good that they think exclusively about didactic matters; that is why there are so few didactic poems.[42]

Motoori believed that the importance of poetry consisted in being the vehicle for man's deepest emotions. Like Arimaro, he considered the *Shin Kokinshū* to be the supreme collection of Japanese poetry, not merely because of the exquisite polish of the diction, but because its poets best expressed their sensitivity to the world.

The key expression in Motoori's aesthetic judgments was *mono no aware*. The word *aware* was found in the *Manyōshū* as an expression of wonder or awe. Motoori defined the word in terms of this original meaning:

> When we speak of knowing *mono no aware* we refer to the cry of wonder that comes to our lips when our mind is moved by the realization that something we have seen, heard or touched is *aware*. Even in our common speech today people say *aa* or *hare*. When they have been impressed by the sight of the moon or the cherry blossoms they will say, "*Aa*, what splendid blossoms!" or "*Hare*, what a lovely moon!" *Aware* is the combination of the two cries of *aa* and *hare*.[43]

But the simple exclamation of wonder or delight was of less importance to Motoori than the act of "knowing" *mono no aware*.[44] It is not that a person merely exclaims "Ahh" blankly before some sight of nature; he must distinguish it by means of his senses and emotions.

> One is moved because one has recognized *mono no aware.* This means, for example, if something joyous makes us feel happy, it is because we have recognized the joyful nature of the thing.[45]

Such an act of cognition, by the senses rather than the intellect, revealed to Motoori the essential meaning of literature.

Motoori's "teacher," Kamo no Mabuchi, had unreservedly admired the masculinity of the *Manyōshū* and earlier poetry, but although Motoori devoted many years of his life to elucidating the *Kojiki*, the rugged simplicity of its songs clearly did not please him as much as poetry that stemmed from a sense of *mono no aware.* In *Ashiwake Obune* he presents the question:

> Why, if we imitate poetry that reveals the beauty and truth of feelings of people in the past, should we not adopt the ancient manner of the *Nihongi* and the *Manyōshū*, rather than take as our only model the *Kokinshū*, which is rather ornamented and artificial?

To this he replies:

> The *Nihongi* and *Manyōshū* poems are so extremely plain and simple that many are actually clumsy, provincial, and ugly.[46]

This opinion was expressed before Motoori had come in contact with Mabuchi's teachings, and does not reflect his later preferences, but even in his maturity Motoori could never accept masculinity as the ideal in poetry.[47] Instead, he proclaimed femininity and frailty as the essence of literature:

> When I speak of human feelings I mean those that are frail, like those of children and women. Those that are masculine, correct and severe, do not belong to the domain of human feelings.[48]

Motoori means that women and children openly express feelings that men are obliged by their social position to control or conceal.

> The true feelings of people are awkward and untidy. Supposing a beloved child dies—surely there would be no difference in the depth of the grief of the father and mother. But the father would try to pretend this was not so, even as the mother,

> overcome by lamentations, is blinded by her tears. Why should this be the case? The mother, unable to conceal her true feelings, expresses them exactly as they are. The father unavoidably must worry about how he appears in others' eyes, and he will control or suppress his emotions for fear people will think him softhearted. He will not shed a single tear, nor will he reveal on his face the terrible grief he feels in his heart, but will present a picture of noble resignation. The mother's appearance will be unseemly, distraught and disheveled. But this is what is meant by showing feelings as they actually are. The father's appearance is indeed masculine and severe, and it is admirable that he manages somehow not to appear distraught, but these are not his true feelings. . . . One may see, then, that the real appearance of human emotions is frail, untidy, and foolish. And since poetry is something that describes feelings, it is fitting that it should accord with the feelings and also be untidy, clumsy, and frail.[49]

Motoori believed that poetry was the product of deep emotions, expressed in a manner that might have seemed unmanly or indecorous to Mabuchi. The sensitive person, when overcome by feelings of *aware*, naturally and inevitably expresses himself in poetry.

> The man who "knows *mono no aware*" may attempt when he encounters something that is *aware* not to think about it, but he cannot prevent himself from feeling the *aware*. It is like a man with good hearing who, though he tries not to hear the thunder, hears it and is afraid. . . . The words that naturally burst forth when the poet is unable to resist *aware* inevitably multiply and become decorated, and eventually form themselves into a poem.[50]

It may be wondered why a man, having relieved his feelings by expressing in poetry his intimations of *aware*—"the pity of things," as one translator put it—should still find it necessary to show his poem to other people. Motoori answered this:

> A poem is not merely something composed to describe one's feelings when one cannot bear any longer the *mono no aware*. When the feelings are extremely deep, one's heart still feels dissatisfied and unresigned, even after having composed a poem.

> In order to feel comfort one must read the poem to someone else. If the other person hearing the poem finds it has *aware*, this greatly comforts the poet. . . . Even though reading one's poem to someone else brings no material advantage either to the listener or the poet, it is quite natural that the poet feel compelled to read it aloud to another person; and since this is the intent of poetry, it is a most basic principle and not an accident that poems must be heard by others. Someone who does not understand this might say that a true poem describes one's emotions exactly as they are, whether good or bad, and it has nothing to do with whether or not people hear it. Such an argument sounds plausible, but it betrays ignorance of the true meaning of poetry.[51]

Motoori's description of the poetic process suggests Murasaki Shikibu's famous statement on how a writer comes to compose novels:

> It is a matter of his being so moved by things both good and bad, which he has heard and seen happening to men and women that he cannot keep it all to himself but wants to commit it to writing and make it known to other people—even to those of later generations.[52]

A poem, then, originates as a moment of emotional awareness so intense that it cannot be stifled. The emotion finds expression naturally in the traditional poetic forms, and must then be recited to others in order to satisfy an inner necessity. But no matter how sincere a poet may be, he must clothe his emotions in appropriate language. Even in ancient times poets sought heightened expression for their thoughts, but it was easier then, before words and thoughts had become debased, to write a beautiful poem using ordinary, daily words. Today, however, the poet must study the *Kokinshū*, *Gosenshū*, and *Shūishū* for their language, but the highest achievement in the poetic art is the *Shin Kokinshū*. No age has produced such magnificent poetry as that of the *Shin Kokinshū*, and this collection is particularly valid for modern men because the emotions described and the language employed are still meaningful; men can no longer hope to imitate the innocence and simplicity of the *Manyōshū* or earlier poetry.[53]

Although Motoori's researches on the *Kojiki* are his most

impressive scholarly monument, his writings on *The Tale of Genji* are even more likely to excite our admiration. His love for the work is unmistakable, and it was not philological or ideological. He considered it the supreme masterpiece of literary beauty and the embodiment of *mono no aware.* The medieval commentaries on *The Tale of Genji* had been moral interpretations, whether Buddhist or Confucian; the Nō play *Genji Kuyō* portrays Murasaki Shikibu suffering the torments of hell for having written a novel containing fabrications. Even in the Tokugawa period such men as Kada no Azumamaro or the Confucian scholar Kumazawa Banzan (1619–91) had discussed *The Tale of Genji* in terms of its success in inculcating the principle of "encouraging virtue and chastising vice."[54] Motoori dismissed such interpretations with contempt, declaring that they were responsible for the general inability of readers to understand the true nature of the work:

> It is simply a tale of human life which leaves aside and does not profess to take up at all the question of good and bad, and which dwells only upon the goodness of those who are aware of the sorrow of human existence (*mono no aware*). The purpose of *The Tale of Genji* may be likened to the man who, loving the lotus flower, must collect and store muddy and foul water in order to plant and cultivate the flower. The impure mud of illicit love affairs described in the tale is there not for the purpose of being admired but for the purpose of nurturing the flower of the awareness of the sorrow of human existence.[55]

This for Motoori was the meaning of this great novel. He contrasted it with the didacticism of Chinese literature which, "stripped of its surface ornamentation and polish is totally inept when it comes to describing real emotions." *The Tale of Genji* is a supreme artistic creation because it captures man's deepest feelings directly, without moralizing over them or attempting to rationalize.

The reason for reading *The Tale of Genji* was not to absorb a moral lesson painlessly, as had often been claimed, nor was it simply to kill time. It was necessary in order to cultivate one's sensitivity to *mono no aware,* and beyond *mono no aware* was the Way.

> Every man must be aware of the essence of beauty. If he fails to know it, he will not understand *mono no aware* and will be without feelings. The way to learn the essence of beauty is to compose poetry and read novels carefully. Moreover, when one has absorbed the elegance of feeling of the men of the past and, in general, the elegance of the whole world of long ago, it will serve as a ladder for learning the ancient Way.[56]

This Way, unlike that of the Confucianists, was not an attempt to systematize knowledge or to reduce it to logical patterns. As Yoshikawa Kōjirō put it, for Motoori "reality was infinitely complex, mysterious and marvelous. It was impossible to explain it with human knowledge because human knowledge was limited."[57] Ultimately, one reaches the stage of wonder at the work of the gods, the stage where one can only cry out, "*Aware!*"

The ancient works that describe how the gods created the world, the *Kojiki* and *Chronicles of Japan*, are neither systematic nor didactic. There was no need to teach moral principles in an age when people always acted with sincerity and directness. A knowledge of these two works—not only their meaning but their language—can give people of modern times the same outlook on the world of the ancients. It was the function of the scholar to elucidate the Way in the hopes that someday it might be adopted by the ruler as the principle for governing the nation:

> The scholar should consider that his task is to investigate and elucidate the Way; he should not attempt to put it into practice himself. Then, after he has studied and elucidated the ancient Way and taught its general principles and written them down in books, a day will surely come, even if it takes five hundred years or one thousand years, when the Ruler will adopt and practice it, and promulgate it to the nation. The scholar must wait for that time.[58]

Motoori's reconstruction of the *Kojiki* was a supreme act of "investigating and elucidating the Way." Each phrase of the original was subjected to the utmost scrutiny. Sources were cited for the pronunciations adopted, geographical and historical background material was supplied, and Motoori's own comments interspersed, making *Kojiki Den* less a commentary than a presentation of Motoori's total understanding of the past. Even an apparently simple section in the *Kojiki* often elicited an imposing display of information: for example, a passage in forty-two characters that merely states how the emperor Ōjin ordered the construction of certain waterways and storehouses was provided with six pages of minute annotations.[59] The display of erudition is overwhelming.

Motoori also wrote many waka. Unlike most other waka poets of his day, he recognized the existence of other forms of poetry; early in his career he was even ready to admit that haikai or Jōruri might be better suited to contemporary men than the waka. Later he decided that, since all varieties of Japanese poetry were essentially branches of the same art, it was foolish to devote oneself to minor offshoots rather than to the core, the waka. When Kamo no Mabuchi, who always insisted on the importance of a kokugaku scholar's composing poetry, accepted Motoori as his disciple, he asked him to submit some poems. Motoori's waka, in the *Shin Kokinshū* style, displeased Mabuchi exceedingly. About one, an inoffensive description of cherry blossoms falling at an old temple, Mabuchi wrote, "This is not even a poem." About another, on cherry blossoms "burying the moss," he merely commented, "Disgusting." Mabuchi declared, "If you like this style of poetry, you should give up your studies of the *Manyōshū*."[60]

Motoori dutifully began to compose verse in the *Manyōshū* style, but late in life he wrote, "If a man today writes in the old style of the *Manyōshū*, it will not be his own true feelings but a fabrication written in imitation of the *Manyōshū*."[61] He undoubtedly considered his own poems in this style a fabrication, and that was why he advocated the *Shin Kokinshū* style which permitted him to write from the heart. But whatever style he adopted, his poetry was undistinguished. There is not much to choose between his hackneyed descriptions of cherry blossoms and his Shinto poems, like the following one, phrased in archaic language:

kusuwashiki	How vain it is
kotowari shirazute	For the men of China
Karahito no	To discuss the reason of things
mono no kotowari	When they know not the reason
toku ga hakanasa	Of the miraculous![62]

Despite his failings as a poet, Motoori was unquestionably the greatest of the kokugaku scholars. Yet, paradoxically, he disliked the word *kokugaku* and even attacked it, declaring that Japanese learning should simply be called "learning" without the qualifying adjective "national."[63] The objection is typical of Motoori, yet as he himself was aware, the purity of language and thought he advocated represented a special development. Motoori's knowledge and sensitivity gave to the Japanese learning first advocated by Azumamaro, Keichū, and Mabuchi a dignity commensurate with their high purpose, and established it as a rival to the Confucian and Buddhist thought that had long been dominant.

NOTES

1. Takagi Ichinosuke and Hisamatsu Sen'ichi, *Kinsei Waka Shū*, p. 93.

2. Kamo no Mabuchi wrote, urging the importance of writing prose and poetry in the archaic style: "In the *Kojiki* the events of the Age of the Gods are related chiefly in prose, so unless you yourself write prose you will not understand these writings. In order to write this ancient prose you must also compose ancient poetry. Ability in these two is the most essential part of the learning of our country." (Quoted in Hisamatsu Sen'ichi, *Kinsei Waka Shi*, p. 94.)

3. Grace N. Takahashi, *Kada no Arimaro's "Kokka Hachiron"* (unpublished M.A. essay, Columbia University, 1963), p. 40.

4. Hisamatsu, p. 17.

5. *Ibid.*, p. 16.

6. Matsuda Osamu, *Nihon Kinsei Bungaku no Seiritsu*, p. 95.

7. *Ibid.*, p. 90.

8. Ōkubo Tadashi, "Manyō e no Shibō ṭo Waka," in Imoto Nōichi and Nishiyama Matsunosuke, *Ningen Kaigan*, p. 61.

9. Matsuda, p. 83.

10. Hisamatsu, p. 18.

11. *Ibid.*, p. 19.

12. Fujii Otoo, *Kyohakushū*, p. 6.

13. Matsuda, p. 100.

14. *Ibid.*, p. 105.

15. Chōryū probably derived his name from the first syllable of Chōshōshi, plus *ryū*, meaning "style." (See Hisamatsu, p. 41.)

16. Ōkubo, p. 66.

17. Hisamatsu, p. 51.

18. *Ibid.*, p. 50.

19. *Ibid.*, p. 25.

20. *Ibid.*, p. 28.

21. Ryusaku Tsunoda, *et al.*, *Sources of Japanese Tradition*, pp. 512–13.

22. *Ibid.*, p. 513.

23. Hisamatsu, p. 57.

24. *Ibid.*, p. 55. See also Tani Kanae, "Kada Azumamaro," in Kubota Utsubo and Matsumura Eiichi, *Tokugawa Jidai Waka no Kenkyū*.

25. Tani, pp. 260–61, gives a statistical comparison of imagery in Azumamaro's poetry with those of five contemporaries.

26. Inoue Yutaka, "Kamo no Mabuchi," in Hisamatsu Sen'ichi and Sanekata Kiyoshi, *Kinsei no Kajin*, p. 7.

27. Takagi and Hisamatsu, p. 55.

28. *Ibid.*, p. 57.

29. Saigusa Yasutaka, *Kamo no Mabuchi*, p. 262.

30. See Takagi and Hisamatsu, p. 522. Earlier authorities dated these poems at 1761, but 1764 seems correct.

31. Saigusa, p. 249.

32. Fujimura Tsukuru (ed.), *Nihon Bungaku Daijiten*, II, p. 320.

33. Inoue, p. 42.

34. Takagi and Hisamatsu, p. 113.

35. The *Manyōshū* poems quoted include nos. 4164, 4408, and 3978.

36. Inoue, p. 42.

37. The difficulty of reconstructing the pronunciations is suggested by this example, a poem by Hitomaro in Book One of the *Manyōshū*. The traditional reading of the opening lines was:

azuma no no — In the eastern fields
keburi ni tateru — At a place where
tokoro ni te — The smoke is rising . . .

Mabuchi's reading, still followed today, was:

himugashi no — In the fields to the east
no ni kagiroi no — The flush of dawn
tatsu miete — Can be seen rising.

See Saigusa, pp. 270–71; also Takagi Ichinosuke, *et al.*, *Manyōshū*, I, pp. 34–35.

38. See Ōkubo Tadashi, "Kofū wa Shirotae," in Nakamura Yukihiko and Nishiyama Matsunosuke, *Bunka Ryōran*, pp. 169–71.

39. Saigusa, pp. 256–59.

40. The title is derived from poem no. 2745 in the *Manyōshū*. See Ōkubo Tadashi (ed.), *Motoori Norinaga Zenshū*, II, p. xi.

41. The contents are analyzed in *ibid.*, pp. 81–83.

42. *Ibid.*, p. 3.

43. Nakamura Yukihiko (ed.), *Kinsei Bungakuron Shū*, pp. 104–105.

44. See Tahara Tsuguo, *Motoori Norinaga*, pp. 74–87.

45. Ōkubo, *Motoori*, II, p. 99.

46. *Ibid.*, p. 44. *Nihongi* was a variant name for *Nihon Shoki* (Chronicles of Japan).

47. Ōkubo Tadashi, "Kofū wa Shirotae," p. 175.

48. Ōkubo, *Motoori*, II, p. 35.

49. *Ibid.*, pp. 36–37.

50. *Ibid.*

51. Tahara, p. 53.

52. Ivan Morris, *The World of the Shining Prince* (New York: Knopf, 1964), p. 309.

53. Tahara, p. 61.

54. Tahara, pp. 67–68.

55. Tsunoda, p. 534.

56. Tahara, p. 32.

57. Yoshikawa Kōjirō, "Motoori Norinaga no Shisō," in Yoshikawa Kōjirō (ed.), *Motoori Norinaga Shū*, p. 3.

58. Tahara, p. 38.

59. Motoori Kiyozō (ed.), *Motoori Norinaga Zenshū*, IV, pp. 1821–26.

60. Ōkubo, "Kofū," p. 177.

61. *Ibid.*, p. 178.

62. Tsunetsugu Muraoka, *Studies in Shinto Thought*, p. 155.

63. Tahara, p. 28.

BIBLIOGRAPHY

Fujii Otoo (ed.). *Kyohakushū*. Tokyo: Bunken Shoin, 1930.

Hisamatsu Sen'ichi. *Kinsei Waka Shi*. Tokyo: Tōkyōdō, 1968.

——— and Sanekata Kiyoshi (eds.). *Kinsei no Kajin*. Tokyo: Kōbundō, 1960.

Imoto Nōichi and Nishiyama Matsunosuke. *Ningen Kaigan*, in Nihon Bungaku no Rekishi series. Tokyo: Kadokawa Shoten, 1967.

Kubota Utsubo and Matsumura Eiichi. *Tokugawa Jidai Waka no Kenkyū*. Tokyo: Ritsumeikan, 1932.

Matsuda Osamu. *Nihon Kinsei Bungaku no Seiritsu*. Tokyo: Hōsei Daigaku, 1963.

Matsumoto, Shigeru. *Motoori Norinaga*. Cambridge, Mass.: Harvard University Press, 1970.

Motoori Kiyozō (ed.). *Motoori Norinaga Zenshū*. Tokyo: Yoshikawa Kōbunkan, 1927.

Tsunetsugu Muraoka. *Studies in Shinto Thought.* Translated by Delmer M. Brown and James T. Araki. Tokyo: Ministry of Education, 1964.

Nakamura Yukihiko. *Kinsei Bungakuron Shū,* in Nihon Koten Bungaku Taikei series. Tokyo: Iwanami Shoten, 1966.

——— and Nishiyama Matsunosuke. *Bunka Ryōran,* in Nihon Bungaku no Rekishi series. Tokyo: Kadokawa Shoten, 1967.

Nishishita Keiichi. *Wakashi Ron.* Tokyo: Shibundō, 1944.

Okubo Tadashi (ed.). *Motoori Norinaga Zenshū,* II. Tokyo: Chikuma Shobō, 1968.

Saigusa Yasutaka, *Kamo no Mabuchi.* Tokyo: Yoshikawa Kōbunkan, 1962.

Tahara Tsuguo, *Motoori Norinaga.* Tokyo: Kōdansha, 1968.

Takagi Ichinosuke, Gomi Tomohide, and Ono Susumu. *Manyōshū.* I, in Nihon Koten Bungaku Taikei series. Tokyo: Iwanami Shoten, 1957.

———and Hisamatsu Sen'ichi. *Kinsei Waka Shū,* in Nihon Koten Bungaku Taikei series. Tokyo: Iwanami Shoten, 1966.

Tsunoda, Ryusaku *et al. Souces of Japanese Tradition.* New York: Columbia University Press, 1958.

Yoshikawa Kōjirō (ed.). *Motoori Norinaga Shū.* Tokyo: Chikuma Shobō, 1969.

PART TWO
LITERATURE FROM 1770-1867

CHAPTER 14

HAIKAI POETRY

BUSON AND THE HAIKAI REVIVAL

It did not take long after Bashō's death for his school to fragment into contesting factions, and when the direct disciples died the situation further deteriorated. During the first forty years of the eighteenth century, haikai poetry had none of the dignity and even grandeur that Bashō had imparted to a humble form. Far from attempting to evoke with a bare seventeen syllables a whole world and the poet's understanding of that world, the "grandchildren disciples" of Bashō either reverted to the superficial humor of the Teitoku and Danrin schools, or else wrote verses of such utter simplicity and insignificance that they hardly merit the name of poetry. Haikai was popularized: it no longer was necessary to display depth of feeling or even a knowledge of tradition provided one was clever enough to twist the seventeen syllables into an amusing comment. If the intent of this popularization had really been to bring poetry to the masses, we might forgive the lowering of standards, but the haikai masters of the day were guided by commercial rather than educational aims; the more pupils, the greater their income as "correctors."

Haikai poetry came to be divided between the city style, especially the Edo style of the followers of Kikaku, and the country style, whether Shikō's in Mino province or Ryōto's in Ise. The city style exhibited all the worst features of Kikaku's late manner, imitating his arcane allusions in intellectual exercises that were almost devoid of poetic quality. Sometimes these verses have nothing to distinguish them from the humor of senryū, at other times they were the private jokes of a coterie. As we read these verses today we can easily imagine a group of haikai poets gathering at a restaurant in Edo or Osaka and composing verses that grew more and more eccentric as the saké took effect. There is nothing objectionable about composing poetry as a diversion at a party, but when trivial allusions and quips came to be considered the stuff of poetry, this surely was a betrayal of the art of Bashō.

The country style insisted on simplicity. Shikō once said that a poet should try his haikai on some old woman outside his gate; if she could not understand it, it was not a true haikai.[1] Bashō's doctrine of karumi (lightness) was taken literally, sometimes with unintentionally comic results, as in this inept verse by Iwata Ryōto (1655–1717):

kogarashi no	The winter wind
ichinichi fuite	For one whole day blew
orinikeri	And kept blowing.[2]

On the whole the country style, despite its banality and obviousness, the result perhaps of teaching poetry to badly educated rustics, is less offensive than the smart-alecky manner of the city style. The leader of the Edo poets, Mizuma Sentoku (1661–1726), was like a throwback to the worst of the Danrin poets:

hikuki kata e	Foam on the water
mizu no Awazu ya	Floats toward the Awazu shallows—
hatsu arashi	The first autumn storm.[3]

The waters of Lake Biwa were shallowest at Awazu, and the first storm blowing over the lake would therefore drive the foam in that direction. This unimpressive poetic conception is given its point by the pivot word on *awa* (foam) and the place name Awazu.

Sentoku's typical verses, like those of his master, Kikaku, often require lengthy explanations, and he himself took the trouble to provide some in his essays on haikai composition called *Sentoku Zuihitsu* (1718). This work is otherwise notable for his unfriendly criticism of Bashō, including such remarks as: "Some of Bashō's hokku are good, but they are thin. As a poet he achieved thinness, but it was beyond Bashō's powers to match the strength of Kikaku's poetry."[4] Sentoku's disciple Kishi Senshū (1670–1739) made cleverness of style a crudely humorous technique; he was famous for his salacious second verses supplied to the maeku written by another man. Tachiba Fukaku (1662–1753), despite his high rank within the Buddhist clergy, wrote many verses of notable silliness during the course of a long lifetime. One, entitled "I know about Mount Obasute but . . . ," alludes to the legend of the mountain where an old woman was abandoned:

kyō no tsuki	The moon tonight—
wakashu sutetaru	I wish there were a mountain
yama mo gana	Where they left young boys![5]

Of course, not all the haikai verses composed by these men were bad but, even at their best, their whimsy or ingenious observations do not suggest that Bashō and his school had flourished shortly before. They pretended to take Kikaku as their model, but actually looked beyond him to the frivolity of the old haikai. Perhaps they were intimidated by the thought of writing with such intensity and self-effacement as to involve their entire beings, in the manner of Bashō at his greatest; or perhaps their verses were essentially a thumbing of the nose at tradition and a confession of defeat.

Even in the worst period of haikai a few poets preserved something of the traditions of Bashō. The rustic schools of Mino and Ise continued to pay at least lip service to him, and it was they, rather than the poets of Edo, who eventually paved the way for a revival of haikai poetry. Kaga no Chiyojo (1703–75), the most famous woman haikai poet, deserves special mention among the rustic poets, if only because several of her poems have enjoyed extraordinary popularity:

asagao ni	The well-rope has been
tsurube torarete	Captured by morning-glories—
moraimizu	I'll borrow water.[6]

This verse, similar in conception to Onitsura's expression of reluctance to throw away his bath water and disturb the flowers, had just the right amount of ingenuity to appeal to the general public without falling into the excessive cleverness of the Edo poets. Critics today, however, dismiss it as an inferior poem.[7] Another verse by Kaga no Chiyojo is probably more successful:

chōchō ya	The butterfly—
nani wo yumi mite	What are the dreams that make him
hanezukai	Flutter his wings?[8]

Probably the usual allusion to the story of how Chuang Tzu dreamed he was a butterfly is being made, but with a new twist: the butterfly, dreaming it is Chuang Tzu, restlessly flutters its wings in sleep. The verse is saved by being intelligible even without reference to the allusion; this distinguishes it from the puzzles of Teitoku and Danrin verse. We feel quite sure that Chiyojo had actually observed a butterfly before writing her poem.

Observation of nature (*shasei*) was to be elevated during the Meiji period into a touchstone of excellence in judging the poetry of the past, especially that of the haikai revival. Even a minor poet like Hayano Hajin (1677?–1742) was able to exert considerable influence because he described scenes he had actually witnessed:

sumigama ya	The charcoal kiln—
shika no mite iru	A deer watches
yūkemuri	The evening smoke.[9]

Hajin, a former pupil of both Kikaku and Ransetsu, was repelled by the vulgarity and superficiality of the Edo haikai poetry of his day, and turned instead to simple observation, without neglecting to include a suggestion of beauty. In later years his great pupil Buson recalled:

> We would talk together about haikai, but if ever anything came up of a mundane nature, he would pretend not to have heard and would act as if nothing had been said; he was an old gentleman of the noblest character. One night, sitting perfectly erect, he told me, "In the art of haikai one should not necessarily follow the diction of one's teacher. A poem should be written suddenly, without consideration of before or after, changing and developing with the moment." I experienced sudden enlightenment under the Master's stick, and learned something of what freedom of expression in haikai means.[10]

Hajin was able to detect and foster the poetic talent of the young Buson, who became Hajin's pupil in 1737, when he was twenty-two. The 1730s were the period when the first stirrings of the "back to Bashō" movement occurred. In 1731 a group of Edo poets published the collection *Goshikizumi* (Ink of Five Colors), expressing in it their opposition to the prevailing haikai poetry, with its emphasis on word plays and similes. Their protest and their own poetry were too feeble to bring about a revolution in haikai, but *Ink of Five Colors* provides clear evidence of the growing dissatisfaction with the Edo school.[11]

The haikai revival proper began about 1743, the fiftieth anniversary (by Japanese reckoning) of the death of Bashō in 1694. Hajin had died in 1742, and in the following year a memorial collection of poetry by his pupils was published, testimony to their intention of carrying on his traditions. At about the same time, several haikai poets made journeys to the north of Japan, in the footsteps of Bashō, and buildings dedicated to Bashō's memory were erected. The next forty years, until the premature celebration in 1783 of the centennial of Bashō's death, marked the period of the haikai revival; it was brought to a close by the death of Buson in that year.

The central figure in the revival was Yosa Buson (1716–83), usually ranked as the second greatest of the haikai poets. He was born near Osaka, the son of a well-to-do farmer, and received a good education, including training in both poetry and painting. During most of his life he was known chiefly as a painter, and supported himself on the pictures he sold. Even during the period after his death when his fame as a poet was temporarily eclipsed, his reputation as a painter remained high. For Buson the two arts probably represented essentially the same kind of expression, both being associated with the Chinese ideal of the *bunjin*, or gentleman scholar. Although Buson was deeply devoted to Bashō, as he frequently stated, he was temperamentally incapable of leading a similar life or of consecrating himself to haikai poetry with Bashō's self-effacing intensity. His attitude was closer to that of the dilettante, but he was a brilliantly accomplished dilettante.

The differences between the two great poets came first of all from their personalities. Although Bashō lived in the Genroku era, celebrated for its lively appreciation of the present, he felt closest to the medieval poets, Saigyō and Sōgi especially, and chose a life resembling that of the hermits of the past. Buson felt none of this attraction for the medieval period. He loved Heian literature and the poetry of China, finding in both the pictorial beauty he sought to capture in his paintings. His religious feeling, unlike Bashō's Zen intuitions, was most overtly revealed by his belief in the magical powers of foxes and badgers. Despite his great admiration of Bashō's poetry, Buson wrote that his haikai was "by no means directly imitated from Bashō. I enjoy changing my style from day to day as my fancy dictates."[12] Again, contrasting his life with Bashō's he wrote, "I have no desire to follow the elegant path of Bashō to Yoshino in order 'to display the cherry blossoms to my hat.' I stay at home all the time, occupying myself with worldly matters, unable to accomplish any of the things I plan."[13]

Yet even if Buson had desired nothing more than to become the second Bashō, the times would not have permitted it. At the end of his life—his most productive period—Japan was afflicted with a series of natural disasters, beginning with the great drought of 1770. Fires, floods, epidemics, volcanic eruptions, and famines struck year after year. Perhaps the worst single disaster was the eruption of Mount Asama in 1783, which took the lives of thirty-five thousand people and laid central Japan waste for nearly five years. At the same time, the country was being grossly misruled by the notorious Tanuma Okitsugu, who made bribery his state policy. Any poet who chose to engage himself with society would have had to touch on such matters, but not a suggestion of criticism, or even of interest, can be found in Buson's poetry. Being a bunjin meant removing oneself from such worldly concerns; most of the professed bunjin claimed to despise social involvement and to consider gentlemanly detachment the essential mark of an artist.[14] This attitude naturally imposed serious limitations on Buson's art, but it is precisely because Buson's poetry was so exclusively concerned with his private feelings, tastes, and perceptions that it strikes us as being modern; there is no barrier of time between him and us. Hagiwara Sakutarō, the greatest modern Japanese poet, was attracted to Buson, alone among the haikai poets of the Tokugawa period, because of "his freshness, romanticism, and something akin to Western poetry."[15] He found the coloring of Buson's poetry bright and vivid, like an impressionist painting, and favorably contrasted the youthfulness of Buson's hokku with Bashō's dislike of youth and color.[16] Hagiwara cited this verse as an example of how closely Buson's techniques resemble those of a Western painting:

zetchō no	On the pinnacle
shiro tanomoshiki	The castle stands, confident,
wakaba kana	Among strong young leaves.[17]

The appeal of the poem for Hagiwara lay in the visual contrast of the white walls of the castle and the green of the young leaves, and the underlying impression of vitality in both. The poem succeeds in other terms because of the adroit use of the Sino-Japanese word *zetchō* in the first line, giving a firmness to the sound, and the ambiguity of the adjective *tanomoshiki* (dependable) in the second, applicable either to the castle alone or to both castle and green leaves. The poem is, further, an example of the objectivity Masaoka Shiki so admired in Buson's poetry: it brilliantly portrays a scene (shasei), but makes no comment or deduction from it.

Buson's objectivity has sometimes been exaggerated. Hagiwara himself, characterizing Buson as a poet of nostalgia, cited this verse, "Recalling the Past," to prove his thesis:

osoki hi no	Long, slow spring days,
tsumorite tōki	Piling up, take me far away
mukashi kana	Into the past.[18]

The mood of this hokku, which has been called "romantic," is strengthened by the repetition of the *o* sounds, particularly the long vowel in *tōki*; the poem suggests that, lulled by the drowsy atmosphere of a spring afternoon, Buson has let his daydreams carry him back to the distant past, perhaps his beloved Heian period.[19]

Even his warmest, most romantic poems do not reveal much of Buson's deepest concerns. Recollections of the Heian past did not stab him with the poignancy that the remembrances of dead warriors, induced by the waving summer grass, aroused in Bashō. Buson apparently did not consider that haikai poetry—or bunjin painting—was an appropriate medium for revealing personal griefs. Toward the end of his life, when afflicted by poverty and family troubles, Buson continued to write pictorially exquisite, absolutely unruffled poetry. A letter written to a friend in 1777, describing his daughter's divorce, includes this poem:

samidare ya	The rainy season—
taiga wo mae ni	The swollen river before them,
ie ni ken	Two little houses.[20]

This poem brilliantly evokes the picture of the two houses on the bank, threatened by the turbid river; Japanese critics, praising Buson's skill, have pointed out that only *two* houses would successfully create the desired scene, not one or three.[21] But however moving we may find the poem, it tells us nothing of Buson's anguish at the time, nor does another hokku in the same letter:

suzushisa ya	The cool of morning—
kane wo hanaruru	Separating from the bell,
kane no koe	The voice of the bell.[22]

The poem describes a morning in summer: when Buson strikes the temple bell its voice, leaving the bell, spreads out in the cool morning air. This was the kind of subject matter and mood Buson considered the proper domain of haikai poetry. We can imagine that Bashō, if faced with griefs similar to those of Buson, would have immersed himself in the experience and eventually found light even within the darkness. For Buson, however, poetry itself was the world of light, an escape from harsh realities. His advocacy of a "rejection of vulgarity" meant in fact a turning away of his eyes from the darkness of this world, to find comfort in the world of the senses.[23]

The pleasures of reading Buson's haikai poetry exist almost without reference to the circumstances of their composition. When we read Bashō's poems in chronological order, reinforcing them with the background material in the travel accounts and other descriptive writings, we ourselves create the picture of a great man; but Buson's poems, read in isolation or in the conventional groupings according to season and subject (summer moon, fragrant breeze, peaks of clouds, etc.), are no less effective than when read chronologically. Buson's reticence left us with few details of his personal life. We know that he left his native Osaka as a boy of sixteen to go to Edo, but not the reasons. We know also that in 1751 he moved to Kyoto, and remained there for most of the rest of his life, but he never indicated why he chose this city. He traveled fairly extensively—to the north of Japan (apparently attracted by Bashō's traces), to the Japan Sea coast (where he remained about three years), and twice to the island of Shikoku. His travel accounts are exceedingly meager when compared to Bashō's, and add little to our knowledge of the man. The closest Buson came to giving personal impressions of a journey was in the prefatory notes he wrote for a few of the poems.

yanagi chiri	Willow leaves have fallen, the
shimizu kare ishi	Clear stream dried up, and stones
tokorodoko	Are scattered here and there.[24]

This haiku bears the note:

> Written when I made a pilgrimage to the province of Shimotsuke toward the beginning of the tenth month and, standing under the old tree called the Yugyō Willow, surveyed the scene before my eyes.

The tree was the famous willow associated with Saigyō, who had written a poem while standing in its shade, unable to leave the spot because of the loveliness of the clear stream nearby. Bashō had also described this willow in *The Narrow Road of Oku*. Buson, however, described a contrasting scene: at the approach of winter the willow leaves have fallen, and stones lie bleakly here and there in the bed of the river.

For the most part, Buson's hokku are complete and do not require additional information. This should not suggest that they are impersonal; the superbly evoked scenes are testimony not only to his acute observation but to his compassion, as in this example:

sararetaru	The divorced woman
mi wo fungonde	Plunges into the paddies—
taue kana	It's rice-planting time.[25]

Buson's sympathy obviously is given to the woman who, to forget her despair at having been divorced, throws herself into the back-breaking labor in the wet fields. Perhaps, even, she must work side by side with the husband who has divorced her. The poem is affecting, though not because of any overt comment by Buson.

Buson also excelled at telling a story, whether observed or imagined, in the brief space of seventeen syllables:

Toba dono e	To the Toba Palace
gorokuki isogu	Five or six horsemen gallop
nowaki kana	In the autumn wind.[26]

Probably Buson had no particular historical incident in mind, only a medieval scene of horsemen intently galloping somewhere, and of the wind blowing long after they had disappeared.

oteuchi no	They should have been killed,
fūfu narishi wo	But became husband and wife,
koromogae	And now change their clothes.[27]

Here is the explanation offered by a Japanese commentator for this cryptic verse:

> A young man and woman who should have been put to death by the master of their household for their illicit relations have been spared, thanks to the merciful intercession of the master's wife, and have run off together. They are secretly living as man and wife in a wretched hovel on a back street. Now that they have escaped from the constricting life of service in a great household, they remember it as a bad dream. They throw off the padded clothes they were still wearing when they left the household, and put on unlined summer kimonos, faded from many washings. Suddenly they feel light and full of joy over their new life. They exchange smiles as a faint breeze blows.[28]

Perhaps not *all* of the foregoing is implied in Buson's poem, but each word was chosen with a care that made such an expansion possible.

Often Buson's story is from the world of the Heian romance:

sashinuki wo	This night the young noble
ashi de nugu yo ya	Kicks off his trouser-skirts
oborozuki	Under the misty moon.[29]

The atmosphere is romantic: under a misty moon a courtier has returned to his room, probably after visiting some lady. Too weary—or perhaps too drunk—to unlace the trousers of his court costume, he kicks them off and falls into bed. This romantic tone is an element missing from Bashō's poetry. Both Bashō and Buson had definite views on the proper domain of haikai; but for Buson the exclusion of vulgarity did not imply an exclusion of romantic love.

Ueda Akinari once said that Buson had written Chinese poetry in Japanese. Certainly we find strong Chinese influence present in many poems, even in those that do not suggest their provenance either by loan words or by allusions:

ureitsutsu	Prey to melancholy,
oka ni noboreba	I climbed the hill and found
hana ibara	Briar roses in bloom.[30]

The grief Buson feels is the nameless melancholy of youth. Ishikawa Takuboku, writing almost 150 years later, described the same sensation: "Melancholy sweeps over me/ And, when I climb the hill,/ A bird whose name I don't even know/ Is pecking there/ At the red fruits of the briar." But however genuine the emotion Buson felt when he wrote his poem, every image was borrowed from Li Po.[31] Many other haikai reveal Buson's indebtedness to the Chinese poets, and we sense that he envied their freedom to express themselves in longer forms, despite his love of haikai. On three occasions he wrote poetry in totally unconventional forms, experiments that presage the creation of modern Japanese poetry a century later. The first, written in 1745, at the beginning of Buson's career, consists of nine related poems mourning Hayami Hokuju, a rich saké brewer and amateur haikai poet who had befriended Buson.

MOURNING FOR MY OLD FRIEND HOKUJU

You went away in the morning; in the evening my heart is
torn a thousand ways.
Why have you gone so far?

Longing for you, I went to the hills with nothing to do.
Why have the hills become so sad?

Amid the yellow of the dandelions the purseweed bloomed
whitely.
No one was looking at them.

There must have been a pheasant somewhere—when I heard
it sing so piercingly,
I remembered I had a friend who lived across the river.

A wraith of smoke dropped down all of a sudden and was
caught by the west wind blowing
Fiercely, but in the fields of bamboo and of sedge
It had nowhere to escape.

I had a friend. He lived across the river. Today
Not even the pheasants are calling.

You went away in the morning; in the evening my heart is
torn a thousand ways.
Why have you gone so far?

To the Amida Buddha in my hut I offer no candles,
No flowers, but this evening, as I stand there dejected,
I feel a special holiness.[32]

The poem is signed *Shaku Buson,* Shaku denoting a priest.

"Mourning for My Old Friend Hokụju" is so striking and unconventional that two twentieth-century poets found it more "modern" than any other poetry composed for 150 years.[33] Other examples of "free verse," Japanese approximations of Chinese poetry, antedate Buson, but nothing remotely resembles the quality of this poem. Its elegiac tone and length may suggest the chōka of the *Manyōshū,* and there is certainly Chinese as well as Buddhist influence present,[34] but Buson's irregular lines suggest emotions too powerful to fit into the normal pattern of alternating lines of five and seven syllables. Although he broke every "rule" of Japanese prosody, the result is unmistakably poetry, written according to the rules of internal necessity. It is easy to see why recent poets have been so drawn to Buson.

Buson wrote two other irregular "Chinese poems in Japanese." The first, *Shimpū Batei Kyoku* (Lines on the Kema Banks in the Spring Wind),[35] consists of a preface in Chinese followed by eighteen sections, including four hokku, four quatrains in Chinese, and various passages in Japanese verse that do not fit any established pattern. The preface relates how the poet met a servant girl on *yabuiri*, the day in the first month when domestics were permitted to return home for their annual visit. Buson wrote down what he imagined the girl's emotions were, speaking in her voice to describe the journey—how she looked for fragrant herbs along the riverbanks only to be scratched by thorns; how she gathered watercress, standing on stones in the river to keep her skirts from getting wet; how she stopped at a teahouse on the way; how when she picked a dandelion her fingers were stained with its milk; and finally, the main theme, her longing for her mother. When the girl finally reaches her old house her mother is waiting for her, holding her little brother in her arms.

The meaning of this poem obviously goes beyond what the preface states—that it is the narration of a servant girl's emotions on returning home after long absence. Buson, in a letter written in the spring of 1777, gave a fuller explanation for the poem. He recalled how he used to walk along the Kema embankment as a boy, and what induced him to relate the emotions of the girl returning home:

> It is a michiyuki describing the journey from Osaka to the girl's native village. I have staged it like the manager of a theater—laugh at me if you will. To tell the truth, these were the actual emotions I summoned up painfully, born of uncontrollable nostalgia.[36]

In his old age, Buson, who no longer had any home to return to, wistfully recalled his boyhood and the mother who had died long ago. The strong emotions Buson deliberately excluded from his haikai found an outlet in the longer poems.

Buson composed one other work in irregular poetic form, *Dengaka* (Poems on the Yodo River, 1777). It consists of two quatrains in Chinese and a Japanese poem in four lines.[37]

Spring waters float plum blossoms;
Southward flowing, the Uji joins the Yodo.
Do not unfasten the brocade hawser,
The swift current will carry the boat like lightning.

Uji waters join the Yodo waters,
Flowing into each other like one body;
I wish we could sleep together aboard this boat,
And I could live in Naniwa long years to come.

You are like plum flowers on a stream—
How quickly they float away on the water!
I am like the willow on the riverbank
Whose shadow cannot sink to you in the water.

The entire poem is apparently based on one by Ts'ao Chih (192–232) that includes these lines:

You are like the dust on the clean road,
I am like the mud in the turbid waters.[38]

In both poems the contrast between floating and sinking takes the form of a dialogue between a man and a woman. The romantic strain in Buson is given its most overt expression in the reference to the joining of man and woman like the two rivers. The man, perhaps Buson himself, meets a prostitute aboard the boat from Kyoto to Osaka (Naniwa), and they both regret that their pleasure together must be short-lived. Perhaps, as Andō Tsuguo suggested, there is also a suggestion of Buson's fear of losing his virility with old age. The poem is written in the person of the woman addressing the man, but Andō believed that we must also interpret it as the voice of Buson speaking to the woman, fearing she will be borne away like the blossoms and that his own life is speeding away like lightning, or even that Buson is addressing his own passions.[39]

These three long poems reveal both Buson's indebtedness to Chinese poetry and his ardor, perhaps the two most striking elements in his works. Masaoka Shiki, who interpreted Buson always as a poet of direct observation, falsified our image of Buson; direct observation was of less significance than the blending of literary tradition and the poet's private emotions, though Buson often used for his imagery some apparently impersonal perception.[40] In Buson's poetry, as in his paintings, realistic depiction was of little importance when compared to the nobility of the conception. A poem written in 1774 comes close to his ideal:

yūkaze ya	The evening breezes—
mizu aosagi no	The water splashes against
hagi wo utsu	A blue heron's shins.[41]

The verse seems an objectively described picture: after a hot summer's day the evening breezes stir little waves along the shore, splashing water against the heron's legs. There is at least indirect Chinese influence in the wording, and Buson, in a letter written in 1777, said that the words *yūkaze ya* (evening breezes) imparted a peculiarly noble quality to the poem.[42] The motionless heron stands majestically against the coming of the dusk.

The importance of the haikai revival could be measured in terms of the poetry of Buson alone, even if no other poets were working, so superior was he to his contemporaries. But he was by no means the only one to advocate a "return to Bashō." Both in the provinces and in Edo a general rejection of the frivolous poetry of the early eighteenth century had inevitably favored a revival of the style of Bashō. Tan Taigi (1709–71), Ōshima Ryōta (1718–87), Hori Bakusui (1718–83), Takakuwa Rankō (1726–98), Miura Chora (1729–80), Katō Kyōtai (1732–92), and Kaya Shirao (1738–91) were the most important poets of the revival, and their activities extended to many parts of the country—mainly places where Bashō had traveled and left disciples. These men at almost the same time, but independently, began to rediscover Bashō. In 1742, for example, Ryōta traveled to the north, following Bashō's traces, and in the following year, as part of the fiftieth-anniversary celebration, he joined with other poets in publishing supplementary materials about Bashō's journey. Buson and Taigi made similar journeys about the same time and other poets followed.

Although each of these poets had a circle of disciples in Edo, Nagoya, Kanazawa, or wherever it might be, the center of the revival definitely was in Kyoto. Even though other forms of literary activity in the capital had waned by this time, Kyoto still had outstanding scholars of Chinese (Minagawa Kien, Miyake Shōzan, etc.) and painters in the Chinese style (Sakaki

Hyakusen, Ike no Taiga, Itō Jakuchū, Maruyama Ōkyo, etc.), the two arts most closely associated with the haikai revival. The presence of Buson was also a magnet. Shirao from Kanazawa and Kyōtai from Edo, among others, visited Buson, joined in writing linked verses, and were deeply influenced by his style.

The return-to-Bashō movement for some men was no more than a rejection of the artificiality of the Edo school or the banalities of the Ise and Mino schools, but gradually poets realized that if they really wished to return to Bashō they must familiarize themselves with all his writings and follow what he taught. Kyōtai published *Conversations with Kyorai* in 1774, together with two collections of kasen by Bashō. But the poets differed as to which of Bashō's several styles should be preferred. Bakusui in *Shōmon Ichiya Kuju* (One Night's Oral Teaching of the School of Bashō, 1773) insisted that haikai poets should return to the pre-Genroku Bashō, especially the difficult, elevated manner of *Minashiguri* (Empty Chestnuts, 1683). In 1777 Bakusui published *Shin-Minashiguri* (The New Empty Chestnuts) to exemplify the way he thought modern poets should follow Bashō. Rankō, Ryōta, and Shirao, on the other hand, preferred the "lightness" of style of Bashō's last period, though they sometimes fought among themselves as to what precisely this was. Rankō admired the simplicity of *A Winter's Day*, and went to Shinano, Shirao's home grounds, to criticize the difficulty of Shirao's language. Chora was from Ise, where the old poetic traditions lingered, and liked to think that Bashō's haikai poetry was essentially quite similar to the waka in language and subject matter: "on evenings when the cherry trees were in blossom he clung to the feelings of the butterflies and birds and regretted the passing of the spring."[43] Each man tried desperately to establish his own special competence and authority.

These poets are remembered today for a few haikai each and sometimes for visits with Buson that resulted in a roll of haikai linked verse. They do not compare with Buson as poets and they share little of his popularity. However, before Masaoka Shiki published his celebrated essay *Haijin Buson* (1896–99), most Japanese probably considered Ryōta to have been the outstanding poet of the haikai revival. Ryōta published over two hundred books, boasted some two thousand disciples and, far from leading the life of a hermit in the manner of Bashō, was something of a social lion. Today Ryōta is remembered less for his poetry than for his efforts over the years to secure a "return to Bashō." Hardly a single poem has survived the test of time.[44] Perhaps the best, in Harold Henderson's beautiful translation, is:

samidare ya	All the rains of June:
aru yo hisoka ni	and one evening, secretly,
matsu no tsuki	through the pines, the moon.[45]

Taigi is a more appealing poet, He had almost no influence in the haikai circles of his day (he lived for years in the Shimabara licensed quarter and spurned the company of poets), but as a poet he ranks second to Buson. His poetry, marked by a warm humanity and closeness to ordinary experience, never drifts into vulgar or banal expression.

furimukeba	I look behind me:
hi tobosu seki ya	At the barrier, a light
yūgasumi	In the evening mist.[46]

hashi ochite	The bridge has fallen,
hito kishi ni ari	And people stand on the banks
natsu no tsuki	Under the summer moon.[47]

The second poem effectively depicts a scene: the bridge has been swept away by the river swollen with the summer rains, but now that it has cleared and the moon is shining people stand on the banks surveying the fallen bridge. Nature at its most frightening and most benign join in this city scene.

ne yo to iu	"Let's get to bed," says
nezame no tsuma	The husband who's been wakened:
sayoginuta	Fulling-block at night.[48]

This poem rivals Buson's in its ability to tell a story in seventeen syllables. A husband, wakened at night by the autumnal sound of someone beating a fulling-block, notices that his wife is also awake, and suggests that they both get back to sleep.[49] Or perhaps—the poem is ambiguous—the husband gets out of bed and, going outside, urges whoever is pounding the block to go to bed.[50] However one interprets the poem, it tells its story with economy and humor.

Taigi's poetry foreshadowed Buson's interest in romantic subjects:

hatsukoi ya	First love!
tōro ni yosuru	They draw close to the lantern,
kao to kao	Face next to face.[51]

Under a stone lantern, lit for the Bon Festival in early autumn, two young lovers, drawn to each other, brush face against face.

Finally, a *tour de force* by Taigi that comes off beautifully, an evocation of yellow kerria roses blooming profusely among leaves:

yamabuki ya	Kerria roses!
ha ni hana ni ha ni	Leaves and flowers and leaves and
hana ni ha ni	Flowers and leaves and . . .[52]

The haikai revival demonstrated that the form had not been killed by misuse earlier in the century. Buson developed new capabilities of expression, though at times he seemed to crave even freer forms of poetry. The poets of the revival often spoke of the necessity of returning to Bashō but they never did; no one could mistake their poems for those of the Master or his direct disciples. The "return" was in the attitude toward haikai composition; like Bashō the poets of the revival were sure that haikai could embrace a man's deepest thoughts and deserved the greatest care and intelligence. None of the poets attained Bashō's sublimity, but they never sought it. The qualities that Bashō inherited from medieval poetry no longer interested these poets.

Some attempts were also made to revive the traditions of haibun, prose in the haikai style. The best examples were probably by Buson, found in the prefaces to his collections. The preface to *Shin Hanatsumi* (1777) includes reminiscences of his youth and impressions of Kikaku and other poets, both of great interest, but we search in vain for a new masterpiece worthy of standing alongside Bashō's prose. The most celebrated work of haibun was *Uzuragoromo* (A Patchwork Cloak) by the Nagoya haikai poet Yokoi Yayū (1702–83).[53] Fragments of the manuscript were discovered by Ōta Nampo in Edo, and he eventually managed to piece together the whole work after Yayū's death. It consists of haibun essays written between 1727 and about 1770. The contents are humorous, rather in the manner of *haiga*, the haikai style of painting, with rapidly brushed-in comments on such subjects as ghosts, nightclothes, tobacco, the sadness of old age, borrowing things, and so on. It is the work of a dilettante, a bunjin, like so many other products of the haikai revival, but no less enjoyable for that.

NOTES

1. Quoted in Kuriyama Riichi, *Haikai Shi*, p. 180. Shikō undoubtedly was thinking of the practice of Po Chü-i, who was reputed to have tried all his poems on an illiterate old woman.

2. Abe Kimio and Asō Isoji, *Kinsei Haiku Haibun Shū* (henceforth abbreviated KHHS), p. 131.

3. KHHS, p. 136.

4. Quoted in Kuriyama, p. 179.

5. KHHS, p. 141.

6. KHHS, p. 152.

7. See KHHS, p. 152, and Teruoka Yasutaka, *Kinsei Haiku*, pp. 190–91.

8. Kawashima Tsuyu, "Chiyo-ni," p. 211.

9. KHHS, p. 146.

10. Preface to *Mukashi wo ima* (1774); text in Teruoka Yasutaka and Kawashima Tsuyu, *Buson Shū*, p. 272. Mention of the Master's stick refers to the rod a Zen master uses to startle a meditating monk into enlightenment.

11. See Konishi Jin'ichi, *Haiku*, p. 11, and Shimizu Takayuki, "Bashō ni kaere," pp. 110–13.

12. Ebara Taizō, *Buson Zenshū*, p. 728.

13. The mention of displaying cherry blossoms to one's hat refers to the haiku Bashō composed when he was about to start on his journey to Yoshino, famed for cherry blossoms. Buson's text, written in 1782, is included in Ebara Taizō, *Yosa Buson Shū*, p. 278.

14. See Kuriyama, p. 208.

15. Hagiwara Sakutarō, "Kyōshū no Shijin," p. 477.

16. *Ibid.*, p. 479.

17. Teruoka and Kawashima, p. 122.

18. *Ibid.*, p. 42.

19. See Shimizu Takayuki, *Buson no Kaishaku to Kanshō*, p. 3, for an analysis of what the word *mukashi* meant to Buson.

20. Teruoka and Kawashima, p. 91.

21. See Konishi, p. 159, and Shimizu, *Buson*, p. 81.

22. Teruoka and Kawashima, p. 89.

23. Konishi, p. 160.

24. Teruoka and Kawashima, p. 165.
25. *Ibid.*, p. 148.
26. *Ibid.*, p. 108.
27. *Ibid.*, p. 100.
28. Shimizu, *Buson*, p. 93. See also Teruoka, *Kinsei Haiku*, pp. 221–22.
29. Teruoka and Kawashima, p. 49.
30. *Ibid.*, p. 128.
31. Shimizu, *Buson*, p. 130.
32. Teruoka and Kawashima, pp. 258–60.
33. Andō Tsuguo, *Yosa Buson*, p. 63; Hagiwara, p. 477.
34. Andō has pointed out the significance of the signature *Shaku Buson*, indicating Buson was a priest at the time. Not only does the last stanza refer to his Amidist beliefs, but mention of the west wind earlier in the poem probably had similar overtones.
35. Translated in *Haikai and Haiku*, pp. 133–37.
36. Ebara, *Buson Zenshū*, p. 812.
37. Text in Teruoka and Kawashima, pp. 266–67.
38. *Ibid.*, p. 266.
39. Andō, p. 13.
40. See Konishi, p. 152.
41. Teruoka and Kawashima, p. 116. See also Konishi, p. 157, and Shimizu, *Buson*, pp. 108–109.
42. Ebara, *Buson Zenshū*, p. 688.
43. Shimizu, "Bashō ni kaere," p. 123.
44. Konishi, pp. 139–40.
45. Henderson, p. 111.
46. KHHS, p. 153.
47. KHHS, p. 154.
48. KHHS, p. 155.
49. Konishi, pp. 143–44.
50. KHHS, p. 155.
51. KHHS, p. 155.
52. KHHS, p. 153.
53. Text given in KHHS.

BIBLIOGRAPHY

Abe Kimio and Asō Isoji. *Kinsei Haiku Haibun Shū*, in Nihon Koten Bungaku Taikei series. Tokyo: Iwanami Shoten, 1964.

Andō Tsuguo. *Yosa Buson*. Tokyo: Chikuma Shobō, 1970.

Ebara Taizō. *Buson Zenshū* (revised and augmented). Kyoto: Kōseikaku, 1933.

——— and Shimizu Takayuki. *Yosa Buson Shū*, in Nihon Koten Zensho series. Tokyo: Asahi Shimbun Sha, 1957.

Hagiwara Sakutarō. "Kyōshū no Shijin Yosa Buson," in *Hagiwara Sakutarō Zenshū*, III. Tokyo: Shinchōsha, 1959.

Haikai and Haiku. Tokyo: The Nippon Gakujutsu Shinkōkai, 1958.

Henderson, Harold G. *An Introduction to Haiku*. Garden City, N.Y.: Doubleday, 1958.

Ijichi Tetsuo, *et al*. *Haikai Daijiten*. Tokyo: Meiji Shoin, 1957.

Kawashima Tsuyu. "Chiyo-ni," in *Haiku Kōza*, vol. II. Tokyo: Meiji Shoin, 1959.

Konishi Jin'ichi. *Haiku*. Tokyo: Kenkyūsha, 1952.

Kuriyama Riichi. *Haikai Shi*. Tokyo: Hanawa Shobō, 1963.

Shimizu Takayuki. "Bashō ni kaere," in Nihon Bungaku no Rekishi series, vol. VIII. Tokyo: Kadokawa Shoten, 1967.

———. *Buson no Kaishaku to Kanshō*. Tokyo: Meiji Shoin, 1956.

Teruoka Yasutaka. *Buson*. Tokyo: Meiji Shoin, 1954.

———. *Kinsei Haiku*. Tokyo: Gakutōsha, 1956.

——— and Kawashima Tsuyu. *Buson Shū, Issa Shū*, in Nihon Koten Bungaku Taikei series. Tokyo: Iwanami Shoten, 1959.

CHAPTER 15

HAIKAI POETRY

HAIKAI OF THE LATE TOKUGAWA PERIOD

The haikai revival rapidly distintegrated after the death of Buson in 1783. His chosen sucecssor, Takai Kitō, died at a drinking party in 1789, only forty-eight years of age, and the school thus came to an end. Shirao died in 1791 and Kyōtai in 1792. By 1800 virtually everyone who had been closely associated with the revival was dead. But even before all these poets had disappeared from the scene, a marked change was evident in the style of the haikai poetry being composed. Buson was not merely the best of a group of talented poets, but set the tone for the entire movement; and Kyoto, because Buson lived there, had been the center of haikai writing. After Buson's death, however, the aristocratic tone of the poetry of bunjin quickly gave way to the hearty simplicity of the popularizers. The writing of haikai developed into a nationwide avocation.

In 1783, as we have seen, Kyōtai celebrated the hundredth anniversary of Bashō's death ten years early, perhaps with the premonition that by 1793 most of the best poets (including himself) would be dead. On that occasion imposing ceremonies were conducted at three sites in Kyoto associated with Bashō. The 1793 celebrations were on quite a different scale. Not only did they extend to all parts of Japan, with special Buddhist services and the erection in many places of memorial stones, but they inspired the reprinting of Bashō's various collections, the publication of commentaries, and so on. Haikai masters, taking advantage of the new and widespread interest in in Bashō, began traveling ever more aggressively into remote regions, drumming up trade for their profession. Simple country folk found the composition of haikai a welcome diversion from the tedium of their lives, and gladly paid the traveling expenses of visiting poets. When collections of their haikai eventually were published, these rustic Miltons naturally were proud to share in the expenses.

The adulation offered Bashō also gave rise to a craze for journeying along the Narrow Road of Oku in the footsteps of the master. By the 1790s this journey had become an indispensable qualification for all haikai masters, and so many thronged the well-known routes that they came to be detested by the local people as a worse nuisance even than itinerant gamblers![1]

Ueda Akinari, disapproving of this adulation, declared that the hermit's life advocated by Bashō was a "poisonous" menace to society. He sardonically described the visit of a haikai poet to a remote town:

> Long ago there was a man who loved haikai. He journeyed all the way to distant Michinoku, drawn by nostalgia for the Narrow Road of Oku described by Bashō. One day he found himself at dusk by the foot of the castle of the governor of a certain province. He searched for a house where he might spend the night, but could find none. He had grown quite weary with anxiety when he noticed an old man standing by a gate. Going up to the man, he politely asked to spend the night. The old man looked him over and asked, "Are you a Zen priest?"
>
> "No," replied the man, "I do not follow any priestly disci-

pline. I am a student of the art of Master Bashō, and I have come all this distance hoping to see with my own eyes Matsugaurashima and Kisakata."

The old man's voice grew harsh: "Haikai teachers and gamblers aren't permitted to stay in the castle town of his lordship." Apparently both professions were equally disliked, a most unfortunate state of affairs.[2]

The popularity of haikai poetry nevertheless continued to grow. Unlike the similar movement in the early part of the eighteenth century, it was closely associated, in theory at least, with the name of Bashō, who had acquired the aura of a deity. Indeed, Bashō was given a name as a god in 1793 by the chief of the Department of Shinto, and in 1806 the court bestowed on him the title of Hion Myōjin, literally "Jumping Sound Bright Deity," a reference to Bashō's celebrated poem on the sound of water after a frog jumped in. In 1812 the poet Moro Nanimaru (1761–1837), exclaiming in awe and wonder at the marvelous profundity of the same hokku, declared, "Anyone who wishes to explain the full meaning of this poem should go to the afterworld, meet the Master, and ask him."[3] In 1843, the 150th anniversary of Bashō's death, he was elevated to the rank of daimyōjin in the Shinto pantheon, the same rank as Hitomaro.

Amateur poets from all over the country, from southern Kyushu to Hokkaido, were affected by the craze for haikai and the worship of Bashō.[4] An ability to compose haikai became a social accomplishment, indispensable at parties. This popularization inevitably lowered the standards, but there was no return to the manner of the Danrin poets who carelessly dashed off verse after verse while in their cups, or to the early eighteenth-century poets whose haikai were virtually indistinguishable from senryū; the new poets, however clumsy their style and however obvious their verses, always professed to be following Bashō, and they obeyed the surface requirements of his poetry absolutely, painstakingly including seasonal words, cutting words, and the rest. They were also unlike the amateur poets of the past who were satisfied with amusing friends with their verses; these men wanted to see their names and haikai in print.

Suzuki Michihiko (1757–1819) was a representative poet of the 1790s. He went to Edo from Sendai to practice medicine, and became a pupil of Kaya Shirao before 1790. After Shirao's death in 1791 Michihiko, by astute political maneuvering, managed to gain control of Shirao's school, and from his headquarters in Edo kept up a nationwide correspondence with other poets. Michihiko, never averse to controversy, issued a manifesto in 1798 violently denouncing the poets of the haikai revival. He did not spare even his own teacher; he wrote: "Shirao had all the weapons necessary to intimidate people, but not the deeper virtue of being able to get along with them."[5] Yet Michihiko, for all his arrogance, worshiped the memory of Bashō, and tried to imitate in every way Bashō's manner of living, visualizing himself as one of the faithful ten disciples.[6] He carved with his own hands a statute of Bashō and enshrined it as "the Buddha Tōsei." His verses too attempted to capture the *sabi* (quality of unostentatious beauty) of the Master:

neoki kara	As soon as I get up
uchiwa torikeri	I take my round fan in hand—
oinikeri	How old I've become![7]

This verse effectively evokes the picture of an old man waking on a hot summer's day, picking up the fan lying by his bed, then feeling a terrible weariness as he tries to cool himself. The repetition of the verb ending *-keri* at the ends of the second and third lines intensifies this mood of weariness.

Sometimes, however, Michihiko supplies all the "props" of a haikai in the Bashō manner, but misses the target:

sabishisa ya	What loneliness—
hi wo taku ie no	Irises beside a house
kakitsubata	At fire-lighting.[8]

Michihiko provided the verse with a cutting word (*ya*) and a seasonal word (*kakitsubata*), and he attempted to evoke the lonely atmosphere typical of Bashō's poetry, but irises were an ineptly chosen image for loneliness.

Michihiko was viciously attacked as a perverter of Bashō's teachings. His reputation today is low: he is generally dismissed as an ambitious and unscrupulous politician who popularized haikai as a means of self-aggrandizement. This evaluation is probably unfair; one apologist has claimed that Michihiko was more faithful to Bashō than the poets of the haikai revival.[9]

Whatever our judgment on Michihiko as poet and popularizer, it is clear that he himself was sure he was spreading the true Style of Bashō. Michihiko's poetry has been criticized for its "commonness," but perhaps his fidelity to the ideals of Bashō, despite his position as the leader of a popular movement in haikai, deserves greater praise than he has generally been allowed.

Michihiko was one of three famous poets of the Kansei era (1789–1800), the other two having been Emori Gekkyo (1756–1824) of Kyoto and Inoue Shirō (1742–1812) of Nagoya. Gekkyo, though a favorite pupil of Buson's, rapidly abandoned the Buson style after his master's death. Shirō, a disciple of Kyōtai's, was a kokugaku scholar and also excelled in Chinese and in painting; he was thus perfectly equipped to be a bunjin, but the extraordinarily high reputation he enjoyed during his lifetime soon melted away. It is easy to find quotable poems by these men, and even critics who deplore their flatness and vacuity admit their technical skill. Although these poets had nothing new to offer, they were intelligent and deeply devoted to the craft of poetry. Sometimes, however, in hope of attracting pupils, they adopted an overly facile style.

In the Meiji period Masaoka Shiki bitterly criticized what he termed the *tsukinami* style of the poets of the 1830s. The term *tsukinami* referred to the regular monthly meetings at which poets composed haikai without reference to observation or their actual emotions, relying on well-worn themes. Such poetry lacked the freshness that was always the "flower" of haikai poetry, and when read today little impresses us one way or the other.[10] Haikai became a national pastime, not very different from flower arrangement; it made life pleasanter, especially for retired old gentlemen or housewives with time on their hands, but it no longer served to convey a man's deepest feelings. It was, in the words of a much later critic, a "second-class art," agreeable to compose and publish, but seldom worth the effort to read.

In 1813 a nationwide register of haikai poets was published, containing information on some six hundred men, each with his portrait. Although these poets lived in all parts of the country and belonged to every social class, the largest number were from the Edo school, headed by Suzuki Michihiko.[11] A supplementary register, published in 1821, added another 120 names, the largest number of men from the northern provinces. Poets from Edo and from the north dominated haikai poetry in the nineteenth century. Collections of poetry grew bigger and more varied, and were no longer restricted to a single teacher and his disciples.

For the first time, too, poets who had never studied under any teacher were given recognition. Natsume Seibi (1749–1816), a well-to-do Edo townsman, rejected the professionalism of Michihiko and his followers, and insisted that haikai poetry should be the pleasure of the amateur, not a means of earning a livelihood. One verse may suggest the delicacy of Seibi's art:

haya aki no	Autumn—already
yanagi wo sukasu	The morning sun pierces through
asahi kana	The willow leaves.[12]

Seibi's poor health did not permit him to travel, but he engaged in a wide correspondence with poets throughout Japan; it has been claimed that it would be impossible to find a collection of haikai published anywhere in the country during the early years of the nineteenth century that failed to include at least one verse by Seibi.[13] He was a generous host to many visitors to Edo, including the two best poets of the period, Iwama Otsuni (1756–1823) and Kobayashi Issa (1763–1827).

Otsuni, like Seibi, was an autodidact. He insisted that a study of the poetry of the past provided a better guide to haikai composition than any teacher could. No less than other poets of his age, he worshiped Bashō, but the influence of Buson was also strong; he published in 1833 the first commentary on Buson, based on lectures he had delivered in remote Hakodate on the island of Hokkaido. Otsuni was constantly traveling. His travels, like Bashō's, had for their object a search for the essence of haikai poetry in nature; he was not attempting to "sell" a particular variety of haikai. By training he was a yamabushi priest, and he believed that writing haikai in itself constituted an act of religious discipline. The contrast between Otsuni and the smoothly professional poets of his time is striking: his deep religious convictions formed a bond between him and both Bashō and Buson. He was perhaps their most orthodox follower in the early nineteenth century. Otsuni excelled also at composing haikai no renga in the style of Bashō, giving this dying art a final moment of glory. His poems are filled with the landscapes of his native northeast—logs caught in seaweed drifting toward the shore in the early morning light, smoke rising from the open hearth of a farmhouse, melting snow dripping from the trees. The particularity of so many of his poems makes them difficult to translate, but Otsuni's poetry was even more seriously impaired by his excessive fidelity to his models. His poems lack individuality, though a yamabushi priest writing about distant regions of the country ought to have been able to break through the stagnation of tsukinami versemaking.

The one haiku poet of the period whose verses reveal a distinctive personality ranks in popular favor today with Bashō and Buson—Kobayashi Issa. He was immensely prolific: close to twenty thousand haikai have been preserved, and he also composed many verses of haikai no renga and works in prose.[14] Issa is loved by the Japanese people because of his personal, simply phrased poems, particularly on two subjects, his poverty and his affection for small animals and insects. His prose, especially *Ora ga Haru* (The Year of My Life, 1819), also ranks among the most moving documents of the nineteenth century.

The simplicity of Issa's poems and their strong associations with the mountain country of Shinano have led many readers to suppose that he spent his life in some remote village. He was indeed born in the mountains, to a fairly well-to-do farming family, but he left for Edo to become an apprentice when he was thirteen or fourteen, apparently because his stepmother made life miserable for him at home. It is not clear how Issa spent the next ten years in Edo, but whatever work he performed as an apprentice, his talents as a haikai poet must have revealed themselves. He became the pupil of Chikua (d. 1790), the leader of a fairly important school of haikai with disciples all over the country. After Chikua's death Issa succeeded (at the age of twenty-seven) as head of the school, further evidence of his precocious gifts. He was now a full-fledged marker (*tenja*), and when he set out in 1792 on a journey to the Kamigata region, Shikoku, and Kyushu, he was welcomed everywhere, not only by former disciples of Chikua but by the leading poets; he was especially pleased to have spent one night as a guest in Matsuyama Castle.[15] His style at the time resembled that of the poets of the haikai revival, and contained little of the subject matter that distinguished his mature poetry. A verse written in 1792 is skillful, but might have been written by a dozen other poets:

yūkaze ya	The evening winds—
yashiro no tsurara	Lamplight from inside the shrine
hi no utsuru	Reflects on icicles.[16]

Issa traveled for six years, until 1798. Although his journeys were intended to deepen his art, his poetry was little changed when he returned to Edo.[17] He spent most of the next fourteen years in Edo, eking out a living as a haikai teacher, so poor that he was obliged at times to lodge with his friend Seibi, for want of a house of his own; he frequently referred to himself as "Issa the beggar." In 1801 he returned home to Shinano after a long absence, and while he was there his father was mortally stricken. For a month Issa tended the father, who died that summer. Issa's account *Chichi no Shūen Nikki* (A Diary of My Father's Last Days) is one of his most affecting compositions; he describes not only his love for his dying father but his unpleasant relations with his stepmother and stepbrother. It is written in a strict diary form, with entries for almost every day, and contains only a scattering of poems, unlike Issa's other journals. According to Issa, his father on his deathbed expressed regret that he had sent Issa to Edo as a boy, and urged him to return to Shinano and raise a family. His will apparently divided his property among the three heirs, but the stepmother and stepbrother refused to carry out its provisions. Issa's dispute with them dragged on until 1813, when the stepbrother finally ceded half of the property. From then on Issa had a modest but steady income, and the remaining fourteen years before his death were spent more cheerfully. As a haikai master returned from Edo he attracted many pupils from the region, and was sufficiently prosperous to marry at last, after fifty. He had several children, all of whom died in infancy except for one posthumous daughter. The death of one of his children, a little girl named Sato, is described in the most poignant section of *The Year of My Life*,[18] and occasioned Issa's celebrated verse:

tsuyu no yo wa	The world of dew
tsuyu no yo nagara	Is a world of dew, and yet,
sarinagara	And yet . . .[19]

Issa's most important period as a poet was between the death of his father in 1801 and 1818, especially the last eight years, when he wrote some seventy-three hundred haikai. His verses are an extraordinary mixture of every style—parodies of old poems, imitations of his predecessors, haikai that can hardly be distinguished from senryū, and poems sprinkled with slang, dialect words, and snatches from popular songs.[20] Even though most of these verses were hardly worth preserving, some are unmistakably by Issa and nobody else:

ware wo mite	When he looks at me
nigai kao suru	What a sour face he makes,
kaeru kana	That frog over there![21]

Another haikai on a frog, written in 1816, when Issa went to watch a fight staged between two frogs, is even more famous:

yasegaeru	Skinny frog,
makeru na Issa	Don't get discouraged:
kore ni ari	Issa is here.[22]

Issa's sympathies were always with small and weak animals, perhaps because he identified himself with them, as the victim of his stepmother's cruelty. A poem that appeared in 1814 was signed with Issa's childhood name and a note stating that it was composed when he was a boy of six or eight; perhaps he actually wrote the poem when his father remarried, or perhaps he merely ascribed it to his childhood in retrospect:

ware to kite	Come with me,
asobe yo oya no	Let's play together, sparrow
nai suzume	Without a mother.[23]

Issa even showed sympathy for insects and animals that are normally disliked:

yare utsu na	Hey! don't swat him!
hae wa te wo suri	The fly rubs his hands, rubs his feet
ashi wo suru	Begging for mercy.[24]

Issa ingeniously interpreted the characteristic movements of a fly on alighting in this poem suggestive of a senryū. Another poem on flies, in Harold Henderson's translation, goes:

yo ga yokuba	If the times were good,
mo hitotsu tomare	I'd say: "One more of you, sit
meshi no hae	down, flies around my food!"[25]

Other verses describe mosquito wrigglers, baby spiders and other unattractive creatures, with all of whom Issa managed to feel a bond of sympathy.[26] Issa's poetry is certainly appealing, but it is debatable whether or not his professions of solidarity with frogs, snails, and flies should be called haikai. They have almost no tension, make almost no demands on the reader; they are little more than epigrams, artfully conceived. There is no disputing the freshness and individuality even of verses that disregard the traditional standards of haikai, and Issa on occasion showed that he was quite capable of writing more conventional poems when he so chose:

ariake ya	At break of dawn
Asama no kiri ga	The fog from Asama creeps
zen wo hau	Over my breakfast tray.[27]

This verse beautifully evokes a scene in Karuizawa, near Mount Asama. On a chilly autumn morning the traveler is about to take his breakfast before an early departure when he notices the fog creeping into his room and over his food. Probably the moon still lingers in the sky, lending a bleak light to the scene. This verse, written in 1812, suggests Issa could easily have surpassed Seibi or Otsuni if he had written in the style of the haikai revival.

It is surprising that Issa turned his back on larger aspects of nature to devote himself almost exclusively to trifling observations. Perhaps it is even more surprising that he continued to observe the formal requirements of haikai poetry and also participated in composing linked verse. We may wonder why Issa did not kick over the traces and write poems in forms that were as untraditional as his subjects. Perhaps, as one critic suggested,[28] it is well that he did not; freed of controls he might have given himself to excesses of sentimentality or farce that would surely not have enhanced his reputation.

Issa is an unforgettable poet, but in the end he leaves us unsatisfied because he so rarely treated serious subjects. As a young man he must have known the horrors of the natural disasters that struck his part of the country, especially the eruption of Asama in 1783, but he never refers to them. Even if he felt that haikai poetry was not suited to describing such tragedies, he might at least have expressed his concern for humanity, rather than for mosquito wrigglers; but his poems refuse to treat the world seriously. His earliest reputation was as a comic poet,[29] and his commonplace books, given over to quotations he admired from poets of the past, are filled with extracts from Teitoku's haikai writings, kyōka by various poets, and even the haikai poetry of Hosokawa Yūsai.[30] Certainly Issa was capable of expressing tragedy—no one who has read *The Year of My Life* could doubt this—but he was reluctant to reveal these feelings in his poetry. His enormous success with readers, especially after his rediscovery by Masoaka Shiki in the 1890s, proves that he supplied a want that no other poet filled, even though his subject matter was limited.

Issa had no literary posterity. If he had never appeared the history of haikai would probably not have been much changed.[31] But we are fortunate that there was an Issa; the sincerity and warmth emanating from his poetry were qualities rare in the haikai poetry of any age and unique in their own.

The last group of haikai poets of the Tokugawa period are known as the poets of the Tempō era (1830–43). Three men—there are always three!—were ranked as the masters of the age, Tagawa Hōrō (1762–1845), Narita Sōkyū (1761–1842), and Sakurai Baishitsu (1769–1852). These men were the special targets of Masaoka Shiki; he attacked their tsukinami poetry, the product of cogitation and technique rather than of felt experience or observation. However, their poetry, on one level at least, was far more skillful than Issa's, and they could write haikai hardly inferior to those of the masters of the haikai revival. They in fact represent the full flowering of the art of haikai, and their poems, finished products that reveal a complete mastery of the traditions of Bashō and Buson, were perfect to the last detail.[32] But this poetry has not survived because it possesses no distinctive odor of its own. Anyone can recognize a poem by Issa, good or bad, but it would take a great scholar of haikai poetry to identify a work by one of the three masters of the Tempō era.

At a time when the leading poets of the waka—Kotomichi, Akemi, and Kageki—were preaching the necessity of contemporaneity in poetry and sometimes even achieving this ideal, haikai had become classical and utterly remote from its day; its marble perfection invited the attacks of a Shiki. The poets of the

Tempō era looked back to Bashō and invoked his authority, but they forgot his insistence on ryūkō, the change that is the necessary complement to the eternal.

NOTES

1. Shimizu Takayuki, "Haikai no Taishūka," p. 251.
2. Iwahashi Koyata (ed.), *Ueda Akinari Zenshū*, I, p. 341.
3. Quoted in Kuriyama Riichi, *Haikai Shi*, p. 299.
4. Kuriyama, p. 262.
5. Nakamura Shunjō, *Buson Igo*, p. 14.
6. Suzuki Katsutada, "Suzuki Michihiko," p. 410.
7. Abe Kimio and Asō Isoji, *Kinsei Haiku Haibun Shū*, p. 199.
8. Nakamura, p. 14.
9. Suzuki, p. 415.
10. See Konishi Jin'ichi, *Haiku*, p. 173.
11. Shimizu, p. 242.
12. Abe and Asō, p. 197.
13. Nakamura, p. 17.
14. Itō Masao, *Kobayashi Issa Shū*, p. 1.
15. Shimizu, pp. 252–53.
16. Konishi, p. 166.
17. See Itō, p. 4.
18. Translation by Nobuyuki Yuasa, *The Year of My Life*, pp. 103–104.
19. Teruoka Yasutaka and Kawashima Tsuyu, *Buson Shū, Issa Shū*, p. 462.
20. Shimizu, p. 255.
21. Konishi, p. 169.
22. Teruoka and Kawashima, p. 331.
23. *Ibid.*, p. 457.
24. *Ibid.*, p. 341.
25. Harold G. Henderson, *An Introduction to Haiku*, p. 142.
26. See Kuriyama, p. 268.
27. Teruoka and Kawashima, p. 347.
28. Kuriyama, p. 272.
29. *Ibid.*, p. 274.
30. *Ibid.*, pp. 289–90.
31. Kawashima Tsuyu, in Teruoka and Kawashima, p. 315.
32. Konishi, p. 173.

BIBLIOGRAPHY

Abe Kimio and Asō Isoji. *Kinsei Haiku Haibun Shū*, in Nihon Koten Bungaku Taikei series. Tokyo: Iwanami Shoten, 1964.

Henderson, Harold G. *An Introduction to Haiku*. Garden City, N.Y.: Doubleday, 1958.

Itō Masao. *Kobayashi Issa Shū*, in Nihon Koten Zensho series. Tokyo: Asahi Shimbun, 1953.

Iwahashi Koyata. *Ueda Akinari Zenshū*, in Kokusho Kankōkai series. Tokyo: Kokusho Kankōkai, 1917.

Konishi Jin'ichi. *Haiku*. Tokyo: Kenkyūsha, 1952.

Kuriyama Riichi. *Haikai Shi*. Tokyo: Hanawa Shobō, 1963.

Mackenzie, Lewis. *The Autumn Wind: a Selection from the Poems of Issa*. London: John Murray, 1957.

Nakamura Shunjō. *Buson Igo*, in Nihon Bungaku Shi series. Tokyo: Iwanami Shoten, 1958.

Shimizu Takayuki. "Haikai no Taishūka," in Nakamura Yukihiko and Matsuyama Matsunosuke, *Bunka Ryōran*, vol. VIII of Nihon Bungaku no Rekishi series. Tokyo: Meiji Shoin, 1959.

Suzuki Katsutada. "Suzuki Michihiko," in *Haiku Kōza*, III. Tokyo: Meiji Shoin, 1959.

Teruoka Yasutaka and Kawashima Tsuyu. *Buson Shū, Issa Shū*, in Nihon Koten Bungaku Taikei series. Tokyo: Iwanami Shoten, 1959.

Yuasa, Nobuyuki (trans.). *The Year of My Life: A Translation of Issa's Oraga Haru*. Berkeley: University of California Press, 1960.

CHAPTER 16

FICTION

UEDA AKINARI (1734–1809)

During the hundred years after Saikaku's death only one writer of fiction appeared whose works are still widely read today, Ueda Akinari. He is a difficult writer to classify because his literary production extends into many genres and styles. For most people he is known only as the author of *Ugetsu Monogatari* (Tales of Rain and the Moon), a brilliant collection of stories, mainly dealing with ghosts and other supernatural phenomena. Akinari undoubtedly considered this work to be of small consequence; his commentaries on the Japanese classics and studies of antiquity, the product of his long association with kokugaku scholars, occupied him during most of his mature years, and only at the end of his life did he turn again to fiction, when he wrote *Harusame Monogatari* (Tales of the Spring Rain). Despite the fewness of his stories, there is no mistaking his extraordinary talent, and his life has intrigued many students of eighteenth-century Japan.

Akinari was born in Osaka, apparently the illegitimate child of a prostitute. His mother died when he was three, but soon afterward he was adopted by a prosperous merchant, only to be struck by another misfortune: in 1738, when he was four, he contracted such a severe case of smallpox that one finger on each hand was twisted and shortened out of shape. This affliction did not prevent him from writing voluminously in later years, but he remained sensitive about his misshapen fingers, using a penname for *Tales of Rain and the Moon* that refers obliquely to them.[1] Despite his early misfortunes, he seems to have led a cheerful and even rather wild life as a young man, protected by foster parents who were deeply devoted to him; but he was also interested in his studies, and obtained a better than average education.[2] At the age of twenty-one he first published some haikai, and he continued from then on to associate with leading poets. In 1774 he wrote the essay *Yasaishō*, a discussion of the kireji (cutting words) of haikai; it is graced by a preface by Buson, whom Akinari met in the following year. Seven haikai by Akinari were also included in Buson's collection *Zoku Akegarasu* (1775), to which he contributed a preface. Akinari seemed well on the way to establishing himself as a poet, but he was convinced that writing haikai was no more than a diversion, and refused to allow *Yasaishō* to be published for thirteen years, until he finally succumbed to the pleading of friends.[3]

It was through haikai that Akinari formed some valuable friendships, notably with Fujitani Nariakira and Hattori Seigyo, about 1758, when he was twenty-four. Nariakira, the younger brother of the well-known Confucian literatus (bunjin) Minagawa Kien, was precociously gifted, and from childhood enjoyed reading novels written in colloquial Chinese. Later in life he founded a school of Japanese philology. It was he who stimulated Akinari's interest in kokugaku. Seigyo was not only familiar with colloquial Chinese fiction, but had learned to read it in Chinese pronunciations; he introduced Akinari to these works that so greatly influenced his later fiction.[4]

In 1766, at the age of thirty-two, Akinari published a ukiyo zōshi called *Shodō Kikimimi Sekenzaru* (Worldly Monkeys with

Ears for the Arts), and in the following year a similar work, *Seken Tekake Katagi* (Characters of Worldly Mistresses), both in the vein of the Hachimonji-ya books. He signed these works Wayaku Tarō; this name suggested to some critics that the stories were Japanese translations (*wayaku*) of Chinese works, but there is no evidence of borrowing; *wayaku* was a dialectal word meaning "peculiar" and the name was probably an example of Akinari's drollery.[5] These two books are popular fiction in the tradition of ukiyo zōshi: most of the stories are humorous in conception, and it is hard to detect any deeper purpose than entertainment. Nevertheless, Akinari was so much superior to his predecessors in the genre that critics have found deeper significance in his stories than in similar works. But the modernity, antifeudalism, or cynicism they have read into these two unpretentious collections of stories owes more to their own literary persuasions than to anything Akinari wrote.[6]

Worldly Monkeys and *Worldly Mistresses* are in the tradition of Ejima Kiseki and Tada Nanrei. The sixth story in *Worldly Monkeys*, for example, tells about Yozaemon, the debt-ridden customer of a teahouse run by the fierce Kisuke, known as the Devil. Kisuke goes one day to collect his debts, only to discover that Yozaemon's house has been stripped bare, even to the mats on the floor. He searches the neighborhood until he at last finds his man in another house sitting stark naked in the cold. Kisuke the Devil is so shocked at the sight that he throws down some money and runs off in dismay.[7] The kernel of the story is amusing, and the description of exactly what Kisuke sees when he penetrates Yozaemon's house—"everything had been sold down to the *tatami* and rats had built nests in the bamboo flooring. There was one scrap of paper and a single wooden clog; the only remaining object in sight was a spider's web"[8]—suggests the enumerative skill of the ukiyo zōshi writer. The rest of the story, however, is marked by the typical digressiveness of the genre: it opens with a rather amusing but irrelevant passage describing the varieties of tattooing preferred by dashing young men of Edo, and concludes with Yozaemon, having become a Buddhist priest out of despair at the world, taking part as a drummer in a performance of Nō plays. He wears a wig, to hide his shaven head; but drums so energetically the wig falls off, to his great embarrassment. Nothing in the artistic conception and very little in the style suggests Akinari's superiority to other Hachimonji-ya writers.

His next work, *Worldly Mistresses*, though ostensibly a series of portraits of different varieties of mistresses, deals more with wives than with mistresses. Akinari's preface discloses that he wrote the book not as a keepsake for eternity but in order to raise money to repair his dilapidated house; he also states that his ten stories are sad or funny, depending on how kindly the mistresses were treated. The best story in the collection is definitely sad. It tells of Saitarō, the son of a rich farmer, who loses his fortune gambling on the rice exchange in Osaka. His mistress, a former prostitute named Fujino, is determined to set Saitarō on his feet, and in order to raise money sells herself to a brothel once again. Saitarō gratefully accepts the money and goes to Edo, resolved to win a fortune. He hears of a promising deal in silks and goes to an island to purchase them. On the way back to Edo, however, his ship is intercepted by pirates, and Saitarō is robbed of all his possessions. In despair and humiliation, he commits suicide. When the news reaches Osaka, the master of the brothel where Fujino works shows her the greatest consideration—quite unlike most brothel-keepers of Japanese fiction! He says it is entirely up to Fujino whether she continues to serve as a prostitute or follows Saitarō in death. Fujino, after a suitable period of mourning, bravely decides to show her appreciation to the master by entertaining customers with no suggestion of her personal grief. When her contract expires she becomes a hairdresser in the licensed quarter and, never marrying, spends the rest of her life praying for Saitarō's repose.[9]

Obviously this story is not only markedly superior in every way to the silly tale of Kisuke the Devil, but its tone threatens to break the confines of the ukiyo zōshi. The story opens in the flippant, allusive manner of the Hachimonji-ya books, but once we have entered the main story, it approaches tragedy. The self-sacrificing devotion of Fujino and the decency of Eigorō, the brothel-keeper, belong to a different world from the usual stories about the licensed quarter. At the beginning of the work Saitarō is portrayed as a typical spendthrift, destined to lose the fortune he inherited, but the suicide note he writes to Eigorō, asking him to persuade Fujino to live on without him, is so moving that he seems transformed into an altogether different and superior person. Akinari, evidently much impressed by his heroine, Fujino, remarks at the end that her devotion to Saitarō's memory was "without parallel even in the *Accounts of Virtuous Women* (*Lieh Nü Chuan*) of those damned Chinese." This last foolish jest, referring to the Chinese by the uncomplimentary expression *ketōjin*, in no way alters the serious, almost tragic nature of the tale. Fujino is the first of Akinari's paragons of Japanese womanly virtues. Even if her portrait is incompletely drawn, it has much more depth than anything we would expect of a "character" in a collection of mistresses. It suggests that Akinari already had in mind a different kind of fiction.

The preface to *Tales of Rain and the Moon* bears the date 1768, the year after the publication of *Worldly Mistresses*, but the book was not published until 1776. The style and content are so unlike Akinari's previous writings that most critics find it impossible to believe that *Rain and the Moon* was in fact completed in 1768; perhaps the preface itself was written in 1768 for an earlier draft of the stories, but they were reworked many times before publication eight years later.[10]

Various changes in Akinari's personal affairs had affected his future writings. In 1771 his house was destroyed in a fire, and Akinari lost all his possessions. When it proved impossible to restore the business Akinari had been left by his foster father, he decided in 1773 to begin the study of medicine. He also took up kokugaku, combining these two disciplines like Motoori Norinaga before him. Akinari himself had a very modest opinion of his abilities as a doctor but he prospered in his new profession, apparently because of the unusual conscientiousness he displayed toward patients, even if not fully equipped to deal with their illnesses. In 1788, however, he made a faulty diagnosis that resulted in the death of a small girl; this so upset him that he gave up his practice. Henceforth he devoted himself mainly to kokugaku.

Akinari's studies of kokugaku undoubtedly account for some stories in *Rain and the Moon*, notably the first, "Shiramine," a dialogue between the priest Saigyō and the retired emperor Sutoku, set in the year 1168. But even more conspicuous than the influence of kokugaku were those from Chinese colloquial fiction. Akinari was the first major writer to benefit by an acquaintance with this body of literature.

The knowledge of colloquial Chinese in Japan had been greatly promoted by the activities of Okajima Kanzan (d. 1727), originally a Nagasaki interpreter, who moved to Edo in 1705. The philosopher Ogyū Sorai, believing that colloquial Chinese was of use in understanding the original meanings of the Chinese Confucian texts, organized a study group around Okajima Kanzan, initiating the first serious study of spoken Chinese among the intellectuals. Kanzan himself undertook to punctuate for reading in Japanese the great Chinese novel *Shui Hu Chuan* (All Men Are Brothers). He published the first ten of the hundred chapters of the book in 1727, the year of his death, and another ten chapters appeared posthumously in 1759. Other men pushed on with the Japanese version of this classic of colloquial fiction, and these translations, together with versions of Ming collections of short stories enjoyed popularity among the intellectuals, as a welcome relief from the tedium of the Hachimonji-ya books.

Ogyū Sorai's disciples used various collections of Chinese ghost stories as texts when learning the colloquial language, but they were not expected to show much interest in the subject matter. The disciples of Itō Tōgai (1670–1736), on the other hand, often became devout admirers of Chinese colloquial fiction. Those with literary talent were not satisfied merely with punctuating texts; instead, they made full translations or even Japanese parallel versions to the Chinese stories. In earlier times such men as Asai Ryōi had included Japanese versions of Chinese ghost tales in his collection *Otogibōko* (Hand Puppets, 1666), but the originals were in classical Chinese, not the colloquial. The new wave of translation and adaptation drew on both classical and colloquial materials.

The success of these works was so great that in 1754 a new category appeared in booksellers' catalogues—*shōsetsu*, at first a term designating works translated from the Chinese, but later used for all varieties of fiction.[11] These early shōsetsu were popular mainly because of their well-constructed and ingenious plots.

The first author to earn a reputation for his adaptations of Chinese colloquial fiction was an Osaka physician named Tsuga Teishō (1718–*c.* 1794), who had become familiar with these writings as a disciple of the Ogyū Sorai school of Confucianism.

In 1749 he published *Hanabusa Sōshi* (A Garland of Heroes), a collection of nine stories, all but one derived from the three most famous Ming collections of ghost stories. Teishō's adaptations did not consist merely of rendering Chinese stories in literary Japanese; he recast them completely into tales of the Kamakura and Muromachi periods, adding numerous historical details to lend them a Japanese character. It was, of course, common practice to evade the censorship by shifting contemporary events into the past; *Chūshingura* (The Treasury of Loyal Retainers), to cite one example, was set in the fourteenth century and some characters were given the names of historical personages. Teishō's intent, however, was not to circumvent the edict of 1722 prohibiting the discussion in print of contemporary affairs,[12] but to give greater immediacy to his versions of Chinese stories by associating their events with familiar Japanese landscapes and people. This was essentially thc same attitude of the author of *Nihon Reiiki* (Account of Miracles in Japan), compiled almost a thousand years earlier: by specifying the particular places in Japan where the miracles had occurred he persuaded readers that such extraordinary events were actually much closer to their own lives than they had supposed. This was particularly important in the case of ghost stories. If an author says, "Once upon a time in a distant country a terrible ghost was seen," he certainly does not have the same effect as if he says, "In the village of Saga, not far from the capital, a terrible ghost was seen by—."

Later men sometimes referred to *A Garland of Heroes* as "the ancestor of the *yomihon*."[13] The *yomihon*, a serious form of fiction intended for "reading" (as opposed to picture books, which were meant to be looked at), developed early in the nineteenth century in reaction to the prevailing frivolous works of fiction. In their stylistic mixture of Chinese and Japanese elements these books did indeed follow the traditions established by Tsuga Teishō. The moral purpose of the yomihon was also foreshadowed by Teishō's concern, announced in the preface to *A Garland of Heroes*, "to describe the importance of a spirit of righteousness."[14]

Teishō published two other collections in the same vein, *Shigeshige Yawa* (1766) and *Hitsujigusa* (1786). There is virtually no stylistic difference, despite the long period that elapsed between his first collection and the last—thirty-seven years. It is now believed that Teishō wrote all twenty-seven stories about the same time, when still a young man.[15]

Some evidence suggests that Ueda Akinari studied medicine with Tsuga Teishō during the years immediately preceding the publication of *Rain and the Moon.*[16] This influence might explain Akinari's use of a similar technique in writing—"naturalizing" Chinese popular fiction by setting the stories in ancient or medieval Japan. But Akinari was at even greater pains to conceal his sources, giving his characters such unmistakably Japanese attitudes and backgrounds that it would never have occurred to the ordinary reader that Chinese models had been followed. Unlike the yomihon writers, moreover, Akinari had no Confucian philosophy to expound; indeed, his attitude was anti-Confucian, as we might expect of a kokugaku scholar. His style is also conspicuously less Chinese in vocabulary and construction than Teishō's. Akinari, for all his eminence, was not considered by Bakin and the other yomihon writers as an "ancestor."

Bakin chose, instead, a writer he much admired, Takebe Ayatari (1719–74), as his candidate for "ancestor of the Edo yomihon."[17] Ayatari, a rival of Akinari, was a samurai from the north of Japan who turned to literature as a young man after a scandalous love affair with his brother's wife had resulted in expulsion from his native fief. He studied haikai poetry with Bashō's disciple Yaha, and painting with the bunjinga artist Sakaki Hyakusen, as well as with a Chinese painter in Nagasaki. In 1763 Ayatari formally became a member of the kokugaku school of Kamo no Mabuchi. In his desperate eagerness to make a name for himself, he attempted to revive the archaic poetic form called *katauta*, a "half poem" consisting of five, seven, and five syllables, the first three lines of a waka, or else five, seven, and seven syllables, the first three lines of the ancient poetic form called *sedōka*. These efforts met with scant success, so he turned next to writing a monogatari in the pseudo-Heian style, following the example of such kokugaku scholars as Kada no Azumamaro. His first work in this form was Nishiyama Monogatari (Tale of the Western Hills) published in three volumes in 1768. The story is permeated by the ideals of *bushidō* (the way of the samurai), not surprisingly when we realize that Ayatari was a great-grandson of the foremost exponent of this code, Yamaga Sokō; the manly ideal known as *masuraoburi* was equally appropriate for a disciple of Kamo no Mabuchi. At the same time, Ayatari was trying to inculcate in the samurai of his day a love of the elegant literature of the past. He used archaisms deliberately, explaining them with notes inserted into the body of the text that give both the meaning and the source. This scholarship makes the book rather ponderous, but the style and ideals, if not the literary value, qualify *Tale of the Western Hills* as an ancestor of the yomihon.

The rivalry between Ayatari and Akinari may have led Akinari to date the preface to *Rain and the Moon* 1768, though the book was not published for another eight years. Ayatari published *Tale of the Western Hills* in 1768 and Akinari did not wish to appear to have lagged behind him.[18] There is reason to believe, nevertheless, that Ayatari's archaistic style and themes influenced the writing of *Tales of Rain and the Moon* and Akinari's later works.[19]

Tales of Rain and the Moon consists of nine stories divided into five books. Although Akinari's name nowhere appears in the text, he was identified as the author by Bakin in 1833, and the attribution now seems certain. The collection is generally assigned to the category of ghost stories (*kaidan*). Ghost stories go back very far in Japan, to *Account of Miracles in Japan*, *Konjaku Monogatari* (Tales of Now and Long Ago), and other collections. The prominent attention given to ghosts in the Nō plays and even in such works as *The Tale of Genji* hardly needs mentioning. But ghost stories emerged as a distinct genre only during the Tokugawa period. The first collections seem to have been written under Buddhist inspiration, but the emphasis soon shifted from a pious intent to control devils by revealing their nefarious ways, to an artistic effort to narrate an interesting story. The large number of ghost stories that appeared at this time should not be interpreted as signifying that Japanese of the seventeenth or eighteenth century were especially troubled by the fear of ghosts.[20] The stories were almost always set in the past and in distant parts of the country, unlike the ukiyo zōshi, the product of contemporary urban life.

Three early collections of ghost stories established the characteristic varieties of the genre: *Tonoigusa* (1660) by Ogita Ansei (d. 1669), a haikai poet; *Inga Monogatari* (Tales of

Cause and Effect, 1661) by Suzuki Shōsan (1579–1655), a Zen priest; and *Otogibōko* (Hand Puppets, 1666) by Asai Ryōi, a professional writer. *Tonoigusa*, the prototype of the folk-tale ghost story, consists of sixty-eight stories, mainly about the strange doings perpetrated by animals—rats, foxes, spiders, and so on. *Tales of Cause and Effect*, the prototype of the Buddhist ghost story, was written with the intent of bringing about an awakening to the faith by describing prodigies that had occurred as the result of the inexorable workings of the principle of cause and effect. *Hand Puppets* consists of ghost stories derived from Chinese collections written in the classical language.[21]

Elements from all three varieties of ghost stories are found in *Tales of Rain and the Moon*: in "Shiramine," a tengu, a fabulous beast associated with the folk-tale, appears at the climax; "The Dream Carp" and "The Blue Hood" are Buddhist tales. "The Chrysanthemum Tryst" and "The Kibitsu Cauldron" are adaptations from the Chinese. Akinari's work, however, is most strongly marked by the influence of colloquial Chinese fiction.

The antecedents of each of the nine stories in *Rain and the Moon* have been most carefully investigated by Japanese scholars, yet they have not felt it necessary to explain why Akinari is considered the finest Japanese writer of stories about the supernatural. "Shiramine," the first piece in *Rain and the Moon*, for example, hardly qualifies as a ghost story in the usual sense. It relates how the spirit of the retired emperor Sutoku appears before the poet-priest Saigyō and announces his intention of wreaking harm on the imperial household. Saigyō remonstrates with him at length, urging the emperor to renounce his old hatred and turn his thoughts toward salvation. The intractable emperor predicts the imminent destruction of his old enemies, the Taira family, his rage mounting until his face turns scarlet and he breathes fire. He summons a tengu, a winged demon, and orders it to torture and kill his enemies. Saigyō begs the emperor to remember the inevitable sequence of cause and effect. His words and prayers have effect: the emperor's face calms. He and the tengu disappear, leaving Saigyō alone. The story concludes with an account of the disasters that struck the Taira family thirteen years later, in 1179, when the retired emperor Sutoku's curses came to fruition.

Most of "Shiramine" is taken up with totally unnovelistic argumentation. A Western reader not familiar with Japanese history has difficulty following the story, which has little intrinsic interest. Even a Japanese reader would probably find "Shiramine" insufficiently engrossing if he read it in a modern-language translation; but read in the original, "Shiramine" impresses by its overpowering beauty of style, the essence of Akinari's elegant prose. The first paragraphs describe in language that echoes the poetry of the past the travels of an unidentified person in the autumn of 1168 to the island of Shikoku, where he visits the tomb of the retired emperor Sutoku in the village of Shiramine. The description has the cadences of a michiyuki, and the story as a whole takes its structure from the Nō plays. We only gradually learn the traveler's identity: an unknown man is praying before a tomb that Sutoku will be forgiven his sins, when a voice calls to him, "En'i! En'i!" The learned reader would realize that the unidentified person must be Saigyō, known as En'i when a young man; and the ghost who presently appears before Saigyō, much as in a Nō play, proves to be the former emperor Sutoku.

The Japanese reader with the necessary knowledge of the historical background will be intrigued by the plot and enchanted by the style. But it probably would not occur to anyone reading "Shiramine" in translation that Akinari was a writer of the first quality, considered by the Japanese to be worthy of a lifetime's research. The main theme of "Shiramine" was borrowed from *A Garland of Heroes*, describing the dispute between the emperor Godaigo and his councilor Fujifusa. Other elements were borrowed from a wide variety of sources. Indeed, Japanese scholars have shown that every story in the *Rain and the Moon* can be traced to one or more works of Japanese and Chinese literature. Few elements were invented by Akinari,[22] but thanks to his style, and to an awareness that detected superior literary possibilities in some familiar tale, he produced a work esteemed as a classic.

Probably the most affecting part of *Rain and the Moon* is "Asaji ga Yado" (The House in the Reeds), based directly on a story in the Chinese collection *Chien Têng Hsin Hua* (New Stories after Snuffing the Lamp, 1378) by Ch'ü Yu (1341–1427), called "The Tale of Ai-Ching."[23] A young man named Chao has fallen in love with a courtesan named Ai-ching. He marries her, and they live happily together in the same house with his mother, a widow. One day a letter arrives from an official in Peking, a relative of his father's, offering to prepare the young man for an important position. Chao is reluctant to leave his mother and wife, but they urge him to go, reminding him that it is a man's duty to seize every opportunity to establish himself in the world and bring credit to his family. He is at length persuaded, but when he arrives in the capital he discovers that his patron is out of favor. Chao bides his time, hoping for some improvement in his fortunes, but in the meantime his mother, worried by his absence, falls seriously ill. Ai-ching tends her with great solicitude, but the mother dies. The grief-stricken Ai-ching spends her days and nights weeping by the mother's grave.

In 1356 warfare erupts, and spreads to the village where Ai-ching lives. Her house is occupied by soldiers, and their leader, attracted by her beauty, decides to ravish her. She runs from him and hangs herself with a silken scarf. The soldier, unable to revive Ai-ching, buries her in the garden. Soon afterward peace is restored, and Chao returns home. Everything has changed: the house is in ruins, rats run over the rafters, and owls nest in the trees. Accidentally learning what has happened from an old man, Chao digs under the garden tree and finds Ai-ching's body. She looks alive, and as beautiful as ever. He washes her body, clothes it splendidly, and buries Ai-ching beside his mother.

Ten days later Chao is sitting in his room late at night when he hears weeping. He realizes it must be Ai-ching's ghost, and asks that she show herself. She does, and he sees she is quite unchanged, except for an unfamiliar scarf twisted around her neck. Chao thanks her for having served his mother so faithfully, and for having preserved her chastity, even at the cost of her life. Ai-ching in turn expresses her gratitude for having been rescued from the life of a prostitute. She tells Chao that his mother has already been reborn, but that she herself wanted so badly to see her husband again that she postponed her rebirth until the following day. She reveals that she is to be reborn as a boy in a certain city. They spend the night in each other's arms, but at cockcrow she tearfully says goodbye and disappears.

Chao later goes to the house Ai-ching described, and sees a baby boy who, he is informed, was twenty months in his mother's womb. The baby has been weeping ever since he was born, but at sight of Chao he smiles. From then on Chao and the baby's family never fail to keep in touch.

The same story was adapted by Asai Ryōi in *Hand Puppets.*[24] Almost every detail in the plot exactly follows the Chinese original, though Ai-ching is given the Japanese name Miyagino, and Chao is known as Fujii Seiroku. Here and there Ryōi also added characteristically Japanese details: Seiroku's mother, hearing that her son has ransomed Miyagino from a brothel and made her his wife, is most distressed, because the Fujii family is of great consequence, and she had intended her son to marry a girl of equal distinction. But she relents when she sees how lovely and gentle Miyagino is, and decides that no girl, no matter of what lineage, could make a better wife. From this point on the story follows the Chinese original closely, though details are drawn from the warfare in Japan of the sixteenth century. Only the end is different: unlike Ai-ching, Miyagino's ghost does not sleep with her husband; she vanishes, instead, like the mist after revealing that she is to be reborn imminently. Seiroku goes to Kamakura and finds a baby boy who smiles at him.

Asai Ryōi added extremely little to the plot, but his adaptation is so skillful it reads quite naturally as a Japanese story, and some details are superior to the original. Ueda Akinari's version, on the other hand, transforms the Chinese tale into an infinitely more artistic story.

"The House in the Reeds" opens about 1455 in the province of Shimōsa. In the village of Mama, there lives a man named Katsushirō. Although born into a prosperous family of farmers, he is of a happy-go-lucky disposition, and allows his house to go to rack and ruin, rather than work in the fields. The very fact that one can describe Katsushirō's character places him in an altogether different category from Chao or Seiroku, neither of whom displays any distinctive traits. Katsushirō is eventually obliged to consider seriously how he can earn a living. He asks a silk merchant to take him along to the capital, and the merchant agrees. Katsushirō sells his remaining property to buy silk to sell in the capital.

Katsushirō's wife, Miyagi, is worried about her husband's

new plan, knowing his disposition, but it is useless to argue with him. Soon after his departure warfare breaks out in the region. Miyagi considers taking refuge, like others in her village, but she remembers her husband's command that she wait for his return in the autumn. Ever obedient, she braves the danger. Soldiers come and try to seduce her, but she resolutely repulses their advances and bars the door.

In the meanwhile Katsushirō, having successfully sold his wares in Kyoto, attempts to return to Shimōsa, only to find the roads blocked. Robbers steal his money, leaving him nothing, and he has no means of making his way home. In the province of Ōmi he is suddenly stricken with a fever and must give up all thought of travel. As he recuperates he becomes friendly with the people of the village and before he knows it "seven years have passed like a dream." Akinari's decision to make Katsushirō remain away from home for seven years, instead of the one year of the two earlier versions, may have been in the interests of making more plausible such enormous changes in his village that Katsushirō does not recognize it when he returns; seven years seems an excessively prolonged absence, even for someone who has been described as happy-go-lucky, but it serves to emphasize the contrast between Katsushirō and his wife.

Finally, in 1461, Katsushirō at last begins "to think seriously" about his absence, and feels ashamed he has abandoned his wife for so long. He supposes Miyagi is dead, but decides he must return, if only to erect a funeral monument to her memory. He arrives in Shimōsa some ten days later.

It is the rainy season and the atmosphere evoked perfectly fits a collection called *Tales of Rain and the Moon*. The day is drawing to a close as Katsushirō approaches his village, but he is sure he cannot go astray; after all, he has lived there most of his life. But everything has changed completely. Here and there he sees what appears to be an inhabited house, but it is unfamiliar. As he is wondering what to do, he suddenly notices the lightning-struck pine that had stood before his house. He approaches it, and only then notices the house itself, not in the least altered. To his great surprise he finds Miyagi, alive but much changed: her eyes are hollow, and her complexion looks dark and dusty. They exchange recollections of how each has spent the past seven years. Miyagi concludes by saying, "But the night is short. . . ." The two lie together.

The next morning Katsushirō is awakened by rain falling on him. He sees now that the house is in ruins and the roof is gone. He searches for Miyagi but she has disappeared. He realizes that she was a ghost, and the only trace he can find of her is a scrap of paper with a poem she wrote just before she died. Katsushirō asks in the village what happened, and finally encounters an old man who witnessed the ravages of the warfare and the death of Miyagi. The old man concludes by describing how, many many years ago, there lived in the same village a girl named Tekona who had died of love, and Katsushirō is moved to tears by a tragedy that parallels his own.

In comparing the different versions of the same story we cannot but be struck by Akinari's genius. Not only did he create characters in Katsushirō and Miyagi, in place of the stock figures of an anecdote, but he reorganized the story in an infinitely more effective manner. The crucial change was in not revealing to the reader that Miyagi is a ghost until Katsushirō discovers it. The description of Miyagi, which suggests that the passage of seven years and the hardships she endured have aged her, makes us suppose that she is alive, even though Katsushirō had assumed she must be dead. Her momentary expression of indignation at Katsushirō's long absence not only confirms this impression but suggests a real woman, rather than the effigy of a virtuous wife in the Chinese story. The surprise of Katsushirō's awakening is our own, no less than his; even without any explanations we realize how strong Miyagi's love must have been for her to return as a ghost to spend one more night with her husband.

Miyagi, unlike her predecessors, is not a former courtesan turned wife (perhaps because the virtuous courtesan was all too familiar a figure from the ukiyo-zōshi); she is an ordinary woman who nonetheless embodies the virtues of Japanese womanhood. Katsushirō, on the other hand, is implicitly condemned; his absence is so described as to suggest it was occasioned by his indolent disposition, rather than by internal warfare he was powerless to circumvent. Akinari also made the structure of the story much neater by deleting the unnecessary character of the mother and by giving the narration of what happened in the village during Katsushirō's absence only once, instead of three times. The story is marred only by the ending, the recitation of the *Manyōshū* account of the girl Tekona who came from the village where Miyagi died. Perhaps it was intended to give additional depth to the events, by drawing a parallel with the distant past; in context, however, it is an unnecessary embellishment and seems like a heavy-handed display of scholarship. The inartistic ending of the original story, the rebirth of the wife as a baby boy, was naturally omitted by Akinari.

Akinari in *Rain and the Moon* raised the ghost story to a remarkably high literary level. Some scholars have suggested that this was possible only because he actually believed in ghosts and spirits.[25] Certainly his book of random jottings *Tandai Shōshin Roku* (Courage and Caution), written in 1808, when he was seventy-four, again and again reveals his belief in spirits, foxes, badgers, and the like, and he declared his contempt for Confucian scholars who, in their insistence on rationalism, refused to believe in irrefutable evidence of the supernatural.[26] Perhaps a belief in the supernatural helped to make the stories more effective, but the style, depiction of character, and mastery of construction surely were the principal factors in Akinari's transformation of stories of small intrinsic merit into moving works of art.

It might have been expected that Akinari, having perfected the ghost story, a genre with a long history in both China and Japan, would have continued to explore the vein, like the Hachimonji-ya authors turning out book after book of character sketches after the success of the first, but Akinari never again wrote any ghost stories. Akinari did not explain his reasons for abandoning the genre, but perhaps he found such satisfaction in his kokugaku studies that he had little time for other writing.[27] During the forty years between the preface to *Tales of Rain and the Moon* (1768) and the writing of *Tales of the Spring Rain* (1808), Akinari composed only two minor works of fiction (*Kakizome Kigen Kai* and *Kusemonogatari*),[28] but he wrote many books of kokugaku scholarship, including commentaries on the old classics, discussions of Japanese philology, and descriptions of Shinto theology.

Akinari's interest in kokugaku apparently originated in his middle twenties when he met a kokugaku scholar named

Kojima Shigeie (d. 1760), who urged him to read the works of Keichū. Kojima was a neighbor of the poet Ozawa Roan, and introduced the young Akinari to him, thus beginning a long friendship. Akinari later attended lectures given in Kyoto by Takebe Ayatari, a member of Mabuchi's school; Akinari was disillusioned when he discovered Ayatari's knowledge of Chinese characters was faulty, and his competence in kokugaku so shaky he could only stammer when someone asked him a question.[29] However, it was through Ayatari that Akinari met Katō Umaki (1721–77), about 1765. Akinari was extremely critical of almost every other scholar, but he always showed great respect for Umaki, whom he considered his only teacher.

Akinari's kokugaku writings are no longer widely read, but they are of interest especially because of Akinari's polemics against Motoori Norinaga. In 1785 Motoori published a work expressing his belief in the literal truth of the *Kojiki.* An essay written by Akinari in the following year rejected this view, insisting that the *Kojiki* account of the Age of the Gods applied only to Japan, not to the rest of the world. In the same year Akinari also challenged Motoori on whether or not a final *-n* had occurred in ancient Japanese. Motoori claimed that because there was no symbol for this sound it could not have existed, but Akinari insisted that even if the sound was written as *mu* it must have been pronounced as *-n.*[30] Akinari also took issue with Motoori on his claim that Japan must be superior to all other countries because the sun goddess was born in Japan. Akinari, observing from a Dutch map of the world how small Japan was, saw no likelihood it could have been the first country created or the source of all civilization.[31] In *Courage and Caution* Akinari abused Motoori for making money out of his *Kojiki* studies from his disciples. He even wrote this waka:

higagoto wo	Even though he says
iute nari to mo	The most utter nonsense
deshi hoshi ya	He still wants pupils—
Kojiki Dembei to	Even though people call him
hito wa iu to mo	Dembei the Kojiki beggar.

The point of this verse is the pun on *Kojiki* and *kojiki*, a beggar; Norinaga's great study *Kojiki-Den* is made into the comic name Kojiki Dembei.[32]

Akinari's opposition to Motoori was otherwise expressed in *Yasumikoto* (1792), the most important of his kokugaku studies. This work denied the authenticity of the *Kojiki*, and suggested that it had been drastically edited by later men.[33] Akinari's arguments were intuitive rather than logical, and he was certainly no match for Motoori in scholarly debate, but he was right in his contention that the final *-n* occurred in old Japanese,[34] and his reluctance to accept the *Kojiki* literally was proof of his good sense.

Akinari's devotion to kokugaku, despite his quarrels with Motoori, seems to have originated in his dislike of Confucian philosophy. The rigid, constricting Confucianism favored by the government seemed to him a denial of the wonder of life. His bitterest attacks were directed against such Confucian scholars as Nakai Riken (1732–1817) who rejected, in the name of reason, the evidence that foxes bewitch people and similar prodigies.[35] Akinari repeatedly insisted that the Japanese gods were unlike either Confucius or Buddha because they had never been human beings; they were gods through and through, unknowable to man and not to be measured by his standards.[36] Men sometimes performed completely irrational acts when possessed by a god; Akinari related a horrendous story about a family of woodcutters—a mother, two sons, and a daughter. The children were always well behaved, but one day the eldest son, after cutting down some trees in the forest, suddenly went mad and killed his mother with his ax. The younger son joyfully leaped into the act, hacking his mother's body into pieces, and the daughter chopped up the flesh on a cutting-board. The three of them died in prison, but no stigma was ever attached to their name because it was recognized that they had been possessed when they performed their murderous actions.[37] Akinari does not explain the anecdote, but clearly the horror here, as in the more frightening of the stories in *Rain and the Moon*, is inexplicable in rational terms. Only kokugaku, with its insistence on wonder and its belief in mysteries that cannot be explained, could satisfy Akinari. But he did not find it necessary to accept the nationalistic implications of the *Kojiki*.

Akinari's final work of fiction, *Harusame Monogatari* (Tales of the Spring Rain) was not published in entirety until 1951, after a series of discoveries of missing parts had at last brought to light the entire manuscript. It has since been widely acclaimed; some critics believe *Spring Rain* is even superior to *Rain and the Moon.* Yet surely it is a far less appealing work. A distinguished Akinari scholar wrote, "*Tales of the Spring Rain* is the kind of work whose importance we can first appreciate imprecisely after someone else has logically explained it to us."[38] Perhaps the surprise of the discovery of an important work excited certain critics so much their discrimination was blurred; or perhaps the fact that *Spring Rain* was composed so close to the end of Akinari's life suggested it must contain maturer wisdom and philosophy than in the early *Rain and the Moon.* Judged in purely literary terms, *Spring Rain* lacks the vitality of *Rain and the Moon*; there is such a tired, etiolated quality to many of the stories that one critic wrote, "*Spring Rain*, or at any rate the story 'The Bloodstained Smock,' was the dying gasp of Akinari's wisdom and art."[39]

Akinari did not use Chinese materials in writing *Spring Rain*, nor is the work prevailingly about the supernatural, despite the occasional mention of the wrath of a god or similar themes. Akinari derived inspiration chiefly from works of classical Japanese literature and history, but one story was based on an actual event of 1767, and another may ultimately have been inspired by Saikaku. The stories vary in length from the page or so of "In Praise of Poetry," hardly more than a discussion of some *Manyōshū* poems, to the forty pages of "Hankai." Everywhere there are traces of hasty revisions or of unfinished ideas; an earlier draft of part of the manuscript reveals the kinds of changes Akinari made, and they are not always felicitous. The story "The Pirate," for example, expands and dramatizes the passage in the *Tosa Diary* where Ki no Tsurayuki's ship is pursued by pirates. In this version the pirate boards Tsurayuki's ship, to everyone's dismay, but he proceeds to engage Tsurayuki in a long discussion about poetry and the compilation of anthologies! The pirate criticizes Tsurayuki for the excessive number of love poems in *Kokinshū*, expresses sympathy for Sugawara no Michizane, who was exiled, and finally informs Tsurayuki that his name should really be pronounced Tsuranuki. If the intent had been comic—the fierce pirate spouting the classics and telling the great poet how to pronounce his own name—there might be something to praise in the story, but Akinari seems instead to be parading his knowledge of the classics in peculiarly inappropriate guise.

The most engrossing of the stories is probably "*Nise no en*" (A Bond of Two Generations). A certain rich farmer, hearing a bell ringing in a corner of his garden, decides to dig up the place. His men uncover a stone coffin, and find inside the shriveled mummy of a priest. The farmer supposes the mummy must have been there for at least ten generations, but detects signs of life, and the mummy is given water for fifty days. The color gradually returns to the mummy's face, and finally the eyes open. The farmer naturally expects that this resurrected priest will be some extraordinary, holy being, but to his dismay he discovers the ex-mummy is quite ordinary, or even below average. At first the farmer does not give the man any fish, supposing a priest will not want animal food, but the man's looks reveal all too plainly his eagerness for fish, and when he gets it he devours it bones and all. In place of the words of wisdom the farmer had hoped to receive from a priest who had returned from the dead, he learns nothing at all; the man does not even remember his name. Finally the ex-mummy is put to menial labor, the only work he is capable of. As a result of this experience the farmer's old mother loses her faith in Buddhism, and the people of the neighborhood, also disillusioned, avoid the temples.

"A Bond of Two Generations" has strong anti-Buddhist overtones, but it succeeds not because of the sharpness of its attacks, but because of the amusing central theme: we, like the farmer, are disappointed to discover that even a man returned from the dead may be no wiser than anybody else!

Tales of the Spring Rain stands or falls as a collection on "Hankai"; it is not only by far the longest story, but has generally been treated as the single masterpiece. Daizō, a powerfully built young man, goes on a dare to a mountaintop temple known for the ferocious god who emerges every night. He reaches the temple without incident, and decides to take back a heavy chest as proof he was actually there. To his astonishment, the chest lifts him into the air and carries him many miles away to an island. He makes his way back home much chastened. For a time Daizō leads a virtuous life, but his passion for gambling gets the better of him. In order to pay his gambling debts he compels his mother to hand over the family fortune, then shoves the mother into the money chest. His father and brother run after him, but he pushes them off a cliff into the sea. He goes then to Kyushu and has an affair with a woman in Nagasaki, but she is so terrified of Daizō that she takes refuge in a Maruyama brothel. He pursues her, charging into a room where a Chinese merchant is disporting himself. The Chinese cries out in alarm that Daizō is another Hankai (Fan K'uai, a heroic Chinese general) and Daizō proudly takes this as his nickname.

Adventure after adventure follows. Though occasionally he shows a more amiable side, it is hard to speak of any character development; the most one can say is that, despite Hankai's violence and brutality, he is fairly generous with his money. One day he and his companions are walking along the road when they see a Buddhist priest. Hankai demands his money and is given one coin. Shortly afterward the priest returns and confesses that he had actually had two coins; he is ashamed of this sin of attachment to worldly goods, and insists on giving Hankai the other coin. A wave of awe passes over Hankai as he contemplates a man of such pure, selfless character. He contrasts the priest's ways with his own life and decides to become the priest's disciple. At the end of the story we learn that Hankai subsequently led a life of great holiness and died blessed.

Tales of the Spring Rain has frequently been cited to prove what strong anti-Buddhist and anti-Confucian beliefs Akinari held. Certainly "A Bond of Two Generations" is anti-Buddhist, and "The Bloodstained Smock" has a pronounced anti-Confucian bias, describing (like "Shiramine") the evils that afflicted Japan as the result of the adoption of Confucian political thought. However, the conclusion of "Hankai" is exactly in the manner of a typical Buddhist story and there is no suggestion of cynicism. Perhaps Akinari, remembering the Buddhist fiction of the Muromachi period, decided that a miraculous reform in Hankai's character was the only possible ending for a story of almost unmitigated cruelty and perversion. Nothing has prepared us for the instant conversion of a man who not only killed without a qualm his parents (and many others) but pretended for years to be a priest without noticeable effect; the ending can be accepted only as a miracle, not as a logical development in Hankai's character.

"Hankai," unlike the best stories in *Rain and the Moon*, is long-winded and crammed with useless details. There is no apparent structure and the plot consists merely of a series of incidents. Perhaps Akinari intended it as an elaborate parable demonstrating that even the most evil of men may have some redeeming quality that will gain him salvation, but more convincing Buddhist stories had been written on this theme.

Spring Rain is, nevertheless, far more interesting than most works of ukiyo-zōshi literature.[40] The style, if inferior to that of *Rain and the Moon*, is still that of a master, concise and evocative. It has been said about *Spring Rain* that its characters sometimes display a striking "human" quality anticipatory of modern literature; when we contrast it with other examples of novelistic production in Japan at this time, devoted to trivial incidents of the licensed quarters or to the implausible doings of paper-thin heroes, we can see that despite its relative failure it possesses a literary integrity found nowhere else. The stories were not intended merely to divert readers but to express in some sense the author's view of the world. Akinari was a lonely figure at the end of his life, and something of his bitterness and cynicism comes to the surface in *Spring Rain*. Though it failed to repeat the brilliant success of *Rain and the Moon*, it has qualities of depth and craftsmanship found nowhere else in the popular fiction of the time.

NOTES

1. Teruoka Yasutaka and Gunji Masakatsu. *Edo Shimin Bungaku no Kaika*, p. 110.
2. Morita Kirō. *Ueda Akinari*, p. 15.
3. Teruoka and Gunji, p. 112.
4. Nakamura Yukihiko (ed.), *Ueda Akinari Shū* (henceforth abbreviated UAS), p. 3.
5. Teruoka and Gunji, p. 118. The theory that *wayaku* meant "Japanese translation" was proposed by Takada Mamoru in *Ueda Akinari Kenkyū Josetsu*, p. 38, but was devastatingly refuted by Morita, pp. 67–71.
6. See Morita, pp. 61–71, for a discussion of various theories.

7. Nagai Kazutaka (ed.), *Ueda Akinari Shū*, pp. 40–45.

8. *Ibid.*, p. 42.

9. *Ibid.*, pp. 172–88.

10. Morita, p. 75.

11. Nakano Mitoshi, "Atarashii Shōsetsu no Hassei," p. 82.

12. Teruoka and Gunji, p. 102.

13. Ōta Nampo in *Ichiwa Ichigen*, quoted by Aiso Teizō in *Kinsei Shōsetsu Shi: Edo-hen*, p. 239.

14. Matsuyama Eitarō (ed.), *Gabun Shōsetsu Shū*, p. 1.

15. Teruoka and Gunji, pp. 108–109.

16. Nakamura Yukihiko, *Kinsei Sakka Kenkyū*, p. 161.

17. Quoted in Nakano, p. 84.

18. Shigetomo Ki, *Ugetsu Monogatari no Kenkyū*, p. 137.

19. See Nakamura, UAS, p. 4.

20. Noda Hisao, "Kaii Shōsetsu no Keifu to Akinari," p. 37.

21. *Ibid.*, pp. 38–40.

22. See Morita, pp. 78–85, 104.

23. See Japanese translation by Iizuka Akira in *Sentō Shinwa*, pp. 151–66.

24. Aeba Kōson (ed.), *Kinsei Bungei Sōsho*, III, pp. 62–66.

25. Nakamura Hiroyasu, "Ueda Akinari no Shimpi Shisō," p. 96.

26. See Nakamura Yukihiko, UAS, pp. 258, 268, 276, etc., for examples of fox magic; pp. 258, 268, 270, etc., for condemnations of materialistic Confucianists.

27. Sakai Kōichi, *Ueda Akinari*, pp. 56, 63.

28. For a good discussion of the latter work, see Shigetomo Ki (ed.), *Ueda Akinari Shū*, pp. 30–35.

29. Sakai, p. 60.

30. Morita, p. 20.

31. Takada Mamoru, *Ueda Akinari Kenkyū Josetsu*, pp. 362–81. The original texts are found in Iwahashi Koyata (ed.), *Ueda Akinari Zenshū*, I, pp. 423–64.

32. Nakamura Yukihiko, UAS, p. 254. The fact that Motoori Norinaga came from the region of Ise is alluded to: the inhabitants of Ise depended so much on the income provided by visitors to the shrines that they were known as "Ise beggars."

33. Text in Iwahashi, I, pp. 466–89.

34. See Roy Andrew Miller, *The Japanese Language*, pp. 207–208.

35. Nakamura Yukihiko, UAS, p. 270.

36. *Ibid.*, p. 272.

37. *Ibid.*, pp. 274–75.

38. Uzuki Hiroshi, "Akinari no Shisō to Bungaku," p. 254.

39. Matsuda Osamu, "Chi Katabira no Ron," p. 39.

40. See the complete translation by Barry Jackman, *Tales of the Spring Rain* (Tokyo: Tokyo University Press, 1975).

BIBLIOGRAPHY

Aeba Kōson (ed.). *Kinsei Bungei Sōsho*, III. Tokyo: Kokusho Kankōkai, 1910.

Aiso Teizō. *Kinsei Shōsetsu Shi: Edo-hen.* Tokyo: Asahi Shuppan Sha, 1956.

Araki, James T. "A Critical Approach to the *Ugetsu Monogatari*," in *Monumental Nipponica*, XXII, 1–2, 1967.

Iizuka Akira (trans.). *Sentō Shinwa*, by Ku Yü, in Tōyō Bunko series, Tokyo: Heibonsha, 1965.

Matsuda Osamu. "Chi Katabira no Ron," in *Bungaku*, XXXII (February 1964).

Matsuyama Eitarō (ed.). *Gabun Shōsetsu Shū*, in Yūhōdō Bunko series. Tokyo: Yūhōdō Shoten, 1926.

Miller, Roy Andrew. *The Japanese Language*. Chicago: University of Chicago Press, 1967.

Morita Kirō. *Ueda Akinari*. Tokyo: Kinokuniya Shoten, 1970.

Moriyama Shigeo. *Ueda Akinari*, in Iwanami Kōza Nihon Bungaku Shi series. Tokyo: Iwanami Shoten, 1958.

Nagai Kazutaka (ed.). *Ueda Akinari Shū*, in Yūhōdō Bunko series. Tokyo: Yūhōdō Shoten, 1926.

Nakamura Hiroyasu. "Ueda Akinari no Shimpi Shisō," in *Kokubungaku Kenkyū*, 26, (1962).

Nakamura Yukihiko. *Akinari*, in Nihon Koten Kanshō Kōza series. Tokyo: Kadokawa Shoten, 1958.

———. "Chi Katabira no Setsu," in *Gobun Kenkyū*, XVII (1967).

———. *Kinsei Sakka Kenkyū*. Tokyo: San'ichi Shobō, 1961.

——— (ed.). *Ueda Akinari Shū*, in Nihon Koten Bungaku Taikei series. Tokyo: Iwanami Shoten, 1959.

Nakano Mitoshi. "Atarashii Shōsetsu no Hassei," in Nakamura Yukihiko and Nishiyama Matsunosuke (eds.), *Bunka Ryōran*. Tokyo: Kadokawa Shoten, 1967.

Noda Hisao. "Kaii Shōsetsu no Keifu to Akinari," in Kōza Nihon Bungaku series, VIII. Tokyo: Sanseidō, 1969.

Sakai Kōichi. *Ueda Akinari*. Kyoto: San'ichi Shobō, 1959.

Shigetomo Ki. *Kinsei Bungakushi no Shomondai*. Tokyo: Meiji Shoin, 1963.

———. *Ueda Akinari Shū*, in Nihon Koten Zensho series. Tokyo: Asahi Shimbun Sha, 1957.

———. *Ugetsu Monogatari Hyōshaku*. Tokyo: Meiji Shoin, 1954.

———. *Ugetsu Monogatari no Kenkyū*. Kyoto: Ōyashima Shuppan, 1946.

Shimizu Masao. "Akinari no Haikai," in *Geibun Kō*, 1 and 2 (1967–68).

Takada Mamoru. *Ueda Akinari Kenkyū Josetsu*. Tokyo: Nara Shobō, 1968.

Teruoka Yasutaka and Gunji Masakatsu. *Edo Shimin Bungaku no Kaika*, in Nihon no Bungaku series. Tokyo: Shibundō, 1967.

Uzuki Hiroshi. "Akinari no Shisō to Bungaku," in Nakamura Yukihiko, *Akinari*.

Zolbrod, Leon (trans.). *Ugetsu Monogatari*. London: George Allen & Unwin, Ltd., 1974.

CHAPTER 17
FICTION
GESAKU FICTION

Between 1770 and 1790 the center of literary activity shifted in fiction too from the Kamigata (the Kyoto-Osaka region) to Edo. Even before this time, of course, there were important fiction writers in Edo, and literature elsewhere did not dry up after 1790, but so pronounced a change occurred that from this point on we can speak of pre-modern fiction as being specifically Edo literature.[1]

A great variety of fiction was written during the century between 1770 and the end of the period, but a single term, *gesaku*, is often used to describe the entire production. The term was apparently first used by the jack-of-all-trades genius Hiraga Gennai (1729–79) with reference to his puppet play *Shinrei Yaguchi no Watashi* (The Miracle at the Yaguchi Ferry, 1770).

Gennai, a samurai who dabbled as a playwright, felt obliged to distinguish this work of popular literature from his serious writings, and that is why he qualified it as gesaku, a playful composition. The word "playful" referred not to the subject matter of his drama—a historical tragedy—but to the professed attitude of the author. By preserving a suitable distance from his own creation, Gennai adopted the stance of the dilettante who disclaims responsibility for a composition he never intended to be taken seriously.

An amateur ideal, inspired by the writings of Chinese predecessors,[2] probably first suggested the modest words used by Hiraga Gennai, but by the end of the eighteenth century the term *gesaku* was used uniformly of all works of fiction, even those written by men who were out-and-out professionals. Gesaku writings ranged from booklets of cartoons to immensely long historical novels that extolled the Confucian virtues, and their readers similarly ranged from near illiterates to members of the imperial court. The term *gesaku* at last fell into disrepute during the Meiji era, when novelists, anxious to dissociate themselves from the frivolous and by then worn-out fiction of the immediate past, used it with scorn of writings that lacked the psychological depth of the Western-influenced literature.

Some gesaku writers, particularly in the 1820s and 1830s, were exceedingly earnest about their writings, even though they continued to describe them as "playful compositions," but most gesaku literature was comic, not only in comparison to the philosophical essays of the day, but in the obvious attempts to make the readers laugh. The dilettantish refusal to take themselves seriously that marked the creators of the new literature easily degenerated into an absorption with trivialities, especially the details of the usages of the licensed quarters.[3] Sometimes, it is true, a detachment from mundane activities led to a withdrawal into the serene air of the mountains, but at the end of the eighteenth century it more frequently resulted in prolonged visits to the brothels. Gentlemen of means, distressed by the corrupt government but powerless to alter matters, amused themselves with elegant banter on the latest fashions, and some chose to record their experiences in fiction.

An increased knowledge of Chinese literature promoted their literary efforts. The popularity of Chinese ghost stories during the 1750s, which had so influenced Ueda Akinari, was succeeded by a craze for Chinese fiction of a more erotic nature. Japanese Confucian scholars, in imitation of their Chinese counterparts who had written novels for the diversion of friends and their own amusement, wrote comic poetry in Chinese, or else accounts of the licensed quarters of Edo, using ponderous Chinese phraseology. The humor is pedantic, as if an American classical scholar were to amuse himself by composing Latin verses about a cocktail party or a football game.

Readings in colloquial Chinese fiction, especially such erotic novels as *Chin P'ing Mei*, probably first suggested the possibility of using the Japanese colloquial language to describe the brothels. One Confucian doctor wrote:

> It is hard to describe real feelings accurately if you use the classical language, just as it is harder to write about daily life in a *waka* than in a *haikai* verse. Rarely does anyone succeed. Writers can convey the emotions more easily and accurately by writing their novels in the colloquial. *The Tale of Genji* and *Tales of Ise* are written in the classical language; that is why, even though they are erotic in content, they do not convey feelings as successfully as present-day plays or Hachimonji-ya books.[4]

It was certainly most unorthodox to assert that *The Tale of Genji* was less successful than a contemporary work, but the writer was surely on the right track when he stated that the emotions of the characters seemed much less immediate when described in the classical language than in the colloquial. The use of the colloquial in the novels and plays up to this time had generally been haphazard and even unintentional. A writer's carelessness or his ignorance of the proper literary forms sometimes led him inadvertently to use a colloquial phrase or verb ending, but the characters in the novels of Saikaku or Ueda Akinari do not speak the contemporary colloquial. Even in the dramas of Chikamatsu that are most closely based on current gossip, the dialogue is in a conventional stage language that only intermittently approaches the colloquial. But in the gesaku fiction, seemingly under the influence of Chinese *pai hua* (colloquial) novels, the characters begin to speak something close to contemporary language. The descriptive passages it is true, remained in the literary language, but since the books tended to be composed largely of conversations, the works as a whole have a characteristically colloquial flavor.

The *sharebon*, stories about the licensed quarters that began to appear in the Kamigata around 1745, even borrowed their format from Chinese erotic pamphlets. Before long, the sharebon came to be so closely associated with the Edo brothels that readers probably forgot these origins; nevertheless, the Chinese-sounding titles, the prefaces written in mock Chinese, and the obscure Chinese characters given farcical Japanese readings remained as evidence of their indebtedness.

The sharebon described the manners, language, and clothes of the men who frequented the licensed quarters and were adept in their ritualized etiquette. The word *tsū* designated these connoisseurs, and the sharebon, by detailing what being tsū involved, served as guides to prospective visitors. The books are often devoted largely to satirical comments on the half-baked tsū or the totally non-tsū customers, whose affected and inept behavior was held up to scorn. The readers needed a considerable knowledge of the etiquette if they hoped to appreciate the satire fully; but many sharebon give the impression of having been written for the amusement of the author and his fellow connoisseurs, with no other readers in mind.

Scholars of Chinese who indulged their taste for frivolity by frequenting the licensed quarters and writing about them sometimes justified themselves on the grounds that they were following the traditions of those Chinese gentlemen who had described in poetry their pleasure in wine and women. The Confucian philosopher Kameda Hōsai (1752–1826) wrote: "If Hsi Po-lin and Li Po had not drunk wine they would have been ordinary men; and if we look at the moonlight on the snow at Sarashina or Koshiji without drinking saké, they will look just like ordinary villages."[5] The pleasures of drink lent themselves to poetry, those of the licensed quarters to prose, especially the sharebon and *kibyōshi*.

The kibyōshi originated about the same time as the sharebon and were sometimes written by the same men, but they were distinct literary forms. The kibyōshi were like glorified comic books; the authors often drew their own illustrations, and these were at least as important as the texts in determining their reputation. *Kibyōshi* means "yellow covers," the name referring to the color of a decorative panel on the outer wrapper. As early as about 1670 booklets, mainly children's stories illustrated with crude drawings, had been published with red labels. These were followed about 1750 by booklets with black or blue labels that featured the plots of plays, accounts of military heroes, and ghost stories. At first the two were much alike, but as the black-labeled books grew more serious in tone, perhaps because of their somber labels, the blue ones grew more frivolous. Probably it was the naturally fading of the blue to yellow that first created "yellow cover" books; in any case, the blue books merged almost imperceptibly with the yellow ones. The first kibyōshi was published in 1775: it was *Kinkin Sensei Eiga no Yume* (The Dream of Glory of Master Gold-Gold) by Koikawa Harumachi (1744–1789), a modern-day version of the story of the man who dreamed through a whole life of adventure and glory while his porridge was being cooked in the next room.[6]

A page from any kibyōshi has an extraordinarily crowded look. The human figures, standing or sitting in the elegant room of a brothel or on a public thoroughfare, are much like those in the familiar ukiyo-e prints, but every scrap of blank space is filled with vertical scrawls of kana, hanging like a fringed curtain from above, draping the figures, or even curling between their legs. The men and women in the illustrations are identified by labels on their costumes, and one can generally guess who is speaking the dialogue by the proximity of the script to the figure. But it is not always clear which of the festoons of writing should be read first, or if an inscription on a wall or the text of a letter somebody is reading should be considered a part of the story. The kibyōshi can be properly appreciated only when read with their illustrations, as a special genre halfway between literature and art.

Sharebon and kibyōshi were the two main varieties of early gesaku fiction. Both were frivolous in intent, colloquial in language, and concerned solely with contemporary life even if, to escape the censorship, they were ostensibly set in the Japan of the Kamakura period. Both were appropriate literary products for the age of the corrupt Tanuma Okitsugu, whose lax rule stimulated artistic activity more than the strict Confucianism of more virtuous statesmen. The authors of both sharebon and kibyōshi seem to have been intellectuals of the samurai class who turned to writing as an outlet for their otherwise wasted talents. Whatever bitterness they may have felt toward society, however, their attitude toward their subjects is one of uncritical approval and admiration.[7] They certainly never questioned the morality of women selling their bodies to strangers, nor did they choose to describe, like Saikaku in *The Life of an Amorous Woman*, the misery of an aging prostitute who is doomed to sink ever lower in the hierarchy of lust. Their interest lay chiefly in describing how men in a brothel reveal their true characters in their conversations with the prostitutes and other customers.

These writings, despite the education of the authors, are almost totally lacking in intellectual content. Readers today seldom find gesaku fiction satisfying, even if they can admire the deftness of the style, or the lighthearted humor. The closest this satirical fiction ever comes to criticizing the ills of society is the gentle fun poked, say, at the government's promotion of Confucian learning. Even this was dangerous, as we shall see; the more prudent gesaku writers refrained from all social comment and took refuge in frivolity, pointing out that Confucius had urged men to "seek distraction in the arts."[8]

At this time there was also a conspicuous increase in interest in the Taoist philosophers Lao-tzu and Chuang-tzu. Even some Confucianists expressed the belief that Lao-tzu's teachings were better suited than Confucius's to an age of peace.[9] Taoist influence showed itself also in the writings of such kokugaku scholars as Kamo no Mabuchi, and the doctrine of "no action" appealed to intellectuals as a justification for their happy-go-lucky irresolution. Ōta Kinjō (1765–1825), a Confucianist, wrote:

> Scholars are invariably profligates, but they never can find any authorization for their profligacy in the *Analects* or in Mencius. . . . Repelled by the Confucian sages, they turn instead to Lao-tzu and Chuang-tzu, who scorned benevolence and righteousness and spurned the rites and the law, and they adopt Taoism as their philosophy.[10]

The preference of some Confucian scholars for comic forms of poetry and prose did not imply any rejection of the Confucian ideals; it stemmed instead from a realization that the exemplary actions of the Confucian "superior man" did not take into account all of life. Less noble aspirations also demanded to be heard. The Confucian scholar Minagawa Kien (1734–1807) kept a collection of Jōruri texts in his library. One day they were accidentally discovered, and his disciples were embarrassed for him, but Kien calmly remarked, "None of the countless books that exist between Heaven and Earth but serves as an instrument of 'investigating things and extending knowledge.' "[11] He justified in this manner, using conventional Confucian terminology, owning books that more orthodox scholars would have despised.

SHAREBON AND KIBYŌSHI

Sharebon were written during the period 1745–1830, at first in the Kamigata region, but later mainly in Edo. The form of the future sharebon was set by *Hijiri no Yūkaku* (The Holy Men's Brothel), published anonymously in Osaka in 1757. The theme is startling: Shakyamuni Buddha, Confucius, and Lao-tzu arrive in Japan and at once go to the Osaka brothel run by Li Po, where Po Chü-i serves as a jester. Each holy man is matched with a prostitute whose name suits his philosophy: "Fleeting World" goes with Buddha, "Great Way" with Confucius, and "Great Void" with Lao-tzu.[12] The conversations are filled with phrases borrowed from the sacred writings of the three religions, but we are unlikely to be reminded of the first Japanese "novel," *Indications to the Three Teachings* of Kūkai. The tone throughout is frivolous, and no attempt is made to transcend the surface humor. Certainly it never entered the author's head that he might be committing blasphemy by writing so irreverently about the founders of the three faiths; his object was to titillate and not to make satiric thrusts. The story concludes as Buddha and Fleeting World leave the licensed quarters bent on a lovers' suicide. They go off to the accompaniment of a recitation in the traditional Jōruri style.

Although this sharebon deals exclusively with the licensed quarter, it has little of Saikaku's eroticism and none of his seriousness. Like most later sharebon, it is surprisingly lacking in overt descriptions of what, after all, was the real business of the quarter. A brothel emerges in these pages as a kind of club whose members are more interested in observing and commenting on one another than in lying with the prostitutes. The intent of the author, far from pornography, is to portray the milieu in its most attractive light, extolling the adepts and making fun of the semiadepts and the boors. The greatest ingenuity was directed at creating novel situations, such as the ludicrously implausible visit of the three holy men to the brothel. The conversations are realistically reported in colloquial language and, unlike earlier fiction or Jōruri texts, the speakers are plainly identified.

An even more typical sharebon was *Yūshi Hōgen* (The Rake's Patois), written before 1770 by a man who facetiously signed himself Tada no Jijii (Just an Old Man). The story begins with a description of the protagonists, a man in his thirties and his son. The costume, hair style, accessories and every other aspect of the man's appearance are carefully described, but there is an almost total lack of interest in his character. He falls into an easily recognizable type, and his features, like those of the people in the ukiyo-e prints, are unmarred by intellectual activity. We are told that the man "gazes haughtily around him, sure he is the only 'great lover' in sight." The son, by contrast, is a gentle and polite youth. They accidentally meet, and the father insists on the boy accompanying him to admire the maple leaves at a certain temple. This proves to be a pretext for taking him to the Yoshiwara Quarter. Once they reach the brothel the man flaunts his knowledge of the latest fashions, but his self-confident chatter reveals how flawed his pretensions are, and the courtesans answer sarcastically. His mild-mannered son receives a much friendlier welcome, and at the end it is he, rather than the professed tsū, who is invited to stay for the night.[13]

Other sharebon of the period follow this pattern. The visit of a professed expert and a novice, ending with the expert being shown up as a fraud, was a familiar situation. The kind of special knowledge displayed by the would-be connoisseur was, however, not so very different from that of the real tsū. The exact cut of hair in vogue at the moment, the exact length of the jacket worn by a man of taste, the exact shop in which to buy the most fashionable variety of tobacco or paper handkerchiefs were all necessary pieces of information for the man-about-town. The difference between the real connoisseur and the impostor was often described in terms of the sensitivity shown for the feelings of the prostitutes. The impostor, in order to demonstrate his importance, blusters and swaggers in the brothels, but the connoisseur knows how to please the prostitutes; this skill, in fact, was the most important proof he was tsū.

There is a curious absence of love or desire in these books. The customers, unlike the unhappy heroes of Chikamatsu's tragedies, do not think of the prostitutes as objects of love or seek to obtain sole possession of their favors. They consider such behavior crude and contemptible; for them lightness and detachment, rather than depth of feelings, were the hallmarks of tsū behavior.

The best sharebon and kibyōshi were written by Santō Kyōden (1761–1816), a man with a dazzling array of talents. Kyōden, a typical son of Edo, was not only the leading writer of fiction at the end of the eighteenth century, but was a famous ukiyo-e artist and illustrator, and known also for his comic poetry and even for the advertisements he wrote for the wares sold in his shop. Kyōden's first book appeared as early as 1778, but his period of greatest activity was between 1782 and 1791. His first great success came with a kibyōshi called *Gozonji no Shōbaimono* (The Articles for Sale You Know About, 1782). This work has little literary merit, but it captured the public fancy by the elegance of its illustrations and the novelty of its theme. It opens with a speech of self-identification in Kyōgen style:

> The person who has come before you is a certain man who draws illustrations for comic books every spring. As yet I have found scant favor with children, and I have therefore tried to think of something that might please their tastes. I have just had my first dream of the year, and it was so strange that I have decided to go to the publisher and tell him about it. I have hurried, and here I am already, at the publisher's gate. Is anyone home? Is anyone home?[14]

The illustration to this speech shows the author in the attitude of a Kyōgen actor. Next we see him dozing in the corner of a picture as he dreams of each of the different varieties of fiction appearing before him in human shape. The story, such as it is, describes the jealousies and complaints of the different genres. No attempt is made to impart any order or unity to the presentation, and it is hard to remember anything of the contents after finishing the book. No doubt the comments on the book-and-print business amused readers well aware of the ruthless competition.

Kyōden's masterpiece was the kibyōshi called *Edo Mumare Uwaki no Kabayaki* (Romantic Embroilments Born in Edo), published in 1785. This is the story of Enjirō, the son of an immensely rich family, who aspires to become famous as a great lover. Unfortunately for him, he is grotesquely ugly; Kyōden drew Enjirō with a curious triangular nose that became known as the "Kyōden nose." Enjirō, relying on his money to make up for what he lacks in physical charm, sets about methodically to acquire all the attributes of a great lover.

We are told:

> Enjirō, deciding that tattooing marks the beginning of a romance, had himself tattooed in some twenty or thirty places on both arms and even between his fingers with the names of imaginary sweethearts. He cheerfully endured the pain, rejoicing in his fate.

His adviser reminds him that a few of the tattooings should be blotted out, as a sign he has broken with some of his girl friends, and Enjirō, obliged to suffer more burning, exclaims: "It's certainly painful to become a great lover!"[15]

Next, Enjirō, envious of actors who have women pursuing them, pays a geisha fifty pieces of gold to run after him. She throws herself before his feet and, as requested, declares that if he will not take her for his wife, she will gladly be his scullery maid; if she is refused even that favor, she has determined to kill herself. Enjirō offers her ten additional gold pieces if she will repeat this in a voice loud enough for the neighbors to hear. He has scandal sheets printed about this love affair, and distributes them free throughout Edo.

Enjirō happily supposes every time he sneezes that somebody is gossiping about his love affairs, but in fact no one is taken in. Undaunted, he decides that a courtesan must show jealousy over his affairs if he is to be taken seriously as a great lover. He hires a woman who, true to her contractual obligations, convincingly acts the part of the jealous woman. She reproaches him: "If you dislike being loved so much, you shouldn't have been born such a handsome man."

Enjirō, relentlessly following his program, begs his doting

parents to disinherit him in the manner traditional with great lovers of the past. They reluctantly agree, but continue to provide him with his usual allowance. When the seventy-five days of disinheritance they have agreed on are about to expire, Enjirō begs for an extension, to give him time to commit a lovers' suicide. Of course, he does not really plan to carry out the suicide, but he pays a dramatist to compose a puppet play on the event. He ransoms a courtesan, but pretends he is secretly eloping with her. The menservants in the brothel, playing his game, urge Enjirō to "flee slowly" (*oshizuka ni onige nasarimase*). Plans go awry, however, when Enjirō and the courtesan are set upon by robbers. Enjirō informs the robbers in alarm, "We didn't mean to kill ourselves when we committed suicide." He begs that his life be spared. The robbers agree, but divest Enjirō and his companion of their garments. Clad only in loin cloths, the unhappy "lovers" set out on a traditional michiyuki which is aptly entitled *kyō ga same hada*, a pun on *kyō ga same* (to become disillusioned) and *samehada* (gooseflesh). Enjirō is welcomed back by his family. They gladly agree to allow him to marry the courtesan who accompanied him on his suicide journey. Enjirō, still reluctant to give up his dream of fame as a great lover, asks Kyōden to describe his adventures in a book, as a lesson to all men. The final words are the courtesan's: "I've caught a terrible cold."

After publishing this kibyōshi masterpiece, which is a flawless combination of comic text and pictures, Kyōden shifted his attention to sharebon, writing sixteen works in this genre between 1785 and 1790. His finest sharebon, *Sōmagaki* (The Palace, the name of the leading Yoshiwara brothel), appeared in 1787.[16] The characters are the same as in *Romantic Embroilments*, Enjirō and his companions, but the work produces a quite different impression. Unlike the kibyōshi with its illustrations filling every page, the sharebon has only a frontispiece, but it is otherwise graced by prefaces laden with Chinese allusions. The text itself, in typical sharebon style, consists of conversations broken only by brief descriptions of what the characters are wearing. The work has been praised as the ultimate in realistic descriptions of the Yoshiwara,[17] but its very fidelity to current slang and the whims of fashion makes it tedious to read today. Kyōden seems determined to reveal everything he has learned in his years as a habitué of the licensed quarters. He wrote in the preface to a similar work:

> The courtesans I have described in this book are women I have often amused myself with, whose characters I know well. Some I like, and some I dislike. I have described their accomplishments in detail, even revealing their girlhood names, in the hopes of assisting visitors who may not yet be acquainted with them.[18]

No doubt it was as much as guidebooks—rather like the old "evaluation books" of prostitutes—as for literary value that the sharebon were read. The connoisseurs praised the precise descriptions of the women and of the appurtenances of the brothels, but *The Palace* lacked the appeal of Enjirō's earlier adventures. The work nevertheless reveals Kyōden's determination to pass beyond the comic-strip limitations of the kibyōshi into the domain of fiction.

He was more successful with *Keisei-kai Shijūhatte* (The Forty-Eight Grips in Buying a Whore, 1790), a collection of short stories, rather than the usual formless book of chatter. Kyōden described five, not "forty-eight" different approaches to buying a courtesan; of these the last, the account of "the sincere grip" has been acclaimed as Kyōden's finest work of literature.[19] The story begins with an exchange of banter, but attention quickly shifts to the guest who has remained from the previous night. He confesses to a courtesan that his debts to the brothel now amount to thirty gold pieces. She blames herself for having led him into financial difficulties, but he answers, "Don't talk foolishness. I wouldn't care even if I were disowned and forced to go around in rags. As long as we can be together, that's all I ask."[20]

The unmistakable note of sincere love, quite unlike the usual sharebon playfulness, evokes the world of Chikamatsu. This impression is strengthened when the man sees difficulties for their future because she is a prostitute, and the woman replies, "Do you still think of me as a prostitute? I have long since considered myself to be your wife." She promises to sell her second-best bedding and raise other money for him so that he can pay at least half his debts. The man is overcome with gratitude. Then the woman reveals she has missed her last menstruation; she must be pregnant. The man expresses remorse for the unhappiness he has brought not only his sweetheart but his mother. The woman cries, "I wish I were dead!" and, we are told, "Her cold front lock brushes the man's face." The scene is made sensual, unlike the usual matter-of-fact brothels of the sharebon, thanks to such "stage directions" as: "She blows smoke from her cigarette at the man's face . . . Choking with the smoke he says . . . She puts her hand under the man's pillow and draws his lips to hers . . . She undoes the man's sash and, throwing it outside the bedcovers, unfastens her own sash and presses herself against him."[21] Kyōden, giving his final evaluation of the "sincere grip," states: "When a courtesan is sincere it means her luck has run out." In this story Kyōden, perhaps inadvertently, created real human beings who confront real problems, instead of the caricatures of his earlier works.

Shōgi Kinuburui (The Courtesan's Silken Sieve, 1791) is openly indebted to Chikamatsu: the lovers are named Umekawa and Chūbei, exactly like those in Chikamatsu's *The Courier for Hell*. Kyōden was clearly leaving the conventions of the sharebon behind, in the hope of achieving greater artistry; but at the time he was writing this work other factors were operating to inhibit his literary production: in the fifth and tenth months of 1790 government orders were issued controlling the publication of frivolous books. On the surface these edicts seemed to be no more than repetitions of the usual Confucian admonitions, but this time the government meant business. Matsudaira Sadanobu, reacting against the laxity of the Tanuma regime, was determined to revitalize the samurai class by forcing it to return to the ideals of the past; the military and civil arts were encouraged, and the decadent writings of gesaku authors were condemned. In the autumn of 1790 Kyōden composed three sharebon (including *The Courtesan's Silken Sieve*). He turned the manuscripts over to the printer, the woodblocks were carved, and the censors passed the texts after Kyōden had made some revisions to conform with the new decrees. The books met with instant popular favor when published in 1791, but in the third month an order was suddenly issued confining Kyōden to his house in manacles for fifty days. In addition, half of the publisher's capital was confiscated, and the censors who had approved the books were deprived of office.[22] Kyōden became more famous than ever, but he had to give up his career as a sharebon writer. For some years he ceased to write altogether, depending on the income from his shop, and when he resumed writing, it was in a much more serious vein.

The sharebon did not disappear as the result of Kyōden's misfortune. Umebori Kokuga (1750–1821), among others, continued to write successful sharebon, but they were strikingly unlike earlier examples. His chief work, *Keisei-kai Futasujimichi* (Two Different Ways of Buying a Courtesan, 1798), leads us to believe that an ugly, middle-aged man is more likely than a handsome young man to win the affections of a courtesan, providing his feelings are deeper and purer.[23] This rather sentimental thought indicates how far the sharebon had come from its supreme ideal of being tsū.

LATER GESAKU

The Kansei Reforms, the name given to the edicts issued by Matsudaira Sadanobu's government from 1790, divide the earlier and later gesaku. In the effort to keep intellectuals from diverging from the path of orthodoxy, the government decreed that only the Chu Hsi school of Confucianism would be permitted; and in order to relieve the frustrations of other intellectuals over their inability to obtain suitable employment, it promised new opportunities, providing they devoted themselves to the accepted learning. Some former gesaku writers became officials, others studied science under orders from their clan or the central government.[24] Gesaku ceased to be an outlet for the irritation of cultivated men. Some of the later gesaku writers also belonged to the samurai class, but they were professionals who aimed at pleasing large audiences in hope of making money.

The emphasis placed on education by Matsudaira Sadanobu's reforms increased the potential readership of all kinds of writing, just as those of Yoshimune seventy years before had helped the sales of the Hachimonji-ya books. Lending libraries had begun to operate around 1750 for the sake of readers who could not afford to buy the new books. The number of these lending libraries markedly increased after the Kansei Reforms; by 1808 there were 656 in Edo alone.[25] Particularly notable was the increase in the numbers of women readers. Much of the later gesaku fiction was accordingly aimed specifically at women of the samurai class who, having little opportunity to leave their own homes, found their chief diversion in these books.

The writing of fiction became more and more openly a commercial enterprise. Unlike the publishers in the days of the Hachimonji-ya, who contracted to buy an unseen manuscript for a fixed advanced payment, the Edo publishers now paid writers on the basis of their evaluations of completed manuscripts. In the event that a book was commercially successful, the publisher made additional payments to the author, thus anticipating the modern system of advance and royalties.[26] It was naturally advantageous for both writers and publishers if books appealed to a wide public; this meant that the preferences of the connoisseur were overlooked in favor of mass popularity. The democratization of literature proved beneficial, for it imparted a solid, earthy foundation to humor. The kibyōshi and sharebon of Santō Kyōden are read today only by specialists in the literature of the period, but the works of later gesaku authors like Jippensha Ikku and Shikitei Samba are still popular because their humor is derived not from the peculiar (and now vanished) atmosphere of the licensed quarters but from the lives of the common people. When somebody in a novel has a bucket of excrement dropped over his head the humor is neither subtle nor literary, but the situation remains impervious to the passage of time.

With the change in the system of paying royalties it became possible for some authors to earn a living entirely by their writing, and for others to rely in large part on this income. Kyōden had been a writer mainly by avocation, but Jippensha Ikku (1765–1831) was a thorough professional. He had to produce a steady stream of books, even when there was little originality or inspiration behind them, but Ikku knew how to please the public. Authors rarely wrote out of personal experiences or convictions. Even when an author was ostensibly preaching some moral doctrine like the "encouragement of virtue and the chastisement of vice," his attention was absorbed mainly by the plots and subplots necessary to hold the readers' interest. Nakamura Yukihiko, the great expert on gesaku literature, declared: "What is lacking in gesaku, when compared with modern literature, is any serious confrontation with life."[27]

The later gesaku writers were adept at recording the exact manner of speech of different classes of people, but not at portraying real people or even a real society. The literature, whatever its surface appearance, was essentially frivolous. Even when, as in the writings of Bakin, filial piety and the other Confucian virtues are seemingly the themes, the authors treats them as abstract conceptions handed down from above, rather than as matters of genuine concern. A fantastic or even grotesque story was often "redeemed" by the impeccable sentiments of the moral, but it surely could not be taken seriously.

The reluctance of writers to describe their own society was not only because the readers enjoyed escapist fiction. The example of Santō Kyōden, castigated by the government at the height of his fame, served as a warning to later writers, who were at desperate pains not to share his fate. Gesaku fiction was an obvious medium for satire, but fear of governmental retaliation inhibited the writing; it lacks the intensity of either satire or true didacticism.

The later gesaku writings are divided into various categories, each with its distinctive features and readership, but despite the disparate surfaces, much is common to all varieties. Whatever the period the authors pretend to describe, no attempt was made to achieve historical accuracy. The language is usually a contemporary colloquial in the conversational parts and a standard Tokugawa literary style in the descriptions. Thanks to the simplicity of the language, these stories, unlike those of Saikaku, Kiseki, or Kyōden, are still enjoyed by many readers, who can follow the texts without need for elaborate commentaries. The authors of the later gesaku fiction were far from being literary titans, but they had an unerring touch when they described plebeian life, and enough of that life remains in evidence for readers to respond unaffectedly to these works. They are probably the oldest examples of Japanese prose which average readers peruse with pleasure.

KOKKEIBON

The name *kokkeibon*, or "funny book," was given to one type of gesaku literature about 1820, not because it was conspicuously funnier than all earlier varieties, but so as to distinguish it from the *ninjōbon*, or "love stories," that appeared about the same time in a similar format. There was, of course, a long tradition of humorous writings in Edo, both in prose and in poetry, but it is probably unnecessary to trace the ancestry of the kokkeibon beyond the *dangibon*, books of humorous sermons that reached the height of their popularity in the 1750s.[28] The dangibon were created by priests of the Jōdo sect who tried to instruct their listeners while amusing them. As early as 1735 Ejima Kiseki had published a work in the form of the popular sermon, but only with *Imayō Heta Dangi* (A Clumsy Sermon in the Modern Manner, 1752) by Jōkambō Kōa did the dangibon acquire its distinctive literary character. Because these books had originated in orally delivered sermons, they were colloquial throughout, and the authors distinguished by typical turns of phrase the sex, profession, and age of each character. The dangibon never attained much literary importance, but their faithful evocations of the speech of contemporary Edo influenced the kokkeibon especially, and their appeal to mass audiences, thanks to the liberal admixture of bad or obscene jokes, also relates them to the kokkeibon.

The dangibon tradition is apparent in the fiction of Hiraga Gennai, particularly *Fūryū Shidōken Den* (The Biography of the Jolly Shidōken, 1763). Under the guise of presenting the biography of a famous storyteller of the day, Gennai related fantastic travels and adventures in imaginary countries, the whole colored by his sardonic humor. Although this work was not written in the colloquial, it adheres closely to the form of the recitation. Its descriptions also pointed the way to other books of imaginary voyages.

The work that established the importance of the kokkeibon was without question *Tokai Dochu Hizakuriage* (Travels on Foot on the Tōkaidō) by Jippensha Ikku. The first part appeared in 1802 and for the next twenty years, until the forty-third volume was published in 1822, public demand again and again compelled Ikku to prolong the adventures of his irrepressible heroes, Kitahachi and Yajirobei. These utterly plebeian, typically Edo men are full of a lively if coarse humor, and have a knack of getting involved in comic and usually unsuccessful intrigues with women. The readers' interest in bowel movements was apparently inexhaustible; the number of references to soiled loincloths suggests that the subject was particularly enjoyed, and indicates also the general level of the humor.

Little distinguishes the two heroes, universally known by the abbreviated versions of their names Kita and Yaji, though Kita is said to be younger than Yaji. Both are completely uninterested in considerations of honor or reputation, lust after every woman they see, enjoy nothing more than a fight, and are yet not without a crude charm. They speak the rough language of the Edo man and show immense contempt for what they consider the effeminate speech of everybody else. Their travels take them from Edo along the Tōkaidō road to Kyoto and Osaka, then back to Edo again. The public demanded more, so the obliging Ikku sent the pair on journeys to Shikoku and into the mountains of central Japan.

The Tōkaidō had already been made the subject of fictionalized travel accounts, notably the *Tōkaidō Meishoki* by Asai Ryōi, but the sights along the road and the "famous products" of each of the fifty-three stages were always interesting to the public, as the extraordinary popularity of travel books attests. Yaji and Kita gladly sold their belongings to make the journey, and many readers would have done the same if they could, but few of the adventures described are agreeable. The ability of the Edo man to laugh his way out of difficult and embarrassing situations no doubt endeared the work to its readers.

The humor of *Hizakurige* is typified by a scene in the first book when Yaji takes a bath.[29] The bathtub is in the Kamigata style, a metal cauldron heated from below. The bather must step on a wooden platform floating in the tub to insulate himself from the heat, but Yaji mistakes the platform for a lid and removes it. His feet touch burning-hot metal and he leaps out in wild alarm. Fortunately, he notices a pair of clogs that have been left by the privy, so he slips them on before he enters the tub again. Soon Kita appears, complaining at how long Yaji has been taking. Yaji leaves the tub, but thinking to play a trick on his friend, hides the clogs. Kita jumps in, just like Yaji before him, and is properly scalded. He too eventually finds the clogs and wears them into the bath, but he stamps around so vigorously he kicks a hole in the tub and the water runs out.

The unfamiliar Kamigata bathtub was a typical touch of local color, exploited by Ikku for its comic possibilities. His exceptional familiarity with the countryside, especially the region of Osaka where he had lived as a young man, served him in good stead in writing about travel. His main achievement, however, was to create his two lustful, unscrupulous, but somehow lovable heroes. Even when he borrowed shamelessly from other men's books or plays to bolster his meager powers of invention, he managed always to blend the borrowed materials skillfully into his narration of the adventures of Kita and Yaji.[30] Despite the elementary nature of the humor, the hold *Hizakurige* continues to exert on Japanese readers proves how perfectly Ikku caught the spirit of the common people. Saikaku often wrote about commoners, but they generally aspired to the riches or pleasures of their betters; Yaji and Kita aimed at nothing higher than spending a night in bed with a pretty servant girl. Their gropings in the dark often led them into disasters, but they were ready for more.

Ikku was an exceptionally prolific writer, but whatever talents he may originally have possessed were petrified by the success of *Hizakurige*. Instead of developing as an artist, he was condemned to producing less and less interesting sequels.

Ikku's chief rival as an author of kokkeibon was Shikitei Samba (1776–1822). Like Ikku, he composed in many genres, but his two best works were kokkeibon: *Ukiyoburo* (The Up-to-date Bathhouse, 1809–13) and *Ukiyodoko* (The Up-to-date Barbershop, 1813–14). Samba, the son of a Shinto priest, first gained fame with the publication in 1799 of a kibyōshi that described in comic terms the quarrel that had broken out the previous year between two rival groups of Edo firefighters. The members of one group, considering they had been insulted, charged into the houses of Samba and his publisher. The government threw the firemen in jail for a while, fined the publisher, and put Samba in handcuffs for fifty days. The severity with which Samba and the publisher were treated, though they were guilty of no violence, shows that although the curbs on fiction had been relaxed after Matsudaira Sadanobu's resignation in 1793, they were legally still in force, and at any sign of disorder the government was likely to act against authors and publishers suspected of provoking unruly elements.

His fifty days in handcuffs apparently discouraged Samba from publishing for several years, but in 1802 he began to write again, and soon established a reputation. Samba owed most as a writer to Hiraga Gennai and Santō Kyōden. His style was so closely modeled on Gennai's that contemporary critics spoke of Samba as Gennai's literary heir.[31] With respect to technique, however, he owed even more to Kyōden; the idea for Samba's most famous work, *The Up-to-date Bathhouse*, seems to have come from a kibyōshi written by Kyōden in 1802. Samba's close imitation of Kyōden was normal at a time when professional writers were obliged to turn out many books each year and, in desperation for new themes, often stole from their predecessors. Perhaps even *Hizakurige* influenced Samba, though less directly. In *Hizakurige* the two main characters remain the same, but their constant travels provide them with a great variety of new situations; in *The Up-to-date Bathhouse* the place, a public bath, remains the same, but the customers are constantly changing, producing a similar result.

The public bath and the barbershop, the scenes of Samba's most popular works, served the social functions for townsmen of the lower classes that the licensed quarters served for the more affluent. As people soaked in the hot water or relaxed in the barber's chair, they passed the time in gossip with friends and strangers. The subjects varied but were generally trivial, as we can gather from Samba's faithful evocations of many conversations. Samba never attempted to create individual characters, and he was probably incapable of suggesting any emotions deeper than at surface level, but he could reproduce exactly the manner of speech of the Edo merchant who cannot refrain from advertising his wares even when in the bath; or the Confucian scholar who gives Chinese names even to the most plebeian Japanese objects; or the housewife who speculates about the kind of husband her daughter will marry; or the young lady who exhibits her literary pretensions; or the servant who complains about an unreasonable master. Samba's readers laughed not at the antics of a favorite character like Yaji or Kita, but an anonymous people whose speech, recorded with diabolical accuracy, revealed common human weaknesses.

Samba, unlike Ikku, was uninterested in travel. He confined himself to describing the one society he knew thoroughly, that of the common people of Edo. His only object was to amuse.

In his earliest published work he had complained that comic books had been replaced by "weeping books," referring perhaps to the sentimental sharebon of Umebori Kokuga. Samba rectified this situation brilliantly; his comic works have only slight literary merit, but they are superb examples of Edo humor. It would be pointless to translate them; their interest lies in the words he used to record aimless gossip about incidents of daily life, the theater, and the brothels, perfectly recapturing the speech and spirit of the common people.

NINJŌBON

We have seen how, as the result of the prohibition placed on immoral books in 1790 and the punishment meted out to Santō Kyōden in the following year, the production of sharebon fell off considerably. Even after Matsudaira Sadanobu fell from power there was no immediate resurgence of the old comic spirit. Writers took pains to give their fiction a veneer of respectability, hoping this would excuse the frivolous passages. Umebori Kokuga, by introducing sincerity as a necessary element in the relations between customer and prostitute, provided a transition to the *ninjōbon* (books about human feelings) that became popular in the 1820s and reached full maturity a decade later. In the meantime, other authors, encouraged by the apparent indifference of the government, again tried writing sharebon in the old manner, but without any literary distinction.

The ninjōbon developed from the sharebon, but their differences are more interesting than their similarities. The most important new element was love. The scene was normally set in the licensed quarters, just as in the sharebon, but the hero was no longer the connoisseur who wins admiration by his perfect knowledge of the demimonde. Instead, he was a handsome young man, often the eldest son of a rich merchant family, whose chief distinction was his ability to win the love and devotion of the prostitutes. It was the height of boorishness for the hero of a sharebon to fall in love, but in the ninjōbon he might not only fall in love but even marry. The prostitutes of the sharebon hardly emerged as distinct personalities. They treated upstart customers with disdain, but rarely displayed any real affection even for the tsū. The authors of the ninjōbon, on the other hand, made every effort to impart distinctive traits to their women. Each is in love with a particular man, and shows not only her devotion but her jealousy of other women. The heroes of the ninjōbon are described as men for whom many women are eager to make great sacrifices, but they are not heroic in any other sense. They are generally ineffectual, incapable of earning their living, unashamed to take money from their adoring sweethearts. Obviously, they are masters at making love, but otherwise they are rather effeminate; if ever they are attacked by the villains, they fall easy victims. But this does not disillusion the women. Far from it; the weaknesses of the heroes move them to all the greater love.

The changes in the content and style of the ninjōbon were made in deference to the tastes of the anticipated readers. The sharebon had been intended for men familiar with the licensed quarters, but the ninjōbon were mainly aimed at women of the samurai or upper merchant class, who derived their greatest pleasure from the Kabuki theater and who craved the same romantic atmosphere in the books they read. They preferred above all stories about heroines with whom they could identify themselves—women passionately devoted to their lovers, generous toward their friends, and infinitely ready to sacrifice their own happiness. The women readers, enjoying the vicarious pleasures of romantic scenes, did not object to delicate hints at physical intimacy between the hero and the heroines, but they were shocked by pornography or overt descriptions of sex. As a result, the ninjōbon were extremely erotic, suggesting with rare intensity the claims of physical passion, but rarely pornographic.

The authors of the ninjōbon, unlike the sharebon writers, chose not to expose the weaknesses of their characters; they displayed instead their strongest sympathy, especially for the women. The author's presence is constantly felt as a friendly and understanding observer who from time to time makes comments, lest the reader be misled. He does not stand on a lofty eminence, pointing out moral lessons inspired by the actions, but shares the same plane as the characters. This attitude accounted for the personal popularity of the writers, especially Tamenaga Shunsui (1790–1843).

Shunsui did not originate the ninjōbon, but he raised it to its highest achievements and established its special domain. He was preceded in this genre by Hana Sanjin (Nose Recluse, a pen-name inspired by the famous Kyōden nose). Two sharebon published by Hana Sanjin in 1818 display most of the characteristics of the ninjōbon down to the number and variety of illustrations, but his earliest ninjōbon which is easily recognizable as such appeared in 1821. Hana Sanjin, the first author to appeal deliberately to women readers, enjoyed considerable success until the appearance of Shunsui's masterpiece *Shunshoku Umegoyomi* (Colors of Spring: The Plum Calendar, 1832–33) swept all before it. Hana Sanjin continued to publish until 1836, though overshadowed in his later years by Shunsui.

Not much is known about Tamenaga Shunsui's early life except that he was born into a merchant family of Edo. Apparently he studied writing with Shikitei Samba and assisted Ryūtei Tanehiko, perhaps because he hoped to publish their works.[32] He seems to have founded his publishing company about 1821, but lacking the capital or authority to attract first-class writers, had brought out old works by Samba and Bakin, using the original blocks. The enraged reactions to these acts of piracy may have decided Shunsui to try writing his own books.

Shunsui's first success came with the publication of *Akegarasu Nochi no Masayume* (After the Morning Crow, a True Dream; first three parts 1821, last two parts 1824). It is hard to know how much of the book should be credited to Shunsui; he confessed in 1833 that most of the works he signed at that time were written by disciples.[33] *Morning Crow* was probably written by Shunsui and an assistant, the two men only slightly revising the manuscript of another man.

The success of *Morning Crow* may have decided Shunsui to devote himself to fiction, but he could not depend exclusively on this income. He continued his publishing business until 1829, when his shop was destroyed in a fire. This disaster may have compelled Shunsui to become a professional writer. The skills he had acquired as a reviser and editor of other men's manuscripts served him in good stead; between 1821, when he first used the pen name Somahito II, and 1832, when the first part of *Plum Calendar* appeared, he published about thirty ninjōbon, some of which (despite his confession) he probably wrote himself. During this time his style matured, and he was ready to compose his masterpiece, *Plum Calendar*, which was not only the single first-rate example of a ninjōbon, but perhaps the best work of fiction composed in Japanese between the novels of Ueda Akinari and Futabatei Shimei.

Shunsui's style owes much to his predecessors. The use of a vivid Edo colloquial, for example, follows the tradition of Samba. Not only was Shunsui most comfortable in writing this language, but he anticipated that his readers would be Edo women; he wrote in the preface to a work published in 1825 that he had refrained from having the characters speak the Kamigata language required by the setting for fear of making the work difficult for Edo women and children to understand.[34] *Plum Calendar* consists mainly of conversations, together with brief introductory passages, "stage directions," and occasional comments by the author. The reliance on dialogue and stage directions suggests the importance of Kabuki in the formation of Shunsui's style; two of his early collaborators were in fact Kabuki playwrights. The stage directions are usually in colloquial Japanese, leaving only a very small part of the work in the classical language. It is frequently stated that *Ukigumo* (1887–89) by Futabatei Shimei was the first novel to have been written in the colloquial, but *Plum Calendar*, fifty years earlier, came exceedingly close to earning that distinction. The language of *Plum Calendar* is at times startlingly close to contemporary Japanese; the dialogue is so brilliantly exact we can all but see the characters before us. Even readers of the day must have had some trouble with the specialized language of the licensed quarters; Shunsui from time to time explains such terms in notes. But *Plum Calendar* is so closely connected in mood and atmosphere with the subsequent Japanese literature describing the demimonde—the novels of the Kenyūsha group, of Nagai Kafū and others—that it seems more like a bridge to later fiction than a work bound by language and outlook to 1830. The characters not only live within the world created by Shunsui, but have unmistakable counterparts in the life and literature of modern Japan.

Shunsui originally intended to publish *Plum Calendar* in six volumes, but he extended it by popular demand to twelve. The doubling of the original plan did no great harm to the structure. There is no discernible organization to the story: problems are resolved only for fresh ones to replace them. But however far the author sometimes wanders from his main subjects, he never quite forgets them, and his digressions grow organically from the work. Perhaps Shunsui wrote this book by himself because he had greater literary ambitions for it than for his collaborative efforts.

Plum Calendar is the story of Tanjirō, the illegitimate son of a high-ranking gentleman. As a boy he is sent in adoption to the Karagoto-ya, a brothel in Yoshiwara, but the villainous clerk of the establishment gets rid of Tanjirō by falsely implicating him in the theft of a valuable heirloom. Tanjirō, unable to prove his innocence, goes into hiding.

The book opens as Yonehachi, a geisha in love with Tanjirō, is searching for his hideout. After she finds him we learn bit by bit of Yonehachi's passionate devotion to her lover and of the fierce jealousy she displays at the thought of any other women in his life. She wants the sole privilege of supplying him with money, cooking his meals, and sharing his bed. She is ready to sell all her possessions to help, and Tanjirō is not embarrassed to accept. Yonehachi's jealousy flares up when he asks about Ochō, the daughter of the former owner of the Karagoto-ya. He and Ochō grew up like brother and sister, but Yonehachi accuses him of being in love with her. Tanjirō denies it, and Yonehachi accepts his reassurances, only for doubts to arise again. Tanjirō's attitudes hardly strike us as romantic, and we later learn that he has been deceiving Yonehachi in pretending not to be in love with Ochō, but women readers of the day must have found his studied indifference somehow appealing.

From time to time Shunsui intrudes into the narration:

> My only intent in this story is to describe the feelings (*ninjō*) of Yonehachi, Ochō and the others. I have therefore not written satirically about the Green Houses. In the first place, I am not familiar with the brothels, and for this reason have only cursorily described their atmosphere. I earnestly request that this work not be judged in the same way as a sharebon.[35]

One of the best scenes of the work relates how Tanjirō and Ochō accidentally meet in the street. He invites her into a restaurant, where she soon unabashedly reveals her love. Like Yonehachi, she desires nothing more than to cook for him and provide his needs. Tanjirō is reluctant to disclose his connections with

Yonehachi and tries to keep Ochō at a distance by urging her to be more concerned about her reputation. Ochō, sensing he must have some other romantic attachment, becomes jealous, and Tanjirō, to change the subject, opens the window and looks out into the street. At that moment Yonehachi and a friend happen to pass and catch a glimpse of Tanjirō. He is acutely embarrassed at being caught between the two women and attempts to leave before Yonehachi can reach him. At this point Shunsui speaks an aside:

> What will be the emotions of Tanjirō and Ochō when they go down the stairs and meet Yonehachi? The author still hasn't thought of a good solution. . . . If any readers have good suggestions to make, I beg them to get in touch with the author at once.[36]

The next chapter follows immediately on the previous scene. The two rivals for Tanjirō's love do indeed meet on the staircase, where they exchange angry looks. Yonehachi, addressing Tanjirō with great familiarity, expresses surprise he should be leaving instead of waiting for her. Then, turning to Ochō, she says, "You've certainly become a very pretty girl. And how you've grown in such a short time! It's time for you to think of getting married." So saying, she stares hard at Tanjirō's face.

The three of them drink together. Yonehachi, aware of the danger that Ochō may steal her sweetheart, adopts a bold course of action. She informs Ochō that, even though she still performs as a geisha, she considers herself to be Tanjirō's wife, and reveals that she is working only so as to support her husband. Ochō is young and inexperienced, but no less determined; she politely declares her intention of henceforth providing for Tanjirō. The two women exchange sarcasms until Tanjirō, who has taken little part in the conversation, announces he will escort Ochō home. Yonehachi, seeing him to the door, pinches Tanjirō's back fiercely, and mutters to him, "Leave at once. I can't stand you."

Tanjirō answers with a grim smile, "You're crazy. You're too much for me."

"So I'm crazy, am I?" cries Yonehachi, throwing down the toothpick from between her teeth. Then she adds in a soft voice, "You'd better take Ochō by the hand so she doesn't get lost."

Tanjirō answers, "Say any damned foolishness you please."

Later, when Tanjirō and Ochō are walking alone, she asks bluntly who will be his wife, and he says, "There's a girl ten times prettier and sweeter than Yonehachi."

"Where?"

"Here," he says, throwing his arm around her.[37]

The rivalry between the two women reaches its climax when Ochō, in order to raise money for Tanjirō, becomes a professional entertainer. The owner of the place where she works is constantly nagging Ochō to accept some rich man as her patron, but she resists. In the meantime, Tanjirō continues to live as Yonehachi's kept man. This does not prevent him from having an affair with another geisha, Adakichi. The quarrel between the two geishas is even sharper than that between Yonehachi and Ochō.

Another high point in the story occurs when Ochō and Tanjirō finally make love. The scene is narrated with extreme discretion, but Shunsui nevertheless felt obliged to defend himself from the charge he might be tempting women readers into immorality:

> In general, I write books with the expectation that most of the readers will be women; that is why they are so crude and clumsy. But even though the women I portray may seem immoral, they are all imbued with deep sentiments of chastity and fidelity. I do not write about women who have affairs with many men, or who indulge in lustful pursuits for the sake of money, or who deviate from the true path of morality, or who are wanting in wifely decorum. There are many romantic passages in this book, but the feelings of the men and women I have described are pure and uncorrupted.[38]

Plum Calendar is full of subplots and digressions, but it was so enjoyable that readers clamored for more. Shunsui accordingly wrote a sequel, *Shunshoku Tatsumi no Sono* (Colors of Spring: The Southeast Garden, 1833–35). This novel has never enjoyed the popularity of *Plum Calendar*, but it is a surprisingly effective reprisal of the themes of the earlier work, and its eroticism is heightened by illustrations by the artist Kuninao which skirt the border of "dangerous pictures." The story revolves around the rivalry of Yonehachi and Adakichi for Tanjirō's love. There are effective scenes of jealousy and bickering, but the work ends happily with Tanjirō, his wife Ochō, and his *two* mistresses all living amicably together. It was mainly because of this book that Shunsui obtained the undeserved reputation of being a pornographer.

Shunsui wrote many other ninjōbon, sometimes by himself, sometimes by utilizing a staff of assistants. At the end of 1841 Shunsui, under investigation for some time by the government, was summoned to a magistrate's office and questioned about his books. In the spring of the following year he was put in handcuffs for fifty days, and his illustrator and publisher were fined heavily. The blocks of his books were destroyed, and complete volumes were burned. This action came as part of the Tempō Reforms. After his release from handcuffs Shunsui turned to didactic fiction, but never achieved much success. He died in 1843 at the age of fifty-three, no doubt weakened by the shock of his punishment.

The ninjōbon revived after the effects of the Tempō Reforms had worn off, but they never again reached the level of *Plum Calendar*. The influence they exerted on later Japanese fiction, however, was greater than that of any other variety of gesaku writing.

YOMIHON

The curious name *yomihon* (book for reading) was given to one kind of gesaku fiction to distinguish it from works enjoyed more for their illustrations than for their texts. The yomihon also were illustrated, but the emphasis clearly was on the story. Although they were considered to be gesaku, no less than the most trivial composition, their heavily didactic tone sharply contrasted with the frivolity of the kibyōshi or sharebon. Their plots were burdened with historical materials derived from both Chinese and Japanese sources, and the authors did not hesitate to point out the moral of each episode. But despite the serious intent of the yomihon, they were romances, rather than novels; the characters are schematized, and the incidents are not those of ordinary life but belong to the world of witches, fairy princesses, and impeccably noble warriors. Where they succeeded, as in two or three works by Bakin, they represented the culmination of the art of the traditional storytellers.

The yomihon were often inspired by colloquial Chinese literature, either the novel *Shui Hu Chuan* or one of the collections of ghost stories.[39] They were written in a distinctive mixture of the *gabun* (elegant prose) of the scholars of national learning and allusions derived from Chinese sources. Usually they were set in the age of warfare of the Muromachi period, and they emphasized the samurai ideals, especially those that could be equated directly with the moral principles of Confucianism. Unlike most earlier Japanese fiction, composed seriatim with one episode loosely linked to the previous one, the yomihon were carefully structured. Bakin once listed the seven factors of composition of the novel: the creation of a hero and secondary figures; subplots; underlying themes; comparison; contrast; abbreviation; and unspoken implications. His novels are often garrulous and digressive, or even ponderous in their didacticism, but his sense of literary purpose and the broad canvases he filled with people and incidents earned him the distinction of being considered "the greatest writer of romances in the history of the Japanese novel."[40]

The name Bakin is as closely associated with the yomihon as Kyōden's with the kibyōshi or Shunsui's with the ninjōbon. However, Bakin wrote almost every other kind of gesaku fiction, sometimes with success in his day, though the humor of his lighter works is so contrived as to exasperate rather than divert modern readers.[41] We turn with relief to his sternly moral works.

Takizawa Bakin was born in Edo in 1767, the fifth son of a samurai. He was proud of his ancestry, and throughout his life attempted to restore the family prestige. As a boy he served in various samurai households, but in 1790 he made up his mind to become a professional writer. He took the manuscript of a kibyōshi to Santō Kyōden for his comments. Kyōden was so impressed he arranged for publication with illustrations by the celebrated artist Toyokuni in the following year. That was the year Kyōden was punished for his allegedly immoral sharebon. During the time that Kyōden was kept in manacles Bakin lived in his house and wrote several kibyōshi which he published in Kyōden's name, as an act of gratitude to his master.

Bakin first attracted fame in 1793 when he published seven kibyōshi under the name Kyokutei Bakin. From then on he kept up a fantastic rate of production, often writing as many as thirteen kibyōshi in a single year. His greatest fame, however, came with his yomihon. Two works in particular, *Chinzetsu Yumiharizuki* (Crescent Moon, 1807–11) and *Nansō Satomi Hakkenden* (Biographies of Eight Dogs, 1814–41), are considered his masterpieces. Bakin established his supremacy as a writer of yomihon in 1806 with the first part of *Crescent Moon*. The first part describes the ancestry and childhood of the twelfth-century hero Minamoto Tametomo, his triumphs and defeats, and ends with his exile on the island of Ōshima. In the second part Tametomo leaves Ōshima to conquer other islands, but he is pursued by an imperial army. He and his son are caught at sea in a storm and are separated. In this sequel, written by popular demand, we learn that Tametomo was shipwrecked in the Ryukyus. He subdues an uprising, saves a princess from a corrupt minister with designs on the throne, and in the end he triumphantly proclaims his virtuous rule. The people beg Tametomo to be their king, but when his wife, a Ryukyuan princess, suddenly dies, he goes up to heaven after her, leaving his son to govern the country.

The success of *Crescent Moon* owed much to its heroic scale, the product of Bakin's study of Chinese novels, especially *Shui Hu Hou Chuan*,[42] the sequel to *Shui Hu Chuan*. Tametomo, a man of enormous prowess who embodies the samurai ideals, makes an ideal hero for a romance, and although Bakin based the novel in part on historical fact, he did not hesitate to invent when his story required it. The real Tametomo died on Ōshima and never even saw the Ryukyus, but few of Bakin's readers would have been aware of this violation of fact. Bakin painstakingly studied books on the Ryukyus to provide his romance with a maximum of local color, and occasional graphic touches probably convinced readers of the truth of the narration, despite the implausible transformation of the rough soldier Tametomo described in history books into a model of benevolence and righteousness. Bakin's prose, in the tradition of the medieval romances, was both appropriate to the stirring events he described and melodious, often falling into cadences of alternating phrases in seven and five syllables, as in his mature works.

Crescent Moon was intended to embody the principle of *kanzen chōaku*—the encouragement of virtue and chastisement of vice. Bakin included amorous and exciting incidents in order to attract readers, but he considered that this was merely an expedient; his real purpose in writing fiction was moral and didactic, and the reader was expected to absorb the allegorical implications of the events by the time he finished the novel. The popularity of *Crescent Moon*, especially among the samurai class, owed much to Bakin's lofty purpose, but the moral would not have been so easily swallowed without the fantasy and exotic setting.

Bakin's yomihon appealed primarily to the educated classes. They were printed in editions of about three hundred copies, more than half sold directly to lending libraries.[43] Because sales of the yomihon brought in insufficient money to support Bakin and his family, he was obliged to turn out many potboilers. His serious books were the justification for his career; not only did they bring him satisfaction as an artist, but they embodied the ideals that increasingly obsessed him. Bakin had given up his samurai duties to become a writer, and he had married not a lady of his class but the owner of a *geta* (clog) shop. His own failure to live up to the code of the warrior made him all the more determined that his son would be a true-blue samurai. The son eventually died of the nervous and physical strain, but Bakin never wavered in his resolve to restore the glory of his family. It led him to write in *Eight Dogs* the grand exposition of the ideals of the samurai class.

Bakin began to publish *Eight Dogs* in 1814, at the age of forty-seven. He was still deeply under the influence of Chinese fiction,[44] but he also consulted many Japanese works in order to draw an accurate picture of Japan in the fifteenth century. His original intention may have been no more ambitious than to write a romance similar to his earlier yomihon, but as he wrote, the potentialities of his theme expanded before him. He spent twenty-seven years on the work, which totaled 106 volumes. During the composition of this novel Bakin was beset by every variety of family trouble. Moreover, from 1831 his eyes began to bother him seriously. In 1834 he lost the sight of his right eye and the left eye pained him constantly. He persisted with the manuscript, writing larger and larger characters so that he could see them more easily. In 1840 he lost the sight of his left eye too, and was totally unable to write, but he was determined to complete his great work. He decided to make his daughter-in-law his amanuensis, and she dutifully accepted. But it was not easy dictating his elaborate phraseology, and often he had to teach her the characters as he went along. It was a painful experience for both of them, but Bakin finally completed the text in the autumn of 1841. It is the longest work of Japanese fiction, and perhaps the longest romance ever written anywhere in the world.

Hakkenden means literally "Biography of Eight Dogs." This strange title originates with an incident early in the work. The general Satomi Yoshizane, besieged in his castle, declares in desperation that he will give his daughter Fusehime to whoever brings him his enemy's head. His watchdog, Yatsufusa, bounds off and soon comes trotting back with the enemy general's head in his jaws. Yoshizane is enabled to win a great victory, but he has no intention of bestowing his daughter on a dog. Fusehime, a stickler for promises, insists on accompanying the valiant Yatsufusa, despite all opposition, and the happy couple goes off into the mountains to live in a cave. When a year or so of conjugal life has passed Fusehime finds herself with child. About this time a retainer of Yoshizane's, anxious to rescue Fusehime from her curious fate, makes his way to the cave and shoots at Yatsufusa. The bullet strikes Fusehime instead. Mortally wounded, and aware that she cannot be saved, she stabs herself. A white vapor issues forth from her wound and envelopes the crystal beads of the rosary hung around her neck. Eight beads rise into the sky, each marked with the Chinese character for one of the Confucian virtues. The eight beads are subsequently found in the hands of the newly born sons of eight men whose surnames begin with the word *Inu*, Dog. Each of these eight "dogs" proves to be the incarnation of the virtue whose name is carved on the crystal bead he carries. The eight heroes meet and separate many times, but finally they assemble and by their efforts restore the Satomi family to its former glory. At the end the eight "dogs" withdraw to Yatsufusa's cave and suddenly vanish.

It is obviously impossible to present a fair impression of this immensely long work with a mere summary. Even if the main outlines were adequately stated, it would still not be possible to suggest the prodigious flow of poetic language and the endless variety of incidents that animate the narration and impart to the seemingly cold Confucian themes a vitality that captivated many generations of readers. Again and again the heroes are tested by malignant beings bent on destroying them, or by the claims of affection which, though more agreeable, are no less dangerous to men consecrated to a mission. In a famous episode the hero Inuzuka Shino rebuffs the beautiful Hamaji, who loves him so much she is ready to sacrifice her honor for him.[45] Shino is not insensitive to her charms, but his Confucian training does not permit him to deviate from the strict code of samurai conduct. Here, as elsewhere in *Eight Dogs*, duty triumphs over human weakness, and the dispassionate behavior of the heroes is held up for admiration.

Despite the verbosity of this enormous book, it compels our respect by its magnitude and by the strength of its exposition of the ideals of the Tokugawa period. The main philosophical background was, of course, Confucian, but the popular Buddhism of the time, with its heavy insistence on retribution for evil and reward for good, provided the mechanics for much of the action. The samurai ideals, tarnished by Bakin's day, lived again in this book in pristine glory, and they by no means seem contemptible.

Bakin continued to write until shortly before his death, pushing ahead with his long yomihon, first begun in 1828, called *Kinseisetsu Bishōnen Roku* (Handsome Youths of Our Time, a Record). He was still working on the concluding volumes when he died in 1848, at the age of eighty-one. This novel, describing two handsome youths, one good and the other evil, has scenes of such violence, and even perversity, that some critics have found them incomprehensible in terms of Bakin's normal style.[46] Its greater realism may attract modern readers more than the strange accidents and twists of fate that complicate the plots of *Crescent Moon* and *Eight Dogs*; nevertheless, it is still very far from being a modern novel, and it lacks the commanding sweep that makes of *Eight Dogs* a monument of Japanese literature and of Bakin one of the four or five great Japanese novelists.

GŌKAN

Much as the sharebon gave way to the ninjōbon in response to popular demand for sustained stories with greater depth of characterization, the kibyōshi gave way to the *gōkan* (bound-together volumes). The name designated the format: as many as six pamphlets, each consisting of five double pages, bound together and sold as a unit. The gōkan look much like kibyōshi, with strings of writings ingeniously worked into the design, surrounding the human figures and architectural elements of the illustrations. However, the greater length of the stories promoted not only a changed format but a different kind of subject matter. The gōkan, unlike the humorous kibyōshi, generally treated the tragic events of a vendetta. As early as 1783 Nansenshō Somahito (1749–1807) had published an illustrated vengeance story, a kibyōshi without a trace of humor. It attracted little attention, but the same author was more successful with another vengeance story, *Kataki-uchi Gijo no Hanabusa* (A Hero among Women Wreaks Vengeance), published in 1795 with illustrations by the great Toyokuni.

Some writers, resisting this development in the kibyōshi, tried to preserve the old comic touch. Shikitei Samba, writing in 1805, attacked publishers who insisted on vengeance stories, but he had to admit that he himself had catered to their demands. In 1806 Samba published a vengeance story in two parts, each consisting of five small volumes. These booklets were bound together, starting the popularity of the new format, called gōkan.

Not only was the binding attractive to the public, but the cover illustrations, formerly small panels at the upper-left corner, were expanded to fill the entire page, and often printed in color.[47] The illustrations to the gōkan were of crucial importance in selling the books, and the authors composed texts with them in mind. When, for example, Ryūtei Tanehiko wrote his gōkan version of *The Tale of Genji* he experienced the greatest trouble with the second chapter, the static discussion of the qualities of women, which lends itself poorly to illustration. Tanehiko usually sketched the illustrations he wanted for each page, and gave many specific orders to his collaborator, the artist Utagawa Kunisada. The gōkan, despite its high moral tone (hardly distinguishable from that of the yomihon), remained essentially a picture book.

At the beginning of the nineteenth century almost all the leading prose writers were busily turning out gōkan, mainly on vengeance themes, to satisfy the enormous public demand. Santō Kyōden, hoping to restore his reputation after the crippling blow to his career of 1791, began in 1807 to write gōkan illustrated by Toyokuni. From then on until his death in 1816 Kyōden wrote close to ninety gōkan, all of them well received. His younger brother, Santō Kyōzan, also wrote gōkan, some fifty in all, and ranked second in popularity only to Ryūtei Tanehiko. Even Bakin wrote many gōkan, but the genre is typified by one man, Ryūtei Tanehiko, and by one work, *Nise Murasaki Inaka Genji* (The False Murasaki and the Rustic Genji).

Ryūtei Tanehiko (1783–1842) was a samurai who lived his entire life in Edo. Although he belonged to a fairly important family, he showed little interest in martial pursuits, but devoted himself instead to the theater. Not only was he an expert on Kabuki who enjoyed performing in amateur theatricals, but in his fiction he liberally borrowed the plot devices and characterization typical of the stage.

Tanehiko's first work was apparently *Awa no Naruto*, a yomihon published in 1807 with illustrations by Hokusai; though based on a famous Jōruri play, it was a failure. Bakin, praising a later yomihon by Tanehiko wrote: "I never imagined this author was capable of such skill, but he has shown unbelievable improvement. This is so much better than *Awa no Naruto* that it seems like the work of a different man."[48] But Bakin criticized even this yomihon for its excessive borrowings from Kabuki.

Tanehiko at first hoped to establish a reputation as a yomihon writer, but in face of Bakin's supremacy in this genre, he felt he had to try something else. Perhaps the greater financial rewards of the gōkan also attracted him. As late as 1822 he still nursed ambitions of becoming a yomihon writer; the preface to a gōkan states that he originally intended the work to be a yomihon, but he had been compelled by circumstances to give up this plan. So, he writes, he "eliminated the excessive verbiage, chose only the essentials, and turned the story into one of the usual picture books."[49] Tanehiko, as Bakin sarcastically noted, lacked the learning to write allegorically on the grand moral theme of "encouragement of virtue and chastisement of vice"; his forte lay instead in a pictorial beauty of description that exactly fitted in with the requirements of the gōkan.

Tanehiko's first gōkan was published in 1811. The favorable attention it attracted probably induced him to specialize in this genre. From that year on he wrote a minimum of two or three gōkan, and sometimes as many as nine, each year. He also tried his hand at another variety of fiction: in 1815 he published the first of his *shōhon jitate* (outlines of Kabuki plays). He continued until 1831 to write these booklets, lavishly illustrated with pictures of popular actors. The collaboration with Kunisada, begun at this time, continued to Tanehiko's death, and was indispensable to the success of his books.[50] The combination of Kabuki plots and illustrations in the shōhon jitate went hand in hand with Tanehiko's work as a gōkan writer, and exploited his special knowledge of the theater.

Tanehiko first conceived of writing his masterpiece, *The Rustic Genji*, about 1825. The direct stimulus may have been Bakin's success with some unusually long gōkan published at this time. Tanehiko could not compete with Bakin when it came to adapting Chinese materials, but he was unusually well read in Japanese literature, and had an impressive collection of old books and manuscripts. He had read *The Tale of Genji* with the aid of a commentary and had attended lectures on the Heian classics given by Ishikawa Masamochi. In later years Bakin, irritated by the success of *The Rustic Genji*, expressed his doubts that Tanehiko had ever read the original work.[51] This was unfair, but Bakin was right in supposing that Tanehiko's conception of *The Tale of Genji* lacked the aesthetic or philosophic insights of Motoori Norinaga; his approach was that of the Kabuki dramatist who freely adapted an old classic to fit the requirements of his medium.

Even after Tanehiko had chosen *The Tale of Genji* as his model, he had to decide the setting of his gōkan and how closely he would follow the original. He once described his uncertainties during the early stages of the writing:

> When I first began to write *The Rustic Genji* an aged friend said to me, "You should try to the best of your ability to preserve the language of the original and not alter the story. It will probably then be of some use to young people who haven't read *The Tale of Genji*." But a young friend said, "You should vary the plot. Weave in effects from Kabuki and the puppet theater. Surely there can't be anyone who hasn't read *Genji*."[52]

Faced with such contradictory advice, Tanehiko set the *Genji* during the reign of the shogun Yoshimasa, at the end of the fifteenth century. This age of warfare and disorder was certainly a far cry from the serene world of the Shining Prince, but since Tanehiko intended to write a romance glorifying the samurai ideals, the Muromachi period suited his purpose. Needless to say, he made no attempt to evoke the atmosphere of the shogun Yoshimasa's court, any more than the authors of *Chūshingura* worried about authentic details of the reign of the first Ashikaga shogun.

Tanehiko also had difficulties determining how faithful he should be to the plot of *The Tale of Genji*. His manuscripts are full of crossings out and additions, indicating his uncertainties, especially at the beginning of the work. It was with great reluctance that he finally dropped an opening paragraph directly modeled on Lady Murasaki's famous lines,[53] but as a mark of tribute to the original author he pretended that a woman, a court lady named Ofuji, had written his work. This identification accounts for the first part of the title *The False Murasaki and the Rustic Genji*: Ofuji is an imitation Murasaki. As for the "rustic Genji," Tanehiko explained in a preface: "Although I have described events that occurred in the capital, I have qualified my *Genji* as 'rustic' because of the countrified language."[54] The language is in fact classical, and not colloquial, but being easy to understand is "rustic." Tanehiko's hero, Mitsuuji, is also many cuts below the aristocratic Genji, if not actually rustic.

The story follows *The Tale of Genji* with reasonable fidelity, though sometimes, because of the simplification involved in an illustrated book, the actions of two or three characters are telescoped. On the other hand, in the interests of heightening the Kabuki effects, Tanehiko added characters and episodes that would have been unthinkable in the original. Early in the book a villain named Dorozō makes an attempt on the life of Hanakiri, the "equivalent" of Kiritsubo, Genji's mother. Dorozō inadvertently kills another lady, and is in turn accidentally killed by his own sister. This working out of the Buddhist principle of cause and effect has an embellishment reminiscent of Kabuki: the characters mistake their intended victims in the dark. The sister attempts suicide when she realizes she has killed her brother, but she is stopped and becomes a nun instead. Later in the book she dies at the hands of bandits, a substitute (in the Jōruri manner) for the hero, Mitsuuji.

Mitsuuji is the son of the shogun Yoshimasa by Hanakiri, a woman of inferior rank. He himself has no ambition of becoming shogun, but three treasures, necessary to anyone who would succeed to the post, have mysteriously disappeared, and Mitsuuji resolves to find them. Lost treasures were familiar plot devices from Kabuki and, like Sukeroku, Mitsuuji frequents the licensed quarters in hope of discovering information about the treasures. The love affairs that sprinkle the pages are described with conventional skill and heightened by the charm of Kunisada's illustrations, but there is something unpleasantly cold and deliberate about Mitsuuji's systematic use of the women he sleeps with to further his investigation. Judged in terms of the samurai morality, Mitsuuji is superior to Genji in that his love affairs are occasioned not by fleshly lust but by a higher purpose, recovery of the treasures. But it is hard for us to feel affection for this love machine or, for that matter, for the women of different social stations who vie to become his slaves. Mitsuuji seems incapable of a spontaneous act of generosity or love, and the women who surround him totally lack the vivid personalities so superbly described in *The Tale of Genji.*

Despite the failings of *The Rustic Genji* for modern readers, it enjoyed amazing popularity in its time. It is hard to understand this today, when *The Rustic Genji* has lost most of its charm, and the endless ramifications of the plot bore rather than intrigue. The genteel tone maintained throughout—Tanehiko never shocked the sensibilities of even the most refined ladies—is also likely to exasperate us. Even the illustrations seem rather insipid. But for many years readers eagerly awaited each new installment, curious to discover how *The Tale of Genji* would be altered in this latter-day version.

Tanehiko published the first part in 1829 rather as a trial balloon, neither the author nor the publisher having much confidence in the sales of a modernized version of *Genji.* The first part met with a surprisingly favorable reception, and was followed in 1830 with the second and third parts. For several years Tanehiko published two parts annually, but from 1833 he stepped up the pace to three or four parts a year, continuing at this rate until 1842, when he published the thirty-eighth part, in a total of 152 pamphlets. In the summer of 1841 Tanehiko fell sick, and it was rumored he would be unable to continue the work. So great was the consternation aroused by this danger, even in the women's quarters of the shogun's palace, that innumerable prayers were offered for Tanehiko's recovery. One court lady made pilgrimages to a certain temple for seven days running, and offered a copy of *The Rustic Genji* to the Buddha.[55]

Tanehiko recovered in the same year and published part 38 in 1842. He had also delivered to the illustrator and calligrapher the manuscript of part 39 when he was unexpectedly summoned by an official of his clan and informed that it was improper for him, as a samurai, to write such books. This strangely delayed reaction to a work that had begun to appear twelve years earlier, a book which was moreover not in objectionable taste, was probably a result of the Tempō Reforms rather than a response to anything specific in *The Rustic Genji*, though rumors had it that Tanehiko had portrayed in his work the profligate atmosphere of the court of the shogun Ienari, a notorious libertine.[56]

The action against his book came as a terrible shock to the cautious Tanehiko. Even Bakin, long his enemy, felt intimidated; after expressing thanks that he himself had never had his books banned, he announced his intention of being even more careful in the future.[57] Tanehiko renounced all hopes of publishing parts 39 and 40 (they did not appear until 1928), and agreed to give up his gesaku writings. But the worst was yet to come. He was summoned for a second time to answer charges; their exact nature is not known, but it has been conjectured that someone discovered he had written a pornographic book. This revelation would naturally have been a source of acute embarrassment to a high-ranking samurai, and Tanehiko died soon afterward, a suicide by some accounts.[58]

As soon as the effects of the Tempō Reforms had worn off, *The Rustic Genji* quickly regained its popularity, finding many new readers. Young women in particular delightedly pored over the endless volumes. Tanehiko's gōkan were even known abroad: *Ukiyogata Rokumai Byōbu* (1821) was translated into German as *Sechs Wandschirme in Gestalten der vergänglichen Welt* by the Austrian scholar August Pfizmaier in 1847, the first Japanese novel to appear in a Western language.

The gōkan remained popular until well into the twentieth century. They satisfied a demand for popular fiction which would later be met by even cruder works. The original little volumes, with their dramatic illustrations and long squiggles of writing, graphically suggest the state of Japanese fiction before the wave of the Meiji enlightenment struck.

NOTES

1. Nakamura Yukihiko, *Gesaku Ron*, p. 27.
2. See Joseph R. Levenson, *Confucian China and Its Modern Fate*, vol. I, pp. 20–22, for a discussion of the amateur ideal among Chinese painters. In Japan, too, the bunjinga (paintings of literary men) were closely related to the poetry and prose of the same men. See above, p. 342.
3. See Nakamura, *Gesaku Ron*, pp. 46, 52–53.
4. The statement, by Hattori Seigyo, is quoted in Nakamura, p. 83.
5. Quoted by Takasu Yoshijirō in *Ranjukuki, Taihaiki no Edo Bungaku*, p. 312.
6. The text is found in Mizuno Minoru (ed.), *Kibyōshi Sharebon Shū*, pp. 33–46.
7. Mizuno, p. 251.
8. The quotation is from *Analects*, VII, 6. (See translation by Arthur Waley, pp. 123–24.) London: Allen and Unwin, 1938.
9. Nakamura, *Gesaku Ron*, p. 66.
10. Quoted in Nakamura, *Gesaku Ron*, pp. 69–70.
11. *Ibid.*, p. 84.
12. See Takasu, pp. 314–16.
13. Text in Mizuno, pp. 269–94.
14. Mizuno, p. 88.
15. Mizuno, p. 139. The Japanese original is: *Iro-otoko ni naru mo, tonda tsurai mono da.*
16. Text in Mizuno, pp. 353–86.
17. Aiso Teizō, *Kinsei Shōsetsu Shi: Edo-hen*, p. 120.
18. *Ibid.*, p. 121.
19. Koike Tōgorō, *Santō Kyōden*, p. 259.
20. Mizuno, p. 411.
21. *Ibid.*, pp. 412–13.
22. Koike, pp. 86–87.
23. Text in Mizuno, pp. 441–65. See also Aiso, pp. 136–37.
24. See Nakamura, *Gesaku Ron*, p. 100.
25. *Ibid.*, p. 105.
26. *Ibid.*, p. 120.
27. *Ibid.*, p. 132.

28. See Noda Hisao, *Kinsei Shōsetsushi Ronkō*, pp. 217–35, for a discussion of the dangibon. See also Nakamura, *Gesaku Ron*, p. 251, and Aiso, p. 143.

29. See the translation by Thomas Satchell, *Hizakurige*, pp. 24–26.

30. See Aiso, pp. 171–73, for a detailed list of borrowings.

31. See Nakanishi Zenzō (ed.), *Ukiyodoko*, pp. 29–30.

32. This view is expressed by Jimbō Kazuya in *Tamenaga Shunsui no Kenkyū*, p. 23.

33. Nakamura Yukihiko (ed.), *Shunshoku Umegoyomi*, p. 390.

34. Jimbō, p. 73.

35. Nakamura, *Shunshoku Umegoyomi*, p. 68. By "Green Houses" (*seirō*) he meant brothels.

36. *Ibid.*, p. 89.

37. *Ibid.*, pp. 101–103.

38. *Ibid.*, p. 148.

39. See above, p. 376.

40. Teruoka Yasutaka and Gunji Masakatsu, *Edo Shimin Bungaku no Kaika*, p. 384.

41. See Leon Zolbrod, *Takizawa Bakin*, pp. 23–24; also Zolbrod's translation of *The Vendetta of Mr. Fleacatcher Managorō V*, in *Monumenta Nipponica*, XX, Nos. 1–2, Tokyo, 1965.

42. *Shui Hu Hou Chuan*, by Ch'en Shen (*c.* 1590–*c.* 1670), is discussed by Richard G. Irwin in *The Evolution of a Chinese Novel* (Cambridge, Mass., Harvard University Press, 1953), pp. 184, 204. Bakin was apparently inspired by the descriptions of a successful attack on Siam to write about Tametomo's exploits in the Ryukyus.

43. Teruoka and Gunji, p. 376.

44. See the article by Leon Zolbrod, "Tigers, Boars and Severed Heads: Parallel Series of Episodes in *Eight 'Dogs'* and *Men of the Marshes*."

45. An abbreviated translation of this episode is found in Keene, *Anthology of Japanese Literature*, pp. 423–28. For a fuller summary see Zolbrod, *Takizawa Bakin*, pp. 116–20.

46. Aiso, p. 282.

47. *Ibid.*, p. 344. An edict of 1808 prohibited the use of color (and of the names and crests of samurai who lived later than 1590), but it was not rigorously enforced, and the illustrations grew more elaborate than ever.

48. Quoted in Yamaguchi Gō, Introduction to *Nise Murasaki Inaka Genji*, p. 27.

49. Yamaguchi, p. 29.

50. See *ibid.*, p. 42. Utagawa Kunisada, whose real name was Tsunoda Shōgorō, lived from 1785 to 1864.

51. Yamaguchi, p. 42.

52. *Ibid.*, p. 54.
53. *Ibid.*, pp. 48–49.
54. *Ibid.*, p. 43.
55. *Ibid.*, p. 92.
56. Teruoka and Gunji, p. 391.
57. Yamaguchi, pp. 93–94.
58. *Ibid.*, p. 96.

BIBLIOGRAPHY

Aiso Teizō, *Kinsei Shōsetsu Shi Edo-hen.* Tokyo: Asahi Shuppan Sha, 1956.

Asō Isoji. *Takizawa Bakin.* Tokyo: Yoshikawa Kōbunkan, 1959.

Jimbō Kazuya. *Tamenaga Shunsui no Kenkyū.* Tokyo: Hakujitsusha, 1964.

——— (ed.). *Ukiyoburo.* Tokyo: Kadokawa Shoten, 1968.

Koike Tōgorō. *Santō Kyōden.* Tokyo: Yoshikawa Kōbunkan, 1961.

Levenson, Joseph R. *Confucian China and its Modern Fate*, vol. I. Berkeley: University of California Press, 1958.

Mizuno Minoru (ed). *Kibyōshi Sharebon Shū*, in Nihon Koten Bungaku Taikei series. Tokyo: Iwanami Shoten, 1958.

Nakamura Yukihiko. *Gesaku Ron.* Tokyo: Kadokawa Shoten, 1966.

——— (ed.). *Shunshoku Umegoyomi*, in Nihon Koten Bungaku Taikei series. Tokyo: Iwanami Shoten, 1962.

Nakanishi Zenzō (ed.). *Ukiyodoko*, in Nihon Koten Zensho series. Tokyo: Asahi Shimbun Sha, 1955.

Noda Hisao. *Kinsei Shōsetsushi Ronkō.* Tokyo: Hanawa Shobō, 1961.

Satchell, Thomas (trans.). *Hizakurige.* Kobe: Chronicle Press, 1929.

Takasu Yoshijirō. *Ranjukuki, Taihaiki no Edo Bungaku.* Tokyo: Meiji Shoin, 1931.

Teruoka Yasutaka and Gunji Masakatsu. *Edo Shimin Bungaku no Kaika*, in Nihon no Bungaku series. Tokyo: Shibundō, 1967.

Yamaguchi Gō. Introduction to *Nise Murasaki Inaka Genji*, II, in Edo Bungei series. Tokyo: Nihon Meicho Zenshū Kankōkai, 1928.

Zolbrod, Leon. *Takizawa Bakin.* New York: Twayne Publishers, 1967.

———. "Takizawa Bakin, 1767–1848," in *Monumenta Nipponica*, XXI (1966), 1–2.

———. "Tigers, Boars and Severed Heads: Parallel Series of Episodes in *Eight 'Dogs'* and *Men of the Marshes*," in *Chung Chi Journal*, VII (1967), 1.

CHAPTER 18

DRAMA

EIGHTEENTH-CENTURY KABUKI

During the first half of the eighteenth century Kabuki actors came increasingly to depend on Jōruri. No important dramatists wrote for them, and partisans of Jōruri had reason to suppose that Kabuki no longer counted as a serious rival. The actors nevertheless retained some following, especially in Edo, and at the first signs of faltering in the popularity of the puppet theater Kabuki again emerged as the main dramatic art of Japan. As the eighteenth century drew toward a close the best authors shifted from Jōruri to Kabuki; the final triumph of Edo Kabuki was signaled by the move to Edo in 1796 of the leading Kamigata playwright, Namiki Gohei. From this time until the end of the nineteenth century, Edo (or Tokyo) Kabuki was the fountainhead of all developments in Japanese drama.

Kabuki from its origins had been centered around the actors, not the plays, and the audiences, idolizing the actors, gladly permitted even the most extraordinary liberties with the texts. Unlike Jōruri, a musical art derived from dramatic recitations, Kabuki emphasized physical movements, whether dance or exaggerated displays of histrionics. The Jōruri chanter might interpret passages somewhat differently from his predecessors, or he might even omit whole sections of the plays, but he could not depart from the text without confusing the musicians and puppet operators. The Kabuki actors, on the other hand, were not only free to improvise, but were often specifically required to do so. Jōruri texts were printed even during the formative period of the art, the early seventeenth century, and by Chikamatsu's day the popular Jōruri were available in fairly large editions both as reading material and as practice texts for amateur chanters. Because these texts belonged to a story-telling tradition, they were embellished with high-flown language pleasing to the ear, if difficult to understand. The language was stylized, even in the most colloquial parts, and the audience accepted this poetic but artificial speech as a necessary element in a Jōruri; it would have seemed absurd for a chanter to sing, with the emphasis and emotions appropriate to grand tragedy, the words of everyday life. Kabuki, on the contrary, tended to reproduce with only minimal stylization the contemporary colloquial, and the texts performed today, including those purporting to go back to the Genroku era, are conspicuously easier to understand than any Jōruri. Music plays an important part in the Kabuki theater too, but usually as the accompaniment to dances or as incidental songs and not as the sustaining background to the main dramatic incidents. Jōruri is sometimes performed entirely as a musical and narrative art without puppets, for the benefit of people who find puppets unnecessary or distracting, but surely no one has ever preferred a performance of Kabuki without actors.

The supremacy of the actors implied a position of inferiority for the dramatists. In the seventeenth century the leading actors themselves wrote the plays in which they appeared, naturally making sure there would be roles in which they could display their particular gifts. Even after the functions of actor and playwright had been separated in Chikamatsu's time, the authors were still obliged to satisfy the actors. The story has often been recounted of the lengths to which the first important Kabuki dramatist, Tsuuchi Jihei II (1679–1760), went in order to satisfy the great actor Danjūrō. When he read his new work to Danjūrō, the latter looked displeased. Jihei wrote another play, but this time Danjūrō looked even more displeased. Jihei wrote still another play, but hardly had he started to read it than Danjūrō interrupted, saying, "Any man who can write three different plays must be a great playwright." He apologized. On another occasion Jihei wrote six different plays, all of which were rejected by the actors. On the seventh try he read the first play, merely changing the names of the characters; this time it was accepted.[1]

Jihei once expressed his philosophy:

> The author who gets angry when his play has been rejected is taking a narrow view. Even if he puts the play away for a time, it won't disappear or rot away. The dramatist's profession, in any case, involves deference before the actors; his function is to satisfy everyone. If the actors can make do with an old book they don't need a playwright. Frequently it happens that a play that has all along been rejected scores a great success when it is finally performed.[2]

Jihei wrote in the eighteenth century, when even in Edo Kabuki a text (*daihon*) was necessary, but in the seventeenth century the actors had relied merely on scenarios that indicated no more than the general outlines of the plot. The oldest surviving texts, dating back to about 1685, are in the form of illustrated summaries with occasional snatches of dialogue and indications of stage business. Kabuki texts were not printed in full until the Meiji era, suggesting how little they were valued as literature. The illustrated summaries issued in the seventeenth and eighteenth centuries were rewritings of the plays for readers who wanted to know the stories; they were not intended to be independent works, in the manner of a Jōruri text. The summaries occasionally are detailed enough to suggest that the plays had been written with care, but in their present form most seem childish, if not idiotic. Some Kabuki texts survive in the manuscripts handed down within a family of actors.

A typical example of Genroku Kabuki is the four-act play

Gempei Narukami Denki (1689) by Ichikawa Danjūrō I (1660–1704). It follows in general the tradition of the plays popular earlier in the century describing how four great heroes conquered a terrible demon. The central character in this play is a certain priest who succeeds in stopping the incessant thunder which has alarmed the people. The emperor bestows on him the name Narukami Shōnin (Holy Man of the Thunder). Soon afterward Narukami is angered by the refusal of the emperor to grant his plea for mercy toward a former disciple, and he declares that he will shut the rain god in his cave, causing a terrible drought.

The country is soon afflicted by the threatened drought, and no one is able to induce Narukami to release the rain god. One day, however, a beautiful woman visits Narukami. She provocatively displays her white limbs and seduces the holy man. While he is sleeping she severs the ropes imprisoning the rain god. When Narukami awakens he is understandably annoyed. For reasons not explained in the text, he suddenly turns into a frog but, being embarrassed to be seen in this guise, he bites off his tongue and dies. The play concludes with general rejoicing over the downfall of this superhuman priest.[3]

This infantile mixture of fantasy and crude realism contains elements derived from many sources, including Nō and early Jōruri. The central part, the seduction of the holy man who shut up the rain god in a cave, was directly derived from the Nō play *Ikkaku Sennin* by Komparu Zempō, which in turn was ultimately based on an Indian fable. This part of *Gempei Narukami Denki*, much expanded and improved, attained its final form in 1742 in the play called *Narukami*, a work honored by being included in the Eighteen Famous Plays of Kabuki. In the version currently performed the *aragoto* (posturing and displays of heroic strength) of the original work is preserved, but the interest lies chiefly in the erotic elements. *Narukami* has been acclaimed as "one of the finest of all Kabuki works" though its present high reputation dates only from the twentieth century.[4] Crude as the play seems on the printed page, the seduction scene is foolproof in performance. No audience can resist the moment when the holy man, begged by the lady to cure the sudden pains in her chest, first shows interest in a woman's body. Early Kabuki, for all its brilliance as a theatrical art, can rarely be discussed in terms of literary merits.

The Eighteen Famous Plays, first chosen by the seventh Danjūrō in 1840, represent for most Japanese today the essence of Kabuki, though few could name more than four or five of the eighteen. The collection purports to constitute the favorite vehicles of actors of the Ichikawa family, but it is obvious that the choice was haphazard; eighteen was a lucky number,[5] and once it had been decided that *Kanjinchō* (The Subscription List) was one of the eighteen plays dear to the family, it was necessary to fill up the remainder of the list more or less arbitrarily. Some of the eighteen plays are no more than colorful fragments that cannot be staged independently; others have rarely been performed. Apart from *Narukami*, at least three deserve special mention: *The Subscription List*, the most celebrated Kabuki play; *Sukeroku*, a perennial favorite; and *Shibaraku* (Just a Moment!), a nonsensical but colorful work.

The Subscription List is closely based on the Nō play *Ataka*, and is performed against a modified version of the traditional Nō scene, a large pine painted on a backdrop. Musicians and singers are arrayed across the stage throughout the play, somewhat in the manner of a Nō chorus and musicians. The story is much the same in Nō and in Kabuki, telling how the heroic Benkei managed by his quick wit (rather than main force) to obtain passage through the barrier of Ataka for his master, Yoshitsune, and a small band of followers. He pretends that they are priests soliciting funds for the rebuilding of the Tōdaiji temple in Nara; and when the barrier-keeper Togashi questions Benkei about the supposed subscription of funds, he reads from a blank scroll the details of the contributions. Togashi, impressed by this virtuosity, allows the party to pass through the barrier.

Despite the marked similarities, the effect of *The Subscription List* is strikingly unlike that of *Ataka* because of the importance of the individual actors. In the Nō play the personality of the actor appearing as Benkei or Togashi is of no importance; the actor must be the transparent medium of the words and not call attention to his own skill. But in *The Subscription List* the great moments are of acting, not of poetry. When Benkei has successfully guided Yoshitsune through the barrier of Ataka by the desperate expedient of pretending to beat a laggard porter (Yoshitsune's disguise), he is overcome with horror at the realization that he has lifted his hand against his master. Yoshitsune, seated at the opposite side of the wide stage from Benkei, extends one hand in a gesture of affection and understanding to reassure him; Benkei, overwhelmed, bows in profoundest gratitude. *The Subscription List* is a vehicle for star actors, not only for Benkei but Togashi, the barrier-keeper who, out of admiration for Benkei's bravery and resourcefulness, allows the suspicious travelers to pass, though he knows the consequences for himself will be death. Yoshitsune is also an important role, and even the minor parts provide opportunities for the display of comic talent. Above all, we remember Benkei, the master of every situation, even to a final dance of triumph after he imbibes a whole keg of saké.

Sukeroku (or, more fully, *Sukeroku Yukari no Edozakura*) was first performed by Danjūrō II in 1713. Numerous similar plays about the swaggering hero Sukeroku and the courtesan Agemaki had preceded this work, and new versions continued to be made until the text attained its final form during the Meiji era.[6] A crucial development in the formation of the present play out of earlier materials occurred in 1716 when the character Sukeroku was identified as being "in reality" Soga Gorō, the hero of a twelfth-century vendetta. This contribution of the dramatist Tsuuchi Jihei II, combining in one person characteristics belonging to totally different periods of history—the twelfth-century Soga Gorō and the seventeenth-century Sukeroku—was imitated by innumerable later dramatists. It enabled the actor to display in a single play the two traditional styles of Kabuki acting: *aragoto*, associated with the historical plays and *wagoto*, the tender style associated with contemporary plays about the licensed quarters.

The character Sukeroku represented the Edo ideal—the quick-tempered, swaggering hero, irresistible to women and indifferent to money. He may be penniless, but this is of no importance—courtesans vie for the privilege of being with him. Yet all the time he is amusing himself in the gay quarters, he is merely waiting for the moment to strike his enemy.

The play opens with Sukeroku's mother looking for Agemaki. When at last they meet, she asks Agemaki to give up Sukeroku, not because she disapproves of her son's consorting with a prostitute, but because she fears that his constant quarreling in the licensed quarter will prevent him from avenging his father's death. This is the first hint that Sukeroku is more than the dashing man-about-town he appears. However, Agemaki's expressions of devotion to Sukeroku convince the mother that he is in good hands.

Agemaki has another suitor, the bearded old Ikyū, whom she detests. She contrasts the two men:

> One is like snow, the other like ink. An inkwell is a well, and so is a well in the garden, but there's a big difference in depth, big as the difference between a lover and a mere customer.[7]

Soon afterward Sukeroku makes his great entrance on high wooden clogs with a Japanese-style umbrella held cockily over one shoulder. He immediately attempts to pick a quarrel with Ikyū, but to everyone's surprise Ikyū fails to respond when insulted. Later, Sukeroku fights with two of Ikyū's henchmen, eagerly examining the swords they draw. At last he succeeds in provoking Ikyū, first by placing a clog on Ikyū's head, then by slicing in two the arm-rest against which Ikyū leans. But Ikyū still does not unsheathe his sword.

A rice-wine peddler, who has previously figured in a comic scene, reappears. This time he reveals that he is Sukeroku's elder brother, and uses their real names. He scolds his brother for his incessant quarrels, but Sukeroku discloses that he has resorted to quarreling only as an expedient for forcing his opponents to draw their swords. He is searching for a sword called Tomokirimaru which, he has learned in a dream, he must use when he kills their father's enemy:

> Fortunately I hit upon this plan of quarreling. All kinds of people come to the licensed quarter. I force a likely man into a fight, make him draw his sword, and once we've exchanged a few thrusts I grab his blade and examine it.[8]

The peddler, struck with admiration by his brother's ingenious scheme, urges Sukeroku to keep up his belligerence.

Sukeroku provokes Ikyū again by hiding under the bench where Ikyū and Agemaki are sitting and pulling hairs from his legs. Ikyū cries out in fury, but instead of drawing his sword, he proposes to Sukeroku that he and his brother, whose real identities he has known all along, join him in attacking the shogun Yoritomo. Carried away by his own rhetoric, he draws his sword to illustrate a point, and Sukeroku sees that it is indeed Tomokirimaru. He kills Ikyū and takes the sword, but in doing so is himself wounded. Many pursuers come after him, and Sukeroku hides in a rain barrel. At the end of the play he escapes over the rooftops, ready now to use the sword in carrying out his vengeance. His last words are, "And that's all for today."

Shibaraku (Just a Moment!) is the most frequently performed of the Eighteen Famous Plays; by tradition, it is always part of the *kaomise*, or "showing of the company," program at the start of the new theatrical season. The plot is silly, and the play depends for its effects almost entirely on the presentation. The hero—his name has changed a dozen times in successive versions—makes his appearance wearing an immensely long sword and a cloak whose sleeves alone are almost as big as himself; his face is heavily decorated with geometrical patterns. He arrives just in time to stop some wrongdoing by a bunch of villains, signaling his presence by repeated shouts of *shibaraku!* The actor's ability to suggest such enormous power that he can subdue with an imperious command a stage full of villains is essential to the play. The text now used was established only in 1895; until then it was always expected that the play would be extensively rewritten each year, preserving only the shouts of *shibaraku!* The hero's long monologue (*tsurane*) by tradition was written by the current Danjūrō, who always took the role. This monologue contained topical allusions, current slang, and other proofs of novelty, and in some versions even passages of nonsense language. The intent of the play was clearly not literary, nor even dramatic in a normal sense. In the words of Kawatake Shigetoshi, "The value of *Shibaraku* consists in its fairytale artistic beauty composed of the successive, beautiful tableaux on the stage and the enchanting music."[9]

In addition to plays like *Narukami*, *Sukeroku*, and *Shibaraku*, the inheritance of Genroku Kabuki, the repertory by the middle of the eighteenth century came to include many adaptations of Jōruri, as well as dance plays with only a minimum of dialogue. Plays originally written as Jōruri now constitute half the repertory, but the differences between the same play performed by the Bunraku puppets and the Kabuki actors are often considerable. The actors have never hesitated to alter the texts in the interests of more effective theater, and even a masterpiece like *Chūshingura* has been subjected again and again to drastic revisions, though the general themes survive.

A famous instance of an alteration in the text of *Chūshingura* (The Treasury of Loyal Retainers) occurred in 1766. The great actor Nakamura Nakazō (1736–90), having offended the staff playwright Kanai Sanshō (1731–97) during the previous season, was punished by being assigned the minor role of Sadakurō in *Chūshingura.*[10] Probably the manager expected Nakazō would refuse the role of a minor villain. Sadakurō appears only in the fifth act; he kills the old man Yoichibei and takes his money, but is himself killed immediately afterward by shots intended for a wild boar. In previous interpretations of the role, Sadakurō always wore a straw raincoat and hat, like a hunter or woodsman. He runs behind Yoichibei, pretending at first to be friendly, but soon demands the money he knows Yoichibei is carrying. The old man pleads for his money, then his life, but the pitiless Sadakurō kills him.

Nakazō transformed this part into a major one. He appeared wearing the tattered crested garment of a rōnin and carrying a frayed umbrella, a far more striking figure than as a hunter. Nakazō also resorted to the extraordinary expedient of suppressing all the dialogue for the role. His manner of performance, still followed today by Kabuki actors, was to hide in a haystack as Yoichibei stops to count his money. Sadakurō thrusts out his hand and wordlessly snatches the wallet away. He abruptly emerges from the stack and drives his sword into the old man. Kicking aside the dead body, he returns his sword to the scabbard, brushes the raindrops from his hair, and squeezes the water from his wet kimono. Once he has dried himself, he opens the wallet and counts the money, his lips gleefully forming the words, "Fifty *ryō* in gold." He picks up his battered umbrella, opens it and starts to swagger off when he catches sight of the wild boar. Shutting the umbrella in consternation, he jumps back into the haystack. He appears again as soon as the boar has passed, only to be hit by the hunter Kampei's bullets.[11] This is the entire role of Sadakurō but, thanks to Nakazō's inventions, it ranks among the most important of *Chūshingura*; it provides the actor with opportunities for a superb display of miming. In literary terms, however, the role ceases to exist. This extreme instance illustrates how a Jōruri text could be sacrificed to the interests of the Kabuki stage.

The dance plays are even less literary than original Kabuki works. *Musume Dōjōji* (1753), with a text by Fujimoto Tobun (1716–63), has been immensely popular ever since its first performances, not because of the text, no more than a rough adaptation of the Nō play *Dōjōji,* but because of the dances and costumes. The play begins with the priest of the Dōjōji temple making farcical, largely improvised comments about the bell which is to be hung that day. A girl appears and, after lulling the priests into a daze with her dances, turns into a demon inside the bell. But this demon, instead of being vanquished, as in the Nō play, rides atop the bell in triumph as the curtain is drawn. *Musume Dōjōji* is enjoyed for the dazzling series of dances performed by the *onnagata* in a variety of gorgeous costumes, and is typical of other Kabuki works that can be enjoyed without respect to dialogue or plot. Dance sections even from longer, more serious plays are often performed by themselves, entertaining spectators who may be unfamiliar with the play from which it has been extracted.

Kabuki plays first approached the realm of literature during the second half of the eighteenth century. The decline in Jōruri, largely the result of internal difficulties, fostered a revival of Kabuki, and some dramatists began to write Kabuki plays comparable in plot and structure to Jōruri. The first important dramatist of this revival was Namiki Shōzō (1730–73), the son of the owner of a teahouse in the Osaka theater district. Shōzō had frequented both Jōruri and Kabuki theaters even as a child, and wrote his first Kabuki play in 1748, when only eighteen. In 1750 he shifted his interests to Jōruri, becoming the pupil of the famed Namiki Sōsuke (Senryū). After Sōsuke's death in 1751 Shōzō returned to Kabuki, but during his year of apprenticeship in Jōruri he had collaborated with Sōsuke in several works. The influence of Jōruri style is conspicuous in his later plays, extending even to the introduction of a narrator. The narrator was indispensable, of course, in a puppet theater, but in Kabuki his presence emphasized the lyrical, storybook aspects of a play, serving as a chorus who comments in poetic language on the actions. Shōzō was also a gifted inventor of stage machinery, and is credited with the first use of the revolving stage (in 1758) and other innovations that heightened the spectacular effects of his plays.[12]

Shōzō wrote over one hundred plays. Many were adaptations of Jōruri; by introducing to Kabuki the artistic techniques developed by the Jōruri dramatists, he opened the possibility of Kabuki becoming more than a display of the actors' virtuosity. He wrote chiefly historical plays, the central character often being a powerful villain who tries to seize control of the country. His reputation in his day was exceedingly great; contemporary critics ranked him as high as Chikamatsu Monzaemon.[13]

Osanago no Katakiuchi (The Infants' Vendetta, 1753) was an early but typical work by Shōzō. Like many other Kabuki plays, it combines in one story various nearly unrelated plots. The first, in the tradition of the oiemono (plays about disputed successions), involves Iyonosuke, the young heir of the Arita family. He is infatuated with the courtesan Ōhashi and has absconded with the dowry money of the high-born lady he has agreed to marry. Much is made also, in a familiar manner, of two family treasures—a sword and an incense burner—that have mysteriously disappeared but must be produced for the shogun's inspection. The villainous Kanzō is likewise infatuated with Ōhashi, and under pretext of questioning her about Iyonosuke's whereabouts he arranges to see her every night, though she rejects his advances.

In the third act Ōhashi's jealousy is roused to fever pitch by seeing a document written by Iyonosuke extolling the loyal service of the wife and daughter of a family retainer. She is so angry she throws the letter into a well, and at once the water boils up (infected no doubt by the heat of her passions), lifting to the surface the heirloom sword hidden in the well by the wicked Kanzō. Iyonosuke, who has been disguised as a laborer, rushes up to claim the sword. Since he has already tricked Kanzō out of the incense burner, the other missing treasure, all problems have been solved. It is agreed that Iyonosuke will marry Lady Kaoyo (whose dowry he embezzled) and keep Ōhashi as his mistress.

The play might well have ended at this point, but the remaining acts are given over to a subplot lightly touched on in the previous acts.[14] Shōzō displays in this work his expert knowledge of Kabuki techniques but no great skill as a literary figure. It is interesting to read on an elementary level, but nothing remotely suggests character development or even the creation of believable human beings. For all the realistic dialogue—the language rarely rises above banality—the behavior of the characters is incomprehensible. In the first act alone two people attempt to kill themselves because they have been unable to recover the missing sword, but there is no attempt to suggest any tragic sense of mission; each utters a simple "Goodbye, everybody" (*izuremo osaraba*) and without further ado presses a dagger against his abdomen. Both are stopped in the act, and one later expresses thanks for having been spared *mudabara*, a technical term meaning "a useless seppuku."

It is baffling why anyone should have thought Namiki Shōzō was Chikamatsu's peer. It is true that his plays are full of surprises, but their virtuosity becomes irritating. An overabundance of invention (*shukō*) deprives his plays of underlying seriousness. Any one scene may be in deadly earnest, but the effect of a whole play is cheerful and even comic, the villains suggesting the witches of European fairytales rather than genuinely menacing human beings. Moronao, in *Chūshingura*, is at once simplified and exaggerated, but we can believe in his evil; the villains in Kabuki plays by Shōzō and his contemporaries are so crude that they risk becoming figures of fun.

The play by Namiki Shōzō that has enjoyed the most lasting success was *Yadonashi Danshichi Shigure no Karakasa* (Homeless Danshichi and His Chinese Umbrella in a Downpour, 1767). This is also about a missing sword and the usual complications in recovering it, but it is given particular interest by the scene in which Danshichi, reduced to working as a fishmonger as his penalty for losing the sword, visits a playwright named Heiemon to ask for financial help. He overhears Heiemon discussing a new play with two actors, and is struck in particular by the remark, "The man must kill the woman in order to maintain his self-respect." This piece of advice on stagecraft suggests to Danshichi that he must kill his mistress (though he later changes his mind). The passage, affording the audience a behind-the-scenes glimpse into how a Kabuki play was written, largely accounted for the popularity of the play; when it was revived in 1790 the playwright Heiemon was renamed Namiki Shōzō, giving an even greater immediacy to the role.[15]

Shōzō devoted his ingenuity not only to the plots and the stage machinery but to the titles and subtitles of his plays. It had become traditional to give all titles in five, seven, or nine characters; one mark of an author's virtuosity was his success at alluding to the different themes of the play by complex word plays on the five, seven, or nine characters. The titles of late Kabuki plays are the despair of any translator.

Shōzō's fame in his day was so great that in 1785, the thirteenth anniversary of his death, a biography and a list of his plays were published. He was the only Kabuki playwright so honored during the Tokugawa period.

Shōzō's chief disciple was Namiki Gohei (1747–1808), the son of the doorman at an Osaka theater. He became Shōzō's pupil (and took his surname) when he was about twenty. By the time he was twenty-five (in 1772) he had become a principal playwright, writing Kabuki for a famous actor of the day, and by 1785 he had established himself as the leading dramatist in the Kyoto-Osaka region.

Gohei is today remembered for his decision to move from Osaka to Edo in 1796. This not only signified the triumph of Edo Kabuki but enriched it with the techniques of Osaka Kabuki, especially the logical structure of the well-made play. In Edo Gohei was as popular as in Osaka, and his annual salary, 300 *ryō* in gold (the equivalent of about $10,000 in 1960) was unprecedented. He introduced the innovation of presenting two plays on a bill, the first one about the Soga brothers' revenge, the second a domestic tragedy unrelated to the Soga theme, in this way rejecting the familiar combination of old and new found in *Sukeroku* in favor of a more plausible division. The tradition of staging a play about the Soga brothers at New Year, first begun in Edo during the Genroku era, was too strong for Gohei to break, but at least the nonsensical combination of twelfth- and seventeenth-century Japan in a single play had been modified.

Gohei's most successful play, *Godairiki Koi no Fūjime* (The Love Letter Sealed with the Five Great Guardians, 1794) was written while he was still in Osaka. *The Love Letter* is the tale of the virtuous samurai Gengobei who is searching for a lost sword. While in the licensed quarter of Osaka with a fellow samurai, Sangobei, the latter makes advances toward a geisha named Kikuno. In order to escape him, she falsely pretends she has long been intimate with Gengobei, who feels obliged to confirm her story. Sangobei, furious, arranges that Gengobei be publicly insulted at the theater, and the disgraced Gengobei is forced to leave his master's service. Still determined to recover the sword, Gengobei asks Kikuno to use her charms to induce Sangobei to reveal its whereabouts. Before leaving home she writes the characters *godairiki* ("five great guardians") on her samisen, as a sign she craves divine assistance. However, the wary Sangobei tricks her into sending Gengobei a letter that declares she no longer loves him. Just as Kikuno is writing another letter, one revealing her true feelings, Gengobei charges in and, supposing she has deceived him, cuts off her head and right hand, only for them to cling to him even in death. Gengobei finds Kikuno's unfinished letter and learns of her innocence. He kills Sangobei, recovers the sword, and offers Sangobei's head to Kikuno's spirit. He is about to commit seppuku to atone for his rash act when her head flies at his wrist and prevents him from drawing his sword. Her love has survived a beheading.[16]

The ingenuity displayed in this play recalls Namiki Shōzō, but Gohei went beyond his master in his attempts to startle audiences with weird or violent scenes. One play called for two live horses, a novelty that indeed impressed the spectators. However, on the ninth day of performances one horse made water on the hanamichi and then galloped off with the other horse. The audience raised such a pandemonium that the authorities closed the theater for three days. In another play Gohei used real fireworks and rockets, frightening women and children in the theater so much they fled in panic.[17]

Gohei's plays were often based on a well-known event, but the connections were obscured by his embroidering on the theme —his famed mastery of *shukō*—and by his deliberate alterations of the incidents in order to avoid the censor's wrath. The title *Kanjin Kammon Tekudari no Hajimari* (The Origins of the Wiles of Korean People and Chinese Writing, 1789) referred obliquely to the murder in 1762 of a member of a Korean embassy by the Japanese interpreter, but despite the title, there is not a single reference in the play to Korean people or Chinese writing (or anything resembling the circumstances of the death of the envoy). The setting is Nagasaki, the only city with an exotic flavor, and one of the principal villains (a Japanese) is the boss of the "Chinese gang" (*Tōjin-gumi*) of stevedores.

The play falls within the general category of oiemono. Nagatonosuke, the young lord of the Nagasaki clan, is passionately in love with Nayama, a courtesan of the Maruyama Quarter. On the feast day of the Inari Shrine he goes to place before the god the two treasures of his household, a famous flute and the family genealogical table. He learns that Nayama is to be "ransomed" by Sokurō, the boss of the "Chinese gang," and tries to raise the money to ransom her himself. His various efforts fail, and he is, moreover, swindled out of the treasures. At the end of this extremely long play only one of the treasures has been recovered and, contrary to the custom in oiemono, we are not informed whether or not Nagatonosuke and Nayama will remain together; in fact, Nagatonosuke disappears altogether. Although the play preserves the form of the oiemono, it destroys the original meaning by its ostentatious indifference to the conventions. The young lord Nagatonosuke is not merely amorous and weak, in the tradition of the handsome young man who frequents the licensed quarter, but thoroughly corrupt. Nothing he says or does redeems him in our eyes, and we are given no clue as to why Nayama remains faithful to him. Even when he announces to his retainer Denshichi that he is about to commit seppuku, in the traditional manner, he remains contemptible.[18]

Nagatonosuke is not alone in his corruption. Gohei sneers even at filial piety; in conflicts between parent and child the parent always behaves so contemptibly that the child disowns him.[19] Takao, Denshichi's sweetheart, has a particularly loathsome father who shows no appreciation for her goodness; he sneers at her for being "a fool who doesn't even know enough to be greedy." Her brother is so disgusted with his father that he becomes a priest, but the father, showing no respect for the cloth, plots to kill his son. There is hardly a decent character in the entire work; even the virtuous Denshichi turns out to have falsely promised his love to another woman. And the clown Heiroku, in a peculiarly revolting scene, makes love to a corpse.

It is clear that Gohei used the old form of the oiemono only to destroy it. He makes fun of every convention, even at the risk of undercutting his plot. As a result, his plays are a great deal more intriguing than the familiar stories of struggles between brothers for succession to some great house, lost treasures which must be recovered before the rightful heir can be recognized as such, courtesans who steadfastly protect the wronged hero, and so on. Gohei's cynicism strikes a distinctly modern note. The audience did not object to such irreverent treatment of the old themes. In Edo the popularity of Gohei's Osaka-style plays displaced in public favor the works of such recognized dramatists as Sakurada Jisuke (1754–1806) who continued to write in the Edo tradition. Gohei influenced all later Kabuki dramatists, even a direct disciple of Jisuke like Tsuruya Namboku, who refined Gohei's corruption to the ultimate degree.

NOTES

1. Torigoe Bunzō, "Edo no Gekidan," p. 268.
2. *Ibid.*, p. 269.
3. Text in Takano Tatsuyuki and Kuroki Kanzō, *Genroku Kabuki Kessaku Shū*, vol. I. For a fuller summary, see Appendix, 5.
4. Gunji Masakatsu, *Kabuki Jūhachiban Shū*, p. 43.
5. *Ibid.*, p. 14.
6. The original text has not been preserved. The text edited by Kawatake Shigetoshi (*Kabuki Jūhachiban Shū*, in the Nihon Koten Zensho series) dates from 1779, and the text edited by Gunji Masakatsu (see note 4) from 1872. A random comparison of the texts suggests how many minor changes in language occurred: "Otatsu ya, kyō wa Asakusa e maitta ge na ga, hayai kaeri ja na" (1779 text, p. 185); "Otatsu wa kyō Asakusa e maitta to kiita ga, daibu hayai kaeri datta na" (1872 text, p. 63).
7. Gunji, p. 91.
8. *Ibid.*, p. 109.
9. Kawatake Shigetoshi, *Kabuki Jūhachiban Shū*, p. 31.
10. Kanai Senshō's unusual independence and authority as a dramatist is illustrated by the story that he made it his practice to read his plays to the actors with his hand on the hilt of his sword, ready to draw if anyone objected. (See Torigoe, p. 268.)
11. Nakamura Nakazō, *Temae Miso*, pp. 38–43; Onoe Kikugorō, *Gei*, pp. 58–61.
12. Torigoe, p. 266.
13. See the account in *Kezairoku* (1801), a work of Kabuki criticism by Namiki Shōzō II (d. 1807), p. 421.

14. The remaining acts describe the vendetta by a small boy and an equally small girl which occasioned the title of the play. Text in Urayama Masao and Matsuzaki Hitoshi, *Kabuki Kyakuhon Shū*, I, pp. 107–267.

15. Fujimura Tsukuru (ed.), *Nihon Bungaku Daijiten*, V, pp. 442–43.

16. *Ibid.*, III, pp. 158–60. See also *Engeki Hyakka Daijiten*, II, pp. 488–89.

17. Urayama and Matsuzaki, I, p. 323.

18. *Ibid.*, p. 362.

19. *Ibid.*, p. 335.

BIBLIOGRAPHY

Engeki Hakubutsukan (ed.). *Engeki Hyakka Daijiten.* Tokyo: Heibonsha, 1960–62.

Fujimura Tsukuru (ed.). *Nihon Bungaku Daijiten.* Tokyo, Shinchōsha, 1950–52.

Gunji, Masakatsu. *Kabuki.* Tokyo: Kodansha International, 1969.

———. *Kabuki Jūhachiban Shū*, in Nihon Koten Bungaku Taikei series. Tokyo: Iwanami Shoten, 1965.

Kawatake Shigetoshi. *Kabuki Jūhachiban Shū*, in Nihon Koten Zensho series. Tokyo: Asahi Shimbun Sha, 1952.

———. *Nihon Engeki Zenshi.* Tokyo: Iwanami Shoten, 1959.

Nakamura Nakazō III. *Temae Miso* (ed. Gunji Masakatsu). Tokyo: Seiabō, 1969.

Namiki Shōzō II. *Kezairoku*, in *Zoku Enseki Jisshu*, I, in Kokusho Kankōkai Sōsho series. Tokyo: Kokusho Kankōkai, 1908.

Omote Akira and Yokomichi Mareo. *Yōkyoku Shū*, in Nihon Koten Bungaku Taikei series. Tokyo: Iwanami Shoten, 1960–63.

Onoe Kikugorō VI. *Gei.* Tokyo: Kaizōsha, 1947.

Takano Tatsuyuki and Kuroki Kanzō. *Genroku Kabuki Kessaku Shū.* Tokyo: Waseda Daigaku Shuppanbu, 1925.

Torigoe Bunzō. "Edo no Gekidan," in Nihon Bungaku no Rekishi series, vol. VIII. Tokyo: Kadokawa Shoten, 1967.

Urayama Masao and Matsuzaki Hitoshi. *Kabuki Kyakuhon Shū*, in Nihon Koten Bungaku Taikei series. Tokyo: Iwanami Shoten, 1960–61.

CHAPTER 19

DRAMA

NINETEENTH-CENTURY KABUKI

The Kabuki plays staged during the course of the seventeenth and eighteenth centuries were not considered to be the property of any particular man; effective scenes were plagiarized and repeated until the public wearied of them. On the other hand, even successful plays were often drastically revised for revivals, and no respect was shown the texts. Toward the end of the eighteenth century such dramatists as Namiki Gohei and Sakurada Jisuke acquired a following of their own, as distinct from that of the actors, but their plays, though eminently suited to the Kabuki stage, were hopelessly unliterary and do not make interesting reading today.

Not until the nineteenth century, when many other forms of Japanese literature all but disintegrated, did Kabuki first acquire literary importance, thanks to two dramatists who rank with Chikamatsu as the finest of the Kabuki theater: Tsuruya Namboku IV (1755–1829) and Kawatake Mokuami (1816–93).[1] Namboku was probably the best writer in Japan, regardless of genre, during the first twenty-five years of the century, and his plays rival those being written anywhere in the world at that time. Mokuami, whose career began in 1835, was the only author of consequence to have spanned the Meiji Restoration, but his best-known (and most frequently performed) works were written in the 1850s and 1860s.

In addition to Namboku and Mokuami there were many other dramatists active between 1800 and 1868, and a few deserve mention, but these two men, by their conspicuous and distinctive talents, dominated the Kabuki theater and gave it literary importance.

TSURUYA NAMBOKU

Namboku was born in Edo, the son of a dyer. Almost nothing is known about his private life, whether in his formative days or after he had become the outstanding Japanese dramatist, but it has been conjectured that he was attracted as a youth to the world of Kabuki and began writing for the theater about the age of twenty. His name first appears on playbills of 1777, when he served as an apprentice dramatist under Sakurada Jisuke. His marriage about 1780 to the daughter of the popular actor Tsuruya Namboku III undoubtedly helped his career, but his progress during the next twenty years was slow, probably because so many senior men were still active.

Not until 1801 did Namboku attain the status of a "leading playwright" (*tatesakusha*) with a company; previously he had had to content himself with supplying scenes or acts for other men's plays. His first chance to display his ability in this new capacity came in the summer of 1804 when he wrote *Tenjiku Tokubei Ikoku-banashi* (Tokubei from India, a Story of Strange Countries) for the great actor Onoe Shōroku. Many elements in the story, about a Japanese of Korean descent who is shipwrecked in India and returns to Japan after many adventures, were familiar from earlier Kabuki plays, but Namboku and

Shōroku dazzled the audiences, especially by the quick changes. In one scene Shōroku jumped into a tank, splashing water convincingly, only to reappear a few moments later at the end of the hanamichi attired in a splendid kimono with an elaborate headdress. This *tour de force* scored a sensation, and the theater, normally deserted in summer, was jammed. Rumors even spread that Shōroku's quick changes had been achieved thanks to "Christian black magic," and it was reported that he had been investigated by the local magistrate; but it may be that the rumors of Christian magic and of the investigation were inspired by Namboku himself in the interests of publicity.[2]

Namboku's fame, in any case, was now established, and after the deaths of Sakurada Jisuke I in 1806 and Namiki Gohei in 1808 he was recognized as the outstanding Kabuki dramatist. In 1811, when he took the name Tsuruya Namboku IV, he was fifty-six years old, but his career was only beginning. Between 1804, the year of *Tokubei from India*, and 1829, the year of his death, Namboku was responsible for over one hundred full-length plays, each of which took a minimum of seven or eight hours to perform. It is true that he assigned whole acts to assistants, notably Sakurada Jisuke II (1766–1829), and his plots were frequently derived from those of his predecessors, but each play was marked by his distinctive imprint.

Namboku wrote in a brilliant but decadent age. The illustrated books of the period are superbly executed, but the subject matter is sometimes so grotesque as to make one wonder uneasily about the overdeveloped imaginations of the artists. Namboku's plays are also filled with horrid and macabre scenes. He specialized in the portrayal of the sordid world of blackmailers and murderers, and the ghosts of victims often rise up to torment those who stabbed or poisoned them. Humor, often crude, enlivens his scenes, and there is a generous helping of sex, but the prevailing atmosphere is dark. Namboku derided the old conventions, giving each of the familiar elements an unexpected and sinister twist. He wrote in close collaboration with the actors, tailoring the roles to fit their special skills. The most spectacular instance of such collaboration was the play *Osome Hisamatsu Ukina no Yomiuri* (Osome and Hisamatsu, a Scandal Sheet, 1813), which included seven different roles for the same actor. The great success of this play, despite its ruthless treatment of the story of the lovers Osome and Hisamatsu, indicates what measures Namboku was prepared to take in order to win the favor of a public whose tastes were jaded by works of extreme sensationalism.

A critic, writing in 1816 about the decline of morals, declared:

> Up to seventy or eighty years ago the amorous play of men and women was suggested by an exchange of glances; if the man ever took the woman's hand, she would cover her face with her sleeve in embarrassment. That was all there was to it, but even so, old people of the time are said to have been shocked by what they deemed to be an unsightly exhibition. Women in the audience were also very modest, and would blush even at the famous scene in *Chūshingura* in which Yuranosuke takes Okaru in his arms as he helps her down the ladder. Nowadays sexual intercourse is plainly shown on the stage, and women in the audience watch on, unblushing, taking it in their stride. It is most immoral.[3]

Namboku's eroticism certainly surpassed anything attempted by his predecessors. Perhaps his most perversely original work in an erotic vein was *Sakura-hime Azuma Bunshō* (Lady Sakura, Documents from the East, 1817). Inspiration for this play—or, at any rate, for the central character—was apparently provided by an incident that had occurred ten years earlier. A prostitute in an Edo brothel claimed that she was the daughter of a Kyoto nobleman and acted the part, wearing a court lady's robes and composing poetry which she presented to her customers. An investigation revealed that the alleged princess was an impostor. The story got around and all but begged to be enacted on the stage, but Namboku waited ten years before making his dramatization, knowing it was strictly forbidden to draw on contemporary scandals for the theater.[4]

Namboku's first task in writing *Lady Sakura* was to establish the *sekai*, or "world," of the work. He borrowed the names of the priest Seigen and Lady Sakura, characters in a long series of plays dating back to the 1670s.[5] Namboku took virtually nothing else but the names, his plot breaking completely with tradition. Using characters from an earlier work was a familiar practice, known as *kakikae*, related to the even older practice of identifying contemporary persons in a play as being "in reality" the historical Soga Jūrō and the like. Kakikae was not only a useful dodge around the censors, but apparently intrigued audiences, who wondered what Seigen and Lady Sakura would be up to this time.[6]

Namboku next considered his actors. In order to exploit the many talents of the brilliant Danjūrō VII, he wrote for him not only the role of Seigen, the priest destroyed by illicit love, but the brutal yet captivating role of Gonsuke, a new character in the story. Playing these two roles did not involve spectacular quick changes, but Danjūrō gave a virtuoso display of contrasting personalities. The role of Lady Sakura, performed by Iwai Hanshirō V, itself involved a great range of expression, from the attitudes appropriate to a demure princess to those of a brazen prostitute. The roles were written for virtuoso actors, but the play was more than a vehicle; *Lady Sakura* is in fact a brilliant drama.

Like many other plays by Namboku, *Lady Sakura* observed, on the surface at least, the conventions of the oiemono, such as the story of the stolen heirloom that must be recovered if a noble family is not to perish. Neither Namboku nor his audiences could have taken such hackneyed themes seriously, but he preserved them as a harmless and possibly amusing convention, much like the "love interest" in many twentieth-century plays. The real subject was Lady Sakura's degeneration.

Lady Sakura opens with a brief prologue. The priest Jikyū and the young acolyte Shiragiku are about to commit suicide by throwing themselves from a cliff into the sea. Jikyū recalls that he first became a priest after his younger brother had turned to crime. He and Shiragiku fell in love at the temple, but fearful of others' gossip, they have decided to die together. As pledges of fidelity in the world to come, each takes in his hand half of an incense box with the other's name written on it. The boy leaps into the sea. Jikyū starts to follow but hesitates, frightened by the dizzying height. At length he jumps, but his fall is arrested by a pine tree, and he is soon rescued.

The first act opens seventeen years later. Jikyū, now known as Seigen, has risen to become the religious adviser of the shogun and the abbot of a great temple in Kamakura. Various persons connected with the loss of a precious scroll appear, among them young Matsuwaka, who cannot succeed to his father's estates without this heirloom. The father was killed by unknown assailants and the scroll stolen, but as yet it has been reported to the government only that he died of illness. The villainous Iruma Akugorō, the culprit behind the murder, was at one time engaged to marry Matsuwaka's sister, Lady Sakura, but he broke off the engagement when he learned she cannot open her left palm.

So far everything has followed the plots of innumerable other plays, and it does not surprise us when Lady Sakura enters and announces her intention of becoming a nun, to expiate whatever sin has made her a cripple. Seigen expresses regret at her decision, and urges all to pray for her. Suddenly a miracle occurs: Lady Sakura's hand opens and the broken lid of a small incense box falls out. Seigen instantly recognizes it, and realizes that Lady Sakura must be a reincarnation of Shiragiku. But even after this miracle Lady Sakura is still determined to become a nun. As preparations are being completed Gonsuke, the henchman of Iruma Akugorō, arrives with a message from his master asking Lady Sakura to resume their engagement, now that her hand has opened. She refuses to consider the offer. Gonsuke, to relieve the tension, tells a joke, baring his arms to lend vigor to his recitation. Lady Sakura stares in fascination at the tattoo on his arm: a bell and cherry blossoms.

> SAKURA: What is that tattoo? (*Gonsuke hears this.*)
>
> GONSUKE: Oh—please excuse me. (*He covers his arms. Sakura stares at Gonsuke's face.*)
>
> SAKURA: Then, was it you? (*She gestures in surprise. Without realizing it, she drops her rosary.*)[7]

Lady Sakura dismisses her woman, saying she must purify herself after the defilement of worldly talk. Gonsuke starts to leave, but she goes up to him and, rolling back her left sleeve, reveals a tattoo exactly like his. We learn that in the previous spring he broke into her house one night, intending to burgle it, and profited by the opportunity to rape Lady Sakura. Far from resenting his wanton act, she fell passionately in love with her unknown assailant. Her narration rises into poetry as she describes the experience:

SAKURA: It was March, and still rather chilly. Late at night a man crept secretly to my pillow, his face hidden by a hood that masked his features. I trembled in fear.

GONSUKE: I pulled you to me, not asking yes or no. . . . Later, I was startled by the morning cockcrows and slipped away, without further ado. . . .

SAKURA: I didn't hear them. I tried to stop you. By chance I caught a glimpse in the dawn light of the tattoo on your arm, a bell framed in cherry blossoms. I did not know your face, nor what manner of man you might be, but ever since we parted . . . .[8]

She goes on to describe how, as the result of this encounter with Gonsuke, she has given birth to a child, unknown to anyone except her lady-in-waiting, Nagaura. In despair of ever meeting her lover again, she had planned to become a nun, but now she has changed her mind. She asks to become his wife, and Gonsuke accepts her offer, commenting, "We certainly make a crazy couple!" The stage directions indicate at this point: "Lady Sakura and Gonsuke fondle each other in various ways." They retire to a bedroom and discreetly lower the blinds, but Lady Sakura's cries of pleasure give the pair away. Gonsuke escapes, and people accuse Seigen of being Lady Sakura's lover. She does not deny this. Seigen, still feeling guilty about Shiragiku, and convinced that Sakura is his reincarnation, accepts this charge, though he is totally innocent.

The first act ends at this point. It is brilliantly constructed, combining striking realism in the character portrayal and language with stylization and even fantasy in the action; it is hard to imagine a better-written act of Kabuki.[9] Three clearly defined and unusual characters have been presented—Lady Sakura, Seigen, and Gonsuke—and each commands our attention. The dialogue, at once colloquial and stylized, is exceedingly difficult to render adequately into English, but in the original Japanese it carries the play forward with remarkable verve. The rare sections in poetry, intended more as a burlesque of the old tragedies than as genuine heightened expression, contribute to the variety. Reading this act after any play by Namiki Gohei or Sakurada Jisuke is to leave the world of posturing for the world of drama.

The second act takes place in the mean setting of an outcast's hut where Lady Sakura and Seigen are to live. Her infant is brought to her, and the others leave. One outcast lingers long enough to urge Lady Sakura and Seigen to settle down as man and wife. Sakura expresses coy surprise, but Seigen is horrified by the suggestion. When she sees that Seigen is not to be won by lust, she begs him to help a distressed woman, and Seigen, remembering her mysterious connection with Shiragiku, at length consents. He gives up his faith, not because of overpowering love, in the familiar manner of many earlier plays, but because of a nagging sense of guilt. He breaks his rosary and throws down the beads, to show he has renounced the priesthood. At the end of the act Sakura is carried off by the villainous Akugorō. Seigen, attempting to save her, is knocked into the river. When he emerges, dripping wet, he discovers she is gone. He calls her name in vain. Then it occurs to him that she may have deceived him and voluntarily run off with Akugorō. He cries, "I won't let you go! It's all because of you that I became depraved!" He searches for Sakura. Just at this moment the infant cries.

> SEIGEN: Look! There's Lady Sakura's baby. Who could have left it lying there? If I don't take care of it, the baby's sure to be eaten by wild animals. (*He takes the baby in his arms.*) I know, the baby's father is my enemy. But as long as I have the baby with me, I have a good way of finding out where Lady Sakura has gone. (*At this point the first strokes of the hourly bell sound. Startled, he falls back. The infant, frightened by his gesture, begins to cry. Seigen, clutching the child, stares into the distance. The wooden clappers are struck to signal the end of the act.*) Lady Sakura, *yaai*![10]

We realize from this forlorn passage that Seigen, despite his words, has fallen in love with Sakura. The effect is melodramatic, but superbly theatrical.

The third act, though skillfully written, is a digression from the main plot, involving characters who do not otherwise appear. Signposts describing Lady Sakura and her brother Matsuwaka have been set up throughout the country; the two are wanted for having deceived the government about the missing heirloom. Two faithful retainers of the family sacrifice their own son and daughter to substitute for Sakura and her brother, in the usual manner of such substitution scenes. The act is given its interest not by this far-fetched theatrical device but by the vivid portrayal of the shy, stuttering girl who is sacrificed to save Sakura.

The fourth act, though short, is carefully composed. Sakura and Seigen, coming from opposite directions, approach an embankment in the dark. Neither sees or hears the other, but their words, spoken in poetic monologues, blend together. The baby begins to cry. Sakura, remembering her own child, wonders if this baby needs milk. She decides to offer her own and approaches Seigen, only to turn back, embarrassed. Sakura and Seigen catch a glimpse of each other, but too dimly for recognition, and they leave on separate ways.

The fifth act is set in the shabby temple building where Nagaura, Sakura's old lady-in-waiting, is living with Zangetsu, formerly a priest at Seigen's temple. Nagaura, a frumpish harridan, still hangs onto some of her old finery, despite Zangetsu's demands that she sell them, because she is planning to wear these clothes when she and Zangetsu are properly married. Seigen is in the same house, lying in a sickbed hidden behind a screen. From time to time the crying of Sakura's baby punctuates the gloomy atmosphere. Seigen awakens from a delirious sleep. He has been dreaming about Sakura and takes from his wallet the incense box, the fateful memento of the past. Zangetsu, catching a glimpse of the box, supposes it is money. He and Nagaura decide to poison Seigen. Zangetsu adds, "If poison doesn't work there are lots of other ways. He's old and decrepit. If we don't kill him, he's sure to croak soon anyway. It's better even for him if we kill him, rather than let him lie around here, day after day, sponging on us."[11] Nagaura makes a deadly brew from blue lizards and offers it to Seigen. He refuses to drink the "medicine," saying he doesn't want to be cured.

> NAGAURA: I understand, but after I've gone to all the trouble of brewing this medicine . . .
>
> ZANGETSU: Please just take a sip.
>
> SEIGEN: No. Medicine won't do me any good. I've told you again and again, I don't want it.
>
> ZANGETSU: You won't drink it? (*Seigen nods. Zangetsu takes the cup and thrusts it under Seigen's nose.*) Seigen, drink it or else![12]

In the struggle to force Seigen to drink the poison, some falls on his face, and a horrible purple stain spreads over his cheek. Zangetsu, abandoning the poison, chokes Seigen until he stops moving. Then Zangetsu and Nagaura eagerly open Seigen's wallet. They find not money but the incense box, and are understandably furious—"after all the trouble we took!" Now they have the problem of disposing of the corpse. Nagaura goes to get the gravedigger, who turns out to be none other than Gonsuke. In the meanwhile Sakura is guided to the temple. She has been found wandering along a road by a sideshow operator who lives nearby. He and Zangetsu decide to sell Sakura to a brothel, and she raises no objections.

Gonsuke arrives and, finding Sakura, claims her as his wife. She joyfully confirms this: "Yes, it's just as you say. I'm your wife, and a wife's a wife. And you're my precious husband, sworn to me for two lifetimes."[13] Gonsuke draws his knife and orders Zangetsu and Nagaura out of the house. When they are alone Sakura throws herself into Gonsuke's arms and begs him never to leave her again.

> GONSUKE: Please don't worry, lady. Why should I want to leave you? I know that's what used to happen in the old days—men were always leaving women. But in those days a man didn't rate as a lover unless he was a handsome boy with a pale complexion and wore a purple cloak, two swords, and a flat cap. Nowadays gravediggers are surprisingly popular as lovers, which shows you how times have changed.[14]

Gonsuke orders Sakura to comb her hair and put on more attractive clothes, handing her Nagaura's precious kimono. Gonsuke leaves for a moment and, as Sakura combs her hair before the mirror, Seigen rises from behind the screen, not dead after all. He bitterly reproaches Sakura and finally declares he intends to kill her and then himself. In the ensuing struggle he falls on his knife and is killed. Gonsuke returns, ready to escort Sakura to the brothel.

In the sixth and final act we learn that Sakura, known as Wind Bell in the licensed quarter because of her tattoo, has not enjoyed much success as a courtesan because a ghost always appears at her pillow whenever she lies down with a man. She returns to Gonsuke's house and finds the baby he has "adopted," intending to use it to extort money. He knows, but she does not, that it is their own child. Sakura is indifferent to the baby, and even expresses her dislike for all children. Gonsuke leaves and at once Seigen's ghost appears (a quick change for the actor playing both roles). Sakura addresses the ghost with familiarity: "Is that you, ghost? You over there, the ghost of Seigen!" She accuses him of interfering with her business and declares that she is now so accustomed to him that he no longer frightens her. The ghost points to the baby, and Sakura realizes for the first time that it is hers. She also learns that Gonsuke is Seigen's dissolute younger brother. She strikes at the ghost with a sword, but it vanishes.

Gonsuke returns, so drunk he babbles away his secrets, revealing how he killed Sakura's father and stole the heirloom. She plies him with more drink, and when at last he falls into a stupor, she searches his body until she finds the scroll. Now that she knows Gonsuke was her father's murderer, her love has turned to hatred. She cannot even allow their child to live. She covers the baby with a cloak and, shutting her eyes, stabs him. Next she kills Gonsuke. Then she cuts her hair, to signify she has become a nun. The curtain is drawn as a crowd rushes in shouting, "Murder!" In the final scene we learn that the scroll has been restored to its rightful owners and Sakura acclaimed.

Lady Sakura is not Namboku's most famous play; indeed, it is usually omitted from lists of his four or five "masterpieces." Nevertheless, as a work of literature it seems to me to be his finest work. Sakura is a new and startling creation. Unlike the delicate princesses of most Kabuki plays, she lusts after the burglar who raped her, is ready to take a priest as a lover when that seems advisable, and raises no objection to being sold to a brothel. She even mocks Seigen's ghost, though ghosts in Kabuki are normally sacrosanct. No matter how brutally Gonsuke behaves, she loves him all the more, but Seigen's sacrifice makes little impression on her. Yet, despite her waywardness, she is by no means the conventional evil woman of Kabuki; her depravity even gives her allure. For that matter, Gonsuke, whose only emotions are produced by the cravings of money and sex, is not a stage villain (like Akugorō) but a fascinating if terrifying man. Seigen, for his part, sacrifices himself to Lady Sakura because he considers this to be his duty to the reincarnation of his old love; but his actions, undertaken for noble motives, are the cause of his downfall. All the important characters in the play, down to Zangetsu and Nagaura, fall from good fortune into miserable depravity. We accept this as normal, and when we are told at the end that Sakura's family has been restored, thanks to the recovery of the heirloom, we do not believe it. Sakura's murder of her lover Gonsuke does not impress us as the act of a heroic woman but as a final brutality. But the play is satisfying as an artistic whole in a manner rare in Kabuki. The failure of *Lady Sakura* to win wider recognition as Namboku's masterpiece is puzzling. Probably it suffers in comparison with even more sensational plays, but none of Namboku's other works surpasses the literary accomplishment of *Lady Sakura.*

Osome and Hisamatsu, a more popular work, must be quite thrilling in the theater, thanks to the innumerable quick changes, but it seems hopelessly contrived as literature. The most effective scenes in the play do not involve the lovers Osome and Hisamatsu, but a blackmailing couple, Oroku and Kihei. In the first act a vegetable peddler is beaten by a pawnshop clerk, but the owner of the pawnshop, a kindly man, gives the peddler another cloak to replace the one torn in the beating. The peddler takes the cloak to the seamstress Oroku and asks her to alter it to fit him. She and her husband listen attentively to his story.

Soon afterward Oroku goes to the pawnshop to ask if in fact her brother was given the cloak he has brought home; she is afraid he may have stolen it. The pawnbroker assures her that the cloak was indeed a gift. A palanquin is brought to the pawnshop door, and when it is opened a dead body falls out. Oroku declares that it is her brother, who has died from the beating he got from the clerk. The corpse is in fact another man clothed in the torn cloak. Kihei appears and demands, "What do you propose doing about this?" The pawnbroker, horrified at the possible scandal, offers more and more money, but each time Kihei sneeringly asks if that is all a human life is worth. The scene is masterfully contrived, particularly in Kihei's mock humility as he taunts the pawnbroker: "Of course, the life of a simple man like my brother isn't worth very much. . . ." But the scene disintegrates into farce when the "corpse" revives.

Kokoro no Nazo Toketa Iroito (The Riddles of the Heart Unraveled in Colored Threads, 1810), another play in the oiemono tradition, is about the lost heirloom of the House of

Akagi. It is given peculiar vitality by the character Oito, a geisha, perhaps the most attractive figure Namboku ever created. She is high-spirited and generous, ready to do anything for the man she loves, the very model of an Edo geisha. Early in the play she has an amusing scene with her worthless brother Kurobei. He has just been caught with some stolen goods, but he explains to her that he has been planning to reform and earn an honest living. He promises to "ransom" her, even if it takes thirty years.

> OITO: Do you suppose I can stand another thirty years of being a geisha?
>
> KUROBEI: No, that's not what I mean. But anyway, it would be something for you to look forward to. To tell the truth—
>
> OITO: You want money again, I suppose.[15]

When Oito seems disinclined to give Kurobei the money he needs, he threatens to plunge head-first into a barrel of rainwater.

> OITO: So we're going through that again!
>
> KUROBEI: And if that doesn't kill me, maybe I'll cut my belly with a rock. Or maybe the best thing'd be to strangle myself with my towel. (*He takes out a towel and wraps it around his neck.*)
>
> OITO: All right, that is enough. Once you start talking that way I know you'll never leave empty-handed. Take this. (*She pulls out her silver hairpins and gives them to him.*)[16]

Oito is ready to risk her life for her lover, but in order to help recover the missing heirloom she becomes intimate with the villain who stole the heirloom. The lover, imagining she has really deceived him, kills her in a rage, only to discover her sacrifice from the note she left behind. Namboku shamelessly borrowed this situation from Namiki Gohei's *Godairiki*.

A second plot involves Ofusa, a geisha at the same house with Oito, who is forced by her mother into a marriage with a man she does not love. On her wedding day she drinks a poison that apparently kills her, but she is actually only in a coma. She is buried in her wedding finery. Her Romeo visits her tomb, not out of love but because he has been told one hundred *ryō* of gold were buried in her coffin, and he desperately needs the money. When he opens the coffin she comes back to life. Eventually, as we might have predicted, the missing heirloom (all but forgotten in the course of the play) is recovered.

Namboku's masterpiece is generally considered to be *Tōkaidō Yotsuya Kaidan* (Ghost Story of Yotsuya on the Tōkaidō, 1825). Critics have claimed that all of Namboku's previous plays were preparation for this work,[17] and even that it is the supreme masterpiece of all Kabuki.[18] It is the one play of Namboku still frequently performed, not only by Kabuki actors, but in modern adaptations for the theater and films. The character Oiwa has become the archetype of horribly ugly women, though she has also been enshrined officially as Oiwa Daimyōjin. There can be no disputing that *Ghost Story* is a classic of the Kabuki stage.

The world (*sekai*) of the play is that of *Chūshingura*; the various characters are all identified as retainers, loyal or disloyal, of Enya Hangan, or as friends and enemies of Kō no Moronao. Certain events are made to dovetail with the plot of *Chūshingura* because *Ghost Story* was first performed as part of a curious double-bill with the older work. The performances were spread out over two days; on the first day the actors performed half of *Chūshingura* plus the first three acts of *Ghost Story*, and on the second day the remainder of both plays, saving the finale of *Chūshingura* for the end. Just as *Chūshingura* itself portrayed life in the eighteenth century, though ostensibly set in the fourteenth century, *Ghost Story* belongs wholly to its own time; no attempt was made to fuse its expression or morality with those of *Chūshingura*.

Ghost Story is concerned mainly with Oiwa and her philandering husband, Iemon. Even today, when the actors no longer perform the quick changes Namboku intended, and when large sections of the play are normally deleted, it still captivates spectators as a horror story. The disfiguring stain that spread over Seigen's face in *Lady Sakura* is developed into the unspeakable deformation of Oiwa's face after she drinks poison (each actor taking the role tries to outdo his predecessors in the horrible effects he achieves), and every other means is employed to frighten the audience. Small wonder that *Ghost Story* is customarily performed in summer, to chill the spectators! But as a work of literature it cannot be rated very high. Unlike the vivid characters of *Lady Sakura*, those of *Ghost Story* lack depth or complexity. Oiwa is of no interest before drinking the poison, and once she has imbibed it she is a hideous monster, not a deformed woman. The other characters might just as well be played by puppets as by actors. If *Ghost Story* deserves to be ranked as Namboku's finest work, the measuring rod can only be its theatrical effectiveness. It is amazingly successful in its variety of scenes and situations; no one could drowse through a performance. It suggests, however, not so much the ripe maturity of a great dramatist as a master craftsman adroitly displaying his professional cunning.

KABUKI AFTER NAMBOKU

The twenty-five years after Namboku's death were a lean period for Kabuki. Few new plays of distinction were presented, and the very existence of Kabuki was threatened by the drastic program of reforms instituted in 1841 by Mizuno Tadakuni, the chief adviser to the shogun. The purpose of the Tempō Reforms, named after the era, was high-minded; they were intended to reform customs and morals by encouraging thrift and simplicity, and by forbidding waste and extravagance. In order to diminish the appeal of Kabuki, the theaters were ordered to move from the central part of Edo to an outlying area, cutting down on the attendance. The actors were reminded of their base social position and enjoined against transactions with ordinary citizens. They were further ordered to live in a segregated section, to refrain from all ostentation, and to give up their tours of country playhouses. One of Mizuno's trusted associates even proposed in 1843 that the theater be abolished altogether.[19]

Fortunately for Kabuki, other men close to Mizuno opposed the prohibition on Kabuki. They pointed out its long history (always a powerful argument in a society governed by precedent) and asserted that it was "useful" to the government to maintain the theaters. Kawatake Shigetoshi interpreted the ambiguous word "useful" as meaning that the theaters were expected to serve as a "lubricating oil" for society.[20] However, it was urged that only plays explicitly promoting the time-honored doctrine of "encouraging virtue and chastising vice" should be performed. Kabuki was granted a reprieve, but the danger remained great; if the government insisted on restricting the repertory to plays of didactic intent, the most popular works, from Namboku's on down, could not be performed.

Mizuno fell from power in 1843, not because of these unpopular controls on Kabuki, but because of his inept economic policies.[21] The reign of terror of the Tempō Reforms was brief but intense. The most celebrated actor in the country, Danjūrō VII (then known as Ebizō), was arrested in 1842 on the charge of extravagance and banished from the city of Edo; he was not officially pardoned and allowed to return until 1849. The well-known Osaka actor Nakamura Tomijūrō was banished in 1843 and died in 1847 without obtaining a pardon.[22]

The revival of Kabuki was slow, not only because of uncertainty as to future governmental policies, but because the new crop of dramatists was still not ready. The first to emerge into prominence was Segawa Jokō III (1806–81), known for two works, *Higashiyama Sakura Zōshi* (1851) and *Yowa Nasake Ukino no Yokogushi* (1853). The former play, usually called *Sakura Sōgo* after the principal character, combines the story of *The Rustic Genji* by Ryūtei Tanehiko with an account of the quasi-historical personage Sakura Sōgorō, a champion of the peasants against cruel taxation. The theme of a peasant revolt no doubt appealed to audiences especially at this time, when such revolts were frequent.

Segawa Jokō's masterpiece, however, was the later play, popularly known as *Kirare Yosa* (The Slashed Yosa) after the central figure, or else as *Genyadana* after the most famous scene.[23] The lurid story tells of lovers who have been separated by a gang of gamblers. The high point is the scene when the man visits the woman many years later. He intends to extort money from her as the mistress of a prosperous merchant, not realizing that she is his old sweetheart. The realism of the dialogue and the many opportunities provided for virtuoso acting, rather than the plot or characterization, have endeared this play to many generations of theatergoers.

KAWATAKE MOKUAMI

Mokuami was the last great figure of Edo Kabuki. In the opinion of many critics, he elevated Kabuki to its highest level of artistry.

Tsubouchi Shōyō, the outstanding authority on drama during the Meiji era, wrote of Mokuami, "He was truly the grand wholesaler of the Edo theater, the Western Roman Empire of Tokugawa popular literature. His work was a metropolis, a period of several centuries."[24] Mokuami's plays are still frequently performed, though the world he so realistically portrayed is now remote from the experience of most Japanese. His plays, instead of reflecting contemporary life as he intended, are now evocations of a distant, nostalgic past.

Mokuami was born in 1816 in the heart of Edo. His family for some generations had been wholesale fish merchants, but his father shifted professions several times, finally becoming a pawnbroker. The boy had only the minimal education needed to keep accounts for the pawnshop, but in one respect he was quite precocious: at the age of thirteen or fourteen he was disowned by his straitlaced father when he discovered that the boy was already amusing himself with geishas. The next few years were spent as a vagabond; no doubt Mokuami was still supported by his family even after being disowned. At sixteen he took a job as delivery boy for a lending library, and seems to have profited by the opportunity to read the books which he delivered. His life among the lower classes at this time would provide him with invaluable materials for his plays.

Mokuami also began to study Japanese dance, but apparently showed no aptitude. His lessons, however, had an unexpected consequence: his dancing teacher introduced him to the backstage world of the theater, and Mokuami became a pupil of the dramatist Tsuruya Namboku V. His name first appeared on playbills in 1835. Deaths in his family obliged Mokuami to assume duties at home for a time, but in 1841 he returned to the theater and never left it again until he died (1893). During this long period of activity he composed a total of 360 plays, long and short, including 130 domestic plays, 90 historical plays, and 140 dance plays. Although Mokuami did not write every act, relying on assistants for much of the work, he sketched the scenarios and bore full responsibility for the whole.

Mokuami became the leading playwright of the Kawarasaki Theater in 1843, the same year that the company was obliged by the Tempō Reforms to move from the center of the city. He was known at the time as Kawatake Shinshichi, a name he used until he officially retired in 1880, when he took the name Mokuami. His first great success came in 1854, the year after Commodore Perry's visit to Japan, when he wrote for the great actor Ichikawa Kodanji (1812–66) the play commonly known as *Shinobu no Sōda*. Mokuami was obliged to rewrite the play three times to satisfy Kodanji, an actor of unprepossessing appearance and voice who well knew his own strengths and limitations.[25] Mokuami built up the murder scenes, a specialty of Kodanji, and, to please this actor who had grown up in the Kamigata region, Mokuami included passages accompanied by the music typical of the puppet theater, an innovation in a play written originally for Kabuki actors. The play was a great success. Kodanji, now thoroughly aware of the talent of the hitherto inconspicuous dramatist, began a collaboration that lasted until 1866, the year of his death. The scenes Mokuami emphasized in *Shinobu no Sōda* became the hallmarks of his style. The musical accompaniment and the poetic passages declaimed in the traditional rhythm of alternating lines of seven and five syllables especially distinguished Mokuami's plays from those by Namboku and other predecessors.

Mokuami wrote mainly domestic dramas for Kodanji, including *Nezumi Kozō* (The Rat Boy, 1857), *Izayoi Seishin* (The Love of Izayoi and Seishin, 1859), and *Sannin Kichisa* (The Three Kichisas, 1860). He also wrote plays for other actors, including the famous *Benten Kozō* (1862). These works almost all deal with the lives of people of the lower classes, and generally have for their heroes thieves, blackmailers, or swindlers. These antisocial characters were portrayed unsentimentally—by no means as Robin Hoods robbing the rich to help the poor—but their exploits delighted the audiences, who could more readily identify with such minor figures of the underworld than with the great heroes or villains of the past. Becoming a thief may even have seemed a desirable way of life to townsmen caught in the throes of poverty and unable to escape from their fate.[26]

Mokuami was famous also for his explicit love scenes that went even beyond Namboku's in suggestiveness. Probably the change signified not so much temperamental differences between the two dramatists as increased demands for such stimulation from the audiences of a later, more decadent day. But Mokuami's works of violence or eroticism were tempered by their poetic language;

a scene that might have been unpleasant to watch if performed realistically was given artistry by the stylized gestures and the rhythms of the dialogue. For example, the scene in *The Three Kichisas*, in which the three heroes swearing eternal brotherhood by drinking one another's blood was so stylized that this sanguinary action gave no offense. Indeed, one passage in that play had such poetic beauty that people recited it as they walked along the streets.[27]

Mokuami's plays are usually badly constructed, sometimes consisting of two almost unrelated plots, one in the tradition of the jidaimono, devolving on a stolen sword or incense burner, the other a sewamono about the lives of contemporary people in Edo. Only casually do the two plots coincide. The plays are sometimes disconcerting also because they deliberately call attention to their peculiarities as works for the Kabuki theater. Again and again, after some particularly unbelievable coincidence or stroke of fate, a character will remark that it is exactly like a scene from Kabuki. The actors sometimes identify themselves by name, or pick up scraps of paper from the street which turn out to be announcements of the play being performed.

But even more striking than such stylization or unreality was Mokuami's ability to capture exactly the lives of people in the lower classes. The scenes perform superbly, even when the dialogue itself is unimpressive. Occasionally, especially in the poetic sections, the writing rises to the level of literature, but this was not necessarily by design of the playwright.

Mokuami had no literary or social principles he wished to incorporate in his plays, nor had he any intention of criticizing or mocking society.[28] It is hard to detect any important change in his work from the beginning of his career until the end of the Tokugawa period. Some critics even assert that Mokuami failed to change between his earliest works and those of the 1880s.[29] He was a faithful heir to the Edo traditions of the stage, including in his plays whatever his audiences desired, providing it did not get him in trouble with the censors. In 1866 a government edict was issued forbidding excessive realism in the portrayal of thieves and prostitutes as likely to tempt the spectators into corrupt ways and make a mockery of the principle of encouraging virtue and chastising vice. Kodanji was so enraged that his illness took a sudden turn for the worse and soon afterward he died, but

Mokuami was not greatly disturbed. Indeed, he suggested to Kodanji that they might try something new in the way of historical plays if contemporary subjects were dangerous.[30] Mokuami has been characterized as a "timid moralist submissive to the policies of the authorities."[31]

Mokuami's plays have nevertheless kept the stage and deserve their high reputations. It is appropriate that a discussion of Tokugawa theater conclude with this figure, a man who literally obeyed the Confucian principles as they were understood by the lower classes, even though his works in fact exalt vice and sneer at virtue. One senses in his plays the corruption of the times, the petering out of a dynasty. A year after Kodanji's death the Meiji Restoration would change the entire picture.

NOTES

1. I have referred to these playwrights throughout by the names they used at the end of their careers (the names invariably used by scholars today), but each used other names earlier in his life.

2. See Kawatake Shigetoshi, *Tsuruya Namboku Shū*, p. 32.

3. *Ibid.*, pp. 40–41. The quotation is from *Seji Kembun Roku*, a book of gossip on contemporary matters written by someone known only by his pen name, Buyō Inshi.

4. Tsubouchi Shōyō and Atsumi Seitarō, *Ō Namboku Zenshū*, VIII, pp. 1–3.

5. Engeki Hakubutsukan (ed.), *Engeki Hyakka Daijiten*, III, pp. 349–50, gives the names of Kabuki plays built around these two characters.

6. See the article by Atsumi Seitarō, "Namboku no Kakikae Kyōgen," in Tsubouchi and Atsumi, III, pp. xxiv–xxxvi.

7. Tsubouchi and Atsumi, VIII, pp. 48–49.

8. *Ibid.*, p. 52.

9. The act is signed Sakurada Jisuke II, but it is hard to know how to divide the credit for this act between him and Namboku. Sakurada Jisuke II was a distinguished dramatist in his own right.

10. Tsubouchi and Atsumi, VIII, pp. 98–99.

11. *Ibid.*, p. 163.

12. *Ibid.*, p. 164.

13. *Ibid.*, p. 175.

14. *Ibid.*, p. 180.

15. Tsubouchi and Atsumi, III, p. 324.

16. *Ibid.*, p. 325.

17. Takida Teiji, *Dentō Engeki Sadan*, p. 185.

18. Takeuchi Michitaka, "Tōkaidō Yotsuya Kaidan," in Engeki Hakubutsukan (ed.), *Engeki Hyakka Daijiten*, IV, p. 130. For a summary, see Appendix, 6.

19. Kawatake Shigetoshi, *Kabuki Sōkō*, pp. 19–20.

20. *Ibid.*, p. 23.

21. G. B. Sansom, *A History of Japan*, III, pp. 221–27.

22. Kawatake, *Kabuki Sōkō*, pp. 65–73.

23. There is an English translation of the "Genyadana" scene by A. C. Scott.

24. Quoted in Yamamoto Jirō, *Mokuami*, p. 23. The somewhat florid, Western imagery was typical of Tsubouchi Shōyō rather than of Mokuami!

25. Kawatake Shigetoshi, *Nihon Engeki Zenshi*, p. 725.

26. Yamamoto, p. 12.

27. Teruoka Yasutaka and Gunji Masakatsu, *Edo Shimin Bungaku no Kaika*, pp. 424–26.

28. Yamamoto, p. 9.

29. *Ibid.*, p. 22.

30. Kawatake, *Nihon Engeki Zenshi*, pp. 729–30.

31. Yamamoto, p. 13.

BIBLIOGRAPHY

Brandon, James. *Kabuki: Five Classic Plays*. Cambridge, Mass.: Harvard University Press, 1975.

Engeki Hakubutsukan (ed.). *Engeki Hyakka Daijiten*. Tokyo: Heibonsha, 1960–62.

Ernst, Earle (ed.). *Three Japanese Plays*. London: Oxford University Press, 1959.

Kawatake Mokuami. *The Love of Izayoi and Seishin*, trans. by Frank T. Motofuji. Rutland, Vt.: Tuttle, 1966.

Kawatake Shigetoshi. *Kabuki Sōkō*. Tokyo: Chūō Kōron Sha, 1949.

———. *Kawatake Mokuami*. Tokyo: Yoshikawa Kōbunkan, 1961.

———. *Nihon Engeki Zenshi*. Tokyo: Iwanami Shoten, 1959.

———. *Tsuruya Namboku Shū*. Tokyo: Chiheisha, 1948.

Sansom, George B. *A History of Japan*. Stanford: Stanford University Press, 1958–63.

Scott, A. C. (trans.). *Genyadana, a Japanese Kabuki Play*. Tokyo: Hokuseidō Press, 1953.

Takida Teiji. *Dentō Engeki Sadan*. Tokyo: Shomotsu Tembō Sha, 1943.

Teruoka Yasutaka and Gunji Masakatsu. *Edo Shimin Bungaku no Kaika.* Tokyo: Shibundō, 1967.

Toita Yasuji (ed.). *Kabuki Meisaku Sen,* VI. Tokyo: Sōgensha, 1954.

Tsubouchi Shōyō and Atsumi Seitarō. *Ō Namboku Zenshū.* Tokyo: Shun'yōdō, 1925.

Urayama Masao and Matsuzaki Hitoshi. *Kabuki Kyakuhon Shū,* II, in Nihon Koten Bungaku Taikei series. Tokyo: Iwanami Shoten, 1961.

Yamamoto Jirō. *Mokuami,* in Iwanami Kōza Nihon Bungaku Shi series, vol. X. Tokyo: Iwanami Shoten, 1959.

CHAPTER 20

WAKA POETRY

WAKA OF THE LATE TOKUGAWA PERIOD

The waka of the Tokugawa period were of two main varieties: poems by men who sought to recapture the sincerity, grandeur, or elegance of the past, and poems by men who were determined to express their own experiences in their own language. The division can be made more or less chronologically, soon after the death of Kamo no Mabuchi in 1769. This does not mean that most poets after 1769 turned their backs on the past. Even the most "revolutionary" of the new poets drew their inspiration, and often their vocabulary, from a preferred collection, whether the *Manyōshū*, the *Kokinshū*, or the *Shin Kokinshū*. Moreover, no major school or tradition of poetry ever vanished completely. In Kyoto the court poets continued to turn out conventional verses in the Nijō style, oblivious to change and to criticism, as firmly convinced as ever of the importance of the secret teachings. The disciples of Kamo no Mabuchi, still strong in Edo, wrote pseudo-*Manyōshū* verse, exalting the simple, masculine virtues; and the *Shin Kokinshū* tastes of Motoori Norinaga were echoed in the poetry of his disciples. Nevertheless, the most interesting waka written after 1769 were not by the defenders of the precedents of the past, but by men who advocated a new kind of poetry.

The literary pronouncements of these new poets are often striking. The sharpness of their judgments, the vigor with which they denounced the dead weight of the past, and the urgency of their calls for a new and vital poetry make us turn eagerly to their poetry, only to be disappointed. We expect poetry that will closely reflect the writer's anguish or ecstasy, his deep concern with the world he lives in, or at least the quirks of personality that distinguish him from other waka poets; but the poems may seem at first glance almost indistinguishable from those of the rejected past. And even if the sentiments or the language surprise us by an unaccustomed earthiness or novelty of subjects, the level of the poem is apt to be trivial: a waka about a mouse is certainly an unusual departure from the normal range of elegant subjects, but it probably will have little else to recommend it. Saigyō wrote about cherry blossoms as if their tiny, quickly faded petals could stand for the world and all of man's deepest concerns; but the Tokugawa poets, whether they wrote of cherry blossoms or of mice, rarely suggest the intensity of the distillation of a powerful experience. A touch of freshness or a suggestion of anger or disappointment is all the individuality we can hope for.

In part, the severe censorship may have been to blame. A poet who was indignant about the Tempō Reforms of the 1840s would hardly have dared to publish poetry criticizing the government's policies. It is true that poetry was written expressing devotion to the emperor and therefore, by implication, something less than total allegiance to the shogun, but with a few exceptions the waka poets were not politically or socially involved, whether because of fear of the censor or simply out of indifference.

The persistence of the old poetic diction had a far more inhibiting effect than the censorship or any other external factor. Even those poets who insisted they wrote as men of the present time continued to use a dead language. The priest Ryōkan is famous today for his guileless sincerity, displayed especially in poems about children and flowers of the field; nevertheless, he usually wrote in an idiom deliberately borrowed from the *Manyōshū*, employing the most hackneyed makurakotoba (pillow words) and archaisms, a manner incongruous in a poet of unaffected simplicity. The classical language retained certain advantages even for such modern poets as Ishikawa Takuboku: it allows greater flexibility of expression, and the direct connections with the body of classical poetry also make it possible to expand the meaning of a phrase by its associated overtones. It is small wonder the nineteenth-century waka poets were reluctant to abandon so effective a medium. Yet it would be hard indeed to imagine any of their contemporaries in England or America professing to describe themselves and their time, but in Chaucer's language. Even if they studied Chaucer's vocabulary and syntax so thoroughly they could write in his style without great effort, it would certainly seem a *tour de force* rather than an expression from the heart.

Ryōkan was perhaps the best of the archaizing poets of the early nineteenth century. Other poets insisted on a strict adherence to the *Kokinshū*, admitting no words or concepts less than a thousand years old. Tachibana Akemi in a satirical essay derided the old poetry:

> In early spring one writes of the morning sun gently shining and the spreading mists; at the end of the year one speaks of the "waves of years crawling shorewards" and of waiting for the spring. For flowers there is "the blessing of rain" and for snow "regret over leaving footprints." Poetic language has come to mean such phrases and nothing else. A hundred out of a hundred poets, the year before last, last year, and this year too have merely strung together the same old phrases. How depressing![1]

Poets could go on writing in the same vein about the fragrance of plum blossoms or the reddening of the autumn leaves not only because of the conservatism of the poetic diction, far more rigorous than any European parallel, but because so many elements in Japanese life had remained essentially unchanged for centuries. It would be strange if a city poet wrote without irony about the fragrance of plum blossoms today, when the occasions for catching a whiff of fragrance through the fumes of industrial pollution are rare; but in 1800, no less than in 800, the poet, even in the city, could experience the pleasure of the scent of plum blossoms announcing the spring. The scent would also recall to him, in an equally traditional way, his friends of long ago. If poetic decorum forbade the poets of 1800 to describe what were actually the dramatic pleasures of their lives—sex, liquor, a good dinner, a promotion or other recognition of their work, etc.—it encouraged them to describe, in much the same terms as their predecessors, the secondary pleasures—the sights and sounds of the changing seasons, the bittersweet remembrances of love, the pleasures of travel to places with poetic associations. These did not change much over the years, and the poets sincerely believed that even if they avoided direct imitation, their poetry would inevitably come to resemble the masterpieces of the past, as they acquired sensitivity and understanding of life. They were sure that the unchanging truths were the only important subjects of poetry, and however new and unconventional the ways of describing them, there was basically no difference between themselves and the men of a thousand years before.

Readers today tend to prefer the poems that deviate most from the conventions. It comes as a surprise and even as a relief when Tachibana Akemi describes the pleasure of having fish for dinner, or when Ōkuma Kotomichi reveals his pride in his grandchild, subjects unthinkable in a court poet. But unless a waka, regardless of subject, evokes more than it actually says—is more than a charming description in thirty-one syllables—it will surely not be remembered long. Elegance of tone, the goal of the court poets, was rejected by the "new" poets of the Tokugawa period, and they insisted that poetry involve more than giving a slightly new twist to a familiar old poem. But their verses are often so plain and bare they do not seem like waka at all. This may explain why Ryōkan clung to the old language, or why a quite different poet like Ozawa Roan, despite his advocacy of "ordinary speech" was unable to abandon the *Kokinshū* diction. The requisite of a great waka, in the Tokugawa period as before, was that it be filled with passion: without this passion, however suggested, no beauty of language, nor for that matter no startling ugliness, could make of the thirty-one syllables much more than a lovely miniature.

Of course, all poets of the period, regardless of school, paid at least lip-service to the dictum stated in the preface to the *Kokinshū*, that the waka had for its seed the human heart. No one advocated dispassionate objectivity or insincerity, but in fact very little of the human heart was involved in the poetic production. The poems, even by the most boring aristocrats, exhibit a professional competence that earns our grudging admiration, but it is to the unorthodox poets that we must turn for the depth of human feelings that is the true hallmark of the waka.

Five poets, very different in background and style, typify the best in the late Tokugawa waka: Ozawa Roan, Kagawa Kageki, the priest Ryōkan, Ōkuma Kotomichi, and Tachibana Akemi.

OZAWA ROAN (1723–1801)

Roan was born in Osaka, the youngest son of a minor samurai. He himself served in various posts in Kyoto as a young man before taking up employment in his early thirties with a prominent noble family. About 1753 he was accepted as the pupil of Reizei Tamemura (1712–74), a leading figure among the dōjō (court) poets, and gradually he began to acquire a reputation. This may have inspired the jealousy of Tamemura's other disciples; in any case, Roan was expelled from the school about 1773, apparently after having been denounced as a betrayer of its principles.[2] He now became much more independent both in his views on poetry and in his poetry itself. He had already, for almost ten years, been making a living as a poet, ever since he was dismissed for unknown reasons from his samurai duties in 1765. Roan lived very quietly in Kyoto, almost as a hermit, gradually attracting disciples. In 1788, when he was sixty-five, a great fire swept through Kyoto, and Roan was forced to take refuge at a temple in the lonely Uzumasa district, where he remained until 1792. During this period he composed much of his most affecting poetry, including such verses as:

Uzumasa no	The roar of the wind
fukaki hayashi wo	Fiercely resounds as it comes
hibikikuru	From the recesses
kaze no to sugoki	Of the Uzumasa woods
aki no yūgure	This lonely autumn evening.[3]

Hisamatsu Sen'ichi commented, "The poem is descriptive, but it successfully evokes, beyond the surface description, the stillness of late autumn. This is one of Roan's masterpieces. Roan's best works generally tend to treat the season of year from late autumn to early winter."[4] Roan wrote a number of waka ending with the line *aki no yūgure* (evening in autumn), the conclusion of several famous poems in the *Shin Kokinshū*; indeed, only an expert in the development of Japanese poetic traditions could recognize that this was the poem of a man professedly in revolt against the old traditions, written at the end of the eighteenth century. Clearly, the manner of poetic expression learned from Reizei Tamemura had become a part of Roan. Modern or not, the poem effectively conveys the autumnal atmosphere at the lonely temple where Roan was living. Even if this poem was inspired as much by Saigyō as by direct experience, it attains an intensity rare in Roan's work. More typical is the following example:

yama tōku	Even the sunlight
tanabiku kumo ni	Shining on the bank of clouds
utsuru hi mo	In the distant hills
yaya usuku naru	Gradually grows fainter
aki no yūgure	This evening in autumn.[5]

The coloring of this verse is pale: the loneliness of the autumn evening is suggested but without the intensity of the previous verse. But this relatively weak example of Roan's poetry at least accords with his insistence on simplicity and clarity. The language is transparent, and the poet claims no more for his expression than that it is sincere. This was the distinctive feature of his *tadagoto-uta* (poems on ordinary things), a term Roan borrowed from the preface of the *Kokinshū* and used to describe his preference in poetry: "By *uta* I mean the poet's expression in an intelligible manner, using his ordinary speech, of things that have just occurred to him."[6] This statement, from his book of poetical criticism *Ashikabi*, written in 1790, while Roan was living in Uzumasa, represented his basic convictions.

Perhaps because of his unfortunate experiences as the pupil of a dōjō poet, Roan strongly attacked the secret traditions. In his discussion of "secret traditions, oral traditions, and family traditions" evolved by the court poets, he wrote:

> They suppose that a knowledge of such traditions makes for skill and erudition, and they claim that a man who is ignorant of them, being immature and inexpert, will not write poetically and will be unaware of the principles of the art. But see what incomprehensible poems are written by people who have acquired the secret traditions and oral traditions! Consider too how much narrower the art has steadily become, and how much better poetry was in the old days before there were any traditions! Such people have now reached a point where they have not the faintest inkling that in poetry the very first thing is the meaning.[7]

Roan went on to deny altogether the necessity not only of traditions but of teachers of poetry:

> When, having let one's thoughts roam beyond heaven and earth, one encapsulates them inside a mustard seed, one is in communication with all things, and the verses that express what one has just thought make a poem. . . . Nothing takes precedence over one's own heart. One doesn't learn from others how to write poetry, nor does one learn from models. This proves that there are neither rules nor teachers.[8]

Despite his announced rejection of the post, Roan was deeply influenced by his predecessors, notably the poets of the *Kokinshū*. He made fun of Mabuchi and his disciples, who employed the archaic language of the *Manyōshū* to describe their contemporary, sometimes mundane thoughts, but he himself tended to observe the orthodox poetic diction established by Ki no Tsurayuki. His main targets of attack were not the old poems and conceptions of poetry themselves, but the commentators and exegetors who stood between the *Kokinshū* and the modern poets:

> There were no ancient books describing how to write poetry. The first was the preface to the *Kokinshū*. Although one could

not possibly count all the books that have been written by teachers of poetry in the generations since, based on this work, people still go on writing them. . . . It is far better, instead of perusing all their words, to try to understand the preface to the *Kokinshū*.[9]

The poetry of the past was valuable even to the man who sought to express what was in his own heart; this was justified by Roan in terms of universality and particularity of emotions. He gave the name *dōjō* (same emotion) to those feelings aroused in the hearts of all men, regardless of time or place, by certain experiences or perceptions—the dejection of an unsuccessful love affair or the appreciation of the beauty of flowers. He contrasted this with *shinjō* (new emotions), the particular sentiments aroused in a given person from moment to moment; these are his own and, in a sense, absolutely new. But the sum of all the new, never-before-experienced emotions is an unchanging ocean of universal experience. In Roan's words:

Let me try again to describe the difference between dōjō and shinjō. Ever since the heavens and earth first divided it has been true that although the hundred rivers keep flowing into the sea, the sea never overflows. This is a general principle, true of every age. For each river the water from its springs bubbles forth uninterruptedly, day and night, never failing. The water changes, together with heaven, earth, and nature, and is never the same water as in the past. The way these springs gush forth, even as one watches them now, is like human emotions responding inevitably and afresh to each contact with external things.[10]

Each poem must be truly felt by the poet and expressed in his own words. If it successfully communicates his emotions to other people, it will be effective as poetry; otherwise it fails. In order for a poem to be effective, the poet must practice. He must draw from the sea of common experience and feelings; the supreme model for this is the *Kokinshū*. He will then be able to express himself freely and distinctively, but intelligibly, because he will be touching on the common poetic experiences: "When I say that one's expression of one's thoughts should be interesting, it in no way conflicts with my teachings that one should try in one's poetry to write about feelings that no one has ever written about before."[11]

The poet, then, writes not about conventionally admired sights and experiences but what he has *that moment* experienced; but even though his experience is quite distinct from that of any poet of the past, the times having changed, it shares certain basic human qualities. A knowledge of how the *Kokinshū* poets most effectively describe their experiences will enable the contemporary poet to rise above the particular to the universal.

Roan's own poetry usually falls short of his ideals, but occasionally a poem seems to combine the particular and the universal effectively:

MOON OVER THE RUINED TEMPLE

iraka kuchi	The roof-tiles have rotted,
tobari yaburete	The curtains inside are broken;
mi hotoke no	The holy image
mikage arawa ni	Of the Buddha stands exposed
tsuki zo sashiiru	In the moonlight pouring in.[12]

Roan's life in a ruined temple occasioned this poem, rather than any formally imposed subject, but it suggests, if not the *Kokinshū*, the medieval poetry. An even more affecting example is:

VILLAGE MOON

sato no inu no	Only the baying
koe no mi tsuki no	Of the village dogs rings clear
sora ni sumite	In the moonlit sky:
hito wa shizumaru	People have fallen still
Uji no yamakage	In the shade of the Uji hills.[13]

About 15,000 poems in manuscript were left by Roan. Selections were published by his disciples in the collection *Rokujō Eisō* in 1811, and in a supplementary volume of 350 poems published in 1849, some fifty years after his death. He was acclaimed as the waka poet of the age of Rai Sanyō,[14] but it is likely that his greatest importance was as the pioneer of a kind of poetry he himself could rarely write. His disciples and acquaintances were numerous, and his name was often invoked in the late Tokugawa period as the authority for change.

KAGAWA KAGEKI (1768–1843)

The central figure in Kyoto poetic circles in the early nineteenth century, and a major influence until the close of the century, was Kagawa Kageki. He was born in Tottori, the son of a minor samurai, and began his poetic training very early. By the time he was fourteen he had composed a commentary on *A Hundred Poems by a Hundred Poets*, and was recognized as a genius. About the age of twenty-five he went to the capital for further study. He became a pupil of the Nijō-school poet Kagawa Kagemoto, who was so impressed by the young man that he adopted him as his son. In 1804 Kageki broke his relations with Kagemoto, but he continued to use the surname Kagawa. His poetry was recognized and respected even by the dōjō poets, normally unfriendly to anyone from the country, especially a self-styled innovator. He himself stated that he respected two poets especially: Ki no Tsurayuki among the ancients, and Ozawa Roan among the moderns.[15] The influence of Roan on Kageki's poetry was critical in the development of his characteristic style.

Kageki met Roan in 1796, when he was twenty-eight and Roan seventy-three. Despite the great disparity in age and accomplishment, Roan was impressed by the young man, and although Kageki never formally became a pupil, Roan gave him instruction and on occasion severely criticized his poetry.[16] Kageki's preference for the *Kokinshū* and for clear, ordinary language (as opposed to the archaisms of Mabuchi's school) undoubtedly owed much to Roan. Their friendship ended with Roan's death in 1801. On this occasion Kageki wrote:

shitashiki wa	Among my dear ones
naki ga amata ni	So many have disappeared,
narinuredo	But you, above all,
oshi to wa kimi wo	I think of with regret.[17]
omoikeru ka na	

This is a bad poem because it fails totally to suggest a real sense of loss. Even Kageki's admirers are hard put to defend it, and his detractors, like the modern poet Saitō Mokichi, declared it was the expression of shallow, glib feelings.[18] But perhaps the poem represents a failure of expression rather than of feeling: Kageki was as yet unable with the techniques at his command to express grief over the death of a beloved master, though he was adept at composing the usual poems on the seasons. Even in later years Kageki rarely attempted to touch the harsh edges of emotion; he preferred, like the *Kokinshū* poets, to suggest, rather than declare, his feelings.

Kageki's friendship with Roan may have been the cause of his break with Kagemoto; it was certainly a cause of the charges leveled at him by the Edo followers of Kamo no Mabuchi, especially Katō Chikage and Murata Harumi who published a bitter attack called *Fude no saga* (Evils of the Pen) in 1803. Annoyed by Kageki's rising fame, and especially by his advocacy of simple, contemporary expression, in Roan's manner, they branded him a goblin (*tengu*) and a Christian, strong terms of abuse indeed.[19] But the result of their attacks was to confirm Kageki more deeply than ever in his beliefs, as expressed both in his poetry and in his critical work *Shingaku Iken* (Divergent Views on the New Learning, 1811), which included an attack on Mabuchi's *Niimanabi* (New Learning).

The most productive period of Kageki's career was the fourteen years from 1804 to 1818, when he established himself as the leading poet in Kyoto. This was when he wrote most of the poetry in his representative collection *Keien Isshi* (1828). The end of this productive period was marked by his journey to Edo in 1818 to propagate his style; the attempt ended in utter failure, and he never again attempted to secure a foothold in the bastion of his enemies. Mabuchi's disciples continued to attack Kageki, and they may even have tried to have him assassinated.[20] He was also subjected to attacks by the Kyoto court poets, who sought in 1811 to have him legally restrained from teaching poetry. Their suit failed, and only increased Kageki's reputation in the capital. His reputation grew, even in court circles, and in 1841, in recognition of his contribution to the restoration of the art of the waka, he was given junior fifth rank at court and the honorary title of Governor of Higo.[21]

Reading his poetry today it is hard to imagine why Kageki should have been the center of such controversy. Of course, the existence of any successful new rival school posed an economic threat to the established schools, whether the dōjō poets in Kyoto or the *Manyōshū*-style poets in Edo. The fact that Kagawa Kageki was exceptionally intelligent and competent also aroused dislike. But the differences go deeper: Kageki's critical writings prove that he had a distinctive sensibility that went beyond Roan's criticisms of the abuses of the past. Kageki's poetry rarely lives up to his own standards, but it is also rarely bad; *Keien Isshi* is famous for its high proportion of excellent poems.[22] In the Meiji era, under the attacks of Masaoka Shiki and others, Kageki's poetry was discredited, but his critical opinions, the most advanced of the Tokugawa poets,[23] are surprisingly close to modern attitudes. In his own time his outspoken views earned him enmity, but his more conventional skills as a poet attracted huge numbers of disciples—the estimates run as high as ten thousand men—and made his school, known as Keien, the dominant force in late Tokugawa waka. In 1848 Kageki was given the status of a divinity, and in 1907 the emperor Meiji raised his court rank to the senior fifth grade, probably the only instance in history of a man receiving such honors solely on the basis of his poetry.[24] It is small wonder that the poets and critics of the Meiji era, led by Masaoka Shiki, were so determined to destroy Kageki's reputation!

When we read Kageki's critical works today, free of the prejudices of the Meiji period, we cannot fail to be struck by their acumen and good sense. Unfortunately, the vocabulary of his criticism was insufficiently precise, and it is therefore difficult sometimes to be sure how modern an interpretation we should give to his pronouncements. Kageki's most famous statement of poetical principles means literally, "A waka is not something reasoned, but something tuned." This has been interpreted as meaning that literary quality, rather than intellectual content, is of primary importance in the waka.[25] But elsewhere the word *shirabe* (tuning) was used not so much for literary quality as for a characteristic tone. Kageki wrote that the same words could acquire different meanings, depending on the prevalent tone of a poem. He insisted that the tone be exactly appropriate to the subject, so that "the cuckoo will be like the cuckoo, the song thrush like the song thrush, Fuji like Fuji, a garden hillock like a garden hillock, a man like a man, a dog like a dog."[26]

In *Kagaku Teiyō*, a collection of Kageki's literary opinions edited by his disciple Uchiyama Mayumi (1786–1852) and published in 1850, we find the strongest statement of the importance of shirabe:

> He taught us, "a poem is not reasoned, it is tuned (*shiraburu*). It is still possible to write a poem even if it has no intellectual content, but one must not pretend that an intellectual idea without literary quality is a poem." As long as it has shirabe, it is a poem, and if it has no shirabe, it is not a poem. In short, shirabe is a way to designate a poem.[27]

Kageki's discussion occurs in a section of his work devoted to *shukō* (ingenuity of effect), and he contrasted the natural, spontaneous reaction he associated with shirabe and the artificiality of shukō:

> The best thing is to stop searching for shukō and to describe your sincere reactions. Moreover, the use of kakekotoba in general lowers the tone of a poem, and since it makes it seem inferior, it weakens the emotional effect.[28]

This is clearly an attack on the ingenuity of the followers of the *Shin Kokinshū*, but he was no less scornful of the followers of Mabuchi who used the archaic language of the *Manyōshū* under the impression it was more suitable language for poetry:

> The common words of ancient times are today considered dignified old language. The common words of today will be the dignified old language of future generations. One should learn the old words, but not use them in one's poetry. Common words are properly used in poetry, but they need not be studied. In recent times, however, something has developed called "the *Manyōshū* style." This is the eccentric practice of using language that most people find unintelligible. The poetry of the *Manyōshū*, the semmyō and norito, was perfectly intelligible to people of their times because it was written in the common speech of the day. . . . To consider only the old language elegant and to refuse to use ordinary speech because one despises it as vulgar, is disgraceful; it is like hating oneself. No matter how much you may hate yourself, you can't get rid of yourself; and even if you despise the common language, you can't escape it. Poems are written while one is living among commonplace surroundings. If you flee the world to live in deep mountains and dark

valleys, study the mysteries of Taoism and Buddhism, permit no vulgar thought to enter your mind, or you take Buddhist orders and keep yourself utterly detached from this world, what kind of poetry do you think you will write? . . .[29]

Elegance and vulgarity are determined by the shirabe and not by the words. It is not worth answering anyone who despises the common language and supposes only old language is elegant. . . . Poetry is entirely a matter of describing your own feelings. If you fail to stand on the actual ground where you are, you will lose your honesty; and if you think that by letting your mind soar to some lofty distance, and decorating your language with pretty ornaments you will achieve elegance, you are seriously mistaken.[30]

Of course, Kageki did not believe in an artless expression of the emotions. One particularly effective section of *Kagaku Teiyō*, on "Actual Sights," must be quoted in full:

If you feel sorrow or joy over what you see or hear, and then write down your first inspiration, when still addressing yourself to whatever has stirred the first response, the result will be a poem. If you resort to the secondary principle [of rationalization] your poem will fall into mere logic and be without feeling. But when a poet describes "actual scenes," should he write nothing more than what he sees or hears, exactly as perceived? If he were to write about experiences just as they happened, it would be like asking two or three people to describe a song thrush alighting in the plum blossoms overhanging a fence and singing. They would all be sure to say nothing more than, "A song thrush is singing in the plum tree by the fence." But will that do? On hearing the singing of the song thrush, some may be entirely overcome by the beauty of its voice; others may hope for a visit, even if none has been promised; the poet may be startled at how quickly time has passed; the traveler may think of his own house, far away, going to rack and ruin: each person will choose to express himself in a different way. Just as people's faces are all different, why should their emotions not also be different? That is why my teacher always advised us, "It is hard to talk with the kind of poets who, when they see the moon and blossoms, write about nothing but the moon and blossoms." Nevertheless, many poets

> suppose that writing about "actual scenes" consists in describing exactly what they have seen and heard, or that describing their feelings as they actually are, means saying whatever first comes to one's lips. This is a serious error. What is meant is that one should write a poem describing one's actual feelings without falsifying or decorating them.[31]

In other words, the poet must be sincere when he describes his experiences, but he must also bring to the writing of the poem techniques learned in practice, and an experience of life that illuminates the bare experience. He should write about his daily life and not about famous landscapes he has never seen. He should use his own language rather than attempt to achieve elegance by a use of archaic or "poetic" words; Kageki at one point denied that there was any particular language appropriate to the waka. His criticism of shukō, the bane of most late waka, of the tedious kakekotoba and meaningless makurakotoba, and of all other kinds of traditionally accepted elegance comes as a welcome breath of common sense. But his own poetry did not live up to the expectations aroused by these outspoken views. His admiration for the *Kokinshū* unfortunately involved an admiration for its rather artificial stylistic features, including a language which, though far more comprehensible than that of the *Manyōshū*, was certainly not the contemporary colloquial. As we read Kageki's poetry we again and again catch a whiff of something fresh and appealing, but it is always within the elegant framework of *Kokinshū* ideals, and not the slap in the face of a startling new experience. Kageki's insistence on poetry being the vehicle of emotion (or literary quality) and not of thought has reminded some commentators[32] of the statement by Itō Sachio: "The uta is a cry and not a story"; but Kageki's poetry seldom has the force or the surprise of a shout.

His admiration for *Kokinshū* was stated often, but perhaps best in these terms:

> There is nothing to compare with the *Kokinshū*. The uta in *Kokinshū* are like natural blossoms. The uta in *Shin Kokinshū* are like blossoms seen through the leaves of twisted branches. The *Sōanshū* and similar collections are like artificial flowers. [*Sōanshū*, by Ton'a, was especially revered by Nijō poets in the Tokugawa period.]

Saitō Mokichi summed up Kageki's poetry: "He was, after all, a worshiper of *Kokinshū*, and Tsurayuki was his ideal poet. His own poetry consequently rarely went beyond that domain, but his nervous system had a kind of delicacy that was set a-tremble by nature. This was where he showed originality and freshness."[33] A few examples will suggest the typical tone and subject matter of Kageki's poetry.

COLD MOON

teru tsuki no	It feels as if light
kage no chirikuru	From the shining moon
kokochi shite	Is pouring down on me;
yoru yuku sode ni	How the snow piles on my sleeves
tamaru yuki ka na	As I walk along tonight![34]

The poet's momentary misapprehension that the flakes of snow, catching the moonlight as they fall, are flakes of moonlight gathering on his sleeve is at once poetic and believable as an experience; but it suggests the many poems in the *Kokinshū* professing inability to distinguish moonlight and snow (or mountains and clouds). Even Saitō Mokichi grudgingly admitted the beauty of this poem, its naturalness and freshness, but he refused to accept it as the product of a direct, powerful inspiration; he believed it was nature seen through the filter of *Kokinshū* poetry, a weakness not only of this poem but of most by Kageki.

ON HEARING A NIGHTINGALE ON THE BARRIER ROAD

futatabi wa	I am sure that never
koeji to omou	Will I pass this way again:
Michinoku no	In Michinoku,
Iwade no seki ni	At the barrier of Iwade,
uguisu no naku	The nightingales are singing.[35]

There are obvious overtones of Saigyō's famous waka on Saya no Nakayama, but the poem captures the haunting beauty of a moment so beautiful the poet knows it can never recur.

AUTUMN EVENING ON THE BRIDGE

akikaze no	On an evening
samuki yūbe ni	When the autumn wind was cold,
Tsu no kuni no	I made my way across

Sahie no hashi wo	The lonely bridge of Sahie
watarikeru ka na	In the province of Tsu.[36]

This poem is said to have impressed the emperor Kōkaku so profoundly that with his dying breath he commanded that Kageki be given court rank. Although the effect depends on the overtones of the place name Sahie, which suggests *hie*, cold, and *sabi*, loneliness, the poem surely ranks among Kageki's masterpieces.

imo to idete	The spring rain falls,
wakana tsuminishi	And I remember with yearning
Okazaki no	Okazaki and the fence
kakine koishiki	Where I went with my sweetheart
harusame zo furu	And gathered the young shoots.[37]

The poem is about Kageki's wife, who died in 1820. They lived together in the Okazaki section of Kyoto, and he remembers the past with yearning. The language is simple, and the mention of the spring rain falling gives the poem a delicate, nostalgic beauty.

Almost any poem in *Keien Isshi* gives the same pleasure as the ones quoted above: beautiful language, skillfully handled, that presents a touching, evocative scene. But having read Kageki's poetic criticism, one expects more. His poems, though elegantly phrased, are honest, yet the truth they reveal can surely have been only a small part of his life. And even though the language is unaffected, it was hardly the language Kageki employed in daily life; it gives less an impression of immediacy than of gracefulness. Despite his insistence that poetry must be the reflection of personal experience, his poem on the nightingale singing on the barrier road suggests less a cry of wonder than the continuation of a long poetic tradition. The revolution in modern Japanese poetry that began about 1895 would start from a rejection of Kageki; to that degree he seemed the pillar of the Tokugawa-period waka. The attacks by Masaoka Shiki and the others were successful, and Kageki and his school were discredited, but his importance, especially as a critic, can surely not be denied.

RYŌKAN (1758–1831)

The priest Ryōkan is remembered today with great affection, more as a lovable man who played with children than as a poet. He is sometimes thought of as a simple, even untutored country priest, but in fact he was born into a distinguished land-owning family in Echigo province. His father, a fairly well-known haikai poet who preferred literature to the family business, committed suicide in 1795, perhaps because his activities on behalf of a restoration of imperial authority had aroused suspicion. This family background should suggest that Ryōkan was far more complex a man than is popularly supposed.

Ryōkan received a good education from a leading Confucian scholar of the region, learning Chinese well enough to write *kanshi* (poems in Chinese) with exceptional skill.[38] In 1779, at the age of twenty-one, he took orders as a Buddhist monk of the Sōtō Zen sect. There are large gaps in our knowledge of his career, but a particularly fruitful period of his activities as a poet began about 1804, when he moved to a small temple on Kugamiyama, a mountain northwest of the Echigo plain. He remained there until about 1816, studying the *Manyōshū* and the poetry of Han Shan, the dominating influences on his waka and kanshi respectively. In 1826 he was given lodgings in the house of a rich farmer, where he met a young nun named Teishin, the daughter of a samurai of the Nagaoka clan, aged twenty-eight at the time. She served him until his death, and after his death compiled *Hachisu no Tsuyu* (Dew on the Lotus, 1835), an anthology of some 110 of Ryōkan's verses, together with a few of her own.

Although Ryōkan had virtually no contact either with the court poets in Kyoto or with the followers of Mabuchi in Edo, he reveals in style and language how deeply he was influenced by his study of the *Manyōshū*. He apparently was less interested in Hitomaro, Akahito, and the other major poets, the objects of special attention by Mabuchi and his school, than in the lesser poets represented in volumes 7, 10, 11, and 12.[39] One of the few anecdotes of a purely literary nature related about Ryōkan consisted of this question-and-answer exchange with a disciple:

> I asked what book I should read in order to study poetry. My teacher replied, "You should study *Manyō*." I said, "I can't

make any sense of *Manyō*." My teacher said, "Whatever you can understand is enough." He also said at the time, "The *Kokin* is still of value, but the poetry after *Kokin* is not worth studying."[40]

Ryōkan's indebtedness to the *Manyōshū* did not preclude the composition of occasional verses in the *Kokinshū* manner, and his poems are dotted with archaisms, including *makurakotoba* (pillow words) such as *ashibiki no* for mountains, etc. It may be wondered why Ryōkan used such language in poetry intended to describe his personal experiences. It definitely was not because he wished to seem like a professional poet. The same disciple recorded: "My teacher disliked the calligraphy of calligraphers, the poetry of poets, and writing poems on assigned topics." Yet his verses are anything but the spontaneous cries of a humble priest; they are the product of serious self-study of the *Manyōshū*. Eventually Ryōkan was able to employ the old language naturally, as a part of his personal idiom, but the question remains why he resorted to the poetic devices of a thousand years earlier. Perhaps he felt a need to join his verses to the roots of Japanese poetic tradition, or perhaps he even felt something of the original magic behind a makurakotoba.

The following two waka, like dozens of others by Ryōkan, begin with the *ashibiki no*, "foot-dragging," a makurakotoba used as an epithet for mountains:

ashibiki no	A moonlit evening
kono yamazato no	In this village in the mountains,
yūzukuyo	So weary to cross—
honoka ni miru wa	What I faintly discern
ume no hana ka mo	Are plum blossoms, I am sure![41]

This poem not only has the makurakotoba but the archaic, redundant expression *yūzukuyo* (a night of evening moon), and the final exclamatory *ka mo* associated with *Manyōshū*. A similar poem runs:

ashibiki no	A moonlit evening—
katayama kage no	On one side is a mountain,
yūzukuyo	So weary to cross;
honoka ni miyuru	In its shadow, faintly visible,
yamanashi no hana	Blossoms of the mountain pear.[42]

Ryōkan is universally acclaimed for his sincerity and deep feelings, but such poems as these seem pretty rather than deeply felt, and the overtones of their archaisms, though praised by scholars, may elude the modern reader. This is especially true of a poem like the following, acclaimed a masterpiece:

muragimo no	What joy in my heart
kokoro tanoshi mo	On a day in spring
haru no hi ni	When I see the birds
tori no muragari	Cluster and play![43]
asobu wo mireba	

The problem begins with the opening line, the makurakotoba modifying *kokoro* (mind, or heart); *muragimo* meant originally "the internal organs," a term hard to fit into a translation. Even more disappointing is the content of the verse, which seems to be no more than, "It makes me happy to see birds cluster and play." There is nothing wrong with the sentiment, but it hardly seems memorable. Yet Saitō Mokichi wrote the following about this poem:

> One can say that this is the pinnacle of Ryōkan's poetry. The makurakotoba *muragimo* is definitely not useless; if he had used instead another word that had a full meaning, it would surely have encumbered the poem. When he speaks of "birds clustering" and "playing," he creates a distinctive picture with the barest of means, and the tightness of "on a day in spring" reveals a truly unusual talent. . . . If we examine the poem carefully, we can feel a rhythm and elegiac melody that have much in common with the Buddhist classics and hymns (*wasan*). There is no harm in noting correspondences between this poem and those in the *Ryōjin Hishō*, but Ryōkan had probably not seen *Ryōjin Hishō*, so there can be no connection. This poem can be taken as a welling up of the emotions that permeated him as a priest. I believe that in the future a time will surely come when Ryōkan's waka will be appreciated by Europeans and Chinese, and that is why I have discussed this poem in such detail.[44]

The Western critic can only listen in respectful silence. Despite what we are constantly told, much poetry is in fact communicable in translation; but here is an instance when the translation obviously fails to convey what a Japanese senses in this poem. I must confess that even in the original this does not impress me as a good poem.

More appealing to a Western reader are those poems that tell us something specific about Ryōkan. He wrote this poem on a portrait of himself:

yo no naka ni	You mustn't suppose
majiranu to ni wa	I never mingle in the world
aranedomo	Of humankind—
hitori asobi zo	It's simply that I prefer
ware wa masarekeru	To enjoy myself alone.[45]

He wrote the next poem on Mount Kōya (called here Takano, an alternate reading of the characters) when he went to pray for his father:

Ki no kuni no	At an old temple
Takano no oku no	In the depths of Takano
furudera ni	In the province of Ki,
sugi no shizuku wo	I spent the night listening
kiki akashitsutsu	To raindrops through the cedars.[46]

Another poem bears the title "Having Been in a Sickbed for a Long Time":

uzumibi ni	I stretch out my legs
ashi sashikubete	And warm them in the embers,
fuseredomo	But as I lie here
koyoi no samusa	The cold of this night
hara ni tōrinu	Stabs the pit of my stomach.[47]

Ryōkan is known popularly for his love of violets, for his fondness for the annual Bon dances, and for his playing with children. He especially enjoyed bouncing a ball, and one poem consists mainly of his counting from one to ten and starting again as he bounces a ball. All of this is endearing, but Ryōkan's poetry seems to belong to Japan rather than to the world.

ŌKUMA KOTOMICHI (1798–1868)

The writing of poetry in Japan was traditionally the activity of men working within a society of poets. Secrets of the art were transmitted directly from teacher to pupil, and there were frequent meetings of fellow disciples and of poets belonging to opposing schools. This was true especially at the imperial court, for many centuries the heart of all poetry-making, but as other centers of cultural activity were created in the provinces by local potentates during the Muromachi period, poets naturally formed groups. Because the vocabulary and subject matter of their poetry were determined by a preferred classical anthology, generally the *Kokinshū*, local poets rarely displayed individuality or any distinctive regional flavor. But in the late Tokugawa period, with the growing insistence on the necessity for poets to describe their own emotions in their own language, we find the most interesting waka poetry tended to be produced not in Kyoto or Edo but in remote parts of the country. Ryōkan hardly ever left his native Echigo, and was never in correspondence with the famous poets of his day, even those whose admiration of the *Manyōshū* closely resembled his own. His poetry was hardly known in his lifetime and only in the twentieth century became famous.

Ōkuma Kotomichi, perhaps the most enjoyable poet of the late Tokugawa period, came from Fukuoka on the island of Kyushu. Although he spent ten years in Osaka late in life, his main period of creative activity occurred while he lived in Kyushu, completely out of touch with the main poetry-making societies of the day. His views on poetry were undoubtedly influenced by the writings of Kagawa Kageki, but they otherwise shared the same impulse toward self-expression found in all the good poets of the day, regardless of where they lived. Although many of his poems are commonplace, hardly distinguishable from the competent hackwork of the court poets of the preceding thousand years, he also wrote poems of an arresting freshness and originality that earned him a place in the history of the waka.

Kotomichi was born in Fukuoka in 1798, the distant descendant of a court noble who had been exiled to Kyushu. His family had been distinguished for generations for its scholarship. His father, though a merchant, had literary tastes and wrote waka of some distinction. Kotomichi studied waka and calligraphy as a young man, and for a time studied Chinese poetry with the famous scholar Hirose Tansō (1782–1856). Kotomichi seems to have devoted himself entirely to his poetry, to the neglect of his family; his wife died young, in 1843, apparently the victim of her husband's indifference to creature comforts. But nothing seems to have swerved Kotomichi from his study of waka. He began to acquire a local reputation while in his late forties, and his disciples steadily grew more numerous.

Kotomichi's first grandson was born in 1849, a period of extraordinary creativity when Kotomichi was writing a minimum of one hundred waka a day. He doted on this grandson, as he did on all small things: his poems are about ants, snails, wrens, crabs, mosquito wrigglers, and other tiny animals and plants.

In 1857, when he was fifty-nine, Kotomichi went to Osaka, where he met the leading scholars, and made some disciples. Apparently this journey was motivated by a desire to extend his fame nationally, and in particular by his hopes of publishing in Osaka a collection of his poetry. In 1863 a selection made by himself of his best verses was published under the title *Sōkeishū* (Collection of a Grass Path). It seems to have attracted very little attention in its day, and was completely forgotten until 1898 when the scholar of Japanese literature Sasaki Nobutsuna found it by chance in a Tokyo second-hand bookshop, and brought it to the attention of the world.

Kotomichi returned to Fukuoka in 1867, in response to the urgent appeals of his Kyushu disciples, and died there in the following year.

Kotomichi's failure to attract wide attention during his lifetime undoubtedly originated in the very qualities that we admire most today—his unconventionality, freedom from the restraints of a school, and his readiness to describe the most unpoetic subjects in a form which, unlike haikai, had always been associated with beauty. His views on poetry are found chiefly in the essay *Hitorigochi* (Talking to Myself), apparently written in 1844. Although badly organized and disjointed in expression, it is full of striking opinions. It begins with an attack on conventional poetry, which he called "puppet poetry" (*deku uta*):

> There is something which I have for the moment called "puppet poems." They are soulless, and belong to the past, both in form and in meaning. Even if a man wrote one thousand or ten thousand such poems, it would be like trying to dip water with an open-work basket. Few poems written by people today do not leak. How many years will it take before

these puppets acquire a soul? I have carefully examined the poems written by men in the country; most of them end their days as puppets.

The next passage is not directly related, but it implies a contrast between "puppet poems" and those written on the basis of direct, immediate experience:

> The masters of the past are my teachers, but they are not myself. I am a person of the Tempō era, not a man of old. If I were indiscriminately to ape the men of old, I might forget that I am something-hachi or something-bei.[48] The surface meaning might suggest the grandeur of a minister of state, and my poems would surely look impressive, but they would be like merchants in noblemen's attire. It would be an act of pure imitation, like a performance of Kabuki.
>
> I once advised a certain poet, "Imitation is easy. Even a Kabuki actor can pretend he is Sugawara no Michizane. But if a man really wanted to *be* like Sugawara no Michizane, should he behave like an actor? And if a man wanted to write poems truly like the ancient ones, should he do it as a matter of virtuosity? If a man wishes to be good he must begin with his heart. If he wishes to write his own poetry, using his heart as the seed, he will of course use common thoughts and words, but he will not yet be able to suggest poetic style. With the passage of time he will gradually, bit by bit, come closer to the men of old. I will consider him close to the men of old if he does not resemble them in the least, and remote from the men of old if he resembles them too much.[49]

Mention of the human heart as the seed of poetry of course immediately suggests the preface to the *Kokinshū*: this, together with the writings of Kageki, seem to have been the point of departure for Kotomichi. His insistence on being a man of the Tempō era (1830–43) had already been antedated by Kageki's remark: "A man of the Bunka era should write in the Bunka style,"[50] and sometimes Kotomichi even quoted Kageki, especially his rejection of the intellectualizing of poetry.

Kotomichi's poetry does not always live up to his prescriptions, but he was more successful than Kageki in this respect. Again and again we are struck in reading his poems by their contemporary quality. He was by no means free of the conventional poetic diction, but Kageki would not have attempted to write about the humble, almost insignificant sights that catch Kotomichi's attention. His poetry is light and generally cheerful. Very few poems are about abstract or intellectual subjects, and almost none displays interest in the crises of his times. Kotomichi proclaimed himself to be a man of the Tempō era, but his only concerns were what of life he could observe in his house and garden, not the political and other disasters of the times.

Kotomichi's poetry attracts us because of its individuality. His rejection of the classic ideals in favor of individual expression may have been influenced by readings in the eighteenth-century Chinese poet Yüan Mei, whose discussion of poetry *Sui-Yüan Shih Hua* was widely read at the time by scholars of Chinese literature like Hirose Tansō. But, as we have seen, an insistence on individuality was common to all the outstanding poets of the period.

Sometimes this individuality took on the coloration of self-caricature:

LAMENTING THE WORLD

wa ga mi koso	As far as I'm concerned,
nani to mo omowane	It doesn't bother me a bit,
me kodomo no	But when my wife and kids
ushi chō nabe ni	Complain how hard things are,
uki kono yo ka na	It really seems a hard life.[51]

Presumably this was written during the period when Kotomichi was neglecting his family in favor of his unswerving pursuit of poetry. Another poem, also self-satirical, is more humorous:

OLD AGE

nanigoto mo	It doesn't matter what—
kikoe higamete	I never get anything straight;
oi no mi no	The only sure thing
koto tashika naru	Is that I have become old,
omowaku mo nashi	Without an idea of my own.[52]

His poems on children are among his best.

RETURNING GEESE

kaeru kari	The returning geese
kaerite haru mo	Have returned and even the spring
sabishiki ni	Has become lonely;
warawa no hirou	A boy in the rice paddy
oda no kobore hane	Picks up a fallen feather.[53]

kotae suru	It is so much fun
koe omoshiromi	To hear his voice answer him
yamabiko wo	The boy shouts and shouts
kagiri mo nashi ni	Endlessly summoning
yobu warawa ka na	The echo from the mountains.[54]

His poverty also figures in many of Kotomichi's poems, but neither with bitterness nor as part of the pose of the otherworldly poet living in uncorrupted poverty.

SWEEPING THE GROUNDS OF A POVERTY-STRICKEN HOUSE

mazushikute	In this house where I have lived
toshi furu kado wa	In poverty all these years
waza mo nashi	There is nothing to do;
haraishi niwa wo	I sweep the garden again,
mata haraitsutsu	The garden I have already swept.[55]

PAINTINGS

yo no naka ni	I'm the kind of man
wa ga mono nashi no	With nothing I can call my own
mi naredomo	In all this wide world;
e ni utsushite zo	But I have seas and mountains,
motaru umi yama	The ones shown in my pictures.[56]

His pleasures included not only writing poetry but drink, as we know from numerous poems, but the virtual absence of any love poetry suggests that his rather cross-grained temper did not appeal to women. He seems in any case to have preferred being alone when not in the company of infants.

LOOKING ALONE AT THE MOON

tsudoi shite	Do you need a crowd
mono sawagashiku	Making a great commotion
medamashi ya	To admire the moon?

hitotsu no tsuki wa	There's only one moon in the sky—
hitori koso mime	It should be seen by oneself.[57]

A rare philosophical poem suggests that, despite the financial hardships and the public indifference Kotomichi had suffered, he considered himself to be a happy man:

THINKING OF THE FUTURE LIFE

shina takaki	I have no desire
koto mo negawazu	For loftiness of rank;
mata no yo wa	In the world to come
mata wa ga mi ni zo	I hope I can come back again
narite kinamashi	Exactly as myself.[58]

Kotomichi's poems have intelligence, humor, compassion, and charm, but little passion. This lack alone makes of him an interesting second-rate poet rather than a master. His poetry is refreshing, but it suggests also the limits of the Tokugawa waka.

TACHIBANA AKEMI (1812–68)

The last important poet of the Tokugawa waka was Tachibana Akemi. He was born in 1812, the eldest son of a prosperous paper merchant in Fukui. The family believed it was descended from the ancient statesman Tachibana no Moroe, and Akemi, as the thirty-ninth descendant, took the surname Tachibana. He grew up in an unhappy household, marked by the early deaths of his parents, and as a young man went to a local Nichiren temple intending to become a priest. He changed his mind, but the poetic training he received at the temple helped to determine his career.

In 1833 Akemi went to Kyoto and for several months studied with a disciple of Rai Sanyō; his burning feelings of loyalty to the imperial family may have germinated at this time. He returned to Fukui and pursued the family business, but his heart was still set on becoming a scholar and poet. In 1844 he became a pupil of Tanaka Ōhide, a disciple of Motoori Norinaga who lived nearby. Akemi's kokugaku studies strengthened both his patriotic and poetic tastes. In 1846, after the birth of his eldest son, Akemi turned over the family business to his half-brother and went to live in a retreat, devoting himself solely to poetry, both his own works and the study of the *Manyōshū*. He lived in poverty, but his humble circumstances were to provide him with the material for some of his most endearing poems, those describing the little pleasures of a poor scholar's life.

Akemi's first noteworthy sequence of poems was written in 1860. A friend, Tomita Iyahiko (1811–77), a bakufu official and fellow disciple of Tanaka Ōhide, was ordered by the government to take charge of a newly opened silver mine in Hida province, and Akemi, after visiting him there in the spring, wrote eleven poems. Needless to say, the subject of the poems, a silver mine, was hardly envisaged by the orthodox poetic diction of *Kokinshū*; but Akemi may have been influenced by the *Manyōshū* poem celebrating the discovery of gold in Mutsu. The poems are a curious blend of graphic, realistic description and uncompromisingly archaic diction. One, for example, bears the headnote "Hito amata arite, kono waza mono shi oru tokoro mimeguri arikite" which, despite its archaic language, means merely "There were a great many people, and I walked around the excavation site." The poem runs:

hi no hikari	Inside a cavern
itaranu yama no	In the mountains where sunlight
hora no uchi ni	Never penetrates,
hi tomoshi irite	Lighting lanterns they go in
kane horiidasu	To dig out the precious metal.[59]

The next poem of the sequence is even more powerful, suggesting the world of Goya as much as Japan:

mahadaka no	Stark naked
onoko mureite	The men cluster together;
arakane no	Swinging great hammers,
marogari kudaku	They smash into fragments
tsuchi uchifurite	The lumps of unwrought metal.[60]

In 1861 Akemi went to worship at Ise, and took the opportunity to pay his respects at Motoori Norinaga's grave. He also visited Kyoto, where he worshiped the imperial palace and met various poets. His patriotic convictions are reflected in such poems as these two from his sequence *Solitary Pleasures*:

tanoshimi wa	It is a pleasure
kami no mikuni no	When, as a subject of
tami to shite	The land of the gods,
kami no oshie wo	I ponder deeply
fukaku omou toki	The teachings of the gods.

tanoshimi wa	It is a pleasure
emishi yorokobu	In these days of delight
yo no naka ni	In all things foreign,
mikuni wasurenu	I come across a man who
hito wo miru toki	Does not forget the divine land.[61]

Akemi's poetry gradually became known within the fief, and in 1865 the daimyo of Echizen paid a visit to Akemi's retreat. Two years later he granted Akemi a stipend. The news of the restoration of imperial power in 1867 understandably delighted Akemi, but he died in the following year, less than a month before the era name was officially changed to Meiji.

Akemi's major collection of poetry, *Shinobunoya Kashū*, was published in 1878 by his son, but his first major recognition as a poet came about thanks to the efforts of Masaoka Shiki, who contrasted Akemi's blunt, manly poetry with the refinement of Kagawa Kageki. In many ways his poetry resembles Kotomichi's, though there was no connection between them. Both men chose to write about the ordinary events of life, rather than the conventionally admired "poetic" themes; both led lives of self-imposed poverty and enjoyed little recognition beyond their immediate neighborhood. But Akemi's poetry has a coarseness foreign to Kotomichi; his first collection was called not "The Grass Path" but "The Diaper Collection" (*Mutsukigusa*), and there are many other examples of his crude humor. Unlike Kotomichi, too, he was obviously interested in women, and wrote some outspoken poems about his relations:

SNOW AT A BROTHEL

miwa no yuki	Young ladies
tawaremarogasu	Having fun rolling snowballs,
otomedomo	With the garden snow,
sono te wa tare ni	Who will warm for you
nukumesasuran	Your cold little hands?[62]

LOOKING AT SNOW WITH A WOMAN

imo to ware	My sweetheart and I,
negao narabete	Sleepy face side by side,
oshidori no	Look out at the pond
ukiiru ike no	Covered with snow and watch
yuki wo miru kana	The mandarin ducks floating.[63]

Akemi's sense of humor, unlike Kotomichi's, is not directed at the "lovable" little things of nature but, rather, at pretension, vulgarity, and the conventional kinds of poetry.

itsuwari no	Don't write clever poems
takumi wo iu na	Compounded of falsehoods—
makoto dani	As long as they excel
sugureba uta wa	In sincerity, your poems
yasukaran mono	Will be easy to compose.[64]

IN JEST

wa go uta wo	Tonight, at my window,
yorokobi namida	I hear the weeping voices
kobosuran	Of devils—no doubt
oni no naku koe	They are shedding tears of joy
suru yoru no mado	To hear my poetry.[65]

This oblique reference to the statement in the preface of the *Kokinshū* that poetry can move even gods and demons is echoed by others in the sequence.

hito kusaki	Mine are not poems
hito ni kikasuru	For the ears of people smelling
uta narazu	Of humankind,
oni ni yo fukete	But if a devil would come
koba tsuge mo sen	Late one night, I'd tell him all.[66]

tadabito no	My poems will not enter
mimi ni hairaji	The ears of ordinary men;
ame tsuchi no	They are intended
kokoro wo tae ni	To transmit, with mystery,
morasu wa ga uta	The heart of heaven and earth.[67]

Other sequences of waka are conspicuously patriotic, especially one with the general title "Rendering Thanks to Our Country with Sincere Hearts." The first of this sequence runs:

masurao ga	A man of Yamato,
mikado omoi no	Thinking, in true sincerity,
mamegokoro	Of the imperial court,
me wo chi ni somete	His eyes, bloodshot with staring,
yakiba misumasu	Readies his blade for action.[68]

The telltale word *masurao*, rendered here as "man of Yamato," suggests the influence of the *Manyōshū*. Akemi, though not in direct contact with the School of Mabuchi, as a patriot and Shinto believer inevitably turned to the *Manyōshū*. His poems, however, were not paralyzed by this influence, which was usually spiritual rather than lexical.

Akemi's best poems are undoubtedly the sequence *Solitary Pleasures*. The waka does not lend itself easily to patriotic sentiments, and Akemi's righteous indignation, expressed in many verses, seems constricted and inadequate. But in his descriptions of ordinary life he attains a kind of simplicity and sincerity closer to *Manyōshū* ideals than his more overtly archaic poems.

One other late Tokugawa period poet, like Akemi a patriot and admirer of the *Manyōshū*, deserves some attention. Hiraga Motoyoshi (1799–1865), a samurai of Okayama, studied the *Manyōshū* and devoted himself to kokugaku. His poetry is larded with archaisms, including makurakotoba, and is often almost unintelligible in its obscure references. (Saitō Mokichi expressed an inability to understand Motoyoshi's poetry without a commentary.[69]) His poetry was discovered by Masaoka Shiki, who marveled at Motoyoshi's unique devotion to the *Manyōshū* at a time when the other Okayama poets were all under Kageki's influence. Some poems still attract us today:

kiyotaki wo	When I arrive and see
wa ga mi ni kureba	The clear cascades
ashibiki no	Among the trees of the mountain
yama no ki goto ni	So difficult to cross,
semi zo naku naru	The locusts are singing.[70]

But Motoyoshi's most typical poetry is of the martial, patriotic kind. One bears the headnote:

> The first day of the first month of the seventh year of Kaei [1854]. This spring day, my little girls, hearing reports that

bandits from America in the West have arrived, were in a dither.

emishira wo	The spring has come
uchitairagete	When, raising our voices
kachitoki no	In a shout of triumph,
koe agesomen	We will first celebrate
haru wa kinikeri	The destruction of the barbarians.[71]

This poem, reflecting Motoyoshi's distrust of the Americans, is typical of his patriotic fulminations. It proves that it was technically possible to describe even such sentiments in a waka, but we must surely be struck by the inappropriateness of the form. The waka had been given contemporary content at last, after years of urging by the poets, but it lost everything else. By the end of the Tokugawa period all the traditional qualities of the waka—tone, overtones, evocation of mood—had been sacrificed in the interests of sincere expression. The vocabulary of a poet like Motoyoshi remained archaic, but this was a last gesture in the direction of poetry.

It is idle to speculate what might have happened to the waka if Western influence had not made itself felt at this point. Perhaps still another new wave of *Kokinshū* influence would have brought it back to its traditional functions. But more likely, impatience with the limitations of the old classical form would have destroyed the last vestiges of its beauty and glory.

NOTES

1. Quoted in Keene, *Modern Japanese Poetry*, p. 14.
2. Kagawa Kanematsu, "Ozawa Roan," p. 76.
3. Takagi Ichinosuke and Hisamatsu Sen'ichi, *Kinsei Waka Shū*, p. 282.
4. *Ibid.*
5. *Ibid.*
6. Kagawa, p. 66.
7. *Ibid.*, p. 64.
8. *Chirihiji* (1790), quoted in Kagawa, p. 63.
9. *Ibid.*, p. 65.
10. *Wakumon* (1790), quoted in Kagawa, p. 70.
11. Quoted in Kagawa, p. 68.
12. Takagi and Hisamatsu, p. 285.

13. *Ibid.*, p. 286.
14. See Teruoka Yasutaka and Gunji Masakatsu, *Edo Shimin Bungaku no Kaika*, p. 244.
15. *Ibid.*, p. 245.
16. Kagawa, p. 79.
17. Takagi and Hisamatsu, p. 368.
18. Saitō Mokichi, *Kinsei Kajin Hyōden*, p. 67.
19. Kuroiwa Ichirō, "Kagawa Kageki," pp. 97–98.
20. *Ibid.*, p. 102.
21. Teruoka and Gunji, p. 246.
22. Kuroiwa, p. 99.
23. Nakamura Yukihiko, *Kinsei Bungakuron Shū*, p. 24.
24. Kuroiwa, p. 105.
25. Nakamura, p. 151.
26. Quoted in Kuroiwa, p. 108.
27. Nakamura, p. 151.
28. *Ibid.*
29. *Ibid.*, p. 145.
30. *Ibid.*, p. 147.
31. *Ibid.*, pp. 152–53.
32. See Teruoka and Gunji, p. 246.
33. Saitō, p. 55.
34. Takagi and Hisamatsu, p. 349.
35. Kuroiwa, p. 142.
36. Takagi and Hisamatsu, p. 385.
37. *Ibid.*, p. 353.
38. Usami Kizōhachi, "Ryōkan," p. 149. See also Tōgō Toyoharu, *Ryōkan Shishū.*
39. Takagi and Hisamatsu, p. 15.
40. *Ibid.*
41. Usami, p. 165.
42. *Ibid.*; Saitō, p. 193.
43. Saitō, p. 187.
44. *Ibid.*, pp. 187–88.
45. Takagi and Hisamatsu, p. 189.
46. Usami, p. 193.
47. *Ibid.*, p. 188; Saitō, p. 209.
48. Names ending in *-hachi* or *-bei* were usually plebeian, like Kitahachi in *Hizakurige* or Chūbei in Chikamatsu's *Courier for Hell.* Kotomichi is saying, in other words, that if he pretends to be a poet like Teika he would forget his plebeian status.

49. Quoted in Ueda Hideo, "Ōkuma Kotomichi," pp. 296–97.
50. Quoted in Kuroiwa, p. 118.
51. Takagi and Hisamatsu, p. 503.
52. *Ibid.*, p. 485.
53. *Ibid.*, p. 460.
54. Ueda, p. 305.
55. Takagi and Hisamatsu, p. 511.
56. *Ibid.*, p. 486.
57. *Ibid.*, p. 489.
58. *Ibid.*, p. 503.
59. *Ibid.*, p. 406.
60. *Ibid.*
61. *Ibid.*, p. 432.
62. Yamazaki Toshio, "Tachibana Akemi," p. 239.
63. Takagi and Hisamatsu, p. 401.
64. Yamazaki, p. 248.
65. Takagi and Hisamatsu, p. 424.
66. *Ibid.*
67. *Ibid.*
68. *Ibid.*, p. 441.
69. Saitō, p. 79.
70. Teruoka and Gunji, p. 250.
71. Saitō, p. 111.

BIBLIOGRAPHY

Hisamatsu Sen'ichi and Sanekata Kiyoshi. *Kinsei no Kajin*. Tokyo: Kōbunkan, 1960.

Kagawa Kanematsu. "Ozawa Roan," in Hisamatsu and Sanekata, *op. cit.*

Keene, Donald. *Modern Japanese Poetry*. Ann Arbor: University of Michigan Press, 1964.

Kuroiwa Ichirō. "Kagawa Kageki," in Hisamatsu and Sanekata, *op. cit.*

Nakamura Yukihiko. *Kinsei Bungakuron Shū*, in Nihon Koten Bungaku Taikei series. Tokyo: Iwanami Shoten, 1966.

Saitō Mokichi. *Kinsei Kajin Hyōden*. Tokyo: Kaname Shobō, 1949.

Sasaki Nobutsuna (ed.). *Ōkuma Kotomichi Shū*. Tokyo: Kaizōsha, 1942.

Takagi Ichinosuke and Hisamatsu Sen'ichi. *Kinsei Waka Shū*, in Nihon Koten Bungaku Taikei series. Tokyo: Iwanami Shoten, 1966.

Teruoka Yasutaka and Gunji Masakatsu. *Edo Shimin Bungaku no Kaika*, in Nihon no Bungaku series. Tokyo: Shibundō, 1967.

Tōgō Toyoharu. *Ryōkan Shishū*. Tokyo: Sōgensha, 1962.

Ueda Hideo. "Ōkuma Kotomichi," in Hisamatsu and Sanekata, *op. cit.*

Usami Kizōhachi. "Ryōkan," in Hisamatsu and Sanekata, *op. cit.*

Uyehara, Yukuo and Marjorie Sinclair. *A Grass Path: Selected Poems from Sōkeishū by Kotomichi Ōkuma*. Honolulu: University of Hawaii Press, 1955.

Yamazaki Toshio. "Tachibana Akemi," in Hisamatsu and Sanekata, *op. cit.*

CHAPTER 21
WAKA POETRY
COMIC POETRY

Ever since the first ventures at renga composition poetry had served as a medium for communal social activity. The *uta-awase* (poem competitions) of the Heian period had also involved the participation of many persons in the creation of poetry, but they provided less the pleasure of cooperation than the excitement of rivalry. Renga, on the other hand, resembled the traditional football game called *kemari*, a joint effort to keep the ball in the air, rather than a competition to determine who can kick the ball farthest or fastest. The pleasure that Sōgi and his associates experienced when composing an extended renga sequence together was like that of an exalted conversation, the topic shifting slightly from man to man, according to his temperament and poetic sensibility.

We have seen that there existed from the beginnings of renga a humble form, comic in tone and therefore considered unworthy of being recorded. The rise of haikai no renga, the comic linked verse, brought this variety of renga to the fore again but, as so often in the history of Japanese literature, artistry usurped the place of earthy vigor, and (just as sarugaku gave way to Nō, or the puppet shows of the early Tokugawa period to Chikamatsu) haikai poetry was taken over by Bashō and his school. Comic verse was again assigned an inconspicuous place in the world of poetry.

Nevertheless, there was still a need for light verse, suitable for communal composition as an after-dinner entertainment. Although almost nothing remains of such verse, we know that gentlemen of leisure continued to turn out large quantities of impromptu compositions. But even this new style of comic verse, begun as a protest against hampering conventions, soon developed rules and experts. The Japanese seem never to have felt satisfied with any diversion until they had codified it and given it a pedigree.

Each form of serious poetry came to acquire its comic counterpart. The waka masters, even the dōjō poets, composed *kyōka* (mad waka); the haikai poets composed different forms of light verse known collectively as *zappai* (miscellaneous haikai); and the kanshi poets wrote *kyōshi* (mad Chinese poems). Sometimes such poetry was justified as practice for writing the serious variety of the particular poetic art, but more often it was merely a pleasant relaxation after a strenuous session of poeticizing, and no thought was given to excellence. Only two features were essential: that the verses be composed in the company of other poets, and that they be humorous, whether at the sophisticated level of parody or crudely obvious.

KYŌKA

The different forms of comic verse not only developed rules, standards, and even elaborate codes as time went on, depriving them of the fun of informal verse-making, but their authenticity as age-old forms was stressed. Kyōka, for example, was traced back to the comic verse in the *Manyōshū*, the haikai poems in the *Kokinshū*, and to various distinguished poets of the Kamakura period. Some of these claims were true. The priest Jakuren, we know from a work written before 1239,[1] excelled at kyōka, and there is other evidence that as far back as the Heian period comic poems were composed impromptu at parties to amuse the guests.[2] The oldest surviving collection of kyōka is *Hyakushu Kyōka* (Comic Verses on a Hundred Kinds of Liquor), compiled in the fourteenth century. The reputed author was the priest Gyōgetsubō (1265–1328), a grandson of Teika and son of Abutsu-ni, but this attribution is doubtful.[3] The poems, arranged in the conventional manner according to the four seasons and miscellaneous topics, display considerable technical skill, but the humor (at least by modern standards) is faint. Another early collection, *Mochisake Uta-awase* (Poem Competition on Rice Cakes and Saké), is attributed to the prime minister Nijō Yoshimoto (1320–88). It consists of ten pairs of comic poems on rice cakes and saké, together with the poet's comments; we can imagine that the harried prime minister might have enjoyed the momentary escape provided by such kyōka. The period of warfare also occasioned the compilation of *Mongrel Renga Collection* and other collections of humorous poetry and prose. A kind of desperate frivolity brought solace to men tormented by the unrest of their times.

The creation of the haikai style of poetry opened a channel for those who sought to describe the ordinary or humorous experiences of daily life. Kyōka, on the other hand, tended to be the diversion of upper-class poets. The collection compiled by the Zen priest Yūchōrō called *Ei Hyakushu Kyōka* (One Hundred Kyōka, 1589?) is typical of the rather pedantic humor of the kyōka composed at this time. An understanding of the meaning of a poem generally depends on a knowledge of the particular waka that is being parodied.[4]

Hosokawa Yūsai and his pupil Matsunaga Teitoku also indulged in this form of humorous composition. Although Teitoku was hardly proud of his skill at kyōka, considering it virtually beneath his attention, he published one hundred kyōka in 1636 under the title *Teitoku Kyōka Hyakushu* (One Hundred Kyōka by Teitoku). Teitoku's kyōka lack the sharpness or bite of true wit; they consist mainly of ponderous plays on words or else frivolous references to the classics. His kyōka on the *aoi*, or hollyhock, is typical:

fukabuka to	The dew that has formed
aoi no ue ni	Thickly, ever so thickly,
oku tsuyu ya	On the hollyhocks
miyasundokoro no	Must surely be the tears
namida naruran	Of Lady Rokujō.[5]

Reference is made in this verse to the hostility between Lady Rokujō (*miyasundokoro*) and Aoi (hollyhock), Genji's wife, in *The Tale of Genji*. Without a knowledge of the source (it was assumed that no educated person could be ignorant of the famous passage where Aoi's carriage jostles Rokujō's), the poem would be unintelligible. Even with this knowledge, it hardly provokes a smile.

Some of Teitoku's disciples were more attracted than he to the kyōka. Ishida Mitoku (1587–1666), easily surpassing his master, became the most successful of the early kyōka poets. His collection *Gokin Wa ga Shū* (My Collection of Poetry, 1648–52) has a title that parodies *Kokin Waka Shū*, and its preface follows Ki no Tsurayuki's almost word for word, deftly twisting the original meanings. Another disciple of Teitoku, Nakarai Bokuyō (1607–78), was a physician who eventually served the shogunate court in Edo. He was instrumental in promoting a taste for kyōka among upper-class samurai. His own collection *Bokuyō Kyōka Shū* (1682), published posthumously with illustrations by Hishikawa Moronobu, went through many editions,[6] but is hardly readable today; the humor consists mainly of puns and plays on words.

The first important collections of kyōka were published by the disciple of a disciple of Teitoku's, the Buddhist priest Seihaku-dō Gyōfū: *Kokin Ikyoku Shū* (Collection of Barbarian Songs Old and New, 1666), *Gosen Ikyoku Shū* (Later Collection of Barbarian Songs, 1672), and *Gin'yō Ika Shū* (Collection of Silver Leaves and Barbarian Songs, 1678). The first collection included kyōka from all periods, but the later two consisted of contemporary kyōka, mainly by poets close to the style of the compiler. These collections marked the emergence of kyōka as a popular verse form.[7]

The first professional kyōka poet, Nagata Teiryū (1654–1734), another "grandson disciple" of Teitoku, was the son of a prosperous Osaka cake-maker, and the elder brother of Ki no Kaion. Teiryū began publishing kyōka when only seventeen, gradually building up a reputation. His bakery was chosen in 1700 as the official purveyors to the imperial court in Kyoto,[8] and Teiryū profited by the opportunity to exchange kyōka with the nobles. He gained fame with one especially apt verse; when a Chinese-ink merchant from Nara presented the court with an unusually large stick of ink, Teiryū wrote these lines:

tsuki narade	Although not the moon,
kumo no ue made	It has risen so high it dwells
sumi*noboru*	Above the clouds;
kore wa ika naru	I wonder what reason
yuen *naruran*	There can be for this?[9]

The entire interest of this poem stems from the puns on *sumi* ("to dwell" and "Chinese ink") and on *yuen* ("reason" and "lamp black"). This display of wit so enchanted the court, even the emperor, that Teiryū adopted the name Yuensai (from *yuen*, lamp black). He soon gave up his cake business to devote his energies exclusively to kyōka, publishing his own verses and correcting those of other people.

Teiryū once defined kyōka as a poem composed while wearing a robe decorated with gold leaf that has been tied with a rope.[10] He meant that the basic material of a kyōka was the elegant poetry of the past (the robe decorated with gold leaf), but that it must be given a new twist by tying it together with the coarse rope of common speech or irreverent perceptions.

A typical example of Teiryū's kyōka pokes fun in a genteel manner at the conventional waka imagery:

chireba koso	It is precisely because
itodo sakura wa	The cherry blossoms scatter
medetakere	That we prize them so;
saredomo saredomo	That's true, I know, it's true,
sō ja keredomo	It's true all right, but still . . .[11]

The publication of Teiryū's anthology *Iezuto* (Souvenirs) in 1729 established kyōka as a recognized literary genre.

The Kamigata style of kyōka, associated with Teiryū, continued to be composed until the 1920s by poets who carefully preserved the faded charms of their chosen medium. Groups of kyōka poets, known as *ren*, would periodically gather to exchange poems, and from time to time they published collections illustrated by well-known artists. The various ren also made it a practice to send out New Year's greetings on illustrated woodblock sheets known as *surimono*, a minor but delightful branch of the ukiyo-e prints. The center of kyōka composition shifted to Edo about 1760, and the Kamigata kyōka was never again of literary consequence.

No direct connection existed between the Edo kyōka and the earlier kyōka; it developed as a quite distinct art. The founder was a kokugaku scholar named Uchiyama Gatei (1723–88), an important waka poet in his day who had a penchant for humorous verse. The group of younger poets he gathered around him created the Edo kyōka and gave it what literary merits it would possess. Most of these poets were of the samurai class, ranging in status from daimyos down to lowly foot soldiers, but a few cultivated townsmen also participated. The samurai status of the poets inevitably affected the nature of the movement: the Edo kyōka was surrounded by an air of gentlemanly detachment quite unlike the professionalism of Teiryū, and the participants could never permit their sense of humor to carry them into open expressions of disrespect. The government censors were alert to dangerous or immoral writings, but even if the writings were perfectly harmless, samurai might be forbidden to compose them if, for example, kyōka were considered a base poetry that did not accord with samurai dignity. Without the active participation of the fun-loving Edo townsmen, kyōka might have remained a polite literary diversion, rather than an effective medium for displaying wit.

The most important of Gatei's disciples was Ōta Nampo (1749–1823), known also as Yomo no Akara and as Shokusanjin. He came of the humblest samurai stock, and grew up in poverty, but his unusual abilities attracted Gatei's attention. Nampo studied Chinese poetry and prose composition with the noted scholar Matsuzaki Kankai (1725–75) and, like most well-educated men of the period, he had an excellent knowledge of Chinese literature, both classical and modern. His first published work appeared in 1766, when he was seventeen; it was a classification of the vocabulary used in Ming poetry.[12] Although Nampo respected Kankai and his traditional kind of Chinese learning, he was drawn irresistibly to comic writing. In 1767 he published *Neboke Sensei Bunshū* (Essays of Teacher Sleepy-head), with a preface by Hiraga Gennai, a friend of the young Nampo. This collection was written in classical Chinese, but it captured exactly the excitement of contemporary Edo, as seen through the eyes of a young man not yet twenty. Nampo's satirical comments on such subjects as the poverty of the samurai, who were theoretically a privileged class, won the book great popularity and started a craze for comic poems in Chinese. Nampo ranks with Hatanaka Dōmyaku of Kyoto as a master of the kyōshi.

Despite his exceptional ability in Chinese, Nampo was attracted even more strongly by the kyōka. His kyōka first appeared in the collection *Meiwa Jūgoban Kyōka-awase* (Fifteen Pairs of Competing Kyōka of the Meiwa Era, 1770), edited by Uchiyama Gatei and the waka poet Hagiwara Sōko. Other contributors included Karagoromo Kisshū (1749–89), for a time the leading kyōka poet, and Hezutsu Tōsaku (1726–89), a learned tobacconist who was a close friend of Nampo's.

These kyōka poets soon shifted their activities from Gatei's house to Kisshū's, and meetings became more frequent. Kisshū, rejecting the style of Teiryū and his disciples, praised the refined and elegant humor of the early kyōka poets, especially Hosokawa Yūsai and Ishida Mitoku. He began holding kyōka sessions at his house in 1769. The participants at first were few, but their ranks gradually grew. About 1772 the important kyōka poet Akera Kankō (1740–1800) joined the group. Kankō and Nampo both wrote kyōka that were more openly humorous than Kisshū's, and before long they outstripped his popularity. The three men eventually each led a ren, attracting both samurai and chōnin poets.

The popularity of the kyōka by this time surpassed that of any other comic verse, but exceedingly few collections were published. The participants still clung to the belief that kyōka should be composed in fun, with no thought to preservation.[13] Kisshū nevertheless decided about 1780 to prepare a collection for publication, ushering in the great period of kyōka. During most of the decade 1780–90 the leading political figure was Tanuma

Okitsugu. His regime was characterized by corruption and administrative laxity, but somehow it fostered literary activity. Some scholars have suggested that poets turned away in disgust from the society around them and wrote comic verse as the sole outlet for their impotent rage. Perhaps this is true. However, when compared with the severe policies of Matsudaira Sadanobu, Tanuma's successor, the laxity of Tanuma was conducive to the arts, and the kyōka poets may have looked on their times more with pleasure than with disgust. Their fascination with trivialities, shared by the authors of the kibyōshi and sharebon, was clearly the result of a disinclination or inability to face the world seriously. Even under the worst of the censorship it should have been possible to describe the pleasures and griefs of the individual, if not of the society, but in the kyōka we can rarely detect a personal note, a voice that betrays real feelings under the cover of a jesting surface. We are apt to form the impression that the kyōka poets lacked subjects of their own; that was why they so often resorted to parody. This was true particularly of Kisshū. He parodied many famous waka, including this one by Saigyō:

kokoro naki	This sadness would be
mi ni mo aware wa	Apparent even to the man
shirarekeri	Devoid of feelings;
shigi tatsu sawa no	Night in autumn over
aki no yūgure	A marsh where a snipe rises.

Kisshū's parody went:

sai mo naki	This sadness would be
zen ni aware wa	Apparent even on a tray
shirarekeri	Devoid of vegetables:
shigiyaki nasu no	Night in autumn over
aki no yūgure	Eggplant fried snipe-style.[14]

Kisshū published his collection *Kyōka Wakana Shū* (Kyōka Seedlings) in the first month of 1783, with prefaces by himself and his old teacher, Gatei. He included poems by Nampo and Kankō, but very few, considering their importance. The collection *Manzai Kyōka Shū* (Kyōka of a Myriad Years), compiled by Nampo, appeared in the same month. Unlike Kisshū's uninspiringly edited collection, *Manzai Kyōka Shū*, a parody of

Senzai Waka Shū, was cleverly arranged by categories that parallel exactly the old anthology. The authors included "old masters" of kyōka, from Gyōgetsubō and Yūchōrō down to recent times, and a generous selection of over two hundred contemporary poets. In the competition between the two rival anthologies Nampo's scored so conspicuous a triumph that Kisshū was silenced for some years; the promised sequel to his *Kyōka Wakana Shū* never appeared.[15]

The great success of *Manzai Kyōka Shū* initiated the craze for kyōka that swept Edo. Writers of kibyōshi, ukiyo-e artists, Kabuki actors, courtesans—almost every kind of entertainer tried to write kyōka, and different ren, some consisting of samurai and some of chōnin, flourished. Many collections were published, illustrated by the leading artists. Ōta Nampo became a literary celebrity. In 1783, in honor of his mother's sixtieth birthday, Nampo sent out invitations to a birthday party, specifying that everyone should bring his own lunch.[16] Over 180 poets appeared anyway, with presents of kyōka and comic prose. The sales of *Manzai Kyōka Shū* encouraged the editors to begin work immediately on a sequel, *Toku Waka Go Manzai Shū*, published in 1785. In the same year Akera Kankō published the collection *Kokon Baka Shū* (Collection of Fools Ancient and Modern). He and Nampo had similar literary tastes, but Kankō's sense of humor was somewhat earthier. Publication of these Edo collections completed the eclipse of the Kamigata school.

The success of the Nampo-Kankō style of kyōka was more than they had bargained for; they discovered that poets who lacked the background in the waka that Kisshū had insisted on were following in their path, and writing not comic waka but doggerel. At this juncture, in 1786, Tanuma Okitsugu fell from power, and one of Nampo's patrons, a high-ranking official and henchman of Tanuma's, was executed for his outrages under the fallen regime. Nampo, who had been leading a rather dissolute life, became apprehensive, fearing he might be implicated in his patron's crimes, and decided to give up kyōka, an avocation that poorly befitted a samurai. This decision occurred in 1787, and although Nampo in later years wrote kyōka under the name Shokusanjin, he never again associated with the main body of kyōka poets or formed a group of his own. Instead, he took the required examinations in the Confucian classics, passed with highest honors, and eventually was rewarded with posts of some importance within the administration.

The withdrawal of samurai from the kyōka societies was a result of the new policy of Matsudaira Sadanobu's government: samurai were required to be proficient not only in arms but in letters (meaning Confucian learning). The expression *bumbu* (letters and arms) figures in the titles of several satirical kibyōshi written before the authors realized how seriously the government meant its policy. Ōta Nampo felt it expedient to deny specifically that he was the author of a satirical kyōka that was making the rounds:

yo no naka ni	In all the wide world
kahodo urusaki	There is nothing quite so
mono wa nashi	Exasperating:
bumbu to iute	Thanks to that awful buzzing
yoru mo nerarezu	I can't sleep, even at night.[17]

The point of this verse is the play on the word *bumbu*, used to express irritation with the government's encouragement of "letters and arms," though on the surface it represents onomatopoetically the buzzing of a mosquito that keeps the speaker from sleeping. Nampo did not suffer from the false association of his name with this anonymous verse, but two kibyōshi authors were less fortunate: one was ordered by his clan never to write any more fiction, and the other committed suicide.

As a result of Sadanobu's reforms the leadership in kyōka reverted to the conservative Karagoromo Kisshū. Even Nampo's old associate Kankō, intimidated, began to speak of kyōka as a somewhat lighter variant of the serious art of the waka; he taught his pupils that the art of the kyōka consisted in "describing one's ordinary emotions in contemporary language, using the normal form of the waka."[18] Shikatsube no Magao (1753–1829), a merchant, eventually became the chief exponent of this view. His genteel kyōka exercised a surprising appeal on people living outside Edo; no doubt their unfamiliarity with city life had made them despair of imitating the wit of Nampo or Kankō. Magao was so popular that he gave up his business to become a professional kyōka poet, charging one *ryō* in silver for each hundred verses he corrected.[19] In his old age, as further proof of his great dignity and of the refinement of his poetry, Magao customarily appeared at kyōka gatherings dressed in formal court costume.[20]

Magao's effete style of kyōka was opposed by a learned innkeeper named Ishikawa Masamochi (1753–1830), a scholar of kokugaku who published such works as *Gagen Shūran*, a dictionary of classical terms.[21] Masamochi was banished from Edo in 1791 for a suspected violation of lodging-house regulations and was therefore not in Edo during the severest period of Sadanobu's reforms. Under the name Yadoya no Meshimori (Servant at the Inn) he began publishing kyōka in Nampo's anthologies, and proved himself to be a true disciple. When he returned to Edo from banishment in 1805, he attempted to revive the Nampo-Kankō style of kyōka, placing himself squarely in opposition to Magao. His kyōka have the wit of Nampo at his best, but the quarrel between Yadoya no Meshimori and Magao dragged on for so long that the dignity of kyōka was destroyed. After the death of Magao in 1829 and of Meshimori in 1830, kyōka ceased to be of literary importance.

Kyōka appealed primarily to samurai and upper-class merchants who enjoyed displaying their erudition and skill at parody. It was fun to take an elegant waka and, by a deft twisting of the language, totally alter the content, giving it a most plebeian meaning. In order to ensure that their humorous efforts could be fully appreciated, the kyōka poets most often parodied poems from *A Hundred Poems by a Hundred Poets*, the best known of all collections. Nampo's parody of a famous waka by Shunzei made a pun on *naku*, "to cry," and *naku naru*, "to be no more":

yū sareba	It is evening and the
nobe no akikaze	Autumn wind through the fields
mi ni shimite	Bites into my flesh;
uzura naku nari	The quails are crying now
Fukakusa no sato	In Fukakusa Village.

hitotsu tori	First I caught one,
futatsu torite wa	Then, having caught a second,
yaite kui	I fried and ate them:
uzura naku naru	Soon there were no quails crying
Fukakusa no sato	In Fukakusa Village.[22]

Another clever parody of a well-known source, the preface to the *Kokinshū*, incurred the wrath of Hirata Atsutane and other Shinto zealots:

utayomi wa	It's best for a poet
heta koso yokere	To be clumsy:
ame tsuchi no	If heaven and earth
ugokiidashite	Started to move in sympathy,
tamaru mono ka wa	Do you suppose we could stand it?[23]

The poet's ability to move heaven and earth, proclaimed in the preface to the *Kokinshū*, is held up by Yadoya no Meshimori as a potential menace to human tranquility!

Other kyōka are humorous because of their content, rather than because they parody a specific classical waka:

yo no naka wa	In this world, they say,
iro to sake to	Sex and saké
kataki nari	Are our enemies;
dōzo kataki ni	I hope and pray I'll be brought
meguriaitai	Face to face with my enemies![24]

itsu mite mo	Humiliating—
sate o wakai to	The age when everybody
kuchiguchi ni	Praises you, saying,
homesoyasaruru	"No matter when we see you,
toshi zo kuyashiki	You never seem to age!"[25]

Kyōka sometimes depended for their effect on their use, in a pseudo-elegant context, of the typical slang of Edo or the special language of the brothels or the Kabuki theater.[26] Puns and verbal dexterity were also valid excuses for writing a kyōka. Here is a famous example by Karagoromo Kisshū:

izure make	Which one will lose
izure katsu wo to	And which one will be the winner?
hototogisu	The bonito or the cuckoo?
tomo ni hatsune no	The first notes of both of them
takō kikoyuru	Sound awfully high.[27]

This verse, unfortunately, loses everything in translation. There is a pun on *katsu wo*, "the winner," and *katsuo*, "the bonito," and another pun on *hatsune*, "the first notes" (of the cuckoo) and *hatsune*, "the first price" (of bonito coming onto the market).

Sometimes the humor is childish, as in a famous kyōka by one Kabocha Gennari, whose name means "Fed Up with Pumpkins." His verse, entitled "A Palindrome," bears the prefatory note: "Once, when a man broke wind, the person standing next to him laughed so much he was urged to write a palindrome on the subject." The kyōka consists of thirty-one repetitions of the syllable *he* (meaning "fart"), carefully arranged in the traditional waka pattern.[28]

Kyōka was a minor form of poetry, but considering how little humor there is in Japanese literature, we should be grateful for the work of some gifted poets who occasionally approached the realm of genuine comic art.

KYŌSHI

Ōta Nampo's first success, as we have seen, was scored at the age of eighteen with the publication of a small volume of kyōshi, comic poems in Chinese. He continued to write kyōshi, as well as serious poems in Chinese, for the rest of his life, even after fear of punishment had made him abandon kyōka. The writing of Chinese was considered a suitable accomplishment for a samurai, and at one time Nampo not only wrote Chinese himself but tutored young samurai in the composition of Chinese poetry.[29] Nampo's kyōshi look like Chinese poetry: they are arranged in lines with the proper number of characters, and sometimes reach dozens of lines in length. Most of these kyōshi, however, would be incomprehensible to a Chinese. They make sense only if read according to the pronunciations given in kana next to the characters. One long poem begins:

> The echo of the drum from the tower,
> The low "mouse hole" of the entrance:
> If you haven't seen the glory of the theater,
> How can you know how grand Edo is?
> The Morita, Ichimura, and Nakamura Theaters,
> At Fukiya, Sakai Street, and Kobiki Street,
> The actors, names ranged together, gather at the Three
> Theaters.[30]

Nampo deliberately used as many non-Chinese names and terms as possible and, although he observed in general the rules of Chinese prosody, it was solely for comic purposes. Such poems are funny in almost exactly the way a Latin translation of *Winnie the Pooh* is funny: the reader, accustomed to thinking of Chinese (or Latin) as a learned tongue, suitable for the expression of lofty thoughts, is tickled by the unfamiliar combination of the extremely humble and the stiff phrases of a classical language.

Nampo's second solo collection, *Ameuri Dohei Den*, published in 1770 with illustrations by Suzuki Harunobu and with a preface by Hiraga Gennai,[31] attracted many other dilettantes to kyōshi. Hatanaka Tanomo (1752–1801), a Kyoto poet three years younger than Nampo, was his most accomplished rival; he wrote under the pseudonym Dōmyaku Sensei. A collection of kyōshi exchanged by the two men was published in 1790 under the title *Nitaika Fūga* (Elegant Compositions by Two Masters). Dōmyaku was perhaps the best of the kyōshi poets, as well as an outstanding writer of satirical fiction.[32] He is generously represented in the kyōshi anthologies, along with Nampo. Kyōshi, by its very nature, could hardly be more than the diversion of a pedant; for this reason it occupies only a minor place in pre-modern literature.

SENRYŪ

To say that senryū is a comic form of haikai is accurate but puzzling. Haikai poetry, after all, began as an avowedly comic form, and even after Bashō had elevated it into a medium capable of expressing a man's deepest feelings, his disciple Kikaku still used it for its original purposes. After Bashō's death another disciple, Kagami Shikō, broadened the popular base of the School of Bashō by interpreting karumi, the lightness advocated by Bashō in his final period, as meaning common or plain. The countrified variety of Bashō's karumi propagated by Shikō bore less and less resemblance to the poetry of the Master, but tended to aim instead at humorous effects.[33]

The disciples descended from Kikaku departed even more radically from Bashō's ideals and favored a superficial humor depending on tricks of language familiar from the days of Teitoku and the Danrin school. The leading figure of this group in the middle of the eighteenth century was Matsuki Tantan (1674–1761). His two chief claims to fame were his advocacy of the single verse in seventeen syllables as a complete unit, rather than as the opening verse of a linked-verse sequence, and his ability as a marker (tenja) of other men's verses. His preference for independent haikai at first ran counter to current tastes, but eventually he founded a new and popular form of light verse.

Among the lesser haikai poets there long had been a craze for capping verses known as *maekutsuke*. This involved adding a long (seventeen-syllable) or short (fourteen-syllable) tsukeku to the previous verse composed by another man (maeku). A variant, called *kasazuke*, involved adding twelve syllables to the five syllables given by the previous man.

The origins of maekuzuke have been traced, not very convincingly, as far back as 1660, but it is certain that by the 1680s it was enjoying a vogue in the Kamigata region, and before long spread to Edo. By the beginning of the eighteenth century it had become the most popular form of verse composition.[34] The oldest surviving collection of maekuzuke is *Saku ya Kono Hana* (1692). In this collection both the maeku and tsukeku are given, and the content does not differ from other books of haikai poems. A 1701 collection shifted the emphasis entirely to the aptness or novelty of the tsukeku; the maeku was deliberately made simple, sometimes to the point of insignificance, so as not to choke the imagination of the writers of the tsukeku. Tantan elevated the tsukeku to being the sole object of attention. No longer was the success of the tsukeku judged by its effectiveness in "capping" the original verse; it had to stand on its own.

The next development was the appearance of collections of tsukeku treated as independent verses. The earliest goes back as far as 1702,[35] but a far more influential example was *Mutamagawa*, edited by Kei Kiitsu (1695–1762) in fifteen volumes, the first of which appeared in 1750. In the preface the compiler explained that the book was being printed at the urgent request of the publisher; he added: "We should really have supplied the maeku to which these tsukeku were given, but we omitted them to save trouble."[36] *Yanagidaru*, the first collection of senryū, was published in 1765; the connections between it and *Mutamagawa* were extremely close, even though the latter professed it was following the haikai traditions, and *Yanagidaru* opened with an assertion that each verse was complete in itself, without reference to a maeku.

The differences between a comic haikai and a senryū are hard to define, but we might say that in general, haikai poetry deals with nature and senryū with human beings. This choice of subject matter is reflected by the insistence on seasonal words (kigo) in haikai poetry, but not in senryū. Haikai, at its best, tries to capture in seventeen syllables both the eternal and the momentary, but senryū is content with a single sharp observation. The importance of the "cutting words" (kireji) in haikai stemmed largely from the division they established between the two elements they contained, but a senryū needed no cutting words, since only one element was present. The language of senryū is generally that of the common people, and is sometimes even vulgar, but haikai, despite its occasional daring uses of such words, was essentially restricted to the vocabulary of the man of taste. Parts of speech that were considered inconclusive in a haikai often ended a senryū, as if to signify it was a flash of wit rather than a rounded-off poem.

Another important difference between haikai and senryū is that the latter are normally anonymous. The famous collections are known not by the names of the poets but of the editors. Matsuki Tantan was famous for his skill at evaluating other men's senryū, rather than for his own poems. The same was true of Momen (d. 1788), the compiler of the first *Yanagidaru*. For that matter, the term *senryū* itself, though not commonly used until the Meiji period, was taken from the personal name of Karai Senryū (1718–90), for thirty years the leading marker (tenja) in Edo. Senryū used to award a certain number of points to each verse submitted to him, and the best were included in the successive collections called *Yanagidaru*, twenty-four of which had appeared by 1791. It has been estimated that Senryū in his lifetime marked over 2,300,000 verses![37]

But the differences between haikai and senryū should not be exaggerated. Many verses that had appeared in *Mutamagawa* were taken over unchanged or only slightly modified in the *Yanagidaru* collections. Senryū for many years was considered a vulgar, debased form of haikai poetry, and was dismissed as being zappai (miscellaneous haikai), meaning that it was unworthy of classification. Haikai poetry itself occupied a relatively humble position with respect to waka or renga, but zappai ranged at the very bottom of verse composition.[38] As late as 1843 a defender of senryū felt it necessary to state: "Perhaps the reason why some people look down on zappai as a sloppy kind of verse is because they have not discovered the basic purposes of this art. It does not differ from haikai; in fact, it is *the* haikai of haikai."[39]

The contempt displayed by haikai masters for what was clearly an offshoot of their own art derived in part from the unpretentious nature of these "miscellaneous verses." It reflected also the anonymous, communal nature of senryū composition. One authority has written: "It is generally impossible to discuss the style of individual zappai poets. The style was the result of the collaboration between the poet and the marker."[40] In the nineteenth century some senryū poets began to affix their names to their compositions, but senryū was still considered more as a kind of entertainment than as poetry. The tsukeku supplied by one man to the maeku of another was generally much modified by the marker before it appeared in print; this no doubt is why the art is known by the name of a marker.

The distinctive feature of a senryū is its deft observation of a single scene or human trait. It does not pretend to suggest larger concepts, but focuses on some detail in such a way as to evoke a flash of recognition:

kome tsuki ni	If you ask directions
tokoro wo kikeba	From a man pounding rice,
ase wo fuki	First he wipes the sweat.[41]

This is the simplest variety of senryū; it makes us smile by its exactness in capturing an unimportant, but "human" moment. The senryū, however, can go beyond simple observation to an intellectually perceived situation:

ofukuro wo	As a weapon
odosu dōgu wa	To intimidate his Ma,
tōi kuni	Distant employment.[42]

The word used for mother, *ofukuro*, is still used by young men talking of their mothers to friends. The verse, then, is about a young man who boasts to his pals that he got his mother to raise his allowance by threatening otherwise to take a job in some distant province. The use of words is certainly spartan, but each one is a key to a familiar situation.

The effect of many senryū is dependent on a familiarity with the society of the time, particularly the city of Edo, the home of the art. Sometimes a verse reveals a naïve pride in that city:

gobamme wa	They all look alike,
onaji saku de mo	But the number five statue
Edo umare	Was born in Edo.[43]

This verse would be baffling to anyone not familiar with the six statues of Amida Buddha supposedly carved by the priest Gyōgi; five of the six were enshrined in temples outside Edo, but the fifth, being a "child of Edo," was superior to the others, though all looked alike.

To understand even a random selection of senryū a reader would have to be familiar with such matters as the punishment of customers who violated the etiquette of the licensed quarters; the custom of praying at a certain Yoshiwara shrine for a successful marriage; the custom of ringing a bell when making an offering of the first fruits or vegetables to the family Buddha; the clothes in which a dead man was normally buried; the appearance of certain varieties of puppets.[44] Few people possess such informaion today, but these subjects in their time required as little explanation to readers as the penalties on drunken driving or the significance of Cupid to us.

Some senryū depend for effect on a rather more elevated kind of information:

aruji no en	Marriage with the master's daughter
hitoyo herashite	Cuts short by one lifetime
sōzoku su	One's future relations.[45]

The reader of this verse is expected to be familiar with the belief that the ties of parent and child last for one lifetime, those of husband and wife for two lifetimes, and those of master and vassal for three lifetimes. Marrying the master's daughter thus cuts short the relations of the couple from three lifetimes to only two. When explained in this prosaic manner the humor becomes ponderous, but to people who accepted this expression of the conditions of reincarnation as common knowledge, the verse must have been effective. Other senryū are distinctly literary in content:

Kiyomori no	Kiyomori's doctor
isha wa hadaka de	Took his pulse
myaku wo tori	Stark naked.[46]

Reference is here made to the episode in *The Tale of the Heike* describing the incredibly high temperature Kiyomori ran in his final illness: it was so high that water thrown over his body to cool him turned to steam. According to the senryū the doctor was obliged to shed his robes in face of the heat.

Sometimes a senryū parodied a well-known haikai:

niuriya no	The fence post
hashira wa uma ni	Of the saloon was eaten
kuwarekeri	By his horse.[47]

This is a parody of Bashō's famous:

michinobe no	Rose of Sharon
mukuge wa uma ni	By the side of the road—
kuwarekeri	Eaten by my horse.

The senryū shifts the scene to a drinking joint. The owner of the horse ties it to a post outside while he drinks, and the horse, tired of waiting for its master, gnaws through the post.

The most common variety of senryū pokes fun at human weaknesses and foibles. Irony or sarcasm may be employed, but the satire is rarely sharp or intense. Even when making fun of a bribe-hungry official the tone is whimsical:

yakunin no	The official's baby
ko wa niginigi wo	Has mastered the art
yoku oboe	Of closing his fist.[48]

Sometimes too, for all the satirical intent, the effect borders on the sentimental:

kuni no haha	Mother in the country
umareta fumi wo	Cradles and walks the letter
dakiaruki	Telling of a birth.[49]

The story is clear: a woman in the country, learning from a letter of the birth of a grandchild in the city, holds the letter in her arms and walks with it, exactly as if she cradled a baby. In order to convey so much information in the seventeen syllables the poet had to resort to extreme abbreviations in the language;

umareta fumi means literally "a letter which has been born," but its meaning is undoubtedly *umareta to iu fumi*, "a letter which says (the baby) has been born."

The senryū could go beyond sentimental expression to something touching on tragedy:

chi morai no	Stuck in his sleeve
sode ni tsupparu	When he goes begging for milk,
katsuobushi	A dried bonito.[50]

We must suppose that a man's wife has died shortly after childbirth. Her husband goes to the neighbors' begging for milk to give the infant, and he takes along in his sleeve a dried bonito to offer as a return present. Or perhaps, as some commentators have suggested, the bonito was to pacify the infant, who sucks on it while waiting for its milk.

The senryū might, on the other hand, be farcical or even bawdy, though the extreme examples were not included in the anthologies. The following verse is about the prostitutes of the Maruyama Quarter in Nagasaki, frequented by the Dutch:

Maruyama de	In Maruyama
kakato no nai mo	Once in a while babies are born
mare ni umi	Without any heels.[51]

It was commonly believed that the Dutch traders in Nagasaki (unlike the Japanese) wore heels on their shoes because their feet lacked heels of their own.[52]

Senryū, no less than other forms of literature, was subjected to the surveillance of the administrators of the Kansei Reforms. The publishers of senryū, fearful that their books might be censored or confiscated, deleted any verses that might be considered immoral or otherwise objectionable.[53] The bawdier senryū, describing instances of rape, illicit intercourse, streetwalking, pornographic pictures, and so on had first been assembled in a separate collection of 1776 called *Suetsumuhana* (from the word *sueban*, "last choice," used of indecent senryū, but transformed into the name of the red-nosed lady Suetsumuhana in *The Tale of Genji*). Subsequent collections of a similar nature were published in 1783, 1791, and 1803, but during the height of the Kansei Reforms publication was discontinued. Senryū lost its impetus during the reforms, though new collections of *Yanagi-*

daru appeared until 1838, when the fifth-generation Senryū edited the 167th edition. By this time senryū were being signed by their authors, and the original spirit of the form was lost.

Senryū survives to this day in etiolated form. The fourteenth Senryū assumed the name in 1948, and there are still enough enthusiasts to warrant the publication of specialized senryū magazines. But senryū was a product of a particular place, the city of Edo, and of a particular time, the late eighteenth century; the humorous compositions turned out today lack the special flavor of the early *Yanagidaru* verses. The age of frivolity, the Tanuma regime, that gave birth to the kibyōshi, the sharebon, the kyōka, kyōshi and senryū, was a Japanese rococo. Modern imitations are bound to seem either superficial or plain silly. The humor is to be prized, but its literary value should not be overrated. The comic verse of the Tokugawa period was a minor form of literature, though a delightful one.

NOTES

1. *Gotoba-no-in Kuden.* See Hisamatsu Sen'ichi and Nishio Minoru, *Karon Shū, Nōgakuron Shū*, p. 147.
2. *Ibid.*, p. 265.
3. Hamada Giichirō, "Kyōka," p. 19. See also Koike Tōgorō, "Kyōka, Senryū," pp. 40–41.
4. Hamada, "Kyōka," p. 21.
5. *Teitoku Kyōka Hyakushu*, p. 58.
6. Hamada, "Kyōka," p. 23.
7. Teruoka Yasutaka and Gunji Masakatsu, *Edo Shimin Bungaku no Kaika*, p. 34.
8. Hamada, "Kyōka," p. 25.
9. *Ibid.*
10. *Ibid.*, p. 26.
11. *Ibid.*
12. Hamada Giichirō, *Ota Nampo*, p. 14.
13. Sugimoto Nagashige and Hamada Giichirō, *Senryū, Kyōka Shū*, p. 273.
14. *Ibid.*, p. 283. "Snipe-style frying" (*shigiyaki*) is an unpretentious way of frying eggplant in oil, usually served on a skewer, like *yakitori*.
15. Hamada, "Kyōka," p. 29.
16. Hamada, *Ota Nampo*, pp. 90–91.

17. Teruoka and Gunji, p. 263.
18. Hamada, "Kyōka," p. 31.
19. *Ibid.*, p. 31.
20. Teruoka and Gunji, p. 265.
21. He also wrote fiction under the name Rokujuen; one story, *Hida no Takumi Monogatari*, was translated into English by F. V. Dickins in 1912 under the title "The Story of a Hida Craftsman."
22. Sugimoto and Hamada, p. 283. For the poem by Shunzei, see Robert H. Brower and Earl Miner, *Japanese Court Poetry*, pp. 298–99.
23. Sugimoto and Hamada, p. 284.
24. *Ibid.*
25. *Ibid.*
26. See examples in Sugimoto and Hamada, p. 285.
27. *Ibid.*, p. 286.
28. *Ibid.*, p. 440.
29. Hamada, *Ota Nampo*, p. 138.
30. *Senryū Kyōshi Shū*, p. 363.
31. Hamada, *Ota Nampo*, p. 26.
32. See Nakamura Yukihiko, *Kinsei Sakka Kenkyū*, pp. 187–200.
33. Teruoka and Gunji, pp. 27–28.
34. Sugimoto and Hamada, pp. 6–7.
35. *Ibid.*, p. 10.
36. Quoted in Sugimoto and Hamada, p. 10.
37. *Ibid.*, p. 20.
38. Miyata Masanobu, "Zappai to Senryū-fū Kyōku," p. 12.
39. *Hama no Tsuki*, quoted in Miyata, p. 3.
40. Miyata, p. 12.
41. Sugimoto and Hamada, p. 30.
42. *Ibid.*, p. 35.
43. *Ibid.*, p. 29.
44. *Ibid.*, pp. 30–31.
45. *Ibid.*, p. 31.
46. *Ibid.*, p. 41.
47. *Ibid.*, p. 32.
48. *Ibid.*, p. 33.
49. *Ibid.*, p. 35.
50. *Ibid.*, p. 37.
51. *Ibid.*, 52.
52. See Donald Keene, *The Japanese Discovery of Europe*, pp. 170–71.
53. Teruoka and Gunji, p. 275.

BIBLIOGRAPHY

Brower, Robert H. and Earl Miner. *Japanese Court Poetry.* Stanford: Stanford University Press, 1961.

Hamada Giichiro. "Kyōka," in Kōza Nihon Bungaku series, vol. VIII. Tokyo: Sanseidō, 1969.

———. *Ōta Nampo.* Tokyo: Yoshikawa Kōbunkan, 1963.

Hamada Giichirō, Suzuki Katsutada, and Mizuno Minoru. *Kibyōshi, Senryū, Kyōka,* in Nihon Koten Bungaku Zenshū series. Tokyo: Shogakkan, 1971.

Hisamatsu Sen'ichi and Nishio Minoru. *Karon Shū, Nōgakuron Shū,* in Nihon Koten Bungaku Taikei series. Tokyo: Iwanami Shoten, 1961.

Keene, Donald. *The Japanese Discovery of Europe.* Stanford: Stanford University Press, 1967.

Koike Tōgorō. *Edo Joryū Kyōka Hyōshaku.* Tokyo: Ōfūsha, 1971.

———. "Kyōka, Senryū," in Nihon Bungaku Kōza series, vol. IV. Tokyo: Kawade Shobō, 1952.

Miyata Masanobu. "Zappai to Senryū-fū Kyōku," in Kōza Nihon Bungaku series, vol. VIII. Tokyo: Sanseidō, 1969

Nakamura Yukihiko. *Kinsei Sakka Kenkyū.* Kyoto: San'ichi Shobō, 1961.

Senryū Kyōshi Shū, in Yūhōdō Bunko series, vol. XC. Tokyo: Yūhōdō, 1928.

Sugimoto Nagashige and Hamada Giichirō. *Senryū, Kyōka Shū,* in Nihon Koten Bungaku Taikei series. Tokyo: Iwanami Shoten, 1958.

Teitoku Kyōka Hyakushu, in Nihon Meicho Zenshū series, vol. XIX. Tokyo: Nihon Meicho Zenshū Kankōkai, 1929.

Teruoka Yasutaka and Gunji Masakatsu. *Edo Shimin Bungaku no Kaika,* in Nihon no Bungaku series. Tokyo: Shibundō, 1967.

CHAPTER 22

POETRY AND PROSE IN CHINESE

During the Muromachi period the Buddhist monasteries were the repositories of Chinese learning, both religious and secular. The study of Chinese, like the study of Latin in Europe of the time, involved not only reading classical texts but also writing poetry and prose in the language. Sometimes the monks produced works of literary merit, but more often their compositions were little more than exercises in the grammar and metrics of a difficult foreign language. In the Tokugawa period the cultural importance of Buddhism rapidly waned, as the result of the adoption of Confucianism as the state philosophy. The Buddhist temples still prospered financially—the government, in the effort to wipe out Christianity, required every Japanese to be affiliated with a temple—but they ceased to be centers of learning, even though some priests still maintained the traditions of Chinese studies.

The rise in Japan of Confucian philosophy, particularly the variety of Neo-Confucianism associated with the great scholar Chu Hsi (1130–1200), began with Fujiwara Seika (1561–1619), a twelfth-generation descendant of the great Teika. As a child he enjoyed the reputation of a prodigy. He took orders as a Buddhist priest at the Shōkoku-ji in Kyoto, one of the Five Temples, and rose to be the leader of Zen meditation there. He seemed well on his way to rising in the Buddhist hierarchy, but at twenty-eight he left the Shōkoku-ji, finding himself more attracted to the Confucian works he had studied than to Buddhism. Although the study of the Confucian classics had been pursued for many years at the Zen monasteries, by this time few monks were seriously concerned with philosophical matters; the Chinese texts were studied mainly for literary purposes, in order to write Chinese poetry and prose.[1]

Seika's increasing absorption with Confucian doctrine made him feel restless in such an atmosphere. He traveled to Kyushu in 1593 to meet a Chinese envoy, and on this occasion also made the acquaintance of Tokugawa Ieyasu, leading to the invitation to lecture in Edo later that year on *Chen-kuan Cheng-yao*, a text of Confucian statesmanship.[2] Seika, convinced that no one in Japan could teach him about Confucianism, decided he would go to China. He left Kyoto in 1596 and made his way as far as southern Kyushu, but was prevented by a shipwreck from continuing his journey. While waiting for another ship he happened to find a copy of the Confucian Four Books punctuated for reading in Japanese by the Zen monk Bunshi Genshō (1555–1620); Seika was so impressed that he decided there was no need to travel all the way to China for instruction available in Japan. He returned to Kyoto, where he devoted himself to the study of the Chu Hsi interpretation of the Confucian classics, convinced now that "the sage never needs a teacher; it is quite enough for him to peruse the Six Classics."[3] In 1598 he met the Korean official Kang Hang, who had been captured in Korea and was being held at a town south of Kyoto. Kang had been asked by the warlord Akamatsu Hiromichi to write a fair copy of the Confucian Four Books. When this was completed, Akamatsu asked Seika in 1599 to punctuate the texts for reading in

Japanese. This seemingly minor request in fact marked a dramatic break with the medieval traditions of esoteric transmission of such knowledge, and signaled the emergence of a new kind of scholarship.[4]

Seika's direct disciples included Hayashi Razan and Matsunaga Sekigo (1591–1657), the son of Matsunaga Teitoku; almost all the important Confucian scholars of the seventeenth century were "grandchildren" or "great-grandchildren" disciples. Seika's central position as the founder of Neo-Confucian studies in Japan is beyond question. His efforts were devoted mainly to elucidating the Confucian canon according to the interpretations of Chu Hsi, although he did not exclude the views of Wang Yang-ming and other scholars. These philosophical matters are not of immediate relevance to the history of Japanese literature, but Seika, like others in the Confucian tradition, felt he had to state his views on the functions of literature. He believed that literature should serve as a means of teaching the Way; he considered that it was little more than the honey on the lip of the cup that made it easier for a patient to swallow bitter medicine.[5] This typically Confucian opinion denied that literature had any value as an expression of individual feelings. In China such an interpretation of the functions of literature was deeply rooted, though the opposite view, of literature as inspiration, also had a long history. Yüan Hung-tao (1568–1610), a Ming poet whose critical writings particularly influenced the writing of poetry in Chinese by Japanese, declared in the strongest terms that inspiration (*hsing-ling*) and the direct expression of the poet's emotions were of prime importance.[6] In Japan the didactic value of literature had at times been insisted on by Buddhists, who justified literature as an expedient (*hōben*) for gaining enlightenment, but few literary works were in fact composed specifically for this purpose. It was possible, of course, to write beautiful poetry even with a didactic purpose, but on the whole the poems written by the Japanese Confucian scholars to satisfy their professional qualifications were of slight artistic value.[7]

Seika's reputation as a poet is dismal. No one has much praise for the many poems he dutifully wrote as a good Confucianist. Yet the standard forms of expression in Chinese poetry were such that it was hard to go totally wrong as long as one kept to the traditional themes and images. A bad waka is glaringly bad;

its insipidity is apparent without explanation. But a mediocre kanshi (poem in Chinese) often possesses, at least in translation, greater charm than a waka masterpiece. Here is a typical *zekku* (quatrain) by Seika:

AN EXCURSION TO WAKANOURA

When I journeyed with my guests to the castle by the sea
Light from the surging waves joined the light of the sky.
Flying fish leapt from the nets, fresh and quivering with life;
A boatman's song gave chase to the setting sun.[8]

This poem, admittedly, has little or perhaps no individuality. Apart from the rather conventional descriptions of a pleasant outing there is little content; nevertheless, it fares better in translation than most of the great waka by Saigyō. This may prove nothing more than that Chinese poetic expression is closer and more congenial to English than the shorter Japanese forms. Perhaps translating even improves Seika's poem by eliminating the pedantic allusions and stiffness of language; but however one may criticize the poem, it unquestionably has a dignity of tone worthy of a gentleman and scholar. Seika and his many spiritual descendants found it far more congenial to write poetry of this impersonal variety than to follow the injunctions of the *Kokinshū* and base their poetry on their emotions. Even though Seika's poem on his excursion to Wakanoura says nothing about Confucianism, it suggests the calm pleasures of a scholarly life, quite detached from the turbulent feelings listed in the preface to the *Kokinshū* as appropriate occasions for the writing of poetry.

Most kanshi written during the Tokugawa period were in four or eight lines. The difficulty in handling the longer Chinese forms probably accounted for the reluctance of poets to attempt the *ku-shih*, but they may have suffered also from a lack of suitable subject matter. They had no desire to unburden themselves of powerful emotions; they were usually satisfied to describe an outing, or a mountain village in autumn leaves, or the melancholy aroused by a temple bell at dusk. These subjects were not altogether dissimilar to those of the waka, suggesting how strongly Japanese tastes persisted even among Confucian scholars. Only occasionally did they venture into more ambitious themes that risked failure. However, a few men became so interested in poetry as to neglect their philosophy; they were not only the best of the Confucian poets but became the prototypes of the bunjin, the men of letters who so greatly influenced Japanese poetry and painting in the eighteenth century.

Ishikawa Jōzan (1583–1672) was perhaps the first "specialist" at writing kanshi.[9] As a young man he had served in Tokugawa Ieyasu's army with distinction, but at thirty-two he became a monk at the Myōshin-ji in Kyoto. Later he studied with Seika, served a daimyo, and finally withdrew at fifty-eight to the house he built at the foot of Mount Hiei and called Shisendō (Hall of the Immortals of Poetry). The building was decorated with the portraits of the thirty-six immortals of Chinese poetry, ranging from the Former Han to the Southern Sung dynasties. Jōzan lived very quietly in the Shisendō, as we know from a letter he wrote Hayashi Razan:

> Sometimes I pick flowers in the garden and make them the companions of my heart. Or I listen to the first wild geese and treat them as my guests. Sometimes I open my brushwood gate and sweep out the leaves, or I look into the old garden and plant chrysanthemums. Sometimes I climb the eastern hill and sing to the moon, or I draw my chair to the northern window and read books and recite poetry. Apart from these pursuits I do nothing.[10]

There was more than a touch of the dilettante to Jōzan. His poetry is dotted with self-contented and rather excessively self-congratulatory references to his withdrawal from the strife and ambitions of the world:

THOUGHTS

For long I have rejected worldly dust to live in this secluded
quiet;
How many years it has been since I forgot about fame or
disgrace!
Thirty springs I have spent sitting late at night under my lamp;
I am not drunk with crimson skirts, I am drunk with words.[11]

Jōzan's poetry was extravagantly admired in his time; the preface to one collection quotes a Korean scholar's opinion that Jōzan was the "Li Po and Tu Fu of Japan."[12] This clearly was gross overpraise, but at least indicates Jōzan's preference for the mid-T'ang poets, rather than the late T'ang poets who inspired most other kanshi poets of the time. Jōzan was otherwise influenced by the views of Yüan Hung-tao, who rejected the imitation or even plagiarism of old poetry that was so prevalent, and insisted that any influence a modern poet received from the past must be completely absorbed.[13] Jōzan's readings in this near-contemporary Chinese poet refutes the charge once made by Ogyū Sorai that the kanshi poets were always two hundred years behind the Chinese,[14] but Jōzan's poetry, unlike the romantic poetry of Yüan Hung-tao and his brothers, which captured the imaginations even of the common people, remained the avocation of a hermit. Read today, it is pleasing but by no means remarkable.

Another seventeenth-century poet of some literery distinction was a high priest of the Nichiren sect named Gensei (1623–68). He became a close friend of Ch'en Yüan-yün (1587–1671), a refugee from the disturbances attending the fall of the Ming Dynasty, who had reached Japan in 1638. The two men joined in composing poetry and in reading together (from 1659 to 1662) the works of the outstanding late Ming poets, Yüan Hung-tao in particular.[15] Gensei's own poetry had strong moral overtones; he attempted to fuse Buddhist and Confucian thought, clothing it in the graceful language of the traditional Chinese poetry. His poems were so popular, even during his lifetime, that, in the old phrase, the price of paper went up, especially after he published in 1656 this poem:

MY NEW HOUSE

Nobody knows yet about my new house.
This spring I came here alone, quite by chance.
When I washed my pots I discovered the spring water was hot;
When I read the sutras I noticed how much time I had
before evening.
Haze and clouds shut in my quiet door;
Fragrant grasses sprout outside my rough gate.
Pines and bamboos have found their own place;
Now in the woods and hills the snow begins to melt.[16]

Many of the next generation of scholars of Chinese wrote kanshi of great competence. The best poets were probably Arai

Hakuseki (1657–1725) and Gion Nankai (1677–1751), both disciples of Kinoshita Jun'an (1621–98). The volume of Hakuseki's collected poems includes prefaces and afterwords by Koreans, testimonial to his competence. The same book was taken by a man from the Ryukyus to China, where the Confucian scholar Cheng Jen-yüeh read it with such admiration that he made a copy for himself and wrote a preface; when a copy bearing this preface reached Hakuseki in Japan he was naturally overjoyed.[17] Hakuseki admired Tu Fu most of the Chinese poets, but his own poetry rarely exhibits the intensity of that of Tu Fu, who lived in an age of warfare and disasters.

OFFERED AT THE GRAVE OF MY TEACHER, JUN'AN, ON A WINTER'S DAY

A cold day—I go down the hill slope
And recall the unbearable grief of the elegy;
Now, when I come before your grave,
I only see the many white clouds.[18]

The poem indirectly describes Hakuseki's emotions on visiting Kinoshita Jun'an's grave at the foot of a hill. He recalls the unbearable grief he felt when he composed the funeral elegy; but as he stands by the grave, he notices that it is deserted—only insentient clouds visit it now. The poem, appropriately for a Confucian scholar, gives no overt statement of his emotions; but it is nevertheless more personal than most kanshi of the period.

Gion Nankai was an even better poet, as Hakuseki himself recognized. He was also an accomplished artist, and is considered one of the founders of bunjin painting. Nankai led a rather turbulent life as a young man. In 1692, as a boy of sixteen, he dazzled everyone by composing in a single night one hundred kanshi.[19] However, once he had obtained a post as a Confucian scholar his profligate habits soon led to his dismissal. Nankai became famous both for his love of saké and for his literary performances while in his cups. He was a facile writer, excelling especially at *renku,* the Chinese equivalent of renga. Acclaimed by his contemporaries as a genius, he was chosen in 1711, the year he was restored to his position as a Confucian scholar, to join with a Korean envoy in composing poetry. Nankai's poems most closely resemble those of Li Po, not too surprising, considering his love of drink! The language he employed was noticeably more difficult than that of most of his contemporaries, perhaps because of his conviction that a poem must be the vehicle for elegant language and thoughts.

In his guide to the writing of poetry in Chinese, *Shigaku Hōgen* (In Quest of the Sources of Poetics, published 1763), Nankai insisted that poetry must be a "voice"; unlike other kinds of writing, it does not relate moral truths or admonish people, though when a man hears this "voice" it naturally will stir such sympathetic understanding that his evil thoughts will cease and virtuous ones burgeon instead. "The Sung Confucianists, not understanding this, explained poetry in terms of reasons, a great mistake."[20] "Poetry is not a tool for explaining principles or discriminating truths. It is song that depicts human emotions. When men hear poems they are moved, and as a result they somehow acquire understanding. This wonderful, mysterious quality is restricted to poetry and is innate in poetry."[21]

The particular features Nankai distinguished in poetry were poetic elevation, rhythm (including internal rhythm), and inspiration. He disliked any form of unadorned expression: he traced the expression of a single thought "I would like you to come visit me" from the flattest, most banal remark to a statement on a poetic level of which he could approve—indirect, elegant, and witty. Plain expression was vulgar, but sometimes vulgar thoughts were merely clothed in prettified language that concealed their barrenness. Only a perfect congruence of elevated language and thought was worthy of the name "poetry."[22]

Nankai has been described as a kanshi poet of the first magnitude, but his poetry does not seem as markedly superior to that of other men as do his writings on poetics. This poem describes a shrine at Wakanoura, near the spot of Seika's poem:

> Wind across the wide night sighs in the river reeds;
> The goddess is wandering in the autumn moonlight and has
> not yet returned.
> Sharp strings of biwas cry to the parting geese;
> Frost glitters dreamlike above the cold sea mist.[23]

Nankai's poem is more elegant than Seika's, but it may not be immediately apparent why Nankai was acclaimed as a master and Seika dismissed as an incompetent poet. Nankai's reluctance to state his emotions plainly gives his poem a refined detachment, but it is not very moving. The impersonality of the tone does not, of course, mean that Nankai remained impassive before the sight he described, but he refused to name the emotions that the autumn scene stirred in him. The same holds true of many fine poems, in both Japanese and Chinese, and is not necessarily a failing; but the quiet appreciation of a lovely scene, expressed in highly poetic language, does not seem to possess the individuality of a "voice."

Nankai's poetry appears so bland, despite the refinements, that we may wonder what he considered to be his artistic purpose. He declared that his ideal was the high T'ang poetry:

> The poems about nature written during the T'ang Dynasty have a kind of thought, quite apart from the sights or circumstances described, that cannot be conveyed in words. It can be comprehended only by the mind and spirit. That is why later poets could not match those of the T'ang.[24]

He sought to portray nature in elegant language with the object of evoking real, if hard to define, emotions in the reader. This was also the ideal of the bunjin artists and haikai poets, though it was quite foreign to many important Chinese poets, who used powerful and direct language.

Nankai's insistence on elegance made him dislike especially the poetry of Po Chü-i, who treated "vulgar" subjects in simple language. He once wrote:

> People praise Po Chü-i as a great poet, but they are mistaken. When one examines the hundreds of poets during the three hundred years of the T'ang, one will see that he belongs far down on the list.[25]

Nankai was particularly incensed by the story that Po Chü-i, rejecting the difficulty of elegant poetry, had written so plainly that even an illiterate old woman could understand his poetry. Nankai considered this as an example of how the art of poetry, perfected in the mid-T'ang, had been destroyed by later men.[26]

Nankai's ideals were otherwise expressed by the word *eisha* (reflection), and he gave as examples of the effect he most admired flowers seen reflected in a mirror or the moon reflected in the water, visible but beyond the immediacy of touch.[27] The quiet beauty achieved in his poetry has charm, and his skill in manipulating the Chinese language deserved the praise it received, but for those who seek an individual voice, Nankai's poetry may seem like many bunjin paintings—lovely but remote.

Gensei and Jōzan represent the first period of Tokugawa kanshi, from 1596 to 1687, as Hakuseki and Nankai represent the second period, from 1687 to 1771. In both periods the writing of kanshi was predominantly an activity of Confucian scholars. The followers of the orthodox Chu Hsi school wrote rather differently from those of the Ogyū Sorai school, but in neither case was the writing of poetry much more than a gentlemanly accomplishment. In the third period (from 1771 to 1868), however, not only was there a great increase in the number of poets, but the best ones were mainly professionals who earned their living as writers and not as philosophers.

During this third period, the summit of the Tokugawa kanshi, many theoretical works on Chinese poetics were published. The increased interest in kanshi was reflected also in the organization of societies of kanshi poets, much along the lines of the haikai and kyōka societies. Each group would be headed by an important poet, but the majority of the members were amateurs.[28] At first there was a surprising freedom in the composition of these societies: anyone was allowed to join as many as he pleased and, a miracle in Japanese literary circles, there was no trace of factionalism. The sole intent was to share in the pleasure of composing kanshi and to benefit by the criticisms of others. Toward the end of the eighteenth century, however, the predictable splits into violently opposing schools developed.

The general spread of interest in kanshi helped also to foster a marked improvement in the competence of the poets. Kanshi poets, no longer confined to themes and subjects they could comfortably describe in Chinese metrics, filling the slots in a zekku with words in the appropriate tones, now could treat their experiences, even if unpoetic, in a variety of extended forms. Sometimes the more adventurous of the poets went too far, at least in the eyes of their contemporaries. Emura Hokkai (1713–88), noted as the compiler of several important collections of kanshi, denounced as "criminals" poets who addressed poems to prostitutes, wrote poetry while staying in a brothel, or used phrases suggestive of immoral relations. To us, living in a less moral age than Hokkai's, such "criminal" poems are certainly more attractive than Hokkai's hackneyed descriptions of dusk falling over the sea or of lonesome crows in a withered willow.[29] Two poems by Minagawa Kien (1734–1807), whose poetry was known for its "spirit," rather than for its philosophic overtones, suggests some of the new criminality:

PARTING

Near the south ferry in Edo, just as the rain was stopping,
You and I tied our horses and went up to a room over the river.
When I got so drunk I quite forgot the way back to Osaka,
You laughed and pointed at the long river flowing to heaven's edge.

WATCHING DISTANT RAIN FROM AN INN ON THE WEST BANK OF THE KAMO RIVER

In an upstairs room, a cup of saké in hand, I look out at the sky;
The bamboo mats and coarse reed blinds look cool against the distant rain.
Over the river, through breaks in the clouds, evening appears—
Ten miles of embankment are caught in the setting sun.[30]

Such poems were not as deeply felt as the best by Gion Nankai, but they are appealing because they have the ring of actual experience. Their expression is also relaxed, even if the poet felt compelled to refer to Edo as Buryō (Wu-ling) and to allude to a poem by Li Po; obviously, there was no longer any question of poetry being intended as a means of teaching doctrine. The poets of the late Tokugawa period advocated, in place of the stale (but lofty) conventions of the past a more realistic poetry, and looked especially to the Sung poets for inspiration.[31] The leader of this movement, Yamamoto Hokuzan (1752–1812), condemned Ming poetry as being nothing more than plagiarism of T'ang poetry, and he was so suspicious of the past that he even denounced the celebrated *Selection of T'ang Poems* as a forgery.

Hokuzan insisted that the essential characteristics of poetry were freshness and inspiration, rather than technical proficiency or "spiritual resonance," as was often claimed. Despite his harsh rejection of Ming poetry, his attitudes were unquestionably colored by the critical writings of Yüan Hung-tao;[32] but he pointed the way to a kind of kanshi that would be just as Japanese and just as true to the poet himself as any other type of poetry. The plagiaristic borrowings, fake archaisms, hackneyed expressions, and rigid compliance with metrics and diction expected of kanshi poets had imprisoned the poetic spirit of the earlier men, but the late Tokugawa kanshi have a notable freshness, as in this poem by the Tendai monk Rikunyo (1734–1801):

FROSTY DAWN

When I awoke on my dawn pillow, the frost was half evaporated,
And the clear sunshine, filling the window, was already
faintly warm.
From my bed I watched cold flies cluster on the other side
of the panes,
Rub their legs together, fall, then fly up once again.[33]

This description of a winter morning suggests direct observation; we feel sure that Rikunyo actually saw the flies through the translucent paper of the shōji as they dropped to the floor, then flew up to the shōji again. Even if he borrowed from some Chinese poet, the experience was his, and not the stereotyped evocation of a conventional scene. The preceding poem in a plebeian vein may remind us of a haiku; in other cases the resemblances are startling:

I have planted the well morning-glories in a different place;
The wild vines, climbing up the sides, had spread sideways
and across
Until they surprised me by taking possession of the rope.
Of late I have been going to a neighbor to ask for water.[34]

This kanshi seems little more than a translation and expansion of the famous poem by Kaga no Chiyojo:

asagao ni	The well-rope has been
tsurube torarete	Captured by morning-glories—
moraimizu	I'll borrow water.

Rikunyo does not refer to Chiyojo's poem, but the similarity could hardly have been a coincidence; if nothing else, it demonstrates how Japanized his kanshi are, and how close in spirit to haikai.

The new style in kanshi was perfected by Kan Chazan (1747–1827).[35] Unlike most kanshi poets of earlier times, Chazan was not a samurai, but came from a wealthy farming family. Although he spent most of his life in his native town, Kannabe in Bingo province, he frequently visited Kyoto and Osaka, where he studied the Confucian classics and medicine. The school he later founded in Kannabe became widely known and attracted pupils even from distant places. Chazan's poetry has been said to be in Rikunyo's tradition, but he was not a disciple; the men did not meet until 1794, when Chazan was already an established poet.[36] Rikunyo's influence is nevertheless apparent everywhere, and Chazan's first collection has for its preface two letters sent him by Rikunyo. Both men were inspired by Sung poetry to describe in their poetry the scenes of daily life and the feelings they inspired. In a poem like the following Chazan perfectly evoked a hot summer afternoon in his village:

> More than twenty days without rain in this valley town;
> The river is beginning to dry in the shoals and shallows.
> At noon the whole town buzzes with locusts from under the
> pagoda trees;
> A mountain boy, keeping close to the houses, is selling
> sweetfish.[37]

The elements of the picture are effective: the sleepy town in the heat, the dinning of the locusts, and the boy, keeping under the shade of the eaves as he goes from door to door selling fish.

A winter poem describes the same village with equal vividness:

> Cold stars brilliantly frame my hut in the woods;
> The lonely cloud at the crest of the cedars is frozen and
> motionless.
> What are they making a fuss about in the house next door?
> Men from the village have shot a deer and brought him back
> on a pole.[38]

Chazan's poetry struck most people of the time as unconventional or even perverse. Hirose Tansō (1792–1856), later famed as a scholar and kanshi poet, wrote:

> The first I ever heard that there was someone named Kan Chazan was when I was fourteen. I enjoyed the Sung style, and that is how I happened to read his quatrain in seven-character

> lines including the verse, "I love to watch a great moon climb, embracing the pines." At the time I really thought this was unorthodox, if not heretical. Later, when I went to Chikuzen [in Kyushu] I heard his name from time to time, but there too people only sneered and attacked him. However, the Zen master Don'ei told me that Chazan was a great poet, and I realized for the first time that he was by no means to be rejected out of hand. By the time I was twenty-six I had decided to send a couple of dozen of my recent compositions through a friend to Chazan for his corrections.[39]

This was the poem that had so startled the young Tansō:

> In the southern hall, waiting for someone, I do not light the
> lamps;
> Insect cries from the four walls sound clear in the night air.
> Pointing at the peak ahead, I keep my guest sitting with me—
> I love to watch a great moon climb, embracing the pines.[40]

The image of the full moon embracing the pines as it rises must have been bewildering to most readers. When Tansō got to know Chazan's poetry better, however, he was moved to write:

> Chazan's poetry derives its style from Rikunyo's. The poems of Rikunyo are rich in descriptions but convey few emotions, and they are excessively dense. Even if one can at first enjoy them, one is apt to dislike them later on. Chazan's poetry is half emotion and half description; he strikes a balance between thin and dense. That is why, as I discovered, one does not dislike it even after long acquaintance.[41]

Chazan's skill at finding a happy medium between the startling and the familiar probably made him a better poet than Rikunyo, though he lacked some of Rikunyo's excitement.

Chazan's poems often describe with great charm the scenes around the town of Kannabe, especially near his school:

> The lazy houseboy still hasn't swept the gate;
> The snow of pear blossoms, circling the eaves, is warm in
> the afternoon breeze.
> A pair of delirious butterflies pass, chasing each other;
> Out from the south hall they go, then into the north.[42]

Other poems describe his visits to Yoshino, Edo, Osaka, and Kyoto. There can be no doubt that these poems reflect personal experience: the sharpness of the details contrast with the conventionally admired sights, generally borrowed from some Chinese poet, in the kanshi written by poets earlier in the Tokugawa period. Of course, Chazan often alluded to Chinese poetry, but his kanshi are also close to haikai poetry in their themes and even in their techniques, perhaps because of his friendship with Buson. One zekku in five-character lines is especially close to a famous haikai:

The rough wind brushes the flowering tree;
Blossoms fall and strike the poet's chair.
One petal suddenly returns to the branch:
I notice then it is a butterfly.[43]

The conception is identical with the haikai by Arakida Moritake:

rakka eda ni	The fallen blossom
kaeru to mireba	Returns to the branch; I look—
kochō kana	It is a butterfly.

Chazan, however, sometimes used the kanshi for purposes quite beyond the scope of either haikai or waka, as in this ironic comment on social conditions:

A STORY HEARD FROM SOMEONE ON THE BITCHŪ ROAD

People are running frantically around the village;
They say the official has come to inspect the rice fields.
Day after day in the mayor's house
The kitchen fills with rare and delicious food.[44]

This poem refers to the fear of the villagers that the official, after inspecting their fields, will raise their taxes; they call each day at the mayor's house, where the official stays, to leave presents for him. Similar criticism is found in some *Manyōshū* poetry, but not in the later collections; that was one reason why nineteenth-century poets with criticisms to make of society often chose to write kanshi. Other poets indirectly attacked present conditions by writing about great historical figures, implicitly contrasting their actions with the ineffectuality of contemporary men. Chazan's poetry sometimes treats such themes, but his best works tend to be in the quiet vein of the Sung poets:

READING ON A WINTER NIGHT

Snow has engulfed the mountain house; shadows of trees lie deep.
Bells at the eaves are motionless; the night is perfectly still.
As I quietly put away my pile of books, I ponder what I have read:
One thread of blue lampwick and ten thousand years of thoughts.[45]

Ichikawa Kansai (1749–1820) enjoyed in Edo a reputation as a kanshi poet almost as great as Chazan's in the Kamigata region. At first he studied at the Shōheikō, the school of Confucian studies of the Hayashi family. After this school was reorganized in 1790, on the heels of the Kansei Reforms, he left, and for some twenty years earned a living as a teacher to the Toyama clan, frequently visiting Edo. While in Edo his main activity was running the Kōkosha, the poetry society he founded. Kansai and others of his society in general favored the style of the Sung poets, and the use of unaffected language. Their themes tend to be the hackneyed ones of Chinese poetry with little of Chazan's individuality.

Many exceptionally gifted kanshi poets were active at the beginning of the nineteenth century. The greatest was undoubtedly Rai Sanyō (1780–1832), the son of the eldest of the famed three Rai brothers, all distinguished kanshi poets. His father, Rai Shunsui (1746–1816), joined the Kontonsha, a kanshi society in Osaka, when he was twenty, and wrote poetry of surprising freshness and directness; but he was best known as an exceptionally orthodox follower of the Chu Hsi school of Confucianism. The son, Rai Sanyō, had little to do with Confucian philosophy, but he became the outstanding writer of Chinese poetry and prose of the Tokugawa period,[46] and perhaps of all Japanese literary history. Sanyō's extraordinary proficiency in writing Chinese undoubtedly reflects the heritage from his father and uncles. He began his studies of Chinese at six and made rapid progress. At seventeen he was taken to Edo by his uncle Rai Kyōhei (1756–1834), where he studied at the Yushima Seidō, the center of Confucian learning. He was acclaimed as a boy prodigy, but apparently he suffered from fits of depression that drove him into erratic ways.

When Sanyō was twenty (in 1800) he suddenly, without permission from his clan, left Hiroshima for Kyoto, where he indulged in a wild and dissipated life. He was brought back to Hiroshima and confined to his quarters for three years. Fortunately, the daimyo recognizing Sanyō's literary gifts, allowed him to read and write freely during this imprisonment, and Sanyō used the time to study history and government. Even after his release from confinement, he was officially disinherited, and he spent several lonely years at his studies. In 1807 he completed the first draft of *Nihon Gaishi*, an "unofficial" history of Japan written in Chinese.[47] Sanyō's proficiency in Chinese attracted the attention of Kan Chazan, who invited him in 1809 to become the chief disciple (*tokō*) at his school in Kannabe. Sanyō spent a year and a half studying Chinese poetry under Chazan, whose tutelage proved crucial in Sanyō's development as a poet. While Sanyō was in Kannabe, Chazan's most important collection of kanshi, *Kōyō Sekiyō Sonsha Shi* (Poems Written at Sunset in a Cottage among Yellow Leaves), was published, and Chazan entrusted Sanyō with reading the proofs.

In 1811 Sanyō left for Kyoto, moved by a patriotic desire to serve his country with his writings. His studies of Japanese history had made him a loyalist—a partisan of the emperor, as opposed to the shogun—at a time when the open profession of such beliefs was dangerous. In Kyoto he attended meetings of the kanshi societies but, as a letter to an uncle reveals, he was disillusioned by the incompetent poets. He sought distraction with geishas; Kan Chazan had occasion to rebuke him for his dissolute life. But already in this early period Sanyō had begun to write the poems on historical subjects that would bring him unique distinction.

In the spring of 1818 Sanyō left on a year's journey through Kyushu. He visited scholars everywhere, leaving behind evidence of his heightened poetic abilities. His poem on the Dutch ship he saw in Nagasaki, for example, was important not only for its unusual subject but because Sanyō had brilliantly employed a long verse form that demanded a mastery of overall structure, always a problem for Japanese poets.[48] The poem also reveals Rai Sanyō's freedom to treat a subject not already provided with conventional imagery, and his concern with the moral issues which he reveals in the conclusion.[49] The subject was clearly much too complex for either a waka or a haikai, and the development of the thought demanded an ampler form. Some kanshi, as we have seen, had become so naturalized that they seem little more than expansions of the traditional Japanese poetic forms, but the content of Rai Sanyō's poetry perfectly accorded with the various kanshi styles he employed.

Even the shorter poems composed on Sanyō's journey to Kyushu are revelatory of his new mastery. Two poems describe foreigners he encountered in the southern part of Kyushu: descendants of Korean craftsmen captured over two hundred years earlier, and some merchants from the Ryukyus:

On the road I met some descendants of Korean prisoners;
They make a living as potters in a village of their own.
How touching to think they can mold from Japanese clay
The Korai bowls they fashion in our time.

I met some visitors from the south in the marketplace;
They gabbled away in a mixture of Chinese and barbarian.
But they knew the prices of the emperor's ink and brushes,
For they claimed they had twice visited Peking.[50]

While in Kyushu Sanyō also met Hirose Tansō, who later expressed both criticism and admiration:

> Sanyō is arrogantly confident of his talent. He is ambitious and without manners. When he was young he ran away from his province because it was not big enough to hold him. By the time he came to Kyushu he was close to forty, but everywhere people disliked him; there wasn't a place he wasn't driven from. I gather that even in Kyoto he had been widely attacked. However, his talents are truly outstanding. In China there are literati like him; people take them as a matter of course, and nobody is suspicious of them. The ways of our country, however, are unsophisticated, and when people notice anybody reading books they consider it their duty to attack him. That is why a man like Sanyō cannot find a place for himself in society. It is a shame.[51]

Sanyō was the first scholar of Chinese in Kyoto to make a living as a writer rather than as a Confucian philosopher. His return to Kyoto from Kyushu in 1819 opened a period of extremely fruitful literary activity in both poetry and prose; he sold his published works and lived on the income.[52] Not only were his kanshi popular but his prose, unlike the stiff compositions of the Confucianists, was enjoyable to read and won many readers. *Nihon Gaishi*, though written in classical Chinese, was the most popular history of Japan during the nineteenth century, both because of its vivid style and its exciting handling of the material.

Sanyō's poetry also became increasingly concerned with Japanese history. Probably his most famous composition was *Nihon Gafu*, sixty-six poems in the *yüeh fu* style, an archaic Chinese form; with lines of irregular lengths they describe the course of Japanese history from ancient times to the sixteenth century.[53] Not all sixty-six poems were successful, but the best have a unique vigor:

THE MONGOLS ARE COMING!

The whirlwind over the sea of Tsukushi looms black against
the sky.
Who are these brigands who approach, covering the sea?
The Mongols are coming! They have come from the north,
And to east and west have steadily grown more voracious.
They managed to intimidate the old widow of the Chao family,
And with this behind them, they come to challenge the Land
of Men.[54]
Sagami Tarō's heart is huge as some great cauldron,[55]
And his warriors, defending the sea, are all on their mettle.
The Mongols are coming! We are not afraid!
We fear the orders from the East, imposing as a mountain.[56]
Advancing directly ahead, we slash the brigands and give no
quarter.
We topple their masts. We climb the captive ships.
We make prisoners of their generals. Our army shouts in
triumph.
But the hateful east wind with one blast has driven their fleet
into the sea,
And kept us from wetting Japanese swords with the fresh
blood of those sheep.[57]

Sanyō chose his form adroitly: broken lines in six characters like "The Mongols are coming! We are not afraid!" give a sense of urgency, and the two long lines at the end (in nine characters) give a final weight of utterance to the poem. The conclusion, though typical of Sanyō's patriotic thought, is most unusual: the Japanese warriors express hatred of the famed *kamikaze* because, by blowing the Mongol fleet out to sea, it has deprived them of the opportunity to slaughter their enemies; gratitude was the normal reaction to the "divine wind." The extremely nationalistic sentiments found in all sixty-six poems of the sequence would mark the kanshi composed by many patriots toward the end of the Tokugawa period.

Sanyō's rival in Edo, Yanagawa Seigan (1789–1858), wrote kanshi with even more nationalistic sentiments toward the close of his career, but his early life had been free of such serious concerns. Seigan went from his native province of Mino to live in Edo in 1807 so that he might enter the Chinese school of Yamamoto Hokuzan, but he ran up such enormous debts at the brothels that he escaped prison only by shaving his head and becoming a Buddhist priest. Even then, as he recalled in a poem written many years later, he still could not forsake his old haunts:

> Gaunt of frame, like a starving priest,
> I wander a thousand leagues, staff in hand.
> But don't be surprised if I still smell of powder and paint:
> I have gone again, as a beggar, to the singing girls.[58]

Seigan, dressed perhaps as a komusō priest, with a basket over his head, is drawn again to the brothels, and even as he accepts alms, the odor of cosmetics clings to him.

After a visit home to Mino, Seigan returned in 1810 to Edo, this time to establish himself as a poet. Even at this juncture he was not permanently domiciled anywhere; he continued his wanderings, never staying long in one place. Many poems describe his travels or his nostalgic remembrances of home. In 1819, learning that Kashiwagi Jotei (1763–1819), an Edo kanshi poet he especially admired, had died in Kyoto, Seigan hurried there in hope of finding any poems Jotei might have left behind. He arrived in time for the burial, and wrote a moving description of what he saw:

> Outside the city of Kyoto the spring stretches like the sea;
> You only loved songbirds and flowers, and never craved office.

In vain you prided yourself on the grandeur of your poetic
soul, your intransigence,
Could you endure the poverty, the traveler's thin clothes?
Mist envelops the withered grass, your ghost has gone far away.
Rain soaks the ravaged mountains, your white bones must be
cold.
I remember the chilly wind the day you were buried,
And the withered wisteria vines they tied around a coffin thin
as bark.[59]

It was on this occasion that Seigan first met Sanyō, and the two men became friends. In the following year, 1820, Seigan married a woman much younger than himself who, under the name Yanagawa Kōran, later established something of a reputation as a kanshi poet. The marriage was unusually happy; unlike most Japanese poets, Seigan took his wife with him everywhere.

In 1822 Seigan and his wife traveled to Kyushu, perhaps at Sanyō's suggestion. The journey, as in Sanyō's case, occasioned much excellent poetry. Unlike Sanyō, Seigan did not see all of Kyushu, but he remained there four years. The most interesting poems were composed in Nagasaki. Seigan described the local restaurant and brothels where he drank "barbarian wine" (Dutch and Chinese liquors), and referred on occasion to the exotic ships and buildings:

NAGASAKI

A myriad layers of peaks surround the expanse of sky;
Clouds from the sea, trees on the cliffs, are blue in the mist.
Houses of the town cover the ground, leaving no empty land;
Buddhist temples ring the mountains, so close they almost touch.
At sunset a gong sounds in the Dutch factory,
And a breeze flutters the pennants on the Chinese ships.
The times are peaceful, no invader threatens us;
For two hundred years barbarians have come and barbarians
have gone.[60]

On the way back Seigan stopped in Kannabe to show Kan Chazan the poetry he had composed in Kyushu.

During the next five years, until 1832, when he at last settled down in Edo, Seigan kept wandering, sometimes stopping in

Mino, or Kyoto, or Hikone. It was while on his way to Edo in 1832 that he learned of Rai Sanyō's death. He was moved to write this poem:

> When autumn wind and evening rain filled the capital
> We chatted of my departure; I wrote lines to match your
> sickbed poems.
> The lamplight on yellow flowers—it seems a dream of yesterday;
> When the news reached me in the East, before me was only dust.
> Surely no one will ever rival your knowledge of history;
> And your poetry, stripped to the bones, had more soul than ever.
> Now you will be idle—Yen Hui, lend him your brush!
> From now on let him keep the records in the other world.[61]

Toward the end of his life, while living in Edo, Seigan grew increasingly agitated over the state of the country, perhaps under the influence of the philosopher Sakuma Shōzan, who became his pupil in kanshi. Seigan's distrust of the shogun is revealed in the following poem:

> You, whose ancestors in the mighty days
> Roared at the skies and swept across the earth,
> Stand now helpless to drive off wrangling foreigners—
> How empty your title, "Queller of Barbarians"![62]

This attack suggests that Seigan's sudden decision in 1845 to leave Edo was inspired by reluctance to remain close to the seat of the shogun's power. He returned for a time to Mino, but in 1846 moved to Kyoto, probably to be near the emperor, and spent the remainder of his life there. The poems of his last years frequently touch on patriotic themes, and Seigan came to be known almost as much for his devotion to the emperor as for his poetry. Leaders of the loyalist movement—men like Yoshida Shōin, the priest Gesshō, and Rai Mikisaburō (the youngest son of Sanyō)—associated with him. Seigan died in 1858, the year before the shogunate ordered wholesale arrests of the loyalists; wags of the time commented that Seigan had been clever at *shi*, meaning either "poetry "or "death."[63]

The loyalist poets of the end of the Tokugawa period provided a marked contrast to the Confucian poets of the seventeenth century calmly observing the quiet beauty of a spring day. A note of fierce urgency gives their kanshi something of the strength of the T'ang poetry written in the midst of national disasters. However, their poems, unlike the masterpieces of Tu Fu, are of interest almost exclusively for their content, not for the beauty of their expression, whether they decry the "rank barbarian stench" of the Westerners, praise the achievements of Western science, or lament, like Rai Mikisaburō, that the author must die in prison.[64] The language is still classical Chinese, and allusions to Chinese poetry are still evident, but the poets lacked the skill to convert their experiences into poems that could survive the crises that inspired them.

The kanshi of the pre-modern period began as the literary accomplishment of the gentleman scholar and ended in a chorus of angry shouts. It served a unique purpose, giving the strength of an imposing tradition to the poet's utterances, unlike the more intimate, elusive waka or haikai. For a short time, notably with Rai Sanyō, it acquired the character of a most important Japanese verse form; so far was it from being considered alien that the loyalists, even those of the most fanatic sort, normally composed in Chinese, to clothe their sentiments in an appropriately dignified language. The kanshi survived well into the twentieth century. Not until the Japanese turned their backs on their Chinese heritage in favor of the West would it perish as a medium of serious poetry. It is a paradox of literary history that in the nineteenth century, when the Japanese at last became capable of writing Chinese as if the language were their own, they decided to reject the ties to the traditional Chinese culture formed at the beginning of their history.

At the beginning of the pre-modern period literature belonged to the upper classes, the people who could afford expensive manuscripts; they were privy to the secret traditions of poetry and scrupulously followed the precedents set by the masters of the past when composing their own works. The 250 years of Tokugawa peace, when the country was isolated by official policy from the rest of the world, may at first glance seem to be a period of deliberate resistance to all forms of change, the expression of the policy of stability and order advocated by the Confucian advisers to the regime. Yet when we examine the literature, what extraordinary changes we find! The gratitude of Matsunaga Teitoku to the Tokugawa family for having brought peace to the nation was replaced, by the end of the period, by veiled expressions of hatred toward the family which had usurped power from the emperor. The elegance of the courtly waka in the traditions of the *Kokinshū* gave way to waka describing the sights and smells of plebeian life. In the theater the stage came to be occupied by gamblers, thieves, and their murderous mistresses. Even in the Chinese poetry, seemingly the last refuge of the old Confucianism, there are unmistakable signs of impatience with the existing order.

Changes would occur, and very rapidly, once Japan was opened to the West, but even without this external factor the Japanese were ready to jettison much of the past. Certainly every aspect of the literature suggests this, from the faded rococo trivialities of the late fiction and comic verse to the earnestness of the kanshi poets. This judgment may be hindsight, but one cannot escape the feeling that the literature which had flourished so long within the walls erected by the Tokugawa rulers had finally used up the nutriments in the Japanese soil and needed fresh stimulation from abroad. This came from the West, and the manner in which Japanese literature responded to this stimulation would be its history in modern times.

NOTES

1. Yamagishi Tokuhei, *Gozan Bungaku Shū, Edo Kanshi Shū*, p. 28.
2. See Tsunoda, *Sources of Japanese Tradition*, pp. 345 ff.
3. Yamagishi, p. 29.
4. See above, p. 28.
5. See Matsushita Tadashi, *Edo Jidai no Shifū Shiron*, pp. 193–210.
6. See Yang Chia-lo (ed.), *Yüan Chung-lang Ch'üan Chi*, pp. 5–6.
7. Yamagishi, pp. 30–33.
8. *Ibid.*, p. 170.
9. Matsushita, pp. 261–67.
10. *Ibid.*, p. 262.
11. *Ibid.*, p. 263.
12. Toda Hiroaki, *Nihon Kambungaku Tsūshi*, p. 90.
13. Matsushita, pp. 273–75.
14. See Burton Watson, "Some Remarks on the *Kanshi*," p. 17.
15. Matsushita, p. 248.
16. Toda, p. 107.

17. *Ibid.*, p. 93.
18. Yamagishi, pp. 200–201.
19. See Nakamura Yukihiko, *Kinsei Bungakuron Shū*, p. 27.
20. *Ibid.*, p. 227.
21. *Ibid.*, p. 228.
22. See *ibid.*, pp. 233–37.
23. Watson, p. 16.
24. Quoted in Matsushita, p. 386.
25. *Ibid.*, p. 381.
26. Nakamura, p. 247.
27. Matsushita, p. 390; Nakamura, p. 237.
28. See Fujikawa Hideo, *Edo Kōki no Shijintachi*, pp. 16 ff. Fujikawa describes in detail one society, the Kontonsha, founded in Osaka by Katayama Hokkai (1723–90). Most societies were in Edo, but they had branches in the provinces.
29. Yamagishi, pp. 245–47.
30. *Ibid.*, pp. 256–57. Mention of the "long river" is a reference to a poem by Li Po. The Kamo River is in Kyoto.
31. Fujikawa, p. 5.
32. Matsushita, pp. 564–70.
33. Fujikawa, p. 7.
34. *Ibid.*, p. 12.
35. The name is also read Sazan by some scholars.
36. Fujikawa, p. 28.
37. *Ibid.*, p. 29.
38. *Ibid.*, p. 30.
39. *Ibid.*, p. 31.
40. *Ibid.*
41. *Ibid.*, p. 32.
42. *Ibid.*, p. 34.
43. *Ibid.*, p. 45.
44. Yamagishi, p. 283.
45. Toda, p. 111.
46. Yoshikawa, "Chinese Poetry in Japan: Influence and Reaction," p. 892.
47. The completed work was not published until 1827.
48. Watson, p. 19.
49. For a translation by Burton Watson see Keene, *Anthology*, pp. 436–37.
50. Fujikawa, p. 218.
51. *Ibid.*, p. 219.

52. *Ibid.*, p. 221.

53. The number 66 was apparently based on the number of provinces in Japan. See Fujikawa, p. 222.

54. Chao was the surname of the Sung imperial family. The "widow" refers to Yang T'ai-hou, the empress dowager, who ruled for the last of the Sung emperors, a minor. "The Land of Men" means, here, Japan; it is used by contrast to China, ruled by a woman when the Mongols invaded.

55. Sagami Tarō was the name used when a young man by Hōjō Tokimune (1251–84), the regent (*shikken*) at the time of the Mongol invasion.

56. "Orders from the East" would refer to orders from Tokimune's government in Kamakura.

57. Toda, p. 108.

58. Itō Makoto, *Yanagawa Seigan Zenshū*, I, p. 598.

59. *Ibid.*, I, p. 74.

60. *Ibid.*, I, p. 164.

61. Yamagishi, p. 303. The last two lines refer to the legend that Yen Hui, the beloved disciple of Confucius, became after his death a scribe in the world of the dead; Rai Sanyō, according to Seigan, should succeed Yen Hui in this capacity.

62. Translated by Burton Watson in Keene, *Anthology*, p. 439.

63. Fujikawa, p. 281.

64. See Keene, *Anthology*, pp. 439–40.

BIBLIOGRAPHY

Fujikawa Hideo. *Edo Kōki no Shijintachi.* Tokyo: Mugi Shobō, 1966.

Itō Makoto. *Yanagawa Seigan Zenshū.* Gifu, 1956.

Keene, Donald. *Anthology of Japanese Literature.* New York: Grove Press, 1955.

Matsushita Tadashi. *Edo Jidai no Shifū Shiron.* Tokyo: Meiji Shoin, 1957.

Nakamura Yukihiko. *Kinsei Bungakuron Shū*, in Nihon Koten Bungaku Taikei series. Tokyo: Iwanami Shoten, 1966.

Toda Hiroaki. *Nihon Kambungaku Tsūshi.* Tokyo: Musashino Shoin, 1957.

Tōgō Toyoharu. *Ryōkan Shishū.* Tokyo: Sōgensha, 1962.

Tsunoda, Ryusaku, *et al.*, *Sources of Japanese Tradition.* New York: Columbia University Press, 1958.

Watson, Burton. "Some Remarks on the *Kanshi*," *Journal-Newsletter of the Association of Teachers of Japanese*, vol. V, no. 2 (July 1968).

Yamagishi Tokuhei. *Gozan Bungaku Shū, Edo Kanshi Shū,* in Nihon Koten Bungaku Taikei series. Tokyo: Iwanami Shoten, 1966.

Yang Chia-lo (ed.). *Yüan Chung-lang Ch'üan Chi.* Taipei: Shih-chien Shu-chü, 1964.

Yoshikawa, Kōjirō. "Chinese Poetry in Japan: Influence and Reaction," in *Cahiers d'Histoire Mondiale,* vol. II, no. 4 (1955).

Yoshikawa Kōjirō. *Gemmeishi Gaisetsu.* Tokyo: Iwanami Shoten, 1963.

APPENDIX
SUMMARIES OF PLAYS

1. *Keisei Mibu Dainembutsu* by Chikamatsu Monzaemon (see p. 251 for explanation of title of play). This Kabuki play has an exceedingly complicated plot, though it follows familiar patterns. Tamiya, the scion of the house of Takatō, has fallen in love with a prostitute from the Shimabara Quarter and disappeared. His wicked stepmother and her brother decide to take advantage of Tamiya's absence to seize the domain, but a faithful retainer, Hikoroku, is determined to prevent this.

An impostor, pretending to be Tamiya, has visted the house of Lady Katsu, Tamiya's fiancée, and given directions for the disposal of the statue of Jizō, possession of which is an absolute qualification for anyone desiring to wield authority within the family. The real Tamiya appears in mean attire, pretending to be a buyer of saké dregs. He delivers a long monologue on the art of buying prostitutes, and is recognized by Lady Katsu. Soon afterward a former mistress of Tamiya's is killed by the false Tamiya, and at once turns into a vengeful spirit, vowed to torment the real Tamiya, whom she supposes to be her murderer. All this takes place in the first act.

In the second act a rich man attempts to "ransom" Michishiba, Tamiya's girl friend from Shimabara. Tamiya lacks the money to block this, but his faithful retainer Hikoroku, knowing that a courtesan's maid named Koden is carrying a large sum of money, kills her and delivers the money to Tamiya. But when Tamiya presents the money to the brothel-keeper in order to "ransom" Michishiba, he is accused of robbery and murder. It turns out, however, that Hikoroku killed his own daughter, Koden, sacrificing her so as to aid his master, Tamiya. All are impressed, and the rich man yields Michishiba to Tamiya. In the final act the bodhisattva Jizō restores Koden to life, taking her place, and the play ends with the display of the sacred image of Jizō at the Mibu Temple.

2. *Kokusenya Kassen* (The Battles of Coxinga) by Chikamatsu Monzaemon. This play opens at the Chinese court. The villainous Ri Tōten, urging the emperor to accept humiliating conditions of peace with the Tartars, gouges out his left eye as proof of his absolute loyalty. Later we learn that this gesture was in fact a signal to the Tartars that he would betray the country to them. The Tartars soon arrive in force. The loyal minister Go Sankei attempts to defend the emperor and empress, but he stands alone against the enemy hordes. The empress, who is momentarily expecting to give birth, is struck by a bullet and dies. Go Sankei is so determined to preserve the succession that he performs a caesarean operation on the dead empress and delivers the baby. Realizing, however, that the Tartars will never relent in their search for the missing heir if they find the empress's body without an infant in her womb, he kills his own baby and pushes it into the empress's abdomen. "Noble child," he cries, "you have been blessed by fortune! You were lucky to have been born at a time when you could die in place of the prince destined to become our emperor." In the meantime, Go Sankei's wife has safely escorted the emperor's sister, Princess Sendan, to the coast, before she herself is killed by the Tartars.

In the second act we see Watōnai, the future Coxinga. He is a fisherman who lives on the coast near Hirado. The boat bearing Princess Sendan is washed ashore on that very coast, and she informs him (he understands Chinese because his father came to Japan from China) of the disasters she has witnessed. Watōnai and his parents leave at once for China, resolved to oust the usurpers. In the second scene Watōnai and his mother struggle through a bamboo forest in China, heading for the castle where his half-sister lives. Suddenly a great tiger springs out on them. Watōnai grapples with the beast, but it is subdued only when his mother points at the tiger a sacred charm from the Great Shrine of Ise. A force of Chinese soldiers appears, and this time Watōnai and the tiger join to conquer them.

The third act, by contrast, is devoted mainly to a "human" situation and involves little fantasy. Watōnai's half-sister, Kinshōjo, is the wife of General Kanki, the lord of the Castle of the Lions. At first she is delighted to learn that her long-lost family has arrived from Japan, but before long she is forced to mediate between Watōnai's insistence that Kanki join him, and Kanki's refusal to be swayed by a request emanating from his wife's family. She kills herself, freeing Kanki to join Watōnai. Kanki gives Watōnai the new name of Coxinga, Lord of the Imperial Surname.

The fourth act is taken up with supernatural doings. Go Sankei, wandering in the mountains with the baby prince he has saved, encounters two immortals who reveal to him in a vision the triumphs Coxinga has won all over China. Five years flash by in a moment. Now Go Sankei is joined by Coxinga's father and by Princess Sendan, who has returned from Japan. They are quickly surrounded by Tartars, but a miraculous bridge of clouds spans the gorge before them and they cross safely. When the Tartars follow them onto the bridge it collapses, and they plunge to their deaths.

The last act depicts Coxinga's decisive battle with the Tartars and his victory. Ri Tōten is killed and the young prince is enthroned as the emperor. The play concludes: "This joy they owe to the divine, and the saintly virtues of the Emperor of Great Japan, a land endowed with perpetual blessings which will prosper forever."

3. *Ōtō no Miya Asahi no Yoroi* (The Prince of the Great Pagoda) by Takeda Izumo. This play is loosely based on the *Taiheiki*. It involves Saitō Tarozaemon, a retainer of the Hōjō regents in Kamakura, whose son-in-law has decided to support the rival cause of the Prince of the Great Pagoda, the son of the emperor Godaigo. He sends his wife to ask Tarozaemon to join him. Tarozaemon at heart sympathizes with the prince, but out of giri to the Hōjō family refuses. The son-in-law, who has secretly been listening in on the conversation between Tarozaemon and his daughter, thereupon commits seppuku to atone for his wife's having revealed the plot to an enemy. Tarozaemon sounds the alarm drum to summon the Hōjō forces, and in the ensuing struggle his daughter is killed.

The third act is the best-known part of the play. The prince's young son has been captured and given into the custody of Nagai

Umanokami. The governor of Suruga, a Hōjō adherent, orders Tarozaemon to kill the young prince, but Umanokami, learning this, decides to substitute his own son. It is the time of the Bon Festival, and village children join in the dances with the young prince and Umanokami's son. Tarozaemon arrives and, to the astonishment of Umanokami, kills neither the prince nor the intended substitute but an unknown village child. Tarozaemon then reveals that the slain child is his own grandchild, the son of the son-in-law who committed seppuku. In the final act the Prince of the Great Pagoda, learning of Tarozaemon's sacrifice, offers him a large province as a reward, but Tarozaemon, still bound by giri to the Hōjō family, refuses. He kills the wicked governor of Suruga and, as a last gesture, cuts off his own head.

4. *Imoseyama Onna Teikin* (Household Teachings for Women at Imo and Se Mountains) by Chikamatsu Hanji. The first act opens in the palace of the seventh-century emperor Tenji. He has become blind, to the dismay of his subjects. However, the evil Soga no Emishi, who harbors plans of rebellion, uses an opportunity to denounce his enemy, the loyal Fujiwara no Kamatari, and forces him to withdraw from the court.

We learn that Koganosuke, the son of the minister Daihanji, and Hinadori, the daughter of Sadaka, the widow of another minister, have fallen in love, despite the enmity prevailing between their two families. Koganosuke, who is in the service of the emperor's mistress, Uneme (the daughter of Kamatari), learns that she is being subjected to unwanted advances from Emishi's son Iruka. He helps her to escape, giving out that she has drowned herself in Sarusawa Pond in Nara. In the next scene Iruka, who has led people to believe that he is immersed in Buddhist meditation, sends proof to the court of his father's disloyalty. The men of the court confront Emishi with the document. Emishi is naturally furious that his son has betrayed him, but his wrath is cut short by an arrow that strikes and kills him. Iruka appears and discloses to Daihanji that he himself intends to seize the throne; he killed his father because the latter was incompetent at sedition. Iruka has obtained possession of the sacred sword, one of the three imperial regalia. The mirror, another of the regalia, has disappeared. At the end of the act Iruka, resplendently attired, leaves for the imperial palace to discover, by force if necessary, where the other regalia are hidden.

These complications—and there are more—were intended to arouse in the spectators curiosity as to what would happen next. Will the emperor regain his sight? Will the loyal Kamatari be able to stop Iruka? Will Koganosuke marry Hinadori? Such questions suggest melodrama rather than tragedy; indeed, however pathetic some of the events, however beautiful the presentation, the play is effective as a dramatic, but not as a literary, work. The foregoing questions are answered one by one in the course of the following acts, but not before fresh complications arise. In the second act Kamatari reveals his strategy for conquering Iruka: it is based on the unusual circumstances of Iruka's birth. Emishi, despairing over not having a son, consulted a diviner and was told that if his wife drank the living blood of a white doe she would conceive a son. The blood was obtained, and the son was accordingly named *iru* (to enter) and *ka* (deer) because a deer's blood had entered his mother's womb. The diviner also disclosed that Iruka could always be overcome if blood from a deer with black hooves and blood from a jealous woman were mixed in a flute. Kamatari orders his men to obtain these two kinds of blood. Later in the act the emperor's sight is restored when Kamatari, discovering where the sacred mirror was buried, digs it up and returns it to the emperor.

The third act, the most important one of the play, shows the lovers, Koganosuke and Hinadori, in their houses on opposite sides of the Yoshino River. Koganosuke has refused Iruka's command that he become his vassal. His father, alleging that Koganosuke is unwell, sends him to his country estate at Se Mountain to recuperate. Across the river Hinadori is celebrating the doll festival in her house on Imo Mountain. Soon the parents of the lovers arrive. Each pretends to be eager to have his child enter Iruka's service, but both children refuse. Koganosuke commits seppuku and Hinadori dies at her mother's hand rather than become Iruka's bride. The mother, as proof that the two young people were really married, despite the enmity between their families, sends Hinadori's head floating across the river to be presented to the dying Koganosuke.

In outline this act sounds unspeakably crude. Even when read, the exaggerations are dismaying. But when performed, either by puppets or by actors, the effects are magnificent. The two houses, one austere and the other bright with dolls, the pink blossoms of Yoshino above and the blue river flowing between the mountains, make for a set of dazzling beauty. The use of a divided stage, emphasized in Kabuki by entrances being made over two runways through the audience, was a brilliant stroke of theater. The fairytale atmosphere is so pervasive that even the unspeakable moment when the head is sent across the river becomes not only tolerable but moving.

It might appear that the play must come to an end with such a scene, but even though blood from a black-hooved deer has in the meantime been obtained, blood from a jealous woman is still needed to make the magic potion needed to destroy Iruka. The jealous woman proves to be the simple girl Omiwa, who falls in love with Kamatari's son (who is disguised as a commoner). The son, Motome, loves Tachibana, Iruka's younger sister. In one famous scene Motome, determined to find out where Tachibana lives, follows her by means of a thread unraveled from a spool attached to her kimono. Omiwa follows Motome wth the same device. In the end Omiwa, consumed with jealousy when she learns Motome and Tachibana are to be married, rushes into the palace, where she is wounded by one of Kamatari's attendants. He catches her blood, which is boiling with jealousy, in a flute, and when this is mixed with the blood of the black-hooved deer Iruka at once becomes as timid as a fawn. His downfall is described in the brief concluding act.

5. *Gempei Narukami Denki* by Ichikawa Danjūrō I. This play is in the tradition of plays celebrating the Four Great Heroes who conquered the demon Shutendōji of Ōeyama. It begins with the discovery of a mysterious votive offering to the Great Dragon God of Japan. When it is revealed that the donor was Minamoto no Yorichika, Kintoki (one of the heroes) immediately announces his intention of subduing this villain, though the text fails to indicate what villainy he suspects. The second act opens as incantations are being offered at the imperial palace to overcome the thunder god, who has alarmed the court by incessant claps of thunder. A priest named Kaizan is summoned, and he declares that the thunder must be the work of Shutendōji. Kaizan's magic eventually halts the thunder, and the grateful emperor bestows on him the name Narukami Shōnin (Holy Man of the Thunder). At this point Yorichika is dragged in, a prisoner. A sentence of execution is pronounced, but Narukami pleads for his life, revealing that Yorichika was formerly his disciple. His plea is refused, and Narukami declares in enraged tones, "I will go to the dragon god's cave and seal in the dragon god. A terrible drought will afflict the realm."

Narukami fulfills his threat, to the dismay of all. Some time later the beautiful Lady Kumo no Taema (Break in the Clouds) visits Narukami, provocatively displaying her white limbs. The startled holy man asks who she is. "I am a widow," she replies. "I was separated by death from the husband I loved." She adds, "But you look exactly like him."

The holy man, by now in her power, joins with her in the "pledges of husband and wife." She also succeeds in getting him drunk. While he is sleeping she reveals to the audience that she is the wife of Watanabe Tsuna, another of the Four Heroes, and that she has come by imperial command to rescue the country from the drought. She severs the sacred ropes imprisoning the dragon god, and hurries back to the capital. When the holy man awakens from his stupor and discovers what has happened, he is furious.

The third act opens as the apoplectic Narukami drinks some water. Instantly he turns into a frog. His former sweetheart, Lady Yaegaki, comes to call, and the frog informs her that he has been undone by Kumo no Taema. Yaegaki is enraged that he should have proved to be so susceptible to the charms of another woman after having refused to marry her. The holy man bites off his tongue and dies, but not before leaving behind a note explaining that he was ashamed to be seen in animal shape by Lady Yaegaki. General rejoicing greets the news of Narukami's death, but his spirit appears once again to place a curse on his enemies. The spirit also explains that he took the form of a thunder god as an expedient for saving mankind. With these words he disappears.

The fourth and final act presents still another demon, who declares that it was he who entered the body of Yorichika and caused him to act disloyally. The play concludes with festivities and dances.

6. *Tōkaidō Yotsuya Kaidan* (Ghost Story of Yotsuya on the Tōkaidō) by Tsuruya Namboku IV. This play is usually referred to merely as *Yotsuya Kaidan*. It contains two related plots. The first and more important deals with Oiwa and her evil husband, Iemon; the second is about Oiwa's step-sister Osode and her unwanted lover, Naosuke. The play opens as Iemon asks Oiwa's father for his formal consent to their marriage, pointing out that they have been living together and that she is expecting a child. The old man refuses brusquely, knowing that Iemon was disloyal to Enya Hangan, the daimyo they both served. The enraged Iemon kills him. In the next scene Naosuke, in love with Osode, kills a man he supposes to be her fiancé. Both Iemon and Naosuke successfully pretend that they had nothing to do with these crimes, and even declare their intention of exacting vengeance. Oiwa and Osode, having no one else to whom they can turn, decide to endure their respective "husbands."

Oiwa gives birth to a child. The infant, far from warming Iemon's heart, infuriates him with its squalling. Iemon also complains about Oiwa's bedraggled appearance, and is only too glad to leave the house when invited to the mansion of a neighbor, a retainer of Moronao named Kihei. This old man's granddaughter, Oume, has fallen in love with Iemon. Kihei, reminding Iemon that he is not legally married, urges him to marry Oume, and after some hesitation Iemon agrees. Kihei is determined to eradicate any last trace of affection Iemon may have for Oiwa. He sends her a poison that will horribly disfigure her, under the pretense that it is a healing broth to fortify her after childbirth. Oiwa takes the poison and is at once transformed into an ogress. Iemon is naturally horrified when he returns home and, as a pretext for getting rid of her, he cries that he has trapped her with a lover. Oiwa is accidentally killed, and Iemon also kills his servant, Kohei, whom he had caught stealing some valuable medicine earlier that evening. He ties Oiwa's body to one side of a plank and Kohei's to the other, as if they were lovers discovered together, and pushes the plank into the river.

Oume and her father come to visit Iemon. The newlyweds go to bed, but when Oume lifts her head from the pillow and tenderly looks at Iemon, he sees Oiwa's ravaged face. He snatches up his sword and beheads her, only to discover, as soon as the head strikes the floor, that it is Oume's. He rushes into the next room to inform Kihei what has happened, but sees not the old man but Kohei. Again he beheads the apparition, only for the severed head to become that of the old man. Thus concludes the second act.

The play is full of terrible prodigies. Perhaps the most frightening scene is one which takes place by the river, where Oume's mother and a waiting woman see the plank floating in the water, showing now Oiwa's corpse, now Kohei's, as it turns in the waves. Oiwa makes her presence known in the form of rats— she was born in the Year of the Rat—which prey on and finally kill the old women.

Osode has agreed in the meanwhile to marry Naosuke, believing that he is her only hope for avenging her father and sister; but no sooner does she yield herself to him than her old fiancé returns. She learns that Naosuke killed another man, mistaking him for the fiancé. Caught betwen the two men, Osode kills herself. Before she dies she shows them her birth certificate. Naosuke discovers to his horror that Osode was his sister and that their relations were therefore incestuous. He also kills himself.

The fifth act opens with the most artistic scene of the play. Iemon, visiting a farmer's house, falls in love with the farmer's daughter, who strikingly resembles Oiwa in happier days. When at last he takes her in his arms, she turns into a loathsome apparition, and suddenly we are made aware that the entire scene has been a dream. The final scene of the play shows Iemon being tortured by Oiwa's vengeful spirit. Villagers try to exorcise her ghost, but it defies them. Swarms of rats surround Iemon, and he seems likely to be devoured by them, but the play ends inconclusively with Iemon fighting Osode's fiancé. Apparently Namboku, planning to end the evening with the last act of *Chūshingura*, deliberately avoided any resolution to his own drama.

GLOSSARY OF JAPANESE TERMS AND CERTAIN JAPANESE AND CHINESE NAMES

ARAGOTO A style of Kabuki acting characterized by exaggerated posturing and displays of superhuman strength; contrasted with wagoto.

ASHIBIKI NO A fixed epithet (makurakotoba), meaning something like "foot-dragging," used to modify the word "mountain."

ASHIGARU The lowest rank of samurai, a foot soldier.

AWARE Originally an exclamation of surprise or awe, it came to be used to express feelings of being moved or touched.

BASHŌ The plantain tree, a variety of banana tree which bears no fruit. Prized for its broad leaves, whose fragility in the wind suggested the poet's sensitivity.

BIWA A musical instrument, the Chinese *p'i-pa,* used in Japan not only in court music (*gagaku*) but to accompany certain forms of dramatic recitation.

BUMBU "Letters and arms"—the accomplishments expected of a samurai.

BUNJIN "A man of letters" (the Chinese *wen-jen*), the dilettante ideal of many Japanese painters and poets, especially of the eighteenth century, who rejected professionalism.

BUNJINGA The paintings of the bunjin.

CHŌKA A long poem in Japanese. The form, seen to best advantage in the eighth-century anthology *Manyōshū*, was revived in the seventeenth century after long neglect.

CHU HSI Chinese Confucian philosopher (1130–1200) whose interpretations of the Confucian classics were followed most widely in Tokugawa Japan.

CHUANG TZU Chinese philosopher (d. *c.* 300 B.C.) whose Taoist philosophy appealed to many Japanese poets of the pre-modern period.

DAIHON The script of a Kabuki play.

DAIMYŌJIN A Shinto god of special importance; the title bestowed on certain persons of conspicuous qualities after their death.

DAMMONO Passages of special beauty selected from Nō or Jōruri plays, often chosen for their dramatic quality.

DANGI A sermon on a Buddhist text; used also of works in this form, even though frivolous in content.

DANGIBON A book of sermons; but used especially of the satiric writings, often cast in the form of sermons, popular between 1750 and 1770.

DANRIN Originally a Buddhist term, meaning something like an academy of doctrinal experts, but used sardonically of a popular form of haikai poetry characterized by its spontaneity and wit.

DŌJŌ A term used of court poets of high rank. In the pre-modern period it often referred specifically to court poets who had received the *Kokin Denju*.

EDO The city now known as Tokyo. The Tokugawa shoguns ruled the country from their castle in Edo, and the pre-modern literature is therefore sometimes called Edo literature, although it was the center of literary production only after 1770 or so.

ENGO A related word, that is, a word connected to one or more others by overtones as well as meaning. "The airlines instituted a crash program" contains an engo on the word "crash."

FUEKI The ideal, espoused by Bashō, of unchanging value or meaning in poetry, the eternal component of haikai.

GABUN Elegant writing, either by people at the court or by others imitating the poetic, purely Japanese style of the Heian past.

GESAKU A general term for the prose fiction composed from about 1770 to 1870; it means literally "playful composition," a term originally intended to indicate that the author disclaimed responsibility for a frivolous work.

GIRI Duty or social obligation, an important theme especially in the plays of Chikamatsu and his successors.

GŌKAN A form of gesaku writing; it means "bound together" and originally designated the pamphlets composing a work which were sewn together, rather than sold separately. These lavishly illustrated works, popular from about 1820 onward, were intended mainly for women readers.

HAIBUN Prose writing characterized by the ellipses and other stylistic features of haikai poetry. Bashō's travel diaries are examples of haibun.

HAIGA Paintings, often by haikai poets, which suggest by their swiftly executed outlines and their humor the haikai poetry.

HAIGON Words peculiar to haikai poetry. Matsunaga Teitoku insisted that each haikai poem must contain a haigon, which was a word not permitted in the older poetry because of its vulgarity, novelty, or foreign origins.

HAIKAI The word was used originally of the comic poetry found in the *Kokinshū*, and later of the comic style of renga. Its chief importance as a literary term was as a designation of the poetry, originally humorous, that grew out of haikai no renga, and reached its culmination with Bashō.

HAIKAI NO RENGA The comic style of renga, practiced by even the serious poets by way of diversion. With Matsunaga Teitoku it became a full-fledged genre practiced by many poets.

HAIKU A term invented late in the nineteenth century to designate a poem which is complete in seventeen syllables and is not thought of as a hokku (opening verse of a comic linked-verse sequence). Now generally used when referring to any haikai verse which is not specifically part of a sequence.

HANAMICHI The raised walkway through the audience to the stage of a Kabuki theater.

HITOMARO The greatest poet of the *Manyōshū* (d. *c.* 708), revered during the pre-modern period especially by the kokugaku scholars and poets.

HŌBEN A Buddhist term designating an expedient for achieving a higher goal; literature was often considered as a hōben that permitted persons of limited intellectual capacity to understand the higher Buddhist truths.

HOKKU The opening verse of a renga sequence. It came, especially during the seventeenth century, to stand on its own without any necessity of continuing it; in this sense it is identical to the more modern term haiku.

HOTOTOGISU A bird often translated as "cuckoo" or "nightingale" though it bears slight resemblance to either. Frequently mentioned in poetry, especially waka describing the season of early summer rain.

HYŌBANKI Books of evaluations of prostitutes and actors, one form of kana zōshi writing.

JIDAIMONO Plays, generally based (however loosely) on historical facts, which depict the grandiose actions of people of the past.

JŌDO The Pure Land, or Paradise, to the West; believers in Jōdo Buddhism expect to be guided to this paradise after death by Amida Buddha.

JŌRURI The puppet theater, called Bunraku since the early ninteenth century. Originally the name of a lady whose misfortunes were the subject of dramatic recitations.

KABUKI The most popular form of Japanese theater. It originated with the dances performed by one Okuni early in the seventeenth century, but developed during that century into a serious form of theater, the rival of Jōruri.

KABUKI ODORI The dances performed by the priestess Okuni of the Izumo Shrine. *Kabuki* meant "unusual" or "deviant" and *odori* was a lively form of dance.

KAKEKOTOBA A "pivot word"; that is, a word with a double meaning, one related to the previous word, and the other to the following word. "What do I seaweed on the shore?" is a crude example of a pivot word, "seaweed," which shifts in meaning from "What do I see?" to "seaweed on the shore."

KAMIGATA The general region of Kyoto and Osaka.

KAMO The name of a river flowing through Kyoto.

KAMPAKU The highest state office under the emperor; sometimes translated as "chancellor."

KAN A unit of currency, consisting of one thousand copper coins (*zeni*).

KANA The Japanese syllabary, forty-eight phonetic symbols each representing a syllable, such as *ka*, *ki*, *ku*, *ke*, *ko*, etc. Used from the ninth century together with, or in place of, Chinese characters.

KANA ZŌSHI Works of fiction or of didactic intent composed mainly in kana; a general term for literary works in prose of the early seventeenth century.

KANSEI REFORMS The name given to the edicts issued in 1790 by Matsudaira Sadanobu which were intended to restore the prestige of the samurai class. The best-known provision of these reforms was the prohibition on unorthodox varieties of Confucianism and the insistence on a strict adherence to the Chu Hsi interpretations of Confucius.

KANSHI Poetry in Chinese composed by Japanese.

KANZEN CHŌAKU "Promotion of virtue and chastisement of vice"—the ostensible object of many works of fiction and drama.

KAOMISE A "showing of the faces" of a Kabuki troupe before the opening of its spring season; these were traditionally the best performances of the year.

KARAKURI Use of stage machinery and similar devices to obtain trick effects.

KARUMI "Lightness"—a principle advocated by Bashō toward the end of his life.

KASAZUKE A form of comic linked verse which involved adding twelve syllables (one verse of seven and one of five) to the five syllables supplied by the previous man.

KASEN A sequence of comic linked verse in thirty-six links, called "poetic immortals" because there were thirty-six such.

KATAGI Character sketches; a form of fiction made popular by Ejima Kiseki.

KATAUTA An archaic poetic form which was revived (unsuccessfully) by Takebe Ayatari in the eighteenth century. It consisted of the first three lines of a waka (five, seven, five syllables) or the first three lines of a sedōka (five, seven, seven syllables).

KAWAZU A kind of frog prized for its beautiful voice.

KECHIMYAKU "Blood lineage"—a criterion of haikai poetry espoused by Morikawa Kyoriku.

KEIEN The school of poetry founded by Kagawa Kageki, so called because this was his literary name (*gō*).

KEMARI A kind of football, the purpose of which is to keep the ball in the air.

KIBYŌSHI "Yellow-covered books"—a form of gesaku literature popular at the end of the eighteenth century which featured many illustrations.

KIGO A seasonal word which designates directly or indirectly the season of a haikai poem.

KIREJI A "cutting word," such as *ya*, which has as its function dividing the two component elements of a haikai verse.

KIYOMIZU The name of a famous temple of the Hossō sect situated in the Higashiyama district of Kyoto. The central object of worship of this temple, the statue of Kannon, was often referred to in literature.

KOKIN DENJU The secret transmission of traditions about the meanings of poetry in the *Kokinshū*.

KOKKEIBON "Funny books"—the designation of a variety of humorous gesaku works of the early nineteenth century.

KOKUGAKU "National learning"—the study of the Japanese classics, especially *Manyōshū* and *Kojiki*; flourished in the eighteenth century.

KŌSHOKU Literally, "to love love," a term used in the titles of many ukiyo zōshi to indicate the erotic content.

KŌSHOKUBON Works of erotic content in the tradition of such novels as Saikaku's *Kōshoku Ichidai Otoko*.

KU-SHIH A form of Chinese poetry going back to the Han Dynasty which was freer in form and generally longer than later varieties of Chinese poetry. It was not widely adopted in Japan until the nineteenth century.

KYŌGEN The farces that accompany Nō plays; also, the interludes within a Nō play in which a "man of the place" relates the history of a place or some legend.

KYŌGOKU-REIZEI A school of poetry, opposed to the Nijō, which was known for its advocacy of novel, sometimes even eccentric, theories of waka composition. The chief figure of the school was Kyōgoku Tamekane (1254–1332).

KYŌKA A comic variety of waka.

KYŌSHI A comic variety of kanshi.

LI PO The great Chinese poet (701–762) much admired in Japan.

MAEKU The "previous verse" in a linked-verse sequence.

MAEKUZUKE A kind of "verse-capping," the object of which was to demonstrate one's wit in adding seventeen syllables to another man's maeku, the ancestor of senryū.

MAGOKORO The "true feelings" of people; these were believed to be unchanging. An ancient poem was therefore still valid thousands of years later.

MAKOTO "Truth"—the ideal in poetry of such different men as Kamo no Mabuchi and Uejima Onitsura; it was opposed to artifice or ingenuity.

MAKURAKOTOBA A "pillow word"—a kind of fixed epithet standing generally at the head of a poem and modifying place names, features of the landscape, etc. Many had become unintelligible and were used mainly to impart dignity to a poem.

MARUYAMA The licensed quarter in Nagasaki.

MASURAOGOKORO "Manliness"—an ideal of some kokugaku poets of the eighteenth century, as opposed to the femininity of most waka compositions.

MIBU KYŌGEN A form of comic play staged at the Mibu Temple in which all actions are mimed, without recourse to words.

MICHIYUKI The journey section of a play or work of fiction, often relating, with references to places passed on the way, the feelings of suicidal lovers on their way to death.

MINAMOTO The family name of one of the great clans. The Kamakura shogunate was founded by Minamoto Yoritomo; and Tokugawa Ieyasu, the founder of the Tokugawa shogunate, claimed to be a member of the same clan.

MONO NO AWARE The "pity of things"—a term used especially by Motoori Norinaga to describe the sensitivity of people to emotional experiences.

MUDABARA A term designating a meaningless seppuku.

MURASAKI SHIKIBU The author of *Genji Monogatari* (The Tale of Genji).

MUSHIN A term used of the comic form of renga.

NICHIREN An important Buddhist leader (1222–1282) who founded a militant, nationalistic sect.

NIJŌ The name of a conservative school of waka, which advocated simplicity and plainness of expression; founded by Nijō Tameuji (1222–86). Most court poets were affiliated with this school.

NINJŌ "Human feelings"—often contrasted with giri, or social obligations. These were the natural, spontaneous feelings which often conflicted with a man's sense of duty.

NINJŌBON Works of gesaku fiction which emphasized romantic attachments.

NIOI "Fragrance"—used especially of the overtones of the previous verse which were echoed by the continuer of the sequence of renga.

NŌ The dramas evolved in the fourteenth century which in the premodern period were considered to be the state "music" of the shogunate.

NORITO The texts of Shinto prayers.

ŌHARAI A great purification ceremony; a rite of Shinto.

OIEMONO Plays describing discord within some great household, often devolving on the succession to a fief.

OTOGISHU Companions to the military nobles who amused them with stories, poetry, etc.

PAI-HUA Used of Chinese fiction written in the colloquial language.

PO CHÜ-I A Chinese poet (772–846) who enjoyed a uniquely high reputation in Japan.

REN An association of amateur poets.

RENGA The art of linked verse.

RENKU Linked verse composed in Chinese, rather than in Japanese.

RŌNIN A samurai who serves no master, either because he himself has been deemed unworthy or because his master has been deprived of his retainers by the order of the government.

RYŪKŌ "Up to date"—used by Bashō when he insisted that poetry must not only be eternal but of the moment.

SABI A quality of unostentatious beauty prized by tea masters, etc.

SAIKAKU Ingenuity, a virtue of comic poets or merchants.

SAMISEN (or SHAMISEN). A three-stringed musical instrument popular since the sixteenth century, used to accompany Jōruri.

SARUGAKU An old name for Nō, meaning literally "monkey music."

SEDŌKA An archaic poetic form, rarely used after the eighth century, consisting of six lines in five, seven, seven, five, seven, seven syllables.

SEI SHŌNAGON The celebrated author of *Makura no Sōshi* (The Pillow Book).

SEMMYŌ An imperial edict, composed in Japanese.

SENRYŪ A comic verse form written in five, seven, five syllables, usually poking fun at human foibles.

SEPPUKU Ritual disembowelment.

SEWAMONO Domestic tragedies, written by Chikamatsu and others, describing events in the contemporary world, especially those relating to the townsmen and lower ranks of samurai.

SHAKU A term placed before a man's name to indicate he has become a Buddhist priest.

SHAREBON A form of gesaku fiction largely devoted to describing the licensed quarters.

SHASEI "Depiction of life"—the ideal of writers who aimed especially at fidelity to nature.

SHINJŪ Originally a kind of pledge or other sign expressing feelings within a person's heart for his beloved; later used with the special meaning of a double suicide, the supreme indication of love.

SHIORI A quality in haikai poetry espoused by Bashō suggestive of the delicacy of feelings in the poet's heart.

SHIRABE The "melody" of poetry, a quality advocated by Kagawa Kageki.

SHŌHON JITATE A form of gōkan consisting of summaries of Kabuki plays.

SHŌSETSU Originally used to designate novels based on Chinese colloquial fiction, it has come to be used for the novel in general.

SHŪ A collection or anthology.

SHUI HU CHUAN A Chinese novel, known in Japan as *Suikoden*, which exercised considerable influence on gesaku fiction, notably the novels of Bakin. Translated into English by Pearl Buck with the title *All Men Are Brothers*.

SHUKŌ A device of plot used by dramatists. Familiar shukō include substitution of one person for another, the revelation that a person's motives are quite different from what we had supposed, etc.

SUGAWARA NO MICHIZANE A statesman and poet (846–903) who has been deified as the god of learning.

TADAGOTO "Ordinary things"—the poetic ideal of Ozawa Roan, who favored the use of ordinary language to express ordinary experiences.

TAIRA An important military family. The fighting between the Taira and the Minamoto occasioned many works of literature, and the fall of the house of Taira is chronicled in *Heike Monogatari* (The Tale of the Heike).

TEMMANGŪ The shrines dedicated to the memory of Sugawara no Michizane.

TEMPŌ REFORMS Reforms instituted between 1841 and 1842 by Mizuno Tadakuni, a high shogunate official, with the intent of improving morals, ending extravagance, and otherwise restoring the country to its former samurai standards. The theaters and the writing of fiction were particularly afflicted by these reforms.

TENGU A fabulous creature, believed to live in the mountains, recognizable by its extremely long nose and its feathers.

TENJA A corrector of poetry who often charged fees for this service.

TŌKAIDŌ The road between Kyoto and Edo. There were fifty-three stages along the road, and each was known for some "famous product" and scenic feature.

TOKUGAWA The name of the family of shoguns who ruled Japan, in reality or in name, between 1600 and 1867.

TORIAWASE "Juxtaposition"—a principle of poetry enunciated by Morikawa Kyoriku.

TSUKEKU The verse appended to a maeku by another poet.

TSUKINAMI A term used to designate the regular monthly gatherings of poets; later used in a derogatory sense to designate the uninspired poetry composed at such gatherings.

TSURANE A long monologue delivered by a Kabuki actor, often describing the history of some practice, with many references to place names, etc.

TU FU The great Chinese poet (712–770), revered by Bashō.

UGUISU A kind of song thrush often described in poetry, especially in conjunction with plum blossoms.

UKIYO The "floating world" of uncertainty, a term much in vogue from the seventeenth century.

UKIYO ZŌSHI The fiction composed between 1683 (the year of *Kōshoku Ichidai Otoko*) and 1783.

UKIYO-E "Pictures of the floating world"—woodblock prints which depicted courtesans, actors, and others of the world of pleasure; later used for almost all varieties of woodblock prints produced before 1868.

USHIN The serious variety of renga.

UTA A general name for Japanese poetry and songs, often used as a synonym for waka.

UTA-AWASE A poem competition: two groups of poets were required to compose waka on prescribed subjects, and their respective merits were judged.

WAGOTO "Tender business"—the romantic scenes in Kabuki plays, a specialty of actors from Osaka; contrasted with aragoto.

WAKA The classic Japanese verse form, thirty-one syllables arranged in lines of five, seven, five, seven, seven syllables. Commonly called *tanka* (short poem) in recent years.

WAKASHU A young man; sometimes used specifically of young men who appeared in wakashu Kabuki in the seventeenth century, taking the parts of women as well as men.

WAKI The secondary actor in a Nō play, generally a priest or a courtier, who serves to introduce the main actor. Also, the second verse in a renga sequence.

WASAN Buddhist hymns composed in Japanese.

YAKAZU A rapid-fire composition of haikai no renga, likened to firing arrows in quick succession into a target.

YAMABUKI A kind of wild rose called "kerria," yellow in color; often appears in poetry.

YAMABUSHI A priest who lives in the mountains and practices rites of austerity.

YAMATO The ancient name for Japan; also, the name of the region around the city of Nara.

YOMIHON A variety of gesaku fiction, generally serious in tone. The term means literally, "a book for reading," as opposed to a picture book.

YOSHINO A mountainous region southeast of Nara, celebrated for its cherry blossoms.

YOSHIWARA The licensed quarter in Edo.

YUDAN Carelessness, the cardinal sin for a merchant, according to Saikaku.

ZAPPAI "Miscellaneous haikai"—a variety of comic poetry.

ZEKKU A quatrain of Chinese poetry, composed in lines of five or seven characters.

ZUIHITSU "Follow the brush"—miscellaneous jottings supposedly written as the writer's brush moved him, a term used in general for short essays on unrelated subjects.

INDEX

ABOUT THE AUTHOR

Donald Keene began his study of Japanese at Columbia in 1941, just before the outbreak of war with Japan. Soon afterward he entered the U.S. Navy Japanese Language School, and after graduation served for three years as a translator and interpreter. When the war ended he pursued his studies of Japanese literature at Columbia, Harvard, and Cambridge. In 1948 he became Assistant Lecturer in Japanese at Cambridge, and remained there for five years. From 1953 to 1955 he studied at Kyoto University, and he has spent part of every year since then in Japan. He is now Professor of Japanese at Columbia.

Professor Keene began his history of Japanese literature in 1966 and this has been his principal concern since then. His other publications include *Anthology of Japanese Literature*, *Modern Japanese Literature*, *The Japanese Discovery of Europe*, *Landscapes and Portraits*, and a dozen volumes of translations of both classical and modern Japanese literature. He received the Order of the Rising Sun in 1974 for his services to Japanese literature.